Temperament in Childhood

Temperament in Childhood

Edited by

GELDOLPH A. KOHNSTAMM
University of Leiden,
The Netherlands

JOHN E. BATES
Indiana University, USA

MARY KLEVJORD ROTHBART
University of Oregon, USA

JOHN WILEY & SONS
Chichester · New York · Brisbane · Toronto · Singapore

Other Wiley Editorial Offices

John Wiley & Sons, Inc., 605 Third Avenue,
New York, NY 10158-0012, USA

Jacaranda Wiley Ltd, G.P.O. Box 859, Brisbane,
Queensland 4001. Australia

John Wiley & Sons (Canada) Ltd, 22 Worcester Road,
Rexdale, Ontario M9W 1L1, Canada

John Wiley & Sons (SEA) Plc Ltd, 37 Jalan Pemimpin #05-04
Block B, Union Industrial Building, Singapore 2057

Library of Congress Cataloging-in-Publication Data:

Temperament in childhood / edited by Geldolph A. Kohnstamm, John E.
    Bates, Mary Klevjord Rothbart.
        p.   cm.
    Includes bibliographies and indexes.
    ISBN 0 471 91692 7
    1. Temperament in children.   I. Kohnstamm, Geldolph A., 1937-   .
    II. Bates, John E., 1945-   .   III. Rothbart, Mary Klevjord.
    [DNLM: 1. Child Development.   2. Cross-Cultural Comparison.
    3. Personality — in infancy & childhood.   4. Psychophysiology.   BF
    798 T2819]
    BF723. T53T46   1989
    155.4'182—dc20
    DNLM/DLC
    for Library of Congress   89-14788
                                                               CIP

British Library Cataloguing-in-Publication Data:

Temperament in childhood.
    1. Children. Temperament
    I. Kohnstamm, Geldolph A.
    II. Bates, John E.
    III. Rothbart, Mary Klevjord
    155.4'18

    ISBN 0 471 91692 7

Typeset by Witwell Ltd, Southport.
Printed and bound in Great Britain by Courier International Ltd, Tiptree, Essex.

Contents

Section Three: Temperament and Development

Section Four: Applications of Temperament Concepts

Section Five: Cross-Cultural, Socioeconomic Status, Sex and Other Group Differences

Contributors

GRAZIA ATTILI: *Istituto di Psicologia del Consiglio Nazionale delle Ricerche, Rome, Italy.*

GENEVIÈVE BALLEYGUIER: *University Francois Rabelais, Tours, France.*

JOHN E. BATES: *Indiana University, Bloomington, IN, USA.*

DYMPHNA C. VAN DEN BOOM: *Department of Psychology, University of Leiden, The Netherlands.*

ARNOLD BUSS: *University of Texas, Austin, TX, USA.*

WILLIAM B. CAREY: *Division of General Pediatrics, Children's Hospital of Philadelphia; and Private Practice of Pediatrics, Media, PA, USA.*

STELLA CHESS: *New York University Medical Center, New York, NY, USA.*

NATHAN A. FOX: *Institute for Child Study, University of Maryland, USA.*

WILLIAM FULLARD: *Temple University, Philadelphia, PA, USA.*

SUSAN GOLDBERG: *Psychiatric Research Unit, The Hospital for Sick Children; and Faculty of Medicine, University of Toronto, Toronto, Ontario, Canada.*

H. HILL GOLDSMITH: *Department of Psychology, University of Oregon, Eugene, OR, USA.*

MEGAN R. GUNNAR: *Institute of Child Development, University of Minnesota, Minneapolis, MN, USA.*

BERIT HAGEKULL: *University of Uppsala, Department of Clinical Psychology, Uppsala, Sweden.*

J. D. HIGLEY: *Laboratory of Comparative Ethology, National Institute of Child Health and Human Development, Bethesda, Maryland, USA.*

ROBERT A. HINDE: *MRC Unit on the Development and Integration of Behaviour, Madingley, Cambridge, UK.*

GAIL S. HUNTINGTON: *University of North Carolina at Chapel Hill, USA.*

JEROME KAGAN: *Department of Psychology, Harvard University, USA.*

BARBARA K. KEOGH: *University of California, Los Angeles, CA, USA.*

GELDOLPH A. KOHNSTAMM: *Department of Psychology, University of Leiden, The Netherlands.*

JACQUELINE V. LERNER: *Pennsylvania State University, USA.*

RICHARD M. LERNER: *Pennsylvania State University, USA.*

SARAH MANGELSDORF: *Department of Psychology, University of Michigan, USA.*

SHARON MARCOVITCH: *Developmental Evaluation Unit, The Hospital for Sick Children; and Faculty of Medicine, University of Toronto, Canada.*

ROY P. MARTIN: *University of Georgia, Athens, GA, USA.*

ADAM P. MATHENY, JR: *Department of Pediatrics, University of Louisville, School of Medicine, Louisville, KY, USA.*

MICHEL MAZIADE: *Centre de Recherche Laval Robert-Giffard, Hôtel-Dieu de Sacré-Coeur, Quebec; and Département de Psychiatrie, Université Laval, Quebec, Canada.*

HANS-JÜRGEN MEYER: *Institut für Psychologie der Technischen Hochschule Darmstadt, BRD.*

KATHERINE NITZ: *Pennsylvania State University, USA.*

FRANK OBERKLAID: *Department of Ambulatory Pediatrics, Royal Children's Hospital, Melbourne, Australia.*

MARGOT R. PRIOR: *Department of Psychology, La Trobe University, Melbourne, Australia.*

J. STEVEN REZNICK: *Department of Psychology, Yale University, USA.*

MARY KLEVJORD ROTHBART: *Department of Psychology, University of Oregon, Eugene, OR, USA.*

MICHAEL RUTTER: *MRC Child Psychiatry Unit, Institute of Psychiatry, London, UK.*

ANN V. SANSON: *Department of Psychology, University of Melbourne, Australia.*

RUNE J. SIMEONSSON: *University of North Carolina at Chapel Hill, USA.*

NANCY SNIDMAN: *Department of Psychology, Harvard University, USA.*

CYNTHIA A. STIFTER: *Department of Individual and Family Studies, Pennsylvania State University, USA.*

JAN STRELAU: *University of Warsaw, Poland.*

S. J. SUOMI: *Laboratory of Comparative Ethology, National Institute of Child Health and Human Development, Bethesda, MD, USA.*

RACHNA TALWAR: *Pennsylvania State University, USA.*

ALEXANDER THOMAS: *New York University Medical Center, New York, NY, USA.*

ANNE MARI TORGERSEN: *University of Oslo, Norway.*

MARC WEISSBLUTH: *Department of Pediatrics, Northwestern University Medical School and Children's Memorial Hospital, Chicago, IL, USA.*

Preface

In this book, co-authored by 43 researchers from 11 countries, we hope to communicate to you some of the fascination of present-day research on temperament in childhood. The book's authors share the idea that there are important individual differences that can be labeled 'temperamental' and are at least partly rooted in constitutional variables.

The book's authors also share an involvement in a developmental program of research. In the words of the late Ron Wilson – to whose memory this book is dedicated:

> the general expectation is that if temperament is rooted in constitutional and genetic variables, there must be some continuity in its expression over the developmental history of the child ... The problem, and the challenge, is one of determining when dissimilar behaviours over time may reflect the same characteristics of temperament. The behavioural criteria would therefore be age-specific, and the thread of continuity would be educed from a coherent patterning of behaviours during childhood. (Wilson, 1982, pp. 122–123)

Responding to this challenge further unites the contributors to this volume.

As shown by the increasing stream of scholarly books and journal articles, temperament research in the 1980s has been a vital scientific program. In addition, recent growth in the field has been strongly international in character. In the early 1960s the English psychiatrist Michael Rutter casually suggested to the principal investigators of the New York Longitudinal Study, Birch, Chess and Thomas, that they adopt the word 'temperament' for the individual differences they had begun to study. The label temperament has served well as a unifying term for the domain, bringing together people of many nationalities at a number of international conferences. The idea for this book was born during one of these conferences, held at Leiden University in The Netherlands, and its international composition is characteristic of the field.

STRUCTURE AND CONTENT OF THE BOOK

Most handbooks in psychology provide the reader with long, integrative reviews of theory, method and research; each major issue is treated by only one author. In this volume, we are adopting a different format. Each of the six sections of the book is introduced by a major chapter, and each of these major chapters is followed by shorter contributions from active researchers and theorists in the field. The hope of the editors is that this format will give the reader a good view of the field as a whole. Some of these introductory chapters are attempts at a major integration of the topic.

The first section is devoted to *Concepts and measures*. Although the term temperament is unifying for the field, there are important differences in conceptual and operational approaches, and these need to be made explicit. The chapters of the first section consider what temperament is and how it can be measured. In the first chapter, Bates provides an integrative overview of the major theories and measures of temperament in children, emphasizing the value of being explicit about the level of conceptualization – overt behavior vs neurological factors vs underlying constitution – and the importance of evaluating specific temperament dimensions rather than thinking of temperament as a monolith. Subsequent chapters describe the current theoretical and measurement directions of four leading theorists. Hinde, from an ethologist's perspective, emphasizes the search for coherent patterns across time and situation, and cautions that we should not expect to find isomorphic links between behavior patterns and neuroendocrine systems. Strelau reviews work on his regulative theory of temperament, with emphasis on reactivity as a dimension of response to stimulation and activity as a way of regulating arousal, and with attention to the ways in which level of reactivity predicts how individuals will respond to varying situations. Buss extends his conceptualizations of the three variables he regards as temperament, by considering subcomponents of the variables, motivational aspects of temperament, the role of learning in temperament traits, and sex differences. Finally, Rothbart presents her latest framework of temperament, in which she considers not only reactivity and self-regulation, but also stimulus properties and the role of effort. She also considers general criteria for defining a specific dimension of temperament.

The second section is devoted to the search for the *Biological bases of individual differences in temperament*. Physiological work on temperament in childhood is in its own early stages of development, but promises to be a source of important information in illuminating the psychological work on temperament. There are two introductory chapters in this section, Rothbart's general review of research in the area, the Goldsmith's description of behavior genetics approaches to the study of temperament. These introductory chapters are followed by Kagan, Reznick and Snidman's discussion of basic issues in the study of temperament. These issues are related to their research on the physiology of inhibition and lack of inhibition to the unfamiliar. In the fourth chapter, Gunnar and Mangelsdorf discuss the dynamics of temperament–physiology relations with a focus upon the study of neuroendocrine correlates of temperament. Temperament is a construct which can be equally well applied to other animals as well as human beings, and Higley and Suomi summarize some very important work with non-human primates on temperament. Finally, Fox and Stifter conclude this section with a discussion of reactive and self-regulative aspects of temperament that reviews their research on temperament and vagal tone.

The third section has its focus on *Developmental issues*. The section begins with a long review of research on temperament during the course of early development.

Thomas and Chess then discuss the relation between temperament and personality, presenting their approach to thinking about temperament in the context of functional behavioral adaptation. The Louisville Twin Study has been one of the major contributors to our understanding of temperament and development, and in the third chapter, Matheny presents a review of the twin study's research on the relation between temperament and mental test scores across the early years of life. Berit Hagekull then reviews the work of herself and her collaborators in applying the behavioral style approach to the study of early temperamental development. In the final chapter of this section, van den Boom makes a contribution to the current discussion of the relation between temperament and attachment by presenting her data relating early individual differences in irritability to the development of attachment.

The fourth section is on the *Applications of temperament research in clinical and educational settings.* In the introductory chapter Bates considers not only how temperament concepts can be applied but also gives an intensive review of the crucial empirical question of what role temperament actually does play in children's interactions with caregivers and the development of behavior problems. In the subsequent eight chapters of the section a distinguished group of pediatricians, psychologists and psychiatrists present a rich array of theoretical, empirical and practical insights concerning the practical value of temperament. Weissbluth provides a detailed analysis of the way in which sleep deficits intersect with temperament. Thomas and Chess use their infancy-to-adulthood longitudinal study for insights about the ways in which temperament affects life course and how the concepts can be used in treating behavioral and emotional problems. Goldberg and Marcovitch consider the ways in which temperament concepts help one to understand and deal with developmentally disabled children of several types. Carey not only describes a very wide variety of practical applications, but also suggests ways in which future research can better facilitate practice. Maziade addresses the question of the role of temperament in behavior problems with data from this longitudinal research and points the way to future research valuable to the clinician. Two separate chapters, one by Keogh and the other by Martin, consider how temperament and its role in children's learning and conduct can be assessed and dealt with in elementary school. Finally, Rutter provides insightful comments not only on the clinical uses of temperament but also the other major issues of the book — definitional, theoretical, and empirical.

The fifth section is on *Sociocultural and other group factors* influencing the expression and assessment of temperament, including social class, ethnic group and sex. This section of the book considers temperament measures of groups of individuals who share specific constitutional, cultural or subcultural characteristics. The central question is: what empirical associations have been found between group characteristics such as social class, ethnicity and sex and the distribution of temperamental phenotypes in children? The data currently available in the literature are in no way sufficient to answer this question with certainty. However, an inventory of progress in the field can serve both to attract young researchers to research in the area and to help them avoid the methodological shortcomings of the past.

In the introductory chapter Kohnstamm first summarizes the results from cross-cultural studies and then focuses on what is known of sex differences in motor activity and emotionality. In the second chapter, the Lerners and their co-workers give an overview of their recent research done in a developmental contextual framework and using the concepts 'developmental niche' and 'ethnotheory', as formulated by Super and Harkness. In the third chapter Fullard, Simeonsson and Huntington review American and Canadian studies in which socioeconomic status of the family has been related to child temperament. In the last chapter Prior, Sanson and Oberklaid give an overview of results obtained in a large-scale longitudinal temperament study done in Australia. Several aspects of this study make it fit well in this section: the ethnic differences in the population sampled, the social class influences on the temperament ratings, and the gradually emerging sex differences.

The last section is on *Historical and European perspectives*. The study of individual differences in personality presently enjoying revival as 'temperamental' has a long and respectable history. In this last section, part of that history is described, notably the history of publications in German, French and Italian in chapters by Meyer, Balleyguier and Attili. These authors focus on the history of thought about temperamental differences in infants and children. It is evident, however, that this cannot be done without paying attention to the history of thought on temperamental differences in adults.

Following these excursions into history, overviews are given of present-day research in Germany, France, Italy and the Scandinavian countries. Torgersen, one of the pioneers of modern temperament research in infancy and childhood, reviews the Scandinavian research.

Many countries, languages and cultures are *not* represented in this section. Although some of the studies done in Australia, Canada, Great Britain, Holland, Japan and Poland have been mentioned in foregoing chapters, we did not ask these writers to give historical and national overviews of the field. We expect an increase of Asian temperament research, notably from India and Japan. In India, the psychiatrist Malhotra and her associates have published several studies on temperamental differences in normal and emotionally disturbed children (Malhotra, Malhotra & Randhawa, 1983a,b; Malhotra & Randhawa, 1982; see Chapter 30, by Kohnstamm, for full details of these references), which would have been described in this section had we known about them in time.

The present order of the sections is somewhat arbitary. If we could have made a book with a circular organization, connecting the last section to the first, this would probably have been a better representation of our material.

This applies in particular to the sixth and last section. To close the book with the historical roots of the study of temperament is unusual. The discussion of issues in temperament provides a necessary perspective for the history, which in turn provides an important perspective for viewing current issues.

Do we imply that the study of temperament in childhood is also circular? Certainly not. We believe that real progress has been made, though slowly, and that additional and speeded progress is to be expected in the last decade of this century. We do not expect this to be an easy job. The main issues are complicated enough to demand great effort and clarity of thought and availability of resources for longitudinal research. Since money for behavioral and social science research is very limited – and since there are no signs of important future increases in funding temperament research – only intensive communication and cooperation can help us to produce the progress we seek.

Sharing information, using the same or comparable instruments, agreeing on standards of measurement and on criteria for accepting results as important, should become a general practice for this field of research. This book, we hope, illuminates what might be possible if we follow this road, both in the communication and cooperation it demonstrates among workers in psychology, medicine and biology, and in the communication and cooperation among workers of different nationalities.

Working together on this project has been a great joy to us. We are grateful to our publisher, for his sympathy, patience and support, and we are equally grateful to our colleagues who reacted so promptly and in such good spirit to our editorial suggestions.

DK, JB and *MR*

REFERENCE

Wilson, R.S. (1982). Intrinsic determinants of temperament. In R. Porter & G.M. Collins (Eds), *Temperamental differences in infants and young children* (pp. 121–140). Ciba Foundation Symposium No. 89. London: Pitman.

Section One
Concepts and Measures

1

Concepts and Measures of Temperament

JOHN E. BATES
Indiana University

Temperament is an ancient concept in philosophy (Rothbart & Derryberry, 1981), but only very recent in empirical research on human development. Current temperament concepts and measures are the focus of this chapter. The goal of the chapter is not to provide the final word on the issues, but rather an advanced point of entry – a context for appreciating the contributions of the many authors writing about children's temperament, both in this volume and in the literature in general.

In the last few decades the child-development literature has shown an exponential increase in the use of temperament concepts. This expansion can be attributed to the conceptual and empirical groundwork laid by the ancient and modern temperament theorists. It can also be attributed to the seminal contributions of Thomas and Chess and their colleagues (e.g. Thomas, Chess, Birch, Hertzig, & Korn, 1963), who pioneered the systematic application of temperament concepts to the measurement of children's individuality. Finally, it must also reflect broader scientific movements – increased support for research in general, the systems *Zeitgeist* in the behavioral sciences, and the discovery of new ways of conceptualizing and observing competencies developing from the earliest infancy.

Social-developmental researchers had for many years put heavy emphasis on questions about the influence of environmental variables. With the appearance of works such as those of Bell (1968) and Thomas *et al.* (1963), researchers began to work more diligently toward understanding how children's own tendencies affect transactions with caregivers and, ultimately, personality development. Children's behavioral tendencies are very often described in terms of temperament.

DEFINING TEMPERAMENT

What does the term temperament mean? I would assume that most readers share similar intuitive definitions of the term. This assumption of commonality is partly

Temperament in Childhood   Edited by G.A. Kohnstamm, J.E. Bates and M.K. Rothbart
© 1989 John Wiley & Sons Ltd

based on the similar usages of the term one can see in the literature. However, it is also based on a common set of folk meanings. Temperament is a concept serving to tie together a variety of primary behavioral dispositions commonly used to distinguish one individual from another. One might apply a temperament term in talking about infants, children, or adults, especially when talking about the characteristic mixture of activity, moods, and emotional responses. One might apply it in talking about pets and livestock, too. There are many varieties of temperament concept. Goldsmith and Rieser-Danner (1986) captured the sense of the panoply of temperament traits when they referred to temperament as a *rubric*.

Beyond intuitive meanings, the term temperament becomes much more complex. It carries a number of interesting connotations, and it is defined in different ways by different users. The term temperament links a moderately large group of scholars and practitioners in the field of child development, including psychologists, psychiatrists, pediatricians, and educators, with interests ranging from psychophysiology to the processes of social interaction and the development of clinical disorders.

At this point it is probably impossible to establish a fixed definition of temperament in scientific application, as Hinde has remarked (in Goldsmith *et al.*, 1987). Temperament is not a thing, even a complex thing. Like most psychological terms, it is a set of hypothetical constructs. One would still want to try to comprehend the major points of agreement and disagreement in the concepts of temperament. Both the points of clarity and confusion could ultimately advance our comprehension of the natural phenomena of behavior and development.

The most general definition of temperament across these varied constituencies is that it consists of biologically rooted individual differences in behavior tendencies that are present early in life and are relatively stable across various kinds of situation and over the course of time (Bates, 1987; Goldsmith *et al.*, 1987; Kohnstamm, 1986). Furthermore, there is general agreement that temperament is manifest largely in the context of social interaction, although one might imagine temperament playing a role in even a hermit's existence.

The term is most often applied to behavioral qualities of emotion, attention, and activity. These are big areas of behavior. Only an exceedingly grandiose temperament theory would try to encompass them in whole. It is necessary to specify what particular aspects are allocated to temperament. Frequently cited ones in the developmental area include the following: (a) the positivity vs negativity of emotional responses in general, emotional responses to novel stimuli in general, emotional responses to familiar and unfamiliar people in particular, and emotional expression in response to internal states such as hunger and boredom; (b) attentional orientation patterns, such as soothability when distressed and distractability of attention; and (c) motor activity's vigor and frequency and appropriate self-modulation of activity.

Although it would lighten our conceptual baggage if we could assume that these emotion, attention, and activity variables are highly distinct from one another, they are probably not so distinct. For example, the behavior pattern that we would call high activity level could be based on temperamentally positive emotional response to novel stimuli, need for a high level of stimulation to maintain optimum arousal, distractability of attention, and internal-symbolic controls on behavior, all in addition to the various physiological variables that must control motor activity level more directly. Much of the recent research and writing in temperament has been focused on the need to simplify the list of temperament variables, or at least to describe the complex systems in more efficient language. The results have been noticeable. There have been advances in conceptual clarity of temperament as a general rubric, as well as in empirical and theoretical comparisons and contrasts between specific temperament variables. However, there are still many points of disagreement and confusion in the temperament area.

MAJOR CONCEPTUAL ISSUES

Where the general agreement about temperament breaks down is in the precise nature of the phenomena that are considered to be temperament. Let us consider some aspects of this complexity, and see if there might be some way of organizing the conceptual variables.

Surface Behavior Versus Underlying Organization

Is temperament a particular behavior itself, or is it something underlying the behavior? Most writers who make the effort to define it think of it as the latter – a property of the organism that organizes interactions with the environment over a wide range of situations. It is inferred from consistencies in behavior aggregated over many situations. However, within this general agreement there is room for some ambiguity in what is meant by the underlying organization. This sometimes leads to confusion in discussing issues such as stability vs change in temperament. Here is a way of defining temperament suggested by the advanced thinking in the literature (e.g. see Bates, 1986, 1987; Buss & Plomin, 1984; Goldsmith & Rieser-Danner, 1986; Goldsmith, in Goldsmith *et al.*, 1987; Hinde, in Goldsmith *et al.*, 1987; Rothbart, 1986; Rothbart in Goldsmith *et al.*, 1987; Strelau, 1983, 1986; I am also indebted to an informal discussion with T. Wachs in September 1987): I find it helpful to think of the concept of temperament as having three different levels.

Levels of Temperament Definition

The first level is temperament as a *pattern in observed behavior*. This is the level of conceptualization in most uses of the term. Consider for example the construct of negative emotionality, a broad-band dimension represented in all major conceptualizations of temperament. Any given behavioral event expressing negative emotion would not generally be considered as temperament in itself. (However, at least one writer has explicitly taken a position that temperament is the behavior itself, not an underlying pattern (McCall, in Goldsmith *et al.*, 1987). I have seen numerous examples of a tacit acceptance of this non-distinction.)

One would compare individuals on negative emotionality as a first-level temperament characteristic on the basis of patterns of specific emotions expressed through particular actions in particular contexts: e.g. crying, screaming, or fretting;

expressed, e.g. intensely vs moderately, with fear vs anger, or in quick vs slow reaction; and shown, e.g. when fatigued vs rested, in a conflicted vs calm social atmosphere, or under high vs low sensory stimulation. In other words, *who*, in the sense of the attributes of an individual, is a function of *what* behaviors occur *how* and *where*.

Of course, temperament would not be the only factor underlying such patterns of behavior. Situational factors would also influence any given behavioral event in relatively direct ways, e.g. a child would be more likely to cry in a situation threatening neglect of basic needs than in one offering gratification. In addition, the behavioral pattern would be partially attributable to more indirect experiential factors. These would include what the child has learned about basic opportunities, preferences, and limits of his/her environment, as well as the child's basic perceptual, cognitive, and motor abilities. Such factors would influence how environmental contexts are seen by the child, which of course would influence responses. It is also possible that some of the child's accumulating experience could itself be based on the effects that individual children have upon their environments, such as in the case of an active, stimulus-hungry child prompting his/her parents to provide a more stimulating environment than they might for a less energetic child.

The next conceptual level on which one could think of temperament is in terms of *factors of neurological individuality*. This would include differences in anatomical and functional patterns of the central nervous system (CNS). It is clear that there can be variations in the numbers and patterns of organization of particular kinds of neurons in particular locations, in the amounts of the various neurotransmitter chemicals in various brain centers, and in the patterns of nervous system reaction to various stimulus situations, and that these correspond in somewhat understandable ways with behavior (Greenough, Black, & Wallace, 1987; Nowakowski, 1987; Strelau, 1983, 1986; Tucker & Williamson, 1984; and see Chapter 6, by Rothbart). For example, at the level of neurological individuality, the construct of negative emotionality might consist of tendencies toward sympathetic nervous system dominance, perhaps due to relative and absolute amounts of various neurotransmitters or numbers of particular kinds of neurons and ancillary cells. The specifics here are few relative to the complexity of the systems being described, although the facts are multiplying. The literature suggests that there is not a simple pattern of physiological events underlying a particular kind of behavior, and that the same systems might underlie a number of different temperament patterns (Buss & Plomin, 1984; Strelau, 1986). There is also another, even less well specified complicating factor: it has been suggested by a number of leading writers that structures and processes at the CNS level can be lastingly altered through environmental influences and through the experiences of the nervous system – e.g. how often and intensely the environment activates the arousal systems (Goldsmith, in Goldsmith *et al.*, 1987; Hinde, in Goldsmith *et al.*, 1987; Strelau, 1983). However, empirically based specifics of this hypothetical process are not well established, especially in relation to human development.

The final level of the concept of temperament contains the earliest biological roots of the patterns of behavior, *constitutional factors*. These would include especially the individual's genetic inheritance, and also other aspects of the constitution rubric such as prenatal exposure to maternal stress hormones, prenatal nutrition, etc.

Some definitional statements are radically neutral on the issue of whether there are constitutional substrates to individual differences in temperament. These restrict the definitional focus, in effect, to the first level of the concept of temperament, and leave open the question of the precise origins of the patterns of behavior (Goldsmith & Campos, 1982). Nevertheless, most statements (including ones by Goldsmith, e.g. in Goldsmith *et al.*, 1987) do presume some combination of biological and environmental origins for temperament, including genetic inheritance and other aspects of constitution.

Is Heritability Necessary?

Buss and Plomin (1984) have taken the position that behavior traits we call temperament ought to have a clear genetic basis. I have agreed with them (Bates, 1987). There is evidence for an early-appearing genetic component in a number of temperament variables (e.g. Buss & Plomin, 1984; Plomin, 1987; Wilson & Matheny, 1986). However, the position has been criticized (Goldsmith, in Goldsmith *et al.*, 1987; Hinde, in Goldsmith, *et al.*, 1987; Stevenson-Hinde, 1986; Strelau, 1986) as being overly restrictive in what phenomena it encompasses and as ignoring complications in the developmental, temporal patterns of gene action, as well as ignoring the plausible influence of the pre- and postnatal environments on the nervous system and behavioral systems. In considering some trait as having a genetic basis, one does not necessarily have to think of a genetic code as completely and precisely programming the trait. One could take a dynamic systems perspective, in which behavioral organization is less programmed than it is emergent (Thelen, 1989), and thus see the genetic code as shaping only the broad outlines and the initial parameters of the individual's response to environmental conditions. In any event, the ultimate value of the strict definition will turn on discoveries of particular processes of genetic influence.

Would defining temperament as personality traits with some genetic heritability necessarily divert scientific interest away from any important behavioral phenomena of young children, as some have worried? I would argue that it would not; it might, on the contrary, influence the development of new descriptive rubrics for early individual differences. There may be a tendency to try to assimilate too many aspects of child personality to the concept of temperament. We might well benefit from developing some new, non-temperament concepts – they might help us see important distinctions in our behavioral 'snow'. Nor do I think that a strict definition would limit interest in non-inherited biological processes underlying behavior; again, maybe new concepts would arise to help us see important distinctions.

It does seem likely now that the part of the Buss–Plomin definition concerning early appearance of traits will have to be revised. This is suggested by evidence that genes might turn on and off at different times over the course of development, and that features of the nervous system relevant to temperament are configuring themselves through principles of dynamic self-organization (Thelen, 1989). Thus, the constitutional basis of temperament could change. As empirical examples of the hypothetical phenomena emerge in the literature, we will be in a better position to judge the usefulness of calling later-emerging traits 'temperament'. In Chapter 12 Rothbart reviews evidence for one such trait: impulsivity vs self-restraint, a temperament-like dimension whose biological underpinnings in the CNS do not mature until late in the first year. Another possibility mentioned increasingly is that there is environmental action upon the functioning of the gene system, e.g. influencing hypothetical regulator genes. This could be important, depending on how often and in what behavior systems this kind of process occurs, but again, I do not know of relevant empirical examples. Section Two of the present volume will consider this and related issues in greater detail and with greater authority than I could.

Coping with Definitional Ambiguities

The genetic-basis controversy has been valuable to me in learning to appreciate the importance of the levels of temperament definition. The levels represent vantage points for judging the value of the various suggested attributes of the construct. There is a healthy tension between interest in the natural phenomena of child behavior and in the abstract grids we put over those phenomena for the sake of description. The meanings of words are by convention, in science just as in any social enterprise. Unproductive conventions in the meanings of the term 'temperament' can be avoided by remaining somewhat open to contrasting concepts. This increases ambiguity in communication, but does not have to be crippling; any living language is constantly evolving. One might prefer, at any one time, a temperament concept that is narrow in its hypothesized biological bases and behavioral dimensions of manifestation; one might prefer a concept that is broad in its range of behaviour dimensions, but largely restricted to the first level of definition; or one might prefer some other set of concept attributes. As long as it is well recognized that the word temperament might be used from several different perspectives, it can be a viable term. It is also useful to remember that the behavior pattern referred to as temperament can in theory be only partially derived from the deeper, constitutional layers of temperament, being obviously also the product of experience with the environment, even in the early months of life.

Having addressed what I see as the central definitional issue in temperament, the comparative emphasis placed on the different levels of organization, I will now list some other, somewhat overlapping, issues. The questions have been addressed in a number of recent publications (Bates, 1987; Goldsmith *et al.*, 1987; Kohnstamm, 1986).

Development

How is temperament a developmental concept? Does it describe behavior systems that all individuals have or eventually develop, e.g. the capacity to respond with fear to a stranger, or does it refer to individual differences in the action of such systems, e.g. the timing of onset or intensity of stranger fear? Generally, temperament is used as an individual differences concept. Normative developmental functions are occasionally spoken of in terms of temperament, e.g. as in the development of sociability; usually they are described as independent of temperament *per se*, but affecting the ways in which temperament is expressed. In resolving this issue, the question of conceptual level should be kept in mind. For further consideration of this interesting issue see Chapter 12 by Rothbart.

Change in Temperament

Along the same lines, one could ask whether the name temperament should be reserved for characteristics that are quite stable. Or would one logically expect change, either due to environmental pressures (e.g. see Chess & Thomas, 1984; Thomas, Chess & Birch, 1968) or due to ontogenetic shifts in behavioral organization (Rothbart & Derryberry, 1981) and delayed gene action (e.g. see Goldsmith & Campos, 1982). Although no one has indicated precisely how stable a trait should be if it is truly temperament, most temperament writers say it should have high stability relative to other personality variables (e.g. see Buss & Plomin, 1984; Strelau, 1983). At the same time, most writers explicitly include a notion that temperament is also changeable.

It makes sense to think of temperament defined on the first, behavioral organization level as subject to many environmental forces for change. It also makes sense that there could be changes at the second, neurological organizational level. One type of change could be due to endogenous development. For example, it is quite clear that there is much change in the neurological organization of infants' behavior in the first months postpartum (Emde, Gaensbauer, & Harmon, 1976). Temperamental behaviors based on these systems would probably show some change.

In fact, studies, e.g. of negative emotionality, find only very modest stability for neonatal measures at best (Isabella, Ward, & Belsky, 1985; Matheny, Riese, & Wilson, 1985; Riese, 1987; St James-Roberts & Wolke, 1986; Worobey, 1986). This is much less than the stability of such variables after the first few months. Some writers still regard these neonatal indexes as temperament (Riese; Worobey), while others would prefer not to classify them as such (Bates; Isabella *et al.*; St James-Roberts & Wolke). Another possible type of change on the neurological organization level concerns response to exogenous forces. Strelau (1983) feels that changes in a person's level of sensitivity to stimulation could result from chronic over- or understimulation. This scenario, first advanced perhaps by Strelau's associate Eliasz (Strelau, 1983), has not been well studied but has received empirical support in at least one recent study: Sankowski (1985) found that decreases over time in children's levels of reactivity were associated with living in a large family and with an increase in the amount of physical activity. In related vein, Weissbluth (1987) has clinically observed improvements in children's characteristic irritability and social demandingness when parents finally manage to establish routines promoting adequate child sleep.

I doubt the prevalence of change in the third level, genetic inheritance, but am trying to keep an open mind about emerging changes in the action of genes.

Discussion at the recent meetings in Leiden (Kohnstamm, 1986) made me realize that, while we speak of stability as a criterion for temperament, the related criterion of *continuity* is more important. One would not necessarily expect the exact same behavior pattern to be present across intervals of development, but one would expect some continuity in age-appropriate manifestations of the pattern (Thomas & Chess, 1977). There are likely to be genetic influences on many aspects of behavior, and some of these influences might occur past early childhood (Plomin, 1987). However, just because individual variations in a behavior pattern have a genetic root does not mean that the pattern must be designated temperament. One could refer to those late-emerging patterns of variation as temperament, or, following Buss and Plomin (1984), not regard them as temperament. One, somewhat late-emerging dimension that I have been thinking of as temperament is variation in the inhibition system (mentioned above), which does not emerge until late infancy, but which otherwise seems an important aspect of temperament.

In short, when thinking of temperament on the behavior-system level, one would tend to expect some stability, but also at least moderate amounts of change. At the neurological system organization level, one might expect even greater stability, but still some change. For the sake of conceptual simplicity, temperament in the sense of genetic roots should be not just relatively stable, but highly stable. However, we must remember that this set of expected features is not necessarily an accurate reflection of the real phenomena we seek to understand, and eventually we will judge it on how well it has helped us to see new features of the phenomena.

Does the multi-level concept of temperament provide so much complication that it is an impediment to potential measurement of temperament-related phenomena? To the contrary, it might actually help organize our research analyses more effectively. Theoretically, the social environment's major behavior-shaping efforts and major changes in stimulus situations could be assessed, and statistically held constant, yielding a truer estimate of the deeper temperament components of the behavior pattern. As a partial example, Crockenberg and Acredelo (1983) have suggested that temperament be measured in terms of the frequency of a certain kind of child response, e.g. positive affect, relative to the frequency of stimuli that would elicit such a response, e.g. playful surprises. I say such methods would yield truer, rather than true, estimates of the temperament component; there is at least one other component that would be difficult to estimate, the influence of the child's characteristics upon the environment. For example, Plomin (1987) has emphasized the possibility of correlations between genetic tendency and environmental characteristics. This could happen through passive linkage in that a child with an active temperament might tend to have parents who are active themselves, thus affecting the environment; it could also happen through active influence, where the child's tendency causes others to provide events they might not otherwise provide. However, it appears possible that general parameters for these kinds of influence may be established through future research. For example, Plomin, Loehlin, and DeFries (1985) included parameters for gene–environment correlation in their empirical study of adoptive vs non-adoptive families.

Of course, it must be recognized that we will never precisely measure the abstract, pure concept of temperament (Bates, 1986). However, the abstract notion is still useful, especially in thinking about questions of endogenous vs environmental origins of social behavior dispositions and their stability vs instability. In advocating this somewhat more purified, abstract rubric of temperament, I am talking about what should be referred to by the particular hypothetical construct, temperament, not about what natural phenomena should be of interest to researchers. A behavioral disposition could be very useful in describing development and well worth measuring, yet not to be considered a reflection of temperament.

The Conceptual Advantage of Temperament Concepts

The roundtable on temperament organized by Goldsmith (Goldsmith *et al.*, 1987) asked six major questions of the participants, most of which focused on definitional issues mentioned above. One very interesting question was what insights temperament concepts give that other concepts do not. The answers to this question were generally not as organized and compelling as those to the other questions, probably because it is hard to achieve the vantage from which one can imagine temperament being absent from the descriptive/explanatory landscape. Perhaps the question will be better answered in relation to specific dimensions of temperamental behavior than in a general sense. However, before turning to specific constructs, I will add my own, still inadequate attempt to place the general construct of temperament in the arena with competing constructs.

The temperament concept offers advantages especially in discussing the origins of children's personality differences. It is a shorthand way of postulating that there are endogenous forces shaping the child's individual, social characteristics. In doing so, it is rooted in good empirical research on animal behavior (Buss & Plomin, 1984), and does not invoke the exceedingly general notion of 'instinct'. It is also a very useful, almost indispensible way of summarizing individual differences in socially relevant behavior in the earliest part of life, especially basic social communications like emotion. Temperament is an element in models of development. It guides the selection of variables for measurement in a study of the origins of individuality, along with other major concepts like intellectual competence, environmental pressures, and acquired personality.

In addition, however, temperament concepts are enriching our view of the behaviors we have conventionally regarded as part of cognitive development, not personality. There is evidence, for example, that the temperament variable of activity level moderates the effect of environmental deprivation upon cognitive development (see Chapter 17, by Bates).

The concept of temperament also guides the way clinicians formulate children's behavior problems. Having a biological attribution for a child's behavior is sometimes very helpful to parents who are trying to cope effectively with children's characteristics. Such attributions could keep parents more relaxed and appreciative of children's unique qualities, yet more steadily poised for prevention of negative side-effects of the fit between temperament and environment (see Chapter 17, by Bates).

As indicated earlier, however, we recognize that the concept also has its deficiencies; one uses temperament measures as indexes of biologically rooted individual differences only with the aid of highly tentative assumptions. It is clear that any given measure has a number of components, including situational context, past learning, etc., that do not fit the simpler abstractions of temperament. Nevertheless, as a class of personological attributions for behavior, temperament occupies a crucial part of our contemporary, systems models of the ontogeny of behavior.

Specific Temperament Concepts

The conceptual advantage of temperament is not just in the general concept, but also in the specific concepts used to describe individual differences in behavior. Indeed, it has been argued that specific concepts are of more fundamental importance than the general construct (Bates, 1986; Goldsmith & Rieser-Danner, 1986). The following is a list of specific temperament concepts for which there exist relatively extensive construct validational findings. The specific operational variables used to assess a given construct probably do not correlate highly with one another (Rothbart & Goldsmith, 1985); the precision of definition is not that far advanced. However, there is high conceptual similarity, and in many cases some empirical convergence, enough to provisionally group the concepts together. No concept is highly crystallized in relation to its definition and validation, and the distinction between the concepts is not exactly crystalline, either. However, there is an emerging coherence in the major temperament variables, one with both conceptual and empirical bases. I have grouped the constructs, loosely corresponding to my impressions of their meanings, based on my reading of the literature and our own research data.

(1) *Negative emotionality.* There is a negative emotionality concept in all schemes of temperament used to describe children. It generally refers to the disposition to show various forms of negative affect, such as generalized distress, fear, and anger. Buss and Plomin (1984) include negative emotionality (in addition to activity and sociability) in their EAS scheme of temperament. They suggest that emotionality differentiates over the first year into anger, fear, and general distress. The very widely used, nine-scale scheme of Thomas and Chess (1977) puts negative and positive mood on the same continuum, with scores at one end describing children showing more negative, unfriendly behavior and scores at the other end showing more joyful, friendly behavior. Buss and Plomin define emotionality on the basis of how strongly the child responds, the intensity of stimulus eliciting the response, and how easily the child is pacified. Thomas and Chess include the first of these aspects in a more general dimension of intensity (i.e. concerning intensity in a wide variety of other behaviors besides emotional expression), the second in a more general dimension of threshold of response, and the third in a general dimension of distractibility. Rothbart (1981) differentiates negative emotionality into separate fear, distress, and soothability constructs. Buss and Plomin (1984) conclude that there is evidence for inherited emotional traits. I do not have a clear conception of what the key processes are on the neurological level, but they may be related to those discussed under adaptability (below), including the brain system inhibiting behavioral response.

(2) *Difficultness*. A concept closely related to negative emotionality, and perhaps even best seen as subordinate to that concept, is the concept of difficult temperament. Thomas *et al.* (1968) were the first to operationalize a concept of difficult temperament, defined as the sum of five of their nine variables. In addition to negative mood, the variables are withdrawal and poor eventual adaptation to new situations, high intensity, and low regularity of biological rhythms. This definition has been the most widely used. However, the five variables do not all cluster empirically, and some researchers have attempted to establish more coherent definitions of difficultness. For example, we have defined it in infants, based on factor analysis of parent ratings, as primarily involving frequent and intense expression of negative affect, and having possible connotations of both sensitivity to stress and social demandingness (Bates, 1987). Alternatively, the core cluster of parentally defined difficultness in the Thomas–Chess variables appears to be both mood and adaptability (Hubert & Wachs, 1985). While my own position (e.g. Bates, 1987) is that it is worthwhile to include difficultness under the rubric of temperament, there are some who have argued that the concept suffers from negative value connotations and a lack of definitional precision, and that it should not be used (G. A. Kohnstamm, personal communication; Rothbart, 1982).

(3) *Adaptability*. Also related to the negative emotionality concept is the notion of adaptation to novelty. Initial approach and eventual adaptability are separate variables in the Thomas–Chess system , but empirically they always tend to cluster together. The core idea is that there are individual differences in the extent to which children respond positively vs negatively to new people and other new stimuli. It is not clear that the child's adaptability to one kind of stimulus would always covary with adaptability to another kind of stimulus; for example, a child could be positive in response to new physical settings yet shy with new people; but our own work supports some covariation in responses to different kinds of novelty (Bates & Bayles, 1984). Kagan and his colleagues have focused sharply on shyness or behavioral inhibition in the face of novelty (Kagan, Reznick, & Snidman, 1986; Rosenberg & Kagan, 1987). They have established that children at the extremes of this dimension differ on physiological processes involving response to stress, and have even identified a quite imperfect, but statistically significant, physical marker: children who are highly inhibited in the face of novelty tend to have the sympathetic nervous system dominant and are most often blue-eyed, while highly uninhibited children show parasympathetic dominance and are more often brown-eyed. Consistent with these findings and a model of inhibition as reflecting inclination toward anxiety, our own longitudinal work shows that unadaptability perceived in infancy tends to predict anxiety-type, internalizing behavior problems perceived in later childhood better than it predicts externalizing problems (Bates & Bayles, 1988; Bates, Maslin, & Frankel, 1985).

(4) *Reactivity*. The Thomas–Chess dimension of threshold of responsiveness (Thomas & Chess, 1977) touches on the concept of reactivity. And Buss and Plomin's (1984) emotionality includes it as part of the definition. However, as articulated by Strelau (1983) and Rothbart (Rothbart, 1986; Rothbart & Derryberry, 1981) reactivity is a variable that is theoretically central to all of the above dimensions, as well as quite a few other ones, including introversion–

extraversion, sensation-seeking, and other dimensions often used in studies of personality, as well as even other elements of temperament. There seems to be a CNS-based individual variability in patterns of response to stimuli. Some people are highly sensitive, reactive to low levels of stimuli, while others define the opposite, relatively insensitive end of the dimension.

Reactivity is related to the Pavlovian concept of strength of the nervous system. However, Strelau (1983) has carried the important neo-Pavlovian tradition of individual differences research into a new context. Reactivity has deep roots in studies of psychophysiological and respondent conditioning phenomena. At the same time, it has strong roots in studies of social adaptation or major personality dimensions. Strelau offers empirical support for the belief that there are systematic patterns of neuroendocrine functioning beneath psychological traits and behaviors relevant to reactivity. He thinks it likely to have to do with CNS activity that augments or suppresses stimulation, especially activity in the reticular formation and cortex (see also Tucker & Williamson (1984) for a well-integrated formulation of the brain's arousal and activation systems). There is corresponding evidence that psychophysiological indexes have some meaningful connections to temperament-like behavior.

However, the connection of psychophysiological individuality to behavioral individuality is not yet clearly detailed. Strelau (1983) accepts a considerable amount of unexplained complication in the psychophysiological system. He has purposely sacrificed some of the psychophysiological roots of this traditional concept for the sake of attaining a more integrative, psychologically meaningful construct of temperament-like behavior. The result is a construct that can be assessed by self-report (the Strelau Temperament Inventory), while still having some theoretical and empirical links to psychophysiological processes.

Reactivity, in Strelau's (1983) definition, is a variable that, in effect, has two, interacting components. These are stimulus intensity and response intensity. There are individual differences in how intense a stimulus must be to evoke a reaction, as well as in how intense the reaction is (e.g. in magnitude of a conditioned response) to a stimulus of a given intensity. Strelau points out that at low stimulus intensity, high-reactive people will be more intensely reactive to the stimulus than low-reactive people. However, at higher levels of stimulus intensity the high-reactive people would tend protectively to inhibit reactivity, showing a decrease in strength of response, while the low-reactive people would not show this protective inhibition or loss of endurance until the intensity of stimulation became still greater. Thus, the low-reactive group would be more responsive to moderately high levels of stimulation than the high-reactive group. At medium levels of stimulus intensity, the response intensities of high- and low-reactive persons would not differ. Of course, at the very lowest and highest levels of stimulus intensity, both kinds of person would show low or no response. It is possible that in many cases inhibitory tendencies, although moderately related to reactivity, function independently (see Chapter 6, by Rothbart; Strelau, 1983). So one might wish to list strength of inhibition of response to stimuli as a separate temperament variable, as have, e.g., Kagan *et al.* (1986) and Reed, Pien, and Rothbart (1984).

Strelau (1983) implicity writes of temperament as a multi-level concept, analogous to that outlined earlier in the chapter. Temperament is manifested in the formal properties of behavior, but it must also have biological roots, even if the neuroendocrine processes are conceivably influenced by characteristics of the environment such as chronic over- or understimulation. Strelau (1983) recognizes that the behavior from which temperament is inferred does not simply reflect temperament. Concerning the concept of reactivity, Strelau distinguishes 'trait' reactivity from 'state' reactivity. Trait reactivity is the stable, temperament variable. State reactivity is dependent on such things as transient levels of stimulus intensity, the individual's current state of arousal, the meaning of the stimulation to the individual, and motivation.

In the typical temperament concept in developmental research, temperament is revealed in particular domains of behavior, especially emotional responses. However, in contrast, Strelau (1983) argues that temperament consists of formal properties of behavior in any domain, including intellectual functioning. The formal characteristics of behavior that are temperament are energetic variables, including the most central concept of reactivity, as well as activity (discussed below), and temporal variables, such as reaction time and mobility (also discussed below).

(5) *Activity*. All the temperament schemes include the concept of activity, and activity is often a target of study apart from other kinds of temperament. Typically it refers to frequency and intensity of motor activity. For example, Eaton and Enns (1986) define it as 'the individual's customary level of energy expenditure through movement' (Eaton & Enns, 1986, p. 19). In most usages activity is spoken of as if it were a dimension independent of other temperament concepts. However, Buss and Plomin (1984), Rothbart and Derryberry (1981), and Strelau (1983) have pointed out the possible role that activity plays in arousal. Activity can discharge CNS tension as well as contribute to the augmentation or prevention of tension (Strelau, 1983). When a child is at an uncomfortably low level of arousal, motor activity can bring the child a more stimulating situation as well as provide afferent feedback to the CNS; and when arousal is uncomfortably high, activity could theoretically be used to reduce or avoid stimulation (Strelau, 1983). (In this sense, activity comes near the concept of impulsivity. Buss and Plomin (1984) argue that impulsivity is not temperament in itself – there is insufficient evidence for infancy and genetic origins. However, they leave open the possibility that the excitement-seeking component of impulsivity might be temperament. Harburg, Gleibermann, Gershowitz, Ozgoren, and Kulik (1982) provide some interesting suggestions that there may be an inherited basis for impulsivity – there are blood markers for the trait.) For Strelau, activity partially overlaps with the reactivity concept: the low-reactive person tends to seek out highly stimulating activities more than the high-reactive person. That temperamental activity could condition the activity choices of a person seems likely. For example, Strelau suggests that low-reactive individuals are more likely to seek out competitive sports than high-reactive individuals. (And in some instances the causal direction might be reversed – regular, vigorous sport could perhaps reduce one's reactivity on the neurological and behavioral levels, through the action of endorphins or some other physiological system. Sankowski (1985) offers a bit of empirical support for this.

The biological bases of the temperamental aspect of activity are not clear at this time. It appears that it has a heritable component (Buss & Plomin, 1984). It also is conceivable that the neuroendocrine factors contributing to individual differences in reactivity could influence the types, intensity, and amounts of activity the child engages in. Perhaps androgens play some role (see Chapter 26, by Kohnstamm). However, on the other hand, Strelau (1983) has argued that activity differences do not reflect differences in psychophysiological processes, in contrast to the variable of reactivity. Individual differences in activity are operant behaviors, according to Strelau, acquired as a result of their ability to regulate arousal.

(6) *Attention regulation.* There are several temperament variables conceptually linked in that they concern regulation of interest and other kinds of affect; they are not necessarily empirically related to each other. Most questionnaires developed out of the Thomas–Chess system include scales for distractibility. The concept refers to the extent to which the child will shift attention from his/her distress in response to external stimuli. Rothbart (1981) refers to this as soothability. The concept also refers sometimes to distraction from other kinds of activities, e.g. to attention span and task persistence in a schoolchild. Rothbart calls this duration of orienting. In either instance, the child's propensity to shift attention is the temperamental component of the behavior. Strelau (1983) has invoked the concept of mobility, seen as a temporal aspect of temperament (as opposed to the energetic aspects, activity and reactivity). Mobility describes how easily one shifts behavior in response to changing environment. Strelau does not see the mobility variable as being functionally orthogonal to the level of reactivity. There is a suggestion that, as the concepts are currently measured, the low-reactive person might be more stimulus-hungry, and would thus change quickly in response to environmental cues. It would also be logical, however, to look for high-reactive people to show fast mobility. What might make the difference in whether the high- or the low-reactive people show the highest mobility is the intensity level of the environmental changes (see discussion under reactivity, above). The common meaning in soothability, distractibility, and mobility is regulation of the individual's arousal/affect through attention deployment.

The biological roots for the attention regulation variables may be related to those for the reactivity-type variable, involving the receptivity-to-stimulation properties of the reticular and related systems deep in the brain, as well as cortical systems, especially the frontal cortex (Tucker & Williamson, 1984). One would suppose that such tendencies would also have neurological origins somewhat distinct from those for reactivity.

(7) *Sociability and positive emotionality.* Buss and Plomin (1984) include sociability as meeting criteria for definition as temperament, but explicitly exclude positive emotionality. However, it seems likely that the two concepts do overlap. Sociability refers to appreciation of the company of other people, in the form of responsive interchange, such as might be provided by either strangers or familiars. Positive emotionality refers to tendencies to express enjoyment, e.g. as measured by Rothbart's (1981) smiling and laughter scale or the positive vs negative mood scale of Thomas and Chess (1977). The conceptual overlap with sociability is that the child's expressions of joy in social interactions are probably the most important determinant of sociability ratings. However, according to Buss and Plomin (1984)

the evidence for the heritability of sociability is more solid that that for positive emotionality. While positive emotionality may indeed be an important characteristic of children, it may actually be a function of another, more basic temperament variable – emotionality/adaptability. Perhaps high-emotionality, low-adaptive, difficult children create a social climate less supportive of or evocative of joy, and thus have fewer opportunities for positive interchanges (cf. Buss & Plomin, 1984). The extent of sociability would also depend to a large extent on the environment, e.g. the warmth and responsiveness of an infant's mother influencing the infant's attachment security and thus the tendency to explore (Lamb, 1982).

MEASURING TEMPERAMENT

How does one turn the above concepts into operational measures? This is an important question, ultimately determining the value of the abstract concepts themselves. Measurement is usually spoken of as a consequence of defining an abstract concept, but measures can apparently also be a cause of the concepts. The concrete measures we use sometimes shape the way we think about the phenomena of interest. We sometimes confuse the measures with the abstractions. And we sometimes limit our working glossary of concepts to the things for which we have established measurement instruments. One example of the natural tendency to forget ambiguities in measures would be implicitly or explicitly regarding parent ratings of a child's temperament as tantamount to the endogenous temperament construct, often seen in temperament articles in the 1970s (Bates, 1980) and still seen sometimes.

Internal Versus External Validity

One would like to have a measure which is conceptually simple and highly reliable. One could do this by choosing highly 'objective' criteria as measures of temperament, e.g. operationally define emotionality as the frequency of observed crying by a baby. This would result in a conceptually simple, reliable measure. However, if the main criterion for success is that the measure be externally valid as a representative of the more general temperament construct, the highly objective measure would not be so successful. It captures only one aspect of only the first level of definition of the emotionality concept. There is a trade-off between internal validity or objectivity in a measure and its validity as a measure of the inherently abstract and multi-level concept of temperament. This difficulty is not cause to despair or abandon the concepts of temperament, but one must keep in mind the conceptual and measurement issues (Bates, 1986). Measures can be used to good advantage as long as users remember to note explicitly their assumptions about the meanings of the measures, and at least occasionally test those assumptions. The particular problems the main types of temperament measure are prone to have been considered in recent articles and chapters (representative examples are Bates, 1986, 1987; Bornstein, Gaughran, & Homel, 1986; Hubert, Wachs, Peters-Martin, & Gandour, 1982; Rothbart & Goldsmith, 1985). These sources review general psychometric principles and mention specific findings on a variety of parent-report instruments as well as direct observation measures, addressing issues such as reliability, stability over ages, and convergent and discriminant validity.

There are three main ways in which temperament concepts have been operationalized for measuring children's individual differences. The first is *parent report*, including questionnaire (the most widely used) and structured interview of the parent. Second is *naturalistic observation* in the home (although so far used mainly as a benchmark for validating the parent-report measures). Third is observation in structured *laboratory situations* (not used widely, but recently adding important information to the study of temperament). A fourth method for studying temperament is the use of *psychophysiological* measures as indexes of response to particular stimuli. This is not at all prevalent in current research on children's temperament; however, it does occur in personality/temperament research in adult subjects (Strelau, 1983), and would appear to be a good future direction for work with child subjects, especially for the sake of exploring the second level of meaning in the temperament concept, the hypothetical organization of neuroendocrine processes.

The next question might be: 'What is the most valid way to measure temperament?' The researcher wants to employ temperament concepts in an economical way, considering the practical costs of collecting data on children's development. What measures deliver the most meaning for the cost? I think parent reports would be the answer to a question put this way. However, thinking of the choice in this way can be seriously misleading: psychological assessment devices are not just little trucks carrying informational nuggets to the refinery – the more trucks and nuggets the better. Some of the information we are seeking in science and clinical work is of that sort. But, ultimately, the value of the information depends on what *novel* processes in development it enables us to see and understand.

The thoughtful use of naturalistic and structured observations tends to be very expensive, but it also tends to provide very rich confirmations and challenges for the field's concepts. The purposes of the investigation are essential guides for choices of temperament measures. As initial explorations of the possible temperamental basis of some aspect of personality, parent-report questionnaires or interviews are probably the best first probe. Parent reports have some roots in objectifiable reality in the child's behavior, despite the possible biases in a parent's perceptions of the child's behavior and its context (Bates & Bayles, 1984). However, as one's research questions reach further into the finer qualities of the temperament-like behavior patterns and into the biological roots of the behavior, one would want to compare the questionnaire information with more objective observations, whether naturalistic, structured, or psychophysiological.

For some years the critical focus was on the methodological limitations of the parent-report instrument, but in the past several years, the problems in interpreting data from the more direct observation methods have also been considered. The area of temperament research has become increasingly sophisticated about the psychometric limitations of *all* of the types of measure (e.g. Bates, 1986, 1987; Rothbart & Goldsmith, 1985; Strelau, 1983). The limitations might be considered to be an impediment to progress. However, increasing awareness of the specifics of the limitations actually offers the possibility for meaningful advances. If ways can be found to control for the potential bias factors, and to know which potential factors actually cause appreciable measurement bias, the conceptual clarity of temperament measures could be significantly increased. This kind of bootstrap method has had some successes in personality research (Wiggins, 1973).

There are many possible targets for methodological control. Rothbart and Goldsmith (1985) provide an especially well-organized and comprehensive review of the methodological biases of parent report, home observation, and laboratory observation in assessing infants. Their Table 1 is the essence of the present Table 1. I have altered the table by adding several possible sources of bias not listed by Rothbart and Goldsmith. Many of the sources of bias are potentially measurable themselves. For example, the cognitive–perceptual biases of the parent can be evaluated for impact on the temperament score itself, as well as for impact on the score's relation to various important criterion variables. Advanced statistical models could control to some extent for the effects of the 'nuisance' variables.

Concomitant to the increased awareness of the spectrum of measures and their limitations as realizations of theoretical concepts about children, there is an increasing reliance on triangulation among a multivariate network of parent-report and observational measures. For example, a number of recent studies consider child behavior patterns as seen by the parent in relation to those seen by an observer (e.g. Bates, Olson, Pettit, & Bayles, 1982) and a few consider behavior patterns in relation to neuroendocrine processes (e.g. Kagan *et al.*, 1986). Through this kind of research, the concepts of temperament have been both challenged and enriched.

An Example of Recent Measurement Research

A study of Matheny, Wilson, and Thoben (1987) provides a good example of the kinds of studies that are advancing the measurement and concepts of temperament. Matheny *et al.* evaluated the objective and subjective components in mother reports of temperament in children's second year. They compared mother report and laboratory observation on conceptually similar main scales, named Tractability. Tractability included variables such as positive emotional tone and attentiveness, and was derived via factor analysis of the mother-report questionnaire scales (of the Toddler Temperament Scale) and of the battery of laboratory situations. They found modest- to moderate-sized correlations between mother report and laboratory observation.

Previously, the hypothesized objective component of parent temperament reports was established much more solidly in relation to home observation than laboratory observation (Bates & Bayles, 1984). Naturalistic observation support is helpful, but it is insufficient as a demonstration of temperament because it assesses temperament in the presence of the mother, and could be merely a function of the structure the mother provides in the home environment. With the Matheny *et al.* (1987) data, however, there is also strong support for temperament as something that can be perceived in quite different situations by both parents and independent observers.

Matheny *et al.* (1987) also added to understanding of the hypothesized subjective factor in parent reports. They showed that mother personality variables, e.g.

Table 1 Potential sources of measurement error in three infant temperament assessment methods

	A. Rater characteristics relatively independent of infant behavior	B. Bias in assessment as a function of infant behavior or rater–infant interaction	C. Method factors relatively independent of both infant and rater characteristics
I. Parent questionnaires	1. Comprehension of instructions, questions, and rating scales 2. Knowledge of infant's behavior [and general impression rater has of the infant] 3. Inaccurate memory: recency effects, selective recall 4. State when completing rating task, e.g. anxiety 5. Response sets, e.g. social desirability and acquiescence 6. For ratings, knowledge of implicit reference groups 7. Accuracy in detecting and coding rare but important events 8. Kind of impression (if any) rater (mother) wants baby/self to make on researcher	1. Observed infant behavior occurring in response to parental behavior 2. Parents' interpretation of observed behavior a function of parental characteristics	1. Need to inquire about rarely observed situations 2. Adequacy of item selection, wording, and response options

II. Home observation measures (*in-vivo* coding)	1. Limited capacity of coder to process all relevant behavior 2. Coding of low-intensity, ambiguous behaviors 3. State of coder during observation 4. Limits of precision of coding 5. For ratings, knowledge of implicit reference groups 6. Accuracy in detecting and coding of rare, but important events	1. Caregiver–infant interaction moderating behavior coded [including I.8] 2. For ratings, halo effects	1. Change in infant and caregiver behavior due to presence of coder (e.g. decreased conflict) 2. Difficulties of sensitively coding the context of behavior 3. Limitations of number of instances of behavior (esp. rare ones) that can be observed 4. Lack of normative data 5. Lack of stability in reasonable-length time windows – limited sample of behavior
III. Laboratory measures (objective measures scored from videotape in episodes designed to elicit temperament-related reactions)	1. Scoring of low-intensity, ambiguous reactions 2. For ratings, knowledge of implicit reference groups 3. Limited capacity of coder to process all relevant behavior 4. State of coder during observation 5. Limits of precision of coding 6. Accuracy in detecting and coding of rare, but important events	1. Effects of uncontrolled caregiver behavior or other experience prior to/during testing 2. Selection of sample, including completion of testing on the basis of infant reactions (e.g. distress-prone infants not completing procedures) 3. Subtle variations in experimenter reactions to different infants (e.g. more soothing behavior directed toward distress-prone infant)	1. Lack of adequate normative data 2. Limitations on number of instances of behavior that can be recorded 3. Carryover effects in repeated testing 4. Constraints on range of behavioral options 5. Novelty of laboratory setting 6. Adequate identification of episodes appropriate to evoking temperamental reactions

Adapted from Rothbart and Goldsmith (1984). Comments in square brackets and items I. A7 and 8, II. A6 and C5, and III. A3–6 have been added to the table.

emotional stability, have modest correlations with not only the mother reports of tractability, which had been fairly well appreciated previously (Bates & Bayles, 1984), but also, to a lower degree, with the laboratory tractability. This suggests that some of the correlation between parent personality variables and parent ratings of child temperament reflects actual parent–child resemblance, and not subjective bias alone. Plomin and DeFries's (1985) data on adopted vs non-adopted parents and children also suggest this. Aside from providing an excellent example of thoughtful interlacing of parent report and observational indexes of attachment, the Matheny *et al.* work is exciting in its potential for probing the relevance of these measures of temperament to the third level of the general model: estimates of genetic inheritance will be forthcoming eventually, since it is a twin study.

Survey of Instruments

A complete review of the many measures of temperament is beyond the scope of this chapter. However, I will list some major representatives of the different types. Parent- and teacher-report instruments have been developed to tap the package of nine Thomas–Chess dimensions from early infancy, to toddlerhood, to school age. The most widely used here are those developed by Carey and his associates, including the Infant Temperament Questionnaire (Carey & McDevitt, 1978), the Toddler Temperament Scale (Fullard, McDevitt, & Carey, 1984), and for older children, the Behavioral Style Questionnaire (McDevitt & Carey, 1978). Other questionnaires, predominantly used for parent report, have some basis in the Thomas–Chess system, but also introduce other concepts of temperament, focus on fewer than the nine dimensions, or refine the boundaries of dimensions based on psychometric considerations. Widely used questionnaires include three closely related forms of one questionnaire developed by Bates and his associates for infants from 6 to 24 months, the Infant Characteristics Questionnaire and the Child Characteristics Questionnaire (Bates, no date; Bates, Freeland, & Lounsbury, 1979) and revised for preschool children (Finegan & Hood, 1988; Kohnstamm, 1984). Other widely used questionnaires are the Dimensions of Temperament Scale of Lerner and his associates (Lerner, Palermo, Spiro, & Nesselroade, 1982) with one form designed to assess temperament in all ages, and the Infant Behavior Questionnaire of Rothbart, for infants from 3 to 9 months of age (Rothbart, 1981, 1986). The Rothbart instrument has inspired a related questionnaire for toddlers, the Toddler Behavior Assessment Questionnaire (Goldsmith, 1987), and forms for other ages are being developed by Rothbart and her colleagues (H.H. Goldsmith, personal communication, 29 December 1987). Parents are the most frequent respondents on temperament questionnaires, but teacher perceptions are also assessed frequently. Instruments for teacher report are described in Section Four of this volume.

Structured observation techniques have been advanced the furthest by Goldsmith and Rothbart (1988) and Matheny and Wilson and colleagues (e.g. Matheny *et al.*, 1987). So far, these techniques have been primarily applied to infants and toddlers. Naturalistic observation measures are not primary means of assessing temperament, but deserve mention as a backdrop against which other measures of temperament are appraised. One project that has used such measures extensively for this purpose is the Bloomington Longitudinal Study (Bates & Bayles, 1984; Bates *et al.*, 1982; Lee & Bates, 1985; Pettit & Bates, 1984). The measures have ranged from simple frequency counts of temperament-relevant events such as crying, to complex sequences such as resistance to control of particular trouble behaviors, to somewhat impressionistic ratings by observers on the same scales used in the parent-report questionnaires.

For further detail on and critiques of the existing psychometric and validity data the reader may wish to refer to sources cited above, especially Bates (1987), Buss and Plomin (1984), Hubert *et al.* (1982), and Rothbart and Goldsmith (1985).

CONCLUSION

This chapter has addressed core issues in the definition of temperament. I have suggested that the concept has three levels: patterns of behavior, neurological organization, and constitutional origins. Awareness of these levels should help in considering the major issues of definition, especially issues concerning the level of stability expected in a temperamental trait and the roles of experience and development in continuity of temperament. One would expect the biggest roles for experience and development at the first level of definition, the behavior patterns. However, it is also possible that there would be change at the neurological organization level. Change at the third level is not inconceivable, but harder to imagine than change at the first two levels. Ultimately, the ways in which one uses temperament concepts will depend on the purposes. Researchers who are interested in the ontogeny of individual differences in social behavior will probably tend to prefer a concept of temperament that reaches down into the second and third levels, while those who are merely looking for coherent descriptions of early individual differences might prefer not to make any assumptions about the deeper levels of temperament. In either case, however, I recommend that writers be clear about how they are using the construct.

The chapter has also addressed measurement issues in a very general way. It was designed to orient the reader to the most general considerations in choosing operationalizations of temperament constructs and sources in the literature for further information. There is no one 'best' way of measurement. What is best depends certainly on psychometric adequacy of instruments (Hubert *et al.*, 1982), but also on what particular concepts one wishes to assess, and how much time one is willing to spend in describing temperament-like behavior. In general, one would expect that a more extensive description would result in a more generalizable picture of temperament than a shorter one. However, within the limits considered by temperament research so far, this has not yet been shown clearly to be true. It will most likely prove to be so for observational assessments, but it has not yet been proved for questionnaire methods. For example, our temperament questionnaire (Bates *et al.*, 1979), which asks relatively few and relatively general questions, has typically achieved psychometric and validational results comparable in strength of relationships to those achieved by much longer instruments.

The temperament area represents the study of human social development and psychobiology at the same time. It must deal with the enormous conceptual complexity of attempting to integrate these traditionally disparate foci of interest.

Nevertheless, much progress has been made toward mastering the complexities in a relatively few years.

The exciting research trends of today, evident in the chapters of the present volume, will advance understanding of individual differences in the developing child even more rapidly in future years, I would predict. The further consideration of definitional and measurement issues will be the first step toward this goal.

We have asked four of the most prominent conceptualizers of temperament to present their own approaches to defining and measuring temperament. These explications are in the following four chapters.

ACKNOWLEDGMENTS

The author gratefully acknowledges the comments of Dolph Kohnstamm, Mary Rothbart, Jan Strelau, and Ted Wachs on earlier drafts of this chapter.

REFERENCES

Bates, J.E. (no date). Information on the Infant Characteristics Questionnaire. Dept of Psychology, Indiana University, Bloomington, IN 47405.

Bates, J.E. (1980). The concept of difficult temperament. *Merrill-Palmer Quarterly*, **26**, 299–319.

Bates, J.E. (1986). The measurement of temperament. In R. Plomin & J. Dunn (Eds), *The study of temperament: Changes, continuities and challenges* (pp. 1–11). Hillsdale, NJ: Erlbaum.

Bates, J.E. (1987). Temperament in infancy, In J.D. Osofsky (Ed.), *Handbook of infant development*, 2nd edn (pp. 1101–1149). New York: Wiley.

Bates, J.E. & Bayles, K. (1984). Objective and subjective components in mothers' perceptions of their children from age 6 months to 3 years. *Merrill-Palmer Quarterly*, **30**, 111–130.

Bates, J.E. & Bayles, K. (1988). The role of attachment in the development of behavior problems. In J. Belsky & T. Nezworski (Eds), *Clinical implications of attachment* (pp. 253–299). New York: Erlbaum.

Bates, J.E., Freeland, C.A.B., & Lounsbury, M.L. (1979). Measurement of infant difficultness. *Child Development, 50*, 794–803.

Bates, J.E., Maslin, C.A., & Frankel, K.A. (1985). Attachment security, mother–child interaction, and temperament as predictors of behavior problem ratings at age three years. In I. Bretherton & E. Waters (Eds), *Growing points in attachment theory and research. Monographs of the Society for Research in Child Development*, Serial No. 209, 167–193.

Bates, J.E., Olson, S.L. Pettit, G.S., & Bayles, K. (1982). Dimensions of individuality in the mother–infant relationship at six months of age. *Child Development*, **53**, 446–461.

Bell, R.Q. (1968). A reinterpretation of the direction of effects in studies of socialization. *Psychological Review*, **75**, 81–95.

Bornstein, M.H., Gaughran, J., & Homel, P. (1984). Infant temperament: Tradition, critique, new assessments, and prolegomena to future studies. In C. Izard & P.B. Read (Eds), *Measurement of emotions in infants and children*, Vol. 2. New York: Cambridge University Press.

Buss, A.H. & Plomin, R. (1984). *Temperament: Early developing personality traits*. Hillsdale, NJ: Erlbaum.

Carey, W.B. & McDevitt, S.C. (1978). Revision of the Infant Temperament Questionnaire. *Pediatrics*, **61**, 735–739.

Chess, S. & Thomas, A. (1984). *Origins and evolution of behavior disorders: From infancy to early adult life*. New York: Brunner/Mazel.

Crockenberg, S. & Acredolo, C. (1983). Infant temperament ratings: A function of infants, or mothers, or both? *Infant Behavior and Development*, **6**, 61–72.

Eaton, W.O. & Enns, R. (1986). Sex differences in human motor activity level. *Psychological*

Bulletin, **100**, 19–28.

Emde, R.N., Gaensbauer, T.J., & Harmon, R.J. (1976). Emotion expression in infancy. *Psychological Issues Monographs,* No. 37.

Finegan, J.K. & Hood, J. (1988). Factor structure of the Preschool Characteristics Questionnaire and the stability of difficult temperament from 7 months to 4 years. Unpublished paper, Dept of Psychology, The Hospital for Sick Children, Toronto.

Fullard, W., McDevitt, S.C., & Carey, W.B. (1984). Assessing temperament in one- to-three-year-old children. *Journal of Pediatric Psychology,* **9**, 205–216.

Goldsmith, H.H. (1987). The Toddler Behavior Assessment Questionnaire: A preliminary manual. Unpublished, Dept of Psychology, University of Oregon.

Goldsmith, H.H., Buss, A.H., Plomin, R., Rothbart, M.K., Thomas, A., Chess, S., Hinde, R.A., & McCall, R.B. (1987). What is temperament? Four approaches. *Child Development,* **58**, 505–529.

Goldsmith, H.H. & Campos, J.J. (1982). Toward a theory of infant temperament. In R.N. Emde & R.J. Harmon (Eds), *The Development of attachment and affiliative systems* (pp. 161–193). New York: Plenum.

Goldsmith, H.H. & Rieser-Danner, L. (1986). Variation among temperament theories and validation studies of temperament assessment. In G.A. Kohnstamm (Ed.), *Temperament discussed* (pp. 1–10). Lisse (Neth): Swets & Zeitlinger.

Goldsmith, H.H. & Rothbart, M.K. (1988). The Laboratory Temperament Assessment Battery: Locomotor version. Unpublished, Dept of Psychology, University of Oregon.

Greenough, W.T., Black, J.E., & Wallace, C.S. (1987). Experience and brain development. *Child Development,* **58**, 539–559.

Harburg, E., Gleibermann, L., Gershowitz, H., Ozgoren, F., & Kulik, C.L. (1982). Twelve blood markers and measures of temperament. *British Journal of Psychiatry,* **140**, 401–409.

Hubert, N.C. & Wachs, T.D. (1985). Parental perceptions of the behavioral components of infant easiness/difficultness. *Child Development,* **56**, 1525–1537.

Hubert, N.C., Wachs, T.D., Peters-Martin, P., & Gandour, M.J. (1982). The study of early temperament: Measurement and conceptual issues. *Child Development,* **53**, 571–600.

Isabella, R.A., Ward, M.J., & Belsky, J. (1985). An examination of the convergence between multiple sources of information on infant individuality: Neonatal behavior, infant behavior, and temperament reports. *Infant Behavior and Development,* **8**, 283–291.

Kagan, J., Reznick, J.S., & Snidman, N. (1986). Temperamental inhibition in early childhood. In R. Plomin & J. Dunn (Eds), *The study of temperament: Changes, continuities and challenges* (pp. 53–65). Hillsdale, NJ: Erlbaum.

Kohnstamm, G.A. (1984). Bates' Infant Characteristics Questionnaire (ICQ) in the Netherlands. ERIC reports, ED 251 179.

Kohnstamm, G.A. (Ed.) (1986). *Temperament discussed: Temperament and development in infancy and childhood.* Lisse (Neth.): Swets & Zeitlinger.

Lamb, M.E. (1982). Individual differences in infant sociability: Their origins and implications for cognitive development. In H.W. Reese & L.P. Lipsett (Eds), *Advances in child development and behavior,* Vol. 16. New York: Academic Press.

Lee, C. & Bates, J. (1985). Mother–child interaction at age two years and perceived difficult temperament. *Child Development,* **56**, 1314–1326.

Lerner, R.M., Palermo, M., Spiro, A., & Nesselroade, J. (1982). Assessing the dimensions of temperamental individuality across the life-span: The Dimensions of Temperament Survey (DOTS). *Child Development,* **53**, 149–160.

Matheny, A.P., Jr, Riese, M.L., & Wilson, R.S. (1985). Rudiments of infant temperament: Newborn to 9 months. *Developmental Psychology,* **21**, 486–494.

Matheny, A.P., Wilson, R.S., & Thoben, A.S. (1987). Home and mother: Relations with infant temperament. *Developmental Psychology,* **23**, 323–331.

McDevitt, S.C. & Carey, W.B. (1978). The measurement of temperament in 3- to 7-year-old children. *Journal of Child Psychology and Psychiatry,* **19**, 245–253.

Nowakowski, R.S. (1987). Basic concepts of CNS development. *Child Development,* **58**, 568–595.

Pettit, G.S. & Bates, J.E. (1984). Continuity of individual differences in the mother–infant relationship from 6 to 13 months. *Child Development*, **55**, 729–739.

Plomin, R. (1987). Developmental behavioral genetics and infancy. In J.D. Osofsky (Ed.), *Handbook of infant development.* New York: Wiley.

Plomin, R. & DeFries, J.C. (1985). *Origins of individual differences in infancy: The Colorado Adoption Project.* New York: Academic Press.

Plomin, R., Loehlin, J.C., & DeFries, J.C. (1985). Genetic and environmental components of 'environmental' influences. *Developmental Psychology*, **21**, 391–402.

Reed, M.A., Pien, D.L., & Rothbart, M.K. (1984). Inhibitory self-control in preschool children. *Merrill-Palmer Quarterly*, **30**, 131–147.

Riese, M.L. (1987). Temperamental stability between the neonatal period and 24 months. *Developmental Psychology*, **23**, 216–222.

Rosenberg, A. & Kagan, J. (1987). Iris pigmentation and behavioral inhibition. *Developmental Psychobiology*, **20**, 337–392.

Rothbart, M.K. (1981). Measurement of temperament in infancy. *Child Development*, **52**, 569–578.

Rothbart, M.K. (1982). The concept of difficult temperament: A critical analysis of Thomas, Chess & Korn. *Merrill-Palmer Quarterly*, **28**, 35–40.

Rothbart, M.K. (1986). Longitudinal observation of infant temperament. *Developmental Psychology*, **22**, 356–365.

Rothbart, M.K. & Derryberry, D. (1981). Development of individual differences in temperament. In M.E. Lamb & A.L. Brown (Eds), *Advances in developmental psychology*, Vol. 1. Hillsdale, NJ: Erlbaum.

Rothbart, M.K. & Goldsmith, H.H. (1985). Three approaches to the study of infant temperament. *Developmental Review*, **5**, 237–260.

Sankowski, T. (1985). Reaktywnosc dzieci i mlodziezy szkolnej a oddzialywania stymulacyjne. (Reactivity of school children and youth and stimulative action.) *Psychologia Wykchowawcza*, **28**, 377–385. (Abstracted in Pyschinfo Database.)

St James-Roberts, I. & Wolke, D. (1986). Bases for a socially referenced approach to temperament. In G.A. Kohnstamm (Ed.), *Temperament discussed.* Lisse (Neth.): Swets & Zeitlinger.

Stevenson-Hinde, J. (1986). Towards a more open construct. In G.A. Kohnstamm (Ed.), *Temperament discussed.* Lisse (Neth.): Swets & Zeitlinger.

Strelau, J. (1983). *Temperament, personality, activity.* New York: Academic Press.

Strelau, J. (1986). Do biological mechanisms determine the specificity of temperament? In G.A. Kohnstamm (Ed.), *Temperament discussed.* Lisse (Neth.): Swets & Zeitlinger.

Thelen, E. (1989). Self-organization in developmental processes: Can systems approaches work? In M. Gunnar (Ed.), *Systems in development: The Minnesota Symposium in Child Psychology*, Vol. 22. (pp. 77–117). Hillsdale, NJ: Erlbaum.

Thomas, A. & Chess, S. (1977). *Temperament and development.* New York: Bruner/Mazel.

Thomas, A., Chess, S., & Birch H.G. (1968). *Temperament and behavior disorders in children.* New York: New York University Press.

Thomas, A., Chess, S., Birch, H.G., Hertzig, M., & Korn, S. (1963). *Behavioral individuality in early childhood.* New York: New York University Press.

Tucker, D.M. & Williamson, P.A. (1984). Asymmetric neural control systems in human self-regulation. *Psychological Review*, **91**, 185–215.

Weissbluth, M. (1987). *Healthy sleep habits, happy child.* New York: Ballantine.

Wiggins, J.S. (1973). *Personality and prediction: Principles of personality assessment.* Reading, Mass.: Addison-Wesley.

Wilson, R.S. & Matheny, A.P. (1986). Behavior genetics research in infant temperament: The Louisville Twin Study. In R. Plomin & J. Dunn (Eds), *The study of temperament: Changes, continuities and challenges.* Hillsdale, NJ: Erlbaum.

Worobey, J. (1986). Convergence among assessments of temperament in the first month. *Child Development*, **57**, 47–55.

2

Temperament as an Intervening Variable

ROBERT A. HINDE
*MRC Unit on the Development and
Integration of Behaviour, Cambridge*

The current debate about the concept of temperament is in part a consequence of the acquisition by one discipline (developmental psychology) of a concept proving valuable in another (psychiatry), which in turn acquired it from everyday speech. Whilst a rapprochement between these two disciplines is a crucially important goal, it cannot necessarily be assumed that the practical requirements of the clinician mesh precisely with the developmentalist's need for hard theoretical concepts. Temperament has been useful to clinicians in part because it can be used to identify children who pose problems to the caregivers who provide the information for the assessment: the probability that the children so identified will also pose problems in other relationship contexts is a further, but often secondary, consideration. The concept is also of use to the clinician in distinguishing between the possible sources of a problem: Thomas and Chess (in Goldsmith *et al.*, 1987) use as an example the question of whether a child's tendency to cling to mother is due to motivation, ability or temperament.

Developmentalists would like to use temperament primarily to refer to characteristics of, or differences between, individuals that are consistent across situations or over time, usually with the ultimate goal of understanding the causal bases of developmental consistencies or changes in behaviour or the genesis of individual differences. In addition, they often add the requirements that, to be included as 'temperamental', the characteristic in question should appear early and (according to some workers) be 'genetically based'. These secondary requirements are presumably covertly linked to the first, in that characteristics that appear early and are 'genetically based' are thought to be less likely to be influenced by experience and thus to show both cross-situational consistency and continuity over time. The debate arises in part because the instruments devised for measuring 'temperament' both by clinicians and by developmentalists are diverse and measure

Temperament in Childhood   Edited by G. A. Kohnstamm, J. E. Bates and M. K. Rothbart
© 1989 John Wiley & Sons Ltd

very different characteristics, so that it is not at all clear where the boundaries of temperament lie (see also Rutter, 1987).

The following paragraphs have two aims. First, it is suggested that an ethological perspective may pour oil on the turbulence produced by the diverse and partially conflicting requirements of the clinicians and the developmentalists. The second involves consideration of the extent to which the nature of the concept of temperament places limits on its usefulness in 'explaining' the stability of behaviour across situations and over time; and it also emphasizes the importance of considering not just stability or consistency, but also the *coherence* of behaviour.

To those developmentalists who see temperament as a tool for counteracting the heavy emphasis they have put hitherto on environmental variables (Bates, see Chapter 1 in this volume) the first aim will seem a dubious one: ethologists have had to travel in the opposite direction. But perhaps an ethological perspective can soothe the problem just because ethologists are so familiar with comparable ones. In their endeavours to produce simplifying generalizations about the almost infinite diversity of nature, ethologists had to come to terms with the fact that nature could not be crammed into the neat pigeonholes desired by the research worker. Not only is the behaviour of different species organized in different ways, but the labels for types of behaviour such as 'aggressive', even when applied to one species, cover heterogeneous phenomena (e.g. Moyer, 1968). Even more relevant to the present context is the fact that the mechanisms underlying behaviour are diverse: 'motivation' is a useful term to pose the *problem* of the mechanisms underlying changes in responsiveness to a constant stimulus, but the answers depend upon the particular problem under study. Bates acknowledges this in saying that there will always be tension (a 'healthy tension') between interest in natural phenomena and the abstract grids we put over them for the sake of description (Chapter 1). Let us therefore reject once and for all the implication that there ever could be an 'abstract, pure concept of temperament' (Bates, Chapter 1) even if it could never be measured. Let us be clear from the start that the search for that pure concept would be as frustrating, and as dangerous, as hunting the Snark. As Bates emphasizes, research workers see temperament 'from several different perspectives'. Whilst it is useful to see what, if anything, they have in common, evangelical fervour in pursuing the 'pure concept' will be wasted.

Over one issue there is general agreement. Dimensions of temperament are *inferred* from behaviour, and refer to behavioural dispositions or tendencies rather than specific acts. This is intrinsic to all instruments used for measuring temperament, for assessment of any one dimension always depends on data on more than one response or type of behaviour. Temperament thus has some of the status of an intervening variable, though the independent variables that affect it remain hazy. As an intervening variable, its usefulness depends on the number of dependent variables that it ties together, and the success with which it does so (Miller, 1959).

In some cases the intervening variable is inferred not only from behavioural indices, but also from physiological ones (e.g. Kagan, Reznick, & Snidman, 1986; Rothbart, in Goldsmith *et al.*, 1987). Ultimately the bases of each temperament dimension may be identifiable in terms of physiological mechanisms, and temperament may thus also have the status of an hypothetical construct (MacCorquodale & Meehl, 1954).

Because the indices of a temperament dimension, and the variable or mechanism 'underlying' those indices, are correlated, there is a tendency to include both in the same concept. Thus Rothbart (in Goldsmith *et al.*, 1987) includes reactivity in both behaviour and endocrine, etc., systems, and Bates (see Chapter 1) sees the temperament concept as having three levels – behavioural, neurological and constitutional (including genetic). For the sake of conceptual purity, however, it is preferable to resist this tendency, for it could lead to the postulation of mechanisms isomorphous with behaviour. Although it now seems a long time since the instinct concept was laid to rest, ethologists are still very conscious (some will say here hyperconscious) of the dangers of isomorphism. Those mechanisms responsible for aspects of temperament are likely to affect also other types of behaviour, some of which we would be unwilling to refer to as temperament (see also Buss & Plomin, 1984). We can be reasonably sure that what Bates (Chapter 1) refers to as 'the deeper, biological layers of temperament' also have other jobs to do. Whilst differences in 'temperament' may, and indeed must, depend on differences in physiological mechanisms, we could be in difficulties if we included specific mechanisms in our concept of temperament. We hope, of course, that the nature of the temperament variables will eventually be explicable in terms of (probably multiple) physiological mechanisms, but in the meanwhile we would be well advised to avoid begging questions by maintaining conceptual purity. And, as a further point, there is no reason to think that the wide variety of physiological differences on which individual differences in the several aspects of temperament depend share common mechanisms.

We may now return to the two basic issues with the concept of temperament. First, if temperamental dimensions are to be useful in the study of individual differences, they must have some cross-situational consistency and some temporal continuity. Second, if temperament is to have explanatory value for a category of phenomena, its members should have some common properties and its boundaries should be capable of at least approximate definition. These two requirements have become interrelated.

Stability implies a lack of environmental lability, and it is presumably for this reason that 'genetically based' is often advanced as a useful criterion for temperament (e.g. Buss & Plomin, 1984; and see Chapter 1, by Bates). This, however, raises a number of problems. In the first place, all behaviour has genetic bases, and we can make attributions about the genetic bases only of differences between or variance in behaviour: we must not be led back into the old nature–nuture morass by any hint that behaviour can be divided into that which is genetically influenced and that which is not (see also McCall, in Goldsmith *et al.*, 1987). It is for that reason that a definition of temperament in terms of individual differences (or, for that matter, species differences – contrast McCall in Goldsmith *et al.*, 1987) is to be preferred over one in terms of behavioural characters. Other reasons for rejecting 'genetically based' as a criterion have been listed elsewhere (Hinde, in Goldsmith *et al.*, 1987): (a) the cut-off point for heritability required for the criterion of 'genetically based' to be reached is arbitrary; (b) heritability estimates vary with age and with the sample or environment studied; (c) influences on development may be genetic but not heritable; (d) perinatal influences may be neither and (e) the biological contribution includes constraints on and pre-dispositions concerning what is learned, as well as more direct influences on behaviour. Of course some differences in behaviour can be ascribed to genetic differences more readily than others, but that in itself is an unsatisfactory criterion for temperament. Furthermore, as with physiological mechanisms, there is no isomorphism between genes and behaviour, and the genes that affect those items or aspects of behaviour that we like to label as temperament may well also affect aspects of behaviour that we do not label in that way, so we certainly must not be led into supposing that genes can be divided into those that have to do with temperament and those that do not. Finally, on this issue, if we are using temperamental dimensions as tools for assessing individual differences, behavioural differences resulting from environmental influences can be just as stable as those resulting from genetic differences.

Thus the 'genetically based' criterion for temperament must be deemed unsatisfactory. Other criteria that have been suggested – early appearance, the stylistic component of behaviour, individual differences in reactivity and regulation or in the probability of experiencing and expressing the primary emotions and arousal, or clinical relevance – have been discussed elsewhere (Goldsmith *et al.*, 1987). All are useful in some contexts, but none have found ubiquitous acceptance.

Whilst one must agree with Goldsmith (in Goldsmith *et al.*, 1987, p. 506) that the concept should not be 'a repository for all dimensions of individual difference noted in early development', the fact remains that 'just which phenomena define a coherent package remains an unsolved matter'. The concept's usefulness seems to reside in the fact that temperament researchers can identify themselves as having a

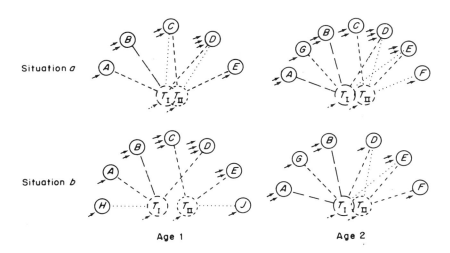

FIGURE 1 Diagrammatic representation of the relations between two temperament dimensions (T_I and T_{II}) in two situations (a and b) at two ages (1 and 2). A, B . . . J represent behavioural outcomes. See text.

common interest in 'investigating the biological bases of personality, in the structure of covariation in behaviour across situations and time, and in other issues' (Goldsmith, in Goldsmith *et al.*, 1987, p. 516).

Given the haziness in the boundaries of the concept, let us return to the question of the dependence of the utility of temperament as an intervening variable on its stability. Diagrammatic representations inevitably simplify nature, but Figure 1 may help to pinpoint the issue. It represents the relations between two temperament dimensions (T_I and T_{II}) in two contemporaneous situations (*a* and *b*) and at two points in time (1 and 2). Each temperament dimension (shown dotted, as it is only an inferred variable) is based on data from a number of actually observed behavioural items (*A, B, C,* etc., continuous circles). The strength of the correlations differ between each case (though shown here by lines of only three degrees of discontinuity). Each of the behavioural items is influenced also by many other factors (continuous arrows). Whether the underlying temperament dimension is also to be thought of as influenced by other factors is unclear at present (discontinuous arrows). The figure is intended to emphasize that:

(1) The correlations between the actually observed items of behaviour and the temperament dimensions, and hence the utility of the latter, vary with time and situation: this is illustrated by the differing degrees of continuity in the temperament circles.
(2) The same item of behaviour may be related to two or more temperament dimensions (e.g. *Ca*1, *Da*1, *Da*2, *Db*2).
(3) A change in situation or age may lead to a given temperament dimension being inferred from additional items of behaviour (e.g. at age 1, T_I is related to *H* at *b* but not *a*; T_I is related to *G* at age 2 but not age 1).
(4) The diversity of behavioural items related to a given temperament dimension may increase (or decrease) with age (age 2 versus age 1).
(5) The several temperament dimensions may be correlated with each other to an extent that varies with age and situation (illustrated by the extent of overlap between the temperament circles).

Thus the relations between temperament dimensions in one situation may differ with age, between boys and girls, or for either sex between home and school. Indeed, in any one situation there may be rather poor correlations between temperament as assessed by two interactants (e.g. mother and father). In addition to characteristics of each parent, such as negative emotionality, affecting perceptions of the child's temperament (reviewed by Bates, 1987), there is suggestive evidence that discrepancies are also related to differences between the relationships of the two interactants with the child (Hinde & Tobin, 1986). This is in harmony with the view that although temperament is derived from behaviour, that behaviour differs according to the characteristics of the interactant and the child's relationship with him/her. Stevenson-Hinde (1988) has suggested that measures of individual characteristics could be arranged along a continuum from person characteristics to relationship characteristics, with height and weight but few psychological characteristics at the person end, and the various temperament dimensions close to, but at varying distances from, it.

Table I Spearman correlation coefficients between temperamental characteristics and behaviour with mother and with adults/peers in preschool. Items selected to illustrate different types of relations between home and school correlations

	Home			School
Intense (42 months) with				
Child friendly mother	.36*		Child interacts peers	.31*
Child hostile mother	.34*		Child plays interactively	.35*
Mother reactive hostile child	.32*			
Active (50 months) with				
Child neutral speech	−.43**		Child active hostile peers	.39*
Mother friendly child	−.38*		Adult active hostile child	.32*
Mother expresses pleasure	−.46**		Adult reactive hostile child	.37*
Shy (50 months) with				
Boy hostile mother	.50*		Boy reactive hostile peers	.26
Girl hostile mother	−.33		Girl reactive hostile peers	−.50*
Moody (50 months) with				
Mother friendly child	−.43**		Child interacts peers	.49**
Mother reactive hostile child	.33*		Child controls peers	.34*
			Adult reactive hostile peers	.32*

* $P < .05$, ** $P < .01$, two-tailed.

Table 1, taken from Hinde & Tobin (1986), illustrates some different ways in which temperament at home may relate to behaviour at home and school. *Intense* children showed generally similar behaviour in the two situations: they tended to show both more friendly and more hostile behaviour to the mother at home, and at school interacted more with peers, though the proportions of hostile and friendly interactions were not proportionately changed. The characteristic *Active* was related to similar but different behaviour: at home Active children had fewer friendly interactions with their mothers than non-Active children, but at school they showed more hostility to teachers and peers. In the case of *Shy* children, Shy girls tended to have better relationships with their mothers than non-Shy girls, but Shy boys tended to have worse ones. This can be interpreted as a consequence of the value system of the mother (Hinde & Stevenson-Hinde, 1986; Simpson & Stevenson-Hinde, 1985). But it appears to have carried over into the personality of the child, because Shy boys tended (non-significantly) to be more hostile to peers in school than non-Shy boys, whereas Shy girls were significantly less hostile. Finally, *Moody* seemed to be 'expressed' directly in school whereas its correlates at home concerned items indicating the mother's response to its expression (Hinde, Stevenson-Hinde, & Tamplin, 1985).

We can thus speak about the coherence of temperament across situations, an issue beyond that of cross-situational consistency or what is 'age appropriate' for the individual. But this requires us to address the dialectical relations between the level of individual behaviour and those of interactions and relationships (Hinde & Stevenson-Hinde, 1987).

Clearly the safe course, though an apparently difficult one, is to stick to the view that temperament is what the instrument measures. Each instrument uses several items to infer each temperament dimension. For the clinician, the utility of the dimensions depends on their ability to discriminate problem and no-problem children, and to localize the sources of the former's difficulties. For the developmentalist, their utility depends on the extent to which they provide *coherent* explanations of the behaviour of individuals across situations or over time, and thus pave the way for the understanding of process. The search for physiological mechanisms is an important further step, involving yet another level of analysis.

REFERENCES

Bates, J.E. (1987). Temperament in infancy. In J.D. Osofsky (Ed.), *Handbook of infant development*, 2nd edn. New York: Wiley.

Buss, A.H. & Plomin, R. (1975). *A temperament theory of personality development*. New York: Wiley.

Buss, A.H. & Plomin, R. (1984). *Temperament: early developing personality traits*, Hillsdale, NJ: Erlbaum.

Goldsmith, H.H., Buss, A.H., Plomin, R., Rothbart, M.K., Thomas, A., Chess, S., Hinde, R.A., & McCall, R.B. (1987). Roundtable: what is temperament? Four approaches. *Child Development*, **58**, 505–529.

Hinde, R.A. & Stevenson-Hinde, J. (1986). Relationships, personality, and the social situation. In R. Gilmour & S. Duck (Eds), *The emerging field of personal relationships*. Hillsdale, NJ: Erlbaum.

Hinde, R.A. & Stevenson-Hinde, J. (1987). Interpersonal relationships and child development. *Developmental Review*, **7**, 1–21.

Hinde, R.A., Stevenson-Hinde, J., & Tamplin, A. (1985). Characteristics of 3- to 4-year-olds assessed at home and their interactions in preschool. *Developmental Psychology*, **21** (2), 130–140.

Hinde, R.A. & Tobin, C. (1986). Temperament at home and behaviour at preschool. In G.A. Kohnstamm (Ed.), *Temperament discussed*. Lisse (Neth.): Swets & Zeitlinger.

Kagan, J., Reznick, J.S., & Snidman, N. (1986). Temperamental inhibition in early childhood. In R. Plomin & J. Dunn (Eds), *The study of temperament: changes, continuities and challenges*. Hillsdale, NJ: Erlbaum.

MacCorquodale, K. & Meehl, P.E. (1954). Edward C. Tolman. In W.K. Estes *et al.* (Eds), *Modern learning theory*. New York: Appleton-Century-Crofts.

Miller, N.E. (1959). Liberalization of basic S–R concepts. In S. Koch (Ed.), *Psychology, a study of science: study 1*, Vols 1 and 2. New York: McGraw-Hill

Moyer, K.E. (1968). Kinds of aggression and their physiological basis. *Commun. Behav. Biol.*, **2**, 65–87.

Rutter, M. (1987). Temperament, personality and personality disorder. *British Journal of Psychiatry*, **150**, 443–458.

Simpson, A.E. & Stevenson-Hinde, J. (1985). Temperamental characteristics of three- to four-year-old boys and girls and child–family interactions. *Journal of Child Psychology and Psychiatry*, **26**, 43–53.

Stevenson-Hinde, J. (1968). Individuals in relationships. In R.A. Hinde & J. Stevenson-Hinde (Eds), *Relationships within families: mutual influences*. Oxford: Oxford University Press.

3

The Regulative Theory of Temperament as a Result of East–West Influences

JAN STRELAU
University of Warsaw

The environmentalistic approach by which personality psychology was dominated for many years meant that there was no, or only marginal, attention to theories stressing the importance of biological factors in co-determining individual differences.

Facts collected in the last two decades show that there are individual differences in behavior characteristics that cannot be completely explained by the social factor. It has also become clear that many human behavioral traits must be partly accounted for by physiological mechanisms regulating the level of arousal.

To describe individual characteristics present since the first weeks of life and with a biological background (whether genetically determined or shaped during development), and at the same time not belonging to the sphere of abilities, many researchers use the notion of temperament. There are differences in defining temperament, but there seems to be agreement that this concept refers to basic behavioral characteristics in which individuals differ, these differences being to a high degree determined by endogenous factors, as primarily suggested by the ancient Greek philosophers and physicians, Hippocrates and Galen.

Despite agreement in the very broad understanding of the concept of temperament, it has to be said that there exist many theories of temperament that differ, sometimes essentially, from each other. These differences concern, among other things, definitions of temperament, views regarding the number and structure of temperament traits, and the importance of specific factors determining individual differences in temperament. Some temperament theories have a descriptive value only, these being mainly based on a psychometric approach. However, others claim to explain what temperament is and what its underlying mechanisms are. Some of the theories, mainly those developed in the United States, are child-centered, whereas others center mainly on adults.

Temperament in Childhood   Edited by G.A. Kohnstamm, J.E. Bates and M.K. Rothbart
© 1989 John Wiley & Sons Ltd

The theory of temperament to be presented in this chapter is termed the Regulative Theory of Temperament (RTT). It derives from at least three sources:

(1) The author's studies conducted over a long period within the framework of the Pavlovian typology of higher nervous activity (Pavlov, 1951–52) as modified by Nebylitsyn (1972a) and Teplov (1964).

(2) The theories of arousal (activation), with special attention to the concepts of optimal level of arousal (Hebb, 1955) and arousability (Gray, 1964), the latter being understood as a trait that refers to relatively stable individual differences in the level of arousal.

(3) The theory of action as developed by Leontev (1978) and modified by Tomaszewski (1978), according to which human activity has to be considered as the main way the individual regulates his/her relationship with the external world.

PAVLOV'S TYPOLOGY

Since the Pavlovian typology, with the modification introduced by neo-Pavlovian typologists, was the starting point of the RTT, a short presentation of this theory is needed.[1]

Pavlov's research on the efficiency of conditioning in dogs drew his attention to the fact that there exist properties of the processes of excitation and inhibition of the central nervous system (CNS) that are responsible for individual differences in behavior. The combination of these properties, which refer mainly to the cortex, constitutes the types of CNS regarded as the physiological basis of temperament. Pavlov often used the terms type of nervous system and temperament interchangeably.

There are three fundamental properties of the CNS – strength, balance (equilibrium), and mobility of the nervous processes (excitation and inhibition). The strength of the nervous system refers to the functional capacity (endurance) of the CNS, manifested in the ability to withstand prolonged or strong excitation (or inhibition). The occurrence of protective (transmarginal) inhibition, expressed in decrease of performance (reaction) under strong or prolonged stimulation, was regarded by Pavlov as the main indicator of strength of excitation. The strength of excitation is indexed by how intense stimuli must be in order to develop the state of transmarginal inhibition. As assumed by Nebylitsyn (1972a) and Teplov (1964) there exists a reverse relationship between strength of excitation, understood as the functional capacity of the CNS, and sensitivity, as measured by sensory threshold. According to these authors, the dimension of strength of excitation comprises both endurance and sensitivity, regarded as two extremes of this CNS property.

Equilibrium of nervous processes was regarded by Pavlov as the property which results from the ratio between strength of excitation and strength of inhibition. Nebylitsyn (1972a), as well as most neo-Pavlovian typologists, considers equilibrium to be a secondary property.

For Pavlov, the essence of mobility consists in 'the ability to give way – according to external conditions – to give priority to one impulse before the other, excitation before inhibition and conversely' (Pavlov, 1952, p. 540). Mobility of the nervous system manifests itself in the speed and adequacy of reactions to changes in the surroundings. On the basis of research showing that the ability to react quickly and adequately to changes in the surroundings does not correlate with the speed with which the nervous processes are initiated and terminated, Teplov (1963) identified a new property of the CNS, which he called lability. This property is supposed to be orthogonal to mobility, but refers, together with mobility, to the temporal characteristics of behavior. It is expressed in the speed with which reactions are initiated and terminated.

In spite of the many possible configurations of the three basic nervous-system properties, Pavlov, being under the influence of the ancient Greek typology, limited his classification of the CNS types to the following four:

(1) the strong, balanced, and mobile type, treated as equivalent to the sanguine temperament;
(2) the strong, balanced, and slow type – equivalent to the phlegmatic temperament;
(3) the strong, unbalanced type with predominance of excitation over inhibition – equivalent to the choleric temperament;
(4) the weak type – similar to the melancholic temperament.

In describing the nature of the three fundamental properties of the CNS Pavlov did not refer to the neurophysiological or biochemical mechanisms underlying these properties. He and his followers mostly concentrated on the functional aspects of excitation and inhibition by showing the role of CNS properties in the individual's ability to adapt to the environment. Pavlov conceptualized the types of CNS, as well as the separate properties, as being innate, and relatively immune to environmental influences. This position has been shared by neo-Pavlovian typologists (see Merlin, 1973; Nebylitsyn, 1972a; Teplov, 1964).

In the 1930s two of Pavlov's students – Krasnogorsky and Ivanov-Smolensky – transferred the application of the CNS typology from studies on animals to those on children. Krasnogorsky (1953), who used the conditioned response (CR) method for diagnosing CNS type in children, gave the first systematic psychological description of the four Pavlovian temperaments. In contrast to most of the Pavlovians, Krasnogorsky stated that the types of CNS are changeable.

Ivanov-Smolensky (1935) used speed of conditioning as the main criterion for diagnosing CNS properties in children. He drew attention to the important fact that children may be ascribed different types of CNS depending on the kind of unconditioned stimuli used in the CR procedure. Thus he was the first to discover that traits (in this case CNS properties) established in laboratory settings are stimulus- and reaction-specific. Later research has confirmed this rule, e.g. in CNS properties in adults (Nebylitsyn, 1972b; Strelau, 1972), in resistance to stress (Lacey, 1967), and in emotionality or neuroticism (Fahrenberg, 1987).

In the RTT, advantage was taken of many of the considerations of Pavlov and the neo-Pavlovians, as well as of the more than 50 years of research on types of the CNS. First of all, the idea that temperament traits have a biological background and that they should be treated in a functional way has been one of the basic assumptions of the RTT. Use has been made of many of the methods aimed at diagnosing the Pavlovian properties. This was possible because some of the temperament traits as presented in the RTT (reactivity and mobility of behavior) are comparable on the operational level with the Pavlovian properties.

Using Hebb's (1955) terminology one may say that the Pavlovian typology of the CNS is a theory that refers mainly to the conceptual nervous system. The guiding principle of the RTT was to develop a psychological concept of temperament in which human behavior, activity, would be the core of the theory. One of the consequences of the switch from physiology to psychology was the use of a psychological terminology for labeling the temperament traits, instead of the physiological notions of strength, balance, and mobility of the nervous processes (excitation and inhibition). In the RTT Pavlov's old-fashioned typological thinking has been rejected, as well as his constitutional approach, according to which the type of CNS (temperament) should be treated as a genotype, insusceptible to changes under environmental influences.

THE REGULATIVE THEORY OF TEMPERAMENT

Basic Assumptions

The basic assumptions of the RTT were formulated in the late 1960s and early 1970s (Strelau, 1969, 1970, 1974). The theory is however, still in a state of development (Strelau, 1983, 1985b), with essential contributions by my students and co-workers (see e.g. Eliasz, 1974, 1985; Klonowicz, 1974, 1985; Matysiak, 1985).

In our theory *temperament* is defined as *a set of relatively stable features of the organism that reveal themselves in such formal traits of behavior as energetic level and temporal characteristics. Being primarily determined by inborn physiological mechanisms, temperament is subjected to slow changes caused by maturation and by some environmental factors.*

Stability

The separate components of the definition need brief explanation. In speaking about relatively stable features, we assume that temperament, in comparison with other psychological phenomena, is less susceptible to change. However, temperament, like other psychological and physiological characteristics, does change in the process of maturation (Leites, 1972; Strelau, 1984; Thomas & Chess, 1977; Troshikhin, Kozlova, Kruchenko, & Sirotsky, 1971). These changes are mainly due to developmental and life-span changes (progressive and regressive) in the physiological mechanisms underlying temperament. Some changes in temperament characteristics may also occur under the influence of environmental factors, such as nutrition, long-lasting or strong stimulation, chronic deprivation, climate, population density, etc. Changes in temperament under environmental influences do not occur from moment to moment or from day to day. In one of the studies conducted in our laboratory, Eliasz (1981) gives some empirical support for the hypothesis that reactivity, considered in our theory as one of the basic temperament traits, may change over several years in adolescents under such conditions as loud traffic noise and high density of population in the district.

Formal Characteristics

The statement that temperament traits reveal themselves in the formal characteristics of behavior means, among other things, that temperament traits manifest themselves in every behavior, in all human actions, independent of their content and direction. Any behavior may be characterized by its intensity (magnitude) as well as by its speed or duration. Contrary to the traditional approach, we assume that temperament manifests itself not only in emotions (cf. Goldsmith & Campos, 1982) or in motor reactions, or in both, as many psychologists claim, but also in all other kinds of mental activities. This position has support in the literature (Leites, 1956, 1972; Malkov, 1966; Merlin, 1973) as well as in our studies (Klonowicz, 1979; Matczak, 1985; Strelau, 1983, 1984). In speaking about the formal characteristics referring to temperament, we want also to stress that temperament traits do not exist as isolated phenomena. They appear, as a rule, only as given characteristics of reactions and behaviors. This means that the assessment of temperament is always involved in a given kind of behavior from which the energetic and temporal features have been extracted.

Energetic Traits

According to the RTT there are two basic dimensions of temperament responsible for individual differences in the energetic characteristics of behavior – reactivity and activity.[2] Both these traits, specifically defined in our theory, have a tradition in temperament research. For example, reactivity was one of the main concepts in Thomas, Chess, and Birch's (1968) theory of temperament. In the first stage of their conceptualizations in this area they used the term reactivity as a synonym of temperament. Activity also belongs to the energetic traits, which occupy an important position in the structure of temperament in most theories (see e.g. Buss & Plomin, 1984; Guilford & Zimmerman, 1956; Nebylitsyn, 1976; Thomas & Chess, 1977). For the pioneers in studying temperament (Heymans & Wiersma, 1906–09), activity was regarded as one of the three dimensions (besides emotionality and perseverance) constituting the structure of temperament. According to these Dutch authors, activity is revealed in the way people perform tasks when using free time or working. This understanding of activity, which refers to goal-directed behavior, is very close to our conceptualization.

The concept of reactivity was introduced to our theory at the end of the 1960s (Strelau, 1969, 1974) and adapted by Rothbart to her developmental theory of temperament in a similar way (Derryberry & Rothbart, 1984; Rothbart, 1986). It is based on findings from experimental research that individuals differ in the intensity or magnitude of their reactions to stimuli (situations). Reactivity understood as a temperament trait reveals itself in a relatively stable and characteristic way for a given individual intensity (magnitude) of reactions. It co-determines, among other things, sensitivity (sensory and emotional) as measured, for example, by sensory threshold, and endurance (capacity to work). The latter reveals itself in the ability to react adequately to strong or long-lasting stimulation. The reactivity trait closely resembles the neo-Pavlovian concept, discussed above, of strength of the nervous system in regard to excitation, especially at the level of operational measurement.

The physiological mechanism of reactivity includes probably all the physiological systems responsible for the regulation of level of arousal (activation). Certain features of the endocrine system, autonomic nervous system, the brainstem, and subcortical and cortical centers should be mentioned here. These systems operate as a functional unit with a fairly stable structure. Depending on the behavior or reaction being measured, the significance of each system within this unit in determining the energetic level of responses (behavior) may vary. There exist intra- and interindividual differences in the level of functioning of each separate system included within the unit. These differences are probably one of the main sources of the modality- (stimulus-) and/or reaction-specific temperament characteristics. In order to stress the individual-specific configuration of systems responsible for the level of activation and determining the level of reactivity I prefer to use the concept *neuroendocrine individuality*.

Individuals who occupy extreme positions on the reactivity dimension differ essentially in the level of arousal. In high-reactive individuals, characterized by high sensitivity and low endurance, the physiological mechanism of reactivity enhances (augments) stimulation. Using Gray's (1964) concept of arousability we may say that these individuals have a high level of arousability. Low-reactive individuals, whose physiological mechanism suppresses (reduces) stimulation, have a low level of arousability. This explains their low sensitivity and high endurance.

Considering the intensity (magnitude) of reaction as the main indicator of reactivity we should differentiate between state-reactivity and trait-reactivity. State-reactivity is a resultant of the intensity of acting stimuli (this intensity being determined by their physical parameters as well as by their meaning), the actual level of activation, and the individual's trait-reactivity. It means that in experimental conditions we are always measuring state-reactivity which is co-determined by trait-reactivity, understood as a relatively stable tendency to react to stimuli (situations) with given intensity or magnitude (Strelau, 1983).

The second temperament trait which belongs to the energetic characteristic of behavior is activity, introduced to the RTT at the beginning of the 1970s (Strelau, 1969, 1970, 1974; see also Eliasz, 1974). Activity has in our theory a specific meaning and special significance: activity regulates the stimulative value of behavior and/or situations, in correspondence with the individual's need for stimulation, the latter being co-determined by his/her level of reactivity. According to our theory, activity is a temperament trait which reveals itself in the amount and range of undertaken actions (goal-directed behaviors) of a given stimulative value.

As follows from the concept of optimal level of activation introduced by Hebb (1955) and adapted to the RTT by Eliasz (1974), individuals supply themselves with stimuli until they attain an optimal level of activation (arousal). When excessively stimulated, activities are undertaken to reduce activation to an optimal level.

Maintenance of an optimal level of arousal is one of the individual's basic needs. Activity is regarded as the temperament trait that plays the primary regulatory function in providing an optimal level of arousal. Reactivity and, especially, activity maintain arousal at an optimal level by regulating the stimulative value of behavior and situations the individual is confronted with. This crucial role was one of the main reasons for labeling our conception as the regulative theory of temperament.

The regulation of stimulation by means of activity takes place in two different ways: (a) activity by itself is a source of stimulation; (b) by means of activity the individual may avoid or approach situations of a given stimulative value.

There are at least three reasons to consider activity as a *direct* source of stimulation:

(1) Motor (physical) activity result in arousal of the receptors which transmit this arousal to higher nervous centers. This is the well-known mechanism of afferent feedback.

(2) Most human behaviors have an emotional connotation. The emotional state accompanying a given action comprises the activating factor; activities which carry risk or threat may be mentioned as examples here.

(3) Activities differ in stimulation depending on the degree of difficulty and complexity in their performance. The more difficult and more complex the activity, the higher the stimulation being generated.

Activity regarded as an *indirect* source of stimulation plays the role of an 'organizer' of sources of stimulation. By means of activity the individual approaches or avoids stimulation delivered from the environment – surroundings, situations, settings, tasks, social demands, etc.

Reactivity and activity are functionally related. High-reactive individuals, whose physiological mechanism enhances stimulation (with high arousability), tend to perform activity of low stimulative value in order to ensure an optimal level of activation. Thus we may say that they are characterized by low activity understood as a temperament trait. Low-reactive individuals are characterized by high temperament activity. This results from the fact that their physiological mechanism suppresses stimulation (low arousability). To ensure an optimal level of activation, activity of high stimulative value has to be performed by the low reactives.

Any kind of activity, regardless of its specificity and direction, has a given stimulative value – shaking a rattle, climbing, playing football, driving a car, solving a puzzle, or robbing a bank. Temperament activity does not determine the kind of behavior an individual performs. In determining the kind and/or direction of activity the social environment plays the crucial role. Temperament, however, does determine to a large extent whether the individual prefers activities of high or low stimulative value. Several studies conducted in our laboratory on schoolchildren, students, and professional people showed that, depending on the level of reactivity, individuals prefer activities differing in stimulation load (Eliasz, 1974, 1981; Klonowicz, 1985; Strelau, 1983, 1984).

In the early stage of development, activity, understood as the regulator of stimulation, is unspecific. During the process of learning and socialization the individual acquires activities which serve, among other things, as stimulation regulators. There are essential differences between reactivity and activity, and two of them are of special importance.

(1) Reactivity, being a primary temperament trait, is directly determined by the physiological mechanism which modulates stimulation. In the case of activity the physiological mechanism is only a starting point. It means that the individual has a biologically determined tendency to develop activity of a stimulative value for which the physiological mechanism of reactivity is adequate. Since the social environment has an essential influence on the development of the child's activity, it happens that the stimulative value of temperament activity does not necessarily correspond with the biologically determined level of reactivity. For example, a high-reactive child may be forced by parents to perform highly stimulating activities which exceed his/her capacity determined by the level of reactivity. A long-lasting discordance between the stimulative value of activity (too low or too high) and the individual's reactivity may result in behavioral disorders. It has been shown in two of our studies (Strelau, 1984), conducted on 8- to 9-year-old children, that behavior disorders occur in high-reactive individuals whose level of activity is over their biologically determined need for stimulation. In one of the groups the disorders were expressed in psychomotor hyperarousal, whereas in the other one emotional hyperarousal was observed.

(2) Reactivity reveals itself primarily in the intensity (magnitude) of reactions which are responses to given stimuli. In other words, this trait is expressed mainly in reactive behavior. However, activity is concerned with operant, goal-directed behavior, which is often not directly bound to actual stimuli. In most concepts of temperament, in which no distinction between operant and reactive behavior is made, both these kinds of behavior are put together under one label 'activity' (Buss & Plomin, 1984; Guilford & Zimmerman, 1956; Nebylitsyn, 1976; Thurstone, 1951). Without differentiating between these two phenomena, it is impossible to show how important activity, as understood in our theory, is in regulating the stimulative value of human behavior.

Temporal Traits

As mentioned above, temporal traits are also part of the structure of temperament as seen from the perspective of the RTT but will not be fully discussed here. However, among the six traits referring to the temporal characteristics (see Strelau, 1983, 1985a) it is worth mentioning that mobility of behavior has a distinguished place in our theory. This is due to the importance it plays in human life. As shown in our studies (Gorynska & Strelau, 1979; Strelau, 1983), mobility, understood as the ability to react quickly and adequately in response to environmental changes, is a secondary trait. It comprises such first-order factors as persistence, recurrence, regularity, speed, and tempo of reactions.

Some Regularities Based on Empirical Evidence

During the almost 20 years of research on temperament aimed at developing the RTT, many experiments and field studies have been carried out (Eliasz, 1974, 1981; Klonowicz, 1974, 1985; Matczak, 1985; Strelau, 1969, 1983, 1984, 1985b). Most of them, conducted on adults or adolescents, were centered on the relationships between temperament traits, mainly reactivity, and:

(1) *efficiency* of performance under behavior or situations of different stimulative value (Strelau, 1988);
(2) *style of action* aimed at modifying the stimulative value of behavior or situations;
(3) *preference* of activity or surroundings of a given stimulative value.

Also many studies were aimed at examining the interrelationships between temperament, understood, broadly speaking, as a result of biological evolution, and personality, conceived as a product of the social environment.[3] Findings important for temperament research in children are presented very briefly below.

Efficiency

Efficiency of performance in situations of very high stimulative value decreases in high-reactive individuals as compared with low reactives. High-reactive individuals are also less efficient in situations of very high stimulation value than in normal situations. If they do not show a performance decrement under intense stimulation, high-reactive individuals pay higher psychophysiological costs, e.g. in the form of elevating the level of state-anxiety. Low-reactive individuals are at a similar disadvantage, in efficiency of performance as well as in psychophysiological costs, in situations of extremely low stimulative value (e.g. deprivation).

Style of Action

Depending on their level of reactivity, individuals differ in their style of action. The style of action is defined as the typical manner in which an action is performed. Taking as a point of departure the distinction between basic and auxiliary actions introduced by Tomaszewski (1978), we were able to show that high-reactive individuals perform essentially more auxiliary actions as compared with low-reactive persons. Whereas *basic* actions lead directly to the attainment of a certain goal, the function of *auxiliary* actions is to organize conditions for the performance of basic ones. For example, to summarize the content of a given book (basic action), the pupil checks several times which book has to be summarized, he/she cleans the desk, tests now and again whether the summary corresponds with the text of the book, makes a first draft, asks the parents or somebody else to read the summary before making a clean copy of it, etc. These behaviors belong to the category of auxiliary actions, which play the role of safeguarding, facilitating, or simplifying the performance of basic actions. Auxiliary actions lower the stimulative value of the activity or of the situation in which the activity is performed. This explains why high-reactive individuals, in order to decrease the stimulative value of performed activity, or of the situation in which performance occurs, undertake more auxiliary actions as compared with low reactives. Thus one may say that, depending on the level of reactivity, individuals use different strategies (styles) aimed at modifying the intensity of stimulation. This pattern has been observed in individuals differing in age (from 3-year-old children to adults) and performing different tasks, such as, for example, playing games, taking part in a school play, doing a professional job, etc. (see Friedensberg, 1985; Strelau, 1983, 1984, 1988).

Preference

When given a choice among behaviors or situations differing in intensity of stimulation, according to our studies, high-reactive individuals prefer situations (behaviors) of lower stimulative value than do low-reactive people. Among individuals performing risky or demanding activities (e.g. sportsmen, pilots, parachutists, steelworkers) there are significantly more low-reactive than high-reactive individuals.

Temperament and Personality

Taking into account the relationship between temperament and personality we have concentrated our research on selected personality traits on the one hand, and on reactivity on the other. In general, we have found that the behavioral characteristics of personality traits ascribed to high-reactive individuals have a lower stimulative value as compared with the characteristics typical for low reactives. Some examples may be given to illustrate this pattern. Whereas high-reactive individuals have a rather cautious attitude, low-reactive persons are characterized by a hazardous attitude. This has been found in two studies conducted on high-school students performing decision-making tasks during hazardous games (Kozlowski, 1977; Przymusinski & Strelau, 1986). Another experiment with high-school students has shown that, whilst high reactives are submissive to group pressure, low reactives in the same situation are resistant to group pressure (Strelau, 1983). In the above-mentioned experiments the assumption was made that a hazardous attitude and resistance to group pressure are expressed in activities of higher stimulative value in comparison with a cautious attitude and with submissiveness to group pressure. Detailed descriptions of the studies presented here as well as of other research on personality–temperament relationships may be found elsewhere (Eliasz, 1974, 1981; Strelau, 1983, 1984).

Measurement

To finish the presentation of the RTT, some information regarding the diagnostic tools measuring temperament traits is needed. The method most often used in our laboratory is the Strelau Temperament Inventory (STI), which has gained international popularity (see Strelau, Angleitner, and Ruch (1989) for its use in some studies in Western countries). The STI contains 134 items with a three-point rating scale. Primarily aimed at measuring the Pavlovian properties – strength of excitation, strength of inhibition, mobility, and balance of nervous processes – this inventory also measures reactivity and mobility as understood in the RTT. The details of the STI as well as reliability and validity data are described elsewhere (Strelau, 1983; Strelau *et al.*, in press).

For measuring reactivity a special diagnostic tool was elaborated, i.e. the Reactivity Rating Scale (RRS), in three equivalent versions: RRS_1 (for preschool children), RRS_2 (for primary school children), and RRS_3 (for secondary school pupils) (Friedensberg & Strelau, 1982; Strelau, 1983). The RRSs are used by school and nursery teachers and are based on samples of typical behavior in preschool and school situations. The kinds of behavior selected are concerned with tasks and social situations. The nine items of the RRS_1 (rated on five-point scales) are given as examples.

(1) Is capable of concentrated attention
(2) Is resistant to setbacks
(3) Shows initiative in organizing joint play with others
(4) Does not abandon current activity on encountering obstacles
(5) In the presence of an unknown adult behaves as usual
(6) Shows no tension when confronted with an important task
(7) Willingly carries out tasks demanding considerable exertion
(8) In an unknown group of persons behaves as usual
(9) Seeks the company of other children

Temperament traits, especially reactivity, can also be measured in experimental settings. Some of the neo-Pavlovian methods aimed at diagnosing the CNS properties are used in our laboratory. As mentioned before, this is possible due to the fact that some of our temperament traits (reactivity and mobility), when considered on the operational level, are comparable with the Pavlovian CNS properties (strength and mobility of nervous processes). Among these methods the measures based on reaction-time (RT) experiments have gained the highest popularity: for example, slope of the RT curve and simple RT under repeatedly applied stimuli.[4]

CONCLUSION

The RTT presented above in a very short and schematic way, is an outcome of many influences which stem from the East and the West, but also from our own conceptualizations. Together with the neo-Pavlovian typology, as elaborated by Soviet researchers, the RTT belongs among the most popular theories of temperament developed in Eastern Europe.

ACKNOWLEDGMENTS

Preparation of this chapter was supported by the Ministry of National Education (Grant: RPBP III. 25).

NOTES

[1] A detailed description of the concept of types of nervous system and of the nervous system properties as developed by Pavlov and his followers may be found in many publications (Mangan, 1982; Nebylitsyn, 1972a; Strelau, 1975, 1983, 1985a; Teplov, 1964).

[2] Because of limitations on space I will concentrate in the presentation of the RTT only on the energetic characteristics of temperament.

[3] The differences and similarities between the two concepts – temperament and personality – have been presented in detail elsewhere (Strelau, 1987). The realization of possible interrelationships between temperament and personality seems to be of special importance for the developmental approach in temperament.

[4] These methods as well as all the other diagnostic procedures used for assessing the CNS properties are thoroughly described by Nebylitsyn (1972a) and Strelau (1969, 1983).

REFERENCES

Buss, A.H. & Plomin, R. (1984). *Temperament: Early developing personality traits.* Hillsdale, NJ: Erlbaum.

Derryberry, D. & Rothbart, M.K. (1984). Emotion, attention, and temperament. In C.E. Izard, J. Kagan, & R. Zajonc (Eds), *Emotion, cognition and behavior* (pp. 132–166). Cambridge: Cambridge University Press.

Eliasz, A. (1974). *Temperament a osobowosc* [Temperament and personality]. Wroclaw (Poland): Ossolineum.

Eliasz, A. (1981). *Temperament a system regulacji stymulacji* [Temperament and system of stimulation regulation]. Warszawa (Poland): Panstwowe Wydawnictwo Naukowe.

Eliasz, A. (1985). Transactional model of temperament. In J. Strelau (Ed.), *Temperamental bases of behavior: Warsaw studies on individual differences* (pp. 41–78). Lisse (Neth.): Swets & Zeitlinger.

Fahrenberg, J. (1987). Concepts of activation and arousal in the theory of emotionality (neuroticism): A multivariate conceptualization. In J. Strelau & H.J. Eysenck (Eds), *Personality dimensions and arousal* (pp. 99–120). New York: Plenum.

Friedensberg, E. (1985). Reactivity and individual style of work exemplified by constructional-type task performance: A developmental study. In J. Strelau (Ed.), *The biological bases of personality and behavior: Theories, measurement techniques, and development*, Vol. 1 (pp. 241–253). Washington: Hemisphere.

Friedensberg, E. & Strelau, J. (1982). The Reactivity Rating Scale (RRS): Reliability and validity. *Polish Psychological Bulletin*, **13**, 223–237.

Goldsmith, H.H. & Campos, J.J. (1982). Toward a theory of infant temperament. In R.N. Emde & R.J. Harmon (Eds), *The development of attachment and affiliative systems* (pp. 161–193). New York: Plenum.

Gorynska, E. & Strelau, J. (1979). Basic traits of the temporal characteristics of behavior and their measurement by an inventory technique. *Polish Psychological Bulletin*, **10**, 199–207.

Gray, J.A. (Ed.). (1964). *Pavlov's typology.* Oxford: Pergamon Press.

Guilford, J.P. & Zimmerman, W.S. (1956). Fourteen dimensions of temperament. *Psychological Monographs*, **70**, 1–26.

Hebb, D.O. (1955). Drives and the C.N.S. (conceptual nervous system). *Psychological Review*, **62**, 243–254.

Heymans, G. & Wiersma, E.D. (1906–09). Beitraege zur speziellen Psychologie auf Grund einer Massenuntersuchung. *Zeitschrift für Psychologie*, **42**, 81–127; **43**, 321–373; **45**, 1–42; **46**, 321–333; **49**, 414–439; **51**, 1–72.

Ivanov-Smolensky, A.G. (1935). The experimental investigation of higher nervous activity in children. *Fiziologicheskii Zhurnal SSSR*, **19**, 133–140 (in Russian).

Klonowicz, T. (1974). Reactivity and fitness for the occupation of operator. *Polish Psychological Bulletin*, **5**, 129–136.

Klonowicz, T. (1979). Transformation ability, temperament traits and individual experience. *Polish Psychological Bulletin*, **5**, 129–136.

Klonowicz, T. (1985). Temperament and performance. In J. Strelau (Ed.), *Temperamental bases of behavior: Warsaw studies on individual differences* (pp. 79–115). Lisse (Neth.): Swets & Zeitlinger.

Kozlowski, C. (1977). Demand for stimulation and probability preferences in gambling decisions. *Polish Psychological Bulletin*, **8**, 67–73.

Krasnogorsky, N.I. (1953). Typological properties of higher nervous activity in children. *Zhurnal Vysshei Nervnoi Deyatelnosti*, **3**, 169–183 (in Russian).

Lacey, J.I. (1967). Somatic response patterning and stress: Some revisions of activation theory. In M.H. Appley & R. Trumbull (Eds), *Psychological stress: Issues in research*. New York: Appleton-Century-Crofts.

Leites, N.S. (1956). An attempt to give a psychological description of temperaments. In B.M. Teplov (Ed.), *Typological features of higher nervous activity in man*, Vol. 1 (pp. 267–303). Moscow: RSFSR Academy of Pedagogical Sciences.

Leites, N.S (1972). Problems of interrelationship between typological features and age. In V.D. Nebylitsyn & J.A. Gray (Eds), *Biological bases of individual behavior* (pp. 74–85). New York: Academic Press.

Leontev, A.N. (1978). *Activity, consciousness and personality*. Englewood Cliffs, NJ: Prentice-Hall.

Malkov, N.E. (1966). The manifestation of individual-typological differences of nervous processes in intellectual abilities. *Voprosy Psikhologii*, **1**, 38–48 (in Russian).

Mangan, G.L. (1982). *The biology of human conduct: East–West models of temperament and personality*. Oxford: Pergamon.

Matczak, A. (1985). The role of temperament in cognitive functioning: Reactivity and cognitive style. In J. Strelau (Ed.), *Temperamental bases of behavior: Warsaw studies on individual differences* (pp. 116–140). Lisse (Neth.): Swets and Zeitlinger.

Matysiak, J. (1985). Need for sensory stimulation: Effects on activity. In J. Strelau (Ed.), *Temperamental bases of behavior: Warsaw studies on individual differences* (pp. 141–180). Lisse (Neth.): Swets & Zeitlinger.

Merlin, V.S. (Ed.). (1973). *Outline of the theory of temperament*, 2nd edn. Perm: Permskoye Knizhnoye Izdatelstvo (in Russsian).

Nebylitsyn, V.D. (1972a). *Fundamental properties of the human nervous system*. New York: Plenum.

Nebylitsyn, V.D. (1972b). The problem of general and partial properties of the nervous system. In V.D. Nebylitsyn & J.A. Gray (Eds), *Biological bases of individual behavior* (pp. 400–417). New York: Academic Press.

Nebylitsyn, V.D. (1976). *Psychophysiological research in individual differences*. Moscow: Nauka (in Russian).

Pavlov, I.P. (1951–52). *Complete works*, 2nd edn. Moscow & Leningrad: SSSR Academy of Sciences (in Russian).

Pavlov, I.P. (1952). *Dwadziescia lat badan wyzszej czynnosci nerwowej (zachowania sie) zwierzat* [Twenty-five years of objective study of the higher activity (behavior) of animals]. Warszawa: Panstwowy Zaklad Wydawnictw Lekarskich.

Przymusinski, R. & Strelau, J. (1986). Temperamental traits and strategies of decision-making in gambling. In A. Angleitner, A. Furnham, & G. van Heck (Eds), *Personality psychology in Europe: Current trends and controversies*, Vol. 2 (pp. 225–236). Lisse (Neth.): Swets & Zeitlinger.

Rothbart, M.K. (1986). A psychobiological approach to the study of temperament. In G.A. Kohnstamm (Ed.), *Temperament discussed: Temperament and development in infancy and childhood* (pp. 63–72). Lisse (Neth.): Swets & Zeitlinger.

Strelau, J. (1969). *Temperament i typ ukladu nerwowego* [Temperament and type of nervous system]. Warszawa: Panstwowe Wydawnictwo Naukowe.

Strelau, J. (1970). Indywidualny styl pracy ucznia a cechy temperamentalne [Individual style of pupil's work and temperamental traits]. *Kwartalnik Pedagogiczny*, **15**, 59–77.

Strelau, J. (1972). The general and partial nervous system types: Data and theory. In V.D. Nebylitsyn & J.A. Gray (Eds), *Biological bases of individual behavior* (pp. 62–73). New York: Academic Press.

Strelau, J. (1974). Temperament as an expression of energy level and temporal features of behavior. *Polish Psychological Bulletin*, **5**, 119–127.

Strelau, J. (1975). Pavlov's typology and current investigations in this area. *Nederlands Tijdschrift voor de Psychologie*, **30**, 177–200.

Strelau, J. (1983). *Temperament, personality, activity*. London: Academic Press.

Strelau, J. (1984). *Das Temperament in der psychischen Entwicklung*. Berlin: Volk und Wissen Volkseigener Verlag.

Strelau, J. (1985a). Pavlov's typology and the regulative theory of temperament. In J. Strelau (Ed.), *Temperamental bases of behavior: Warsaw studies on individual differences* (pp. 7–40). Lisse (Neth.): Swets & Zeitlinger.

Strelau, J. (Ed.) (1985b). *Temperamental bases of behavior: Warsaw studies on individual differences*. Lisse (Neth.): Swets & Zeitlinger.

Strelau J. (1987). The concept of temperament in personality research. *European Journal of Personality*, **1**, 107–117.

Strelau, J. (1988). Temperamental dimensions as co-determinants of resistance to stress. In M.P. Janisse (Ed.), *Individual differences, stress,and health psychology* (pp. 146–169). New York: Springer Verlag.

Strelau, J., Angleitner, A., & Ruch, W. (1989). Strelau Temperament Inventory (STI): General review and studies based on German samples. In C.D. Spielberger & J.N. Butcher (Eds), *Advances in personality assessment*, Vol. 8 (pp. 187–241). Hillsdale, NJ: Erlbaum.

Teplov, B.M. (1963). New data for the study of nervous system properties in man. In B.M. Teplov, (Ed.), *Typological features of the higher nervous activity in man*. Vol.3 (pp. 3–46). Moscow: RSFSR Academy of Pedagogical Sciences (in Russian).

Teplov, B.M. (1964). Problems in the study of general types of higher nervous activity in man and animals. In J.A. Gray (Ed.), *Pavlov's typology* (pp. 3–153). Oxford: Pergamon.

Thomas, A. & Chess, S. (1977). *Temperament and development*. New York: Brunner/Mazel.

Thomas, A., Chess, S., & Birch, H.G. (1968). *Temperament and behavior disorders in children*. New York: New York University Press.

Thurstone, L.L. (1951). The dimensions of temperament. *Psychometrica*, **16**, 11–20.

Tomaszewski, T. (1978). *Taetigkeit und Bewusstsein: Beitraege zur Einfuehrung in die polnische Taetigkeitpsychologie*. Weinheim & Basel: Beltz Verlag.

Troshikhin, V.A., Kozlova, L.N., Kruchenko, Z.A., & Sirotsky, V.V. (1971). *Shaping and development of the basic properties of the type of higher nervous activity in ontogenesis*. Kiev: Naukova Dumka (in Russian).

4

Temperaments as Personality Traits

ARNOLD BUSS
University of Texas

Investigators of temperament approach the topic from different perspectives, some emphasizing the study of infant behavior, others focusing on clinical aspects, and still others concentrating on emotion. As a personality psychologist, my perspective (which is shared with Robert Plomin) leads to a focus on temperaments as personality traits. Viewed in this light, temperaments are the subclass of personality traits that are inherited, though they are subject to modification through socialization and individual experience; an appropriate analogue would be body build, not eye color. Temperaments also differ from other personality traits in their initial appearance during the first year of life. The combination of inheritance and early appearance suggests that they are basic building blocks for personality.

The three temperaments that meet the criteria of inheritance and early appearance have been given the acronym of EAS: emotionality, activity, and sociability (Buss & Plomin, 1984). Activity is defined as the sheer expenditure of physical energy. Emotionality is defined as primordial distress, which is assumed to differentiate into fear and anger during the first six months of life. Sociability is defined as a preference for being with others rather than being alone.

These three temperaments are linked to our evolutionary heritage and the development of human personality. All three traits have been observed in primates (Chamove, Eysenck, & Harlow, 1972; Goodall, 1986; Stevenson-Hinde, Stillwell-Barnes, & Zung, 1980). And all three temperaments are observed as personality traits in older children and adults. Activity and sociability are important elements of extraversion, and emotionality is central to neuroticism (Eysenck, 1947).

Evidence bearing on the heritability and factorial unity of these temperaments may be found in earlier works (Buss & Plomin, 1975, 1984). This chapter constitutes a further theoretical analysis of the three temperaments. Their components are specified in greater detail, and the motivational aspects of each are discussed. In the service of comprehensiveness, the measures appropriate to the

Temperament in Childhood   Edited by G.A. Kohnstamm, J.E. Bates and M.K. Rothbart
© 1989 John Wiley & Sons Ltd

various components, discussed in Buss and Plomin (1984), are repeated here with some additions. The last two substantive sections of the chapter deal with the role of learning in shaping each temperament and with sex differences and their origins.

COMPONENTS

Activity

Energy is expended faster when the pace of movements is rapid, and a major component of activity is *tempo*. Highly active children often gallop instead of walking, skip and hop frequently, run up and down stairs, talk faster, and generally move a quicker pace than those who are low in activity.

An alternative means of expending energy is through *vigor*, responses of high amplitude or great intensity. Highly active children tend to push open doors with force, bang hard on toys, talk louder, yell more often, and generally move with greater force than those who are low in activity.

These examples reveal that activity is mainly a *stylistic* trait, the only one of the EAS temperaments to be stylistic. As defined here, style refers to the manner in which responses are delivered, not their content: the *how*, not the *what* of behavior. Thus a handshake is a greeting response (content), but it can be delivered with a quick movement (tempo) or the hand can be grasped in a vise (vigor). This kind of style is usually called *animation*. Like other stylistic personality traits (no other temperament is included, but the trait of formality is an example), activity is a salient feature of individuals and, at the extremes, one of the most recognizable features of one's personality.

Another characteristic of highly active children is their tendency to continue high-energy pursuits long after those lower in activity have slowed down or sat down. Active children tend to have more *endurance*, the third (and minor) component of the trait of activity. It must be added that there may be other reasons why some children have more endurance – physical condition, for example – but, other things equal, active children tend to keep going when others are ready to stop.

The two major components may appear in equal measure in very young children, but as they mature, tempo and vigor are believed to differentiate. Thus some children reveal their high activity in the fast pace of their movements and some, in their vigorous movements, though there are also some children who are both quick and vigorous. Differentiation into tempo or vigor occurs mainly among children who are high in activity. At the low end of this personality dimension, there is too little expenditure of energy for an observer to distinguish tempo from vigor. Said another way, the dimension of activity is asymmetrical with respect to differentiation into its major components.

Emotionality

The primordial emotionality will be ignored here in favor of the products of its differentiation: fear and anger.

Fear

The first component of fear, by definition, is *affective*. There is a strong autonomic arousal, specifically activation of the sympathetic division of the autonomic nervous system. Such arousal is ordinarily accompànied by feelings of apprehension and worry, which comprise the *cognitive* component.

Socialization has only just begun when children are young, and so they express their emotions freely, especially in the face. The *expressive* component of fear, which can be distinguished from the facial appearance of other emotions (Ekman & Friesen, 1971) is believed to have evolved from the primate grimace (Andrew, 1963; Redican, 1982). Aside from the face, this component may be seen in fidgeting, touching oneself, pacing, restlessness, and related kinds of disorganized movements that are regarded as motor spillover of intense arousal.

When afraid, children shrink back, inhibit motor activity, or run away from the threatening stimulus. If the fear is sufficiently intense, children may subsequently avoid the fear stimulus. These various responses comprise the *instrumental* or motor component of fear. It is the most observable aspect of fear and the one most studied by clinical psychologists and psychiatrists. Fearful children are here regarded as being predisposed to become phobic as they mature.

When frightened, some children display all four components, but in most children, some of the components are salient and others can hardly be observed. Thus, for any given child, the dominant component may be autonomic arousal; for another child, motor spillover; and so on. Adult phobics can be divided into *synchronizers*, who reveal their anxiety in all four components, versus *desynchronizers*, who show anxiety in only one or two components (Hodgson & Rachman, 1974). The impact of therapy was different for synchronizers and desynchronizers, which suggests that it may be important to analyse fear into its components.

Anger

As with fear, anger is primarily an *affect*. Its physiological reactivity is here regarded as the same as that of fear. The empirical basis and logic of this conclusion are spelled out elsewhere (Buss & Plomin, 1975, 1984) and need not concern us here. The *expressive* component, especially the facial aspect, appears to be universal in our species (Ekman & Friesen, 1971) and may well have evolved from the primate facial expression in anger, which it resembles (Darwin, 1873). The *cognitive* component is transient dislike of others and negative attributions to them, which comprise the reactions often labelled *hostility*.

The *instrumental* component is aggression, specifically the kind of attack that has been labelled *angry aggression* (Buss, 1961). As its name implies, such agression is accompanied by anger. It ordinarily occurs as a reaction to threat, and unlike fear, the response to threat is to eliminate it. Its usual consequence, which allows us to infer intent, is hurt or harm to a victim. There is some evidence that such aggression can reduce autonomic arousal (Buss, 1961), a phenomenon called *catharsis*.

Sociability

The major component of sociability is *instrumental*: movement in the direction of others. Sociable children strongly prefer to play with others rather than playing by themselves. They do not want to eat alone and, when with others, they want to play interactive games in which there is give and take. When siblings or playmates are not available, sociable children may complain that there is nothing to do. It must be added that children low in sociability do not prefer complete isolation. Like other primates, we are a strongly affiliative species, and no normal human is a hermit.

The minor component of sociability is *responsiveness* to social stimulation. Other things equal – the trait of activity, for example – sociable children react enthusiastically to the overtures of others, whereas children low in sociability do not. Sociable children are happy to be engaged in interpersonal pursuits and reveal it by facial expressions, tone of voice, and general excitement. In this respect, their behavior is a mirror image of what they seek, which is responsiveness from others.

In brief, each of the EAS temperaments consists of two or more components, which may be regarded as subtraits. The various components are summarized in Table 1. The analysis of fear and anger into similar components is not surprising in light of their being the two elements of emotionality. They are more complex than activity, which has three components, and sociability, which has two components. Children are expected to display individual differences not only in these three temperaments but also in their components. Thus one fearful child might be observed to worry a lot but not have a strong avoidance response; another child might display motor spillover but little physiological arousal.

Table 1   Components of the temperaments activity, emotionality, and sociability

Temperament	Components
Activity	Tempo
	Vigor
	Endurance (minor component)
Emotionality	
Fear	Sympathetic activation
	Apprehension, worry
	Fear face
	Escape, avoidance
Anger	Sympathetic activation
	Transient hostility
	Angry face, pout
	Angry aggression
Sociability	Tendency to affiliate
	Responsivity when with others

MOTIVATION

Activity

When teachers or parents are asked about their observations of highly active children, they often mention that such children become frustrated and restless when they are confined and cannot expend their profligate energy. They like to keep busy and chafe at enforced idleness. Clearly, these children are motivated to engage in actions that have a fast tempo or require considerable vigor. They pose few problems in nursery schools, which provide opportunities for energetic play. In grammar school, however, children are expected to sit quietly for some time, and an active child can mark the end of the school day with a burst of pent-up energy.

Their motivation is also reflected in the kind of play they prefer: noisy play that requires running, jumping, hopping, climbing, skipping, and wrestling, and in older children, the more vigorous organized games of football, basketball, and soccer. Other things equal, children low in activity avoid such energetic pursuits and opt for quieter table games, puzzles, or television.

Emotionality

Fear

Fear is one reaction to perceived threat, whether real or imagined. Thus fear involves aversive motivation, as reflected in escape and avoidance behavior. Virtually by definition, fearful children are expected to react more intensely to any threat; a fearful child might react with panic to a mild threat that elicits only wariness in other children. Also fearful children have a lower threshold for anxiety, reacting with fear to a stimulus that may not affect other children. A lower threshold and a more intense reaction are, of course, hallmarks of motivation.

Anger

There appear to be two closely related motives in anger. The first, which is observed in angry aggression, consists of attempting to hurt or harm another person. When young children become enraged, they tend to strike out at the nearest available target, usually the instigator of the rage, with the intent of causing pain. In older children the motive may be to cause psychological hurt by rejecting, ridiculing, taunting, or yelling or screaming at another person. The second motive is destruction of property, not the mindless destructiveness of a young child who does not know better, but the intentional ripping, tearing apart, and smashing of an enraged child.

Parenthetically, anger can occur in the absence of any apparent motive. Young children, especially, may have temper tantrums during which they writhe, wail, scream, and throw themselves on the floor. The anger appears not to be directed at any person or thing and therefore must be regarded as without motivation. There may be a parallel in some kinds of panic attacks, in which the child cannot verbalize the nature of the threatening stimulus nor can it be specified by the observations of adults. Conversely, some temper tantrums are motivated by a desire to annoy parents or caretakers.

Sociability

The motive to affiliate with others is here regarded as the seeking of a particular class of social incentives, *stimulation rewards*. The weakest is the presence of others, which serves only to prevent loneliness. A step up in stimulation and arousal is sharing activities, such as watching television together or playing side by side, without there being any back-and-forth interaction. More arousing is attention from others. And the peak of social arousal is responsivity: when the other person responds in such a way that a conversation or non-verbal interaction can continue in a way analogous to a ping-pong or tennis match. It is assumed here that highly sociable children prefer the highest level of social stimulation, responsivity, though they may settle for weaker incentives. Presumably, the weaker the trait of sociability, the weaker the social stimulation preferred by the child. Less sociable children may find that responsivity is too arousing or too intrusive and prefer not to be bothered by the interference of others. The seeds of aversiveness – boredom, being bossed around, or intrusiveness of others – are present in all social interaction. Highly sociable children, being strongly motivated to attain the stimulation rewards, are willing to put up with social aversiveness; less sociable children are not.

MEASURES

The analysis of these temperaments into components and into varying motives is of more than theoretical interest, for it has implications for measurement of the temperaments. The following measures derive mainly from chapter 7 in Buss and Plomin (1984). Notice the one measure common to all three temperaments: frequency.

Activity

Tempo must be assessed by the rate of responding (frequency per unit time): speed of walking, talking, or climbing stairs and the observed tendency to hurry. Vigor can be assessed by the child's loudness of voice, amplitude of gestures, pressure exerted in opening doors, and the force used in pounding with a hammer or other tool. Endurance can be determined by timing how long the child remains active while others are resting. Most measures of activity, however, do not distinguish between tempo and vigor. Thus the actometer tracks just the total amount of movement of an arm or leg (Bell, 1968; Schulman & Reisman, 1959), and squares can be marked off in a room or at a playground to assess the amount of ground covered by a moving child. Less direct measures are a preference for high-energy or low-energy play and games, and the child's reaction to enforced idleness.

Emotionality

Fear and anger will be treated together. A major measure is the frequency of the fear reaction (crying, shrinking back, wariness, or hiding) or the anger reaction (temper tantrums, destructiveness while angry, and angry aggression). The intensity of these responses is also an indicator of the trait, especially with the inclusion of breathing rate, heart rate, blood pressure, and galvanic skin response (measures of sympathetic activation). Individual differences have been reported early in infancy (Lipton & Steinschneider, 1964), and fearful children have been shown to have a higher and more stable heart rate (Garcia-Coll, Kagan, & Reznick, 1984).

The threshold of the emotional response offers another measurement option: the intensity of the feared stimulus (visual cliff, stranger, or threat of punishment) or the anger stimulus (being blocked or attacked by another person) required to elicit a fear or anger reaction.

Sociability

A good index of sociability is the number of times (frequency) the child attempts to get together with others. Also important is the amount of time spent with others. The degree of social responsiveness is a good supplementary measure, although both degree and duration of responsiveness may not only be determined from sociability but also from the trait of shyness (for data on sociability and shyness, see Cheek & Buss, 1981). Less direct measures involve choice of activities (with others versus alone) when options are available and reaction to enforced social isolation.

LEARNING

There is evidence that activity, emotionality, and sociability are inherited (see Buss & Plomin, 1975, 1984, for reviews), but the same behavioral genetics research that demonstrates heritability also shows that environment is influential. The immediate concern here is the mechanisms of learning by which the environment has an impact. The study of temperament focuses mainly on childhood, especially early childhood. Therefore, the kinds of learning at issue here are those that might have an impact on personality traits during the first 2 years or so of life: habituation, classicial conditioning, and instrumental conditioning.

Habituation plays a role mainly in fear. Many infants become wary of social novelty late in the first year of life, but this stranger anxiety gradually wanes, as infants discover that strangers do not pose a threat. Such waning of an emotional reaction to a neutral stimulus is the essence of habituation. This kind of learning may also influence sociability. Young children may learn to be around many people and can endure even crowded conditions because they simply habituate to the close presence of others.

Fear is especially affected by classical conditioning. There are only a few innate fears, and most of the stimuli that frighten children must be learned. When neutral stimuli are linked with threatening stimuli, the originally neutral stimuli come to be conditioned stimuli for fear. Thus when children suffer pain in a dentist's office, they may subsequently become afraid of the sight of the dentist, the office, or even the waiting room. Fearful children are expected to be especially susceptible to such conditioning, and classical conditioning is assumed to be a major mechanism in the development of the most common fears of children – of snakes and dogs, for example.

Classical conditioning may also affect anger. Initially neutral stimuli, after being linked with stimuli that induce anger, eventually come to elicit a rage response. Thus when another child regularly ridicules or taunts, the sight of this child can become a conditioned stimulus for an anger reaction by the recipient. Or the sight of a disliked food may evoke anger and pushing it away. Though there has been no specific experiment demonstrating classical conditioning of anger, it has been observed by parents and caretakers. And, logically, it would be surprising if anger could not be classically conditioned when fear is so easily conditioned.

The most common mechanism of learning is instrumental conditioning. It affects activity by channelling the urge to expend energy into particular kinds of pursuits. This kind of learning is also essential to the development of phobias, which involves *avoidance* conditioning. The child initially is strongly reinforced for escaping the situation by the sharp drop in aversive arousal. Subsequently, avoidance of the feared stimulus is reinforced by the absence of a fear response, and therefore the avoidance response is not given the opportunity to extinguish. Again, children high in the temperament of fearfulness are at the greatest risk for such conditioning.

Angry aggression often pays off in getting rid of the anger-eliciting stimulus – a threat, for example. Ridding oneself of such aversiveness is a powerful reinforcer, which inevitably strengthens the tendency for a child to aggress when angry.

Instrumental conditioning affects sociability by a pay-off matrix that determines which of the stimulation rewards will be pursued. Thus even a highly sociable child, who initially prefers the highly arousing incentive of responsivity from others, might settle for attention from others if this were the only available reward in social interaction. Instrumental conditioning is especially important in determining the level of the child's responsiveness. If a sociable child's natural enthusiasm were not reinforced by others, it might wane. If a less sociable child's responsiveness were strongly reinforced, the child might become enthusiastic in social contexts.

SEX DIFFERENCES

Boys are more active and more angry than girls; girls are more fearful and more sociable than boys. Thus sex differences prevail for all three temperaments (fear and anger comprising emotionality), but there is a mitigating issue. The distributions of the two sexes overlap, but the statistically different means require explanation.

Two kinds of explanation have been offered for the sex diffferences. One *biological* explanation assumes that prenatal hormones make males more angry (and aggressive) and less fearful (Ellis, 1986). A variation on this theme is that male infants are innately more active than female infants, with the precise biological mechanism not specified (Eaton & Enns, 1986). The only biological explanation for females being more sociable is based on the concept of a *primate biogrammar* which programs each sex differently (Tiger & Fox, 1971).

The major alternative approach is *socialization*. In each society, boys and girls are offered models and given direct training in the sex roles that they will eventually assume as adults. In our society, girls are allowed to express fear openly, just as they are allowed to cry, but they may be punished for expressing anger, for it is not 'ladylike'. Boys are not allowed to express fear (it is considered cowardly), but some anger is tolerated. Boys' games and toys encourage vigorous activity, whereas girls' games are more sedentary. Girls are encouraged to cooperate and to interact closely with one another; boys are encouraged to compete and to strive for individual attainment. The outcome is that girls are more sociable.

Given the slightness of the sex differences in the temperaments, especially in young children, can we draw any conclusions? There is hardly any time for socialization practices to act during infancy, which means that if there is a sex difference in this developmental era, the biological explanation is favored. If sex differences do not show up until after infancy, they would be consistent with the socialization explanation. A fair reading of the developmental evidence leads one to conclude that a sex difference in temperaments has not been established in infancy. The evidence for sex differences in the temperaments is at best equivocal until children reach the age of preschool or kindergarten (see Buss, 1988, for a review). Thus the evidence tilts in the direction of the socialization explanation, but the biological explanation is not necessarily ruled out.

CONCLUDING COMMENTS

This chapter has analyzed the EAS temperaments by specifying their components, motivation, measures, impact of learning, and sex differences. The questions asked and perhaps their answers may provide a deeper and more detailed understanding of the EAS temperaments. Regardless of whether one adopts the EAS approach, temperaments represent individual differences in young children, which means that they are personality traits. It follows that the issues discussed here, which are relevant to any personality trait, take on special importance when temperaments are regarded as a subclass of personality traits, for they may also help investigators with other perspectives to achieve a better understanding of temperaments.

REFERENCES

Andrew, R.F. (1963). The origin and evolution of the calls and facial expressions of primates. *Behaviour*, **20**, 1–109.

Bell, R.Q. (1968). Adaptation of small wrist watches for mechanical recording of activity in infants and children. *Journal of Experimental Child Psychology*, **6**, 302–305.

Buss, A.H. (1961). *The psychology of aggression*. New York: Wiley.

Buss, A.H. (1988). *Personality: Evolutionary heritage and human distinctiveness*. Hillsdale, NJ: Erlbaum.

Buss, A.H. & Plomin, R. (1975). *A temperament theory of personality development*. New York: Wiley.

Buss, A.H. & Plomin, R. (1984). *Temperament: Early developing personality traits*. Hillsdale, NJ: Erlbaum.

Chamove, A.S., Eysenck, H.J., & Harlow, H. (1972). Personality in monkeys: Factor analysis of rhesus social behavior. *Quarterly Journal of Experimental Psychology*, **24**, 496–504.

Cheek, J.M. & Buss, A.H. (1981). Shyness and sociability. *Journal of Personality and Social Psychology,* **41**, 330–339.

Darwin, C.R. (1873). *The expression of emotions in man and animals.* New York: Appleton.

Eaton, W.O. & Enns, L.R. (1986). Sex differences in human motor activity level. *Psychological Bulletin,* **100**, 19–28.

Ekman, P. & Friesen, W.V. (1971). Constants across cultures in the face and emotion. *Journal of Personality and Social Psychology,* **17**, 124–129.

Ellis, L. (1986). Evidence of neuroandrogenic etiology of sex roles from a combined analsysis of human, nonhuman primate and nonhuman mammalian studies. *Personality and Individual Differences,* **7**, 519–552.

Eysenck, H.J. (1947). *Dimensions of personality.* London: Routledge & Kegan Paul.

Garcia-Coll, C.T., Kagan, J., & Reznick, J.S. (1984). Behavioral inhibition in young children. *Child Development,* **55**, 1005–1019.

Goodall, J. (1986). *The chimpanzees of Gombe.* Cambridge, MA: Belknap Press.

Hodgson, R. & Rachman, S. (1974). II. Desynchrony in measures of fear. *Behaviour Research and Therapy,* **12**, 313–326.

Lipton, E.L. & Steinschneider, A. (1964). Studies on the psychophysiology of infancy. *Merrill-Palmer Quarterly,* **10**, 102–117.

Redican, W.K. (1982). An evolutionary perspective on human facial displays. In P. Ekman (Ed.), *Emotion in the human face,* 2nd edn. New York: Cambridge University Press.

Schulman, J.L. & Reisman, J.M. (1959). An objective measure of hyperactivity. *American Journal of Mental Deficiency,* **64**, 455–456.

Stevenson-Hinde, J., Stillwell-Barnes, R., & Zung, M. (1980). Subjective assessment of monkeys over four successive years. *Primates,* **21**, 66–82.

Tiger, L. & Fox, R. (1971). *The imperial animal.* New York: Holt, Rinehart & Winston.

5

Temperament in Childhood: A Framework

MARY KLEVJORD ROTHBART
University of Oregon

In this chapter I discuss a methodological approach to the study of temperament (one widely implemented in the field) and describe the current version of a developmental model for thinking about temperament. In our model for temperament, we have defined temperament as constitutionally based individual differences in reactivity and self-regulation, with 'constitutional' referring to the person's relatively enduring biological make-up, influenced over time by heredity, maturation, and experience (Rothbart & Derryberry, 1981). *Reactivity* refers to the arousability of motor activity, affect, autonomic and endocrine response. Reactivity can be assessed through parameters of threshold of reaction, latency, intensity, time to peak intensity of reaction, and recovery time. *Self-regulation* refers to processes that can modulate (facilitate or inhibit) reactivity, and these processes include attention, approach, withdrawal, attack, behavioral inhibition, and self-soothing. Although developed independently, our constructs of reactivity and self-regulation are very similar to Strelau's (1983, Chapter 3, this volume).

The distinction we pose between reactivity and self-regulation is not an absolute one. Thus, processes described as self-regulative also have a reactive aspect, as when a child becomes inhibited in response to the presence of a stranger. Reactive processes can also be seen to serve regulative functions, as when an infant's arm-waving or banging serves to release motor tension. We feel, however, that this distinction is an especially useful one for thinking about the development of temperament, in that self-regulative processes can be seen increasingly to modulate and organize reactivity as the child develops (Rothbart, in press, and Chapter 12 in this volume; Rothbart & Derryberry, 1981; see also Chapter 11, by Fox & Stifter).

Behaviorally, temperament can be studied in the individual's emotional, attentional, and motor activity. Most of our own work has been at the behavioral level. However, our general framework and its specification of parameters of

Temperament in Childhood   Edited by G.A. Kohnstamm, J.E. Bates and M.K. Rothbart
© 1989 John Wiley & Sons Ltd

response including latency, peak intensity, rise time, and recovery time (Rothbart & Derryberry, 1981) allow for investigation of reactivity and self-regulation at physiological levels as well. A major advantage of having a point of contact between the behavioral and physiological domains is that increased understanding of the behavioral structure of temperament aids in our understanding of its neural structure, and our understanding of biological structure in turn influences our decisions about the major dimensions of behavioral individuality (see Chapter 6).

Emotions are especially interesting processes in our model, in that they can be seen to include both reactive (facial expression, affective, motor, autonomic, and neuroendocrine arousal) and self-regulative aspects (approach, withdrawal, inhibition, attack, etc.). Given this framework, individual differences in temperament can be assessed at many different levels. It is possible to assess individual differences in affect, facial expression, or autonomic or neuroendocrine arousal, *and* to assess individual differences at more general levels of emotional organization such as fear and frustration, or still more general dimensions such as negative emotionality.

MEASURING TEMPERAMENT

We and many others in the field assess temperament at a behavioral or physiological level by aggregating information gathered about an individual across a number of items. These items may be from a questionnaire or an interview, and they can refer to the child's behaviors as observed by a parent, teacher, or peer. For older children, they may involve self-report about the subject's inner states and feelings. Items may also be psychophysiological assays, such as measures of heart rate, galvanic skin response, or cortisol excretion. In all of these measures, we expect that an individual's response to a particular situation as assessed by a single item will be multi-determined. That is, we recognize that many influences operate upon a given behavior or physiological response or feeling, with temperament being only one. One set of possibly biasing influences on questionnaire responses and on relatively subjective observational ratings includes the observer's attitudes, skills, and opportunity to observe the behaviors relevant to each item. An excellent discussion of these biases is given by Bates in Chapter 1, and we have also discussed relevant biases in a previous paper (Rothbart & Goldsmith, 1985). In my current discussion, however, I will set these biases aside to discuss additional influences upon item responses independent of observer bias.

Consider a questionnaire item assessing the child's most recent reaction to a stranger. Children's negative reactions to a stranger may have been influenced by a recent experience with an intrusive person who frightened them or made them feel uncomfortable, or by the fact that they didn't get enough sleep the previous night or were hungry at the moment, or were getting a new tooth, or were offered a toy by the stranger at the time they were being observed. Nevertheless, our assumption is that *one* of the many influences on such an item of behavior is the temperament of the child. We may then view the other influences as 'noise' with respect to the temperamental information, in some conditions facilitating the temperamentally influenced reaction, in other conditions inhibiting it.

When we gather information across a broad set of items, aggregating an overall score across those items, our expectation is that the temperamental 'signal' will become enhanced, while the 'noise' from other influences of mood, need state, and personal history will tend to cancel each other out. The example I have used here involves observers' reports of a child's temperament-related behavior, but the rationale for assessing temperament via multiple items also applies to self-reports about feelings and experiences, episodes designed to elicit temperamental reactions in the laboratory, field observations, and psychophysiological measures such as heart-rate reactivity.

Following this measurement strategy, we expect only low to moderate correlations across items, but with aggregation of adequate numbers of items we will be able to construct a measurement device with relatively high internal reliability. Once we have computed an aggregate measure, we can then investigate its relation to other measures of temperamental characteristics, and its normative stability and changes over time (see Chapter 12).

A Basic Level of Measurement

Questions about the nature of temperament already arise, however, at this basic level of measurement or scale construction: if we find it impossible to construct a scale with adequate internal reliability for a temperamental characteristic, it may be because we have written bad items, but it may *also* be the case that the 'signal' we expected to find across items is missing. For example, let us consider the temperamental construct of 'intensity', defined as energy level of responsiveness, irrespective of the quality of the response or its direction (Thomas & Chess, 1977). Following the rationale described above, we construct a scale of intensity by writing items reflecting intensity of response across the behavioral domains of activity, emotionality (including fear, frustration, and smiling and laughter), and attention or interest.

These items are then administered to a large sample of subjects, and we can assess whether they share a common 'signal' by evaluating the internal reliability of our measure. In fact, we and others (Martin, 1984; Rothbart, 1981; also Rowe and Plomin (1977) using factor analytic methods) have attempted to do this for intensity, but we were not able to develop a basic-level measure, because the items from different behavioral domains were not positively correlated with each other. Thus, we could find related clusters of items assessing intensity within the fear domain or within the smiling and laughter domain, but a child who showed a high intensity of fear did *not* necessarily show high intensity of smiling and laughter (Rothbart, 1981). If researchers continue to attempt to measure intensity at the basic level and fail to do so, then we must consider whether it is proper to include the dimension in our working list of temperament constructs. It may be the case that by defining 'intensity' in a different way, we could find evidence for intensity at a basic measurement level, but this would require at the least a change in the current meaning of the construct.

Soviet and Eastern European researchers encountered a similar problem to that of basic-level constructs when they attempted to assess temperament in the laboratory. In operationalizing their constructs, they found that measures which conceptually *should* have tapped the same 'signal' were in fact unrelated to each other (the 'partiality' phenomenon; see Strelau, 1983). This discovery led to basic changes in their approach to the study of temperament (for a discussion of some of these changes, see Chapter 6). In order for temperament constructs to be helpful, they must be empirically sound, and as researchers we must be prepared to move on to better constructs when the old ones do not work at a basic measurement level.

In another paper we have reviewed evidence from numerous questionnaire studies of infant temperament, finding conceptual and factor-analytic support for the dimensions of reaction to novelty, other distress proneness, positive affect, activity, rhythmicity, and attention span (Rothbart & Alansby, in press).

Breadth Versus Narrowness of Temperament Constructs

Once we have established a basic level of measurement for a temperamental construct, we can then often vary the breadth or generality versus the narrowness of the temperament characteristic we are studying. Thus, we have been able to develop internally reliable measures of fearfulness and frustration in infancy, but we also find that they are positively correlated, so that they can be combined into a larger composite such as negative emotionality (see Rothbart, 1986). Or we may identify even broader temperamental units, either on the basis of factor analysis of basic-level measures (probably the most commonly employed method), or on the basis of theoretically driven predictions about relationships across dimensions (again requiring adequate empirical support in order to be accepted). A good example of a very broad composite temperament construct is the 'tractability' construct of Matheny, Wilson, and Nuss (1984) discussed by Matheny in Chapter 14. In the present chapter I will propose some constructs that can be seen as an attempt to organize the temperament domain at both narrow and broad levels. Research questions about the relations among constructs can be derived from this structure, and the answers to these questions can then be used to revise the model.

A GENERAL FRAMEWORK FOR TEMPERAMENT

Reactivity

A general framework for temperament is depicted in Figure 1. It specifies multiple reactive processes (somatic, autonomic, cognitive, and neuroendocrine), organized into two general categories of positive and negative reactivity. *Stimulus qualities* influencing reactivity include stimulus intensity, signal qualities or the meaning of a stimulus, and expectations, with signal qualities including the powerful affective influences of self-evaluation.

The first of these stimulus qualities, *stimulus intensity*, is expected to lead chiefly to positive reactions at lower intensity levels. At moderate levels of stimulus intensity, both positive and negative reactions will be strengthened (without necessarily reaching a threshold for behavioral expression) and the individual may

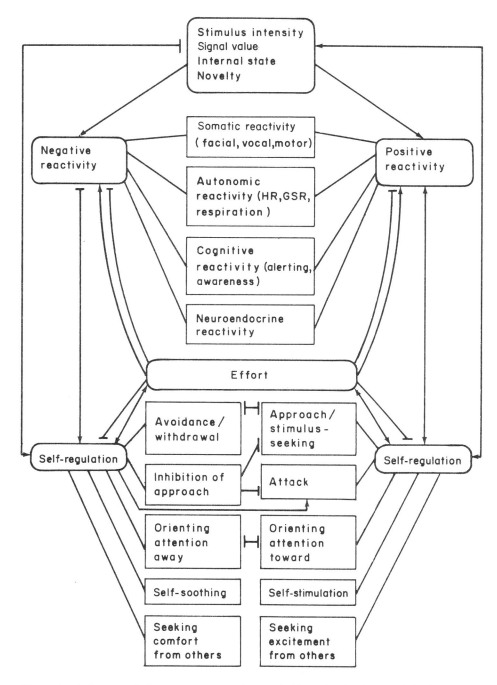

Figure 1 A framework for temperament. Arrows indicate facilitation; straight lines at the end of connecting lines, inhibition; direct connecting lines from larger to smaller boxes, more specific instances of a more general category. The figure does not describe all possible connections, but is designed to illustrate a general framework.

be observed to alternate between expressions of positive and negative affect. At high stimulus intensities, negative reactions become so strong that positive reactions are inhibited (see Berlyne, 1971, 1973).

Individuals are then posited to differ in their thresholds for and intensity of positive and negative reactions, and the rise and recovery time of these reactions, so that the effect of a stimulus will be stronger for some individuals than for others. We can now consider the effects of varying stimulus intensity on individuals who vary in reactivity. Let us say that one set of parents likes to stimulate their babies gently, talking quietly to them, and stroking their faces. Some infants will find these low levels of intensity positive, and will smile and coo, whereas others will require more intense stimulation in order to experience and express pleasure. Consider another set of parents who like to stimulate their babies by jostling them, tossing them in the air, and generally playing roughly with them. Some babies will find this level of stimulation to be unpleasant and show distress to it, whereas others will squeal and laugh, finding these situations to be quite positive. Thus, a stimulus of moderately high intensity, such as a stranger approach, may result in chiefly positive reactions from some individuals and chiefly negative reactions from others, depending upon their temperamental characteristics.

We can also consider some additional factors that may contribute to the reaction. Reactivity will be influenced by the individual's *internal state*, including need states. Hunger, thirst, cold, fatigue, etc. will generally potentiate negative reactions, and the satisfaction of those needs, positive reactions. Achievement of a desired goal will contribute toward positive reactivity; blocking of a goal (frustration) and loss of a valued object to negative reactivity. *Novelty* or surprise (Berlyne's 1970, 1971 collative variables) will also influence both positive and negative reactions. Current models for constructs of behavioral inhibition (see Chapter 8, by Kagan, Reznick, & Snidman) stress the more negative reactions to novelty. However, research on humor and laughter suggests that novelty can also result in smiling or laughter, depending upon the context in which it is experienced (Berlyne, 1970; Rothbart, 1973; Sroufe & Waters, 1976).

Signal value refers to the meaning ascribed to events, including symbolic meanings that may be highly emotionally laden as well as the individual's expectation or anticipation of motivationally relevant events. Positive reactions (and also positive self-regulatory action such as approach: see the lower part of Figure 1) will be potentiated by the anticipation of possible rewards (hope). Negative reactions (and also negative self-regulatory action such as avoidance) will be potentiated by the anticipation of possible punishments (fear). Stimuli can of course be simultaneously positively and negatively anticipated and/or evaluated, as when a person meets a stranger or considers a ride on a roller coaster, where both positive anticipation and fear may coexist, and both approach and avoidance may occur.

Experience will influence positive and negative reactions due to signal value from the earliest months. Children whose cries are readily responded to by the caregiver will come to anticipate relief (and they may become angry when caregiver response is not forthcoming); infants whose cries are ignored will not have such positive expectations. Angry reactions may be more likely in those children whose signals have been responded to in the past, because they have developed positive expectations that can now be blocked. Children who have had repeated successes in school will feel positive anticipation while going to school in the morning; children whose experiences have been chiefly ones of failure will have negative expectations. For most children, both positive and negative reactions (and self-regulatory inclinations such as the impulse to truancy) will be potentiated. An important question about temperament is the extent to which experiences such as these will over time affect the child's general activity and emotionality.

Both positive and negative reactions are expressed via *somatic, autonomic, cognitive,* and *neuroendocrine reactions* and can be experienced as bodily feelings of distress and pleasure. We expect individuals who are more susceptible to negative reactions to experience more feelings of distress, and individuals less susceptible to negative reactions to experience more feelings of pleasure under moderately high stimulus intensity situations. This model differs from several other theories of temperament in childhood which consider only behavioral aspects of emotionality to be temperamental (Goldsmith & Campos, 1982; Thomas & Chess, 1977). Buss and Plomin (1984) argue that emotional behavior involves arousal, while feelings do not, and they consider only high arousal (and by implication, emotions, and not feelings) as reflective of temperament. However, aside from the fact that feeling states are frequently accompanied by high arousal (Tucker & Williamson, 1984), studies of adult temperament rely almost wholly upon individuals' self-reports of positive and negative feelings and motivation. To the extent that we expect some continuity between child and adult temperament, we must consider the possibility that self-report of experienced feelings and preferences may be an expression of individual differences in temperament. We therefore include consideration of feelings as well as overt behavior as temperamental, and allow for the study of self-report of temperament in older children (Rothbart & Derryberry, 1981).

In situations where both positive and negative reactivity is elicited, we expect facial expressions of simultaneous positive and negative affect, where blends are possible, and these have been observed by Izard (1977) and others. In addition, rapid switching between positive and negative facial expressions and vocalizations is expected when one system is activated, followed by the other. In our laboratory, some infants move from intense positive to negative facial expressions and vocalizations over time periods as short as one-tenth of a second.

Reactive patterns involve multiple arousal processes which may follow differing time courses (Rothbart & Derryberry, 1981). Consider, for example, the rapid alerting of attention versus the much slower engagement of the sympathetic–adrenomedullary neuroendocrine axis in response to an exciting event. One reaction is measured in milliseconds (Posner, 1978); the other, in minutes and hours (see Chapter 9, by Gunnar & Mangelsdorf). Although I have identified two broad categories of reactivity, we expect that there will nevertheless be individual variability at multiple levels, including differential sensitivity to varying stimulus modalites and differential reactivity across and within different channels of expression (somatic, autonomic, neuroendocrine; within autonomic, heart rate, and galvanic skin response, etc.; Rothbart & Derryberry, 1981).

If it is true that there are many sources of variability in individual differences in temperament, what does this mean for how we conceptualize temperament? The answer to this question is in part an empirical one, and it is related to the arguments above about basic-level measurement. If we find that reactivity within a given motivational system does not appear to be related to reactivity in other situations, and measures of reactivity in those other situations are positively intercorrelated, then we may want to leave that response system out of our temperament construct. For example, factor analyses of temperament scales have frequently extracted a 'food factor', in which items that might have been expected to be distributed across a variety of temperament dimensions instead are related to other food items but not to the general dimensions of temperament (see Chapter 15, by Hagekull, for an example). In this case, we may decide to exclude hunger reactivity from the temperament domain. Similarly, I have argued above that putative temperament dimensions such as intensity may need to be eliminated or constrained because they do not empirically hold together.

The second consideration has to do with our ability to vary the breadth or narrowness of our temperament measure at any given time. This flexibility in the grain of our analysis allows us to use a temperament construct at a breadth appropriate to the issue we are studying. For example, let us say that we wish to obtain a broad overall estimate of the stability of temperament over time. Here, we may wish to take advantage of aggregation of items across multiple dimensions when each dimension is related to the others in an organized way. We may therefore choose to assess very broad dimensions containing both reactive and self-regulative components. Thus, children who are more easily distressed are also likely to be regulating their reactions by avoiding rather than approaching novel or intense situations and by not attending to possibly distressing stimuli for very long at a time. By using a broad temperament assessment that takes advantage of this organization of temperamental dimensions, we are likely to achieve a higher degree of stability than if we used the component dimensions separately. If we are studying the relation of heart-rate reactivity to temperament, on the other hand, we might wish to look at a much more narrow assessment, e.g. the time course of the smile or the switching of visual attention, rather than a broad set of temperamental characteristics whose time course is not commensurate with our heart-rate measure. Given this approach, temperament is seen as a broad field of study, with both empirical considerations and our choice of research questions determining how we shall study it at any given time.

Self-Regulation

In addition to the reactive elements of temperament, there are also temperamental individual differences in the ease with which self-regulatory motor and attentional reactions are initiated. Some self-regulatory behaviors serve to soothe or excite the person, and these include built-in responses such as thumb- or finger-sucking, hand-clasping, or touching the ear or head. In our laboratory, we have recently been studying some of these behaviors in infants seen longitudinally at 3, 6.5, 10, and 13.5 months of age. Self-soothing behaviors such as sucking and hand-clasping are present at 3 months, show an increase in frequency at 10 months of age, and a later decrease at 13.5 months (Rothbart & Ziaie, 1988). We have found longitudinal stability of thumb- or finger-sucking and other hand–mouth activities, from 6.5 months to 10 and 13.5 months of age.

Self-regulatory processes also include the selective orientation of the person toward or away from the source of the excitement or the orientation of the person's attention toward or away from an environmental or internal location. Self-regulation is influenced by at least two major sources. First, positive and negative affective reactions in themselves (components of reactivity) will influence the individual's need to withdraw from the source of stimulation or to come closer to it and the energy level of that response. The signal value of a stimulus, that is, the extent to which it serves as a cue for positive or negative consequences of a particular response, will also influence the individual's regulatory behaviors and direction of attention, including *stimulus-seeking* versus *avoidance*. In turn, self-regulation can be seen to modulate reactivity. Thus, avoidance of a potentially difficult situation or not thinking about an upcoming threat decreases negative reactions, and approach toward a loved one or thinking about an upcoming pleasurable event increases positive reactions. In addition, behavioral inhibition can be seen in a freezing of the individual's motor response within a given situation. Finally, effortful direction of response can allow an individual actually to approach an event of which the individual is terrified. It is in this effortful level of control that our theory differs from Strelau's (see Chapter 3). With effort, regulation of behavior is no longer driven by the pleasure or distress associated directly with the experience, and a homeostatic model such as Strelau's need not apply.

The direct experience of affect and the signal value of stimulation are only two of many influences on self-regulation. Thus, Haith (1980) has described a set of built-in controls of very early visual orienting in the newborn, and Posner (1988; Posner & Presti, 1987) has identified a set of controls upon orienting and attention in adults and brain-lesioned patients that make it clear we are dealing with multi-determined processes when we discuss self-regulation. However, this model asserts that one set of influences upon variability in individual orienting is temperamental in origin.

Interactions among self-regulatory systems also constitute important aspects of the model. Thus, approach and withdrawal oppose one another, as do stimulus-seeking and avoidance. Behavioral inhibition opposes approach and attack and is not seen until the last half of the first year of life, whereas approach and withdrawal can be observed from birth (McGuire & Turkewitz, 1979).

Our framework allows for the simultaneous potentiation of both motor approach and avoidant self-regulatory tendencies as well as both sensory pleasure and distress (reactivity). Under conditions when both self-regulating directions (toward and away from the stimulus) are strongly potentiated, rapid shifts in the orientation of behavior toward and away from the stimulus may occur, and we have observed such shifts in children's reactions to novel toys (Pien & Rothbart, 1980). Rapid alternation of approach and withdrawal, termed 'conflict' by the ethologists (Berridge & Grill, 1984a,b), is congruent with other two-process models (e.g. Fox & Davidson, 1984). Simultaneous activation of both positive reactivity and negative self-regulation is also seen in such reactions as the coy smile, which combines smiling (a positive facial expression) with averting of gaze (a self-regulatory behavior that decreases excitement or arousal).

In the framework described here, other individuals, especially caregivers, siblings, and peers during the early years, will also influence reactivity and self-regulation. Direct stimulation from others can result in excitement in the child, and others may also act to regulate the child's state, as in providing soothing when the child is distressed. The seeking of excitement from others can be seen in some children at an early age. At a later age, children can also appeal directly to others in asking their help to overcome an obstacle or to soothe an upset. As more highly developed cognitions are added in the course of development, older children can also protect the self from negative information (and thereby negative feelings) by defensive strategies such as seeing the self as the victim of others' actions and responsibilities. Thus, at the most simple as well as the most complex levels, the operation of an individual's temperament is closely tied to the actions and perceptions of others.

Effort occupies a special status in this model, because effortful (conscious) control is capable of regulating both approach and avoidance, and, probably to a lesser degree, positive and negative reactivity. Examples of the conscious generation of reactivity include individuals' thinking about something happy in order to feel better or purposefully focusing upon an injustice in order to steel themselves for a difficult action. The controls of conscious effort upon self-regulatory activity are very important in our consideration of temperament because they make possible purposeful action that is counter to feeling. Thus, we can effortfully approach a stimulus that will create pain for us (e.g. an examination) in order to bring about a career goal, or withhold approaching a positive stimulus (e.g. a piece of chocolate cake) in order to avoid gaining weight. In anorexic individuals, such effortful control can assume life-threatening proportions. As described above, we can also, within limits (and these limits need also to be empirically explored), control the direction of our own attention, or we can effortfully attempt to influence others to provide the regulatory influences upon our own reactivity (soothing, support, etc.) that we desire.

Effort creates complications for the study of temperament. If we were *only* creatures of our likes and dislikes of the moment, then our orientation would be more directly the result of positive and negative reactivity. Effort or will allows us to behave in accordance with rules that require us to oppose these predispositions. Effects of effort will only be seen, however, when there is *conflict* between our inclinations and the prescribed action. Similarly, we will only see the effects of behavioral inhibition when conditions of novelty or challenge conflict with approach tendencies.

Effort affects both our reactive state and the other regulative strategies we employ. Effort can also be combined with both positive and negative affect, as when feelings of anger accompany planned attack, feelings of fear accompany planned withdrawal, or feelings of positive anticipation accompany working toward a distant positive goal.

Research Implications of the Model

A number of research questions can be derived from this model. For some of these questions, suggestive research data has already accumulated; for others, evidence is needed to clarify the model further. One empirical question concerns the relationship between the experience of sensory pleasure or distress (reactivity) in a given situation and the strength of actions undertaken to achieve pleasure or avoid distress (self-regulation). Can a person experience positive or negative sensations easily, but not have much inclination toward doing anything about them?

In parents' reports about their infants (Bates, Freeland, & Lounsbury, 1979; Rothbart, 1981) and in mothers' reports about their 3- to 7-year-old children (using the Children's Behavior Questionnaire now under development), we have found children's smiling and laughter and activity level to be positively related. In the laboratory, we have also found that infants who approach toys more quickly also tend to smile and laugh more (Rothbart, 1988). The correlations are low, however, and it is possible that these dimensions are functionally related (that is, children who derive active enjoyment from situations also approach sources of stimulation more rapidly because they enjoy them) rather than being a part of the same biological system. Evidence from neuropsychology suggests that motor responsiveness is based on a different biological system than sensory pleasure (Tucker & Williamson, 1984). We would hope that future research at both behavioral and physiological levels will allow us to determine the nature of the association between these two temperamental characteristics.

Evidence of a positive relation between infants' fearfulness and their susceptibility to distress from overstimulation (Rothbart, 1987) is congruent with our findings from the Children's Behavior Questionnaire that children more susceptible to discomfort also tend to be seen by their parents as more fearful. Again, the extent to which these two characteristics share common biological mechanisms or a functional relationship where children who are more easily discomfited are more likely to avoid potential dangers is also a question for future research.

Another research question is whether the parameters of motor reactivity in the young infant (e.g. the latency, intensity, and duration of motor excitement shown by the 3-month-old infant in reaction to social stimulation) are predictive of the response parameters of the child's later self-regulatory motor actions (approach and avoidance). In the young infant, motor activity is not goal-directed but is nevertheless elicited by exciting stimuli from the environment (Kistiakovskaia, 1965). It is possible that the early reactive aspects of the motor system will contribute to timing and/or intensity of a later motor response, but that cues of reward versus punishment will guide the *direction* of this response relatively independently (Posner & Rothbart, 1981, 1985).

An additional research question has to do with the relation between fear and frustration across different developmental periods. Our results with adults find the experience of fear and frustration to be positively correlated, and they are also positively correlated with other measures of negative reactivity (sadness and discomfort; Derryberry & Rothbart, 1984, 1988); during infancy we have found fear and frustration to be positively correlated for most of our samples, but not all.

In the laboratory, measures of fear and frustration are positively correlated for infants at 6.5 months but not at 10 and 13.5 months; fear and frustration are each independently positively related to the tendency to become overstimulated (distress to high intensities of stimulation) at *all* of these ages (Rothbart, 1987).

There are theoretical reasons for believing that fear might oppose frustration in strange situations such as the laboratory. Thus, if one component of fear is behavioral inhibition or the inhibition of approach responses, then in the laboratory, more fearful children would be less likely to mount strong approaches upon the stimuli presented than would less fearful children. For both infants and older children, we also regularly find a positive relation between activity level and distress to limitations or anger/frustration (Derryberry & Rothbart, 1984), suggesting that the *stronger* the behavioral approach tendency, the more susceptible the individual will be to frustration reactions. With less strong approach, there will be less strong frustration experienced, and probably even the expression of feelings of frustration would be inhibited.

In the home, frustration reactions should be likely even for fearful children (unless they are directly punished), because feelings of security in the home environment do not set up the conflict between fear and frustration that can exist in the laboratory. In self-report, we might expect to find the strongest relations between felt (but not necessarily behaviorally expressed) fear and frustration. We expect some children to show a good deal of consistency across situations (those less susceptible to fear) and others to look (and probably feel) quite different depending upon whether they are at home or in a strange or demanding place. This would constitute a temperamental example of *lack* of consistency for some individuals across situations as has been suggested by Bem and Allen (1974).

Differentiating between the strength of reactive sensory experiences and the strength of self-regulatory tendencies is also important when we think about behavioral inhibition or the inhibition of approach (Rothbart, in press). In inhibition of approach, the motor aspects of approach are inhibited, but the individual can continue to *feel* attracted to the goal and may become distressed at not being able to achieve it, even though inhibiting tendencies within the individual are preventing its achievement. Such an individual will thus be suceptible to both anger and fear reactions, and this combination of reactions may be related to the interesting mix of anger and fear items found in most anxiety scales (Watson & Tellegen, 1985).

Other research questions have to do with the relation between emotional reactivity and attentional self-regulation. The review in Chapter 12 suggests that high susceptibility to distress is related to low focused attention, but these characteristics have not been assessed in different situations. When they are assessed at the same time, high distress may preclude externally focused attention because the infant's eyes are often closed at high levels of crying. The correlation between distress and low attention (congruent with our adult research in which persons who report greater control over attentional shifting also report less susceptibility to distress; Derryberry & Rothbart, 1988) suggests that attentional self-regulation may involve direction of attention away from the disturbing stimulus (as indicated in Figure 1), but we must note that attention is also sometimes directed *toward* the threatening stimulus with the function of getting rid of it. Research will be necessary to explore the possibility that some individuals are more likely to focus upon negative stimuli than others.

In addition to these research questions, many additional developmental questions remain unanswered. Some of these involve the relation between different self-regulatory behaviors over time. Lipsitt and his associates have found that a measure of avidity in sucking a sweet liquid during the neonatal period (a form of approach) positively predicts behavioral inhibition during the toddler period (Lagasse, Gruber, & Lipsitt, in press). This finding may be related to a previous version of our model which posited that sensory sensitivity leads to positive reactions at low stimulus levels and negative reactions at higher stimulus levels for more sensitive individuals (Rothbart, in Goldsmith *et al.*, 1987).

This sensitivity constraint is not built into the model presented here, but if it should receive empirical support, it could be easily reincorporated into the framework. Our work has suggested an association between perceptual sensitivity and appreciation of pleasure at low stimulus intensities for both children and adults (Derryberry & Rothbart, 1984, 1988). We have found a negative relation between perceptual sensitivity and susceptibility to negative affect only for one sample of adults, however (Derryberry & Rothbart, 1984, 1988), so its status in the model is currently questionable.

CONCLUSIONS

In this chapter, I have laid out a methodological and conceptual approach to thinking about temperament. Although the framework provided can be used to derive empirical questions about temperament, the results of research from other sources can also be used to support or restructure the framework. In general, strategies for learning more about the detail of the organization of temperament will involve asking questions at different levels of breadth or narrowness about relationships among sets of reactive and regulatory processes. Our own approach has been to look for broad outlines of temperament by employing many temperament variables at a fairly gross level of analysis, but it is to be hoped that addressing increasingly more precise questions will allow us to come to understand temperament in its important fine details.

ACKNOWLEDGMENTS

I greatly appreciate the critical comments of Jack Bates and Susan Green on previous versions of this chapter.

REFERENCES

Bates, J.E., Freeland, C.A.B., & Lounsbury, M.L. (1979). Measurement of infant difficultness. *Child Development*, **50**, 794–803.

Bem, D.J. & Allen, A. (1974). On predicting some of the people some of the time: The search for cross-situational consistencies in behavior. *Psychological Review*, **81**, 506–520.

Berlyne, D.E. (1970). Novelty, complexity, and hedonic value. *Perception and Psychophysics*, **8**, 279–286.

Berlyne, D.E. (1971). *Aesthetics and psychobiology*. New York: Appleton-Century.

Berlyne, D.E. (1973). The vicissitudes of aplopathematic and thelematoscopic pneumatology (or The hydrography of hedonism). In D.E. Berlyne & K.M. Madsen (Eds), *Pleasure, reward, preference* (pp. 1–34). New York: Academic Press.

Berridge, K.C. & Grill, H.J. (1984a). Alternating ingestive and aversive consummatory responses suggest a two-dimensional analysis of palatability in rats. *Behavioral Neuroscience*, **97**, 563–573.

Berridge, K. C., & Grill, H. J. (1984b). Isohedonic tastes support a two-dimensional hypothesis of palatability. *Appetite*, **5**, 221–231.

Buss, A.H. & Plomin, R. (1984). *Temperament: Early developing personality traits*. Hillsdale, NJ: Erlbaum.

Derryberry, D. & Rothbart, M.K. (1984). Emotion, attention, and temperament. In C.E. Izard, J. Kagan, & R. Zajonc (Eds), *Emotion, cognition and behavior* (pp. 132–166). Cambridge University Press.

Derryberry, D. & Rothbart, M.K. (1988). Arousal, affect and attention as components of temperament. *Journal of Personality and Social Psychology*, **55**, 953–966.

Fox, N.A. & Davidson, R.J. (1984). Hemispheric substrates of affect: A developmental model. In N.A. Fox & R.J. Davidson (Eds), *The psychology of affective development* (pp. 353–382). Hillsdale, NJ: Erlbaum.

Goldsmith, H.H., Buss, A.H., Plomin, R., Rothbart, M.K., Thomas, A., & Chess, C. (1987). Roundtable: What is temperament? Four approaches. *Child Development*, **58**, 505–529.

Goldsmith, H.H. & Campos, J. (1982). Genetic influences on individual differences in emotionality. Paper presented at the International Conference on Infant Studies, Austin, Texas.

Haith, M.M. (1980). *Rules that babies look by*. Hillsdale, NJ: Erlbaum.

Izard, C.E. (1977). *Human emotions*. New York: Plenum.

Kistiakovskaia, M.I. (1965). Stimuli evoking positive emotions in infants in the first months of life. *Soviet Psychology and Psychiatry*, **3**, 39–48.

Lagasse, L., Gruber, C., & Lipsitt, L. (in press). The infantile expression of avidity in relation to later assessments of inhibition and attachment. In S. Reznick (Ed.), *Perspectives in behavioral inhibition*. Chicago: University of Chicago Press.

Martin, R. (1984). The Temperament Assessment Battery Manual. University of Georgia, unpublished manuscript.

Matheny, A.P., Jr, Wilson, R.S., & Nuss, S.M. (1984). Toddler temperament: Stability across settings and over ages. *Child Development*, **55**, 1200–1211.

McGuire, I. & Turkewitz, G. (1979). Approach–withdrawal theory and the study of infant devlopment. In M. Bortner (Ed.), *Cognitive growth and development*. New York: Brunner/Mazel.

Pien, D. & Rothbart, M.K. (1980). Incongruity, humour, play and self-regulation of arousal in young children. In A. Chapman & P. McGhee (Eds), *Children's humour*. New York: Wiley.

Posner, M. I. (1978). *Chronometric explorations of mind*. Hillsdale, NJ: Erlbaum.

Posner, M.I. (1988). Structures and function of selective attention. In T. Boll & B.K. Bryant (Eds), *Clinical neuropsychology and brain function: Research, measurement and practice* (pp. 173–202). Washington, DC: American Psychological Association.

Posner, M.I. & Presti, D.E. (1987). Selective attention and cognitive control. *Trends in Neuroscience*, **10**, 12–17.

Posner, M.I., & Rothbart, M.K. (1981). The development of attentional mechanisms. In J. Flowers (Ed.), *Nebraska symposium on motivation* (pp. 1–52). Lincoln, NE: University of Nebraska Press.

Posner, M.I., & Rothbart, M.K. (1986). The concept of energy in psychological theory. In R. Hockey, A. Gaillard, & M. Coles (Eds.), *Energetical aspects of human information processing* (pp. 23–42). Boston: Martinus Nijhoff.

Reznick, J.S., Kagan, J., Snidman, N., Gersten, M., Baak, K., & Rosenberg, A. (1986). Inhibited and uninhibited children: A follow-up study. *Child Development*, **57**, 660–680.

Rothbart, M.K. (1973). Laughter in young children. *Psychological Bulletin*, **80**, 247–256.

Rothbart, M.K. (1981). Measurement of temperament in infancy. *Child Development*, **52**, 569–578.

Rothbart, M.K. (1986). Longitudinal observation of infant temperament. *Developmental Psychology*, **22**, 356–365.

Rothbart, M.K. (1987). Laboratory observations of infant temperament. Paper presented at the Meetings of the Society for Research in Child Development, Baltimore.

Rothbart, M.K. (1988). Temperament and the development of inhibited approach. *Child Development*, **59**, 1241–1250.

Rothbart M.K. (in press). Behavioral approach and inhibition. In S. Reznick (Ed.), *Perspectives on behavioral inhibition*. Chicago: University of Chicago Press.

Rothbart, M.K. & Alansby, J.A. (in press). Questionnaire approaches to the study of infant temperament. In J.W. Fagen & J. Colombo (Eds), *Individual differences in infancy: Reliability, stability and prediction*. Hillsdale, NJ: Erlbaum.

Rothbart, M.K. & Derryberry, D. (1981). Development of individual differences in temperament. In M.E. Lamb & A.L. Brown (Eds), *Advances in developmental psychology*, Vol. 1 (pp. 37–86). Hillsdale, NJ: Erlbaum.

Rothbart, M.K. & Goldsmith, H.H. (1985). Three approaches to the study of infant temperament. *Developmental Review*, **5**, 237–260.

Rothbart, M.K. & Posner, M.I. (1985). Temperament and the development of self regulation. In L.C. Hartlage & C.F. Telzrow (Eds), *The neuropsychology of individual differences: A developmental perspective* (pp. 93–123). New York: Plenum.

Rothbart, M.K. & Ziaie, H. (1988, March). Infant behaviors that may modulate distress. In J. L. Gewirtz (Chair), *Development and control of infant separation distress*. Symposium conducted at the meeting of the International Conference on Infant Studies, Washington, DC.

Rowe, D. & Plomin, R. (1977). Temperament in early childhood. *Journal of Personality Assessment*, **41**, 150–156.

Sroufe, L. & Waters, E. (1976). The ontogenesis of smiling and laughter: A perspective on the organization of development in infancy. *Psychological Review*, **83**, 173–189.

Strelau, J. (1983). *Temperament, personality, activity*. New York: Academic Press.

Thomas, A. & Chess, S. (1977). *Temperament and development*. New York: Brunner/Mazel.

Tucker, D.M. & Williamson, P.A. (1984). Asymmetric neural control systems in human self-regulation *Psychological Review*, **91**, 185–215.

Watson, D. & Tellegen, A. (1985). Toward a consensual structure of mood. *Psychological Bulletin*, **98**, 219–235.

Section Two
Temperament and Biological Processes

6

Biological Processes in Temperament

MARY KLEVJORD ROTHBART
University of Oregon

Relating temperament to biology is an activity with both an ancient history and, given recent rapid advances in the neurosciences, a promising future. In this chapter, some historical attempts to link the psychology of temperament to the biology of individual differences are discussed. Much of this work has focused upon adult temperament, but it is also highly relevant to the study of temperament in childhood. Contributions considered in this brief history include early Greco-Roman approaches, the theories of Pavlov, and the British approaches of Eysenck and Gray. The history is followed by a review of some current perspectives on the biology of temperament, with models based upon central nervous system (CNS) development, studies of autonomic and endocrine processes, and approaches to the development of hemispheric control of emotion and action. A separate chapter in this section (Chapter 7), written by Hill Goldsmith, is given over to a discussion of behavior-genetic approaches to temperament in childhood.

HISTORY

The Fourfold Typology

Concepts of temperament have their roots in centuries-old attempts to link individual characteristics to variations in physiological structure. These ideas are present in both Eastern (Needham, 1973) and Western intellectual traditions (Diamond, 1974). The term temperament itself comes from the Latin *temperamentum*, meaning a mixture (of the bodily humors), from *temperare*: 'to mingle in due proportion'. Thus, the idea of multiple biological influences upon an individual's characteristic behavior is central to even ancient uses of the term.

Although Galen (second century AD) is usually given credit for identifying the fourfold typology of the sanguine, choleric, melancholic, and phlegmatic types of

Temperament in Childhood   Edited by G.A. Kohnstamm, J.E. Bates and M.K. Rothbart
© 1989 John Wiley & Sons Ltd

individuals and relating them to the person's relative mixture of bodily humors, in fact he did not (Diamond, 1974). The syndrome of melancholia and its association to a predominance of black bile was present as early as the fourth century BC in the writings of Theophrastus, and Diamond (1974) argues that the work of Vindician (fourth century AD) portrayed the first complete fourfold typology of temperament associated with the Hippocratic bodily humors.

Although Galen is not responsible for the fourfold typology, his writings are appropriate to this brief history, because he used the existence of individual differences in the very young child to argue for the study of temperament: 'The starting point of my entire discourse is the knowledge of the differences which can be seen in little children, and which reveal to us the faculties of the soul. Some are very sluggish, others violent; some are insatiable gourmands, others quite the contrary; they may be shameless, or shy; and they exhibit many other analogous differences' (Diamond, 1974, p. 604). Galen goes on to argue that if the souls of the young were interchangeable, we would expect them to act in similar ways from the earliest days; the presence of early behavioral differences indicates that 'the nature of the soul is not the same for all' (Diamond, 1974, p. 604). Thus, both ideas about the organization and physiology of temperament and the importance of temperamental differences among children were present in early writings.

The fourfold typology persisted through the Middle Ages and the Renaissance (Burton, 1621; Culpeper, 1657) and was later to be found in the writings of Kant (1798). By the time of Wundt (1903), a shift had occurred from positing typologies of temperament to dimensions of individual variability. Wundt proposed the temperamental dimensions of strength and speed of change of feelings, and Ebbinghaus proposed the dimensions of optimism–pessimism and emotionality (Eysenck & Eysenck, 1985). Each of these two-dimensional models could be used to generate four quadrants corresponding to the ancient typology.

Constitutional Psychology

The attempt to link psychological characteristics to body structure also has an ancient history. Sheldon and Stevens (1942) note that, as early as the fifth century BC, Hippocrates identified two physical types, *habitus apoplectus* (thick, muscular, and strong) and *habitus phthisicus* (delicate, thin, and weak). Hippocrates argued that the two types differed temperamentally, and that muscular individuals were more prone to apoplexy (high blood pressure) and thin individuals to tuberculosis. French and German typologies incorporating three physical body types were developed in the nineteenth century, and Kretschmer (1925) linked body typology to both temperament and mental illness.

Again forsaking a typology, Sheldon and Stevens (1942) measured the endomorphic (soft, rounded), mesomorphic (hard, rectangular), and ectomorphic (linear, fragile) components of five different areas of the body. A revision of this measurement system was offered in 1969 (Sheldon, Lewis & Tenney, 1969). They also identified three temperament clusters:

> *viscerotonia* (sociable, gluttonous for food and affection, appreciative of comfort, relaxed, even-tempered, slow, and tolerant);

somatotonia (need for muscular and vigorous activity, risk-taking and adventure, aggressive, noisy, courageous, and callous toward others);

cerebretonia (inhibition, restraint, secretiveness, fearfulness, self-consciousness, and need for solitude).

Sheldon and Stevens (1942) linked these clusters to corresponding body components (viscerotonic to endomorphy, somatotonic to mesomorphy, and cerebretonia to ectomorphy).

Since much less work has been done in this area than in other domains involving temperament and biological processes, constitutional psychology will only be briefly mentioned in this historical section. It should be noted, however, that, although Sheldon and Stevens' (1942) approach is usually introduced in the literature chiefly in order to dismiss it, research with children as subjects has found correlations of a moderate size between somatotype and teachers' ratings of 2- to 4-year-olds' behavior patterns (Walker, 1962), behavior ratings of classmates for 7-year-olds (Hanley, 1951), and adolescents' self-reports (Cortes & Gatti, 1965). These findings are likely influenced by the strong stereotypes that exist about body types (Lerner, 1969), but studies have also linked delinquency positively to mesomorphy and negatively to ectomorphy, where the effect of stereotypes would need to be more indirect (Cortes & Gatti, 1972; Glueck & Glueck, 1950, 1956).

These relationships between physique and behavior are more well established for males and they tend to be stronger for mesomorphy and ectomorphy than for endomorphy measures. Greater longitudinal stability has also been found for mesomorphy and ectomorphy than for endomorphy, with stability for mesomorphy and ectomorphy from age 8 to 18 being as high for males as is stability for measures of height (Walker & Tennes, 1980). Considerable stability of somatotype has also been found for girls as well as boys from the preschool period to late adolescence (Walker, 1978). In addition to work following directly in Sheldon and Stevens' (1942) tradition, a current research approach relating constitution to behavior is the study of Type A behavior and heart disease, which has been applied to children as well as to adults (Matthews, 1980, 1982; Matthews & Avis, 1983; Steinberg, 1986; Whalen & Henker, 1986).

Pavlov and the Soviet Schools: Properties of the Nervous System

There is a strong and highly physiologically oriented temperament research tradition in Eastern Europe, and schools of thought within this tradition are described in some detail in Jan Strelau's (1983) book, *Temperament, personality, activity*. Work in this tradition stems from Pavlov's ideas about individual differences in properties of the nervous system, although Strelau (1983) points out that Pavlov actually defined these differences in terms of behavioral functioning. The most important of the nervous system properties was seen to be strength of excitation of the nervous system. This property was originally assessed in laboratory measures of 'transmarginal inhibition', i.e. decrements of conditioned responding at high levels of stimulus intensity. Pavlov argued that individuals who were able to continue to function under high intensity or prolonged exposure to stimulation before inhibition set in were characterized by 'strong' nervous systems; those with low thresholds for decrement, by 'weak' nervous sytems.

Later research in the laboratory of Teplov and Nebylitsyn (Nebylitsyn, 1972) indicated that individuals with weak nervous systems also demonstrated lower sensory thresholds than individuals with strong nervous systems. Thus, individuals with weak nervous systems tended to demonstrate thresholds, peak responses, and response decrement at lower stimulus intensity levels than did individuals with relatively strong nervous systems. Additional nervous system properties in Pavlov's model included strength of inhibition, equilibrium between excitation and inhibition, and mobility, i.e. the rapidity with which the altered signal value of a stimulus is reflected in the individual's behavior. Soviet laboratories added other nervous system properties: lability (speed of initiation and termination of nervous system processes; Teplov, 1964) and dynamism (the speed with which conditioned responses are formed).

Later workers in the Pavlov tradition abandoned the notion of nervous system properties and referred instead to traits seen as inborn and stable (Nebylitsyn, 1972; Teplov, 1964). Serious problems developed for the Nebylitsyn school when laboratory indices of presumably global nervous system properties proved to be highly dependent on the nature of the stimulus and response employed (the 'partiality' phenomenon; see Strelau, 1983). This problem led researchers to move out of the laboratory and into the development of broad questionnaire measures (Rusalov, 1987; Strelau, 1972) or, when they continued laboratory work, to limit the number of psychophysiological measures employed (Bodunov, 1985).

Pavlov's model was based upon observations in conditioning research and emphasized reactivity to the signal value of stimuli and the ease of formation, performance, and extinction of conditioned responses. Strelau (1983) and his associates in the Eastern European tradition have additionally recognized self-regulative, motivational, and motor-tempo aspects of temperament, while laboratory work on individual differences in Moscow came to be interpreted in terms of a cybernetic model involving motor programming, tempo, and variability of motor function (Bodunov, 1985).

The British Tradition: Factor Analysis, Temperament, and the Nervous System

Whereas the Soviet tradition in temperament began with ideas about a conceptual nervous system and related them to dimensions of temperament, the tradition in Great Britain began by deriving temperament factors from self-report instruments and only later relating these to the nervous system. Using the techniques of factor analysis originally employed in the study of intelligence, Webb, a student of Spearman, and Cyril Burt each undertook the factorial study of temperament in 1915. Factor analyzing items assessing emotionality, activity, self-qualities, and intellect, Webb identified a factor w, which was defined as 'consistency of action resulting from deliberate volition or will' (Webb, 1915, p. 34). Later reanalyses of Webb's data also yielded introversion–extraversion factors (Burt, 1937; Cattell, 1933; Garnet, 1918; Studman, 1935).

At about the same time, Burt (1915) introduced a factor called emotionality, or emotional stability–instability, which was later also identified by Eysenck and titled Neuroticism. By 1939, Burt had also identified the factor of introversion–extraversion and had used the two dimensions of emotionality and introversion–extraversion to derive the ancient typology: melancholic, the emotional introvert; choleric, the emotional extravert; phlegmatic, the less emotional introvert; and sanguine, the less emotional extravert. A number of studies in the 1930s and 1940s in Great Britain had also identified factors of introversion–extraversion and emotionality (see review by Eysenck, 1947). In a study of 700 patients in an army neurosis unit, Eysenck (1947) also reported evidence for an emotionality factor (neuroticism or N) and introversion–extraversion (E) factors, along with a psychoticism (P) factor.

What Eysenck added to these temperament factors in 1957 was a possible physiological base. His biological model was originally inspired by the work of Pavlov and by Hull's (1943) applications of Pavlov's constructs to learning theory in the United States. Eysenck's (1957) first model related introversion–extraversion to the balance between cortical excitation and inhibition, arguing that relatively weak excitatory potentials predisposed the individual to extraversion and hysterical–psychopathic disorders, and strong excitatory potentials to introversion and dysthymic disorders. Eysenck also described neuroticism in terms of the 'drive' concept of Hull (Gibson, 1981), and he predicted that introverts would be more conditionable than extraverts.

In 1967, with the intervening discovery of the ascending reticular activating system (ARAS) (Moruzzi & Magoun, 1949), Eysenck modified his biological theory into an arousal-based one. He now noted that non-specific externally driven arousal of the cerebral cortex could be inhibited or facilitated by corticoreticular loops allowing the cortex to regulate its own level of arousal. Extraverts were understood to have stronger corticoreticular inhibitory processes so that their level of cortical arousal would be tonically lower than that of introverts. Eysenck believed that introverts had weaker inhibitory processes, resulting in higher tonic cortical arousal levels that would exceed optimal levels of arousal at lower stimulus intensities than for extraverts. Thus, introverts were expected to experience as unpleasant and to avoid situations involving stimulation that an extravert might find pleasant. Extraverts, being tonically underaroused, were seen as more likely to seek stimulation that would bring them to an optimal level of arousal. In 1967, Eysenck related neuroticism to the functioning of the limbic system, postulating that neuroticism increased as the sympathetic division of the autonomic nervous system gained dominance over the parasympathetic division. As of 1967, no neurophysiological basis for psychoticism had been proposed.

Within the last two decades, Jeffrey Gray (1971, 1979, 1982) has undertaken a major revision of Eysenck's principal dimensions and neurophysiology. First, Gray (1970) argued that introverts are not generally more conditionable than extraverts, but that they are especially likely to show conditioning in situations involving threat. In Gray's model, introverts are seen as more susceptible to punishment or non-reward; extraverts, as more sensitive to reward or non-punishment. Neuroticism is viewed as the result of increasing sensitivity to both reward and punishment, or as a combination of arousing aspects of introverted and extraverted tendencies. Gray's theoretical model rotates the axes of Eysenck's model 45 degrees, making anxiety (behavioral inhibition) and impulsivity (behavioral activation) the basic dimensions of temperament rather than neuroticism and introversion–extraversion.

Criticism of Gray's model as it relates to Eysenck's theory has been raised in connection both with its failure to satisfy criteria of simple factorial structure (Fahrenberg, 1987) and with its assumption of a relationship between E and N in the anxiety dimension (Robinson, 1986). Whether Gray's model can be viewed as a variant of Eysenck's or a radical alternative (the latter characterization is made by Robinson, 1986), his view of behavior as representing a balance between an approach and an inhibition system is an intriguing one for the developmental psychologist (Rothbart, 1988).

In Gray's neurophysiological model, the approach or behavioral activation system (BAS) is traced through structures previously identified in the self-stimulation literature (Olds & Olds, 1963), including the medial forebrain bundle and lateral hypothalamus, and involving the influences of the neurotransmitters dopamine (DA) and norepinephrine (NE) (Stein, 1980). The anxiety or behavioral inhibition system (BIS) is seen as including the ARAS, the orbital frontal cortex, the medial septal area and the hippocampus, and involving the neurotransmitters NE and serotonin. The BIS is seen to be involved in passive avoidance and extinction. When the individual responds to signals of punishment or non-reward, the ARAS activates the medial septal area (which is also monitored and modulated by the orbital frontal cortex). The medial septal area in turn leads to hippocampal theta rhythm, resulting in inhibition of reticular activity and of ongoing behavior. The BIS and BAS are seen as being mutually inhibitory, so that they compete to control the individual's motor functioning (Gray, 1975).

GRAY'S MODEL: BEHAVIORAL ACTIVATION AND INHIBITION

Gray's model (1979, 1982) holds integrative promise for students of development, and will be described here in some detail. As described above, the BAS responds to cues signalling reward, and the BIS to signals of punishment. Individuals are seen to differ in the strength of each, with the balance indicating differences in introversion (BIS greater than BAS) and extraversion (BAS greater than BIS). Fowles (1984) has provided a clear outline relating Gray's model to studies on the effects of reward and punishment, and I follow this outline here.

First, consider a situation in which a response is rewarded every time it occurs. In this situation, the BAS is operating, and stimuli present in the situation become conditioned to signals that a given response will be rewarded. Now, what will happen when a response that has been consistently rewarded is instead punished? The BIS will now decrease the likelihood of the response, and stimuli present in the situation will become cues for punishment of the response. Since the BAS and BIS oppose one another and both are now operating, a situation of conflict is created. Whether an approach will occur depends upon the relative strength of the two systems. To the extent that individuals differ in the relative strength of BAS and

BIS, they will differ in the extent to which the now-punished response will be performed.

There are direct applications of the situation described above to child socialization. For example, consider that a child has just performed an act with pleasurable consequences (e.g. tearing the pages from a book or magazine and chewing on them). The caregiver gives a sharp command for the child to stop. Will this punishment be effective in inhibiting the child's activity? Although other variables will also influence the outcome, it is likely that the resolution of the behavioral conflict created by imposing punishment upon a previously rewarded act will be related to the relative strengths of the BAS and BIS systems.

Another laboratory situation in which both systems operate is one in which a response has been rewarded but now is no longer rewarded (an extinction condition). When a reward fails to appear when expected, frustration (a form of punishment) occurs, so that both BAS and BIS are again seen to be operating. As cues indicating non-reward or punishment are repeatedly experienced over extinction trials, the BIS comes to dominate the BAS and approach is inhibited.

An interesting effect can be observed in connection with partial reinforcement, i.e. a situation where during training a response is sometimes rewarded and sometimes not. Animals will persist in responding over a longer period during extinction when they have been trained under partial reinforcement than when they received only reward. Amsel (1986) interprets this effect as occurring because cues signalling the punishment of non-reward which precede both non-rewards and rewards, come to signal reward as well. Thus, when reward is no longer forthcoming, the BAS will continue to operate even in the presence of cues signalling non-reward, and the animal will show greater persistence. Changing from a larger reward to a smaller reward also leads to weaker responding than if the smaller reward alone had been presented: in this case the BIS is strengthened and frustration is created by the discrepancy between what was expected and what was experienced, so that extinction occurs more rapidly.

Finally we can consider a situation in which the animal is given both the signal that shock will be forthcoming and the opportunity to avoid the shock by leaving the area. Active avoidance of punishment is thus rewarded, and the BAS will be strengthened. The BIS in this instance is also involved in signalling environmental danger (Gray, 1979), but in Gray's model, the chief involvement of the BIS is in passive, not active, avoidance.

Gray (1977, 1979, 1982) has found that anti-anxiety drugs both disinhibit behavior when passive avoidance is required and also increase resistance to extinction when continuous reinforcement is followed by non-reinforcement. Anti-anxiety drugs do not, however, affect responses that are expected to be chiefly affected by the BAS, such as reward and active avoidance learning. Gray has studied likely physiological sites for behavioral inhibition in rats, identifying in particular the septal–hippocampal areas, where lesions produce changes in behavior similar to effects of anti-anxiety drugs (Gray, 1978).

Gray finds that when animals are exposed to inhibition-inducing conditions, hippocampal theta rhythm centered on a narrow band of 7–8.5 Hz is associated with ensuing behavioral inhibition. Stimulation of the septal area also increases hippocampal theta and behavioral inhibition. Finally, Gray and his colleagues have investigated neurotransmitter functioning, finding that the dorsal ascending noradrenergic bundle from the locus coeruleus to the septal–hippocampal area is involved in the effects of the anti-anxiety drugs (Gray, 1982).

Gorenstein and Newman's Model for Septal–Hippocampal Function

Related work involving human subjects and stemming from a theoretical framework developed by Gorenstein and Newman (1980) suggests the relevance of constructs of behavioral inhibition and activation to a socialization setting. Gorenstein and Newman propose that the effects of septal lesions provide a model for impulsivity exhibited in individuals with psychopathic, antisocial, alcoholic, hyperactive and extraverted tendencies. They note that extraverts and psychopaths will sometimes continue to emit dominant responses in spite of punishment, extinction or the reversal of contingencies (McCleary, 1966).

Newman and his colleagues have assessed the capacity of extraverted and psychopathic subjects to use cues for punishment to withhold inappropriate approach-driven behavior. The paradigm used is a passive avoidance procedure, also called a 'go–no go' situation, where the subject is expected to withhold responses that have been associated with punishment. Newman, Widom, and Nathan's (1985) subjects were given a series of two-digit numbers and learned by trial and error to respond to some of the numbers but not to others. Extraverts made more errors of commission to punished numbers than did introverts.

In a further study, Nichols and Newman (1986) asked subjects to view a visual pattern and match a subsequent pattern against it using a same–different judgment. Rewards and punishments were preprogrammed and non-contingent on the subject's response. Introverts responded more slowly on trials following punishment, while extraverts responded more quickly on trials following punishment. This effect was not found in a reward-only or a punishment-only condition, but extraverts responded more quickly in a reward-only than in a punishment-only condition. Derryberry (in press) has found a similar effect using a paradigm in which the appropriate response to the punishment signal is speeding rather than slowing responding for the subsequent trial. Finally, Patterson, Kosson, and Newman (1987) have found that subjects' tendency to slow down after a punished item was significantly related to their performance on a 'go–no go' task.

This research suggests that it is possible to separate energizing from directional influences of punishment: for introverts, goal-directed responses are inhibited by punishment; for extraverts, goal-directed responses may be activated by punishment. Research on attention also supports the separation of selective and energizing functions (Posner, 1978; Posner & Rothbart, 1981, 1986). Thus, in the context of previously rewarded behavior, punishment may actually *increase* approach in relatively extraverted individuals. Saltz, Campbell, and Skotko (1983) found, in support of Luria's (1961, 1969) observations, that increasing the loudness of a 'no go' command increased 3- to 4- year-old children's likelihood of performing a prohibited act. They also found that increasing loudness decreased the likelihood of responding for children 5–6 years of age, indicating developmental changes in excitatory and inhibitory effects.

This line of research is likely to have important implications for the development of behavior problems in children. In studies of aggressive behaviors, Patterson (1980) has found that parents of non-problem children are effective in stopping their children's aversive behavior on three out of every four occasions when they punish. However, when parents of problem children used punishment, the likelihood that the child would continue the punished behavior increased rather than decreased (Patterson, 1977, 1980; Snyder, 1977). Thus, punishment of aggressive behavior in some children serves to increase rather than decrease its likelihood of occurrence in a manner reminiscent of Newman's extraverts' decreased latency to perform a previously punished act (Nichols & Newman, 1986).

Adaptations of the Newman go–no go paradigms to research with children will be important, because results from them suggest that temperament may place powerful constraints on social learning. For example, the effects of punishment in the context of reward are likely to be more effective with children who are susceptible to behavioral inhibition than with those who are not. Thus, different approaches toward modifying behavior rather than the use of punishment may be needed with at least some young children.

Amsel's Research on Septal–Hippocampal Development and Behavior

For the past decade, Amsel and his colleagues have been engaged in a research program that has increasingly come together with Gray's work (Amsel, 1986; Amsel & Stanton, 1980). In Amsel's research, observation has been made of the age at which developing rats demonstrate frustration effects (e.g. effects of partial reinforcement on extinction, effects of changing reward size), resulting in a timetable for the appearance of these effects. Nicholson and Gray (1972) have also measured susceptibility to frustrative non-reward in children, and found it to be related to measures of neuroticism and introversion. Amsel (1986) found that, although rats as young as 10 days old can learn to alternate responding with non-responding when responding is rewarded only on odd-numbered trials, they do not show the effects of partial reinforcement on extinction until 16–18 days and they do not show the effects of changing from large to small rewards until 25–26 days.

Amsel (1986) relates these changes to development of the septal–hippocampal system: approximately 90% of the development of the granule cells of the dentate gyrus in the hippocampal formation of the rat occurs after the birth of the animal, with the greatest differentiation occurring between days 12 and 14 and with near-adult levels reached by days 25–30. When granule cells are X-irradiated early in development, later effects of partial reward on extinction are reduced. Lesions in adult rats in the septal–hippocampal area also reduce or eliminate these effects.

Amsel (1986) points out that the theta rhythm of the hippocampal electro-encephalogram (EEG) is not demonstrated until around 11–12 days, and that the granule cells of the hippocampal dentate gyrus are theta-producing. He also notes that theta activity is linked not only to the effects of frustration but also to the effects of novel or disruptive stimulation. Amsel cites research by Deadwyler, West, and Lynch (1979a,b) in which an electrode placed within the granule-cell layer does not indicate activity when the animal is responding to a tone that signals only water reward, but when a second tone indicating non-reward is added, the cells in the granule layer respond to both tones. As the rat shows greater discrimination in performance to the two tones, the discharge of granule cells changes in the direction of longer bursts of firing for the tone signalling reward and short bursts for the tone signalling non-reward. Recordings taken higher in the dentate gyrus meanwhile show response to both rewarded and unrewarded tones, with these responses present from the beginning of conditioning. This finding suggests the presence of two processes, one linked to excitatory and the other to inhibitory effects of the signals.

Researchers have also linked hippocampal development to the development of inhibitory tendencies. Douglas (1975) noted that rats with hippocampal lesions show decreases in signs of Pavlovian internal inhibition such as susceptibility to extinction and passive avoidance learning, as well as the tendency to alternate responses to two different locations when neither location is rewarded (spontaneous alternation). Douglas observed that juvenile rats show performance similar to that of hippocampal-lesioned adult rats, but change to more adult behavior by 35 days of age. He notes that these changes occur at a time when major differentiation of granule cells in the hippocampal dentate gyrus had occurred (Altman, Brunner, & Bayer, 1973). Another location related to tasks involving inhibition is the lateral convexity of the prefrontal cortex (Rosenkilde, 1979), which is connected to the dentate gyrus of the hippocampus via the entorhinal cortex.

The maturation of cholinergic systems in the septal–hippocampal areas may be implicated in these changes, and behavioral changes in activity level in juvenile rats have been related to development of cholinergic mechanisms by about 15 days of age. These developmental decreases in activity level can be counteracted by introduction of cholinergic antagonists, but they are not effective until 15–20 days of age (Pradhan & Pradhan, 1980).

Development of Behavioral Inhibition in Infancy

Taking into account Amsel's (1986) argument that hippocampal theta activity is related to the inhibition associated with novelty as well as with punishment, we may consider the development of inhibited approach to novelty and to potential punishment in infancy. In research on the development of inhibited approach, Schaffer and his colleagues have observed the onset of wariness, that is, 'a relative increase in the time taken before contact is made on first exposure to an unfamiliar object' (Schaffer, Greenwood, & Parry, 1972, p. 173). Schaffer argues that one important change occurring at 6–9 months is not the onset of avoidance responses but rather the onset of inhibition of the child's approach responses.

Schaffer *et al.* (1972) conducted a longitudinal study in which 20 children's responses to unfamiliar stimuli were observed monthly from 6 to 12 months of age. Even at the earliest age, infants revealed by their increased looking time to novel stimuli in comparison with familiar stimuli that they were sensitive to the unfamiliarity of objects. Although Schaffer and his colleagues did not find that novelty affected manipulation time, other studies indicated that young infants also differentially manipulate novel and familiar toys (Rubenstein, 1974, 1976; Ruff, 1976). However, at 6 months, infants approached unfamiliar objects 'impulsively and immediately' (Schaffer, 1974, p. 14). Only at 8 months and beyond was latency to reach and grasp influenced by familiarity. At this age, infants showed hesitations, sometimes but not always accompanied by distress and/or avoidance to novel objects. When older infants made contact with the novel object, their action was likely to be abbreviated and cautious.

Schaffer (1974) noted that, during their hesitations, children subjected the stimulus 'to intense and uninterrupted visual inspection – as though appraising it before selecting a response deemed suitable in terms of the individual's past experience of that stimulus. Impulsiveness thus gave way to wariness, and the response that emerged after the period of immobility could take the form of approach or avoidance (i.e. cautious exploration or a fear reaction)' (Schaffer, 1974, p. 15).

We have also found increases in latency to contact an intense and unfamiliar toy for children between 6.5 and 10 months of age in a longitudinal study (Rothbart, 1988). In addition, individual differences in latency to approach low-intensity stimuli at 6.5 months are predictive of latencies at 10 and 13.5 months and 10 month latencies to 13.5 months, but individual differences in latency to approach high-intensity stimuli do not show stability across age. These findings may be interpreted as indicating the development of inhibition of motor activity to novel and potentially punishing stimuli across this period (Rothbart, 1988, in press).

It is important in connection with this discussion of the development of inhibitory controls over approach processes that we recognize that we are discussing processes that: (a) are not operating at birth, but can be observed at a later time, (b) will be variable in the age of onset, and (c) will demonstrate individual variability once the controls have developed. Thus, we can speak of the age of onset of behavioral inhibition related to passive avoidance, and we can also speak of individual differences in this kind of behavioral inhibition in later childhood or adulthood (Gray, 1982).

HEMISPHERIC LATERALITY AND TEMPERAMENT

Developmental changes in hemispheric control of emotion and action have been linked to emotional functioning in ways that may prove important for our understanding of individual differences in temperament and development. Following McGuinness and Pribram's (1982) analysis of attentional systems, Kinsbourne and Bemporad (1984) identify: (a) an activation mechanism supporting motor performance and involving the lateral hypothalamus, basal ganglia, and nigrostriatal pathways, (b) an arousal or stop response to novel, complex, and intense stimuli involving the ventromedial nucleus of the hypothalamus, amygdala, and frontal cortex, and (c) an effort system coordinating arousal and activation and involving the hippocampal circuit. Emotion accompanies activity of the arousal stop system, and motivation accompanies the activational go system. Coordination of activation and arousal involves attentional and emotional sets that operate on the basis of the person's experiences of reward and punishment contingencies. We

(Rothbart & Posner, 1975) have suggested that development of a conscious effort system capable of overriding otherwise dominant reward or punishment related responses allows for a new, active level of control that is not present in the more passive regulation of the 'stop' system.

Kinsbourne and Bemporad (1984) propose that the neural function coordinating these attentional and emotional sets is localized in the brain along hemispheric and anterior–posterior axes, so that the left frontotemporal cortex is seen to control action mediating external change, including the planning and sequencing of acts. The right frontotemporal cortex controls internal emotional arousal. In addition, each of the anterior systems controls the posterior centers which provide it with information. The two hemispheres are seen to complement rather than inhibit each other: 'Thus, whether control is momentarily vested in the left hemisphere "go" or the right hemisphere "no go" system depends on stimulus circumstances, and on the status of the organism's attempt to exert control over its environment or itself' (Kinsbourne & Bemporad, 1984, p. 263).

Kinsbourne and Bemporad's (1984) model stresses the operation of self-regulatory functions that in one case ('go') are associated with actions upon the environment, and in the second case ('no go') with reactions to emotion-producing stimuli. Kinsbourne and Bemporad present evidence suggesting that damage to the right orbital frontal cortex is associated with emotional disinhibition. Luria (1966) has also suggested that the right frontal lobes are associated with the modulation of social behavior in accordance with the context and appropriateness of that behavior. Damage to the left dorsolateral frontal area, on the other hand, is associated with inaction and apathy.

Kinsbourne and Bemporad's (1984) model is interesting in connection with findings on early hemispheric development. Whitaker (1978), reviewing findings from the neurological literature, has concluded that the right hemisphere matures earlier than the left. These findings included observations by Taylor (1969) that seizures are more common in the left than the right hemisphere in infancy, and more likely in immature than mature brain tissue. Frequency of left hemisphere seizures also appears to decline with language acquisition, suggesting that functional development of the left hemisphere occurs at an age when there is protection against seizures.

Electrophysiologic evidence also suggests earlier right hemisphere maturation (Tucker, 1985). The alpha rhythm of brain activity in children is found to be more pronounced over the right hemisphere and theta activity over the left hemisphere (Walter, 1950); the process of brain maturation is associated with a decrease in theta rhythm and an increase in alpha rhythm. More pronounced photic driving over newborns' right hemispheres has also been found, suggesting more mature response from the right hemisphere to stimulation very early in life (Crowell, Jones, Kapuniani, & Nakagawa, 1973). Recent work by Thatcher, Walker, and Giudice (1987) also suggests greater development of the right hemisphere in the first year of life followed by greater development of the left hemisphere during early childhood. If the right hemisphere does mature at a more rapid rate than the left and if we adopt Kinsbourne and Bemporad's (1984) model of self-regulation, then the young infant's attentional and emotional sets toward the world would involve chiefly the arousal of emotional states and actions that do not follow intended sequences. Only later would planned sequential acts related to functioning of the left prefrontal cortex provide control over the environment and over emotional reactions.

Fox and Davidson (1984) have proposed that there are differences in hemispheric specialization for affect, with the left hemisphere associated with positive affect and approach and the right hemisphere with negative affect and avoidance. They suggest that, toward the end of the first year of life, development of commissural transfer permits left hemisphere inhibition of right hemisphere function, attenuating the expression of negative affect, and leading to behavioral alternations between approach and avoidance.

Davidson and Fox (1982) made EEG recordings from left and right frontal and parietal positions for infant girls aged 10 months, evaluating the EEG in connection with the infants' response to video segments depicting positive affect (smiling and laughter) and negative affect (frowning and crying). Infants showed frontal asymmetry with greater left hemispheric activity to the positive segment; parietal asymmetry was not found. In an EEG study with newborns, greater activation was found in both left frontal and parietal regions for a sugar stimulus and the opposite pattern, that is, greater right activation in both areas, for a water stimulus (Fox & Davidson, in press). The authors suggest that these EEG findings in the newborn may have been generated by the activity of other locations, cortical or subcortical.

Both of these hemispheric models predict decreases in the expression of negative affect and increases in the expression of positive affect over early development. In Kinsbourne and Bemporad's (1984) model, this is seen as being due to the development of right frontal inhibition of negative affect; in Fox and Davidson's (1984) model, it is the result of the development of callosal connections allowing inhibition of right hemisphere function by the left. Research results indicate increases in positive affect and decreases in negative affect over the first year of life (Bloom & Capatides, 1987; Rothbart, 1987).

These hemispheric specialization models also predict that differences in the rate of CNS development will underlie differences in the age at which emotional expression becomes modulated, and the age at which sequentially organized action upon the environment emerges as a mode of control. In addition, they predict that the relative strengths of frontal mechanisms of both the right and left hemispheres may underlie temperamental individual differences in motor and emotional behavior.

TEMPERAMENT AND OTHER ASSESSMENTS OF NEURAL FUNCTION

Electroencephalogram Measures and Temperament

Because Eysenck's theory has posited individual differences in tonic arousal level between introverts and extraverts, numerous studies have investigated the relationship between EEG measures of arousal and extraversion in adults. The results of this research have been carefully reviewed by Gale and Edwards (1986) and they are not definitive. More recently, however, two approaches involving EEG measurement appear to show promise in the adult literature. In the first, measures of impulsivity have been found to relate to spontaneous alpha activity for subjects with eyes open and closed, with subjects scoring high on impulsiveness showing less alpha activity (O'Gorman & Lloyd, 1987).

A second approach involves use of the visual or auditory evoked potential. Buchsbaum and his co-workers (Buchsbaum, Haier, & Johnson, 1983; Buchsbaum & Pfefferbaum, 1971; Buchsbaum & Silverman, 1968) have investigated amplitude of evoked response to light flashes varying in intensity by measuring the P100 and N120 components. They defined augmenting (enhancing of stimulus-intensity effects) as a high positive slope of the regression of stimuli of increasing intensity upon event-related potential (ERP) amplitude. In other words, augmenters show increased amplitude of ERPs with increasing intensity, in a fashion similar to what would be predicted for a Pavlovian 'strong' nervous system. Reducers demonstrate either a low-positive or a negative slope, indicating decrements of response to high stimulus intensities similar to what would be predicted for a Pavlovian 'weak' nervous system.

Augmenting–reducing shows stability over time in adults (von Knorring, 1980) and augmenting has been related to extraversion measures (Soskis & Shagass, 1974) and to the Disinhibition subscale of Zuckerman's Sensation Seeking Scale (von Knorring, 1980; Zuckerman, Murtaugh, & Siegel, 1974). Augmenting individuals report themselves as being outgoing, active, and (in the case of the Disinhibition subscale) seeking out intense forms of stimulation, with items such as, 'I often like to get high' and 'I like to date members of the opposite sex who are physically exciting' (Wohlwill, 1980).

Augmenting–reducing in visual evoked potentials has also been studied in the cat. Saxton, Siegel, and Lukas (1987a) reported stabilities of augmenting–reducing over a period of 20 months. Augmenting in cats was also found to be related to greater activity, exploration, and aggressiveness, and reducing to greater withdrawal, less activity (Hall, Rappaport, Hopkins, Griffin, & Silverman, 1970), and greater emotionality and tenseness (Saxton, Siegel, & Lukas, 1987b). In addition, Saxton *et al.* (1987b) found reducer cats to be more successful at performing a task requiring response inhibition when low rates of response were differentially reinforced.

The theoretical picture is not altogether clear within this literature, however, because the studies finding positive relations between augmenting and extraversion have tended to use higher intensity levels of stimulation than those usually employed by Buchsbaum (see review by Haier, Robinson, Braden, & Williams, 1984). Haier *et al.* used moderate intensity levels and found that the relation between augmenting–reducing and extraversion was reversed, that is, extraverts were more likely to be reducers. Similar relationships have been found in research linking the auditory evoked response to low-frequency tones to introversion–extraversion. Stelmack and Michaud-Achorn (1985) found introverts to demonstrate larger N1–P2 amplitudes to the first stimulus in a four-stimulus train, and determined that these effects were not due to habituation or attentional processes. These findings, they argued, may be combined with those showing greater sensitivity of introverts at threshold levels, found across multiple modalities and using varying psychophysical procedures (Eysenck, 1976; Stelmack & Plouffe,

1983), to indicate that introverts show greater sensitivity to stimulation (Stelmack & Michaud-Achorn, 1985). In addition, a positive correlation has been found between introversion and latency to an auditory brainstem evoked response to click stimuli (Stelmack & Wilson, 1982).

Combining these two sets of findings suggests that introverts show greater increments of responsiveness to low-intensity stimuli than extraverts, and smaller increments of responsiveness to high-intensity stimuli, in an inverted-U function. This set of results is congruent with findings in the Soviet tradition on strength of the nervous system, where individuals with 'weak' nervous systems have been found to show both lower thresholds and non-augmenting at high-intensity levels (see discussion above).

Neuroregulatory Amines and Temperament

One of the most exciting yet elusive areas of speculation about neurobiological individual differences relevant to temperament involves the neuroregulatory amines. Thus, Panskepp and Cox (1986) have written:

> The past two decades' intensive research into the behavioral effects of biogenic amines has repeatedly affirmed that these widely ramifying neurochemical systems participate in all behaviors in relatively nonspecific ways. They dictate global shifts in vigilance, attention, and tendencies to act (Panskepp, 1986). These systems are highly responsive to all attention-grasping environmental events (with NE neurons being more responsive than serotonin ones). These systems also exhibit spontaneous rhythmicity, as evidenced by their tendency to sustain characteristic firing patterns *in vitro* (Andrade & Aghajanian, 1984; Jacobs, Heym & Steinfels, 1984). Thus it is to be expected that these systems help generate personality traits which may be best encapsulated by broad concepts such as introversion–extroversion, active–passive, Type A–Type B, impulsive–controlled. As Soubrie (1986) asserts, perhaps a bit too cautiously, the basic functions of the systems should prove to be quite similar in humans and lower animals. (Panskepp & Cox, 1986, p. 341)

Norepinephrine pathways from the locus coeruleus to the neocortex, hippocampus, thalamus, cerebellum, and parts of the hypothalamus and limbic system allow for the possibility of very general effects. Locus coeruleus cells respond to intensity of stimuli across modalities rather than to spatial–temporal information (Robbins, 1986). They also respond to novel stimulation distributed widely across the visual field rather than to specific locations (Watanabe, Nakai, & Kasamatsu, 1982). Activity in the locus coeruleus is highest during waking states, less during slow-wave sleep and lowest during rapid eye movement sleep, so that it also is correlated with states of behavioral arousal (Aston-Jones & Bloom, 1981; Jacobs, 1984). Activation of the locus coeruleus (the main site of NE production) appears to strengthen the effects of other inputs which may be excitatory or inhibitory (Bloom, 1979). Norepinephrine function has been theoretically and empirically linked to sensitivity to novelty and right hemisphere function (Tucker & Williamson, 1984), to attention (Mason, 1980; Mason & Iverson, 1977, 1979), to anxiety (Gray, 1982; Redmond & Huang, 1979), to the effects of a variety of stressors (Robbins & Everitt, 1982), and to general emotional arousal (Panskepp, 1982). Temporary depression of NE activity following chronic exposure to inescapable stress has also been linked to deficits in motor activity and learning called 'learned helplessness'

(Anisman, Kokkendis, & Sklar, 1981) and to depression (Tucker & Williamson, 1984), although revisions of this hypothesis are currently under way (see review by Stone, 1983).

Robbins (1986) has noted the interesting parallel organization of serotonin (5-hydroxytryptamine) pathways to central NE pathways, with the major difference being serotonin innervation of the basal ganglia. Serotonin activity also is related to states of behavioral arousal, and shows a slow and regular discharge during waking movement of the cat (Jacobs, 1984). Because the serotonin systems are also active during stress (Anisman et al., 1981), they were originally linked to anxiety. More recently, however, it has been argued that serotonin activity plays a role in the behavioral inhibition that is linked to cues signalling punishment (Soubrie, 1986). Serotonin function has also been related to the inhibition of general activity (Crow, 1977) and the inhibition of emotional response (Panskepp, 1982).

Central DA projections arise in the ventral tegmental area (VTA), innervate parts of the limbic system associated with the basal ganglia, and project to the prefrontal cortex (Robbins, 1986). Spontaneous activity of DA cells does not vary across states of behavioral arousal, although the magnitude of DA response to stimulation is affected by state (Jacobs, 1984). Wise's (1980, 1982) model for the role of DA in reward identifies DA cells in the VTA as receiving inputs from diverse reward sources, such as those activated by electrical brain stimulation of the lateral hypothalamus and administration of opiates. Stellar and Stellar (1985) note that Wise's view of DA action resembles an incentive motivation model in that it suggests that DA-depleted rats do not move because stimuli in the environment are not attractive and rewarding enough to lead to movement. A second view of DA functioning is that DA processes influence general behavioral activation as measured in open-field locomotion and activity (Kelly & Stinus, 1984; Kelly, Stinus, & Iverson, 1980). These effects operate through activation of the nucleus accumbens. Dopamine depletion from these areas reduces speed and probability of response, but not discrimination accuracy, in a reaction-time study of rats (Robbins, 1986).

Robbins (1986) concludes that DA depletion from striatal and nucleus accumbens areas reduces both speed and probability of responding but does not effect discrimination of visual events. Panskepp (1986b) has also reviewed the literature on DA effects, concluding that 'the general function of DA activity in appetitive behavior is to promote the expression of motivational excitement and anticipatory eagerness – the heightened energization of animals searching for and expecting rewards (Panskepp, 1981, 1985)' (Panskepp, 1986b, p. 91). Thus, DA has been consistently associated with activation and energy level of responses in appetitive situations.

Cholinergic (acetylcholine, ACh) pathways extend to the hippocampus from the medial septum and to the neocortex from the nucleus basalis of Meynert (NbM), (Robbins, 1986). The NbM receives inputs from the septum, nucleus accumbens and hypothalamus. Like the NE effects, ACh appears to accentuate the response of a cell to other inputs (Robbins, 1986). Since selective lesions of ACh projections are not possible, more indirect information must be relied upon. This evidence currently suggests ACh enhancement of vigilance and sustained attention under non-stress conditions (Robbins, 1986).

Several opioid transmitter and receptor systems have been identified that may be of importance to individual differences in temperament, including the endorphins, enkephalins, and dynorphins. Most research to date has been done on the effects of morphine and naloxone within the μ-receptor system (Panskepp, 1986). Panskepp, Siviy, and Normansell (1985) have noted the role of the μ system in the intensity of separation distress. In addition, the system is related to the placebo response (Grevert, Albert, & Goldstein, 1983), modulation of appetite (Morley, Levine, Yim, & Lowy, 1983), selectivity of attention to information (Arnsten, Neville, Hillyard, Janowsky, & Segal, 1984), and other peripheral physiological effects (Panskepp, 1986). Panskepp (1986) suggests that the general function of the μ system may be to counteract stress effects, an interpretation that would fit within an opponent-process theoretical framework (Schull, Kaplan, & O'Brien, 1981). Panskepp (1986) notes that since pleasure is frequently experienced to stimuli associated with a return to homeostasis (Cabanac, 1971), the positive affect to opioids may be the result of associations with anti-stress effects.

Recently, Cloninger (1986, 1987a,b) has developed a tripartite model of personality based upon underlying brain systems and neuromodulator functioning. It specifies (Cloninger, 1987a) the personality characteristics of:

(1) *harm avoidance*, ranging from the individual who is relaxed, confident, uninhibited, optimistic, and energetic to the individual who is cautious, apprehensive, inhibited, shy, pessimistic, and subject to fatigue;
(2) *novelty-seeking*, ranging from being rigid, reflective, orderly, and attentive to details to being impulsive, exploratory, excitable, distractible, and disorderly;
(3) *reward dependence*, ranging from being socially detached, cool, tough-minded, and independently self-willed to being emotionally dependent, warmly sympathetic, sentimental, persistent, and sensitive to social cues.

These characteristics are in turn linked to neuromodulator function, with novelty-seeking (which Cloninger sees as similar to Gray's system of approach or behavioral activation) related to DA functioning; harm avoidance (seen as similar to Gray's system of anxiety or behavioral inhibition) to the functioning of serotonin and the septal–hippocampal system; and reward dependence (Cloninger's addition to the BAS and BIS which is seen as related to behavioral maintenance) to NE functioning.

Although to date a good deal of research has been done on the relation of neuromodulators and their regulating enzymes to psychiatric disorders, only a little research has related these variables to normal adult temperament (see review by Zuckerman, Ballenger, & Post, 1984), and even less research has attempted to relate them to temperament in children. In addition, important methodological questions have been raised about whether assays (plasma, cerebrospinal fluid, urine) taken in this research reflect accurately brain chemistry (see the extensive discussion following the review article by Zuckerman, 1984). In some of the research on adults, there has also been failure to replicate findings across studies (Zuckerman *et al.*, 1984). Nevertheless, the few studies done with infants are related in interesting ways to some of the replicated findings from adult research.

One of these investigations (Sostek, Sostek, Murphy, Martin, & Born, 1981) involved assessment of the enzyme monoamine oxidase (MAO), which regulates the synthesis and concentration of the monoamines NE and DA. Platelet MAO levels show high test–retest reliabilities for up to 10 weeks for adults (Murphy et al., 1976), and similar ranges of variability of MAO are found in adult populations and in newborn infants (Sostek et al., 1981). Females show higher MAO levels than males across ages 18–60 (Murphy et al., 1976) but differences in MAO levels by sex are not found in the newborn (Sostek et al., 1981). Evidence has been found for gonadal regulation of MAO levels, in that estrogen therapy lowers elevated MAO activity in female subjects (Klaiber, Broverman, Vogel & Kobayashi, 1979).

Negative relationships have been found between MAO levels and measures of sensation-seeking in studies of normal subjects and patients, and significant negative correlations also have been found between plasma amine oxidase (AO) and sensation-seeking measures (see review of these studies by Zuckerman et al., 1984). Monoamine oxidase inhibitors are used in antidepressant therapy, where they appear to increase activity level and motivation in depressive patients. Monoamine oxidase has also been found to be negatively related to extraversion in adults (Gattaz & Beckman, 1981). Research on monkeys reports high-MAO monkeys to be relatively inactive, passive and solitary within a colony, and low-MAO monkeys to be active, to make many social contacts, and to more frequently engage in play, aggression, and sexual activity (Redmond & Murphy, 1975; Redmond, Murphy, & Baulu, 1979).

In the research by Sostek et al. (1981) on infants, assays were taken of MAO and AO levels in the cord blood of newborn infants, and the Brazelton Neonatal Behavioral Assessment Scale (Brazelton, 1973; see discussion of this measure and newborn temperament in Chapter 12) was administered. Lower levels of MAO in newborns were found to be related to higher arousal levels (this item ranges from sleep through quiet awake, then active awake state, to distress) and to lower consolability. Lower AO levels were related to greater rapidity of build-up (infants showing irritability earlier in the procedure) and to lower consolability. In addition, infants lower in AO were more active. These findings suggest that MAO and AO are related to alertness, activity, and distress, but the findings are not in the direction that would have been predicted by adult research.

Other studies have measured levels of the enzyme dopamine-beta-hydroxylase (DBH), an enzyme that synthesizes NE from DA. Serum levels of DBH have been found to be negatively related to sensation-seeking (Uberkoman-Wiita, Vogel, & Wiita, 1981), and in studies of augmenting–reducing, patients with high-DBH serum levels have tended to be reducers and patients with low DBH, augmenters (von Knorring & Perris, 1981). Rapaport, Pandari, Renfield, Lake, and Ziegler (1977) have studied plasma levels of DBH in the neonatal period and found positive correlations between neonatal DBH levels and measures of distress at 5 and 12 months. This finding is more in keeping with the adult research than are the results of Sostek et al., (1981), although it should be noted that Rapaport et al., were predicting distress measures taken considerably later than the newborn period.

In animal studies, behavioral change has also been related to development of the amine systems, with research indicating that the earliest maturing systems are catecholaminergic, and related to early high motor activity. Thus, functional development of DA (Phelps, Koranyi, & Tamasy, 1982; Shaywitz, Yager, & Klopper, 1976) and NE pathways in juvenile rats has been related to increases in motor activity during the first days of life, while subsequent development of motor inhibition and lowered activity levels has been related to the development of serotonergic and cholinergic mechanisms. Serotonin antagonists do not increase activity level in developing rats until 15 days of age (Mabry & Campbell, 1974), and cholinergic antagonists do not do so until 15–20 days (Pradhan & Pradhan, 1980). A later-developing motor-inhibitory influence of the DA prefrontal cortex pathway has also been identified (Heffner, Heller, Miller, Kotake, & Seiden, 1983; Shaywitz *et al.*, 1976). If the developmental progression of these neuroregulators were to be the same in humans as in rats, we would expect to see novelty-seeking and reward effects before we see behavioral inhibition, and this appears to be the case (see discussion above and in Chapter 12).

Individual Differences in Autonomic Reactivity

Lacey (1950, 1967) has demonstrated individual differences in the patterning of autonomic reactivity to challenging stimuli or situations. Thus, some individuals tend to react primarily through cardiac response, others through electrodermal reactions, and still others through vasomotor reactions. Little research on infants' and children's autonomic reactivity has focused upon patterning of responding, but children have been found to differ in their responsiveness within single-response channels. Thus, Lipton, Steinschneider, and Richmond (1961, 1966) studied cardiac reactivity to an air puff in infants during the neonatal period and again at 2.5 and 5 months. Although stability in magnitude of individual response was not found between birth and 2.5 months, stability was found from 2.5 to 5 months, and Steinschneider (1973) suggested that this later stability may have been related to maturation of cardiac control mechanisms. Individual differences were also found by Richmond, Lipton, and Steinschneider (1962) in time to peak magnitude and recovery time of cardiac reaction. Additional work on early cardiac reactivity has been done by Richmond and Lustman (1955), Bridger, Birns, and Blank (1965), and Lewis, Wilson, Ban, and Baumel (1970). In her review of heart-rate (HR) research, von Bargen (1983) reported HR reactivity to stimulation to be the most stable and reliable of HR measures.

Lacey and Lacey (1962) carried out a longitudinal study of individual differences in autonomic function that is a model of careful design and analysis. In it, they investigated HR, HR variability, blood pressure, and skin conductance across a 4-year period for children who were 6 to 14 years old at the first testing. They found relatively high stability for blood pressure, palmar conductance, and overall HR reactivity. Moreover, the reactivity measures to stress showed considerably higher stability than did baseline levels. In addition, Lacey and Lacey reported age differences, with general decreases in reactivity with increasing age. Sex differences were also found, with girls showing consistently higher HR at baseline and under stress and consistently higher stress levels for palmar conductance and HR over the 4-year period.

Garcia-Coll, Kagan, and Reznick (1984) have more recently found that groups of children selected for highly inhibited versus uninhibited activity to the unfamiliar could be differentiated in their cardiac reactivity while viewing a set of slides of familiar and unfamiliar objects. Inhibited boys showed higher HR magnitude and less HR variability than uninhibited boys; inhibited girls also showed higher HR magnitude but not less variability than uninhibited girls.

One problem in interpreting HR reactivity differences is that HR magnitude and variability are physiologically multi-determined (Levine, 1986). In an attempt to gather more specific information on neural influences upon HR, Porges (1983) has implemented a method to estimate parasympathetically determined vagal tone. This is done by statistically extracting variance associated with respiratory sinus arrhythmia from the HR pattern. Fox and Davidson (1986) note that the measure of vagal tone thus derived ($\hat{V}$) may reflect the parasympathetic aspect of autonomic balance sought by Wenger (1941) and Gellhorn (1957). Fox (Chapter 11, this volume) and Stifter have found a positive relation at 14 months between $\hat{V}$ and children's latency to approach a stranger. Richards and Cameron (1987) have similarly found respiratory sinus arrhythmia to be positively related to parent-reported measures of approach at 6 and 12 months.

McGuire and Turkewitz (1979) have followed Schneirla (1959, 1965) in describing Withdrawal (W) and Approach (A) responses that can be observed during the early weeks of life. Both are seen as driven by stimulus intensity, with A-responses having lower intensity thresholds than W-responses, and A- and W-responses acting in opposition to one another. Withdrawal processes involve energy expenditure, and are associated with HR acceleration, distress, looking or turning away, and limb flexions. Withdrawal processes overlap with those specified in Sokolov's (1963) defensive reaction and Gellhorn's 'ergotrophic' reactions (Gellhorn, 1968; Gellhorn & Loofbourrow, 1963). In functional terms, these defensive or avoidant reactions can be seen as behaviors that could serve to decrease the child's degree of overstimulation by high stimulus intensities.

Approach processes, on the other hand, include responses such as looking toward, turning toward, and limb extensions, and are similar to Gellhorn's (1968) 'trophotropic' reactions. These behaviors are associated with motor quieting, HR deceleration and regular respiration. Turkewitz and his co-workers have reported that intensities of auditory and visual stimulation appear to summate in influencing the infant's looking toward or away from a visual stimulus (Lawson & Turkewitz, 1980; Lewkowicz & Turkewitz, 1980), with increasing stimulus intensity leading to greater looking away. The findings of Turkewitz and his associates recall factor analytic studies of newborn distress-proneness and self-regulation: higher expression of distress is associated with less focused orienting, just as individual children who demonstrate more distress also show less focused orienting (see review in Chapter 12).

One of the most interesting findings in studies of individual differences in electrodermal responding has been the negative relationship found between galvanic skin response and behavioral expression of emotion. This relationship was noted by Waller in 1919, Prideaux in 1920 and 1922, and Landis in 1932 (see review by Buck, 1979). Jones (1950) studied electrodermal reactivity in infants and preschool children, finding a higher threshold for responding in infants than in the older children. He described three patterns of reactivity in children presented with stimuli including a live rat, buzzers and bells, and a dental examination. One pattern, which he associated with the 'externalizer', showed high facial, emotional, and body expression but low electrodermal response. The second, 'internalizer' pattern, showed little behavioral expressiveness but large or frequent electrodermal response. The third, 'generalizer', showed both behavioral and electrodermal reactions (Jones, 1950).

Jones (1935, 1960) then compared the ten highest and ten lowest electrodermal responders age 11–18 in the Berkeley Adolescent Growth Study. High electrodermal responders were found to be described by psychologists as showing high emotional control, quiet, reserve, and deliberation. They were also seen as being calm, good-natured, and responsible. Low electrodermal responders were rated as more impulsive, active, and talkative, and were seen as more attention-seeking, assertive, and bossy. Buck (1975, 1977) has more recently studied what he calls 'sending accuracy'. Subjects are videotaped while they view emotion-inducing slides. Their videotaped reactions are then judged by 'receivers' who are asked to match the 'sender's response to the slide and rate its strength. Buck (1975) found a positive correlation between children's sending capacity (as assessed in ability to pose emotions and performance in the sending paradigm described above) and nursery school teachers' ratings of the children's impulsivity, bossiness, and expression of hostility, extraversion, and sociability. Posing ability was negatively correlated with ratings of shyness, emotional control, and introversion. In a second study, boys with high scores on expressiveness were found to have lower skin conductance measures, but significant effects were not found for girls (Buck, 1977).

Adult studies have also confirmed the existence of stable individual difference in electrodermal reactivity, and have found it to be negatively related to measures of extraversion (Crider & Lunn, 1971; Stelmack, 1981; reviews by Buck, 1979; and Eysenck, 1967). Fowles (1982) has also found electrodermal responding, but not HR reactivity, to be related to measures of Gray's behavioral inhibition system.

Although the research on autonomic measures and temperament is likely to be widely pursued in the future, researchers should consider Gale and Edwards' (1986) caution that using only one psychophysiological index in a given study neglects possible individual differences in patterning of responding, disregarding Lacey's (1950, 1967) concerns. Combining measures of cardiac and electrodermal reactivity within the same study would be of definite interest, given the correlations found between each measure and assessments of introversion–extraversion. Future research might profitably employ multiple measures of autonomic reactivity, including them within a single statistical treatment. More importantly, in connection with both measures of autonomic function and the neuroendocrine measures to be discussed below, we are badly in need of theory to guide research and to elucidate the meaning of findings (Gale & Edwards, 1986).

Individual Differences in Neuroendocrine Function

Most of the work done to date on individual differences in hormonal response has focused upon the two adrenal systems: the sympathetic–adrenal medullary axis and the pituitary–adrenal cortical axis. The adrenal medulla is an extension of the sympathetic nervous system, which synthesizes and secretes the catecholamines epinephrine and NE (Carter, 1986). The adrenal cortex, embryologically related to gonadal tissue, secretes steroid hormones, including the glucocorticoids cortisol and corticosterone. These hormones increase blood glucose and work with the catecholamines to produce glucose from free fatty acids. They also serve an anti-inflammatory function in connection with injury and disease. The adrenal cortex is regulated by adrenal corticotropic hormone (ACTH) from the anterior pituitary. The secretion of ACTH is in turn regulated by corticotropin releasing hormone from the hypothalamus, and probably other CNS sites (Carter, 1986).

Panskepp (1986) has noted that central administration of corticotropin releasing factor (CRF) can lead to intense arousal (Britton, Koob, Rivier, & Vale, 1982; Sutton, Koob, LeMoal, Rivier, & Vale, 1983), and that the anatomy of the CRF system maps very closely to the anatomy of distress vocalization systems (Herman & Panskepp, 1981; Swanson, Sawchenko, Rivier, & Vale, 1983). He therefore suggests that the CRF system may generally modulate distress reactions to stressful situations.

In reviewing the results of her laboratory, Frankenhaueser (1986) identifies two factors in adult reactions to stress. One she calls an effort factor, which includes feelings of interest, engagement, and determination. The second is a distress factor, which includes feelings of uncertainty, anxiety, dissatisfaction, and boredom. She reports that when effort is combined with distress, both catecholamine and cortisol secretion are observed. Effort without distress is usually associated with catechol-amine secretion, and cortisol secretion may be suppressed. Distress without effort, involving feelings of helplessness and loss of control, is typically associated with cortisol secretion increases, although catecholamine levels may also be elevated (Frankenhaeuser, 1986). In a study of Swedish children, Frankenhaeuser and Johansson (1976) found that children who responded to mental work assignments with higher epinephrine levels tended to perform better than those whose epinephrine levels decreased. The children with higher epinephrine levels were also rated as less aggressive and restless.

Ursin, Baade, and Levine (1978) have also identified a 'cortisol factor' and a 'catecholamine factor' in their studies of parachute jumpers in training. In addition, Henry and Meehan (1981) have identified the amygdaloid/sympathetic-adrenomedullary axis as being involved with a behavioral dimension ranging from 'relaxation' to fight–flight and aggression, and the hippocampal–adrenocortical axis as involved with a dimension ranging from helplessness and depression to security and control.

Most studies of individual differences in neuroendocrine function in children have studied the adrenocortical axis via assays of cortisol excretion. In studies of individual differences in cortisol excretion in infancy, Tennes, Downey, and Vernadakis (1977) have found relatively high stability in urinary cortisol excretion rate on two observation days, one in which the children were separated from their mothers. Infants who showed the most distress to the mother's departure excreted the highest levels of cortisol. A moderate but non-significant stability correlation from 1 to 3 years in these measures was also reported (Tennes & Mason, 1982). Suomi and his associates (Suomi, 1986; and see Chapter 10, by Higley & Suomi) have also reported positive relations between plasma cortisol reactivity and juvenile rhesus monkeys' behavioral reactions to environmental challenge, with stability of cortisol reactivity to challenge found across measurement periods.

The relationship between susceptibility to behavioral distress and heightened cortisol level in infancy is not entirely straightforward, however. Gunnar and her associates (Gunnar, 1986; and see Chapter 9, by Gunnar & Mangelsdorf) report positive correlations between plasma cortisol elevations and evidence of behavioral distress in tissue-damage conditions such as circumcision, but negative correlations between cortisol elevations and evidence of distress during stressful non-tissue-damage conditions such as a hospital discharge exam. Under both conditions, soothing procedures decrease behavioral distress but do not decrease plasma cortisol elevations. It should be noted from studies of neuroendocrine function in adults and other animals that only one kind of distress, that of a helpless variety, is associated with cortisol secretion. Older infants may be more susceptible to such feelings of helplessness than infants during the newborn period.

In studies of older children, Tennes and Kreye (1985) found that cortisol excretion levels were negatively correlated with hostile and aggressive behaviors and positively correlated with social competence in second grade children. In a second study of a subsample of these subjects, cortisol and epinephrine levels were both found to be positively correlated with social affiliative behavior, and NE levels were positively correlated with aggressiveness and attentiveness (Tennes, Kreye, Avitable, & Wells, 1986). Epinephrine levels were positively related to teachers' ratings of task orientation and were negatively related to fidgeting, in a finding replicating the work of Johansson, Frankenhaueser, & Magnusson (1973). On test days, cortisol levels increased and catecholamine levels decreased, in a finding that would not have been predicted by Frankenhaueser's (1986) model.

Recently developed techniques for salivary assay (Riad-Fahmy, Read, Joyce, & Walker, 1981) are likely to greatly increase the research on cortisol reactivity, and the need for theory to organize and elucidate the meaning of findings will become more critical, just as it has in other areas of psychophysiological research (Gale & Edwards, 1986). It is likely that helpful theoretical models will involve multiple systems, as described by Gunnar and Mangelsdorf in Chapter 9, and that behavior will be seen to be functionally related to physiological processes in important ways.

In our theoretical model for temperament, Derryberry and I have specified self-regulatory aspects of behavior in the modulation of reactivity, with stimulus-seeking and avoidance increasing or decreasing reactivity, and self-soothing procedures, including directing attention away from the source of stimulation, decreasing reactivity (Rothbart & Derryberry). Strelau's (1983) model for temperament is organized around very similar constructs of reactivity and activity, with activity including important self-regulative aspects of the behavioral expression of temperament. Such approaches may provide a beginning toward effective theory-building.

A Final Development Note

We will hope eventually to be able to describe the organization of interacting systems of temperament, and this organization will necessarily also be a developmental one. In my review of temperament and development in this volume (Chapter 12), I have attempted to describe some of the ways in which the behavioral expression of temperament changes with development. Our understanding of biological levels of temperament will also require this developmental perspective, as has been argued by Rosenblatt and Lehrman (1963):

> The processes underlying the organization of the behavior of an animal at any developmental age... appear to us to be best illuminated by analyzing the ways in which the age (or stage) influences or gives rise to succeeding ones. The relationships among those processes and influences which persist through several stages, those continuous through the life of the animal, and those specific to different stages are often complex. Their analysis involves the simultaneous consideration of events at different biological and psychological levels. These may include physiological events which are themselves organized at different levels (for example, central nervous regulation, local sensitivities and reactions, regulation of endocrine secretion, specific effects of hormones, and so on), and psychological processes of varying complexity, ranging from reaction to simple forms of stimulation to behavior patterns characterizing interindividual (that is, social) situations. (Rosenblatt & Lehrman, 1963, p. 9)

As Rosenblatt and Lehrman argue, a complete developmental analysis will involve consideration of organization at multiple levels of study, ranging from the physiological to the social. We may hope and expect that future reviews of temperament and development will increasingly involve an integration across these levels.

REFERENCES

Altman, J., Brunner, R.L., & Bayer, S.A. (1973). The hippocampus and behavioral maturation. *Behavioral Biology*, **8**, 557–596.

Amsel, A. (1986). Daniel Berlyne Memorial Lecture. Developmental psychobiology and behavior theory: Reciprocating influences. *Canadian Journal of Psychology*, **40**, 311–342.

Amsel, A. & Stanton, M. (1980). Ontogeny and phylogeny of paradoxical reward effects. In J.S. Rosenblatt, R.A. Hinde, C. Beer, & M. Bushel (Eds), *Advances in the study of behavior*, Vol. II (pp. 227–275). New York: Academic Press.

Andrade, R. & Aghajanian, G.K. (1984). Locus coeruleus activity *in vitro:* Intrinsic regulation by a calcium-dependent potassium conductance but not α_2-adrenoceptors. *Journal of Neuroscience*, **4**, 161–170.

Anisman, A., Kokkendis, L., & Sklar, L.S. (1981). Contribution of neurochemical change to stress-induced behavioral deficits. In S.J. Cooper (Ed.), *Theory in psychopharmacology*, Vol. 1 (pp. 65–102). London: Academic Press.

Arnsten, A.F.T., Neville, H.J., Hillyard, S.A., Janowsky, D.S., & Segal, D.S. (1984). Naloxone increased electrophysiological measures of selective information processing in humans. *Journal of Neuroscience*, **4**, 2912–2929.

Aston-Jones, G. & Bloom, F.E. (1981). Activity of norepinephrine containing locus coeruleus neurons in behaving rats anticipates fluctuations in the sleep–wake cycle. *Journal of Neuroscience*, **1**, 876–886.

Bloom, F. (1979). Is there a neurotransmitter code in the brain? In P. Simon (Ed.), *Advances in pharmacology and therapeutics: Neurotransmitters*, Vol. 1. Oxford and New York: Pergamon.

Bloom, L. & Capatides, J. (1987). Expression of affect and the emergence of language. *Child Development*, **58**, 1513–1522.

Bodunov, M.V. (1985). Typology of mental activity as a temperamental trait and the level of activation of the nervous system. In J. Strelau, F. Farley, & A. Gale (Eds), *The biological bases of personality and behavior:* Vol. II, *Psychophysiology, performance and applications* (pp. 43–57). New York: Hemisphere.

Brazelton, T.B. (1973). *Neonatal Behavioral Assessment Scale*. London: Spastics International Medical Publications.

Bridger, W.H., Birns, B., & Blank, M. (1965). A comparison of behavioral and heart rate measurements in human neonates. *Psychosomatic Medicine*, **27**, 123–134.

Britton, D.R., Koob, G.F., Rivier, J., & Vale, W. (1982). Intraventricular corticotropin-releasing factor enhances behavioral effects of novelty. *Life Sciences*, **31**, 363–367.

Buchsbaum, M.S., Haier, R.J., & Johnson, J. (1983). Augmenting and reducing: Individual differences in evoked potentials. In A. Gale & J. Edwards (Eds), *Physiological correlates of human behavior*: Vol. 3, *Individual differences and psychopathology*. London: Academic Press.

Buchsbaum, M.S. & Pfefferbaum, A. (1971). Individual differences in stimulus-intensity response. *Psychophysiology*, **8**, 600–611.

Buchsbaum, M.A. & Silverman, J. (1968). Stimulus intensity control and the cortical evoked response. *Psychosomatic Medicine*, **30**, 12–22.

Buck, R.W. (1975). Nonverbal communication of affect in children. *Journal of Personality and Social Psychology*, **31**, 644–653.

Buck, R.W. (1977). Nonverbal communication of affect in preschool children: Relationships with personality and skin conductance. *Journal of Personality and Social Psychology*, **35**, 225–236.

Buck, R.W. (1979). Individual differences in nonverbal sending accuracy and electrodermal responding: The externalizing–internalizing dimension. In R. Rosenthal (Ed.), *Skill in nonverbal communication: Individual differences*. Cambridge, MA: Oelgeschlager, Gunn & Hain.

Burt, C. (1935). General and specific factors underlying the primary emotions. British Association Annual Report, 694.6.

Burt, C. (1937). The analysis of temperament. *British Journal of Medical Psychology*, **17**, 158–188.

Burton, R. (1921). *The anatomy of melancholy*. Oxford: Oxford Press.

Cabanac, M. (1971). Physiological role of pleasure. *Science*, **173**, 1103–1107.

Carter, C.S. (1986). The reproductive and adrenal systems. In M.G.H. Coles, E. Donchin, & S.W. Porges (Eds), *Psychophysiology* (pp. 172–182). New York: Guilford Press.

Cattell, R.B. (1933). Temperament tests: I. Temperament. *British Journal of Psychology*, **23**, 308–329.

Cloninger, C.R. (1986). A unified biosocial theory of personality and its role in the development of anxiety states. *Psychiatric Developments*, **3**, 167–226.

Cloninger, C.R. (1987a). Neurogenetic adaptive mechanisms in alcoholism. *Science*, **236**, 410–416.

Cloninger, C.R. (1987b). A systematic method for clinical description and classification of personality variants. *Archives of General Psychiatry*, **44**, 573–588.

Cortes, J.B. & Gatti, F.M. (1965). Physique and self-descriptions of temperament. *Journal of Consulting Psychology*, **29**, 432–439.

Cortes, J.B. & Gatti, F.M. (1972). *Delinquency and crime: A biopsychosocial approach*. New York: Siminar Press.

Crider, A. & Lunn, R. (1971). Electrodermal lability as a personality dimension. *Journal of Experimental Research in Personality*, **5**, 145–150.

Crow, T.J. (1977). In A.N. Davidson (Ed.), *Biomechanical correlates of brain structure and function* (pp. 137–174). New York: Academic Press.

Crowell, D.H., Jones, R.H., Kapuniani, L.E., & Nakagawa, J.K. (1973). Unilateral cortical activity in newborn humans: An early index of cerebral dominance? *Science*, **180**, 205–208.

Culpeper, N. (1657). *Galen's art of physik.* Translated with a glossary by N. Culpeper. London.

Davidson, R.J. & Fox, N.A. (1982). Asymmetrical brain activity discriminates between positive versus negative affective stimuli in human infants. *Science*, **218**, 1235–1237.

Deadwyler, S.A., West, M., & Lynch, G. (1979a). Synaptically identified hippocampal slow potentials during behavior. *Brain Research*, **161**, 211–225.

Deadwyler, S.A., West, M., & Lynch, G. (1979b). Activity of dentate granule cells during learning: Differentiation of perforant path input. *Brain Research*, **169**, 29–43.

Derryberry, D. (in press). Incentive and feedback effects on target detection: A chronometric analysis of Gray's model of temperament. *Personality and Individual Differences.*

Diamond, S. (1974). *The roots of psychology.* New York: Basic Books.

Douglas, R.J. (1975). The development of hippocampal function: Implications for theory and for therapy. In R.L. Isaacson & K. H. Pribram (Eds), *The hippocampus*, Vol. 2, *Neurophysiology and behavior.* New York: Plenum.

Eysenck, H.J. (1947). *Dimensions of personality.* London: Routledge & Kegan Paul.

Eysenck, H.J. (1957). *The dynamics of anxiety and hysteria.* London: Routledge & Kegan Paul.

Eysenck, H.J. (1967). *The biological basis of personality.* Springfield, IL: Thomas.

Eysenck, H.J. (Ed.) (1976). *The measurement of personality.* Baltimore, MD: University Park Press.

Eysenck, H.J. & Eysenck, M.W. (1985). *Personality and individual differences.* New York: Plenum.

Fahrenberg, J. (1987). Emotionality and arousal. In J. Strelau & H. Eysenck (Eds), *Personality dimensions and arousal* (pp. 99–120). New York: Plenum.

Fowles, D.C. (1982). Heart rate as an index of anxiety: Failure of a hypothesis. In J.T. Cacioppo & R.E. Petty (Eds), *Perspectives in cardiovascular psychophysiology* (pp. 93–126). New York: Guilford Press.

Fowles, D.C. (1984). Biological variables in psychopathology. In H.E. Adams & P.B. Suthern (Eds), *Comprehensive handbook of psychopathology* (pp. 77–110). New York: Plenum.

Fox, N.A. & Davidson, R.J. (1984). Hemispheric substrates of affect: A developmental model. In N.A. Fox & R.J. Davidson (Eds), *The psychology of affective development* (pp. 353–382). Hillsdale, NJ: Erlbaum.

Fox, N.A. & Davidson, R.J. (1986). Psychophysiological measures of emotion: New directions in developmental research. In C.E. Izard & P.B. Read (Eds), *Measuring emotions in infants and children*, Vol. II (pp. 13–50). Cambridge: Cambridge University Press.

Fox, N. A. & Davidson, R.J. (1986). Taste elicited changes in facial signs of emotion and the asymmetry of brain electrical activity in human newborns. *Neuropsychologica*, **24**, 417–422.

Frankenhaueser, M. (1986). A psychobiological framework for research on human stress and coping. In M.H. Appley & R. Trumbull (Eds), *Dynamics of stress* (pp. 101–116). New York: Plenum.

Frankenhaueser, M. & Johansson, G. (1976). Task demand as reflected in catecholamine excretion and heart rate. *Journal of Human Stress*, **2**, 15–23.

Gale, A. & Edwards, J.A. (1986). Individual differences. In M.G.H. Coles, E. Donchin, & S.W. Porges (Eds), *Psychophysiology* (pp. 431–507). New York: Guilford Press.

Garcia-Coll, C.T., Kagan, J., & Reznick, J.S. (1984). Behavioral inhibition in young children. *Child Development*, **55**, 1005–1019.

Garnet, J.C.M. (1918). General ability, cleverness and purpose. *British Journal of Psychology*, **9**, 345–366.

Gattaz, W.F. & Beckman, H. (1981). Platelet MAO activity and personality characteristics:

A study in schizophrenic patients and normal individuals. *Acta Psychiatrica Scandinavica*, **63**, 291–304.

Gellhorn, E. (1957). *Autonomic imbalance and the hypothalamus.* Minneapolis: University of Minnesota Press.

Gellhorn, E. (1968). Attempt at synthesis: Contribution to a theory of emotion. In E. Gellhorn (Ed.), *Biological foundations of emotion* (pp. 144–153). Glenview, IL: Scott, Foresman.

Gellhorn, E. & Loofbourrow, G.N. (1963). *Emotions and emotional disorders.* New York: Hoeber.

Gibson, H.B. (1981). *Hans Eysenck.* London: Owen

Glueck, S. & Glueck, E. (1950). *Unraveling juvenile delinquency.* New York: The Commonwealth Fund.

Glueck, S. & Glueck, E. (1956). *Physique and delinquency.* New York: Harper.

Gorenstein, E.E. & Newman, J.P. (1980). Disinhibitory psychopathology: A new perspective and a model for research. *Psychological Review*, **87**, 301–315.

Gray J.A. (1970). The psychophysiological basis of introversion–extraversion. *Behavior Research and Therapy*, **8**, 249–266.

Gray, J.A. (1971). *The psychology of fear and stress.* New York: McGraw-Hill.

Gray, J.A. (1975). *Elements of a two-process theory of learning.* New York: Academic Press.

Gray, J.A. (1977). Drug effects on fear and frustration: Possible limbic site of action of minor tranquilizers. In L.L. Iverson, S.P. Iverson, & S.H. Snyder (Eds), *Handbook of psychopharmacology*, Vol. 8, *Drugs, neurotransmitters and behavior* (pp. 433–530). New York: Plenum.

Gray, J.A. (1978). The neuropsychology of anxiety. *British Journal of Psychology*, **69**, 417–434.

Gray, J.A. (1979). A neuropsychological theory of anxiety. In C.E. Izard (Ed.), *Emotions in personality and psychopathology.* New York: Plenum.

Gray, J.A. (1982). *The neuropsychology of anxiety.* New York: Oxford University Press.

Grevert, P., Albert, L.H., & Goldstein, A. (1983). Partial antagonism of placebo analgesia by naloxone. *Pain*, **16**, 129–143.

Gunnar, M. (1986). The organization of 'stress' responses in the newborn. Paper presented at the International Conference for Infant Studies, Los Angeles, C.A., April 1986.

Haier, R.J., Robinson, D.L., Braden, W., & Williams, D. (1984). Evoked potential augmenting–reducing and personality differences. *Personality and Individual Differences*, **5**, 293–302.

Hall, R.A., Rappaport, M., Hopkins, H.K., Griffin, R.B., & Silverman, J. (1970). Evoked response and behavior in cats. *Science*, **170**, 998–1000.

Hanley, C. (1951). Physique and reputation of junior high school boys. *Child Development*, **22**, 247–260.

Heffner, T.G., Heller, A., Miller, F.E., Kotake, C., & Seiden, L.S. (1983). Locomotor hyperactivity in neonatal rats following electrolytic lesions of mesocortical dopamine neurons. *Developmental Brain Research*, **285**, 29–38.

Henry J.P. & Meehan, J.P. (1981). Psychosocial stimuli, physiological specificity and cardiovascular disease. In H. Weiner, M.A. Hofer, & A.J. Stunkard (Eds), *Brain, behavior and bodily disease* (pp. 305–334). New York: Raven.

Herman, B.H. & Panskepp, J. (1981). Ascending endorphin inhibition of distress vocalization. *Science*, **211**, 1060–1062.

Hull, C.L. (1943). *Principles of behavior: an introduction to behavior theory.* New York: Appleton-Century.

Jacobs, B.L. (1984). Single unit activity of brain monoaminergic neurons in freely moving animals: A brief review. In R. Bandler (Ed.), *Modulation of sensorimotor activity during alterations in behavioral states* (pp. 99–120). New York: Liss.

Jacobs, B.L., Heym, J., & Steinfels, G.F. (1984). Physiological and behavioral analysis of raphe unit activity. In L.L. Iverson, S.D. Iverson, & S.H. Snyder (Eds), *Handbook of psychopharmacology*, Vol. 18, *Drugs, neurotransmitters and behavior*. New York: Plenum.

Johansson, G., Frankenhaueser, M., & Magnusson, D. (1973). Catecholamine excretion in young children and their parents as related to performance and adjustment. *Scandinavian Journal of Psychology*, **14**, 20–28.

Jones, H.E. (1935). The galvanic skin response as related to overt emotional expression. *American Journal of Psychology*, **47**, 241–251.

Jones, H.E. (1950). The study of patterns of emotional expression. In M. Reymert (Ed.), *Feelings and emotions* (pp. 161–168). New York: McGraw-Hill.

Jones, H.E. (1960). The longitudinal method in the study of personality. In I. Iscoe & H.W. Stevenson (Eds), *Personality development in children* (pp. 3–27). Chicago: University of Chicago Press.

Kant, I. (1798). *Anthropology from a pragmatic point of view*. Republished in 1978. Carbondale: Southern Illinois University Press.

Kelly, A. & Stinus, L. (1984). Neuroanatomical and neurochemical substrates of affective behavior. In N.A. Fox & R.J. Davidson (Eds), *Affective development: A psychobiological perspective* (pp. 1–76). Hillsdale, NJ: Erlbaum.

Kelly, A., Stinus, L., & Iverson, S.D. (1980). Interactions between d-ala-metenkephalen, A 10 dopaminergic neurons, and spontaneous behavior in the rat. *Behavioral Brain Research*, **1**, 3–24.

Kinsbourne, M. & Bemporad, B. (1984). Lateralization of emotion: A model and the evidence. In N.A. Fox & R.J. Davidson (Eds), *The psychology of affective development* (pp. 259–292). Hillsdale, NJ: Erlbaum.

Klaiber, E.L., Broverman, D.M., Vogel, W., & Kobayashi, Y. (1979). Estrogen therapy for severe persistent depressions in women. *Archives of General Psychiatry*, **36**, 550–554.

Kretschmer, E. (1925). *Physique and character*. New York: Harcourt, Brace.

Lacey, J.I. (1950). Individual differences in somatic response patterns. *Journal of Comparative and Physiological Psychology*, **43**, 338–350.

Lacey, J.I. (1967). Somatic response patterning and stress: Some revision of activation theory. In M.H. Appley & R. Trumbull (Eds), *Psychological stress: Issues in research* (pp. 14–37). New York: Appleton-Century-Crofts.

Lacey, J.I. & Lacey, B.C. (1962). The law of initial values in the longitudinal study of autonomic constitution: Reproducibility of autonomic response patterns over a four year interval. *Annals of the New York Academy of Science*, **98**, 1257–1290, 1322–1326.

Landis, C. (1932). An attempt to measure emotional traits in juvenile delinquency. In K.S. Lashley (Ed.), *Studies in the dynamics of behavior* (pp. 265–323). Chicago: University of Chicago Press.

Lawson, K.R. & Turkewitz, G. (1980). Intersensory function in newborns: Effect of sound in visual preferences. *Child Development*, **51**, 1295–1298.

Lerner, R.M. (1969). The development of stereotyped expectancies of body build–behavior relations. *Child Development*, **40**, 137–141.

Levine, P. (1986). Stress. In M.G.H. Coles, E. Donchin, & S.W. Porges (Eds), *Psychophysiology: Systems, processes and applications* (pp. 331–351). New York: Guilford Press.

Lewis, M., Wilson, C., Ban, L., & Baumel, L. (1970). An exploratory study of the resting cardiac rate and variability from the last trimester of prenatal life through the first year of postnatal life. *Child Development*, **41**, 799–811.

Lewkowicz, D.J. & Turkewitz, G. (1980). Cross-modal equivalence in early infancy: Auditory–visual intensity matching. *Developmental Psychology*, **16**, 597–607.

Lipton, E.L., Steinschneider, A., & Richmond, J.B. (1961). Autonomic function in the neonate: Individual differences in cardiac reactivity. *Psychosomatic Medicine*, **23**, 472–484.

Lipton, E.L., Steinschneider, A., & Richmond, J.B. (1966). Autonomic function in the neonate: VII. Maturational changes in cardiac control. *Child Development*, **37**, 1–16.

Luria, A.R. (1961). *The role of speech in the regulation of normal and abnormal behavior*. New York: Liveright.

Luria, A.R. (1966). *Higher cortical functions in man*. New York: Basic Books.

Luria, A.R. (1969). The frontal syndrome. In P.J. Vinken & G.W. Bruyn (Eds), *Handbook of clinical neurology*, Vol. 2. Amsterdam: North Holland.

Mabry, P. & Campbell, B.A. (1974). Ontogeny of serotonergic inhibition of behavioral arousal in the rat. *Journal of Comparative and Physiological Psychology*, **86**, 193–206.

Mason, S.T. (1980). Noradrenaline and selective attention: A review of the model and the evidence. *Life Sciences*, **27**, 617–631.

Mason, S.T. & Iverson, S.D. (1977). Effects of selective forebrain noradrenaline loss on behavioral inhibition in the rat. *Journal of Comparative and Physiological Psychology*, **91**, 165–173.

Mason, S.W. & Iverson, S.D. (1979). Theories of the dorsal bundle extinction effect. *Brain Research Reviews*, **1**, 107–137.

Matthews, K.A. (1980). Measurement of the Type A behavior pattern in children: Assessment of children's competitiveness, impatience–anger, and aggression. *Child Development*, **52**, 466–475.

Matthews, K.A. (1982). Psychological perspectives on the Type A behavior pattern. *Psychological Bulletin*, **91**, 293–323.

Matthews, K.A. & Avis, N.E. (1983). Stability of overt Type A behaviors in children: Results from a one-year longitudinal study. *Child Development*, **54**, 1507–1512.

McCleary, R.A. (1966). Response-modulating function of the limbic system: Initiation and suppression. In E. Stellar & J.M. Sprague (Eds), *Progress in physiological psychology*, Vol. 1 (pp. 209–271). New York: Academic Press.

McGuinness, D. & Pribram, K. (1982). The neuropsychology of attention: Emotional and motivational controls. In M.C. Wittrock (Ed.), *The brain and psychology* (pp. 95–140). New York: Academic Press.

McGuire, I. & Turkewitz, G. (1979). Approach–withdrawal theory and the study of infant development. In M. Bortner (Ed.), *Cognitive growth and development* (pp. 57–84). New York: Brunner/Mazel.

Morley, J.E., Levine, A.S., Yim, G.K., & Lowy, M.T. (1983). Opioid modulation of appetite. *Neuroscience and Biobehavior Review*, **7**, 281–305.

Moruzzi, G. & Magoun, H.W. (1949). Brainstem reticular formation and activation of the EEG. *Electroencephalogram and Clinicial Neurophysiology*, **1**, 455–473.

Murphy, D.L., Wright, C., Buchsbaum, M.S., Nichols, A., Costa, J.L., & Wyatt, R.J. (1976). Platelet and plasma amino oxidase activity in 680 normals: Sex and age differences and stability over time. *Biochemical Medicine*, **16**, 254–265.

Nebylitsyn, V.D. (1972). *Fundamental properties of the human nervous system*. New York: Plenum.

Needham, J. (1973). *Chinese Science*. Cambridge, MA: MIT Press.

Newman, J.P., Widom, C.S., & Nathan, S. (1985). Passive avoidance in syndromes of disinhibition: Psychopathy and extraversion. *Journal of Personality and Social Psychology*, **48**, 1316–1327.

Nichols, S. & Newman, J.P. (1986). Effects of punishment on response latency in extraverts. *Journal of Personality and Social Psychology*, **50**, 624–630.

Nicholson, J.N. & Gray, J.A. (1972). Peak shift, behavioral contrast and stimulus generalization as related to personality and development in children. *British Journal of Psychology*, **63**, 47–62.

O'Gorman, J.G. & Lloyd, E.M. (1987). Extraversion, impulsiveness, and EEG alpha activity. *Personality and Individual Differences*, **8**, 169–174.

Olds, M.E. & Olds, J. (1963). Approach–avoidance analysis of the rat diencephalon. *Journal of Comparative Neurology*, **120**, 259–295.

Panskepp, J. (1981). Brain opioids: A neurochemical substrate for narcotic and social dependence. In S.J. Cooper (Ed.), *Theory in psychopharmacology* (pp. 149–175). London: Academic Press.

Panskepp, J. (1982). Toward a general psychobiological theory of emotions. *Behavioral and Brain Sciences*, **5**, 407–67.

Panskepp, J. (1986a). The anatomy of emotions. In R. Plutchik & H. Kellerman (Eds),

Emotion: Theory, research, and experience, Vol. 3, *Biological foundations of emotion*. New York: Academic Press.

Panskepp, J. (1986b). The neurochemistry of behavior. *Annual Review of Psychology*, **37**, 77–107.

Panskepp, J. & Cox, J.F. (1986). An overdue burial for the serotonin theory of anxiety. *Behavioral and Brain Sciences*, **9**, 340–341.

Panskepp, J., Siviy, S.M. & Normansell, L.A. (1984). The psychobiology of play: Theoretical and methodological perspectives. *Neuroscience and Biobehavior Review*, **8**, 465–492.

Patterson, C.M., Kosson, D.S., & Newman, J.P. (1987). Reaction to punishment, reflectivity and passive avoidance learning in extraverts. *Journal of Personality and Social Psychology*, **52**, 565–575.

Patterson, G.R. (1977). Accelerating stimuli for two classes of coercive behaviors. *Journal of Abnormal Child Psychology*, **5**, 335–350.

Patterson, G.R. (1980). Mothers: The unacknowledged victims. *Monographs of the Society for Research in Child Development*, **45** (5, Serial No. 186).

Phelps, C.P., Koranyi, L., & Tamasy, V. (1982). Brain catecholamine concentration during the first week of development of rats. *Developmental Neuroscience*, **5**, 503–507.

Porges, S. (1983). Heart rate patterns in neonates: A potential diagnostic window to the brain. In T. Field & A. Sostek (Eds), *Infants born at risk: Physiological, perceptual, and cognitive processes*. New York: Grune & Stratton.

Posner, M.I. (1978). *Chronometric explorations of mind*. Hillsdale, NJ: Erlbaum.

Posner, M.I. & Rothbart, M.K. (1981). The development of attentional mechanisms. In J. Flowers (Ed.), *Nebraska symposium on motivation* (pp. 1–52). Lincoln, NE; University of Nebraska Press.

Posner, M.I. & Rothbart, M.K. (1986). The concept of energy in psychological theory. In R. Hockey, A. Gaillard, & M. Coles (Eds), *Energetical aspects of human information processing* (pp. 23–42). Boston: Martinus Nijhoff.

Pradhan, S.N. & Pradhan, S. (1980). Development of central neurotransmitter systems and ontogeny of behavior. In H. Parvez & S. Parvez (Eds), *Biogenic amines in development* (pp. 641–662). New York: Elsevier/North-Holland.

Prideaux, E. (1920). The psychogalvanic reflex: A review. *Brain*, **43**, 50–73.

Prideaux, E. (1922). Expression of emotion in cases of mental disorder. *British Journal of Medical Psychology*, **2**, 30–46.

Rapaport, J.L., Pandari, C., Renfield, M., Lake, C.R., & Ziegler, M.G. (1977). Newborn dopamine-beta-hydroxylase, minor physical anomalies, and infant temperament. *American Journal of Psychiatry*, **134**, 676–679.

Redmond, D.E. & Huang, Y.H. (1979). New evidence for a locus coeruleus–norepinephrine connection with anxiety. *Life Sciences*, **25**, 2149–2162.

Redmond, D.E. & Murphy, D.L. (1975). Behavioral correlates of platelet monoamine oxidase (MAO) activity in rhesus monkeys. *Psychosomatic Medicine*, **37**, 80.

Redmond, D.E., Murphy, D.L., & Baulu, J. (1979). Platelet monoamine oxidase activity correlates with social affiliative and agonistic behaviors in normal rhesus monkeys. *Psychosomatic Medicine*, **41**, 87–100.

Riad-Fahmy, D., Read, G.R., Joyce, B.G., & Walker, R.F. (1981). Steroid immunoassays in endocrinology. In A. Voller, A. Bartlett, & J.D. Bidwell (Eds), *Immunoassays for the 80's*. Baltimore: University Park Press.

Richards, J.E. & Cameron, D. (1987). Infant heart rate variability and behavioral developmental status. Paper presented at the meetings of the Society for Research in Child Development, Baltimore, MD, April 1987.

Richmond, J.B., Lipton, E.L., & Steinschneider, A. (1962). Autonomic function in the neonate: V. Individual homeostatic capacity in cardiac response. *Psychosomatic Medicine*, **24**, 66–74.

Richmond, J.B. & Lustman, L.Q. (1955). Individual differences in the neonate. *Psychosomatic Medicine*, **17**, 269–280.

Robbins, T.W. (1986). Psychopharmacological and neurobiological aspects of the energetics of information processing. In G.R.J. Hockey, A.W.K. Gaillard, & M.G.H. Coles (Eds), *Energetics and human information processing* (pp. 71–90). Dordrecht: Martinus Nijhoff.

Robbins, T.W. & Everitt, B.J. (1982). Functional studies of the central catecholamines. *International Review of Neurobiology*, **23**, 303–365.

Robinson, D.L. (1986). A commentary on Gray's critique of Eysenck's theory. *Personality and Individual Differences*, **7**, 461–468.

Rosenblatt, J.S. & Lehrman, D.S. (1963). Maternal behavior of the laboratory rat. In H.L. Rheingold (Ed.), *Maternal behavior in mammals* (pp. 8–57). New York: Wiley.

Rosenkilde, C.E. (1979). Functional heterogeneity of the prefrontal cortex in the monkey: A review. *Behavioral and Neural Biology*, **25**, 301–345.

Rothbart, M.K. (1987). Laboratory observations of the development of infant temperament. Paper presented at the meetings of the Society for Research in Child Development, Baltimore, MD, April 1987.

Rothbart, M.K. (1988). Temperament and the development of inhibited approach. *Child Development*, **59**, 1241–1250.

Rothbart, M.K. (in press, 1989). Behavioral approach and inhibition. In S. Reznick (Ed.), *Perspectives on behavioral inhibition*. Chicago: University of Chicago Press.

Rothbart, M.K. & Derryberry, D. (1981). Development of individual differences in temperament. In M.E. Lamb & A.L. Brown (Eds), *Advances in developmental psychology*, Vol. I (pp. 37–86). Hillsdale, NJ: Erlbaum.

Rothbart, M.K. & Posner, M.I. (1985). Temperament and the development of self regulation. In L.C. Hartlage & C.F. Telzrow (Eds), *The neuropsychology of individual differences: A developmental perspective* (pp. 93–123). New York: Plenum.

Rubenstein, J. (1974). A concordance of visual and manipulative responsiveness to novel and familiar stimuli in six-month-old infants. *Child Development*, **45**, 194–195.

Rubenstein, J. (1976). Concordance of visual and manipulative responsiveness to novel and familiar stimuli: A function of test procedures or of prior experience? *Child Development*, **47**, 1197–1199.

Ruff, H.A. (1976). The coordination of manipulation and visual fixation: A response to Schaffer (1975). *Child Development*, **47**, 868–871.

Rusalov, V.M. (1987). Questionnaire for the Measurement of the Structure of Temperament (QST), Short Manual. Moscow: Moscow University.

Saltz, E., Campbell, S., & Skotko, D. (1983). Verbal control of behavior: The effects of shouting. *Developmental Psychology*, **19**, 461–464.

Saxton, P.M., Siegel, J., & Lukas, J.H. (1987a). Visual evoked potential augmenting/ reducing slopes in cats: 1. Reliability as a function of flash intensity range. *Personality and Individual Differences*, **8**, 499–509.

Saxton, P.M., Siegel, J., & Lukas, J.H. (1987b). Visual evoked potential augmenting/ reducing slopes in cats: 2. Correlations with behavior. *Personality and Individual Differences*, **8**, 512–519.

Schaffer, H.R. (1974). Cognitive components of the infant's response to strangeness. In M. Lewis & L.A. Rosenblum (Eds), *The origins of fear* (pp. 11–24). New York: Wiley.

Schaffer, H.R., Greenwood, A., & Parry, M.H. (1972). The onset of wariness. *Child Development*, **43**, 165–175.

Schneirla, T.C. (1959). An evolutionary and developmental theory of biphasic processes underlying approach and withdrawal. Republished in 1972. In L.R. Aronson, E. Tobach, D.S. Lehrman, & J. Rosenblatt (Eds), *Selected writings of T.C. Schneirla* (pp. 292–339). San Francisco: Freeman.

Schneirla, T.C. (1965). Aspects of stimulation and organization in approach–withdrawal processes underlying vertebrate behavior development. Republished in 1972. In L.R. Aronson, E. Tobach, D.S. Lehrman, & J. Rosenblatt (Eds), *Selected writings of T.C. Schneirla* (pp. 344–412). San Francisco: Freeman.

Schull, J., Kaplan, H., & O'Brien, C.P. (1981). Naloxone can alter experimental pain and mood in humans. *Physiological Psychology*, **9**, 245–250.

Shaywitz, R.A., Yager, R.D., & Klopper, J.H. (1976). Selective brain dopamine depletion in developing rats: An experimental model of minimal brain dysfunction. *Science*, **191**, 305–308.

Sheldon, W.H., Lewis, N.D.C., & Tenney, A. (1969). Psychotic patterns and physical constitution. In D.V. Siva Sanker (Ed.), *Schizophrenia: Current concepts and research.* Hillsdale, NJ: PJD Publications.

Sheldon, W.H. & Stevens, S.S. (1942). *The varieties of human temperament.* New York: Harper & Row.

Snyder, J.A. (1977). A reinforcement analysis of interaction in problem and nonproblem children. *Journal of Abnormal Psychology*, **86**, 528–535.

Sokolov, E.N. (1963). *Perception and the conditioned reflex.* New York: Macmillan.

Soskis, D.A. & Shagass, C. (1974). The relative reliability of average evoked response parameters. *Psychophysiology*, **11**, 175–190.

Sostek, A.J., Sostek, A.M., Murphy, D.L., Martin, E.B., & Born, W.S. (1981). Cord blood amine oxidase activities relate to arousal and motor functioning in human newborns. *Life Science*, **28**, 2561–2568.

Soubrie, P. (1986). Reconciling the role of central serotonin neurons in human and animal behavior. *Behavioral and Brain Sciences*, **9**, 319–364.

Stein, L. (1980). The chemistry of reward. In A. Routtenberg (Ed.), *Biology of reinforcement* (pp. 109–130). New York: Academic Press.

Steinberg, L. (1986). Stability (and instability) of Type A behavior from childhood to young adulthood. *Developmental Psychology*, **22**, 393–402.

Steinschneider, A. (1973). Determinants of an infant's cardiac response to stimulation. In D.N. Walcher & D.L. Peters (Eds), *Early Childhood: The development of self-regulatory mechanisms.* New York: Academic Press.

Stellar, J.R. & Stellar, E. (1985). *The neurobiology of motivation and reward.* New York: Springer-Verlag.

Stelmack, R.M. (1981). The psychophysiology of extraversion and neuroticism. In H.J. Eysenck (Ed.), *A model for personality* (pp. 38–64). Berlin: Springer-Verlag.

Stelmack, R.M. & Michaud-Achorn, A. (1985). Extraversion, attention, and habituation of the auditory evoked response. *Journal of Research in Personality*, **19**, 416–428.

Stelmack, R.M. & Plouffe, L. (1983). Introversion–extraversion: The Ball–Magendie law revisited. *Personality and Individual Differences*, **4**, 421–427.

Stelmack, R.M. & Wilson, K.W. (1982). Extraversion and the effect of frequency and intensity on the auditory brainstem response. *Personality and Individual Differences*, **3**, 373–380.

Stone, E.A. (1983). Problems with current catecholamine hypotheses of antidepressant agents: Speculations leading to a new hypothesis. *Behavioral and Brain Sciences*, **6**, 535–547.

Strelau, J. (1972). A diagnosis of temperament by non-experimental techniques. *Polish Psychological Bulletin*, **3**, 97–105.

Strelau, J. (1983). *Temperament, personality, activity.* New York: Academic Press.

Studman, L.G. (1935). Studies in experimental psychiatry: V, W and F factors in relation to traits of personality. *Journal of Mental Science*, **81**, 107–137.

Suomi, S.J. (1986). Anxiety-like disorders in young nonhuman primates. In R. Gittelman (Ed.), *Anxiety disorders of childhood* (pp. 1–23). New York: Guilford Press.

Sutton, R.E., Koob, G.F., LeMoal, P.E., Rivier, J., & Vale, W.W. (1983). Corticotropin-releasing factor produces behavioral activation in rats. *Nature*, **297**, 331–333.

Swanson, L.W., Sawchenko, P.E., Rivier, J., & Vale, W.W. (1983). Organization of ovine corticotropin-releasing factor immunoreactive cells and fibers in the rat brain: An immunohistochemical study. *Neuroendocrinology*, **36**, 165–186.

Taylor, D.C. (1969). Differential rates of cerebal maturation between sexes and between hemispheres. *Lancet*, 140–142.

Tennes, K., Downey, K., & Vernadakis, A. (1977). Urinary cortisol excretion rates and anxiety in normal one year old infants. *Psychosomatic Medicine*, **39**, 178–187.

Tennes, K. & Kreye, M. (1985). Children's adrenocortical responses to classroom activities and tests in elementary school. *Psychosomatic Medicine*, **47**, 451–460.

Tennes, K., Kreye, M., Avitable, N., & Wells, R. (1986). Behavioral correlates of excreted catecholamines and cortisol in second-grade children. *Journal of the American Academy of Child Psychiatry*, **25**, 764–770.

Tennes, K. & Mason, J.W. (1982). Developmental endocrinology: An approach to the study of emotions. In C. Izard (Ed.), *Measuring emotions in infants and children* (pp. 21–37). Cambridge: Cambridge University Press.

Teplov, B.M. (1964). Problems in the study of general types of higher nervous activity in man and animals. In J.A. Gray (Ed.), *Pavlov's typology* (pp. 3–156). Oxford: Pergamon.

Thatcher, R.W., Walker, R.A., & Giudice, S. (1987). Human cerebral hemispheres develop at different rates and ages. *Science*, **236**, 1110–1113.

Tucker, D.M. (1985). Neural control of emotional communication. In P. Blanck, R. Buck, & R. Rosenthal (Eds), *Nonverbal communication in the clinical context* (pp. 258–308). New York: Oxford University Press.

Tucker, D.M. & Williamson, P.A. (1984). Asymmetric neural control systems in human self-regulation. *Psychological Review*, **91**, 185–215.

Uberkoman-Wiita, B., Vogel, W.H., & Wiita, P.J. (1981). Some biochemical and behavioral (sensation-seeking) correlates in healthy adults. *Research Communication in Psychology, Psychiatry and Behavior*, **6**, 303–316.

Ursin, H., Baade, E., & Levine, S. (1978). *Psychobiology of stress: A study of coping men.* New York: Academic Press.

von Bargen, D.M. (1983). Infant heart rate: A review of research and methodology. *Merrill-Palmer Quarterly*, **29**, 115–149.

von Knorring, L. (1980). Visual average evoked responses and platelet monoamine oxidase in patients suffering from alcoholism. In H. Begleiter (Ed.), *The biological effects of alcohol.* New York: Plenum.

von Knorring, L. & Perris, C. (1981). Biochemistry of the augmenting-reducing response in visual evoked potentials. *Neuropsychobiology*, **7**, 1–8.

Walker, R.N. (1962). Body build and behavior in young children: I. Body build and nursery school teachers' ratings. *Monographs of the Society for Research in Child Development*, **27**, (3, Serial No. 84).

Walker, R.N. (1978). Pre-school physique and late-adolescent somatotype. *Annals of Human Biology*, **5**, 113–129.

Walker, R.N. & Tennes, J.M. (1980). Prediction of adult Sheldon somatotypes I and II from rankings and measurements at childhood ages. *Annals of Human Biology*, **7**, 213–224.

Waller, A.D. (1919). Periodic variations of conductance of the palm of the hand. *Proceedings of the Royal Society*, **91B**, 32–40.

Walter, G.W. (1950). The twenty-fourth Maudsley lecture: The functions of electrical rhythms in the brain. *Journal of Mental Science*, **96**, 1–30.

Watanabe, K., Nakai, K., & Kasamatsu, T. (1982). Visual afferents to norepinephrine-containing neurons in cat locus coeruleus. *Experimental Brain Research*, **48**, 66–80.

Webb, E. (1915). Character and intelligence. *British Journal of Psychology Monographs*, Nos 1 & 3.

Wenger, M.A. (1941). The measurement of individual differences in autonomic balance. *Psychosomatic Medicine,* **3**, 427–434.

Whalen, C.K. & Henker, B. (1986). Type A behavior in normal and hyperactive children: Multisource evidence of overlapping constructs. *Child Development*, **57**, 688–699.

Whitaker, H.A. (1978). Is the right leftover? Comment on Corballis and Morgan, 'On the biological basis of laterality'. *Behavioral and Brain Sciences*, **1**, 1–4.

Wise, R.A. (1980). Action of drugs of abuse on brain reward systems. *Pharmacology, Biochemistry and Behavior*, **13**, 213–233.

Wise, R.A. (1982). Neuroleptics and operant behavior: The anhedonic hypothesis. *Behavioral and Brain Science*, **5**, 39–87.

Wohlwill, J. (1980). Cognitive development in childhood. In O. Brim & J. Kagan (Eds),

Constancy and change in human development (pp. 359–444). Cambridge: Harvard University Press.

Wundt, W. (1903). *Grundzuge der physiologischen Psychologie*, Vol. 3, 5th edn. Leipzig: W. Engelmann. Cited by H.J. Eysenck & M.W. Eysenck (1985).

Zuckerman, M. (1984). Sensation seeking: A comparative approach to a human trait. *The Behavioral and Brain Sciences*, **7**, 413–471.

Zuckerman, M., Ballenger, J.C., & Post, R.M. (1984). The neurobiology of some dimensions of personality. *International Review of Neurobiology*, **25**, 391–436.

Zuckerman, M., Murtaugh, T.M., & Siegel, J. (1974). Sensation seeking and cortical augmenting–reducing. *Psychophysiology*, **11**, 535–542.

7

Behavior-Genetic Approaches to Temperament

H. HILL GOLDSMITH
University of Oregon

In some more logical future, this chapter on the genetics of temperament would be integrated into the previous one on biological approaches. When a biological variable is shown to affect some aspect of temperament, we might expect that a genetic basis for the biological variable is likely. However, research and theorizing have not progressed in such a logical way. Biological variables like those treated in the previous chapter have typically been studied independently of genetic considerations, and vice versa. This chapter, then, complements the previous one; it summarizes the associations that have been demonstrated between genetic differences and temperamental behavior.

After a brief historical overview of animal and human research related to temperament, this chapter explains the key concepts of behavioral genetics and ilustrates those concepts with examples from the temperament and personality literature. These examples serve as a selective review of the literature. The chapter concludes with a discussion of how behavioral genetics can help elucidate explicitly developmental issues in temperament research.

BEHAVIOR-GENETIC STUDIES OF TEMPERAMENT

Early behavior-genetic studies of temperament represent two traditions: animal research on activity, reactivity, and emotionality measured in the laboratory and field; and human family, twin, and adoption studies of a variety of traits, usually assessed via questionnaires. Research interest in the genetics of temperament, broadly conceived, began shortly after the rediscovery of Mendel's principles.

Animal Research

By 1920, strain differences in emotionality and activity had been found in rats and, in emotionality, in mice. Such studies continued through the 1920s and 1930s and

Temperament in Childhood   Edited by G.A. Kohnstamm, J.E. Bates and M.K. Rothbart
© 1989 John Wiley & Sons Ltd

were reviewed by Hall (1941), whose own classic studies demonstrated that rats could be selectively bred for high emotionality, as operationalized by defecation in the open-field test (Hall, 1951). The brightly lit, open field was assumed to be aversive for the photophobic, agoraphobic rat. Beginning in the 1950s, Broadhurst (1960) initiated another selection study for emotionality in rats; the results indicated very high heritability. Later, more sophisticated studies suggested lower heritability, confirmed a strong genetic correlation between emotionality (again assessed by defecation in the open field) and activity level, and showed that a single gene for albinism exerted a discernible effect on activity level, such that the albino gene occurred more frequently in low-activity lines (DeFries & Hegman, 1970). In some studies, defecation scores have not been uncritically accepted as valid indicators of emotional arousal because they are not always associated with motoric indices of emotionality and they may serve other functions, such as marking territories. Nevertheless, recent research has documented that genetic selection for defecation scores leads to differences in plasma norepinephrine concentrations and related indices of sympathetic nervous system arousal (Blizard, 1981). Behavioral differences between selected lines are apparent under stressful but not under non-stressful circumstances (Blizard, Freedman, & Liang, 1983), a finding reminiscent of Chess and Thomas's (1984) longitudinal case studies of difficult children.

In the 1930s, investigators adduced evidence supporting Pavlov's speculation that differences among dogs in ease of conditioning, as well as other emotion-related behaviors, were heritable. Scott and Fuller's (1965) longitudinal studies of the genetics of canine behavior included analyses of emotionality and activity. Various tests of emotional reactivity and behavior during inhibitory training revealed extensive breed differences among beagles, cocker spaniels, Shetland sheepdogs, basenjis, and wire-haired fox-terriers. Genetic crosses of basenjis with cocker spaniels led Fuller and Thompson (1978) to conclude 'These results are compatible with a hypothesis that general emotionality is strongly heritable and that its expression is determined by independent genetic systems which affect the probability of occurrence of specific behavior patterns' (Fuller & Thompson, 1978, chapter 10).

Genetic effects on canine behavior are, of course, not limited to breed differences. Individual variation within breeds was shown by establishing lines of pointers that were either high or low in fearfulness. Besides a number of behavioral differences, the highly fearful line evinced minimal hippocampal theta activity while alert (Lucas, Powell, & Murphree, 1974). Whether this finding relates to the role of hippocampal theta as an indicator of Gray's behavioral inhibition system is uncertain (see Rothbart's discussion in the previous chapter). Although the nervous line of pointer dogs display generally normal behavior in the presence of other dogs, they freeze and show fear when confronted by humans (Reese, Newton, & Angel, 1983). The nervous line of pointers show alterations in various neurotransmitter systems. Reese (1979) proposed that the nervous dogs respond more to aversive events than to positive reinforcement, a suggestion reminiscent of Newman's findings that introverts are more affected by punishment than extraverts (as reviewed by Rothbart in the previous chapter).

Suomi and colleagues have studied anxiety-proneness in rhesus monkeys from both biological and experiential perspectives (Suomi, 1983, 1986). Among many interesting psychobiological results, they found that certain highly anxious adults tended to produce anxious offspring. Half-siblings showed similar patterns of heart-rate change, a correlate of anxiety-proneness, despite differences in rearing experiences. Early results from this program of research suggest very high heritability; if confirmed with increased sample sizes, this will supply a firm behavior-genetic component to one of the most comprehensive psychobiological investigations of temperament. Furthermore, the primate behavioral and physiological patterns indicative of anxiety-proneness are quite similar to those observed in human infants and toddlers (Kagan, Reznick, & Snidman, 1986).

There is, of course, other behavior-genetic research with non-human animals that might prove relevant to temperament. Examples of this other activity include research on strains of rats susceptible to audiogenic seizures, on activity level in mice and other species, on conditionability in various invertebrates, on avoidance learning in rats and mice, and on aggression in mice (see Wimer & Wimer, 1985, for a review). The advantages of animal research are that the genetic basis for behavioral differences can be unambiguously demonstrated and that correlated neurological and physiological variables can be investigated. The disadvantage is that the relevance to human temperament is always open to question. The remainder of this chapter focuses on human temperament.

Human Research

Beginning in the 1860s, Galton published several pioneering works on behavioral genetics; his studies revealed that men of eminence tended to cluster in families, a finding consistent with hereditary transmission of ability. Galton mustered various arguments that the familial clustering was due to heredity rather than environmental advantages, noting, for instance, that the sons of his eminent subjects were more accomplished than the adopted – and privileged – kinsmen of Roman Catholic popes (Galton, 1869). The two major problems in Galton's early work were his reliance on reputation as a measure of eminence and his inability to separate unambiguously genetic and familial environmental effects. To approach the first issue, he established an Anthropometric Laboratory, and to address the second, he initiated the first systematic studies of twins (Galton, 1883).

Until recently, personality questionnaires have dominated the study of temperament. Some of the personality questionnaires devised early in this century were administered to twins and families, but results can be questioned due to inadequate scale construction techniques. Later, more satisfactory self-report personality instruments such as the Minnesota Multiphasic Personality Inventory (MMPI) and other questionnaires developed by Eysenck, Cattell, Thurstone, and others were used in behavior-genetic studies. Some scales on these instruments would be thought reflective of temperament by today's definitions. In particular, most of these questionnaires tap the broad dimensions of introversion–extraversion and anxiety-proneness (or neuroticism). Some core components of both extraversion and anxiety-proneness are temperamental, in most theorists' thinking, although few would endorse all the items on such scales as primarily reflective of temperamental predispositions.

Pooling heritability estimates from various British and North American twin samples, Henderson (1982) found that about 48% of the observed variation in neuroticism was associated with genetic differences; the corresponding value for extraversion was 58%. The estimates are based on 1948 and 2374 twin pairs, respectively. Recent research on large Swedish and Finnish twin samples (each over 10 000 pairs) yielded heritabilities of .58 for neuroticism and .67 for extraversion. Of course, the questionnaire scales and the characteristics of the samples varied substantially across these studies; nevertheless, it seems clear that an appreciable portion of the variation in these major temperamental dimensions is heritable – and that another appreciable portion is not.

Early human behavior-genetic research did include some laboratory assessment of temperament-like characteristics (see review by Fuller & Thompson, 1978). These studies, mostly in the 1930s suggested hereditary influences on such variables as speed and pressure applied in the act of handwriting. Frischeisen-Kohler (1933) found substantial evidence for genetic influences on choice of tapping rate with finger, hand, and foot in studies of twins and other kinships. Exactly how these measures relate to modern conceptions of temperament is unclear; however, a revival of research in this tradition with large samples might substantially advance the field.

BEHAVIOR-GENETIC CONCEPTS AND METHODS

Heritability

The most familiar concept in behavioral genetics is heritability, the proportion of the phenotypic (observable) variance associated with genetic differences among individuals in the population. The concept seems straightforward, yet it has been overinterpreted so often that one almost reflexively lists what heritability within a population does *not* imply. First, even strong heritability does not imply lack of modifiability. A temperamental trait might be highly heritable, but nevertheless modifiable by the environment, particularly by novel aspects of the environment. Second, strong heritability does not imply that a characteristic will be present at birth or even during infancy. Developmental biologists can point to many instances where new genetically based characteristics arise later in the lifespan. Third, heritability estimates do not necessarily generalize to new populations or environments. For example, establishing that distress-proneness is heritable in English infants holds no definite implications for its heritability in Japanese children. Also, the degree of heritability for distress-proneness in the home setting may not generalize to the day-care setting.

If the environment is conducive to the expression of genetic differences, heritability will be relatively higher, and, if the environment restricts the expression of genetic differences, heritability will be relatively lower. For instance, if activity level is moderately heritable, adjusting the environment so that every child's tendencies are matched by appropriate settings and opportunities will increase heritability. On the other hand, adjusting the environment so that the activity of more active children is curtailed and the activity of less active children is increased will reduce heritability.

Another way to think about the relation of genetic and environmental variance is that heritability will decrease when new, relevant, and differential environmental factors are introduced into a population and increase when environmental factors become more nearly uniform. By the same token, heritability will increase when new relevant genes are introduced into a population and decrease to zero when everyone shares the same genes. Thus, the heritability of 'having two arms' is about zero because the genes that specify development of two arms are shared by virtually all humans. This example highlights the lack of correspondence between a characteristic 'being heritable' and 'being due to a biological process'.

In the temperament domain, there are no unambiguously established examples of characteristics for which heritability is near zero or 100%. Instead, heritability estimates from large samples usually fall in a range from 30% to 70%. Understanding how such heritability estimates are derived requires an introduction to the principal methods of human behavioral genetics. Thus, the next three sections provide brief overviews of the twin, adoption, and family designs (see Goldsmith, 1988, for elaboration).

Twin Designs

Identical twins have structurally identical genotypes, whereas fraternal twins are no more similar genetically than ordinary siblings – they share 50% of their genes by descent on the average. Both identical and fraternal twins are age-matched and presumably experience a number of common familial environmental influences. Thus, identical co-twins should be more similar than fraternals if genetic variation affects a behavior. Shared environmental factors (non-genetic factors that influence co-twins to an equivalent degree) should increase identical and fraternal co-twin similarity to the same degree. If only non-shared environmental factors are important, neither identical nor fraternal co-twins should be similar. Thus, accurate measures of twin similarity allow estimates of the magnitude of genetic, shared environmental, and non-shared environmental variance components.

This line of reasoning depends on the assumption that twins are representative of the non-twin population and that identical twin pairs and fraternal pairs share trait-relevant environmental factors to an equal degree. In the domain of adult and late-adolescent personality, both of these assumptions have garnered substantial support (Loehlin & Nichols, 1976; Lytton, 1977; Matheny, 1979; Plomin, Willerman, & Loehlin, 1976; Scarr, 1968). Nevertheless, these assumptions require investigation when new aspects of temperament are explored or when new age groups are used.

Table 1 illustrates some results from twin studies of childhood personality. Despite many differences between the two studies summarized, identical twin correlations exceed those for fraternal twins (with one exception). Twin data afford several perspectives on heritability. In several cases in Table 1, the identical correlations are approximately twice the fraternal values; this implies that almost

Table 1   Illustrative results from twin studies of infant temperament and childhood personality

(a) Twin similarity in 1- to 6-year-olds

	Identical pairs (n = 181)		Fraternal pairs (n = 84)	
	Ratings by:			
Factor	Mother	Father	Mother	Father
Attention	.47	.62	.11	.12
Behavior modulation (activity)	.61	.66	.12	.28
Sociability	.70	.68	.21	.26
Zestfulness (ebullience)	.78	.78	.43	.65
Verbal expressiveness and mood	.51	.60	.38	.46

From Cohen *et al.* (1977).

(b) Twin similarity in infants and children studied longitudinally

	Psychologists' ratings	
	Identical Rs (n = 110–116 pairs)	Fraternal Rs (n = 206–213 pairs)
Eight-month factors		
Activity	.57	.35
Person interest	.28	.20
Four-year factors		
Impulsivity/activity	.41	.37
Goal-orientation/attention	.56	.25
Negative mood	.45	.17
Seven-year factors		
Activity/spontaneity	.55	.22
Fearfulness	.36	.21
Goal-orientation/attention	.29	.24
Agreeableness/cooperation	−.02	.09

From Goldsmith and Gottesman (1981)

all the shared variance has a genetic origin. (The intraclass correlations are direct variance estimates.) Heritability can be roughly estimated as twice the difference between identical and fraternal intraclass correlations. That is, we know that identical twins share 100% of the genetic sources of variance, and fraternals share 50%; assuming shared environmental variance is equal in identicals and fraternals,

$$2(R_{iden} - R_{frat}) = \text{heritability},$$

where R is the intraclass correlation. On the other hand, because identical co-twins share all sources of genetic variance, the identical correlations themselves are upper-bound estimates of heritability in the 'broad sense'. From another perspective, twice the fraternal correlations are upper bound estimates of heritability in the 'narrow sense' (with 'narrow sense' referring to all additive genetic effects). (See textbook treatments for more details, e.g. Falconer, 1981; Fuller & Thompson, 1978; Plomin, DeFries, & McClearn, 1980.)

Adoption Designs

The most common adoption design contrasts the similarity of adoptees and their rearing parents with that of the same adoptees and their biological parents. Thus, the design contrasts the effects of inheritance with the effects of the rearing environment, to the extent that the rearing environment can be captured by assessment of the adoptive parents. Recent adoption studies have included direct measures of the home environment in addition to parental variables. If the adopting families include biological children, additional contrasts of biological versus adoptive siblings are possible. Also desirable is a control group of non-adoptive families studied in the same manner. With a non-adoptive control group, researchers can compare the similarity of biological siblings reared together with that of unrelated children reared together.

A possible bias in adoption studies is selective placement, the tendency of adoption agencies to match certain features of biological and adoptive parents. If present, selective placement inflates estimates of both genetic and family-environmental effects. Another bias in adoption research is the unrepresentativeness of both biological parents who place their infants for adoption and those who adopt them. Fortunately, both the degree of selective placement and possible unrepresentativeness are assessed in most recent adoption studies, and, if indicated, estimates of genetic and environmental parameters can be adjusted.

Large-scale longitudinal adoption studies that include assessment of personality have been undertaken at the universities of Minnesota (Scarr & Weinberg, 1977; Scarr, Weinberg, & Gargiulo, 1987), Texas (Horn, Loehlin, & Willerman, 1979), and Colorado (Plomin & DeFries, 1985; Plomin, DeFries, & Fulker, 1988). The results from these adoption studies are complex, in part because each has a different type sample and different assessment procedures. Only the Colorado Adoption Project includes assessment of infant temperament. The Minnesota samples (actually two studies) consist of adolescents and transracial adoptees, and the Texas adoptees ranged from 3 to 26 years of age at the time of initial assessment. Neither the Minnesota nor the Texas studies reveal any substantial personality resemblance among adoptive relatives, which implies that shared familial environmental factors that are independent of genotype are not influential in personality variation. The degree of resemblance among biological relatives in adoption studies has generally implied lesser genetic influence than the twin-study results. However, Loehlin, Horn, and Willerman (1981) found genetic effects on extraversion comparable to those indicated by twin studies when they confined their analyses to subjects whose extraversion scores were consistent across two methods of assessment.

Family Designs

Family designs involve studying ordinary families. By definition, they confound genetic and shared environmental sources of variation. Although they have been neglected to some extent in studies of temperament, investigating members of intact non-twin, non-adoptive families is important for several reasons. First, twin and adoption results must generalize to the general population to be useful, and family designs test this generalization. For example, to support genetic inference, investigators must demonstrate that fraternal co-twins are no more similar than ordinary siblings measured at the same age and that the similarity of parents and their biological offspring is no different in families containing adoptees versus those without adoptees.

In family studies, larger samples can be gathered, and family members of 1/2 (sibs; parent–offspring), 1/4 (half-sibs; uncle–nephew; aunt–niece; grandparent–grandchild), and 1/8 (first cousins) genetic overlap can sometimes be assessed. Genetic theory predicts a regular (sometimes linear) decrease in temperamental similarity with decreasing genetic overlap.

A key problem with family designs in temperament research lies in distinguishing temperament characteristics from broader personality traits in the parental generation. That is, understanding of the association between a parental personality trait and an offspring temperament trait requires understanding of the nature of developmental continuity for the trait.

Loehlin *et al.* (1981) compiled ordinary biological family similarity data from several studies, most of which used the MMPI or various scales devised by Eysenck, Cattell, or Tellegen. Just how these personality scales relate to temperament is, of course, a matter for theorists to debate. The median parent–offspring correlation was .14 and the median sibling correlation was .17. In one facet of their own study, Loehlin, Willerman, and Horn (1985) found similar degrees of family similarity for self-reports on the Thurstone Temperament Survey. These values imply lower heritability than the results of most twin studies. However, age and generational differences in the meaning of items may attenuate the observed similarity.

Combining Designs

Twin, adoption, and family designs, as described above, do not exhaust the possibilities for human quantitative genetic analyses. The study of twins reared apart combines twin and adoption designs. The similarity of identical twins reared apart estimates heritability directly. The rarity of twins reared apart cautions against generalizing genetic and environmental variance estimates from these designs. However, large-scale studies of twins reared apart are under way in Finland and Sweden, and a study based in Minnesota involves much more intensive assessment of a smaller sample (Tellegen *et al.*, 1988).

Twin and adoption designs can also be augmented by including other family members. For instance, the study of identical and fraternal twins and their parents constitutes a particularly powerful design when age differences are irrelevant (Fulker, 1982). Another extension of twin designs requires assessing identical twins and their offspring (Nance, 1976; Rose, Harris, Christian, & Nance, 1979). The design yields comparison of genetic full-sibs, some of whom are raised in the same family and some raised as 'social cousins' in different families. Maternal genetic effects can also be investigated in this design by comparing the similarity of the full-sib 'cousins' whose mothers are the identical co-twins with those whose fathers are the identical co-twins.

Table 2   Components of observed similarity for various classes of relatives

Class of relatives	Additive genetic variance	Non-additive genetic variance	Assortative mating variance	Shared environmental variance
Identical twins	1	1	1	1
Fraternal twins	.5	<.25	.5	1
Ordinary siblings	.5	<.25	.5	1
Adoptee and biological child reared together	0	0	0	1
Ordinary parent–offspring	.5	~0	.5	_*
Biological parent–adoptee	.5	~0	.5	0
Adoptive parent–adoptee	0	0	0	_*

* Parents and offspring do not jointly experience environments in the same way siblings do, except for broader aspects of the environment such as social class.

When study of a particular domain matures, it is possible to combine the results of various designs into a powerful multivariate analysis. That is, one can think of the problem as one for structural equation modeling. Each design generates one or more equations containing genetic and environmental parameters. Consider the framework given in Table 2.

Neither the variance components nor the kinship classes in Table 2 are an exhaustive list. However, they clearly overdetermine a solution, given a set of observed covariances or correlations. Certain assumptions are embedded in Table 2. For example, it is assumed that no special twin environments exist and that ordinary and adoptive siblings share environments to the same degree. If these assumptions are clearly violated by the data, the resulting models will not fit. In most applications, the relative fits of a few models are compared, and the best-fitting, most parsimonious one is retained.

Extensive model-fitting analyses have been done primarily for paper and pencil assessment of cognitive ability. An exception is the work of Carey and Rice (1983), who fit models to twin, family, and adoption data, all from Minnesota, for the adolescent and adult traits of dominance, social closeness, and impulsivity. Carey and Rice's results were complex and differed from trait to trait. Although some degree of genetic influence was always indicated, sex differences on various parameters were common, a parameter was sometimes needed to account for higher than predicted identical twin similarity, and non-additive genetic effects were encountered.[1] Unless sampling bias was the culprit, the appropriate conclusion is that the genetic and environmental architecture may vary from one rather narrowly conceived personality trait to the next. All personality traits are not narrowly conceived, however. Extraversion may be viewed as a higher order factor subsuming the three traits studied by Carey and Rice. Analyzing extended English kinship data for extraversion, Eaves and Young (1981) found that a simple additive genetic model, with only non-shared environmental effects, fit the data well. When Carey and Rice (1983) combined results from the three lower order traits to simulate results for a broad extraversion factor, they too found that a simple additive model fit the data well.

Analyses of this type should soon become common in behavior-genetic studies of temperament. Heeding the message of Carey and Rice (1983), we should expect that how narrowly or broadly the temperamental dimensions are conceptualized will affect the configuration of genetic and environmental underpinnings that can be estimated. That is, conceptualizing temperament in terms of broad characteristics such as 'negative emotionality' (rather than fearfulness, anger-proneness, tendency to become sad, etc.) and 'activity' (rather than motoric lability, motoric endurance, verbal responsiveness, etc.) may obscure differences in underlying genetic and environmental architecture.

Types of Genetic Variance: Additive, Dominance, Epistasis

With the background already provided on the meaning of heritability and the presentation of the major behavior-genetic methods used to study temperament, some more complex aspects of behavioral genetics can be discussed.

Behavior-genetic analyses parse total genetic variance into components. Some genetic variance is due to the additive effects of genes whereas other variance is due to non-additive, or interactive, effects. Additive genetic effects can be thought of as the total of the average effects of all of the genes that influence a particular trait. The variance due to these additive effects is, of course, additive genetic variance. One can think of the terms 'additive' and 'interactive' as in analysis of variance terminology. The non-additive component can be subdivided according to two sources of interaction:

(1) interaction between alternative genes at the same chromosomal location, called genetic dominance (in the sense that blood antigen A is dominant to antigen O in the ABO system);
(2) interaction among genes at different chromosomal locations, called epistasis.

In human studies, dominance and epistasis are signaled by phenotypic similarity greater than that expected on the basis of additive genetic effects alone, but not attributable to environmental similarity. For instance, if correlations for identical co-twin similarity are reliably more than twice the fraternal correlations (i.e. fraternal correlations are 'too low'), non-additive genetic effects could be the source of the 'excess' identical similarity. Alternative explanations include the possibilities that the excess identical similarity is due to:

(1) something specific to the identical twin relationship or environment that fosters greater similarity;
(2) fraternal twin contrast effects, such that fraternal co-twins (or those who report on their behavior) seek to accentuate the existing differences between them;
(3) negative assortative mating (see below) in the parental generation; or
(4) biased sampling of identical or fraternal twin pairs.

Some twin studies of early temperament have shown high identical twin similarity accompanied by minimal fraternal similarity. In assessing the New York Longitudinal Study dimensions by interview at age 9 months, Torgersen and Kringlen (1978) found a larger difference between identical and fraternal similarity than additive genetic factors could explain. They studied 34 identical and 16 fraternal pairs; the small sample size suggests that random error might account for the pattern suggestive of non-additive genetic effects. However, findings from five different early-childhood samples that employed various versions of Buss and Plomin's parental rating scales all yielded moderately high identical correlations and near-zero fraternal correlations (see Buss & Plomin, 1984; Harris & Rose, 1977). Average twin correlations for four studies conducted by Plomin for Emotionality, Activity, and Sociability were, respectively: for identicals .63, .62, and .53; and for fraternals .12, –.13, and –.03. Because these values were based on a total of 400 twin pairs, random error is unlikely to explain why fraternal similarity is less than one-half the identical value. Plomin (1974) suggested that the most likely explanation for these results is a form of rating bias, similar to explanation (2) in the preceding paragraph.

It may be that some types of rating scales are particularly susceptible to tendencies of mothers of fraternal twins to exaggerate their differences. For instance, our studies of infant and toddler temperament using Rothbart's (1981) Infant Behavior Questionnaire (IBQ) and Goldsmith, Elliott, & Jaco's (1986a) Toddler Behavior Assessment Questionnaire (TBAQ) were free of the 'too low' fraternal correlations (Goldsmith & Campos, 1986; Goldsmith, Jaco, & Elliott, 1986b). However, when we used a preliminary version of Rothbart's Childhood Behavior Questionnaire (CBQ), we did note that aforementioned too-low fraternal correlations for several scales. Unlike the behavioral frequency ratings called for by the IBQ and TBAQ, the CBQ asks the respondent to rate statements in terms of degrees of truth or falsity. Perhaps this response format – also used in the Buss and Plomin scales – is more susceptible to parental rating biases of some types. On the other hand, the CBQ and the Buss and Plomin instruments assess early childhood temperament whereas the IBQ and TBAQ assess younger subjects, so perhaps non-additive genetic factors become apparent only after the first 3 years of life. The issue is unresolved, but it is clear that the resolution of substantive behavior-genetic issues interacts strongly with psychometric properties of temperament assessment instruments (see Goldsmith & Rieser-Danner, in press, for a review of temperament assessment techniques).

Assortative Mating

Assortative mating refers to the tendency of persons to mate non-randomly with regard to some characteristic. Do persons of similar temperament tend to mate (positive assortative mating)? Or might temperamental opposites attract? Data from self-report inventories clearly indicate low-level positive correlations between spouses on a great variety of personality traits (Price & Vandenberg, 1980). Furthermore, spouse correlations arise primarily from initial mate selection rather than the effects of living together (D. Buss, 1984; Mascie-Taylor, 1989).

The reason that assortative mating affects genetic variance may not be intuitively clear. If parents are genetically more similar to one another than randomly mating persons, their offspring will be genetically more similar to one another and the similarity of one offspring to one parent will be greater than expected for randomly mating couples. Also, if genetic similarity tends to concentrate in families due to assortative mating, it follows that genetic differences between families will increase. In conclusion, if parents mate partially on the basis of genetically influenced aspects of temperament, estimates of heritability for those aspects of temperament increase.

Types of Environmental Variance: Shared and Non-Shared

The way environment is defined in behavioral genetics often seems strange to psychologists (Wachs, 1983). Environment is defined by exclusion: reliable variance that is not associated with genetic sources is defined as environmental in origin. Environmental variance is further decomposed into shared and non-shared components. Which aspects of the environment are shared or non-shared is defined in reference to particular kinship groups. For instance, in twin studies, the shared environment refers to factors experienced jointly or equally by co-twins. Thus, shared and non-shared effects are simply what emerges from kinship designs. These effects do not map readily onto the environmental processes or status variables studied by most psychologists.

The bulk of current evidence in the personality domain implies that non-shared environmental factors account for greater observed variance than shared factors (Henderson, 1982; Loehlin & Nichols, 1976). This conclusion follows from the observation that the similarity of fraternal twins, as well as ordinary siblings, is seldom more than one-half the value of identical twin similarity, as mentioned above. On the other hand, certain characteristics have shown patterns of twin similarity consistent with modest shared environmental effects. In four analyses from three samples, we have found suggestive evidence for shared environmental influences on measures of positive affectivity during infancy (Goldsmith & Campos, 1986; Goldsmith & Gottesman, 1981; Goldsmith et al., 1986b). Other twin results showing fraternal correlations greater than one-half the identical correlations are suggestive of the same effect for positive affectivity (for example, see the data of Cohen *et al.*, 1977, in Table 1). However, twin similarity data by themselves cannot be definitive in this matter.

Another approach to the issue involves correlating the degree of shared experience in twins with personality resemblance. For example, Rose and Kaprio (in press) analyzed extraversion and neuroticism (anxiety-proneness) scores on 2320 pairs of identical twins in Finland. The degree of social contact significantly predicted intrapair personality similarity. Thus, shared experiences seem to be influential for these two major domains of personality.

Assessment of the environment is currently being directly incorporated into many other behavior-genetic studies. For instance, measures of parenting have been integrated into twin studies of temperament (e.g. Lytton, 1980; Torgersen & Kringlen, 1978). Perhaps most informative are adoption results. For instance, Daniels and Plomin (1985) used measures of the family environment in their analyses of infant shyness. Two factors from the Family Environment Scale (FES), Personal Growth (which includes components of active-recreational orientation, expressiveness, and low control) and Cohesion (a measure of involvement and togetherness), were related to shyness in both 1- and 2-year-olds. But is the relationship between these measures of the family atmosphere and infant shyness purely environmental in origin? Daniels and Plomin's results suggest not, because the correlations between family atmosphere were stronger in non-adoptive control families (mean $r = -.38$) than in adoptive families (mean $r = -.19$). Possibly, families scoring higher on the FES factors exposed their infants to more novel social situations, a socializing influence that might decrease shyness. However, the greater effect of this socializing influence in ordinary (as opposed to adoptive) families implies that the socialization is partially genetically mediated.

Another valuable approach to the environment within behavior-genetic designs is exemplified by Rowe's (1983) twin studies of *perceptions* of parenting characteristics. He found that adolescent identical twins were more similar than fraternals in their perception of parental emotional warmth. This implies genetic influence on perception of a parenting variable that might affect temperamental development. Perception of another parenting variable, degree of control, showed no genetic underpinnings.

One of the most needed theoretical contributions is some guidance about which environmental factors affect the development of temperamental characteristics. Which aspects of the environment affect activity level? Which affect negative emotionality? The field needs specific theories of environmental influence. When these theories are better developed and incorporated into genetic designs, truly integrated progress will be possible.

Interactions Between Genetic and Environmental Effects

The concept of gene–environment interaction should be familiar to behavioral scientists by analogy with the concepts of trait by situation interaction in personality psychology and of aptitude by treatment interaction in educational psychology. Definitive gene by environment interactions have been difficult to demonstrate. One reason for the elusiveness of interactions is our inability to identify genotypes for temperament independently of observed temperamental phenotypes. Another reason is the difficulty of specifying beforehand just which aspects of the environment should interact with particular dimensions of temperament. A third problem is well known: the potential of scaling irregularities to mimic statistical interaction.

A non-temperamental example illustrates the potential explanatory power of the interaction concept. Data from a Swedish adoption study implicate gene–environment interaction as a factor in petty criminality (Cloninger & Gottesman, 1987). The cross-fostering design had four cells:

(1) observed petty criminality in male adoptees who had both biological and adoptive parents with no record of criminality (2.9%);
(2) adoptees with criminal records among their adoptive but not their biological parents (6.7%);
(3) adoptees with criminal records among their biological but not their adoptive parents (12.1%);
(4) adoptees with criminal records among both their biological and adoptive parents (40.0%).

A similar pattern of findings with lower incidences was observed in females in the same study. Note that the adoptee's genotype is operationalized as the criminal record of the biological parent and the environment is operationalized as the criminal record of the adoptive parent. Both these operational measures are surely imperfect indices of the adoptee's actual genotype and the environmental processes that lead to petty crime. We might imagine that improved measures of genotype and environment would enhance the magnitude of the interaction. Using three different samples and different statistical methods, Cadoret, Cain, and Crowe (1983) reported a similar interaction between genotype and experience in producing adolescent antisocial behavior in adoptees. We shall bypass the substantive question of whether temperament is related to criminality in these studies (see Eysenck & Eysenck, 1977).

Turning to the search for interactions in the temperament realm, we find sparse data. In the Colorado Adoption Project, Plomin and DeFries (1985) conducted the only extensive search for genotype by environment interactions in the determination of early temperament. Using biological mothers' self-report of temperament as a very approximate index of adoptees' genotypes for temperament and various environmental measures in the adoptive family, no more than a chance number of significant interactions were observed. Although the 'right' combination of adequately measured temperamental characteristics and environmental features might have been missed, genotype by environment interactions are apparently not ubiquitous for temperament.

Correlations Between Genetic and Environmental Effects

The effects of relevant genes and environmental factors are not necessarily independent. Intuition and observation strongly suggest that personal traits are correlated with experiences. To the extent that these traits are heritable, gene–

environment correlation is a reasonable expectation. The most exciting aspect of gene–environment correlation is that the concept lends itself readily to interpretation in terms of developmental processes. Plomin, DeFries, and Loehlin (1977) delineated three types of gene–environment correlation:

(1) passive;
(2) evocative or reactive;
(3) active.

These three conceptual types of gene-environment correlations can be illustrated as follows:

(1) The child who is genetically prone to, say, high activity level might have parents who, being highly active themselves, provide a stimulating environment that encourages exploration, active play, and so forth. The correlation between the child's genetic disposition for high activity level and the stimulating environment supplied by the parent is passive in the sense that the parent is not responding to the child.
(2) The child who is genetically prone to high activity level might evoke reactions in significant others, including the parents, that contribute to the further development of high activity.
(3) The child who is genetically prone to high activity level might actively select situations that elicit active behavior.

To the extent that temperamental characteristics are heritable and discernible to others, gene–environment correlations may be pervasive.

Temperament–environment correlations are ubiquitous. Every time a person picks a gift to suit someone's temperament or considers who would constitute a compatible group for a party, s/he is potentially contributing to evocative temperament–environment correlations. When a temperamentally sociable person chooses to engage in social interaction that promotes further development of sociability, s/he is contributing to active temperament–environment correlation. Whether a genotype–environment correlation underlies an observed temperament–environment correlation depends, of course, on whether the temperamental dimension is heritable. As we have seen, evidence for moderate heritability is generally apparent.

DEVELOPMENTAL BEHAVIORAL GENETICS

Given the increasing emphasis on temperament as a developmental phenomenon (see Chapter 12, by Rothbart), it is reasonable to ask how behavioral genetics can contribute to understanding the explicitly developmental nature of temperament. There are at least three types of possible contributions.

Behavior-Genetic Studies as Guides to the Investigation of Gene Action

Demonstration of heritable influences on a temperamental trait encourage the investigation of physiological underpinnings of that trait. Such investigations are likely to begin with physiological underpinnings closely related to the behavioral manifestation of the heritable trait. An example is the investigation of heart-rate variability and other psychological indicators as related to behavioral inhibition (Kagan, Reznick, & Snidman, 1987). Eventually, geneticists may be encouraged to investigate underlying gene action related to heritable temperamental traits, this is, to determine which segments of DNA contribute to variability in the trait and which gene products are involved in the physiological processes. This latter contribution is more a promissory note at our current state of knowledge. The very demonstration of heritability of temperamental dimensions implies gene action, although the gene action may be only indirectly related to temperament. The action of DNA is perhaps the most fundamental developmental process. At present, it seems feasible only to investigate gene action underlying behaviors due to a single gene. However, temperamental variability is due to the action of polygenic systems. When it becomes more feasible to identify the role of single genes in polygenic systems, gene action related to temperamental behavior can be investigated.

Longitudinal Behavior-Genetic Studies

The second type of contribution is much more conventional. Behavior-genetic designs can be extended to cross-sectional or longitudinal data. The most extensive longitudinal, behavior-genetic exploration of temperament is the Louisville Twin Study (e.g. Wilson, Brown, & Matheny, 1971; Wilson & Matheny, 1983). At various times, this study has included neonatal assessment of reactivity, examiners' ratings of infant behavior while being tested with the Bayley scales, conventional parental report temperament questionnaires, and ratings of temperament-related behaviors while the child engages in a series of laboratory-based vignettes. Twins and their younger siblings are assessed every 3 months during infancy and regularly but less frequently thereafter. The Louisville study has yielded identical and fraternal twin correlations for several temperamental dimensions at each age of assessment for each of the methods mentioned above.

If a single generalization – still tentative – is to be drawn from the Louisville study, it is that genetic effects apparently become more salient as the young child matures. To the non-developmentalist, this might seem counter–intuitive. However, developmentalists recognize that the components of early behavioral systems (including temperamental systems) must mature and regulatory mechanisms must begin to coordinate these components before coherent system properties emerge. On both evolutionary and physiological grounds, it seems reasonable that the effect of genes should be stronger once the system becomes established.

The yield of longitudinal data is greater than simply an age-graded series of twin correlations. Some aspects of this yield from the Louisville study can be illustrated with the key temperamental variable from the laboratory measures, emotional tone. Selected results for emotional tone are shown in Table 3.

Section (a) of Table 3 shows the conventional twin correlations for emotional tone. Ignoring the uncertainty created by the small sample size, the correlations suggest increased heritability after the first year. The change is due to increased identical similarity rather than decreased fraternal similarity.

Table 3 Developmental results for emotional tone in the Louisville Twin Study

(a) Twin correlations at various ages

	Age (months)				
	9	12	18	24	30
Identical twin Rs*	.57	.59	.83	.87	.79
Fraternal twin Rs†	.37	.27	.28	.26	.25

* n = 27–33.
† n = 25–32.

The 9-month data are from Wilson and Matheny (1986). All other data are from Matheny (in press).

(b) Twin correlations for patterns of temporal change in emotional tone

	Age periods (months)				
	9–12	12–18	18–24	12–18–24	12–18–24–30
Identical twin Rs	.50	.63	.80	.73	.79
Fraternal twin Rs	.48	.51	.41	.47	.26

Data for the first four age periods are from Wilson and Matheny (1986). The remainder is from Matheny (in press).

Section (b) of Table 3 displays twin correlations for developmental profiles of emotional tone rated in the laboratory. The correlations reflect similarity for both elevation and shape of profile over time. Subject to assumptions of the twin method, the results imply a strong influence of the shared environment on change during infancy and a strong heritable influence during toddlerhood.

In the 9-month phase of another laboratory-based, longitudinal twin study, Goldsmith and Campos (1986) reported identical and fraternal twin correlations of .46 and .09, respectively, for distress during a stranger approach. In the same sample, the twin correlations for the IBQ Fear scale were, respectively, .66 and .46. Both the Louisville and Goldsmith and Campos studies provide twin data for several other temperamental variables. For example, in both the Denver Twin Temperament Study and another twin study based in the Pacific Northwest, we have demonstrated moderate heritability of anger-proneness and activity level, as measured by the IBQ (Rothbart, 1981) and a companion toddler instrument constructed by Goldsmith *et al.* (1986a) (see Goldsmith & Campos, 1986; Goldsmith *et al.*, 1986b).

Longitudinal results can be analyzed in different ways. For example, Goldsmith (1984) used an adaptation of structural equation modeling (McArdle & Goldsmith, in press) to ask, 'To what extent are individual differences in reactivity, conceptualized as a broad temperamental construct, at age 7 years predictable from genetic and environmental components of reactivity measured at age 4 years?' The answer was that genetic influences at age 4 were the only significant predictors of age-7 reactivity. In other words, the stability from age 4 to 7 was associated with genetic but not environmental factors. The same structural modeling analysis indicated that new genetic variance arose between the ages of 4 and 7 (see Goldsmith, 1984, for details).

These examples show that behavioral genetics can address dynamic as well as static aspects of temperament. These quantitative genetic results may be a pale reflection of underlying changes in gene expression relevant to temperament, although competing explanations cannnot yet be excluded. Extension of the behavior-genetic analysis of temperament to the latter part of the lifespan may help clarify the issues (Plomin, Pedersen, McClearn, Nesselroade, & Bergeman, 1988).

Behavior-Genetic Investigations of the Timing of Development

The third type of potential contribution shifts the focus from the level of expression of some temperamental variable to aspects of the timing of temperamental development. A non-temperamental example illustrates the basic idea: in the course of our twin studies, we have observed that the timing of first tooth eruption is highly similar in identical co-twins whereas fraternal co-twins often differ substantially in the time of first tooth eruption. That is, the timing of tooth eruption seems strongly genetically influenced.

Analogous analyses could be applied to temperamental development. For instance, Freedman (1974) observed, in a small sample, that the onsets of social smiling and wariness of strangers were more similar in identical than fraternal twin pairs. If one analyzes temperamental characteristics into components, the appearance of each component could potentially be charted in twins and siblings. Positive results of such studies would encourage the search for neurophysiological underpinnings of milestones of temperamental development.

SUMMARY

Twin studies indicate moderate heritability of several aspects of early temperament; the evidence is strongest for negative affectivity and activity level, measured with questionnaires. More evidence is needed for other aspects of temperament and for other methods of assessment. Also needed is integration of the types of physiological variables discussed by Rothbart in the previous chapter into behavior-genetic designs. Current longitudinal twin, adoption, and family studies promise to make genetic findings more pertinent to theories of socio-emotional development.

ACKNOWLEDGMENTS

The author was supported by Research Career Development Award KO4-HD 00694 from NICHD during preparation of this chapter. Some of the research reported in the chapter was supported by grants from the Spencer Foundation, NIMH (MH41200), and NSF (BNS85-08927). Mary Rothbart contributed valuable comments on an earlier version of the manuscript.

NOTE

[1]Non-additive effects imply that certain genes differ in their effect according to which other genes are present. See the next section for elaboration.

REFERENCES

Blizard, D.A. (1981). The Maudsley reactive and nonreactive strains: A North American perspective. *Behavior Genetics*, **11**, 469–489.

Blizard, D.A., Freedman, L.S., & Liang, B. (1983). Genetic variation, chronic stress, and the central and peripheral noradrenergic systems. *American Journal of Physiology*, **245**, 600–605.

Broadhurst, P.L. (1960). Experiments in psychogenetics. In H.J. Eysenck (Ed.), *Experiments in personality, psychogenetics and psychopharmacology* (pp. 3–12). London: Routledge & Kegan Paul.

Buss, A.H. & Plomin, R. (1984). *Temperament: Early developing personality traits.* Hillsdale, NJ: Erlbaum.

Buss, D. (1984). Marital assortment for personality dispositions: Assessment with three different data sources. *Behavior Genetics*, **14**, 111–124.

Cadoret, R.J., Cain, C.A., & Crowe, R.R. (1983). Evidence for gene–environment interaction in the development of adolescent antisocial behavior. *Behavior Genetics*, **13**, 301–310.

Carey, G. & Rice, J. (1983). Genetics and personality temperament: Simplicity or complexity? *Behavior Genetics*, **13**, 43–63.

Chess, S. & Thomas, A. (1984). *Origins and evolution of behavior disorders.* New York: Brunner/Mazel.

Cloninger, C.R. & Gottesman, I.I. (1987). Genetic and environmental factors in antisocial behavior disorders. In S.A. Mednick, T.E. Moffitt, & S.A. Stack (Eds), *The causes of crime* (pp. 93–109). New York: Cambridge University Press.

Daniels, D. & Plomin, R. (1985). Origins of individual differences in infant shyness. *Developmental Psychology*, **21**, 118–121.

DeFries, J.C. & Hegman, J.P. (1970). Genetic analysis of open field behavior. In G. Lindzey & D.D. Thiessen (Eds), *Contributions to behavior-genetic analysis: The mouse as a prototype.* New York: Irvington.

Eaves, L.J. & Young, P.A. (1981). Genetical theory and personality differences. In R. Lynn (Ed.), *Dimensions of personality.* Oxford: Pergamon.

Eysenck, S.B.G. & Eysenck, H.J. (1977). Personality and the classification of adult offenders. *British Journal of Criminology*, **17**, 213–232.

Falconer, D.S. (1981). *Introduction to quantitative genetics*, 2nd edn. London: Longman.

Freedman, D.G. (1974). *Human infancy: An evolutionary perspective.* Hillsdale, NJ: Erlbaum.

Frischiesen-Kohler, I. (1933). The personal tempo and its inheritance. *Character and Personality*, **1**, 301–313.

Fulker, D.W. (1982). Extensions of the classical twin method. In B. Bonne-Tamir, T. Cohen, & R.M. Goodman (Eds), *Human genetics*, Part A: The unfolding genome. New York: Alan R. Liss.

Fuller, J.L. & Thompson, W.R. (1978). *Foundations of behavior genetics.* St Louis: C.V. Mosby.

Galton, F. (1869). *Hereditary genius: An inquiry into its laws and consequences.* London: Macmillan.

Galton, F. (1883). *Inquiry into human faculty.* London: Macmillan.

Goldsmith, H.H. (1984). Continuity of personality: A genetic perspective. In R.N. Emde & R.J. Harmon (Eds), *The development of attachment and affiliative systems* (pp. 403–413). New York: Plenum.

Goldsmith, H.H. (1988). Human developmental behavioral genetics: Mapping the effects of genes and environments. *Annals of Child Development*, **5**, 187–227.

Goldsmith, H.H. & Campos, J.J. (1986). Fundamental issues in the study of early temperament: The Denver Twin Temperament Study. In M.E. Lamb, A.L. Brown, & B. Rogoff (Eds), *Advances in Developmental Psychology*, Vol. 4 (pp. 231–283). Hillsdale, NJ: Erlbaum.

Goldsmith, H.H., Elliott, T.K., & Jaco, K.L. (1986a). Construction and initial validation of a new temperament questionnaire. *Infant Behavior and Development*, **9**, 144 (Abstract).

Goldsmith, H.H. & Gottesman, I.I. (1981). Origins of variation in behavioral style: A longitudinal study of temperament in young twins. *Child Development*, **52**, 91–103.

Goldsmith, H.H., & Jaco, K.L., & Elliott, T.K. (1986b). Genetic analyses of infant and early childhood temperament characteristics. *Behavior Genetics*, **16**, 620 (Abstract).

Goldsmith, H.H. & Rieser-Danner (in press). Assessing early temperament. In C.R. Reynolds & R. Kamphaus (Eds), *Handbook of psychological and educational assessment of children*, Vol. 2, *Personality, behavior and context*. New York: Guilford Press.

Hall, C.S. (1941). Temperament: A survey of animal studies. *Psychological Bulletin*, **38**, 909–943.

Hall, C.S. (1951). The genetics of behavior. In S.S. Stevens (Ed.), *Handbook of experimental psychology*. New York: Wiley.

Harris, E.L. & Rose, R.J. (1977). Personality resemblance in twin children: Comparison of self-descriptions with mother's ratings. Paper presented at the Second International Congress on Twin Studies, Washington, DC.

Henderson, N.D. (1982). Human behavior genetics. In M.R. Rosenweig & L.W. Porter (Eds), *Annual review of psychology*, Vol. 1 (pp. 403–440). Palo Alto, CA: Annual Reviews.

Horn, J.M., Loehlin, J.C., & Willerman, L. (1979). Intellectual resemblance among adoptive and biological relatives: The Texas Adoption Project. *Behavior Genetics*, **9**, 177–207.

Kagan, J., Reznick, J.S., & Snidman, N. (1986). Temperamental inhibition in early childhood. In R. Plomin & J. Dunn (Eds), *The study of temperament: Changes, continuities, and challenges* (pp. 53–66). Hillsdale, NJ: Erlbaum.

Kagan, J., Reznick, J.S., & Snidman, N. (1987). The physiology and psychology of behavioral inhibition in children. *Child Development*, **58**, 1459–1473.

Loehlin, J.C., Horn, J.M., & Willerman, L. (1981). Personality resemblance in adoptive families. *Behavior Genetics*, **11**, 309–330.

Loehlin, J.C. & Nichols, R.C. (1976). *Heredity, environment and personality*. Austin: University of Texas Press.

Loehlin, J.C., Willerman, L., & Horn, J.M. (1985). Personality resemblances in adoptive families when the children are late adolescent or adult. *Journal of Personality and Social Psychology*, **48**, 376–392.

Lucas, E.A., Powell, E.W., & Mumphree, O.D. (1974). Hippocampal theta in nervous pointer dogs. *Physiology of Behavior*, **12**, 609–613.

Lytton, H. (1977). Do parents create, or respond to, differences in twins? *Developmental Psychology*, **13**, 456–459.

Lytton, H. (1980). *Parent–child interaction: The socialization process observed in twin and singleton families*. New York: Plenum.

Mascie-Taylor, C.G.N. (1989). Spouse similarity for IQ and personality and convergence. *Behavior Genetics*, **19**, 223–227.

Matheny, A.P. (1979). Appraisal of parental bias in twin studies. Ascribed zygosity and IQ differences in twins. *Acta Geneticae Medicae et Gemeilologiae*, **28**, 155–160.

Matheny, A.P., Jr. (in press). Children's behavioral inhibition over age and across situations: Preservation of a trait during change. *Journal of Personality*, in press.

McArdle, J.J. & Goldsmith, H.H. (in press). Alternative common factor models for multivariate biometric analyses. *Behavior Genetics*.

Nance, W.E. (1976). Genetic studies of the offspring of identical twins: A model for the analysis of quantitative inheritance in man. *Acta Geneticae Medicae et Gemellologiae*, **25**, 103–113.

Plomin, R. (1974). A temperament theory of personality development: Parent–child interactions. Unpublished doctoral dissertation, University of Texas, Austin.

Plomin, R. & DeFries, J.C. (1985). *Origins of individual differences in infancy: The Colorado Adoption Project*. New York: Academic Press.

Plomin, R., DeFries, J.C., & Fulker, D.W. (1988). *Nature and nurture in infancy and early childhood*. New York: Cambridge University Press.

Plomin, R., DeFries, J.C., & Loehlin, J.C. (1977). Genotype–environment interaction and correlation in the analysis of human behavior. *Psychological Bulletin*, **84**, 309–322.

Plomin, R., DeFries, J.C., & McClearn, G.E. (1980). *Behavioral genetics: A primer*. San Francisco: Freeman.

Plomin, R., Pedersen, N.L., McClearn, G.E., Nesselroade, J.R., & Bergeman, C.S. (1988). EAS Temperament during the last half of the lifespan: Twins reared apart and twins reared together. *Psychology and Aging*, **3**, 43–50.

Plomin, R., Willerman, L., & Loehlin, J.C. (1976). Resemblance in appearance and the equal environments assumption in twin studies of personality traits. *Behavior Genetics*, **6**, 43–52.

Price, R.A. & Vandenberg, S.G. (1980). Spouse similarity in American and Swedish couples. *Behavior Genetics*, **10**, 59–71.

Reese, W.G. (1979). A dog model for human psychopathology. *American Journal of Psychiatry*, **136**, 1168–1172.

Reese, W.G., Newton, J.E.O., & Angel, C. (1983). A canine model of psychopathology. In A.J. Krakowski & C.P. Kimball (Eds), *Psychomatic medicine* (pp. 25–31). New York: Plenum.

Rose, R.J., Harris, E.L., Christian, J.C., & Nance, W.E. (1979). Genetic variance in nonverbal intelligence: Data from the kinship of identical twins. *Science*, **205**, 1153–1155.

Rose, R.J. & Kaprio, J. (1988). Frequency of social contact and intra-pair resemblance of adult MZ co-twins, or Does shared experience influence personality after all? *Behavior Genetics*, **18**, 309–328.

Rothbart, M.K. (1981). Measurement of temperament in infancy. *Child Development*, **52**, 569–578.

Rowe, D.C. (1983). A biometrical analysis of perceptions of family environment: A study of twin and singleton siblings kinships. *Child Development*, **54**, 416–423.

Scarr, S. (1968). Environmental bias in twin studies. *Eugenics Quarterly*, **15**, 34–40.

Scarr, S. & Weinberg, R.A. (1977). Intellectual similarities within families of both adopted and biological children. *Intelligence*, **1**, 170–191.

Scarr, S., Weinberg, R.A., & Gargiulo, J. (1987). Transracial adoption: A ten year follow-up. Paper presented at meeting of the Behavior Genetics Association, Minneapolis, MN, June 1987.

Scott, J.P. & Fuller, J.L. (1965). *Genetics and the social behavior of the dog*. Chicago: University of Chicago Press.

Suomi, S.J. (1983). Social development in rhesus monkeys: Consideration of individual differences. In A. Oliverio & M. Zappella (Eds), *The behavior of human infants* (pp. 71–91). New York: Plenum.

Suomi, S.J. (1986). Anxiety-like disorders in young primates. In R. Gittelman (Ed.), *Anxiety disorders of childhood* (pp. 1–23). New York: Guilford.

Tellegen, A., Lykken, D.T., Bouchard, T.J., Jr, Wilcox, K.J., Segal, E.L., & Rich, S. (1988). Personality similarity in twins reared apart and together. *Journal of Personality and Social Psychology*, **54**, 1031–1039.

Torgersen, A.M. & Kringlen, E. (1978). Genetic aspects of temperamental differences in twins. *Journal of American Academy of Child Psychiatry*, **17**, 433–444.

Wachs, T.D. (1983). The use and abuse of environment in behavior-genetic research. *Child Development*, **54**, 396–407.

Wilson, R.S., Brown, A.M., & Matheny, A.P., Jr (1971). Emergence and persistence of behavioral differences in twins. *Child Development*, **42**, 1381–1398.

Wilson, R.S. & Matheny, A.P., Jr (1983). Assessment of temperament in infant twins. *Developmental Psychology*, **19**, 172–183.

Wimer, R.E. & Wimer, C.C. (1985). Animal behavior genetics: A search for the biological foundations of behavior. *Annual Review of Psychology*, **36**, 171–218.

8

Issues in the Study of Temperament

JEROME KAGAN, J. STEVEN REZNICK AND NANCY SNIDMAN
Harvard and Yale Universities

Characteristic styles of behavior and mood are among the most obvious facts of our experience, and the presumed bases for this variation have oscillated between external conditions, like climate and early experience, and internal ones, like brain structure and, currently, balance among neurotransmitters. Although contemporary psychological research remains part of a cycle, now almost 75 years old, that has preferred external environmental interpretations of behavioral variation, the majority of scholars working in the immediately prior cycle believed that inherited biological factors, often called temperamental, exerted considerable influence (Jung, 1924; Kretschmer, 1926; Lombroso, 1911).

Issue 1: The Influence of Biological Processes

The most general, and possibly the least controversial, meaning of a temperamental quality is a relatively stable characteristic – affective, motivational or behavioral – that has a partial origin in the person's biology. It is generally understood that species-specific, biologically prepared responses that occur in most, if not all, intact children, like stranger and separation anxiety, sadness, shame and guilt, are not temperamental concepts because their occurrence is universal. Although the presence of these reactions does not differentiate among children, differences in the frequency, intensity and affective quality of these universal reactions might well be influenced by temperamental factors.

Issue 2: The Measurement of Temperamental Constructs

Although the above definition of temperament has a moderate degree of consensus, there is more controversy surrounding the theoretically most important qualities and their referential meaning. Thus, one major issue involves the actual phenomena

Temperament in Childhood   Edited by G.A. Kohnstamm, J.E. Bates and M.K. Rothbart
© 1989 John Wiley & Sons Ltd

whose measurements provide indexes of the temperamental quality. For example, most contemporary psychologists believe that 'ease of arousal of anxiety, apprehension or uncertainty to novelty and challenge' is likely to be a significant temperamental characteristic. But there is considerable disagreement over whether maternal report, laboratory observations of behavior, biochemical assays, heart rate, cortisol or combinations of these variables comprise the most valid index of this temperamental disposition. Our research group believes a combination of observations of behavior in unfamiliar contexts and selected physiological measures comprise the best referents for inhibition and lack of inhibition. However, at the present time we use only extreme values on behavior to define the two groups.

Issue 3: The Generality of Temperamental Constructs

A subtle, but none the less real, difference among investigators is the relative preference for generalizing from a limited corpus of data to a small number of abstract temperamental constructs that apply across varied contexts contrasted with a Baconian frame in which a large number of specific temperamental categories are inferred from patterns of behavior, interview and physiology. Eysenck (1957) and Gray (1982) are moderately good examples of the former strategy; Thomas and Chess (1977) are better examples of the latter. Our investigation of the temperamental categories of inhibition and lack of inhibition to the unfamiliar, which apply to very specific situations, began in an inductive mode and only later did we posit the two theoretical categories (Garcia-Coll, Kagan & Reznick, 1984; Kagan, Reznick, Clarke, Snidman & Garcia-Coll, 1984). One reason for remaining flexible about the number of fundamental categories is that the number of different neurotransmitters and brain peptides is likely to be large – there are about 100 as of this date – and it is not beyond credibility to suggest that many of the unique profiles of these 100 brain molecules may be linked to specific temperamental categories. If that speculative idea turns out to be valid we will have as many temperamental types as there are chemical elements. No current definition of temperament excludes that theoretical possibility.

Issue 4: Categories Versus Dimensions

The return of temperamental constructs resurrects a controversy over the utility of theorizing about qualitative categories of subjects or continuous dimensions. A central element in Paterson's (1930) popular critique of nineteenth century constitutional psychology, which emphasized types, was that continuous dimensions, not qualitative categories, were the preferred psychological constructs. This is not simply a semantic issue. A biological species, which is a fundamental concept in evolutionary biology, is a qualitative category. Each of the many separate dimensions that, considered together, define a species – weight, length, lifespan, number of chromosomes – is of secondary importance in its taxonomic classification to the profile of values on a set of objective features. Biologists recognize that a value on a single dimension, like body weight, has equivocal significance apart from the other correlated dimensions and no biologist would assign an animal to a family, genus or species on the basis of a single dimension. A mouse and a crab have similar weights but belong to different phyla. Further, many characteristics that contribute to the differentiation among closely related species are discrete qualities rather than continuous dimensions; for example, whether a lizard is terrestrial or marine or whether a bird is winged or wingless.

Clarke, Mason and Moberg's (in press) study of the profile of behavioral and physiological reactions to stress in three closely related species of macaques – rhesus, bonnet and crab-eater – suggests the utility of treating the three species as qualitatively different types. For example, among bonnets there was no correlation between behavioral signs of distress and corticosteroid secretion when the animals were taken from their home cage. By contrast, crab-eaters showed both decreased locomotion and increased corticosteroid secretion and rhesus showed a position between both the depressed posture and high corticoid secretion of the bonnets and crab-eaters. Further, each species showed a unique profile to the stress of being immobilized. Rhesus showed the smallest increase in corticosteroids but struggled the most, while among crab-eaters struggling and corticosteroid secretion were positively correlated. The authors suggest that their data cannot be explained by positing continuous dimensions, like degree of fear or arousal, but require the assumption of qualitatively different categories of response to stress.

> Examination of the pattern of results for each species suggests that they differ qualitatively in their responses to the experimental situations ... species may differ widely in their characteristic mode of responding to stressful situations. (Clarke *et al.*, in press, p. 22).

Hinde and Dennis (1986) have also argued for the theoretical utility of categories. Their work with children suggests that categories can reveal relations different from those revealed by correlations among continuous variables. For example, 4-year-olds who experience a great deal of gentle control from their mother can be very high or very low on observed hostility toward peers; hence, the correlation between the degree of gentle control and hostility is only .06. Hinde and Dennis suggest that examination of children who fall at the extremes on some variable can reveal theoretically interesting relations that are lost when the variables, in this case gentle control, are treated as continuous dimensions.

A qualitative perspective is also common in clinical work. Although investigators can place 10 depressed patients and 50 non-psychotic adults on a continuum called 'sadness of mood', most psychiatrists regard the smaller group of patients as qualitatively different from the non-patients because the two groups differ on other significant characteristics, like childhood history, physiology, and the presence of a pedigree of depression in first-degree relatives.

The advantage of the construct of *category of person*, defined as a group of individuals who have a similar profile of values on a set of correlated dimensions, is evident when we acknowledge that the social environment usually acts in predictable ways toward a type of person, not to a single psychological characteristic. Teachers, for example, are much more likely to chastise a restless child whose history contains no stigmata but will be supportive of restless children who have other qualities characteristic of the category called attention-deficit disorder. The suggestion that categories of individuals can be useful units of analysis does not mean that psychologists should ignore study of single dimensions. Chronically restless behavior may have a small number of specific, facilitating conditions and knowledge of those conditions would be useful. But investigations restricted to the correlates of single personological dimensions (e.g. sadness, anxiety, anger) may not permit a deep understanding or successful prediction of patterns of behavior with others.

This conclusion implies that administering to volunteer samples of children or adults questionnaires that do not contain a sufficiently large number of representatives of the basic temperamental categories may restrict discovery. A zoologist is not likely to find a new species by measuring the characteristics of tame animals who happen to live in the vicinity of the laboratory. The samples of middle-class college students and mothers, who are often the subjects in studies of adult or child temperament, may not contain enough subjects who represent the basic temperamental types.

INHIBITION TO THE UNFAMILIAR

Our current work on the temperamental qualities we call inhibition and lack of inhibition to the unfamiliar provides a nice example of the utility of treating temperamental constructs as referring to categories of children rather than assuming a continuous dimension, like sociability or shyness. The young child's initial reaction to unfamiliar events, and especially other people, is one of the few behavioral qualities that is moderately stable over time and independent of social class and intelligence test scores. About 10–15% of healthy 2- to 3-year-old children consistently become quiet, vigilant and emotionally subdued in such contexts for periods lasting from 5 to 30 minutes. An equal proportion are typically spontaneous and social in the same situations (Garcia-Coll, *et al.*, 1984; Kagan *et al.*, 1984). Empirical indexes of related, but not theoretically identical, constructs in adolescents and adults, often called introversion–extraversion, are among the most stable and heritable in contemporary psychology (Eysenck, 1982; Plomin, 1986; Scarr & Kidd, 1983).

Longitudinal Studies

We have been studying in a longitudinal design two cohorts of Caucasian children from working and middle class Boston families who were selected at either 21 or 31 months of age because the child was consistently shy and timid (inhibited) or sociable and emotionally spontaneous (uninhibited) when exposed to unfamiliar people, procedures and objects in laboratory settings. About 15% of a total sample of 400 children surveyed were classified as belonging to one of the two groups. The correlation between our classification based on the children's behavior in the laboratory and the mother's answers to standard questionnaire items describing similar behaviors in their children averaged only .4. Therefore, maternal reports and behavioral observations of children are not interchangeable referents for the temperamental constructs of inhibition or lack of inhibition (Garcia-Coll *et al.*,

1984; Gersten, 1986; Kagan, Reznick & Snidman, 1987; Reznick *et al.*, 1986).

For the children in Cohort 1 selected at 21 months the major behavioral signs of inhibition were prolonged clinging to or remaining proximal to the mother, cessation of vocalization, and either reluctance to approach, or retreat from, the unfamiliar events (Garcia-Coll *et al.*, 1984). The initial selection of children for Cohort 2, which occured at 31 months, was based on behavior in a laboratory playroom with an unfamiliar child of the same sex and age with both mothers present, and a subsequent episode in which the child encountered an unfamiliar woman dressed in an unusual costume (Snidman, 1984). The indexes of inhibition, similar to those used with the first cohort, were long latencies to play, speak and interact with the unfamiliar child and unfamiliar woman, together with long periods of time proximal to the mother. Each of these two cohorts was observed on three additional occasions. Cohort 1 was observed at 4, $5\frac{1}{2}$ and $7\frac{1}{2}$ years of age and Cohort 2 was seen at $3\frac{1}{2}$, $5\frac{1}{2}$ and $7\frac{1}{2}$ years of age (see Garcia-Coll *et al.*, 1984; Kagan *et al.*, 1984, 1987; Reznick *et al.*, 1986 for details). A brief description of the procedures at the later ages follows.

The index of inhibition on the second assessment ($3\frac{1}{2}$ years for Cohort 2 and 4 years for Cohort 1) was based on behavior in two, separate 40-minute laboratory play sessions with an unfamiliar child of the same sex and age with both mothers present. At $5\frac{1}{2}$ years the children in both cohorts were observed in four different unfamiliar situations. The indexes of inhibition for each situation were based on: (a) long latencies to initiate play or interact with an unfamiliar child as well as time proximal to the mother in a laboratory playroom, (b) spatial isolation and infrequent interaction with classmates in the child's school setting, (c) long latencies to talk and infrequent spontaneous comments with a female examiner during the 90-minute cognitive battery, and (d) reluctance to play with novel toys suggestive of risk in an unfamiliar laboratory playroom. The theoretically relevant variables from each situation were aggregated to form a composite index of behavioral inhibition.

Assessment at $7\frac{1}{2}$ Years

The index of behavioral inhibition at $7\frac{1}{2}$ years was based on two situations separated by several months. The first was a laboratory play situation involving 7–10 unfamiliar children of the same sex and age playing games as well as engaging in free play. The two behavioral variables that best differentiated inhibited from uninhibited children were infrequent spontaneous comments to the other children and long periods of playing or standing apart from any other child. In the second situation, an individual testing session with an unfamiliar woman, the two indexes of inhibition were latency to the sixth spontaneous comment to the examiner and the total number of spontaneous comments over the 90-minute testing session. The indexes of inhibition derived from the two situations were positively correlated (r = .40, $p < .001$).

The behavioral differences between the two types of children were preserved, albeit in different form, from the original assessment at 21 or 31 months to the most recent assessment at $7\frac{1}{2}$ years with inter-age stability coefficients for indexes of inhibited behavior ranging from .5 to .7. Significantly more inhibited than uninhibited children were quieter and spent more time apart from any other child in the free-play situation with unfamiliar peers (χ^2 = 15.2, p < .001). In the testing situation with the examiner, significantly more inhibited than uninhibited children took longer to make their sixth spontaneous comment and made fewer spontaneous comments over the session (χ^2 = 20.9, p < .001). When the two standardized indexes were combined into a single aggregate score about three-quarters of the formerly inhibited children had a positive score on this aggregate index of inhibition while only one-quarter had a negative standard score. Complementary proportions held for the uninhibited children. The correlation between the index of inhibiton at 21 months and 7½ years for Cohort 1 was +.67 (p <.001). A comparable analysis of Cohort 2 data revealed a correlation of .61 (p <.001) between the indexes of inhibition at 43 months and 7½ years.

PHYSIOLOGY AND INHIBITION

Intraspecific variation in behavioral withdrawal to novelty in rats, cats and monkeys is often correlated with physiological reactions that imply greater arousal in selective hypothalamic and limbic sites, especially the amygdala (Adamec & Stark-Adamec, 1983; Adamec, Stark-Adamec & Livingston, 1983). If this relation were present in humans, inhibited children should show more activity in biological systems that originate in these sites. Three such systems are the sympathetic chain, reticular formation with its projections to skeletal muscles, and the hypothalamic-pituitary–adrenal axis.

Five potential indexes of sympathetic reactivity are a high and stable heart rate, acceleration of heart rate to cognitive challenge, pupillary dilation and higher levels of norepinephrine. Mean heart rate and variability are always negatively correlated under both relaxed conditions as well as during cognitive activity. Individual differences in heart rate and heart-rate variability were preserved from 21 or 31 months to 7½ years (r = .5 to .6). Further, at every one of the four assessments the children who were consistently inhibited across all four assessments had higher heart rates than the children who were consistently uninhibited across all the assessments. In addition, inhibited children attained their highest heart rates earlier in the testing battery than uninhibited children and were much more likely to show a cardiac acceleration over the course of the battery. For the first time at 7½ years we measured the change in heart rate when the child's posture changed from sitting to standing. Inhibited children showed a significantly larger increase in mean heart rate (about 10 beats/minute over a 1-minute period), despite a slightly higher heart rate during the sitting baseline. This result suggests a brisker sympathetic response to the drop in blood pressure that accompanies the change from a sitting to a standing position.

Sleeping heart-rate data gathered on Cohort 1 revealed a positive correlation with the laboratory heart rates (r = .4). Further, two indexes of inhibition at 5½ years of age – reluctance to play with novel toys suggestive of risk in an unfamiliar room and shy, timid behavior with an unfamiliar peer – were associated with a higher sleeping heart rate 2 years later (r = .48, p < .01; r = .35, p < .05). The two other indexes of inhibition – behavior in a testing situation and behavior at school – were not associated with the sleeping heart rate at $7\frac{1}{2}$ years.

Pupillary dilation, another potential index of sympathetic activity, also differentiated the two groups. The $5\frac{1}{2}$-year-old inhibited children in both cohorts had significantly larger mean pupil sizes than the uninhibited children during test questions as well as during baseline intertrial intervals.

Projections from limbic structures to skeletal muscles of larynx and vocal cords also appear to be at higher levels of excitability in inhibited children. Increased tension in these muscles is usually accompanied by a decrease in the variability in the pitch periods of vocal utterances. The increased muscle tension can be due to discharge of the nucleus ambiguus as well as sympathetic activity that constricts arterioles serving the muscles of the larynx and vocal folds. Inhibited, compared with uninhibited, children at $5\frac{1}{2}$ years of age showed significantly less variability in the pitch periods of single-word utterances spoken under psychological stress as well as less variability in the fundamental frequency of all the single-word utterances in the episode (Coster, 1986).

Samples of saliva were gathered at $5\frac{1}{2}$ years in order to assess activity in the hypothalamic–pituitary–adrenal axis. These saliva samples were analyzed for unbound cortisol using a modification of the standard radioimmunoassay method. Average cortisol level gathered in the morning across 3 days was related to the original index of inhibition at 21 months ($r = .4$).[1]

We created standard scores for eight of the peripheral psychophysiological variables gathered at $5\frac{1}{2}$ years on Cohort 1 to create a composite index of limbic arousal. We found a substantial positive relation between this index and the index of behavioral inhibition at every age ($r = .70$ with the index at 21 months; $r = .64$ with the index at $7\frac{1}{2}$ years). Further, the consistently inhibited children in Cohort 1 had the highest values on the psychophysiological index (Kagan *et al.*, 1987).

A Normative Sample

Reznick and colleagues have completed a third longitudinal study of Caucasian, middle-class children of both sexes who were not selected initially to be extreme on either of these temperamental styles. The children were observed initially at 14 months ($n = 100$) and again at 20 ($n = 91$), 32 ($n = 76$) and 48 months of age ($n = 72$). The indexes of inhibition at 14 and 20 months were based on behavior with an unfamiliar examiner and with unfamiliar toys in laboratory rooms. At 32 months the index was based on behavior in a 30-minute free-play situation with two other unfamiliar children of the same sex and age with all three mothers present (see Reznick, unpublished, for details). At 4 years of age the children were assessed in a testing situation with a female examiner, with their mother in a small room containing toys suggestive of risk, and in a free-play situation with an unfamiliar peer with both mothers present. The original variation in behavior was preserved for the entire group from 14 to 32 months ($r = .44$, $p < .01$) and from 32 to 48 months ($r = .25$, $p < .05$), but was not preserved from the first assessment at 14 months to the last assessment at 4 years ($r = -.03$).

Further, the expected positive association between the index of behavioral inhibition and acceleration of heart rate or cortisol level, which was positive for the children who had been selected to be extremely inhibited in the two longitudinal studies, did not occur in this sample at 4 years of age – correlations for the entire group of children were close to zero. However, if inhibition and lack of inhibition refer to categories of children, rather than a continuous dimension of sociability, the children who were behaviorally extreme on these characteristics might display stability.

In a first analysis, we selected those children whose scores on the index of inhibition at 14 and 20 months represented the top and bottom 20% of the distribution (13 children in each group) and compared these two extreme groups on the aggregate index of inhibition at age 4. The children who had been extremely inhibited at the two early ages had a significantly higher index at age 4 (z = +.02 versus −.37; t (24 d.f.) = 2.69, p < .01). The relation between the behaviorally extreme groups also worked retrospectively. In a second analysis we selected the children whose scores were in the top and bottom 20% of the aggregate index of inhibition at age 4 and asked if they were different on the earlier assessments. The two extreme groups at age 4 consisted of the 9 most inhibited boys and the 9 most inhibited girls compared with the 9 least inhibited boys and the 9 least inhibited girls. Among the extremely inhibited 4-year-olds, 66% had a positive standard score on the index of inhibition at 14 or 20 months, in contrast to only 22% of the uninhibited 4-year-olds (χ^2 = 5.4, p<.05). The difference between the two extreme groups on a mean index of inhibition across 14 and 20 months approached significance (t (34 d.f.) = 1.87, p = .07). These data suggest that the constructs inhibited and uninhibited refer to groups of children rather than a continuous dimension of sociability or shyness.

Animal Studies

Comparative psychologists and behavioral biologists may be studying analogous categories among strains of closely related animals. Scott and Fuller's (1965) extensive investigation of the genetic contribution to these qualities in five breeds of dogs – basenjis, shelties, fox-terriers, beagles and cocker spaniels – revealed that the first three breeds displayed more timidity and had higher heart rates in unfamiliar situations than the last two. A more recent study with different species replicated this result (Goddard & Beilharz, 1985). Intraspecific variation in these qualities is found in many animal groups. Mice, rats, cats, dogs, wolves, pigs, cows, monkeys and paradise fish differ intraspecifically in their tendency to approach or to avoid novelty (Adamec & Stark-Adamec, 1986; Blanchard, Flannelly & Blanchard, 1986; Blizard, 1981; Cooper, Schmidt & Barrett, 1983; Csanyi & Gervai, 1986; Dantzer & Mormede, 1985; Murphey, Duarte & Penendo, 1980; Stevenson-Hinde, Stillwell-Barnes & Zunz, 1980; Suomi, 1987). Insight into these profiles comes from a study of house cats who also vary in the disposition to retreat from or approach the unfamiliar. Avoidant cats, compared with the complementary group that does not retreat from novelty, show greater neural activity in the basomedial amygdala following exposure to a rat and larger evoked potentials in the ventromedial hypothalamus following stimulation of the basomedial amygdala (Adamec &

Stark-Adamec, 1983, 1986; Adamec et al., 1983). The total corpus of evidence, on both animal and humans, suggests that the preferential behavioral reaction to novelty, which appears early in development, might be associated with distinct physiological profiles and, therefore, be a candidate for two distinct temperamental categories.

DISCUSSION AND CONCLUSION

Among 2- to 3-year-old children selected as extremely shy and timid in unfamiliar contexts, and who comprise about 15% of a volunteer sample, about three-quarters become 7- to 8-year-olds who are quiet, cautious and socially restrained with unfamiliar peers and adults. An equal proportion of unusually sociable, spontaneous 2-year-olds become talkative, socially interactive children. The differences in behavior are associated with peripheral physiological reactions implying important differences in the reactivity of limbic structures following encounter with novel context or challenges to which the children do not have immediate coping reactions.

We believe that the children in the temperamental group we call inhibited were born with a low threshold for limbic–hypothalamic arousal to challenge and unfamiliarity. Although the reasons for the lower thresholds in the limbic sites are not clear, and are likely to be complex, one possible contributing factor is tonically higher levels of central norepinephrine or a higher density of receptors for norepinephrine. It is important to suggest, however, that the actualization of inhibited behavior in 2- and 3-year-olds from an original temperamental disposition may require some form of chronic environmental stress interacting with the original temperamental characteristic. Thus, we adopt a diathesis–stress perspective.

One reason why we believe that the actualization of inhibited behavior requires some form of chronic environmental stress acting upon the original temperamental profile is that two-thirds of the inhibited children in the cohorts were later-born, while two-thirds of the uninhibited children were first-born. An older sibling who unexpectedly seizes a toy, teases or yells at an infant who has a low threshold for limbic arousal might provide the chronic stress necessary to transform the temperamental quality into the profile that we call behavioral inhibition.

These data are relevant to the perplexing problem of classification in the natural sciences. Among evolutionary biologists pheneticists argue that similarities in contemporary characteristics are the only important taxonomic criteria while cladists argue that similarities in phyletic origin should be the primary criteria. But evolutionary biologists subscribing to the modern synthesis believe that both evolutionary history as well as current similarities should be used in classification. We suggest this rule is also useful in studies of human development.

Two boys who had been classified as inhibited when they were 21 months old were, at $7\frac{1}{2}$ years, not distinguishable from the boys originally classified as uninhibited on the interactive behavioral variables. Should we ignore our knowledge of their early characteristics and classify them as uninhibited at this later age? We suggest a negative answer because neither boy had a profile of scores that resembled the profile of the modal uninhibited boy on variables that are theoretically relevant to the two constructs. One of the boys showed a consistent loss in memory performance following stress and the other had a high and stable heart rate. Both qualities are typical of inhibited, but not uninhibited, children. No child classified originally as inhibited or as uninhibited at 21 months had a profile on all of the theoretically significant variables gathered at $7\frac{1}{2}$ years that resembled the profile of any child in the complementary group.

Although investigators must remain receptive to the possibility that an individual can change his or her original psychological category, it is not clear what information will permit that judgment so that an individual's past behavior and biology can be disregarded. The pragmatist regards this question as metaphysical because one can never say with certainty that two objects belong to the same category. Someone may discover a feature that had been disguised that distinguishes two groups that were similar. However, many current investigations in personality and development do not try to discover minimal bases for differentiating among individuals who have similar values on the one or two behavioral variables measured. When a quality is considered ahistorically the scientist is tempted to regard the summary predicate as reflecting a stable characteristic. When assessments of change are attempted, or acknowledged, one is less likely to conceive of the predicate as naming a stable essence. No popular construct in contemporary personality communicates accurately the changing profiles of behavior and heart rate displayed by the children in our two longitudinal cohorts from 21 or 31 months to $7\frac{1}{2}$ years. If scientists focus on one set of reactions at one moment in time, it is tempting to conceptualize inhibition as a fixed characteristic of the child. But the addition of historical information thaws the frozen moment and persuades one of the utility of categories that are much more fluid.

We suggest that it will be theoretically useful to invent terms for transitional developmental intervals; that is, periods of time when a child is changing from one classification to another. Scientists in other domains frequently invent such terms; categories like unbound cortisol or neutrino refer to transition states. It is less common, however, to find category terms in personality development that name classes of individuals who possessed all the primary qualities of a category at one time but only some of those qualities at a future date. One reason for the indifference to transition categories is the reluctance on the part of many to gather historical data directly or to obtain information that has indirect implications for the past.

We do not believe that all infants born with an easily excited limbic system become inhibited children; the temperamental disposition requires chronic environmental stressors if the behavioral profile is to be actualized. It is also necessary to differentiate between shy, introverted adolescents who were born with the temperamental disposition and shy adolescents who acquired their behavioral profile during the school years as a result of experiences and do not belong to our temperamentally inhibited category. Finally, we believe that children who have been consistently inhibited for 6 or 7 years can, under certain conditions, develop an automatized response profile that is relatively independent of the physiological states that supported it earlier. If these inhibited children do not experience chronic sources of anxiety after school entrance, their heart rates, muscle tension and cortisol levels might even approximate those of average children. We know of a few 8-year-old inhibited children in our longitudinal cohorts who fit this description. This hypothesis may explain why some extremely introverted adults do not show high levels of physiological arousal. Perhaps an original relation between a physiological state and a behavioral profile can become disassociated if the latter becomes an entrenched habit.

ACKNOWLEDGMENTS

This research is supported by a grant from the John D. and Catherine T. MacArthur Foundation and by a grant from NIMH.

NOTE

[1] Salivary cortisol levels obtained at $7\frac{1}{2}$ years of age in Cohort 1 did not significantly differentiate inhibited from uninhibited children. The differential stress associated with school may have produced selective changes in cortisol in some children that were unrelated to the original temperamental classifications.

REFERENCES

Adamec, R.E. & Stark-Adamec, C. (1983). Partial kindling and emotional bias in the cat: Lasting effects of partial kindling of the ventral hippocampus. *Behavioral and Neurobiology*, **38**, 223–239.

Adamec, R.E. & Stark-Adamec, C. (1986). Limbic hyperfunction, limbic epilepsy, and interictal behavior. In B.K. Doane & K.E. Livingston (Eds), *The limbic system*, (pp. 129–145). New York: Raven.

Adamec, R.E., Stark-Adamec, C., & Livingston, K.E. (1983). The expression of an early developmentally emergent defensive bias in the adult domestic cat in non-predatory situations. *Applied Animal Ethology*, **10**, 89–108.

Blanchard, R.T., Flannelly, K.J., & Blanchard, D.C. (1986). Defensive behaviors of laboratory and wild *Rattus norvegicus*. *Journal of Comparative Psychology*, **100**, 101–107.

Blizard, D.A. (1981). The Maudsley reactive and non-reactive strains. *Behavioral Genetics*, **11**, 469–489.

Clarke, A.S., Mason, W.A., & Moberg, G.P. (in press). Differential, behavioral and adrenocortical responses to stress among three macaque species. *American Journal of Primatology*.

Cooper, D.O., Schmidt, D.E., & Barrett, R.J. (1983). Strain specific cholinergic changes in response to stress. *Pharmacology, Biochemistry and Behavior*, **19**, 457–462.

Coster, W. (1986). Aspects of voice and conversation in behaviorally inhibited and uninhibited children. Unpublished doctoral dissertation, Harvard University.

Csanyi, V. & Gervai, J. (1986). Behavior-genetic analysis of the paradise fish (*Macropodus opercularis*): II. Passive avoidance learning in inbred strains. *Behavior Genetics*, **16**, 553–557.

Dantzer, R. & Mormede, P. (1985). Stress in domestic animals. In Moberg, G.P. (Ed.), *Animal stress* (pp. 81–95). Bethesda: American Physiological Society.

Eysenck, H.J. (1957). *The dynamics of anxiety and hysteria.* London: Routledge & Kegan Paul.

Eysenck, H.J. (1982). *Personality, genetics and behavior.* New York: Praeger.

Garcia-Coll, C., Kagan, J., & Reznick, J.S. (1984). Behavioral inhibition in young children. *Child Development*, **55**, 1005-1019.

Gersten, M. (1986). The contribution of temperament to behavior in natural contexts. Unpublished doctoral dissertation, Harvard Graduate School of Education.

Goddard, M.E. & Beilharz, R.G. (1985). A multi-varied analysis of the genetics of fearfulness in potential guide dogs. *Behavior Genetics*, **15**, 69-89.

Gray, J.A. (1982). *The neuropsychology of anxiety.* Oxford: Clarendon Press.

Hinde, R.A. & Dennis, A. (1986). Categorizing individuals: An alternative to linear analysis. *International Journal of Behavioral Development*, **9**, 105-119.

Jung, C.G. (1924). *Psychological types.* New York: Harcourt Brace.

Kagan, J., Reznick, J.S., Clarke, C., Snidman, N., & Garcia-Coll, C. (1984). Behavioral inhibition to the unfamiliar. *Child Development*, **55**, 2212-2225.

Kagan, J., Reznick, J.S., & Snidman, N. (1987). The physiology and psychology of behavioral inhibition in children. *Child Development*, **58**, 1459-1473.

Kretschmer, E. (1926). *Physique and character*, 2nd edn (trans. W.J.H. Sprott). New York: Harcourt Brace.

Lombroso, C. (1911). *Crime and its causes.* Boston: Little Brown.

McDonald, K. (1983). Stability of individual differences in behavior in a litter of wolf cubs. *Journal of Comparative Psychology*, **97**, 99-106.

Murphey, R.M., Duarte, F.A.M., & Penendo, M.C.T. (1980). Approachability of Bovine cattle in pastures: Breed comparisons and a breed × treatment analysis. *Behavior Genetics*, **10**, 170-181.

Paterson, D.G. (1930). *Physique and intellect.* New York: Century.

Plomin, R. (1986). *Development, genetics and psychology.* Hillsdale, NJ: Erlbaum.

Reznick, J.S., Kagan, J., Snidman, N., Gersten, M., Baak, K., & Rosenberg, A. (1986). Inhibited and uninhibited behavior: A follow-up study. *Child Development*, **51**, 660-680.

Scarr, S. & Kidd, K.K. (1983). Developmental behavior genetics. In M.M. Haith & J.J. Campos (Eds) (P.H. Mussen, Series Ed.), *Handbook of child psychology*, Vol. 2, *Infancy and developmental psychobiology.* New York: Wiley.

Scott, J.P. & Fuller, J.L. (1965). *Genetics and the social behavior of the dog.* Republished in 1974 as *Dog behavior: The genetic basis.* Chicago: University of Chicago Press.

Snidman, N. (1984). Behavioral restraint and the central nervous system. Unpublished doctoral dissertation, University of California, Los Angeles.

Stevenson-Hinde, J., Stillwell-Barnes, R., & Zunz, M. (1980). Subjective assessment of rhesus monkeys over four successive years. *Primates*, **21**, 66-82.

Suomi, S.J. (1987). Genetic and maternal contributions to individual differences in rhesus monkey biobehavioral development. In N.A. Krasnegor, E.M. Blass, M.A. Hofer, & W.P. Smotherman (Eds), *Perinatal development: A psychobiological perspective* (pp. 397-420). New York: Academic Press.

Thomas, A. & Chess, S. (1977). *Temperament and development.* New York: Brunner/Mazel.

9

The Dynamics of Temperament–Physiology Relations: A Comment on Biological Processes in Temperament

Megan R. Gunnar and Sarah Mangelsdorf
Universities of Minnesota and Michigan

THE DYNAMICS OF TEMPERAMENT–PHYSIOLOGY RELATIONS: A COMMENT ON BIOLOGICAL PROCESSES IN TEMPERAMENT

As Rothbart notes in Chapter 6 the concept of temperament has its roots in attempts to link individual differences in behavior to individual differences in physical structure and functioning. Less apparent, although noted by Rothbart, is that impetus for the study of physiological correlates derives from observations of differences among individuals in their behavior, not in their physiology. As Rothbart points out, even the strong biological orientation of the Eastern European school was motivated by observations of differences in behavior. Pavlov's ideas about 'strong' and 'weak' nervous systems were not based on observations of individual differences in the properties of central or peripheral nervous system activity; rather, the 'strength' of an individual's nervous system was defined in terms of behavioral functioning. In short, the concept of temperament is a behavioral concept. Its utility in the study of human development derives from its behavioral focus. Behavior is the 'stuff' of temperament research, not merely the sign or sympton of more fundamental biological differences.

In fact, to contrast biological processes with behavioral processes is misleading. Behavioral processes are as biological as physiological processes, as ethologists have shown us (Hess, 1970). A more appropriate distinction is between behavior and physiology. While this change in terminology may seem academic, it can have major implications for the questions asked and working models employed because it highlights the relations between the study of physiology and temperament and the study of developmental psychobiology more generally.

Temperament in Childhood   Edited by G.A. Kohnstamm, J.E. Bates and M.K. Rothbart
© 1989 John Wiley & Sons Ltd

As an area of inquiry, developmental psychobiology has never been formalized (Levine, 1982). There is no developmental psychobiological theory. However, there is a clear orientation; an orientation rooted in systemic approaches to the study of development (Gunnar & Thelen, in press; Sameroff, 1983). Accordingly, behavior is considered in terms of an organized system composed of interacting subsystems and embedded in larger social and environmental systems. Bidirectional and feedback effects are anticipated, as well as the need for multiple levels of analysis. Fundamental to this orientation is the emphasis on a holistic rather than a reductionistic approach to the study of developmental processes. Development is viewed as involving bidirectional interactions among dynamical systems, rather than as the product of unidirectional influences of physiology on behavior.

As exemplified by many of the contributions to this volume, temperament theorists are sensitive to the bidirectional flow of influence between child and environment. Indeed, part of the impetus for the study of temperament comes from a concern with ways in which children's temperaments may influence their environments, affect their experiences, and thus influence the development of temperament and other aspects of personality and behavior. A concern with the bidirectional flow of influence is far less apparent in theories of physiological processes in temperament. This is a serious limitation in current theorizing as Rothbart has noted (see Chapter 6).

A focus on unidirectional flows of influence tends to result in working models that emphasize linear relations and concordance in activity across systems. This, in part, is related to the tendency to view behavioral organization as arising from unified, centralized processes or states. A particularly apt example comes from the literature on activation or arousal theory. Behavioral arousal was viewed as reflecting an underlying state of physiological arousal (e.g. Duffy, 1962; Lindsley, 1951). Individual differences in physiological arousability were believed to strongly influence individual differences in behavioral arousal. The problem, as Lacey (1967) noted, is that 'nature is not so simple'. Electroencephalographic, autonomic, behavioral and other 'arousal' systems are only imperfectly coupled, leading to the problem of 'dissociations' between somatic and behavioral arousal. Lacey's solution was not merely to study response patterns as typologies, but to view these different systems as reflecting different forms of arousal. In doing so, he rejected the idea of a central, unified state of arousal and opted instead for an examination of 'complexly interacting systems' with an emphasis on feedback and bidirectionality.

The literature in developmental psychobiology is also repleat with examples of dissocation among systems seemingly organized by unified internal states. A good example is the separation response of rat pups. As with the young of other mammalian species, infant rats exhibit an array of behavioral and physiological 'distress' reactions to maternal separation. Work by Hofer (see review, 1987) and Schanberg (see review by Schanberg & Field, 1987), among others, has shown that these responses are not directed by some underlying state of emotional or psychological distress. Instead, different components of the response are regulated by different components of the mother–pup relationship. Furthermore, the components of the relationship regulating the responses may change with development. For example, in the first week of life, distress vocalizations are regulated by thermal cues, while in the second week of life they are regulated largely by olfactory and tactile cues (Oswalt & Meier, 1975, as cited by Hofer, 1987). The regulatory processes may be highly specific, as in the regulation of enzyme activity by maternal licking (Schanberg & Field, 1987), or more general, as in the regulation of sleep–wake states by a combination of milk, periodicity and tactile cues (see Hofer, 1987). Furthermore, bidirectionality appears to be the rule rather than the exception. One elegant example is the role of infant rest–activity cycles in regulating maternal milk letdown which in turn regulates infant rest–activity cycles (Hofer, 1987).

NEUROENDOCRINE CORRELATES OF TEMPERAMENT

As Rothbart notes (see Chapter 6), most of the work to date on temperament and neuroendocrine activity has focused on activity of the two adrenal systems: the sympathetic–adrenomedullary and pituitary–adrenocortical systems. These two systems have been found, at times, to be associated with two, somewhat distinct, psychological factors: effort and distress (see Frankenhaeuser, 1986). Psychological processes summarized as effort include feelings of interest, engagement and determination. These are associated with increased sympathetic–adrenomedullary activity. Psychological processes associated with distress include feelings of anxiety, dissatisfaction and boredom. These are associated with increased pituitary–adrenocortical activity. Both neuroendocrine systems are often activated in situations associated with both effort and distress; they can be uncoupled, however, in situations predominantly associated with one or the other psychological factor. Because elevations in cortisol can be found under conditions associated with anxiety and negative affect in the absence of psychological effort, Henry (e.g. Henry & Meehan, 1981) and others (e.g. Frankenhaeuser, 1986) have come to view adrenocortical activity as reflecting feelings of helplessness and depression. This view is consistent with evidence of cortisol hypersecretion among a percentage of individuals with clinical depression.

Viewed from a static, unidirectional perspective, we might predict individual differences in adrenocortical (cortisol and other corticoids) and adrenomedullary (catecholamines) activity to be related differentially to two major dimensions of temperament. Specifically, individuals who tend to be high sympatho-adrenal responders should be approachers: individuals who exhibit a high degree of interest in, and involvement and engagement with, the environment. Those individuals tending to be high adrenocortical responders should be avoiders: individuals exhibiting a high degree of inhibition and fearfulness in the face of novelty; prone to feelings of helplessness and depression.

Some of the literature on these two systems supports this dichotomy. As cited by Rothbart (see Chapter 6), Frankenhaeuser (1986) and her colleagues have found that during examinations children and young adults who show elevations in catecholamine excretion perform better than those who fail to show elevations or even exhibit decreases in catecholamine excretion rates. (Note, however, that this is true only for boys.) These data support the catecholamine–effort typology. Conversely, Kagan, Reznick and Snidman (1987) have shown that adrenocortical activity is associated with inhibition in children. Although their work is best known for the associations they have found between behavioral inhibition and sympathetic–adrenomedullary activity (cf. Chapter 6, by Rothbart), consistent with the dichotomy just discussed, they have recently argued that measures of salivary cortisol are even better indices of inhibition than are measures of sympathetic activity (Kagan *et al.*, 1987). Their data on human children parallels Suomi's (see Chapter 10, by Higley & Suomi) data on inhibition and adrenocortical activity in juvenile rhesus monkeys.

My colleagues and I also have found evidence supportive of this typology. For example, we (see Gunnar, Marvinney, Isensee & Fisch, in press, for review) have found that crying and increases in cortisol are positively correlated in response to noxious stimulation (heel-stick, circumcision) in human newborns. We (Gunnar, Mangelsdorf, Larson & Hertsgaard, 1989) have also recently found significant correlations between temperament and elevations in salivary cortisol among older infants. Specifically, infants with more negative, distressed temperaments show greater adrenocortical responses to complex situations involving maternal separation, strangers and strange places.

Other data, however, raise questions about this simple dichotomy and the underlying model of a unidirectional flow of influence it implies. As noted by Rothbart (see Chapter 6), we (Gunnar, Connors, Isensee & Wall, 1988) have found that reducing behavioral distress does not affect the newborn's adreno-cortical response to stressors such as circumcision, blood sampling or a discharge examination. We have also found that among extremely healthy infants elevations in cortisol to events such as a discharge examination, weighing and measuring, or the Brazelton Neonatal examination are associated, not with distress, but with increased self-calming activity. More pertinent, Spangler, Meindl and Grossman (personal communication) have recently found that, among healthy newborns, high baseline cortisol concentrations were correlated with positive social orientation and low irritability. Low baseline concentrations were associated with irritability and disorganized behavior on the Brazelton Neonatal examination.

Associations between higher pituitary–adrenocortical activity and competence or effectance is not limited to the newborn and infancy periods. Again, as cited by Rothbart (see Chapter 6), Tennes and her colleagues (Tennes & Kreye, 1985; Tennes, Kreye, Avitable & Wells, 1986) found that cortisol excretion levels were positively correlated with social competence in school-aged children. On test days, cortisol concentrations increased, while catecholamine levels decreased, a finding which Rothbart rightly notes would not have been predicted by the catecholamine-effort and cortisol–distress/helplessness model. In a study of boys with hemophilia, Mattsson, Gross and Hall (1971) also found that the boys who appeared more distressed and less competent when hospitalized for observation had lower cortisol levels, rather than the higher levels that would be predicted by the distress-helplessness model. Finally, Rose, Jenkins, Hurst, Herds and Hall (1982), in a study of air-traffic controllers, found that those with higher cortisol levels were the ones viewed by supervisors as more competent and who reported themselves to feel more competent and effective.

Temporal changes in behavior–hormone associations also complicate simple, unidirectional physiology-to-behavior models of emotional or temperamental responding. For example, two types of data have often been used to support the cortisol–depression argument by Henry (1980): monkey infants often develop despair or depression responses after the initial protest phase of reaction to maternal separation (cf. Kaufman & Rosenblum, 1967), and monkey infants often exhibit striking elevations in cortisol following maternal separation (see review by Coe & Levine, 1981). However, despair reactions have never been noted in conjunction with elevated cortisol levels in separated monkey infants. In fact, among rhesus monkeys who often exhibit the biphasic protest–despair reaction, cortisol concentrations typically return to baseline within 24 hours of separation or before despair reactions would be expected to develop (Gunnar, Gonzales, Goodlin & Levine, 1981; Levine, Johnson & Gonzales, 1985). As in rhesus macaques, the human adrenocortical system also appears to exhibit strong homeostatic tendencies. Even under conditions which produce prolonged psychological distress, cortisol concentrations rapidly return to basal levels (see Rose, 1980, for review).

In summary, the effort–distress dichotomy does not fit all of the data on the sympathetic–adrenomedullary and pituitary–adrenocortical systems. Activation of both neuroendocrine systems appears, at times, to be associated with effort and competence and, at times, with distress and anxiety. What is needed, as Rothbart notes (see Chapter 6), is a theory or at least an approach that can help integrate these findings.

A MORE DYNAMICAL APPROACH

The purpose of the above exposition is not to put ourselves out of business. The search for physiology-temperament relations holds great promise, if for no other reason than that it will undoubtedly extend our appreciation of the complex interplay among the systems which support human life and development. The concern, however, is with the tendency in this area to slip quickly into dichotomies and typologies, even while noting the complexity of the systems under study. The concern is further with the tendency, having dichotomized or typed individuals, to slip equally quickly into a reductionist shorthand; e.g. easily distressed individuals become high-responders, a shorthand for their often imperfectly correlated tendency to exhibit greater increases in the activity of the physiological system being measured. This typing and reducing leads to a comfortable sense of closure. The physiological differences do seem more fundamental, basic or closer to the real 'biological basis' of the differences in behavior that first intrigued us. However, physiology is no more biological than is behavior, and certainly physiological systems are no more fundamental or immutable. Like behavioral systems, physiological systems are open, not closed, to changes in the activity of the other systems in which they are embedded.

As Oyama (1989) might put it, the problem is one of searching for the ghost in the machine: the fundamental organizer of the phenotypes we observe. Organization, however, may not arise from some central orchestrator. It might arise through the dynamical interplay of systems and their surrounds (see Thelan, 1989). This approach taken to the extreme, of course, threatens us with theoretical nihilism: everything affects everything else and it is all too complex to begin to sort out. We need some sort of organizational road-map to thread our way through the dynamics toward some sense of order. Two, related, suggestions have been made to aid our search for order in chaos: more systematic analysis of context and more consideration of function. Fentress (1989) has argued eloquently that context provides an important piece of the road-map. Organisms self-organize within contexts within lifetimes, and over lifetimes organisms evolve to 'interpret' events within the framework of expectable or probable contexts. In a complementary fashion, Woodson (1983) has argued that developmental predictions depend on analyses of function with an eye to the self-righting and self-maintaining properties of living systems. Behavioral responses, to enter the system on one level of functioning, are not merely symptoms of underlying states; behavioral responses may also serve to modify internal states or conditions, thus helping the organism as a whole to self-right.

The combination of contextual and functional analysis may allow us to approach the study of physiology–temperament relations more dynamically. The contexts in which children develop are enormously complex, offering numerous channels through which experience may be transduced or have impact on organism activity. As the example of the rat pups' reactions to separation demonstrates, the activity of different systems in response to an event may be organized not by a central organizer, but by the organization of the context of the event. A sensitivity to context thus shifts attention from the non-specificity (e.g. a distress response is a distress response across systems and across contexts) to the specificity of responding (see for example Levine, Wiener, Coe, Bayart and Hayashi (1987) for an empirical analysis of the specificity of vocalizations in response to different contexts of separation in the squirrel monkey infant and evidence of causal relations between the specificity of adrenocortical responding and specific types of vocalizations). Because naturally occurring contexts are complex, the patterning of individual differences across systems of responding may be organized or orchestrated, in part, through differential sensitivity to different components of the event.

A sensitivity to the stimuli (i.e. context) associated with activation and modulation of the activity of different systems should help us avoid simple classification schemes and the prediction of physiology–behavior associations across situations that should differentially impact the systems under study. However, alone it will not be enough. In addition, we need to focus more attention on the function of the response: what is this behavioral or physiological system doing, what impact does it have on the organism and its surrounds, how might the response feed back and modulate other systems of responding, how might the impact of the response vary as a consequence of the activity of the other systems in which it is embedded, and how might the answers to each of these questions change as a consequence of the organism's developmental status?

In summary, this kind of dynamical approach to the study of physiology–temperament relations should help us maintain temperament as a behavioral construct on equal footing with the analysis of physiological responses and their regulation. It seems reasonable to assume, at the outset, that the child's temperament plays a role in psychobiological organization: both influenced by and influencing patterns of physiological responses to events. A finer grained analysis of context-behavior and context-physiological associations along with attention to the functions of responding should help explicate the dynamic role of temperament in development.

ACKNOWLEDGMENTS

The writing of this chapter was supported by NICHD grant HD-16494 and NIH Research Career Development Award HD-00712 to Megan Gunnar. The authors wish to express thanks to Mary Rothbart for her comments on drafts of this chapter and to Louise Hertsgaard and Mary Larson for their editorial comments. Requests for reprints should be sent to the first author at the Institute of Child Development, University of Minnesota, Minneapolis, Minnesota, 55455, USA.

REFERENCES

Coe, C.L. & Levine, S. (1981). Normal responses to mother-infant separation in nonhuman primates. In D.F. Klein & J. Kaplan (Eds), *Anxiety: New research and changing concepts* (pp. 155–157). New York: Raven Press.

Duffy, E. (1962). *Activation and behavior*. New York: Wiley.

Fentress, J. (1989). Developmental roots of behavioral order. In M.R. Gunnar & E. Thelen (Eds), *Systems and development: Minnesota symposia on child psychology*, Vol. 22 (pp. 35–76). Hillsdale, NJ: Erlbaum.

Frankenhaeuser, M. (1986). A psychobiological framework for research on human stress and coping. In M.H. Appley & R. Trumbull (Eds), *Dynamics of stress* (pp. 101–116). New York: Plenum.

Gunnar, M.R., Connors, J., Isensee, J. & Wall, L. (1988). Adrenocortical activity and behavioral distress in human newborns. *Developmental Psychobiology, 21*, 297–310.

Gunnar, M.R., Gonzales, C.A., Goodlin, B.L. & Levine, S. (1981). Behavioral and pituitary–adrenal responses during a prolonged separation period in infant rhesus macaques. *Psychoneuroendocrinology, 6*, 65–75.

Gunnar, M.R., Mangelsdorf, S., Larson, M. & Hertsgaard, L. (1989). Attachment, temperament and adrenocortical activity in infancy: A study of psychoendocrine regulation. *Developmental Psychology, 25*, 355–363.

Gunnar, M.R., Marvinney, D., Isensee, J. & Fisch, R.O. (in press). Coping with uncertainty: New models of the relations between hormonal, behavioral and cognitive processes. In D. Palermo (Ed.), *Coping with uncertainty*. Hillsdale, NJ: Erlbaum.

Gunnar, M.R. & Thelen, E. (Eds) (1989). *Systems and development: Minnesota symposia on child psychology*, Vol. 22. Hillsdale, NJ: Erlbaum.

Henry, J.P. (1980). Present concept of stress theory. In E. Usdin, R. Kvetnansky & U.G. Kopin (Eds). *Catecholamines and stress. Proceedings of the Second International Symposium on Catecholamines and Stress*. New York: Elsevier/North Holland.

Henry, J.P. & Meehan, J.P. (1981). Psychosocial stimuli, physiological specificity and cardiovascular disease. In H. Weiner, M.A. Hofer & A.J. Stunkard (Eds), *Brain, behavior and bodily disease* (pp. 305–333). New York: Raven.

Hess, E.H. (1970). Ethology and developmental psychology. In P.H. Mussen (Ed.), *Manual of child psychology* , Vol. 1 (pp. 1–38). New York: Wiley.

Hofer, M.A. (1987). Early social relationships: A psychobiologist's view. *Child Development, 58*, 633–647.

Kagan, J., Reznick, J.S. & Snidman, N. (1987). The physiology and psychology of behavioral inhibition in children. *Child Development*, **58**, 1459–1474.

Kaufman, I.C. & Rosenblum, L.A. (1967). The reaction to separation in infant monkeys: anaclitic depression and conservation-withdrawal. *Psychosomatic Medicine*, **29**, 648–695.

Lacey, J.I. (1967). Somatic response patterning and stress: Some revision of activation theory. In M.H. Appley & R. Trumbull (Eds), *Psychological stress: Issues in research* (pp. 14–37). New York: Appleton-Century-Crofts.

Levine, S. (1982). Comparative and psychobiological perspectives on development. In W.A. Collins (Ed.), *The concept of development: Minnesota symposia on child psychology*, Vol. 15 (pp. 29–54). Hillsdale, NJ: Erlbaum.

Levine, S., Johnson, D.F. & Gonzales, C.A. (1985). Behavioral and hormonal responses to separation in infant rhesus monkeys and mothers. *Behavioral Neuroscience*, **99**, 399–410.

Levine, S., Wiener, S.G., Coe, C.L., Bayart, F.E.S. & Hayashi, K.T. (1988). Primate vocalization: A psychobiological approach. *Child Development*, **58**, 1408–1419.

Lindsley, D.B. (1951). Emotion. In S.S. Stevens (Ed.), *Handbook of experimental psychology*. New York: Wiley.

Mattsson, A., Gross, S. & Hall, T. (1971). Psychoendocrine study of adaptation in young hemophiliacs. *Psychosomatic Medicine*, **33**, 215–225.

Oyama, S. (1989). Ontogeny and the central dogma. In M.R. Gunnar & Thelen (Eds), *Systems and development: Minnesota symposia on child psychology*, Vol. 22 (pp. 1–34). Hillsdale, NJ: Erlbaum.

Rose, R.M. (1980). Endocrine responses to stressful psychological events. *Advances in Psychoneuroendocrinology. Psychiatric Clinics of North America*, **3**, 251–276.

Rose, R.M., Jenkins, C.D., Hurst, M., Herds, J.A. & Hall, R. (1982). Endocrine activity of air traffic controllers at work: II. Biological, psychological and work correlates. *Psychoneuroendocrinology*, **7**, 113–123.

Sameroff, A. (1983). Developmental systems: Context and evolutions. In P. Mussen (Ed.), *Handbook of child psychology*, Vol. 1 (pp. 237–294). New York: Wiley.

Schanberg, S.M. & Field, T.M. (1988). Sensory deprivation stress and supplemental stimulation in the rat pup and preterm human neonate. *Child Development*, **58**, 1431–1447.

Tennes, K. & Kreye, M. (1985). Children's adrenocortical responses to classroom activities and tests in elementary school. *Psychosomatic Medicine*, **47**, 451–460.

Tennes, K., Kreye, M., Avitable, N. & Wells, R. (1986). Behavioral correlates of excreted catecholamines and cortisol in second-grade children. *Journal of the American Academy of Child Psychiatry*, **25**, 764–770.

Woodson, R.H. (1983). Newborn behavior and the transition to extra uterine life. *Infant Behavior and Development*, **6**, 139–144.

10

Temperamental Reactivity in Non-Human Primates

J. D. Higley and S. J. Suomi
National Institute on Alcohol Abuse and Alcoholism and
National Institute of Child Health and Human Development, Bethesda.

Non-human primates have been useful research models in studying and understanding human behavior. Researchers have used such models to study
development, stress, and psychopathology. For example, among researchers
interested in development, Harlow's classic studies using terry-cloth surrogate
mothers have been paramount in understanding the mother–infant bond (Harlow,
1958). Social separation of non-human primates has been important as a model to
study the etiology and treatment of depression (McKinney, 1984; Suomi, 1985).
Other researchers have used non-human primate models to study the effects of
stress on immunology and disease (Coe, Rosenberg, Fischer, & Levine, 1987).

One area receiving much research in many different species of animals is
individual differences in temperament, particularly emotional reactivity (Blizard,
1981; Gray, 1971; Scott & Fuller, 1965; Stevenson-Hinde & Zunz, 1978).
Subprimate species, such as strains of rats and mice, have been selectively bred for
levels of reactivity, as measured by exploration and defecation during an open-field
test (Blizard, 1981; Gray, 1971). Such selective breeding has shown that certain
aspects of emotionality can be bred for, and when reactive strains are tested,
researchers have been able to predict behaviors across time and situation (e.g. see
Blizard, 1981, and Gray, 1971, for reviews). Similarly, Stevenson-Hinde and Zunz
(1978) have found that individual differences in emotional reactivity, as measured
by subjectively rating individual monkeys who lived in a large group for levels of
emotionality, can be observed and rated in non-human primates such as rhesus
monkeys, and these ratings of reactivity show continuity across time and situation
(Stevenson-Hinde, Stillwell-Barnes, & Zunz, 1980a; Stevenson-Hinde, Zunz, &
Stillwell-Barnes, 1980b).

Temperament in Childhood   Edited by G.A. Kohnstamm, J.E. Bates and M.K. Rothbart
© 1989 John Wiley & Sons Ltd

Such emotionality has been labeled by other names such as timidity, reactivity, fearfulness, anxiety, introversion, shyness, and more recently behavioral inhibition. For the purposes of this paper, the term reactivity will be used to describe the hypothetical temperament construct described above. However, it should be noted that we have used other terms such as timidity and behavioral inhibition in other reports. Reactivity reflects an affective and behavioral predisposition to respond to novel or challenging stimuli. Individuals rated high in reactivity would be less likely to approach new stimuli, more anxious, more socially inhibited, and less likely to attempt challenging situations. Kagan, Reznick, and Snidman (see Chapter 8) describe temperament traits as a constellation of correlated behaviors mediated by an underlying variable. In a similar vein, we describe reactivity using overlapping Venn diagrams, with each diagram representing a behavioral expression of reactivity, and a central core that incorporates the hypothetical construct reactivity, the trait controlling the behavioral expressions (e.g. see Figure 1). This central core is intrinsic to the individual and affects how he/she responds to novel or challenging stimuli. For example, in general, highly reactive monkeys are also less dominant in social status (but see Suomi, 1987, for an exception); however some monkeys may also be less dominant because of social support, body size, or social skills. Thus, in the Venn diagram, reactivity may overlap with social dominance, but not perfectly. In addition, social dominance would be expected to overlap with a number of other features of reactivity such as proximity to attachment source, latency to approach novel stimuli, or sympathetic nervous system activity.

Using this approach, a number of different paradigms and behaviors have been used to measure reactivity. In general, these involve measurements of anxiety or fearfulness during novel or possible threatening situations, or behavioral

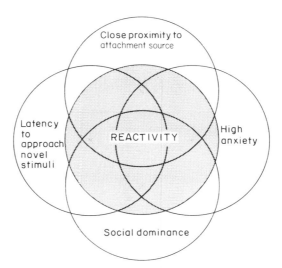

FIGURE 1   The trait reactivity (shaded) can be represented as a number of partially overlapping characteristics; all are a function of the hypothetical central controlling variable reactivity.

withdrawal during social interactions. Some examples are: subjective ratings of fearfulness or emotionality while being handled by an experimenter (Schneider, 1987; Suomi, Kraemer, Baysinger, & DeLizio, 1981), proximity to an attachment source (Suomi, 1983), latency to approach stimuli in a novel setting, initiation of social interactions with unfamiliar individuals (Thompson, Higley, Byrne, Scanlan, & Suomi, 1986), recording of overall distress behaviors during exposure to a novel room (Suomi et al., 1981; Thompson et al., 1986), and physiological reactivity such as levels of cortisol, heart rate, and central amines (norepinephrine, serotonin, etc.) (Higley, 1985; Higley, Suomi, & Linnoila, in press; Suomi et al., 1981; Thompson et al., 1986). Reactivity is most frequently measured during stressful events such as social separation. Reactive monkeys are more likely to show measures of anxiety during social separation such as self-orality, handwringing and self-clasping, distress vocalizations, immobility, and huddling. Anxiety and fear are also prevalent in the presence of stimuli associated with a possible separation (Higley, 1985; Mineka, Suomi, & DeLizio, 1981; Suomi et al., 1981; Suomi, Harlow, & Domek, 1970; Thompson et al., 1986).

While the majority of studies have looked at reactivity during the introduction of a major stressor, other studies have looked at reactivity in response to the day-to-day vicissitudes and demands that occur in normative social challenges and interactions with the environment (Champoux, 1988, Higley, 1985; Stevenson-Hinde et al., 1980a,b), and since anxiety and fearfulness inhibits play (e.g. see Higley, 1985), other studies have used levels of play as an assessment of reactivity, with highly reactive monkeys showing less play than their less reactive counterparts (Higley, 1985). There is also evidence that reactivity is related to other forms of social behavior. Stevenson-Hinde and Zunz (1978) found that their least fearful monkeys were the most social. In terms of day-to-day social interactions, subjects that were less likely to show leadership skills characteristic of monkeys, such as high position in the group's social dominance hierarchy, were later classified as more reactive, based on how they responded to the stressor of social separation: those lacking leadership and social competence showed increased hand-wringing and self-clasping and distress vocalizations during a subsequent social separation (Scanlan, 1987). Thus, reactive monkeys are more likely to acquiesce to other individuals during social interactions or competition for resources (Scanlan, 1987).

While, in general, levels of fearfulness and anxiety are used to rate reactivity, the developmental status of the individual must also be taken into account. Behaviors characteristic of reactivity show age-related changes based on the developmental status of the individual. In general, the types of behaviors shown under states of fear and anxiety at a given age are the characteristic behavioral expressions of this trait. In infancy ventral clinging and nipple contact, self-orality, hand-wringing and self-clasping, distress vocalizations, and social withdrawal are seen in all animals but more often and in more situations in highly reactive animals. By adolescence, increased behavioral withdrawal and immobility or flight as a response to stressful stimuli are behaviors more prevalent during fearful conditions, and occur more frequently in reactive monkeys. Previous experience must also be considered because behavioral regression may occur with repeated exposure to stressors (Higley, 1985; Scanlan, 1984; Suomi et al., 1970, 1981).

In one study, we measured reactivity by temperament ratings and behavior during exposure to a novel room. To facilitate the probability of obtaining monkeys who differed in levels of reactivity, mothers were selectively bred with males who had previously produced offspring that were high or low in reactivity. During the first month of life, neonatal rating scales of fearfulness and consolability were drawn up by two independent researchers and ratings were obtained for each monkey; each researcher was blind to the other's temperament definitions and scoring system, and used different testing conditions. When the two sets of rating scales for emotionality were compared, they correlated .94 (n = 11) (Scanlan; Schneider; unpublished data). When the subjects were 4 months old, they were exposed to a novel environment. We used a paradigm similar to one used by Kagan $et\ al.$ (see Chapter 8), who exposed two children who were unfamiliar to each other, one behaviorally inhibited and the other uninhibited, to a novel but interesting environment. Similarly, we exposed these unfamiliar monkeys, two at a time, one high and one low in reactivity, to a novel environment. Each subject was exposed twice, each time with a different partner. The latency to approach objects and the time spent observing the unfamiliar animal were measured during both sessions.

When these pairs were placed with their respective inanimate surrogate mothers into a novel playroom with interesting objects, subjects that were previously rated as high in reactivity took significantly longer to approach the objects and explore the room, and spent longer in close proximity to their surrogate mother. Also, consistent with Kagan's findings (see Chapter 8), highly reactive infants spent more time observing their partner manipulating the objects and exploring the room, and following such observations, often the highly reactive monkey would approach the same object that its partner had just manipulated and use it in the same fashion (Thompson $et\ al$., 1986).

CONTINUITY AND PREDICTIVE MARKERS

There is evidence that individual differences in reactivity are present early in life. In the Thompson $et\ al.$ (1986) study described above, the neonatal temperament ratings of fearfulness and anxiety predicted individual differences in heart rate during exposure to the novel room previously described, with highly reactive monkeys having higher heart rates (Thompson $et\ al.$, 1986). In another study of reactivity reported by Suomi (1981), heart-rate changes in 22-day-old rhesus monkey infants were recorded as they were repeatedly exposed to a signaled burst of white noise. Monkeys that showed large heart-rate changes to a conditioned stimulus signaling a burst of white noise at 22 days of age demonstrated significantly more anxiety and fearfulness in each quarter of the succeeding 12 months (Suomi, 1981). In a follow-up study of a different group of subjects, heart-rate change at 22 days of age was negatively correlated with activity during a short-term social separation from their social group at 18 months of age (Suomi, 1983).

A recent study by Champoux (1988) assessed individual differences in home-cage behaviors of rhesus monkeys across the first 5 months of life. She found that, for nursery-reared subjects, low levels of neonatal alertness and, for mother-reared subjects, high levels of clinging to the mother were predictive of anxiety during social separation at 6 months of age, as measured by self-clasping and self-orality (Champoux, 1988). Becker, Suomi, Marra, Higley, and Brogan (1984) likewise found that neonatal temperament ratings predicted individual differences in affective state at 6 months of age during the stressor of a social separation. Specifically, subjective rating scales of consolability and fearfulness predicted levels of despair during a 6-month social separation (Becker et al., 1984). In addition, Scanlan and Suomi (1988) found that irritability and crying in the first month of life predicted self-directed behavior during a social separation at 6 months of life.

Several studies have shown measures of reactivity to be highly stable across time. For example, for the previously described 11 monkeys exposed to the playroom, correlations of behaviors across sessions separated by 1 month revealed significant positive correlations for self-scratching and grasping ($r = .69$), activity ($r = .69$), and distress vocals ($r = .60$). There was also a positive correlation for self-mouthing that approached significance ($r = .59$). Correlations of latency behaviors across sessions revealed significant positive correlations for latency to enter room ($r = .79$), latency to touch first toy ($r = .63$), and mean latency to touch all toys ($r = .87$) (Higley & Thompson, unpublished data).

Other studies have found continuity across longer periods. Since fearfulness and anxiety are manifest in response to the day-to-day social challenges and changes in the home environment, some studies have assessed levels of reactivity in the home cage. Higley (1985) found that behaviors that reflect fearfulness and anxiety which are exhibited during home-cage conspecific challenges and day-to-day changes, such as self-directed orality, clasping, and immobility, showed strong continuity from infancy (month 9), to childhood (month 18), and early adolescence (month 30). Subsequent studies have replicated these findings in different monkeys, reared and tested under different conditions (Bush, Steffen, Higley, & Suomi, 1987; Higley, Hopkins, Suomi, Hirsch, & Orman 1985), and with different species studied in different laboratories (Capitanio, Rasmussen, Snyder, Laudenslager, & Reite, 1986). In addition, levels of play in infancy, which as discussed earlier are inhibited by anxiety and fearfulness, were negatively correlated with an aggregate measure of day-to-day home-cage reactivity (defined as immobility while self-clasping and self-mouthing) during subsequent developmental periods. Specifically, levels of play in infancy (9 months of age) during home-cage day-to-day interactions predicted individual differences in home-cage reactivity into childhood (18 months of age; $n = 12$, $r = -.72$) and into adolescence (30 months of age; $n = 12$, $r = -.77$) (Higley, 1985). Stevenson-Hinde et al. (1980a) found that ratings of confidence, excitability, and sociability during day-to-day social interactions were correlated from one year to the next.

REACTIVITY AND AFFECTIVE PROBLEMS

There is evidence that reactivity early in life may be related to subsequent anxiety and despair during future social separations. Higley (1985) measured levels of reactivity exhibited in the home cage 2 weeks prior to a series of social separations. Reactivity, as measured by hand-wringing and self-clasping and by self-mouthing during undisturbed home-cage activity, was strongly correlated with behaviors characteristic of despair during social separation. Furthermore, reactivity during infancy was strongly correlated with behaviors characteristic of anxiety and despair displayed during social separations in adolescence. In the same study, not only were levels of social play negatively related to subsequent home-cage reactivity, but levels of home-cage play in infancy were also negatively correlated with levels of anxiety during social separation in adolescence. In addition, play was negatively correlated with social separation anxiety in adolescence (infants aged 9 months, adolescents aged 36 months; $n = 12$, $r = -.68$).

Champoux (1988) found that social-separation behaviors reflecting differing levels of reactivity, such as grasping and clasping of self, were strongly correlated from the first to the fifth month of age. Scanlan (1987) found that a measure of social competence in monkeys, social dominance, was negatively correlated with anxiety and despair during social separation. Higley, Linnoila, Suomi, Hopkins, and Bush (1987) found that when monkeys were freely provided with an alcohol solution, individual differences in reactivity shown during a social separation (e.g. clasping and immobility) were positively correlated with levels of consumption (Dowd, Highley, Suomi, & Linnoila, 1988; Higley et al., 1987). Thus reactivity may predispose individuals to potential affective problems.

HERITABILITY

There is evidence that both genetic and environmental variables are factors in the development of reactivity. Classic studies using rodents have demonstrated that emotional reactivity can be bred for by selecting males and females that are more reactive to the stressors of an open-field test and breeding them together (Blizard, 1981; Gray, 1971). For non-human primates, there is also evidence that genes play a role in reactivity. These studies have indicated that different species of non-human primates display different levels of reactivity. For example, when gibbons and rhesus monkeys were exposed to a series of novel stimuli, gibbons were more likely to approach and explore the stimuli. Similarly, when exposed to a large open caging area, gibbons were more likely to explore, whereas rhesus monkeys were more likely to remain immobile. Gibbons were also more likely than rhesus monkeys to approach a stranger of their own species and interact with that stranger (Bernstein, Schusterman, & Sharpe, 1963). Under similar test conditions, when rhesus monkeys and langurs were compared, langurs were more likely to investigate novel objects and less likely to urinate and defecate (Singh & Manocha, 1966).

More recently, other studies have shown that even closely related species may vary in reactivity. Clarke, Mason, and Moberg (1988) compared three macaque species – rhesus, crab-eating, and bonnet – in a number of tasks related to emotionality. Across tasks, the crab-eating macaques were the most reactive, showing less exploration and manipulation of novel stimuli, and higher levels of distress cries and behavioral immobility; rhesus monkeys were more active and explorative, and showed more aggression; and bonnet macaques fell in between. When levels of cortisol and heart rate were compared across the different tasks, crab-eaters had the highest levels, rhesus the lowest, and bonnets fell in between, consistent with their behavioral levels of reactivity.

Within species there is also evidence for heritability. In the study described earlier, with heart-rate change at 22 days of age predicting future reactivity, Suomi *et al.* (1981) found evidence for genetic influences on both heart-rate changes and subsequent reactivity. When the subjects were ranked from highest to lowest in levels of both heart rate and behavioral reactivity, half-sibs were more likely to cluster closely together in rank than unrelated individuals in both measures. Similarly, individual differences in levels of cortisol and adrenocorticotropic hormone (ACTH) during the stressor of social separation appear to be highly heritable. Paternal half-sibs reared apart from each other, none of which had seen their father, were correlated more closely in their adrenal response than unrelated individuals (Scanlan, 1987; Scanlan, Suomi, Higley, & Kraemer, 1982). Scanlan (1987) also found that social dominance, a measure previously described as negatively related to reactivity, is heritable.

There is also evidence that reactivity can be specifically bred in non-human primates. In another study, monkeys were specifically bred for reactivity and cross-fostered to mothers differing in maternal skills. Selections of breeding pairs were based on previous male-female pairings producing high-reactive or low-reactive infants. Immediately after birth, the infants were fostered to an unrelated lactating female, which either was nurturant and supportive, or had a previous maternal history indicative of subaverage support and care. Four different cells were possible: high-reactive infant with either a supportive or subaverage foster mother, and low-reactive infant with either a supportive or subaverage foster mother. When the high-reactive infants were compared to the low-reactive infants for their response to social separation, there were no main effects or interactions involving maternal experience. The high-reactive infants were less likely to explore the separation environment and demonstrated more stereotypic locomotion.

After their separation from their mothers, they were placed into a group with other monkeys. Infants with a biologically high reactive background demonstrated significantly more time in close ventral–ventral proximity to other infants in the group. The high-reactive infants were also more likely to initiate aggression to other members of the group (Champoux & Suomi, 1986; Suomi, 1987; Suomi, Champoux, Higley, Scanlan, & Schneider, 1986).

EFFECT OF EARLY REARING HISTORY

While such studies indicate that reactivity may be heritable, there is also evidence that rearing environments affect reactivity. Perhaps the strongest evidence for this comes from studies of infants reared in peer-only groups. Peer-only reared subjects are generally reared for the first 30 days in a neonatal nursery with or without a terry-cloth surrogate mother. Afterward, they are placed together without adults, usually in groups of four, and allowed unfettered daily social interactions. Such rearing largely ameliorates the behaviors seen in subjects that are raised without companionship in social isolation, mainly because peers provide each other with contact comfort, warmth, and contingent daily social interactions that produce social competence and reproductive skills (Harlow, Suomi, & Novak, 1974; Novak & Harlow, 1975).

Nevertheless, peer-only reared subjects display high levels of reactivity relative to their mother reared counterparts. Among mother reared subjects, during the first month of life, infants seldom are out of ventral contact with their mother. After the first month, levels of close ventral contact become less and less frequent, largely because infants spend increasing amounts of time in exploration and social play. Relative to mother reared subjects, over the first 6 months of life, peer-only reared subjects demonstrate more infant-like social clinging (Chamove, Rosenblum, & Harlow, 1973; Harlow, 1969; Hirsch, Higley, & Suomi, 1986). Indeed, these subjects spend much of their day in the infant-like clinging pictured in Figure 2. Mother reared subjects seldom engage in such intimate contact after the ninth month of life, and hardly ever after the first year (Hinde & Spencer-Booth, 1967; Hirsch *et al.*, 1986). Unlike mother reared subjects, peer-only reared subjects continue to show this behavior at high frequencies, even into the second and third years of life (Higley, 1985). The differences are most dramatic under mild challenges such as exposure to novel sounds or the appearance of a stranger in their housing room.

Additional evidence comes from a study in which peer-only reared subjects were exposed to an analogue of the Ainsworth Strange Situation (Ainsworth, Blehar, Waters, & Wall, 1978) designed for rhesus monkey infants. Peer-only reared subjects were more likely to remain in close proximity to their attachment source (a favorite

FIGURE 2 Peer-only reared subject clinging to terry-cloth surrogate mother. Wire surrogate mother, although the provider of nourishment, is rejected in favor of comfort except at feeding times. (Reproduced by courtesy of Harlow Primate Laboratory, University of Wisconsin.)

peer) than were mother reared subjects. Conversely, mother reared subjects were more likely to interact with the stranger and explore the environment (Higley, Danner, & Hirsch, 1988a). Moreover, the effects of peer-only rearing appear to have long-term consequences. Even as adults, when they are exposed to a novel but interesting room, or during social separation, subjects that have been reared in a peer-only group are more likely to show more behaviors characteristic of anxiety (Higley, 1985, and unpublished data). Under the stressor of a new baby, they are also more likely to reject or neglect their first offspring (Suomi & Ripp, 1983). Finally, in terms of their daily behaviors, several studies have indicated that such timidity affects their daily interactions. When both mother reared and peer-only reared subjects have peers with whom to play, peer-only reared subjects demonstrate significantly less play than subjects reared by their mothers (Bush *et al.*, 1987; Chamove *et al.*, 1973; Harlow, 1969; Hirsch *et al.*, 1986).

Several explanations for the effects of such rearing have been put forward. Some have suggested that the deficits these subjects have may be due to non-secure attachment relations (Higley *et al*., 1988a). Indeed, during exposure to the Strange Situation, peer-only reared infants were more likely to maintain close proximity to their attachment source (a favorite peer), and less likely to explore their environment than subjects reared by their mothers. A second explanation, discussed in the next section, indicates that such rearing changes CNS neuro-transmitter activity in both norepinephrine (NE) and serotonin monoamine systems.

BIOLOGICAL CORRELATES

Several studies have shown that differences in sympathetic arousal are positively correlated with levels of behavioral reactivity. For example, in a recent study, two groups of peer-only reared monkeys were reared either in a large noisy room or in a small quiet room. When both groups were exposed to an experimental cage with interesting but novel toys, the subjects reared in the large noisy room adapted to the cage less rapidly and had a higher, less variable heart rate (Byrne, DiGregorio, & Thompson, 1988). Heart rate was also obtained in the subjects described earlier who were exposed to the playroom with an unfamiliar monkey. When their heart rate was correlated with measures such as exploration, there was a significant correlation between heart period and environmental exploration during the first exposure to the playroom ($n = 9$, $r = .67$). Mean heart period of the two sessions also predicted mean levels of environmental exploration during a subsequent series of four, 4-day social separations ($n = 9$, $r = .73$) (Thompson *et al.*, 1986).

For monkeys, one of the most studied indices of sympathetic arousal is the measure of adrenocortical system activity (cortisol and ACTH). As noted by Rothbart in Chapter 6, positive correlations have been found between individual differences in reactivity and cortisol, particularly after stressful conditions. For example, in 24-month-old peer-only reared monkeys, we obtained plasma 1 and 2 hours after social separation, and individual differences in levels of cortisol were correlated with an aggregate measure of distress (immobility, self-directed orality, self-clasping, and huddling; $n = 12$, $r = .60$) (Higley 1985). Champoux (1988) found that, after social separations, individual differences in levels of cortisol for peer-only reared subjects were positively correlated with self-mouthing, and negatively correlated with environmental exploration. Suomi (1983) found that cortisol levels at 22 days of age were positively correlated with levels of self-directed behaviors, and negatively with activity during social separation.

Scanlan (1987, 1988) found that the pituitary hormone responsible for the release of cortisol, ACTH, was positively correlated with measures of reactivity such as self-grasping and distress vocalizations. This positive correlation has been demonstrated in juvenile and adult animals as well as infants (Scanlan, 1984). In addition, social dominance was negatively correlated with ACTH (Scanlan & Suomi, 1986). Other studies have found similar results (Higley, Suomi, Scanlan, & McKinney, 1982; Lande, Hirsch, & Scanlan, 1984; Suomi, 1983). It should be noted, however, that not all laboratories have found such covariance between adrenal cortical measures and behavior (e.g. see Levine, Wiener, Coe, Bayart, & Hayashi, 1987).

There is also evidence that the cortisol response may be a stable trait marker, with cortisol showing strong continuity across time. Several studies from our laboratory have found that individual differences in cortisol levels show continuity over a month of repeated separations (Champoux, 1988; Scanlan, 1986, 1987). Suomi (1983) found that cortisol taken under stressful conditions at 22 days of age demonstrated a correlation of $r = .56$ ($n = 10$) with cortisol obtained at 18 months of age during a brief social separation. In a separate study, the average level of cortisol to the stressor of a series of four, 4-day social separations was positively correlated from the sixth to the eighteenth month of life ($r = .58$) (Higley, Scanlan, & Suomi, unpublished data).

There is also evidence that the activity of the adrenocortical system is controlled at least in part by the neurotransmitters NE and serotonin (e.g. see Feldman & Quenzer, 1984; Ganong, 1974; Scapagnini, 1974). Kagan, Reznick, and Snidman (1987) have hypothesized that reactivity (behavioral inhibition) is controlled by NE. In a recent review, Soubrie (1986) postulates serotonin as a general inhibitory neurotransmitter, with high levels of serotonin correlating positively with levels of inhibition. Thus, it may be that both the activity of the adrenals and behavioral reactivity may be related to the activity of these two neurotransmitter systems. The activity of both NE and serotonin, as measured by levels of their cerebrospinal fluid (CSF) metabolites, are heritable (Sedvall et al., 1980, 1984). Individual differences in both neurotransmitters show stability across developmental epochs (e.g. from the sixth to the eighteenth month of life) (Higley, Suomi, & Linnoila, 1988b).

Several other lines of evidence also indicate a correlation between neurotransmitters and reactivity. Blizard (1981), reviewing studies that used a rodent model of reactivity, found that selectively breeding for high levels of emotionality in specific strains of mice decreased levels of NE in the brain and peripheral nervous system. When he investigated numerous strains differing in levels of emotionality, levels of NE showed a negative correlation with the emotionality in the various strains. It should be noted that the directionality of this correlation is opposite to that proposed by Kagan and others (Higley et al., in press). In addition, he reviewed numerous studies which indicate a positive correlation between levels of serotonin and reactivity (Blizard, 1981).

Among non-human primates, there is also evidence that neurotransmitters are related to reactivity. For non-human primates, rearing conditions that affect reactivity also appear to influence levels of both NE and serotonin. For example, the activity of both neurotransmitters is affected by peer-only rearing. Consistent with Soubrie (1986) and studies of reactive rats, by the second year of life, subjects that had been reared under conditions which produce reactivity, such as peer-only rearing, showed significantly higher CSF levels of the serotonin metabolite 5-hydroxyindole acetic acid (5-HIAA) (Higley et al., in press). In addition, individual differences in CSF 5-HIAA obtained at 6 months of age were positively correlated with levels of reactivity measured previously at 4 months of age in peer-only reared subjects ($r = .65$) (Higley et al., in press). Unlike rats, but consistent with Kagan's findings (see Chapter 8), levels of the NE metabolite 3-methoxy-4-hydroxy-phenylglycol were higher in peer-only reared monkeys during the late phase of chronic social separations (Higley, et al., 1988b). These findings suggest that the noradrenergic and serotonergic systems may play a role in the expression of reactivity. It should be noted, however, that while the studies of the neurotransmitter systems are promising in elucidating the underlying etiology of reactivity, to date those studies are largely correlational in nature. Subsequent studies should pharmacologically investigate the directionality and mechanisms responsible for these correlations.

GENERAL DISCUSSION AND CONCLUSIONS

Through the use of non-human primate models, researchers can ask and answer questions that are very difficult if not impossible to study in humans. However, the use of non-human primate models does have limitations, centering mainly around issues of cross-species generality. The physiology of most of the advanced non-human primate species is highly similar to that of humans. Like humans, they typically live in complex social groups. Some non-human primates such as the great apes share more than 98% of their genetic material with humans; rhesus monkeys, about 92% (Wilson, Carlson, & White, 1977). Nevertheless, that 8% disparity is important (e.g. no non-human primate will obtain a college education), and, in generalizing, this genetic difference should be remembered (e.g. see McKinney, 1984; Suomi, 1986; for discussions of the use of animal models).

With this caveat in mind, our findings suggest several possible similarities between human and non-human primates. We have described a temperamental trait in rhesus monkeys that is related to how individuals respond to challenging stimuli and situations. Like some humans, these individuals are prone to avoid new stimuli, show a more reactive sympathetic nervous system, and tend to over-respond to stressors that cannot be avoided. In rhesus monkeys, this trait is highly stable, especially to identical stressors (as it is for humans; e.g. see Kagan & Moss, 1962; and Chapter 8, by Kagan et al.). One important finding from the non-human primate studies is the relationship between this trait and psychopathology. Our findings suggest that human children should be prospectively followed to assess how much this finding generalizes to humans. In a prospective preliminary follow-up of their longitudinal sample, Chess, Thomas, and Hassibi (1983) have found that negative temperament qualities (difficult temperament, distractability, etc.) in infancy may be related to reative depression in late adolescence.

While central mechanisms cannot directly be assessed in human children, peripheral correlates such as levels of amines or their metabolites in plasma or saliva would be interesting to assess, particularly in children who are extreme in their levels of reactivity. In addition, children who are given pharmacological treatments for childhood illnesses or allergies might be assessed during the treatment regime if the drug is known to affect a certain neurotransmitter system. Because of the difficulty in assessing physiological mechanisms in human children, especially central nervous mechanisms, future primate studies are under way to test causal mechanisms for reactivity. We plan to test directly the relationship of NE and serotonin to reactivity by pharmacologically manipulating their levels and measuring reactivity. Ultimately, the elucidation of etiological mechanisms and outcome of early temperament will be the result.

REFERENCES

Ainsworth, M.D., Blehar, M.C., Waters, E. & Wall, S. (1978). *Patterns of attachment.* Hillsdale, NJ: Erlbaum.

Becker, M.S., Suomi, S.J., Marra, L., Higley, J.D. & Brogan, N. (1984). Developmental data as predictors of depression in infant rhesus monkeys. *Infant Behavior and Development*, 7, 26.

Bernstein, I.S., Schusterman, R.J. & Sharpe, L.G. (1963). A comparison of rhesus monkey and gibbon responses to unfamiliar situations. *Journal of Comparative and Physiological Psychology*, 56, 914–916.

Blizard, D.A. (1981). The Maudsley reactive and nonreactive strains: A North American perspective. *Behavior Genetics*, 11, 469–489.

Bush, D.S., Steffen, S.L., Higley, J.D. & Suomi, S.J. (1987). Continuity of social separation responses in rhesus monkeys (*Macaca mulatta*) reared under different conditions. *American Journal of Primatology*, 12, 333–334.

Byrne, E.A., DiGregorio, G. & Thompson, W.W. (1988). The effect of rearing environment on infant rhesus monkeys' physiological and behavioral adaptation to novelty. *Infant Behavior and Development*, 11, 43.

Capitanio, J.P., Rasmussen, K.L.R., Snyder, D.S., Laudenslager, M. & Reite, M. (1986). Long-term follow-up of previously separated pigtail macaques: group and individual differences in response to novel situations. *Child Psychology and Psychiatry*, 27, 531–537.

Chamove, A.S., Rosenblum, L.A. & Harlow, H.F. (1973). Monkeys (*Macaca mulatta*) raised only with peers: A pilot study. *Animal Behavior*, 21, 316–325.

Champoux, M. (1988). Behavioral development and temporal stability of reactivity to stressors in mother-reared and nursery/peer-reared rhesus macaque (*Macaca mulatta*) infants.

Champoux, M. & Suomi, S.J. (1986). Adaptation to a social group by rhesus monkey juveniles differing in infant temperament. Paper presented at the meeting of the International Society for Developmental Psychobiology, Annapolis, MD, November 1986.

Chess, S., Thomas, A. & Hassibi, M. (1983). Depression in childhood and adolescence: A prospective study of six cases. *Journal of Nervous and Mental Disease*, 171, 411–420.

Clarke, A.S., Mason, W.A. & Moberg, G.P. (1988). Differential behavioral and adrenocortical responses to stress among three macaque species. *American Journal of Primatology*, 14, 37–52.

Coe, C.L., Rosenberg, L.T., Fischer, M. & Levine, S. (1987). Psychological factors capable of preventing the inhibition of antibody responses in separated infant monkeys. *Child Development*, **58**, 1420–1430.

Dowd, B.M., Higley, J.D., Suomi, S.J. & Linnoila, M. (1988). Alcohol consumption as a function of social separation, individual differences in despair, and early rearing experiences in rhesus monkeys. *American Journal of Primatology*, **12**, 417.

Feldman, R.S. & Quenzer, L.F. (1984). *Fundamentals of neuropsychopharmacology*. MA: Sinauer.

Ganong, W.F. (1974). Brain mechanisms regulating the secretion of the pituitary gland. In F.O. Schmitt & F.G. Worden (Eds), *The neurosciences: Third study program* (pp. 549–562). Cambridge, MA: MIT Press.

Gray, J.A. (1971). *The psychology of fear and stress*. Toronto, NY: McGraw-Hill.

Gray, J.A. (1987). *The neuropsychology of anxiety*. New York: Oxford University Press.

Harlow, H.F. (1958). The nature of love. *American Psychiatrist*, **13**, 673–685.

Harlow, H.F. (1969). Age-mate or peer affectional system. In D.S. Lehrman, R.A. Hinde, & E. Shaw (Eds), *Advances in the study of behavior*. London: Academic Press.

Harlow, H.F., Suomi, S.J. & Novak, M.A. (1974). Reversal of social deficits produced by isolation rearing in monkeys. *Journal of Human Evolution*, **3**, 527–534.

Higley, J.D. (1985). Continuity of social separation behaviors in rhesus monkeys from infancy to adolescence. Unpublished doctoral dissertation, University of Wisconsin, Madison, WI.

Higley, J.D., Danner, G.R. & Hirsch, R.M. (1988a). Attachment in rhesus monkeys reared either with only peers or with their mothers as assessed by the Ainsworth Strange Situation procedure. *Infant Behavior and Development*, **11**, 139.

Higley, J.D., Hopkins, W.D., Suomi, S.J., Hirsch, R. & Orman, S. (1985). Peers as attachment sources to reduce separation distress. Paper presented at the meeting of the American Society of Primatologists, Niagara Falls, NY.

Higley, J.D., Hopkins, W.J., Yuill, E.A., Suomi, S.J., Linnoila, M., Kraemer, G.W. & Bush, D.S. (1986). Early roots of affective disorders: Central amine correlates of separation-induced anxiety and despair in rhesus monkeys. Paper presented at the meeting of the International Society for Developmental Psychobiology, Annapolis, MD, November 1986.

Higley, J.D., Linnoila, M., Suomi, S.J., Hopkins, W.J. & Bush, D.S. (1987). Early peer-only rearing increases ethanol consumption in rhesus monkeys (*Macaca mulatta*). *American Journal of Primatology*, **12**, 348.

Higley, J.D., Suomi, S.J. & Linnoila, M. (1988b). Central amine correlates of timidity and affective disturbances in rhesus monkeys. Paper presented at the meeting of the American Society of Primatologists, New Orleans, LA, June 1988.

Higley, J.D., Suomi, S.J. & Linnoila, M. (in press). Serotonin in nonhuman primates: Gender rearing and developmental correlates with behavioral timidity and affective psycholopathology. In E.F. Coccaro & D.L. Murphy (Eds), *Serotonin in major psychiatric disorders*. Washington, DC: American Psychiatric Press.

Higley, J.D., Suomi, S.J., Scanlan, J.M. & McKinney, W.T. (1982). Plasma cortisol as a predictor of individual depressive behavior in rhesus monkeys (*Macaca mulatta*). Paper presented at the meeting of the Society for Neuroscience, Minneapolis, MN.

Hinde, R.A. & Spencer-Booth, Y. (1967). The behavior of socially living rhesus monkeys in their first two and a half years. *Animal Behavior*, **15**, 169–196.

Hirsch, R.M., Higley, J.D. & Suomi, S.J. (1986). Growing-up without adults: The effect of peer-only rearing on daily behaviors in rhesus monkeys. Paper presented at the meeting of the International Society for Developmental Psychobiology, Annapolis, MD, November 1986.

Kagan, J. & Moss, H.A. (1962). *Birth to maturity: A study in psychological development*. New York: Wiley.

Kagan, J., Reznick, J.S. & Snidman, N. (1987). The physiology and psychology of behavioral inhibition in children. *Child Development*, **58**, 1459–1473.

Kraemer, G.W., Ebert, M.H., Lake, C.R. & McKinney, W.T. (1984). Cerebrospinal fluid measures of neurotransmitter changes associated with pharmacological alteration of the despair response to social separation in rhesus monkeys. *Psychiatry Research*, **11**, 303–315.

Kraemer, G.W. & McKinney, W.T. (1979). Interactions of pharmacological agents which alter biogenic amine metabolism and depression. *Journal of Affective Disorders*, **1**, 33–54.

Lande, J.S., Hirsch, G. & Scanlan, J.M. (1984). Social separations involving infant rhesus monkeys with different rearing histories. *Infant Behavior and Development*, **7**, 198.

Levine, S., Wiener, S.G., Coe, C.L., Bayart, F.E.S. & Hayashi, K.T. (1987). Primate vocalization: A psychobiological approach. *Child Development*, **58**, 1408–1419.

McKinney, W.T. (1984). Animal models of depression: An overview. *Psychiatric Developments*, **2**, 77–96.

Mineka, S., Davidson, M., Cook, M. & Keir, R. (1984). Observational conditioning of snake fear in rhesus monkeys. *Journal of Abnormal Psychology*, **93**, 355–372.

Mineka, S., Suomi, S.J. & DeLizio, R. (1981). Multiple separations in adolescent monkeys: An opponent-process interpretation. *Journal of Expermental Psychology: General*, **110**, 56–85.

Novak, M.A. & Harlow, H.F. (1975). Social recovery of monkeys isolated for the first year of life: 1. Rehabilitation and therapy. *Experimental Psychology*, **11**, 453–465.

Scanlan, J.M. (1984). Adrenocortical and behavioral responses to acute novel and stressful conditions: The influence of gonadal status, timecourse of response, age and motor activity. Unpublished master's thesis, University of Wisconsin, Madison, WI.

Scanlan, J.M. (1987). Social dominance as a predictor of behavioral and pituitary–adrenal response to social separation in rhesus monkey infants. Paper presented at the meeting of the Society for Research in Child Development, Baltimore, MD. April 1987.

Scanlan, J.M. (1988). Activity levels, stress responsivity and bodyweight in rhesus monkey neonates. Paper presented at the Biennial meeting of the International Conference on Infant Studies, Washington, DC, April 1987.

Scanlan, J.M., Suomi, S.J., Higley, J.D. & Kraemer, G. (1982). Stress and heredity in adrenocortical response in rhesus monkeys (*Macaca mulatta*). Paper presented at the meeting of the Society for Neuroscience, Minneapolis, MN.

Scanlan, J.M. & Suomi, S.J. (1986). Social dominance as a predictor of behavioral and pituitary–adrenal response to social separation in rhesus monkey infants. Paper presented at the Annual meeting of the International Society for Developmental Psychobiology, Annapolis, MD, November 1986.

Scanlan, J.M. & Suomi, S.J. (1988). Neonatal predictors of separation response in rhesus monkeys. Paper presented at the Annual meeting of the American Society of Primatologists, New Orleans, LA, June 1988.

Scapagnini, U. (1974). Pharmacological studies of brain control over ACTH secretion. In F.O. Schmitt & F.G. Worden (Eds), *The neurosciences: Third study program* (pp. 565–569). Cambridge, MA: MIT Press.

Schneider, M.L. (1987). Neonatal assessment in rhesus monkeys. Unpublished doctoral dissertation, University of Wisconsin, Madison, WI.

Scott, J.P. & Fuller, J.L. (1965). Genetics and the social behavior of the dog. Chicago: University of Chicago Press.

Sedvall, G., Fyro, B., Gullberg, B., Nyback, H., Wiesel, F. & Wode-Helgodt, B. (1980). Relationships in healthy volunteers between concentrations of monoamine metabolites in cerebrospinal fluid and family history of psychiatric morbidity. *British Journal of Psychiatry*, **136**, 366–374.

Sedvall, G., Iselius, L., Nyback, H., Oreland, L., Oxenstierna, G., Ross, S.B. & Wiesel, F. (1984). Genetic studies of CSF monoamine metabolites. In E. Usdin, M. Asberg, L. Bertilsson & F. Sjoqvist (Eds), *Frontiers in biochemical and pharmacological research in depression*. New York: Raven Press.

Singh, S.D. & Manocha, S.N. (1966). Reactions of the rhesus monkey and the langur in novel situations. *Primates*, **7**, 259–262.

Soubrie, P. (1986). Reconciling the role of central serotonin neurons in human and behavioral behavior. *Brain and Behavioral Science, 9*, 319–364.

Stevenson-Hinde, J., Stillwell-Barnes, R. & Zunz, M. (1980a). Subjective assessment of rhesus monkeys over four successive years. *Primates, 21*, 66–82.

Stevenson-Hinde, J. & Zunz, M. (1978). Subjective assessment of individual rhesus monkeys. *Primates, 19*, 473–482.

Stevenson-Hinde, J., Zunz, M. & Stillwell-Barnes, R. (1980b). Behavior of one-year-old rhesus monkeys in a strange situation. *Animal Behavior, 28*, 266–277.

Suomi, S.J. (1981). Genetic, maternal, and environmental influences on social development in rhesus monkeys. In A.B. Chiarelli & R.S. Corruccini (Eds), *Primate behavior and sociobiology* (pp. 81–87). New York: Springer Verlag.

Suomi, S.J. (1983). Social development in rhesus monkeys: Consideration of individual differences. In A. Oliverio & M. Zappella (Eds), *The behavior of human infants* (pp. 71–92). New York: Plenum.

Suomi, S.J. (1985). Ethological approaches to psychiatry: Animal models. In H. Kaplan & B. Sadock (Eds), *Comprehensive textbook of psychiatry*, 4th edn (pp. 226–237). Baltimore: Williams & Wilkins.

Suomi, S.J. (1986). Anxiety-like disorders in young nonhuman primates. In R. Gittleman (Ed.), *Anxiety disorders of childhood* (pp. 1–23). New York: Guilford Press.

Suomi, S.J. (1987). Individual differences in rhesus monkey behavioral and adrenocortical responses to social challenge: Correlations with measures of heart rate variability. In N. Fox (Chair), *Heart rate variability and social behavior: Behavioral and biological correlates*. Symposium conducted at the meeting of the Society for Research in Child Development, Baltimore, MD, April 1987.

Suomi, S.J., Champoux, M., Higley, J.D., Scanlan, J.M. & Schneider, M. (1986). Infant temperament and maternal influences on rhesus monkey biobehavioral ontogeny. Paper presented at the eleventh Congress of the International Primatological Society, Gottingen, FRG, July 1986.

Suomi, S. J., Harlow, H. F. & Domek, C. J. (1970). Effect of repetitive infant–infant separation of young monkeys. *Journal of Abnormal Psychology, 76*, 161–172.

Suomi, S.J., Kraemer, G.W., Baysinger, C.M. & DeLizio, R.D. (1981). Inherited and experimental factors associated with individual differences in anxious behavior displayed by rhesus monkeys. In D.F. Klein & J. Rabkin (Eds), *Anxiety: New research and changing concepts* (pp. 179–200). New York: Raven Press.

Suomi, S.J. & Ripp, C. (1983). A history of motherless mother monkey mothering at the University of Wisconsin primate laboratory. In M. Reite & N. Caine (Eds), *Child abuse: The nonhuman primate data* (pp. 50–78), New York: Alan R. Liss.

Thompson, W.W., Higley, J.D., Byrne, E.A., Scanlan, J.M. & Suomi, S.J. (1986). Behavioral inhibition in nonhuman primates: Psychobiological correlates and continuity over time. Paper presented at the meeting of the International Society for Developmental Psychobiology, Annapolis, MD.

Wilson, A.C., Carlson, S.S. & White, T.J. (1977). Biochemical evolution. *Annual Review of Biochemistry, 46*, 573–369

11

Biological and Behavioral Differences in Infant Reactivity and Regulation

NATHAN A. FOX AND CYNTHIA A. STIFTER
Universities of Maryland and Pennsylvania State

One way of thinking about individual differences in infant temperament is along the dimension of reactivity to stimuli in the environment. In the neurologically intact neonate, individual differences in response to tactile, auditory, kinesthetic and visual stimuli can be seen to reflect variations in nervous system organization. These differences, apparent in infant threshold to response to stimuli and intensity of response, may be the material upon which temperamental characteristics are built. Some infants will have a low threshold for certain sensory modalities (or perhaps multiple modalities), displaying an intense response to low levels of stimulation, whereas infants at the other extreme have quite a high threshold and low intensity of response to sensory stimulation. Note that there are two variables of interest: threshold and intensity of response. These two may or may not be correlated.

The other side of the temperament coin involves infant modulation or regulation of a response. Here again, it is possible to conceive of individual differences in nervous system organization related to the infants' ability to modulate their reaction to stimulation. This modulation may be quite primitive in early infancy, increasing in success with maturation as the infant acquires new skills to deal effectively with his response. Again, one might picture extremes along a continuum of successful modulation or regulation of response. One group of infants may be unable to modulate their response to stimulation, thus appearing to be highly aroused, and another may display overcontrolled, inhibited behaviors in response to stimulation.

Strelau (1983), working from the Pavlovian tradition articulated a theory of temperament emphasizing two dimensions – reactivity and activity. Reactivity is an energetic component which is measured by its temporal characteristics (intensity

Temperament in Childhood   Edited by G.A. Kohnstamm, J.E. Bates and M.K. Rothbart
© 1989 John Wiley & Sons Ltd

and threshold). Activity is the regulator of stimulation. Activity functions to provide and maintain an optimal level of activation and, according to Strelau, develops in accordance with the level of reactivity. Rothbart and Derryberry (1981) have also developed a model for infant temperament involving broad constructs of reactivity and regulation.

Our conceptualization of infant temperament is explicitly a developmental one. To the extent that any physiological variable might be associated with individual differences, there will be changes in the degree to which physiology influences behavior and this influence becomes more stable with age. For example, we know that there are differences at birth in the level of heart-rate variability among normal healthy infants. We also know that these differences are not very stable during the first year and become more stable with development (Fox, 1989; Harper, Hoppenbrouwers, Sterman, McGinty & Hodgman, 1976; Lewis, Wilson, Ban & Baumel, 1970). Thus, the influence of these differences on behavior must be viewed in light of the maturing organism.

Second, the physiological processes influencing reactivity and regulation may not be identical. It seems reasonable both from the developmental data and from our own research to state that differences in reactivity are present early on in the first year but that differences in regulation are more slowly developing (Berg & Berg, 1979; Rothbart & Derryberry, 1981). This may be, in part, a result of maturing physiological systems responsible for regulation (Emde, Gaensbauer & Harmon, 1976). However, environmental factors during this period of development may also have a strong influence on the development of regulation. Consider the simplest example: two infants may both be constitutionally highly reactive to the environment. In one instance, maternal or paternal response might facilitate the development of regulatory strategies for modulating reactivity. For example, a parent who contingently responds to the infant's bids for interaction may directly or indirectly contribute to the infant's sense of control over the environment. In the other instance, caregiver interaction might be less helpful and exacerbate disorganization of response. Tronick (Tronick, Cohn & Shea, 1986) has demonstrated through simulated maternal depression that when a mother did not reciprocate her infant's interactive bids the infant became more distressed and withdrawn. This is not to say that differences in regulation are solely the result of caregiver interventions, but it does argue that differences in developmental pattern will highlight which biological systems are more or less influenced by environmental input.

Physiological Correlates of Temperament

Researchers interested in the physiological correlates or bases of the dimensions of reactivity and regulation have approached the issue in two ways. Many studies have utilized measures of autonomic activity to describe changes in level of arousal. Increases in heart rate, for example, and hence arousal indicate a reactive response, while decreases in heart rate are thought to reflect modulation. A good example are those studies that have measured heart rate during social interaction (Campos, Emde, Gaensbauer & Henderson, 1975; Field, 1981; Waters, Matas & Sroufe,

1975). Heart-rate acceleration or arousal is found to parallel gaze aversion and reaction to overstimulation, while heart-rate deceleration is found to parallel attentive responses following modulation of arousal. The concept of general arousal has been seriously questioned in the literature (Lacey, 1967; Malmo, 1959), however, and no longer seems to be a useful concept for describing physiological changes associated with reactivity. Changes in heart rate, so often used to describe physiological arousal, are multiply determined. Heart-rate acceleration, for example, may be the result of sympathetic activation or parasympathetic inhibition or a combination of these two forces (Levy, 1971). Recent research has thus attempted a second avenue of exploration in which the underlying mechanisms responsible for phasic changes in autonomic activity and behavioral reactivity are specified with greater precision.

Since heart rate has been frequently utilized as a measure of arousal and reactivity it seems a likely candidate for investigation of its underlying mechanisms. There is evidence to suggest that the degree of change in beat-to-beat intervals (heart-rate variability) is related to the heart-rate response (Lacey & Lacey, 1958; Porges, 1972, 1974). Historically, heart-rate variability has been assumed to be a function of the neurally mediated patterning of sympathetic and parasympathetic output. In fact, obstetricians and pediatricians have frequently relied on variation in beat-to-beat intervals as a clinical index of central nervous system functioning (Nelson, 1976). More recently, the relationship between heart-rate variability and individual differences in behavior has been examined (Field, Woodson, Greenberg & Cohen, 1982; Fox & Gelles, 1984; Kagan, 1982; Porges, 1974). Kagan, for example (Kagan, Reznick & Snidman, 1987, and see Chapter 8), in a longitudinal study of behavioral inhibition has shown that extreme groups of children exhibiting shy, withdrawn behavior display faster, more stable heart rate (low heart-rate variability) than extremely outgoing children at 21 months, 4 years and 5½ years. Moreover, Kagan found the indices of behavioral inhibition and autonomic activity to show relative stability across these age periods.

The quantification of heart-rate variability until recently has been with descriptive statistics which have included standard deviation range, variance and mean successive differences. Heart-rate variability, however, is influenced by extraneural factors such as metabolic changes and movement. Thus, interest has turned toward developing new methods for decomposing the heart-rate signal into components which reflect centrally mediated parasympathetic and sympathetic activation (Grossman & Weinthes, 1986; Porges, 1986). These methods rely on evidence that neural modulation of heart rate via vagal afferents is a result of the interrelationship between respiration and vagal influences to the heart. Specifically, respiration acts as a gating mechanism. Inspiration inhibits vagal input to the heart, thus increasing heart rate, while expiration produces maximal vagal output resulting in heart-rate deceleration. It has been demonstrated that the amplitude of the changes in periodic heart rate due to respiration, respiratory sinus arrythmia, reflects the degree of vagal control (Grossman, 1983; Katona & Jih, 1975). Through digital filtering and spectral analysis, Porges (1986) has shown that one can isolate from the complex heart-rate pattern the variance reflecting the influence of respiratory sinus arrhythmia. He has called this variance vagal tone ($\hat{V}$) and has provided empirical support for the relationship between levels of vagal tone and parasympathetic influence on heart rate (Porges, McCabe & Yongue, 1982; Yongue *et al.*, 1982).

In our own work (Fox, 1989, Fox & Gelles, 1984; Fox & Porges, 1985; Healy, Fox & Porges, submitted; Stifter & Fox, in press; Stifter, Fox & Porges, in press) we have made electrocardiogram (ECG) recordings from infants and young children and have utilized Porges' method in analyzing individual differences in resting vagal tone. With just one exception (Fox & Gelles, 1984), each of these studies calculated both heart-rate variability using descriptive statistics and $\hat{V}$. The correlations among the measures ranged from .6 to .8. For conceptual reasons outlined above we chose the $\hat{V}$ measure to represent the degree of parasympathetic influence on the heart. We have also examined relations between vagal tone and reactivity to a variety of elicitors and have found stable and predictive relationships between the level of vagal tone and infant reactivity and regulation.

Vagal Tone and Behavior

The idea that differences in vagal tone may be related to differences in reactivity and regulation is based upon two bodies of literature. The first body of literature reflects the search for a relationship between autonomic patterning and individual differences in behavior. Eppinger and Hess (1915) first pointed out that individuals might differ in the degree to which their autonomic nervous system dominated or regulated behavior. Individuals with low resting levels of heart rate and greater heart-rate variability, both of which reflect parasympathetic dominance, were considered vagotonic. These individuals were described as being depressed, listless and unenergetic. Individuals with high resting levels of heart rate and low heart-rate variability were considered to be more sympathetically dominant (sympatheticotonic) and were described as being highly strung and anxious.

Subsequently, Wenger (1941) renewed interest in the relation between both branches of the autonomic nervous system and proposed a theory in which autonomic balance was the central tendency. Wenger considered five different types of autonomic nervous system response patterns which would be reflected in different patterns of behavior. Lacey and Lacy (1958) reported finding, quite by accident, different patterns of autonomic nervous system activity among adult women who were to be subjects in their laboratory for a reaction-time study. Some women displayed patterns of frequent oscillations in resting heart rate and skin conductance, while others displayed a relatively stable pattern across measures. Lacey and Lacey analyzed the experimental data for the two groups of subjects with respect to their resting baseline patterns and found that individuals with a high frequency of oscillatory patterns were slower in their reaction time but more accurate, while individuals with stable non-oscillatory patterns displayed more impulsive behavior and were less accurate.

More recently, Porges (1976) has speculated that individual variations in parasympathetic influence may be associated with different manifestations of psychopathology. He gave particular emphasis to those disorders which might involve deficits in attention. In this model, individuals with problems in attention or those who cannot make use of attentional strategies to regulate behavioral activity, such as hyperactive children, are characterized as being low in parasympathetic influence, while individuals with an inability to shift attention or respond appropriately to changes in stimuli (autistics) are placed on the opposite end of the continuum.

The second body of literature relating individual differences in reactivity and vagal control is based upon the work of Porges and others which has noted the relation between vagally mediated heart-rate responses and attention (Linnemeyer & Porges, 1986; Porges, 1974; Richards, 1985, 1987). Porges (1972) found that adults with greater resting vagal tone were less likely to make errors on a reaction-time task. Linnemeyer and Porges (1986) found that 9-month-old infants with greater vagal tone were more likely to exhibit a novelty preference on a visual attention task. And Fox and Porges (1985) found that high-risk infants with greater vagal tone were more likely to exhibit positive developmental outcomes than high-risk infants with low vagal tone. Lastly, Richards (1987), in his work with 14- and 20-week-old infants, has found that infants with greater resting respiratory sinus arrhythmia were less distractable and exhibited greater sustained attention to novelty. They also exhibited greater heart-rate deceleration to novel stimuli.

The importance of vagal control to attention has been articulated by Lacey and Lacey (1970), who proposed a feedback loop between the cardiovascular and central nervous systems. They speculated that heart-rate deceleration observed during attention operates afferently, sending messages to central mechanisms. Attention is then prolonged or maintained through the inhibition of centrally mediated physiological (respiration) and behavioral (motor activity) responses. Thus, individuals with greater vagal control are more likely to exhibit greater deceleration and will produce more sustained attentional responses. Empirical research with reaction-time tasks and attentional performance confirm this relationship (Lacey, 1967; Walter & Porges, 1976).

VAGAL CONTROL AND INFANT REACTIVITY

In our own work, to be described below, we have conceptualized differences in vagal influence to reflect two different levels of behavioral control. Individual differences in vagal tone during the neonatal and early infancy period are viewed to reflect general behavioral organization and reactivity to the environment, with greater vagal influence reflective of better organization and increased reactivity. Recent studies with normal (Porter, Marshall & Porges, 1988; Stifter, Fox & Porges, 1986) and high-risk (Fox, 1983; Porges, 1983) infants confirm these associations. In a study of pain cries and vagal tone in the newborn, Porter *et al.* (1981) measured the cardiac activity of healthy term infants undergoing circumcision. Preprocedural vagal tone predicted the level of cardiac reactivity to circumcision and the fundamental frequency of cries emitted to the procedure, with infants with high vagal tone exhibiting greater changes in cardiac response and lower fundamental frequencies. Comparing preterm infants with respiratory distress syndrome (RDS) with healthy preterm infants, Fox (1983) found that at both term and 3 months conceptual age RDS infants displayed lower para-sympathetic tone than healthy infants.

With development, vagal control assumes a specific role in the mediation of attentional responses which may be involved in reaction to novelty and regulation of reactive behavior. Recent work by Richards (1987) illustrates the changes in influence of respiratory sinus arrhythmia over the first year and the increasing relation between this individual difference and sustained attention. Theoretically, then, we would expect individual differences in vagal tone to be associated with reactivity to novel and mildly stressful events and with increasing age to reflect differences in attentional style and regulation.

One of the problems in the area of infant reactivity is the lack of consensual definition as to which behaviors represent the dimension. Historically, researchers have examined responses to discrete sensory stimuli by focusing on the infant's ability to discriminate novel from familiarized events rather than considering variations in stimulus parameters and individual threshold of infant response (Fagan, 1970; Fantz, 1963; McCall & Kagan, 1970; but see Bornstein, Kessen & Weiskopf, 1976). Another problem is the negative connotation often attached to differences in reactivity. A number of temperament questionnaires, for example, ask parents to rate their child's reaction to various stimuli. Children who react intensely to these events are categorized as negative in mood and difficult in temperament (Bates, Freeland & Lounsbury, 1979; Carey & McDevitt, 1978). Reactivity in the first year of life, however, may be a precursor to positive social interactions and more mature exploration of the environment. Haviland (1976) has speculated that infants who are socially responsive to a Bayley examiner are more likely to receive high marks on the exam than those who are non-responsive during the exam. It is not hard to imagine that socially responsive children would receive more attention and interaction than children low in reactivity.

Facial Expressivity as a Measure of Reactivity

Facial expression is an important vehicle for the communication of state or mood, particularly during the first year of life (Izard, 1977). Recent research has demonstrated that the young infant is capable of making different facial expressions during the first year, and that these expressions are read by caregivers as meaningful representations of emotional state (Izard, Huebner, Risser, McGinnes & Dougherty, 1981). Indeed, very early on, parents differentially reinforce facial expressions in their infants (Malatesta & Haviland, 1982). Facial expressions may also reflect the infant's underlying motivational response to the environment. For example, Izard (1977) claims that the infant's facial expression of interest reflects the infant's underlying processing of social and non-social stimuli.

Infant emotional expressions have also been proposed to reflect the infant's active involvement with the environment. Sroufe (Sroufe & Wunsch, 1972), Rothbart (1973) and Kagan (1971) have discussed the meaning of the infant's smile immediately after assimilation of moderately discrepant events. Sroufe and Rothbart view the smile as accompanying reduction in tension produced by a novel event. By reducing tension, smiles enables the child to maintain a positive approach orientation. Kagan views the smile as indicating assimilation of moderate discrepancy. In all these cases, facial expressions may be viewed as having multiple effects: they represent manifestations of the infant's reactivity to novel events and may act as regulators in social interaction. Interest expressions or smiles subsequent to presentation of a novel event may indicate the infant's reaction to novelty and regulation of the tension caused by the initial discrepancy.

During social interactions, smiles and interest expressions may reflect the degree of infant social responsiveness or reactivity, and function to regulate the interaction (Tronick, 1982). For example, young infants will smile in response to adult faces, particularly their mother's face (Stern, 1977) and will turn away or change expression when the level of arousal of the interaction increases (Tronick, Als, Adamson, Wise & Brazelton, 1978). Ten-month-old infants have been found to display different types of smiles to the approach of unfamiliar and familiar adults (Fox & Davidson, 1988) and under certain conditions display wary expressions and gaze aversion to unfamiliar persons (Sroufe, Waters, & Matas, 1974). Thus, facial expression may be viewed as an important behavior reflecting the child's reactivity and his or her attempt to regulate the emotional response.

We investigated the relationship between heart-rate variability and facial expression in a number of studies with children of different ages. In the first study (Fox & Gelles, 1984) we observed 3-month-old children and their mothers in a face-to-face interaction, having previously made ECG recordings in a 3-minute baseline situation. Two findings from this research are of interest. Mothers responded contingently with positive affective behavior (touch, kiss, present toy) to positive infant facial expressions such as interest or smiling, and there was a positive association between heart-rate variability (the mean successive difference measure) and duration of interest expressions. Infants with higher resting heart-rate variability displayed a longer duration of interest expressions. Interestingly, these infants also had mothers who turned toward them and displayed positive affection more often than infants with low resting heart-rate variability. Thus, infants with higher heart-rate variability who displayed facial expressions of interest had more responsive mothers in this situation.

In a second study (Stifter *et al.*, in press), we observed 34 infants (20 5-month-olds and 14 10-month-olds) in a standardized stranger approach/mother approach paradigm, again having previously made 5-minute ECG recordings in a baseline situation. Of interest here are the data relating to vagal tone and facial expression. There was a significant relationship between expression and vagal tone for 5-month-old infants. Infants with greater vagal tone displayed a greater number of positive emotional expressions, especially in response to the approach of the stranger. That relationship, however, was not present for the 10-month-olds. This lack of association may be attributed to a developmental shift in affective organization suggesting that the meaning of facial expression for 10-month-olds may be different from that for 5-month-old infants.

The 5-month data replicate the Fox and Gelles (1984) finding of a relationship between interest expression and heart-rate variability. Five-month-olds displaying interest had higher resting heart-rate variability levels than those with fewer interest expressions. They also exhibited more look-away behaviors. Izard (1977), in his description of differential emotions theory, has conceptualized interest as an expression seen during active attention. The fact that infants in our study displayed greater interest expressions to the stranger than to the mother may indicate that they are actively attending and processing the approach of this unfamiliar person. Taken together, the expression of interest and look-away behaviors during stranger approach may function to regulate the child's emotional response to the novel event.

The association between heart-rate variability and facial expressions denoting attention confirms the relationship between attention and heart rate found by others (Kagan & Lewis, 1965; Porges, 1974). It is interesting to note that in a study of interest expressions and attention, Izard (Langsdorf, Izard, Rayias & Hembree, 1983) found a positive relationship between heart-rate deceleration and interest expressions. Because heart-rate deceleration is vagally mediated (Porges, 1976), it is no surprise that infants with greater resting variability are also those who display greater attentiveness and interest to novel events.

A Longitudinal Study of Infant Reactivity and Regulation

In an attempt to examine differences in heart-rate variability and reactivity we have completed a longitudinal study of 60 infants seen at 2 days, 5 months and 14 months of age (Stifter & Fox, in press). At each age ECG recordings were made and Porges' vagal tone measure, along with a measure of heart period, was computed. At each age infant reactivity was also assessed. At the newborn period a pacifier-withdrawal procedure was administered (Bell, Weller & Waldrop, 1971; see Stifter and Fox (in press) for a detailed explanation of this procedure). At 5 months of age infants participated in a peek-a-boo game with mother and an unfamiliar person, as well as undergoing moderate restraint of the arms. At 14 months of age subjects participated in a session which included a free play with introduction of an unfamiliar adult, presentation of a novel toy, and a separation from mother.

To analyze reactivity at 5 months we computed summary variables representing the dimensions of positive reactivity and negative reactivity. The positive reactivity variable was composed of the measures of frequency, duration and intensity of smiles coded from the mother and stranger peek-a-boo procedures. The summary variable representing negative reactivity was created from the frequency and intensity measures of negative affect, anger and disgust expressions displayed during arm restraint, as well as the latency to cry measure. The correlation between the two summary variables was non-significant (r (62) = .08).

To investigate the relationship between the 5-month autonomic measures and positive and negative reactivity, Pearson product–moment correlations were computed. Several positive relationships emerged between vagal tone and negative and positive reactivity. Infants who exhibited higher 5-month vagal tone showed significantly greater negative reactivity (r (54) = .26) and were more likely to show more positive reactivity (r (54) = .20) than infants with lower vagal tone. A general reactivity score was computed for the 5-month-olds by combining the positive and negative reactivity measures. Correlations with the autonomic measures revealed a significant relationship between vagal tone and reactivity (r (54) = .32).

We next saw these infants when they were 14 months of age. They were tested in our laboratory with a protocol designed to assess their reactivity to novel objects, unfamiliar adults and mildly stressful situations. We made ECG recordings during a baseline situation and during a cognitive task at this visit. In one set of analyses we were interested in determining whether extremes in vagal tone at 14 months were related to social behavior and whether there was any predictive validity from either the neonatal or 5-month assessments to physiology and behavior at 14 months.

Two groups were constructed by performing z-score transformations on each vagal tone measure (there were six different conditions under which ECG recordings were made and the vagal tone measure was computed) and choosing those infants who at 14 months had vagal tone scores above or below the mean on all six recordings. Of the 32 infants in these analyses, data were available on 30 for the pacifier-withdrawal procedure performed at the neonatal assessment. Of these 30 subjects, 17 cried and 13 did not cry. There were no associations between vagal tone group at 14 months and response to pacifier withdrawal.

Of the 32 14-month-old infants, 29 had data available from the moderate restraint task at 5 months. Twelve infants cried to moderate restraint, 17 did not. The relation between responses to arm restraint and group membership at 14 months was significant. Of the 12 criers at 5 months, 9 were in the high vagal tone group, while 13 of the 17 non-criers were in the low vagal tone group at 14 months.

An examination of infant behavior and physiology at 5 months in relation to physiological reactivity grouping at 14 months revealed that the 14-month-old infants with high vagal tone exhibited more negative reactivity at 5 months than infants who at 14 months displayed low vagal tone. The 14-month autonomic measures were also signficantly related to 5-month autonomic activity. Significant group (14-month group) differences were found for heart period and vagal tone. Infants with low and variable heart rates at 14 months had lower heart rates (high heart period) and higher vagal tone at 5 months than infants who had high and stable heart rates at 14 months.

The data relating 5- and 14-month measures revealed that infants who cried to moderate arm restraint displayed greater vagal tone at 5 months and at 14 months of age. There also seemed to be some stability across the 9-month period from 5 to 14 months. Infants at 5 months with high vagal tone continued to exhibit this pattern at 14 months. These findings were our first indication that infants who reacted to a particular set of stressors at 5 months displayed high vagal tone 9 months later. The finding became significant in understanding the meaning of early reactivity when we next examined the relation between 14-month vagal tone and 14-month infant sociability.

A series of one-way analyses of variance with group as the single factor were computed on the dependent measures of latency to approach the stranger, latency to approach the novel toy (a robot) and latency to cry at separation from mother. Results revealed that infants at 14 months with high vagal tone exhibited a significantly shorter latency to approach the stranger than infants with low vagal tone.

In an effort to examine the pattern of behavior of the two groups of infants in approach to the stranger, the infants were divided into three categories: those who approached within the first 3 minutes (when the stranger had her head down and was not interacting), those who approached during the second 4 minutes (when the stranger attempted to initiate interaction) and those who did not approach at all during the 7-minute period. Infants who approached prior to the stranger's overtures included 11 of 15 of the low and variable heart-rate group, and those who subsequently approached when the stranger attempted interaction included 10 of 16 of the high and stable heart-rate group. There was also a tendency for infants with high vagal tone to show a shorter latency to approach the robot than infants in the low vagal tone group. Eight of 16 children approached the robot from the group with high vagal tone, while only 3 of 16 in the low vagal tone group approached at all. There were differences in latency to cry at separation between the two groups; infants with high vagal tone showed a shorter latency to begin crying. The pattern of these findings suggests that infants with high vagal tone at 14 months are more sociable. They were more likely to approach an unfamiliar person and more likely to approach a novel object. Fourteen-month-old children with low vagal tone were more wary and less likely to approach an unfamiliar adult or a novel object.

Inspection of the correlations between newborn autonomic measures and 14-month behavior failed to reveal any significant relations as did those between neonatal and 5-month autonomic and behavioral measures. There were significant associations between 5-month autonomic measures at 14-month behavior. Infants with high vagal tone at 5 months displayed a shorter latency to approach the stranger (r (25) = $-.42$) and a shorter latency to cry at maternal separation at 14 months (r (25) = $-.43$).

Finally, the 14-month behavioral data were examined as a function of infant reactive behavior at both newborn and 5-month assessments. One-way analyses of variance were computed with cry group (cried or did not to pacifier withdrawal) as the single factor and each of the 14-month behaviors as dependent measures. Results revealed a significant group effect for the latency to cry at maternal separation variable. Infants who cried to pacifier withdrawal displayed shorter latencies to cry to maternal separation at 14 months compared to those who did not respond to pacifier withdrawal at the newborn period. There were no other significant results with the newborn measures. Results of the analyses for 5-month data found only a near-significant effect for the latency to cry variable. Infants who cried at arm restraint at 5 months tended to display shorter latencies to cry to maternal separation at 14 months.

DISCUSSION AND CONCLUSIONS

The pattern of results illustrates two important points. First, there is a concurrent relationship between the level of vagal tone and social behavior at 14 months. Infants with high vagal tone are more sociable and outgoing, while infants at the other extreme, with low vagal tone, are less sociable and more inhibited in their interactions. While these data confirm the association between heart-rate variability and social behavior found by others (e.g. Kagan *et al.*, 1987), the methodologies that produced these results are somewhat different across studies. Longitudinal evidence from Kagan's studies is from older children (Garcia-Coll, Kagan &

Reznick, 1984; Kagan, Reznick, Clarke, Snidman & Garcia-Coll, 1984; Kagan *et al.*, 1987), while our data have concentrated on differences within the first year of life. When taken together, however, both Kagan's and our findings suggest that the relationship between biology and behavior is a developmental one which becomes stronger and more stable over time, beginning perhaps as early as 5 months of age. A second difference concerns how the subjects were grouped. Kagan *et al.* (1987) have approached the identification of a subgroup of children with a biologically based behavior pattern by examining *behavior* at the extremes of the distribution. Based on the theoretical history of autonomic patterning and behavior (e.g. Eppinger & Hess, 1915; Lacey & Lacey, 1958), we examined extremes in *autonomic activity* to determine which behaviors might be associated with these groupings. Notwithstanding this difference, significant results were obtained by both studies suggesting that we may be studying two sides of the same coin.

There are, however, two major differences that separate these two lines of research. First, Kagan's interpretation of the significance of high heart rate and low heart-rate variability emphasizes sympathetic excitation rather than parasympathetic control. Use of Porges' vagal tone measure in our work leaves no ambiguity as to the functional meaning of differences in level. Both of Kagan's measures of variability, the standard deviation of heart-period data (e.g. Kagan *et al.*, 1984) and spectral densities below those frequencies for respiration (Kagan *et al.*, 1987), include those influences on the heart that are not neurally mediated. Thus changes in heart-rate variability may represent changes in posture and temperature as well as changes in sympathetic activation. By isolating only those frequencies of heart rate associated with breathing (a period of parasympathetic dominance), the $\hat{V}$ measure is a more accurate assessment of vagal tone.

Second, the data highlighted in this chapter indicate that infants who at 14 months fit the description of either high heart-rate variability and high sociability or low heart-rate variability and inhibited behavior look quite different at 5 months than first expected. Rather than finding that inhibited 14-month-olds were highly reactive as younger infants, the current data support the notion that early positive and negative reactivity, at least to the stimuli which we presented, are precursors of sociability. The 14-month-olds who readily approached the unfamiliar adult and the novel object were the ones who were more likely to cry when restrained at 5 months and exhibit a pattern of reactivity to the peek-a-boo game. The infants who stayed close to mother and were inhibited in their social responses were less reactive as 5-month-old infants to these conditions.

There are a number of possible interpretations of these data that could help explain these across-age relationships. Obviously, the arm-restraint procedure is an aversive stimulus that may elicit frustration rather than response to novelty. It is possible that infants who did not respond to arm restraint would be more reactive to more novel and less frustrating stimulus conditions. In line with these thoughts it is interesting to note that infants who were high in negative reactivity as newborns and 5-month-olds were rated by their mothers (using the Infant Behavior Questionnaire; Rothbart, 1981) as generally more reactive across multiple domains, while those who did not cry to pacifier withdrawal and arm restraint were rated by their mothers as less responsive (see Stifter & Fox, in press).

It is possible that by 5 months, certain infants have learned a passive mode of responding to novel or mildly stressful situations (Gray, 1967). This outward passive avoidance may be accompanied by internal arousal or anxiety in response to novelty. These 5-month-olds may show little overt behavioral response to novelty but display high heart rate and low heart-rate variability. Furthermore, their passive response at 5 months may be translated into their lack of social response to unfamiliar adults or objects at 14 months. Again, they may have learned to avoid these stressors though this avoidance may be accompanied by increases in autonomic activity. Infants who are reactive to the environment and for whom there is not an aversive learning history may be more outgoing and willing to explore their surrounds. They would view novelty as a challenge and not a stressor because they may have at their disposal the strategies for regulating their reactive responses. Thus, infants with high vagal tone at 14 months may be both more reactive to novelty but also able to use attentional strategies to modulate this reactivity.

The data from our laboratory and others indicate that individual differences in vagal tone may be related to the dimensions of reactivity and regulation in infancy. Infants with greater parasympathetic tone are more reactive, more facially expressive and more responsive to the environment. they also seem to develop a wider array of attentional strategies, useful for modulating their reactive response (Fox, 1989; Stifter & Fox, in press). At both 5 and 14 months of age there are strong concurrent relationships between level of vagal tone and behavioral reactivity.

The data also reveal that the origins of inhibition may lie in the apparent lack of behavioral reactivity rather than in extremes of reaction exhibited in early infancy. Passivity in response to stimuli during the first months of life may be a precursor for inhibited social behavior during the toddler years.

ACKNOWLEDGMENTS

The research presented in this paper was funded in part by a grant from the National Institutes of Health (HD 17899) to Nathan A. Fox.

REFERENCES

Bates, J.E., Freeland, C.A.B. & Lounsbury, M.L. (1979). Measurement of infant difficultness *Child Development*, **50**, 794–803.

Bell, R.Q., Weller, G.M. & Waldrop, M.F. (1971). Newborn and preschool: Organization of behavior and relations between periods. *Monographs of the Society for Research in Child Development*, **36** (Serial No. 142).

Berg, W.K. & Berg, K.M. (1979). Psychophysiological development in infancy: State, sensory function and attention. In J.D. Osofsky (Ed.), *Handbook of infant development* (pp. 283–343). New York: Wiley.

Bornstein, M.H., Kessen, W. & Weiskopf, S. (1976). The categories of hue in infancy. *Science*, **191**, 201–202.

Campos, J.J., Emde, R., Gaensbauer, T. & Henderson, C. (1975). Cardiac and behavioral interrelationships in the reactions of infants to strangers. *Developmental Psychology*, **11**, 589–601.

Carey, W. B. & McDevitt, S. C. (1978). Revision of the Infant Temperament Questionnaire. *Pediatrics*, **61**, 735–739.

Di Pietro, J.A., Larson, S.K. & Porges, S.W. (1987). Behavioral and heart rate pattern differences between breast and bottle-fed neonates. *Developmental Psychology*, **23**, 467–474.

Emde, R.N., Gaensbauer, T.J. & Harmon, R. (1976). *Emotional expression in infancy: A biobehavioral study*. New York: International Universities Press.

Eppinger, H. & Hess, L. (1915). Vagotonia: A clinical study in vegetative neurology. *Journal of Nervous and Mental Disease*, **20**, 1–93.

Fagan, J.F. (1970). Memory in the infant. *Journal of Experimental Child Psychology*, **9**, 217–226.

Fantz, R.L. (1963). Pattern vision in newborn infants. *Science*, **140**, 296–297.

Field, T.M. (1981). Infant gaze aversion and heart rate during face-to-face interactions. *Infant Behavior and Development*, **4**, 307–315.

Field, T.M., Woodson, R., Greenberg, R. & Cohen, D. (1982). Discrimination and imitation of facial expressions by neonates. *Science*, **218**, 179–181.

Fox, N.A. (1983). Maturation of autonomic control in preterm infants. *Developmental Psychobiology*, **16**, 495–504.

Fox, N.A. (1989). The biological basis of emotional reactivity during the first year of life. *Developmental Psychology*.

Fox, N.A. & Davidson, R. (1989). Patterns of brain electrical activity during facial signs of emotion in 10-month-old infants. *Developmental Psychology*.

Fox, N. & Gelles, M. (1984). Face-to-face interaction in term and preterm infants. *Infant Mental Health Journal*, **5**, 192–205.

Fox, N. & Porges, S.W. (1985). The relation between neonatal heart period patterns and developmental outcome. *Child Development*, **56**, 28–37.

Garcia-Coll, C., Kagan, J. & Reznick, J.S. (1984). Behavioral inhibition in young children. *Child Development*, **56**, 28–37.

Gray, J.A. (1964). *Pavlov's typology*. Oxford: Pergamon.

Gray, J.A. (1967). Strength of the nervous system, introversion-extraversion, condition-ability and arousal. *Behavior Research and Therapy*, **5**, 151–169.

Grossman, P. (1983). Respiration, stress, and cardiovascular function. *Psychophysiology*, **20**, 284–300.

Grossman, P. & Wienthes, K. (1986). Respiratory sinus arrhythmia and parasympathetic cardiac control: Some basic issues concerning quantification, application and implications. In P. Grossman, K.H. Janssen & D. Vaitl (Eds), *Cardiorespiratory and cardiosomatic psychophysiology* (pp. 117–138). New York: Plenum.

Harper, R.M., Hoppenbrouwers, T., Sterman, M.B., McGinty, D.J. & Hodgman, J. (1976). Polygraphic studies of normal infants during the first 6 months of life. I. Heart rate and variability as a function of state. *Pediatric Research*, **10**, 945–951.

Haviland, J.M. (1976). Looking smart: The relationship between affect and intelligence in infancy. In M. Lewis (Ed.), *Origins of intelligence* (pp. 353–377). New York: Plenum.

Healy, B.T., Fox, N.A. & Porges, S.W. (submitted). The heritability of autonomic patterns and social behavior in young twins.

Izard, C.E. (1977). *Human emotions*. New York: Plenum.

Izard, C.E., Huebner, R.R., Risser, D., McGinnes, G.C. & Dougherty, L.M. (1981). The young infant's ability to produce discrete emotion expressions. *Developmental Psychology*, **16**, 132–140.

Kagan, J. (1971). *Change and continuity in infancy*. New York: Wiley.

Kagan, J. (1982). Heart rate and heart rate variability as signs of a temperamental dimension in infants. In C.E. Izard (Ed.), *Measuring emotions in infants and children* (pp. 38–66). Cambridge: Cambridge University Press.

Kagan, J. & Lewis, M. (1965). Studies of attention in the human infant. *Merrill-Palmer Quarterly*, **11**, 95–127.

Kagan, J., Reznick, J.S., Clarke, C., Snidman, N. & Garcia-Coll, C. (1984). Behavioral inhibition to the unfamiliar. *Child Development*, **55**, 2212–2225.

Kagan, J., Reznick, J.S. & Snidman, N. (1987). The physiology and psychology of behavioral inhibition in children. *Child Development*, **58**, 1459–1473.

Katona, P.G. & Jih, F. (1975). Respiratory sinus arrhythmia: Non-invasive measure of parasympathetic cardiac control. *Journal of Applied Physiology*, **39**, 801–805.

Lacey, J.I. (1967). Somatic response patterning and stress: Some revisions of activation theory. In M.H. Appley & R. Trumbull (Eds), *Psychological stress: Issues in research* (pp. 14–42). New York: Appleton-Century-Crofts.

Lacey, J.I. & Lacey, B.C. (1958). The relationship of resting autonomic activity to motor impulsivity. *Research Publications Association for Research in Nervous and Mental Disease,* **36**, 144–209.

Lacey, J.I. & Lacey, B.C. (1970). Some autonomic–central nervous system inter-relationships. In P. Black (Ed.), *Psychophysiological correlates of emotion* (pp. 205–227). New York: Academic.

Langsdorf, P., Izard, C.E., Rayias, M. & Hembree, E. (1983). Interest expression, visual fixation, and heart rate change in 2-to-8 month old infants. *Developmental Psychology*, **19**, 375–386.

Levy, M.N. (1971). Sympathetic–parasympathetic interactions in the heart. *Circulation Research*, **29**, 437–445.

Lewis, M., Wilson, C.D., Ban, P. & Baumel, M.H. (1970). An exploratory study of resting cardiac rate and variability from the last trimester of prenatal life through the first year of postnatal life. *Child Development*, **41**, 799–812.

Linnemeyer, S.A. & Porges, S.W. (1986). Recognition memory and cardiac vagal tone in 6 month old infants. *Infant Behavior and Development*, **9**, 43–56.

Malatesta, C.Z. & Haviland, J.M. (1982). Learning display rules: The socialization of emotion expression in infancy. *Child Development*, **53**, 991–1003.

Malmo, R.B. (1959). Activation: A neuropsychological dimension. *Psychological Review*, **66**, 367–386.

McCall, R.B. & Kagan, J. (1970). Individual differences in the infant's distribution of attention to stimulus discrepancy. *Developmental Psychology*, **2**, 90–98.

Nelson, N.M. (1976). Respiration and circulation before birth. In C.A. Smith & N.M. Nelson (Eds), *The physiology of the newborn infant*. Springfield, IL: Charles C. Thomas.

Pavlov, I.P. (1955). *Selected works*. Moscow: Foreign Languages Publication House.

Porges, S.W. (1972). Heart rate variability and deceleration as indexes of reaction time. *Journal of Experimental Psychology*, **92**, 103–110.

Porges, S.W. (1974). Heart rate indices of newborn attentional responsivity. *Merrill-Palmer Quarterly*, **20**, 131–154.

Porges, S.W. (1976). Peripheral and neurochemical parallels of psychopathology: A psychophysiological model relating autonomic imbalance to hyperactivity, psychopathy, and autism. In H. Reese (Ed.), *Advances in child development*, Vol. 11 (pp. 35–65). New York: Academic Press.

Porges, S.W. (1983). Heart rate patterns in neonates: A potential diagnostic window to the brain. In T. Field & A. Sostek (Eds), *Infants born at risk: Physiological and perceptual processes* (pp. 3–22). New York: Grune & Stratton.

Porges, S.W. (1986). Respiratory sinus arrhythmia: Physiological basis, quantitative methods, and clinical implications. In P. Grossman, K. Janssen & D. Vaitl (Eds), *Cardiac respiratory and somatic psychophysiology* (pp. 223–264). New York: Guilford Press.

Porges, S.W., McCabe, P.M. & Yongue, B.G. (1982). Respiratory–heart rate interactions: Physiological implications for pathophysiology and behavior. In J. Cacioppo & R. Petty (Eds), *Perspectives in cardiovascular psychophysiology* (pp. 223–264). New York: Guilford Press.

Porter, F.L., Marshall, R.E. & Porges S.W. (1988). Newborn cries and vagal tone: Parallel changes in response to circumcision. *Child Development*, **59**, 495–505.

Richards, J.E. (1985). Respiratory sinus arrhythmia predicts heart rate and visual responses during visual attention in 14 and 20 week old infants. *Psychophysiology*, **22**, 101–109.

Richards, J.E. (1987). Infant visual sustained attention and respiratory sinus arrhythmia. *Child Development*, **58**, 488–496.

Rothbart, M.K. (1973). Laughter in young children. *Psychological Bulletin*, **80**, 247–256.

Rothbart, M.K. (1981). Measurement of temperament in infancy. *Child Development*, **52**, 569–578.

Rothbart, M.K. & Derryberry, D. (1981). Development of individual differences in temperament. In M.E. Lamb & A.L. Brown (Eds), *Advances in developmental psychology*, Vol. 1 (pp. 37–86). Hillsdale, NJ: Erlbaum.

Sroufe, L.A., Waters, E. & Matas, L. (1974). Contextual determinants of infant affective response. In M. Lewis & L. Rosenblum (Eds), *The origins of fear* (pp. 49–72). New York: Wiley.

Sroufe, L.A. & Wunsch, J. (1972). The development of laughter in the first year of life. *Child Development*, **43**, 1326–1344.

Stern, D.N. (1977). *The first relationship: Infant and mother*. Cambridge, MA: Harvard University Press.

Strelau, J. (1983). *Temperament, personality, activity*. London: Academic Press.

Stifter, C.A. & Fox, N.A. (in press). Infant reactivity and regulation: Physiological correlates of newborn and five month temperament. *Developmental Psychology*.

Stifter, C.A., Fox, N.A. & Porges, S.W. (1986). Individual differences in newborn reactivity and regulation. *Psychophysiology*, **23**, 465 (Abstract).

Stifter, C.A., Fox, N.A. & Porges, S. W. (1989). Facial expressivity and heart rate variability in five and ten month old infants. *Infant Behavior and Development*.

Teplov, B.M. (1972). The problem of types of human higher nervous activity and methods of determining them. In V.D. Nebylitsyn & J.A. Gray (Eds), *Biological bases of individual behavior* (pp. 1–10). New York: Academic Press.

Tronick, E.Z. (1982). *Social interchange in infancy: Affect, cognition and communication*. Baltimore: University Park Press.

Tronick, E.Z., Als, H., Adamson, L., Wise, S. & Brazelton, T.B. (1978). The infant's response to entrapment between contradictory messages in face-to-face interaction. *Journal of the American Academy of Child Psychiatry*, **17**, 1–13.

Tronick, E.Z., Cohn, J. & Shea, E. (1986). The transfer of affect between mothers and infants. In T.B. Brazelton & M.W. Yogman (Eds), *Affective development in infancy* (pp. 11–25). Norwood NJ: Ablex.

Walter, G.F. & Porges, S.W. (1976). Heart rate and respiratory responses as a function of task difficulty: the use of discriminant analysis in the selection of psychologically sensitive physiological responses. *Psychophysiology*, **13**, 563–571.

Waters, E., Matas, L. & Sroufe, L. (1975). Infants' reactions to an approaching stranger: Description, validation and functional significance of wariness. *Child Development*, **46**, 348–356.

Wenger, M.A. (1941). The measurement of individual differences in autonomic balance. *Psychosomatic Medicine*, **3**, 427–434.

Yongue, B.G., McCabe, P.M., Porges, S.W., Rivera, M., Kelley, S.L. & Ackles, P.K. (1982). The effects of pharmacological manipulations that influence vagal control of the heart on heart period, heart-period variability and respiration in rats. *Psychophysiology*, **19**, 426–432.

Section Three

Temperament and Development

12

Temperament and Development

MARY KLEVJORD ROTHBART
University of Oregon

Temperament as a construct has an ancient history (Diamond, 1974), but research on temperament in childhood has been carried out over only a relatively brief period. In addition, emphasis upon the trait-like qualities of temperament has often led to a stress upon the stability of temperament over time rather than its development (Buss & Plomin, 1975, 1984). Nevertheless, both our experience and research results to be discussed below lead us to recognize that temperament develops: emotionality, activity, and attention do not have the same organization for the newborn as they do for a 4-year-old or for an adolescent. As we increasingly come to understand developmental change in temperament, we will also be learning more about the organization of emotional and self-regulative processes across age, and these are currently far from understood. This chapter considering temperament and development is only a first approximation to characterizing this complex topic, but perhaps it can also serve as a promissory note to readers: in the future, we hope to be able to describe in some detail the structure of temperament at successive periods of development, to assess the degree of stability or instability of individual differences in the components of temperament over time, and to determine the degree to which temperament at one age may constrain personality and temperament at the next.

It may be argued that taking a strongly developmental approach to temperament puts too little stress upon individual differences. It is true that considering the development of temperament brings a new level of complexity to our thinking. Unless temperamental individual differences are placed within a developmental context, however, our view of them is likely to be superficial at best, and our chance of relating them to other aspects of cognitive and social development will be slight.

In this chapter, I present a selective review of research on the structure of temperament in childhood and the stability and instability of temperamental components over time. The strategy to be followed is to note the ages at which new

Temperament in Childhood   Edited by G.A. Kohnstamm, J.E. Bates and M.K. Rothbart
© 1989 John Wiley & Sons Ltd

dimensions of temperamental variability can be identified in the developing infant and child. In considering the dimensions of temperament to discuss, I define temperament quite broadly to include individual differences in emotionality, activity, attention, and self-regulation, with the last including individual controls on motor activity and emotion, such as behavioral inhibition. This broad definition encompasses the dimensions identified by the four theoretical positions described in a recent *Child Development* roundtable (Goldsmith *et al.*, 1987).

There are several reasons for taking this inclusive approach. A broad approach to temperament allows us to capture developmental transitions that might be missed if we were to define temperament too narrowly. For example, if our definition constrained us to include only emotionality as temperament, as do Goldsmith and Campos (1982, 1986), we could not consider the development of behavioral inhibition as a temperamental dimension. If we constrained emotion- ality to include only negative affect, as do Buss and Plomin (1975, 1984), we could not consider the development of positive emotionality. If we limited ourselves only to characteristics that fall within the nine dimensions identified by Thomas and Chess and their colleagues (Thomas & Chess, 1977; Thomas, Chess, Birch, Hertzig, & Korn, 1963), we could not consider the development of ego-control or effort variables (Block & Block, 1980; Kopp, 1982; Rothbart & Posner, 1985). Knowing that this broad approach has been followed, readers may choose to pursue those aspects of temperament that fall within their own definition of the field.

The chapter begins with a discussion of some of the meanings of developmental stability and instability, and continues with a discussion of temperament during the newborn period, infancy, the preschool, and childhood years, with a short section on temperament and personality in adulthood. After this review of research on the development of temperament, a more speculative attempt is made to relate temper- ament to social development.

DEVELOPMENTAL STABILITY AND INSTABILITY

Questions about the meaning of longitudinal stability have been considered by developmental researchers for the past two decades, beginning with the important contributions of Emmerich in 1964 and 1968. These issues have also been discussed by Kagan (1971), McCall (1981, 1986), Rutter (1983, 1987), and Wohlwill (1980). Most recently, the varieties of developmental stability have been summarized by Rutter (1987) as follows:

(1) *Stability as invariance*, that is, lack of change in development, as in the case of a skill like eating with chopsticks that, once learned, is unlikely to be forgotten, or a skill that has reached an asymptote and will not change much thereafter. This kind of stability is usually *not* expected for temperamental characteristics; to demonstrate invariant stability of negative emotionality, we would expect a 5-year-old to show patterns of crying similar to those of a 2-week-old infant.

(2) *Stability as regularity in a pattern of change*, such as that shown in the Louisville Twin Study's analyses of monozygotic and dizygotic similarities in

patterns of change in measures of intelligence (Wilson, 1977) and temperament (Matheny & Dolan, 1975). Here, a measure at one age may not be predictive of a measure at a subsequent age, but it can be demonstrated that monozygotic twins show similar changes over time. An understanding of this type of stability of change will become increasingly important as longitudinal research with twin populations accumulates, and the reader can consider these issues further in Chapter 7, by Goldsmith.

(3) *Normative stability*, that is, the extent to which individuals maintain their relative position within a group across time. Normative stability can be found in spite of major changes in the average value of a measure at two different times. Rutter (1987) gives the example of height, which undergoes major developmental change in average value, while measures at two different ages are nevertheless highly correlated. Most of the stability of temperamental characteristics to be discussed in this chapter will be normative stability.

(4) *Ipsative stability*, that is, regularity in the predominant characteristics of the individual (in comparison with the individual's other characteristics). A child's predominant mood, one of Thomas and Chess's (1977) temperament variables, may be relatively negative over time even though the frequency and intensity of negative emotionality decreases and positive emotionality increases over that period. Ipsative stability comparisons are made within the individual, not across individuals, and they will not be a major focus of this review. However, this characterization of temperament may prove to be of importance in children's early social relationships with parents and peers.

(5) *Stability of process, structure, or mechanism* across possible behavioral transformations. Here, the researcher has reason to believe that a single process underlies two quite different behaviors. Our ability to predict one measure from another quite different measure taken at an earlier time may demonstrate an underlying continuity of process that obtains even though extensive developmental change has occurred. If shyness, for example, were to prove to be predictable from early negative emotionality, then an underlying characteristic could be seen to be involved in both.

In addition to these five kinds of stability, Hinde and Bateson (1984) have discussed five sources of evidence indicating *instability* over time. All of Hinde and Bateson's instabilities can be seen as changes in the *structure* of temperament. These include normative and ipsative instability derivable from the descriptions above, and in addition, these important varieties of discontinuity in development:

(1) *Instability through the appearance of a new behavior pattern.* Several examples of this kind of instability will be offered in this chapter, such as the emergence of laughter and behavioral inhibition, characteristics that are not evidenced during the earliest weeks of life, but nevertheless may be seen as later-appearing temperamental characteristics.

(2) *Instability through a sudden increase in the frequency of a behavior*, such as the increases in smiling observed at 2–3 months of life (Emde & Robinson,

1978) or in approach through reaching and grasping at 4–6 months.

(3) *Instability through changes in the correlations among sets of behaviors* across age. An example of this kind of instability to be developed below is the positive relationship found between activity level and distress during early infancy, and the later-appearing positive relationship between activity level and positive affect as described by Wolff (1987).

A Cautionary Introduction

In reporting normative stability correlations in this chapter, it must be noted that most of the correlations, although statistically significiant, will be in the .3–.4 range of magnitude, with a few slightly smaller or slightly larger. This means that although 'stability' across time will be frequently reported, in almost all cases it will be of a *very* modest size, accounting for no more than 10–25% of the variance of the measures being predicted. This allows for at least two possibilities in the future. One is that better temperament measures may come to account for more of the variance. As better and more reliable measures are developed, we would expect such an increase to be possible. Given the fact that there are multiple influences on the expression of temperament over time, however, it is likely that longitudinal measures of temperament will never show high stability. A number of important influences on stability or instability have been discussed by Cairns and Hood (1983) and they include: (a) biological constraints, including maturational change, (b) the social network in which development occurs, with greater stability expected when the social network remains constant, (c) consolidation of behavioral patterns and social learning, (d) social evocation effects, such as the effects of one's classification by gender, age, or physical characteristics, and (e) ecological (non-social) constancy, including one's physical setting and the influences of economic factors.

A second possibility for the future is that these other influences upon treatment will be increasingly identified and measured, allowing us to account for both stability and change more adequately. In this connection, the conclusions of Cairns and Hood (1983) about predictability of aggression are of great importance for our consideration of temperamental stability:

> It is not the case that multiple determination necessarily diminishes the level of predictability ... much of the variance that is predictable across ontogeny is not 'in' the organism but 'in' its developmental context, its physical ecology, its relationships, and its likely course of subsequent development. When these factors are identified at the several stages of ontogeny and their role in the behavior to be predicted is assessed, then the prediction of individual differences is markedly enhanced. (Cairns & Hood, 1983, pp. 344–345)

The last section of this chapter and Chapter 13, by Thomas and Chess, describes some additional factors that might be expected to influence the expression of temperament over time.

In describing the structure of temperament at a given age, I will frequently refer to factor analyses of assessment instruments, and Chapter 15, by Hagekull, reports the results of a factor analytic approach in some detail. It should be kept in mind that the results of these factor analyses are always dependent upon the set of items included within the assessment. Thus, if behavioral items or scale scores assessing a given dimension have not been included in a measure, that dimension cannot be expected to emerge from factor analyses of the measure. For a more extended discussion of factor analytic and other approaches to the measurement of infant temperament see Bates (1987) and Rothbart and Goldsmith (1985).

TEMPERAMENT IN THE NEWBORN PERIOD

Two major techniques have been used for assessing individual differences in temperament during the newborn period: the Brazelton Neonatal Behavioral Assessment Scale (NBAS; Brazelton, 1973, 1984; Brazelton, Nugent, & Lester, 1987), an assessment carried out in the context of the newborn neurological examination, and standardized observational and laboratory procedures more specifically designed to assess newborn temperament (Birns, 1965; Matheny, Riese, & Wilson, 1985; Riese, 1987). Neonatal temperamental dimensions to be reviewed in this section include negative emotionality, activity level, distractibility and attention span, and approach–withdrawal.

The NBAS (Brazelton, 1973, 1984) includes observational ratings of autonomic, motor, state, and social attentional variables and 20 reflexes. It is designed as an 'interactive assessment' where the adult who administers the measure and rates the infant's reactions also attempts to promote optimal performance from the infant (Brazelton et al., 1987). Thus, the NBAS differs from other temperament assessments in that the stimulation presented to one infant is not necessarily the same as the stimulation presented to another infant. Questions have been raised about the adequacy of the instrument's psychometric properties (Campos et al., 1983; Kaye, 1978). Nevertheless, the NBAS samples a wide range of the newborn's behavioral repertoire, and it has been used to assess early individual differences in temperamental predispositions (see Crockenberg & Smith, 1982; and Chapter 16, by van den Boom). Standardized observations, on the other hand, typically present fewer but more highly controlled stimuli, such as the application of a cold disc to elicit newborn reactivity (Birns, 1965; Riese, 1987).

Negative Emotionality

Strauss and Rourke (1978) have carried out a factor analysis of ten samples of newborn NBAS scores, and identified four major factors of variability in responsiveness, of which (a) and (b) below involve susceptibility to distress (negative emotionality): (a) irritability, tension, and activity, (b) self-quieting, emotional state lability, and rapidity of build-up, (c) orienting, chiefly to visual stimuli, during quiet alert periods, and (d) response decrement to distal (non-touch) stimuli during sleep and drowsy states. They also report a negative association between orienting and build-up of distress (state lability); that is, newborns who maintain longer periods of orienting toward the environment tend to be infants who are less susceptible to distress (Strauss & Rourke, 1978). Kaye (1978) has also identified an irritability cluster for the NBAS which includes scores from peak of excitement, rapidity of build-up, and irritability, which may combine the two negative emotionality factors from Strauss and Rourke (1978).

Cross-cultural differences in susceptibility to distress as assessed in the NBAS have been reported. Freedman and Freedman (1969) found greater state lability, higher peak distress, and less self-soothing and soothability in European-American than in Chinese-American infants. Garcia-Coll, Sepkoski, and Lester (1982) reported easier consolability in Puerto Rican infants than in North American white and black newborns. Puerto Rican infants also took longer to reach a peak of excitement and more frequently self-quieted or responded to tester soothing procedures. Additional findings on cross-cultural research in newborn temperament are reported by Kohnstamm in Chapter 26.

Birns (1965) developed standardized procedures for assessing neonatal temperament in the laboratory, including application of a cold disc and pacifier removal. In a longitudinal study, these procedures were repeated when infants were 1 month of age, and repeated again with procedures added to elicit positive emotionality when infants were 3 and 4 months old (Birns, Barten, & Bridger, 1969). Birns *et al.* (1969) found that irritability, unsoothability, tension, and sensitivity (the last-mentioned assessed responsiveness to any experimental procedure and to extraneous stimuli such as a door slamming or a telephone ringing) showed interindividual stability for infants from the newborn period to 1, 3, and 4 months of age. In across-age stability of negative emotionality, the neonatal cold-disc irritability measure predicted later irritability pooled across 1–4 months and was also negatively related to later social responsivity (amount and vigor of smiling and vocal responses to social stimulation) pooled across 3–4 months.

The most impressive demonstrations to date of longitudinal stability of susceptibility to distress have employed standardized hospital and laboratory assessments and have been reported by the Louisville Twin Study (Matheny *et al.*, 1985; Riese, 1987). In these studies, stability of negative emotionality was reported from the newborn period to 9 months and more recently to 24 months of age. In the Louisville assessments, neonates are observed in the hospital from one feeding to the next. Episodes include feeding, sleep, orienting, examiner soothing, and application of a stressful stimulus (adapted from Birns: a chilled metal disc placed on the infant's thigh for five 5-second trials). Ratings are made of irritability, resistance to soothing, orienting, reinforcement value, and activity during wake and sleep. Five of the six temperament variables form a cluster during the newborn period: irritability, resistance to soothing, activity awake, low orienting reactivity, and low reinforcement value (reinforcement value is, however, not related to orienting reactivity). Again, a negative relation between orienting and distress is observed, with more irritable infants showing less focused orienting.

At 9 and 24 months, infants in the Louisville Twin Study are observed in the laboratory, and measures of emotional tone, attentiveness, activity, and social orientation are made using age-appropriate episodes. Newborn irritability and resistance to soothing were found to predict negative emotional tone at 9 months, and neonatal reinforcement value of the infant to the tester predicted 9-month positive emotional tone (Matheny *et al.*, 1985). Irritability during the newborn period also predicted 24-month reactions, with more irritable newborn infants more distressed, less attentive to stimuli, less responsive to staff, and more changeable in activity level across situations at 24 months (Riese, 1987).

In considering these findings, it should be noted, however, that the Louisville neonatal ratings showed *little* stability from the newborn period to either 12 or 18 months. Riese (1987) suggests that, during the 24-month period, increased emotionality (perhaps underlying the popular conception of the 'terrible twos') may allow for the expression of individual differences in negative emotionality that could be latent during the more positive ages of 12 and 18 months. This interpretation suggests that later developmental periods of heightened emotionality, such as adolescence, may also be times when a heightened potential for predictability of negative emotionality across age would occur.

In longitudinal research employing the Nebraska revision of the NBAS (NBAS-K), Larson, DiPietro, and Porges (1987) have found some stability of a negative emotionality measure from the newborn period to 15 months. They predicted 15-month fussy-difficult, unsociability, and unadaptability scores on Bates' Infant Characteristics Questionnaire (ICQ; Bates, Freeland, & Lounsberry, 1979) from newborn ratings of irritability, low alertness, and difficulty in testing as assessed in the NBAS-K.

Activity Level

A second major dimension of temperament identified during the neonatal period is activity level. In early research, Fries (1954; Fries & Woolf, 1953) and Escalona (1968) identified activity level as a major dimension of individual differences. Fries developed laboratory assessments of neonatal activity level that included a startle test (dropping a padded weight on the bed close to the infant's head). Infants were designated as quiet if their motor reaction lasted less than 10 seconds, active if it lasted more than 25 seconds, and moderately active at intermediate levels. She also observed the infant's response to removal of breast or bottle after the child had been sucking it. She found that more active infants as defined by the startle test had stronger motor reactions to feeding frustration, whereas quiet infants were likely to continue sucking after nipple removal and to fall asleep. In studies of stability of activity level during the early months, Birns *et al.* (1969) found no stability from the newborn period to ages 3 and 4 months. Some stability was found, however, from 4 weeks of age to the later assessments.

When high levels of waking activity occur in the newborn, they are often correlated with the expression of negative affect (Matheny *et al.*, 1985; Riese, 1987; Strauss & Rourke, 1978). Escalona (1968) observed that newborns engage in their highest motor activity during distress states; more positive states in the newborn are associated with motor quiescence. Later in development, however, the infant becomes motorically aroused while in an alert and non-distressed state, often in connection with orienting toward novel objects or receiving caregiver stimulation (Wolff, 1965).

Distractibility and Attention Span

One of the four factors identified by Strauss and Rourke (1978) from the NBAS was orienting, chiefly to visual stimuli. (Their fourth NBAS factor, response decrement during sleep and drowsy states, has not been identified as temperamental in the theories reviewed by Goldsmith *et al.* (1987) and will not be discussed here.) Osofsky and Danzger (1974) reported that newborns who were alert and responsive to the Brazelton NBAS also tended to be alert and responsive when interacting with the mother in a feeding situation. Bakeman and Brown (1980) found that scores on orientation items in the NBAS for preterm and full-term infants were positively related to measures of social participation and social competence at 3 years of age. In the study by Birns *et al.* (1969), however, longitudinal stability was not found between measures of alertness at the newborn period and at 3 and 4 months.

Approach–Withdrawal

From the earliest days, infants demonstrate that they are not only reacting to environmental and internal stimuli, but are actively influencing and regulating their own experience. McGuire and Turkewitz (1979) have noted that approach associated with the presentation of low-intensity stimuli is already present in the newborn, with looking or turning away (withdrawal) associated with the presentation of high intensities of stimulation. Turkewitz and his associates found that auditory and visual intensities appear to summate in their effects on newborns, with higher intensity levels associated with infants' looking away from a visual stimulus (Lawson & Turkewitz, 1980; Lewkowicz & Turkewitz, 1981). It was previously noted in this chapter that newborn infants demonstrating greater negative emotionality also tend to show less focused orienting. This may represent an adaptive combination of reactive and self-regulative components of temperament, with the infants' looking away serving the function of decreasing the level of visual stimulation the child experiences.

   Although Turkewitz and his associates have demonstrated early approach–withdrawal, and although withdrawal reflexes and rooting, reaching, and grasping reflexes involving approach are all part of the newborn's behavioral repertoire (Prechtl, 1977), individual differences in the latency, intensity, and probability of occurrence of approach–withdrawal reflexes have not been systematically studied in the newborn. Individual differences in avidity as studied by Lipsitt and his collaborators may, however, be seen as a possible index of approach (Lagrasse, Gruber, & Lipsitt, in press). Avidity of positive responsiveness is measured by the slope of the increase of the infant's sucking intensity as the sweetness of the liquid is increased. This measure has been found to predict later *inhibition* of approach rather than approach tendencies, however (Lagrasse *et al.*, in press).

   At later ages, temperament is frequently assessed not only by the nature of the individual's emotional responsiveness or reactivity to a given intensity of stimulation, but also by the kinds of situations the person usually seeks and avoids. Thomas and Chess's (1977) approach–withdrawal dimension thus assesses both distress to novelty and the child's characteristic orientation toward or away from it, and variables such as Zuckerman's (1979, 1983) Sensation Seeking and Eysenck's Extraversion (Eysenck, 1965; Eysenck & Eysenck, 1975) tap similar orientations in adults. Such measures can be seen as assessing two aspects of temperament. The first involves the individual's emotional reaction to environmental stimulation; the second, the extent to which the individual *creates* preferred stimulation levels by seeking out or avoiding high levels of stimulation. It is important to note, however, that internal control which we have called 'effort' (Rothbart & Posner, 1985), similar to the Blocks' (Block & Block, 1980) construct of ego-resiliency, allows an individual to enter a situation which would otherwise *not* be preferred, and this higher level of control would be expected to later add noise to the measurement of a dimension including both emotionality and orientation.

Temperament and Caregiver–Infant Interaction

The infant's temperament regulates and is regulated by the actions of others from the earliest hours. Indeed, social regulation continues to be of major importance throughout development, in attachment relations (Bowlby, 1969) and in the development of individual coping strategies enlisting the intervention of others or involving opposition to others (Horney, 1937, 1945).

Bell (1974) has proposed a homeostatic model for regulatory behaviors in the dyad that is closely related to temperamental analyses of infant and caregiver:

> Briefly, it is assumed that each participant in a social or caregiving interaction has upper and lower limits relative to the intensity, frequency, or situational appropriateness of behavior shown by the other. When the upper limit for one participant is reached, that participant is likely to react in such a way as to redirect or reduce the excessive or inappropriate behavior (upper-limit control reaction). When the lower limit is reached, the reaction is to stimulate, prime, or in other ways to increase the insufficient or nonexistent behavior (lower-limit control reaction). (Bell, 1974, p. 13)

During early infancy, caregivers use the infant's distress reaction as a guide for their soothing interventions, thereby compensating for the relative lack of self-regulatory controls in the very young child. Soothing interventions include picking up the infant, tactile stimulation and rhythmic movement (Ames, Khazaie, Gavel, & Farrell, in press; Bell & Ainsworth, 1972; Korner & Thoman, 1972). Infants often show increases in alert visual orienting when put to the caregiver's shoulder (Korner & Thoman, 1972), and this orienting may also serve to oppose the distress reaction. Observations of caregiver soothing, along with much animal research (Rosenblum & Moltz, 1983), suggest that regulation of the individual is an important aspect of the functioning of the dyad (Hinde, 1983), and the infant's expression of emotions can lead to regulation from the caregiver. Thus, individual differences in temperament will influence dyadic interaction from the earliest days (Rothbart, 1984), and regulation provided by the caregiver will strongly influence the behavioral expression of temperamental characteristics.

We know that the infant's emotional response has predictable effects on the caregiver. Frodi, Lamb, Leavitt, and Donovan (1978) presented parents of newborn infants with a videotape of a smiling or crying infant, and found that parents reported greater feelings of distress with the crying infant and greater feelings of happiness with the smiling infant. Parents' diastolic blood pressure and skin conductance increased for the tape of the crying infant, but not for the tape of the smiling infant. In the view of Frodi *et al.* (1978), the infant's distress creates an aversive stimulus which the parent attempts to terminate.

Initially, there is considerable asymmetry in the caregiver's and infant's contribution to these interactions. Whereas the caregiver can engage in purposeful soothing of the newborn, the young infant is chiefly reacting to its own internal state and to the activating and soothing stimulation provided by the caregiver. Self-regulatory behaviors occur in the newborn, but they occur in response to the stimulus levels the infant is currently experiencing (including discomfort due to hunger, wet, or cold) rather than in anticipation of future events. The infant's emotional expressions have the effect, however, of signaling to the parent the need for increasing or decreasing the stimulation presented to the child (Stern, 1974). Later, children will take a more active and anticipatory role in influencing others to create and maintain situations favorable to themselves.

Table 1 Temperament in development during early childhood

Developmental period	Temperament components
Newborn	Distress & soothability, activity, orienting and alertness (attention), approach–withdrawal
Early infancy	All of the above and smiling and laughter, vocalization, stimulus seeking and avoidance, frustration
Late infancy	All of the above and inhibition of approach, effortful control, fear
Preschool years and beyond	All of the above with continuing development of effortful control

Summary

As indicated in Table 1, components of temperament observable during the newborn period include negative emotionality (susceptibility to distress and soothability), activity level, orienting and alertness, and approach–withdrawal. During this period, expressions of distress are positively related to activity level, and negatively related to focused visual orienting. Infants regulate their levels of distress and pleasure through reflex withdrawal and approach and self-soothing, and caregivers provide external controls upon the infant's behavior by responding to the infant's emotional signals. Signs of positive emotionality during the waking state such as smiling and laughter and positive vocalization are rare or absent during this period (Wolff, 1987). Some stability has been found from the newborn period to later assessments in negative emotionality and to a lesser degree for orienting, but stability of activity level has not been found.

TEMPERAMENT IN EARLY INFANCY

Positive Emotionality

By 2–3 months, infants show a behavioral pattern that includes smiling and vocalization and motor cycling of the limbs, elicited in a social context (Brazelton, Koslowski, & Main, 1974), but also elicited in non-social situations (Bradley, 1985; Kistiakovskaia, 1965; Papousek & Papousek, 1978; Rothbart, 1987). This cluster of reactions was described by Kistiakovskaia in 1965 and termed the 'animation complex', including 'smiling, quick and animated generalized movements with repeated straightening and bending of hands and feet, rapid breathing, vocal reactions, eyeblink, etc.' (Kistiakovskaia, 1965, p. 39). These reactions were observed to appear at the end of the first and the beginning of the second month of life, increasing in duration and decreasing in latency into the second and third months (Kistiakovskaia, 1965). Werner (1988) has more recently reviewed cross-cultural evidence for both an increase in smiling at between 2 and 4 months, and an increase in vocalization at 3–4 months. These responses (smiling and laughter, vocal and motor activity) tend to be positively correlated both in parents' reports and in home observations (Rothbart, 1986). Although this pattern of positive emotionality has been called 'sociability', it is displayed toward exciting and novel objects as well as to people (Bradley, 1985; Brazelton *et al.*, 1974; Kistiakovskaia, 1965; Papousek & Papousek, 1978; Rothbart, 1987). 'Sociability' is likely therefore too narrow a label for this dimension, at least during early infancy, and positive emotionality may be a more appropriate term.

The third factor extracted from Bates' ICQ (Bates *et al.*, 1979) is labeled Dull, although its items assess chiefly positive emotionality, e.g. smiles, happy sounds, and excitement in play. For a sample of infants aged 3–7 months, this scale (Dull) was negatively related to a parent-report measure of activity, that is, infants seen as more positive were also seen as more active. Results from Kistiakovskaia (1965) and our laboratory also indicate that positive affect, vocal reactivity, and activity form a positive emotionality cluster during infancy (Rothbart, 1986). When both positive and negative emotional expressions are measured in the same situation, they tend to be negatively correlated (Rothbart, 1986), but this correlation may result because the occurrence of one set of responses precludes the appearance of the other. When Goldsmith and Campos have measured individual differences in positive and negative emotions independently, using different episodes to assess each, they have found them to be uncorrelated (Goldsmith & Campos, 1986).

Although a cluster of reactions that might be called positive emotionality is not present during the newborn period, it can be assessed by 2–3 months, and shows normative increases in expression across the first year of life. Malatesta, Grigoryev, Lamb, Albin, and Culver (1986) found linear increases in positive affect across 2.5 to 5 to 7.5 months of age, and in our home observations, we have found increases from 3 to 6 to 9 months of age (Rothbart, 1986). Parent reports of smiling and laughter also indicate increases from 3 to 9 months (Rothbart, 1986) and 3 to 12 months of age (Rothbart, 1981). Moss (1967) has reported stability from 3 weeks to 3 months in infant smiling during mother–child interaction, and measures of smiling and laughter and mood have shown some stability from 3 months to beyond a year of age (McDevitt & Carey, 1981; Rothbart, 1981, 1986). We have also found stability for a composite positive emotionality variable including smiling and laughter, and motor and vocal activity as assessed by parent report and home observation across 3–9 months. In addition, we have found stability in a laboratory measure of smiling and laughter from 3 to 13.5 months of age (Rothbart, 1987).

Activity Level

Normative stability in activity level has also been reported during infancy, with mean levels of activity also increasing across this period (Rothbart, 1986). Birns *et al.* (1969) reported some stability of activity level from 4 weeks to 4 months, but not from the newborn period. Hagekull and Bohlin (1981) found that intensity–activity at 3–6 months predicted intensity–activity at 11–15 months. Using parent-report and home-observation measures, we have found stability across 3–12 months (Infant Behavior Questionnaire (IBQ); Rothbart, 1981) and 3–9 months (home observation; Rothbart, 1986), and McDevitt and Carey (1981) have reported stability from 4–8 months to 1 to 3 years and Peters-Martin and Wachs (1984) from 6 to 12 months using the Infant Temperament Questionnaire (ITQ) and the Toddler Temperament Scale (TTS). Huttenen and Nyman (1982) found stability from 6–8 months to 5 years using the first version of Carey's ITQ (Carey & McDevitt, 1978) and Thomas and Chess's (1977) 3–7 year questionnaire on a Finnish sample.

Thomas, Chess, and Birch (1968), however, did not find stability of activity level from the early months to 2 years, and Kagan (1971) found very low correlations from 8 to 27 months on open-field locomotion. On the basis of their review of the literature, Buss and Plomin (1975) concluded that activity level is not stable from infancy, but they argue that from 12 months, activity level shows moderate stability. Thus, ratings of vigor of activity and rapidity (tempo) by Schaefer and Bayley (1963) showed stability across years 1–3 for girls and 2–3 for boys. More longitudinal research across the period in question will be needed to conclude that activity does not show stability from late infancy to later years, however, because the results of McDevitt and Carey (1981) and of Huttenen and Nyman (1982) contradict Buss and Plomin's (1975) conclusion.

Escalona (1968) related early individual differences in activity level to both perceptual and social development in infancy. She compared cross-sectional samples of relatively active and inactive infants at three ages: 1–3 months, 4–5 months, and 6–8 months. At 1–3 months, inactive infants showed more tactile exploration, visual focusing on faces, and non-nutritive sucking than active infants. At 4–5 months, inactive infants engaged in more self-directed behaviors; active infants engaged in more behaviors directed toward inanimate objects. Object stimulation by the mother increased the activity of inactive infants, whereas active infants changed little in response to object stimulation (their level of activity was already high). Social responses occurred more frequently and were more intense for active than inactive infants, with active infants sometimes showing excitement to the 'sight only' of the caregiver at 4–5 months.

At 6–8 months, active infants produced more noise, ranged across more space, and showed more complex behavior than inactive infants when the parent was not present. During object stimulation by the parent, however, inactive infants showed behavior that was just as complex as that of active infants. Inactive infants were less responsive than active infants to low levels of social stimulation, but more responsive to medium levels of social stimulation; high levels of stimulation tended to lead to less focused responsiveness for all infants. As at the earlier ages, active infants directed more attention to the environment; inactive infants to their own bodies (Escalona, 1968).

Distractibility and Attention Span

Although distractibility and attention span/persistence constitute two of the nine categories within Thomas and Chess's (1977) nine dimensions of temperament, little research within the temperament tradition has directly studied individual differences in attention. There is, however, a strong tradition of studying individual differences in attention among cognitive psychologists that may be helpful to our understanding of these variables. In the experimental literature, distinctions between at least two processes involved in visual attention show strong similarities to Thomas and Chess's (1977) distractibility and persistence: Cohen's (1972) attention-getting and attention-holding and Ruff's (1986) alerting and encoding. Cohen's attention-getting process is similar to behavioral aspects of Pavlov's (1927) orienting reaction; attention-holding involves the focused, selective attention that occurs once attention is engaged.

Olson and Sherman (1983) suggest that:

> attention-getting is seen to be under the control of innate mechanisms that orient the infant to such salient properties of the environment as bold patterns, large objects, motion, sudden changes of illumination, and loud sounds. The hypothesis, then, is that attention-getting may not change much with development. However, what holds attention ought to undergo substantial development change, since variables such as the fine details of patterns or their meaningfulness will determine how long patterns are fixated. (Olson & Sherman, 1983, p. 1039)

Olson and Sherman's (1983) argument suggests that measures of distractibility may show greater longitudinal stability than measures of persistence or duration of orienting, and Hagekull and Bohlin (1981) have found stability for a dimension they call 'attentiveness', which contains mainly attention-getting items across a period of 4–13 months.

Ruff's (1986) construct of alerting is operationalized as latency to examine a stimulus, and is similar to distractibility; encoding refers to active processing of information about the stimulus and is similar to persistence. Richards (in press) has been able further to refine measures of attention-holding or encoding by determining that, when heart rate is decelerating, children are not distractible to peripheral events; when heart rate is returning to prestimulus levels, however, infants can be distracted by a peripheral visual probe, even when they are continuing to fixate the stimulus. Thus, only a part of the time when infants are fixating the stimulus do they appear to be processing it in a way that interferes with the movement of attention.

Coldren, Colombo, O'Brien, Martinez, and Horowitz (1987) have reported consistency of rates of looking across three quite different measures in 3-month-old infants: a visual discrimination paradigm, an auditory discrimination paradigm, and a measure of rate of looking toward the mother in social interaction. Colombo, O'Brien, Mitchell, and Horowitz (1986) also reported stabilities of lengths of peak fixation in a visual habituation paradigm from 3 months through 4, 7, and 9 months of age. Byrne, Clark-Touesnard, Hondas, and Smith (1985) reported stability from 4 to 7 months in average looking time and duration of first look in visual habituation tasks.

McDevitt and Carey (1981) have reported stability of attention span/persistence from 4–8 months to 1–3 years, and Huttenen and Nyman (1982) from 6–8 months to 5 years. In our use of the IBQ with infants of 3–12 months (Rothbart, 1981), we have found stability across some age spans but not across others.

Measures of duration of orienting have not shown stability from the newborn period to later infancy, and in part this may be due to the phenomenon of 'obligatory attention' described in very young infants. Friedman (1972) observed mean visual fixations toward checkerboard stimuli of 55 seconds for newborns, and Stechler and Latz (1966) reported 10-day-old infants looking at disorganized face stimuli for minutes at a time, terminated by strong distress. Tennes, Emde, Kisley, and Metcalf (1972) have described obligatory attention in infants of 4–5 to 8 weeks and Cohen (1976) recounts patterns of 14-week-old infants looking at faces: 'they look intently for a while, then become increasingly agitated with their eyes glued to the pattern, and finally avert their gaze in an inconsistent manner. It is almost as if they wanted to turn away earlier but couldn't' (Cohen, 1976, p. 235).

A number of attentional systems contribute to orienting (Posner, 1978), and our ultimate understanding of individual differences in this area is likely to be complex. Through orienting, however, we expect that reactivity can be initiated (e.g. in the visual domain, by looking toward), enhanced (looking intently), maintained (extended orienting), reduced (gaze aversion), or terminated (looking away) (Posner & Rothbart, 1981; Rothbart & Derryberry, 1981). It is interesting to note that most items on Carey and McDevitt's (1978) Infant Temperament Scale assessing distractibility are actually soothability items. In our laboratory research, we blow soap bubbles (from baby shampoo) for soothing infants. These bubbles lead to multiple orienting reactions from the infants and, as the children's heart rates decline to base levels from the high levels associated with distress, the infants are also becoming calmed.

Orienting may increasingly oppose the distress reactions present at birth. Emde and his associates have identified a developmental transition with a strong increase in smiling and interest in the environment and decrease in susceptibility to distress, which they have called the 2–3 month shift (Emde, Gaensbauer, & Harmon, 1976; Emde & Robinson, 1978). In our research, we have also found sharp increases in smiling and laughter and decreases in distress between 3 and 6 months (Rothbart, 1981, 1986).

These developmental changes may be related to stronger orienting reactions observed during this period in the laboratory (Graham, Strock, & Ziegler, 1981). We have found intensity of heart-rate deceleratory orienting reaction at 3 months to be related to the intensity of the child's positive responsiveness in smiling and laughter (Brock, Rothbart, & Derryberry, 1986). Heart-rate reactivity, like orienting, does not show stability from the newborn period to later ages (Lipton, Steinschneider, & Richmond, 1961, 1966; Steinschneider, 1973). Stability is not found until 2.5 months, and it is likely due to the maturation of cardiac control mechanisms (Graham *et al.*, 1981; Steinschneider, 1973).

Approach–Withdrawal

We can now consider individual differences in approach–withdrawal during early infancy. Thomas and Chess (1977) identified approach–withdrawal as a basic dimension of temperament, and McDevitt and Carey (1981) have reported stability of approach–withdrawal from 4–8 months to 1–3 years, Peters-Martin and Wachs (1984) from 6 to 12 months, and Huttenen and Nyman (1982) from 6–8 months to 5 years. Persson-Blennow and McNeil (1980) have found stability of approach–withdrawal from 6 months to 2 years of age. Hagekull and Bohlin's (1981) approach/withdrawal factor also showed stability from 3 to 12 months. It should be noted that the approach–withdrawal dimension in Thomas and Chess's (1977) framework includes emotional reactions (positive or negative) as well as orienting toward or away from new stimuli.

Although Thomas and Chess's work assumes approach and withdrawal to be opposite poles of a single dimension, other research results suggest that approach tendencies can be dissociated from withdrawal tendencies (Berridge & Grill, 1984a, b; Pien & Rothbart, 1980) and that approach tendencies can be dissociated from behavioral inhibition (Rothbart, 1988; in press). In motor approach, control of the limbs and trunk for crawling and coordination of eye and hand for visually directed reaching will be achieved by 4–6 months. We have studied approach as an individual differences measure in infancy, using the infant's latency to reach for and grasp objects as an index of approach (Rothbart, 1988). This measure shows consistency across infants' reaches for different objects, and we find it to be positively related to children's smiling and laughter in the laboratory and as reported by the parent in the IBQ. Our measure of approach to low-intensity, relatively familiar stimuli also shows stability from 6.5 to 13.5 months of age (Rothbart, 1988).

Quickness of approach may be generalized across muscle groups. In an early study with a small number of subjects, Gesell and Ames (1937) found that infants maintained their rank order on measures of grasp time, prone progression step time and length of pauses between steps, and creeping speed. The findings are suggestive that speed of approach may show consistency across muscle groups, but further research will be needed on this question.

The child's ability to develop expectancies so as to anticipate stimulation develops early in the first year, so that the child may act on the basis of the results of past experience as well as in direct reaction to stimulus intensity. The infant can thus seek out stimuli that have been previously associated with positive consequences and avoid stimuli associated with negative consequences. To the extent that some infants are easily overwhelmed by intense stimulation, they may come to avoid situations or persons associated with too high levels of excitement.

Other infants may find such experiences pleasurable and seek them out. Thus, at an early period in development, the terms stimulus-seeking and stimulus-avoidance to *expected* stimulus events can be added to approach and withdrawal to immediately present stimuli in describing individual differences in temperament.

Negative Emotionality

At 3 and 4 months, Birns *et al.* (1969) found infant irritability to be positively related to sensitivity, unsoothability, and tension. Irritability was also negatively related to positive affect and social responsiveness, but since the positive and negative reactions were assessed in the same situation, the occurrence of one response could have constrained the possibility of the occurrence of the other. Research on self-calming during this period has also reported a positive relation between irritability and unsoothability. West, McLaughlin, Rieser, Brooks, and O'Connor (1986) studied self-calming in 6-month-olds to auditory, cold, and tactile stressors. Two days of testing ranged from 1 to 6 weeks apart. Their measures of distress reactivity and soothability showed stability from one session to the next, and the measures were also strongly negatively related: infants who cried more quickly tended to recover more slowly.

Longitudinal studies have also found some stability of distress-proneness from early infancy. In Persson-Blennow and McNeil's (1980) research, parent-report measures of mood showed stability between 6 months and 2 years of age, and McDevitt and Carey (1981) reported stability of mood from 4–8 months to 1–3 years, Peters-Martin and Wachs (1984) from 6 to 12 months, and Huttenen and Nyman (1982) from 6–8 months to 5 years. It is important to note that these mood measures range from positive mood at one pole of the dimension to negative mood at the other, so that either or both positive and negative emotionality may contribute to stability. One of Hagekull and Bohlin's (1981) factors derived from Thomas and Chess's nine dimensions was labeled manageability. This manageability factor included both persistence and affect measures, with children who demonstrated longer periods of interest reported as expressing less negative effect. Scores on manageability showed some stability for children between 4 and 13 months.

In our longitudinal research we have found somewhat less stability across age for distress than for measures of smiling and laughter and activity level. At a given age, more narrow measures of distress-proneness such as fear and distress to limitations (frustrations) tend to be positively related (Rothbart, 1981, 1986, 1987). In the IBQ, fear and frustration measures were positively correlated at 3, 6, 9, and 12 months of age. We were also able to predict later fear and distress to limitations from 6 months to 12 months, but not from 3 months to the later ages (Rothbart, 1981). In a composite measure of negative emotionality in the home observations, we found stability over 3-month, but not 6-month, periods (Rothbart, 1986).

Using laboratory observations of children, we have elicited fear through presentation of novel mechanical toys and stranger interaction, frustration through the presentation of toys out of reach and behind a plexiglass barrier, and suscept-ibility to overstimulation through presentation of intense stimuli across visual and auditory modalities. Infants were seen at four ages between 3 and 13.5 months, and we found overall negative emotionality to decrease across that period. We found stability chiefly across adjacent assessments for composite measures, and less evidence for stability when we assessed fear and frustration separately in the laboratory (Rothbart, 1987).

Bates' longitudinal research has found some stability of measures of 'difficulty' from 6 months to the preschool period (Bates, 1987; Bates, Maslin, & Frankel, 1985), and this research is described in more detail by Bates in Chapter 17. Bates' ICQ (Bates *et al.*, 1979) was developed to assess infant 'difficulty'. The major factor analytic dimension extracted from the ICQ was a measure of negative emotionality, including infants' fussing and crying, negative mood, soothability, and caregivers' rating of the infants' overall difficulty. Home observations made by Bates and his associates at 6 months and observer ratings on relevant ICQ items also yielded measures that were positively related to mothers' ratings (Bates *et al.*, 1979; Bates, Olson, Pettit, & Bayles, 1982; Pettit & Bates, 1984). Difficulty assessed by the TTS was found to predict later mother–child conflict observed at 2 years (Lee & Bates, 1985) and anxious and hostile child behavior problems as reported by the mother at 3 years (Bates *et al.*, 1985).

Summary

All components of temperament observable during the newborn period can also be seen during early infancy. Added to these components during early infancy are the positive reactions of smiling and laughter and vocalization (see Table 1). Activity is now positively correlated with smiling and laughter and vocalization in the 'animation complex'. Now that the child can also begin to anticipate stimulation associated with cues in the environment, the child is no longer only reacting to stimulation immediately present through approach and withdrawal, but can be seen to begin actively engaging in stimulus-seeking and stimulus-avoidance.

TEMPERAMENT IN LATE INFANCY

Inhibition of Approach (Behavioral Inhibition)

During the second half of the first year of life, an important form of self-regulatory control is added, when some infants who previously were approaching now come to inhibit their approach responses to unfamiliar and/or intense stimuli. The resulting state in the infant has been called 'response uncertainty' by McCall (1979), and 'behavioral inhibition' by Garcia-Coll, Kagan, and Reznick (1984), and it has been seen as a prototype for anxiety (Suomi, 1986). Inhibited approach is influenced by perception of the novel or unfamiliar, and Gray (1982) argues that it is also influenced by the intensity of stimulation, with high levels of intensity promoting inhibition of approach. Gray's interpretation is very much in keeping with definitions of behavioral inhibition that refer to responses to novelty and challenge (see Chapter 8, by Kagan, Reznick, & Snidman), which can include both unfamiliar and overly exciting events.

Escalona (1968) noted that, at 6–8 months, only inactive infants showed delays between perception and motor response, and pointed out that these delays may be due either to an inhibitory delay process or to the slow building of an approach response. Schaffer (1974) observed that although infants of 5 months demonstrate via their looking patterns that they can distinguish betwen novel and familiar objects, they reach equally quickly for both novel and unfamiliar objects. At 8 months, however, they show greater hesitancy in grasping the novel toy. In our laboratory, we also find increases in infants' latency to grasp novel and intense toys from 6.5 to 10 months of age (Rothbart, 1988).

A discrepancy or novelty checking process appears to be in place before 7 months, since it influences differential visual orienting to novel versus familiar stimuli. Late in the first year, however, novelty and intensity also come to influence the inhibition of approach responses. Primate studies also report that timidity or anxiety is not in evidence at birth, and that once anxiety is developmentally in evidence, individual differences in anxiety will be shown. Suomi (1984, 1986) reports that although stable individual differences in timidity or anxiety-proneness are not present in newborn rhesus monkeys, by 1 month, individual differences in young monkeys' response to challenging situations begin to show stability across time. For more detail on this research, see Chapter 10, by Higley and Suomi.

Once inhibition of approach is established, longitudinal research suggests that individual differences in the relative strength of approach versus inhibition to novelty or challenge will be a relatively enduring aspect of temperament. Garcia-Coll *et al.* (1984) studied 21-month-old infants' responses to unfamiliar stimuli in the laboratory, noting their tendency to become inhibited (accompanied with distress) or uninhibited. Individual differences in inhibition for extreme groups, that is, highly inhibited versus highly uninhibited infants, showed stability from 21 to 31 months of age, and also from 48 to 66 months, particularly among children who showed high sympathetic tone as assessed by high and relatively stable heart rate and greater pupil dilation (see Chapter 8, by Kagan *et al.*; Kagan, Reznick, & Snidman, in press; Reznick *et al.*, 1986). Stability of inhibition for a less selected sample has also been found between 14 and 32 months of age (Gibbons, Johnson, McDonough, & Reznick, 1986).

Inhibition of Approach: Possible Sex Differences

Although it had been argued earlier that males and females differ from birth on a number of temperamental characteristics (Bardwick, 1971; Garai & Scheinfeld, 1968), research on children younger than 1 year of age demonstrates few temperamental sex differences (Bates, 1987; Maccoby & Jacklin, 1974; Rothbart, 1986; but see Eaton & Enns, 1986, on sex differences in activity level). Using a sample of over 200 infants, ratings of (negative) emotionality, sociability and activity on the Colorado Childhood Temperament Inventory (CCTI; Plomin & DeFries, 1985) demonstrated no sex differences. Sex differences in parent report on the approach–withdrawal dimension of temperament, however, have been found in several cross-cultural samples (Carey & McDevitt, 1978; Hsu, Soong, Stigler, Hong, & Liang, 1981; Miziade, Boudreault, Thivierge, Caperaa, & Cote, 1984), with males reported as showing greater approach than females.

Although the finding of greater approach for boys would constitute only one sex difference among the several dimensions discussed in this review, it could prove to be an important one for social development. If girls demonstrate both greater inhibition of approach and earlier development of language (Schachter, Shore, Hodapp, Chalfin, & Bundy, 1978), they may be more susceptible to early caregiver socialization of impulsive action than boys, on the average. Several studies indicate that young girls are more likely than boys to comply with prohibitions and requests (Minton, Kagan, & Levine, 1971; Pederson & Bell, 1970; Smith & Dagliesh, 1977). These results could clearly have been influenced by differential socialization of self-control in boys and girls, but individual differences in children's susceptibility to inhibition may also contribute to the sex differences.

Since we might also expect approach to be involved in other species typical behavior patterns, such as aggression, if girls demonstrate greater inhibition of approach tendencies, they would be expected to be less susceptible to aggressive and acting-out problems, and this appears to be the case (Achenbach, 1982). We would also expect young girls to be less easily stimulated to excited activity in social situations than boys, and this has been noted in Jacklin and Maccoby's (1978) observations.

Such sex differences could also be related to the greater effect of home environment variables on the development of behavior problems in males than in females (Rutter & Garmezy, 1983). If, in the relative absence of self-regulated controls for behavior of the child, the function of the *family* in providing these controls assumes primary importance (cf. Snow, Jacklin, & Maccoby's (1983) argument that 12-month boys may 'need' more parental control), then a family's failure to provide control as a result of internal discord and disorganization will more likely result in behavior problems for less internally controlled children. The data, reviewed by Rutter and Garmezy (1983), suggest that family variables are generally related to aggression and conduct problems, and that males are more likely to develop such problems.

Negative Emotionality

Turning now to stability of negative emotionality during later infancy and the toddler period, some of the most impressive stability correlations again have come from the Louisville Twin Study. It should be noted, however, that the observations extend only from 12 months to 18 and 24 months and the measures forming temperamental composites include attention and approach–withdrawal as well as composites of both negative and positive emotionality measures (Matheny *et al.*, 1984). In the Louisville infant assessment, the child experiences a set of 2-minute laboratory episodes designed to elicit activity and emotionality. Videotape records are rated at 2-minute intervals for (a) emotional tone or mood, ranging from negative to positive, (b) the degree of focused attention the child directs toward objects, events and persons, (c) the degree of social orientation toward the staff person interacting with the child, and (d) activity. Reaction to restraint (degree of upset) is also assessed when the infant is being measured for weight, recumbent length, and head circumference.

At each age, factor analyses result in a first unrotated factor that shows stability across age: it includes emotional tone, attentiveness, social orientation, and reaction to restraint, and is labeled Lab Tractability. The 'tractable' pole includes positive tone, high focused attention, high social orientation, and low upset to physical restraint. The opposite pole includes negative tone, low focused attention, low social orientation, and high upset to physical restraint. At each age, mothers also complete the TTS (Fullard, McDevitt, & Carey, 1980). The first unrotated factor of the TTS includes mood, adaptability, approach and intensity, and distractibility is also included at 12 months. This first factor is labeled Questionnaire Tractability. At each age, Lab and Questionnaire Tractability scores are positively correlated, and by each method, stability is found from one age to the next, with greater stability from 18 to 24 months than from 12 to 18 months (Matheny, Wilson, & Nuss, 1984). Using a more specific measure of negative emotionality, Plomin and DeFries (1985) have also found stability from 12 to 24 months.

Sociability

In Wilson, Brown, and Matheny's (1971) early work, mothers of same-sex twins compared their twins on 16 behaviors. Analysis of mothers' reports at 12 months yielded two behavioral clusters, one labeled 'temperament' (including temper frequency and intensity, irritable crying, taking toys, and demanding attention), which was found to be positively related to distractibility, and the other labeled 'sociability' (including smiling and laughter, accepting people and seeking affection). The expression of positive affect in parent–child interaction continues to increase across the periods of 6–18 months (Adamson & Bakeman, 1985) and 9–21 months (Bloom, Beckwith, & Capatides, 1987). In later infancy, there is also evidence for longitudinal stability of measures of sociability (see review by Beckwith, 1979; Plomin & DeFries, 1985; Schaefer & Bayley, 1963). Schaefer and Bayley (1963) rated children on the basis of observations during mental and motor tests and found evidence for stability of social responsiveness from 1 through 2 to 3 years of age for girls, with less strong evidence for stability in boys. Using the CCTI, Plomin and DeFries (1985) found stability from 12 to 24 months for their sociability factor.

Activity Level

Plomin and DeFries (1985) also found stability of activity from 12 to 24 months. Schaefer and Bayley (1963), however, reported that early ratings of activity and rapidity (age 10–36 months) were *negatively* related to ratings of positive task-oriented activity through age 12 years for boys and girls. Early activity and rapidity in infancy for girls were also positively related to extraverted and aggressive behaviors in adolescence. Schaefer and Bayley (1963) conclude: 'These findings suggest that high motility may be an innate rather than an acquired characteristic and that high motility during infancy may be predictive of subsequent behavior' (Schaefer & Bayley, 1963, p. 94).

We should note once again that Buss and Plomin (1975) have argued that activity level does not show stability from the first year to later ages. It is possible that if activity serves a different affective system (negative rather than positive) during the period of early infancy, activity during early infancy may predict later inhibited approach (associated with negative emotionality, see Kagan, *et al.*, in press) rather than approach (associated with positive emotionality). Such a finding was reported for boys in a study by Halverson, Moss, and Jones-Kearns (1977; reviewed by Moss & Sussman, 1980). A similar 'inversion of intensity' effect was reported by Bell, Weller, and Waldrop (1971) between the newborn period and age 2½, but this finding was not completely replicated in a study by Yang and Halverson (1976). Nevertheless, the possibility of activity level serving different affective masters from one developmental period to another is an intriguing one.

Attention Span and Effort

In Plomin and DeFries' (1985) Colorado twin study, stability of attention span was found from 12 to 24 months, but at a lower level than stability correlations for sociability, activity, and (negative) emotionality. In research on individual differences in attentional orienting in late infancy, we have studied infants' rate of gaze shifting and fixation time toward small manipulable toys (Kenofer, Rothbart, & O'Curry, in preparation). In this research, we have found stability from 10 to 13.5 months in rate of gaze shifting and duration of orienting. Additional correlates of frequency of gaze shifting included smiling and laughter as assessed by both IBQ and laboratory observation. Infants who shifted their gaze more frequently, i.e. showed shorter visual attention spans, also demonstrated higher rates of activity and more frequent switches of toy play when toys were distributed across an open field at 13.5 months.

Individual differences in flexibility of attention have been studied in adulthood (Keele & Hawkins, 1982), and these measures may be applicable to the study of infants and children with some modifications. In studies of flexibility of attention in adults, however, subjects are usually asked to make an arbitrary connection between a particular environmental event and a particular response, such as pressing a reaction-time key whenever a green light comes on. Subjects then are asked to perform a conflicting response under rarely occurring conditions, so that quick reprogramming of the connection between input and output is required. Individuals appear to reliably differ in how easily these shifts are made (Keele & Hawkins, 1982).

In these attention studies with adults and older children, verbal instructions are given to the subject which result in consciously driven activity, whereas in studies of attention in the young infant, instructions cannot be given. For young infants, we can thus chiefly examine aspects of stimulus engagement, disengagement, and movement of orienting as the child's interest in the stimulus waxes and wanes (although focused attention can also be assessed through heart-rate indicators, as suggested by Richards' work, in press).

A developmental shift in visual orienting appears to occur late in the first year of life. Kagan, Kearsley, and Zelazo (1978) have noted a pattern of fixation times in North American children and in children from rural Guatemala demonstrating a

U-shaped function over time. From 4 to 8 months, there is a steep decline in the amount of time children spend looking at three-dimensional clay faces, with the decline shown for faces both with scrambled features and without. Between 13 and 36 months, however, there is an increase in looking time that is stronger for scrambled than for unscrambled faces.

Kagan *et al.* (1978) suggest that early looking patterns are chiefly a function of alertness, whereas older infants' looking at the faces represents 'richness of hypotheses surrounding representations of humans' (Kagan *et al.*, 1978, p. 80). In addition, they argue, 'It has been our continual assumption that density of hypotheses to discrepant events is a major determinant of duration of fixation after 8 to 10 months of age. The occurrence of continuity from 8 to 13 and 13 to 27 months, without comparable 8 to 27 month continuity suggests that the determinants of fixation time change between 8 and 27 months' (Kagan *et al.*, 1978, p. 81). No continuity was found between 4 months and later measures.

Development of effort, that is, the ability to inhibit responses to stimuli in the immediate environment while pursuing a cognitively represented goal (Posner & Rothbart, 1981; Rothbart & Posner, 1985), may also be linked to the child's developing ability to maintain a focus of attention over an extended period. Sustained attention and the ability to delay are positively related, and both develop over the preschool years. Krakow, Kopp, and Vaughn (1981) studied sustained attention (duration of interest in a set of toys) in 12- to 30-month-old infants, finding that duration of play increased across this period, with interindividual stability between 12 and 18 months, and between 24 and 30 months. Their measure of sustained attention was also positively correlated with self-control measures, independent of developmental quotient, at 24 months. Mothers of children with high sustained attention at 12 months described their children as more quiet and inactive at 24 and 36 months. The research of Krakow *et al.* (1981) suggests that sustained attention may be an additional sign of increasing internal control across the preschool years. Again, as for inhibition of approach, it is important to note that once this normative change in attention has occurred, allowing effortful regulation of activity, children may evidence variability on measures of attention span (related to the ability to delay) that can then demonstrate stability over time.

We might expect that if the capacity for effortful control is relatively lacking in an older child, the child will be functioning at a level where action is more directly driven by the intensity, novelty, or discrepancy of the stimulus or by its signal value (its associations with previous reward and punishment) than by the child's cognitive representations. The child's orienting may then tend to be long or short, but it will not demonstrate the flexibility of response that is possible when effortful levels of control have been added.

Ego-Control and Ego-Resiliency

With the temperamental constructs of behavioral inhibition and effortful control now added to our earlier set of components of temperament, we can consider a major contribution to the study of temperament in childhood: Jeanne and Jack Block's (1980) work on ego-control and ego-resiliency. To understand fully the

Blocks' constructs, it is necessary to read the theoretical discussion in their 1980 paper. However, it is possible to abstract general descriptions of these constructs and relate them to the developmental course of temperament.

The Blocks define ego-control as the characteristic 'expression or containment of impulses, feelings, and desires', so that,

> the ego overcontroller can be expected to have a high modal threshold for response, to be constrained and inhibited, to manifest needs and impulses relatively indirectly, to delay gratification unduly, to show minimal expression of emotion, to tend to be categorical and overly exclusive in processing information, to be perseverative, non-distractible, less exploratory, relatively conforming, with narrow and unchanging interests, to be relatively planful and organized, and to be made uneasy by and therefore avoidant of ambiguous or inconsistent situations. In contrast, the ego undercontroller can be expected to have a low modal threshold for response, to be expressive, spontaneous, to manifest needs and impulses relatively directly into behavior, to tend toward the immediate gratification of desires, to readily manifest feelings and emotional fluctuations, to be overly-inclusive in processing information, to have many but relatively short-lived enthusiasms and interests, to be distractible, more ready to explore, less conforming, relatively comfortable with or undiscerning of ambiguity and inconsistency, to manifest actions that cut across conventional categories of response in ways that are (for better or for worse) original, and to live life on an ad hoc, impromptu basis. (Block & Block, 1980, pp. 43–44)

Ego-resiliency, on the other hand, is defined in terms of adaptation to changing circumstances, allowing persons to modify their usual level of ego-control in order to meet the task demands of the environment. Thus,

> Holding degree of ego-control constant, the ego-resilient person is resourceful before the strain set by new and yet unmastered situations, manifests more 'umweg' solutions when confronted by a barrier, can maintain integrated performance while under stress, is better able to process two or more competing stimuli, is better able to resist sets or illusions, is engaged with the world but not subservient to it, and is capable of both 'regressing in the service of the ego' when task requirements favor such an adaptation and, conversely, of becoming adaptively organized and even compulsive when under certain other environmental presses. With degree of ego-control held constant, the ego-unresilient (brittle) person, according to our conceptualization, is generally fixed in his/her established pattern of adaptation, has only a small adaptive margin, is stereotyped in responding to new situations, becomes immobilized, rigidly repetitive, or behaviorally diffuse when under stress, becomes anxious when confronted by competing demands, is relatively unable to resist sets or illusions, is slow to recover after stress, is disquieted by changes in either the personal psychological environment or the larger world, and cannot modify his/her preferred personal tempo in accordance with reality considerations. (Block & Block, 1980, pp. 48–49)

Given our discussion of temperament thus far, we might expect ego-overcontrol to be related to a high degree of behavioral inhibition, and ego-undercontrol to a low degree of behavioral inhibition coupled with strong approach responses. Ego-resiliency would be related to a high degree of effortful control, and probably also to general flexibility of attention, that is, the capacity to shift readily from one focus of attention to another. Aspects of personality such as self-concept would of course strongly influence expressions of ego-control and ego-resiliency, but the similarity of the ego-control and ego-resiliency constructs to dimensions of temperament is strong.

It should be noted that although Thomas and Chess (1977) identified approach–withdrawal as a temperament dimension, they have no construct that corresponds to behavioral inhibition. Also, although their adaptability dimension gets at the child's recovery time from negative reactions, they do not directly assess more active control processes similar to effortful control. This would be expected, given that the original observations of the New York Longitudinal Study group were made with infants 6 months and younger. These dimensions of individual differences would not be expected to be present or observable in infants at the time the NYLS observations were made. Nevertheless, they are worthy of our consideration, especially in the study of temperament in the preschool years and beyond.

Summary

All components of temperament observable during early infancy can also be seen during late infancy. Added to these are inhibition of approach, that is, inhibition of responses in the presence of novelty and challenge (see Table 1). In addition, effortful control develops, allowing the child to focus upon a goal while inhibiting reactions to immediately present stimuli, including cues indicating potential reward or punishment. Effortful control allows for active planning for future action, and flexibility in reaction to changing circumstances.

TEMPERAMENT IN THE PRESCHOOL YEARS AND BEYOND

More on Ego-Control and Ego-Resiliency

If it proves feasible to relate the Block's ego-control and ego-resiliency constructs to constructs of behavioral inhibition and effortful control, then we will have access to their very carefully conducted longitudinal research (Block & Block, 1980). Children were rated using a Q-sort method by three teachers at age 3 years and independently by three teachers at age 4. At age 7, teachers, and when available, teachers' aides, also completed Q-sort assessments. Ego-control and ego-resiliency were also experimentally defined and measured through a laboratory assessment battery at each age. Ego-control measures included actometer assessments, measures of level of aspiration, delay of gratification, planfulness, and tempo in a motor-inhibition task. Ego-resiliency measures included ability to change tempo under instructions in a motor-inhibition task, performance on a dual-focus task, incidental learning, and ability to generate alternative solutions.

Composites of the experiment-based measures were found to be related to composites of teachers' ratings at ages 3 and 4 in the following ways. Under-controlled children as assessed in the laboratory were rated by their teachers as: 'more active, assertive, aggressive, competitive, outgoing, attention-seeking, extrapunitive, overreactive to frustration, jealous, exploiting, and less compliant, orderly, yielding, and private than children scoring in the over-controlled direction' (Block & Block, 1980, p. 68). In addition, children identified in the laboratory as more ego-resilient were described at both ages as 'more empathetic, able to cope with stress, bright, appropriate in expressions of emotion, self-accepting, novelty-seeking, fluent, self-reliant, competent, creative, and as less anxious, conflicted, suspicious, sulky, imitative, and seeking of reassurance' (Block & Block, 1980, p. 71).

Normative longitudinal stability was found from 3 to 7 years on ego-control measures. Children who scored as highly undercontrolled at 3 were later described as more 'energetic, curious, restless, expressive of impulse, and as less constricted, less compliant, and less relaxed' (Block & Block, 1980, p. 83). Stability was found from age 3 to 4 on ego-resiliency, with more ego-resilient children at age 3 described at age 4 as 'able to recoup after stress, verbally fluent, less anxious, less brittle, less intolerant of ambiguity, and as less likely to externalize or become rigidly repetitive or to withdraw under stress' (Block & Block, 1980, p. 88). Less stability was found for ego-resiliency to age 7, and additional developmental change on this variable may have been occurring across this period.

Verbal Self-Regulation and Effortful Control

Another level of control over temperament is added during the preschool years: the influence of verbal instructions upon behavior. This influence is not a temperamental one, but it has important influences upon the expression of temperament. Soviet research and theory has posited three major levels at which human behavior is regulated (Pavlov, 1928). The first is reflexive, in response to immediately present stimulation. The next level, called the first signal system, functions via conditioned responses that anticipate future events. The final level of control in Pavlov's system, found only in humans, employs the symbolic capacities of language and is called the second signal system. According to Luria (1961), the second signal system developmentally assumes control over the first signal system but does not replace it.

Luria (1966), following Vygotsky (1966), argues that auxiliary stimuli, in the case of the second signal system, words, may be 'artificially introduced into the situation' (Vygotsky, 1966, p. 24) for self-directed control. These words can be used by children to override sensorimotor response inclinations to stimuli and they allow the culture, which shapes the meaning of words and thereby influences the content of the child's semantic associations and rule systems, to exercise powerful control. In verbal control, this influence can operate even when adult representatives of the culture are absent. Thus, in the view of Vygotsky and Luria, society and culture influence the development of the third level of control through the mediating function of language. In the description of effortful control given above, however, control can exist before language develops. Luria argues that, initially, controls of the second signal system are always conscious and verbal. However, with practice, activity that was initially under conscious control can become automatic. Similarities between this higher order control system and internalized moral controls discussed by Freud, Piaget, and Kohlberg (Maccoby, 1980) may be evident to the reader.

Krakow and Johnson (1981), using measures of self-control under verbal instructions with younger children (age 18–30 months), have found a behavioral inhibitory cluster and large age effects. They have also found moderate levels of stablity of inhibitory self-control across the 12-month period. We (Reed, Pien, & Rothbart, 1984) have found strong age effects in two measures of verbally regulated self-control (a pinball game and Simon-says game) in a cross-sectional study of children aged 40-49 months. These studies indicate that there are increases in verbal self-regulation across 18-30 months (Krakow & Johnson, 1981) and also across 40-49 months of age (Reed *et al.*, 1984). Our expectation in a developmental model for temperament is that words come to direct both effortful control and anticipation, thereby influencing the direction of temperamentally based self-regulation. Words are also part of a semantic network of associations, with some of these associations affective ones, so that words will also powerfully affect emotional reactivity.

As noted above, Krakow, Kopp, and Vaughn (1981) found that the ability to delay is positively related to length of sustained attention, and evidence for continuity between ability to delay gratification in the preschool period and later attentional and emotional control has also been reported (Mischel, 1983). In Mischel's work on delay of gratification, the number of seconds delayed by preschool children while waiting for rewards significantly predicted parent-reported attentiveness and ability to concentrate when those children were high-school juniors and seniors. Children who showed a relative inability to delay in preschool also showed a later parent-reported tendency to go to pieces under stress.

Effort and Social Regulation

Verbally regulated effortful control can be used to suppress and redirect emotional reactions, although it is likely that behavioral inhibition (ego-overcontrol) also involves inhibition of the expression of emotions. In the course of socialization, children are instructed as to how they 'should' feel in different situations (Hochschild, 1979), and also come to learn that external expressions of emotions should sometimes be suppressed or exaggerated. Saarni (1979) has studied the 'display rule' knowledge of children from ages 6 to 10 years, and found that with increasing age, children know more rules of display and these rules are more complex than those of younger children. Saarni (1982) also found that children above the age of 6 were more likely to employ an emotion-suppressive display rule in their social behavior. Children's cognitive understanding of possible dissociations between feeling and behavior and their possibly related use of lying (Selman, 1980), poker-face expressions, and the like, are also important changes that may influence the expression, but not necessarily the experience, of temperament-related emotional reactions.

As emotions are becoming increasingly socialized with development, emotionality itself is also employed in the socialization of behavior. Hoffman (1975, 1981) has argued that the empathic experience of another's distress allows the child to develop motivation toward positive behavior to others. Thus, caregivers encourage children to try to feel the way another person might feel, to induce the child effortfully to change behaviors that might cause distress to others. Individual differences in children's temperament are likely to influence the success of this socialization process. First, the child's susceptibility to negative emotions and the time course of this distress will likely influence whether the caregiver can elicit an empathetic response in the first place. Felt emotion can then bring information about how the other person feels and also personal relief when the other is helped (although relief may not follow if distress is high and recovery of distress is low). If an emotional empathic reaction is weak or lacking, socialization via empathy loses an important ingredient for success, although it is possible that responses to another's cognitively perceived suffering could be learned by rote rather than by feeling. The process of empathic socialization also requires the child to be able to apply behavioral inhibition or effortful control to behavior; if both of these controls are weak or lacking, the process will also fail.

Cognitive studies of how children learn to read have profited greatly by a componential analysis of reading skill. This analysis allows a psychologist to identify a number of different ways in which the reading process may go wrong, each of which is likely to require a different treatment (Carr, Brown, & Vavrus, 1985; Coltheart, 1985). A similar analysis can be made of a process like the internalization of socialized rules based upon an empathic emotional response. A child may lack required capacities at cognitive, emotional, or self-control levels, causing the process to fail, given the usual methods for socialization. On the other hand, a lack of emotional feeling may be overcome by invoking a cognitive understanding of situations in which one must be careful and caring. Flexible parents and teachers are often rewarded when they realize that there can be more than one way to instruct a child about reading *or* caring, and that what works for one, or even most, of the children, may not be effective for a particular child.

We (Rothbart & Posner, 1985) have suggested that assessing different components of temperamental variability may aid clinicians in conceptualizing emotional and cognitive disabilities, as in the case of attentional deficit disorder (ADD). Work on children diagnosed with ADD (Douglas, 1980; Kinsbourne, 1984) suggests that high rates of increase and habituation of interest and approach, coupled with deficits in verbally regulated inhibitory control may be implicated in the disorder. High susceptibility to distress (negative emotionality) may be present but it is not critical for the disorder to be diagnosed. Thus, a variety of forms of the disability would be possible depending upon the mix of temperamental components.

Since the findings of Krakow *et al.* (1981) and Mischel (1983) suggest that the capacity to sustain attention and self-control are closely linked, deficits in self-regulated focusing and switching of attention may also be involved in the varying forms of this disorder, but more research in this area is needed. We might also consider the very strong tendency for aggressive and conduct problems to be associated with inattentiveness and/or hyperactivity (Rutter & Garmezy, 1983). As noted above, sustained attention is positively related to internally regulated self-control (Krakow *et al.*, 1981), and the two behavioral variables may be linked to central nervous system maturational events as discussed in Chapter 6.

Sociability and Shyness

In measures of sociability in early childhood, Emmerich (1984) found stability of ratings of interpersonal orientation in his observations of children's nursery school behavior for half-year periods from 1 to 5 years. In addition, Walker (1967) reported considerable stability in ratings of sociability across third to fourth and fifth to sixth grades for a large sample using three different methods: self-report, teacher ratings, and peer nominations. Bronson has also reported stability of extraversion ratings for children from 5 years through adolescence (Bronson, 1966, 1967), in a dimension ranging from reserved, somber, and shy to expressive, gay, and socially at ease.

In reviewing Kagan and Moss's (1962) *Birth to maturity*, Honzik (1965) noted that the Fels subjects' scores on 'spontaneity' versus 'social interaction anxiety' were stable and predictive over long periods for both males (the first 3 years to adulthood) and females (6–10 years to adulthood). She also reported that three other longitudinal studies have found stability on similar dimensions. Bayley and Schaefer (1963) found their most stable and persistent dimension between birth and 18 years to be 'active, extraverted' versus 'inactive, introverted' behavior. Tuddenham (1959) found stability on scales indexing 'spontaneity' versus 'inhibition' for subjects from 14 to 33 years of age in the Oakland Growth Study.

Finally, Honzik (1965) and Bronson (1972) reported that for the period between 21 months and 18 years of age, the two most stable dimensions were 'introversion' versus 'extraversion' and 'excessive reserve' versus 'spontaneity'. Positive correlations have also been reported at 24 months (but not at 12 months) between shyness in infants and their biological mothers' self-report before the infants' birth (Plomin & DeFries, 1985). This finding again supports the development of a relatively late developing component of temperament, one that is not evident in the earliest months, but demonstrates stability once it has developed. Shyness was found to show stability between 1–3 years and 9–12 years in research by Schaefer and Bayley (1963). Stevenson-Hinde and Simpson (1982) have also found stability of shyness from 42 to 50 months in maternal interviews.

These clusters of temperamental characteristics demonstrating normative stability are complex, and a dimension like spontaneity versus inhibition may involve several temperamental components. Highly spontaneous children may combine strong approach with a low self-regulatory 'stop' system (behavioral inhibition) in novel situations or situations where spontaneous behavior may lead to punishment (challenge). In situations that are neither novel nor potentially punishing, the strength of approach itself may chiefly determine the reaction. Inhibition may result when strong approach is combined with a strong 'stop' system, but we must take care that slow approach due to behavioral inhibition is not confused with a general tendency toward slow approach, without any influence of behavioral inhibition. Thus, 'spontaneity versus inhibition' can be seen as involving a complex of temperamental components and one of its poles (inhibition) can be mimicked by individuals low on approach.

MacDonald (1989) has demonstrated how the operation of two major temperamental dimensions, positive and negative emotionality (with the latter including behavioral inhibition), can be seen to generate a single dimension of observed behavior ranging from impulsivity–sociability to caution–reserve. When we observe children only in situations where shyness will prevent expression of a high degree of sociability that might be seen under less novel or challenging circumstances, only a single dimension will be observed. The question nevertheless remains as to whether positive affect and approach and distress and inhibition are necessarily negatively correlated. It was noted above that Goldsmith and Campos (1986) have found positive and negative affect to be uncorrelated when assessed in different situations (so that the occurrence of one reaction does not prevent the occurrence of the other). In the study of approach and inhibition, we have also found that individual differences in rate of approach are evident developmentally before children demonstrate behavioral inhibition, and that these differences show stability across time when children are observed under relatively familiar, non-threatening conditions, suggesting that approach and inhibition can be differentiated (Rothbart, 1988).

Finally, we would expect *variability* of behavior across situations in those children who are both highly approaching and highly inhibited (but only when circumstances of novelty, potential punishment, or other challenge are varied). These children would be expected to behave in an extraverted manner under safe, familiar conditions but to be inhibited under novel or potentially punishing conditions. We might reconsider here Riese's (1987) findings that more irritable newborns showed more variability of activity at 24 months. We might also expect that children who are generally low in approach will appear to be relatively reserved under both sets of conditions (Rothbart, in press). Variability of extraverted behavior across situations that differ in their degree of unfamiliarity or challenge again suggests the operation of two different processes of approach and inhibition.

Activity Level

Interesting correlates of activity level have been reported for preschool and young school-aged children. Buss, Block, and Block (1980) longitudinally assessed activity level at ages 3 and 4 using actometer measures and at ages 3, 4, and 7 using teachers' Q-sort ratings. Correlations were found between actometer-scored behaviors and teacher-rated activity and inhibition items at 3, 4, and 7 years, with more active children by actometer assessment seen as having a rapid personal tempo and being restless and fidgety, and not inhibited, constricted, or physically cautious. A second cluster of items found across ages indicated that active children were seen by their teachers as likely to 'try to stretch limits, try to take advantage of others, try to be the center of attention, like to compete', to be self-assertive and somewhat aggressive, and 'not obedient, compliant, shy or reserved' (Buss *et al.*, 1980, p. 406). A third cluster of items 'seems to involve lack of inhibition and a degree of under-control. Active preschool children, across ages, are not particularly planful or reflective and tend to express their thoughts and feelings openly and without inhibition. Less active children are generally more planful and more able to delay gratification' (Buss *et al.*, 1980, p. 406).

Buss *et al.* (1980) note the consistency of their results with those of Battle and Lacey (1972) and Halverson and Waldrop (1973, 1976). Battle and Lacey (1972) also reported that more active children were more aggressive and dominant with peers, more attention-seeking, more likely to be engaged in social play and less compliant. Halverson and Waldrop (1973, 1976) found that highly active children were more likely to engage in frenetic play, to show an inability to sustain play, to oppose peers, and to be less compliant than less active children. Stevenson-Hinde and Simpson (1982) reported that, at both ages 42 and 50 months, more active children were more likely to show refusals, tantrums, and behavior that was difficult to manage. They were also seen as more attention-seeking at 42 months. Our study of parent-reported temperamental characteristics in the Children's Behavior Questionnaire is also supportive of these relationships. At 3–7 years, activity level is positively correlated with approach, anger, and impulsivity and is negatively correlated with shyness and inhibitory control, even though the shyness and inhibitory control measures are not related to each other.

In research on stability of activity level, Walker's (1967) studies employing self-report, teacher ratings, and peer nominations showed considerable stability from 3 to 4 and 4 to 5 years. Buss *et al.* (1980) found stability across ages 3–4 for both actometer-estimated activity level and teachers' ratings. Both methods at 3 and 4 predicted teacher-rated activity levels for girls at age 7; actometer ratings at age 3 did not predict 7-year measures for boys, but teacher ratings did.

Thomas and Chess (1977) note the alert vigilance necessary for parents of a highly active child, who is likely to be more prone to injury or interference with others' activities. They also suggest that a quiet child may disrupt the household less, but that parents may come to compare the quiet child unfavorably with more active children, seeing slowness as a sign of intellectual inferiority. (In the research literature, we have no reason to believe that a person's preferred rate of speech and motor activity is related to efficiency of mental operations, however.)

D. M. Buss (1981) has completed a longitudinal study linking the child's activity level to parent behavior in a structured parent–child interaction setting. Using composite scores derived from actometer ratings at ages 3 and 4 from the Blocks' study, Buss investigated their relation to mother and father interaction with the children at age 5. In the structured interaction, parents were given freedom to help their children while supervising cognitive and motor tasks such as maze completion and listing of instances of categories. After the interaction, examiners completed a Q-sort to characterize the parent–child interaction and especially the parents' teaching styles.

Buss (1981) found that for girls previously identified as active, both mothers and fathers were likely to engage in power struggles where parent and child competed to perform. Mothers also more frequently used physical means to communicate with more active daughters, talked to them more, and showed more hostility toward them, and fathers were described as having trouble establishing a working relationship with them. Mothers of active sons were more likely to conduct the session 'in unusual ways' and to give the appearance of being confused about their teaching expectations. They also were more talkative and hostile, as with more active daughters. Fathers were more active with their active sons and got into more power struggles with them, but the overall tone of the interaction was more positive than it was with more quiet sons, with fathers more likely to make the situation fun and to show less hostility toward active sons. Less active children tended to be seen as receiving more support and encouragement, especially from mothers. Buss's

(1981) research into parent–child interaction points up the relationship of both child temperament and gender to parental contributions.

Negative Emotionality

In temperament studies of older children, distress-proneness factors have also been extracted. In Martin's (1984) Temperament Assessment Battery for children age 3 through 7, the first factor extracted for both parent and teacher reports is emotionality, chiefly for negative emotions. In Keogh's (Keogh, Pullis, & Caldwell, 1982) Teacher Temperament Questionnaire, the third factor, labeled 'reactivity', includes both negative affect and sensitivity items. This clustering of sensitivity and negative-affect items is of interest in connection with adult work on temperament. Soviet researchers' concept of nervous system 'strength', or endurance under high-intensity stimulation (Nebylitsyn, 1950, 1972), suggests a dimension involving both sensitivity and susceptibility to distress that might also be present in early life. (This dimension is also discussed by Strelau in Chapter 3 and by the present author in Chapter 6.) Thomas et al. (1968) have also reported intensity and threshold to be significantly negatively correlated during years 1, 4, and 5, and Miller and Bates (1986) have found significant correlations between temperature sensitivity and negative emotions. Laboratory research with children would be helpful to test this relationship further.

In research on the stability of distress-proneness beyond infancy, Schaefer and Bayley's (1963) study of children's behavior during mental and motor testing reported stability of ratings of irritability (from excitable to calm) across the first to the third year of life. These ratings may have been affected, however, by the same rater judging children across age. Ratings of unfriendliness minus friendliness in the Schaefer and Bayley study showed stability across 2-year periods from ages 2 to 8 and across 9–12 years for both boys and girls. Negative reactions did not show stability from infancy to adolescence, but shyness (which Kagan et al. (in press) have related to negative emotionality) did show some stability. Stevenson-Hinde and Simpson (1982) have reported stability for moodiness (irritability, sulkiness) from 42 to 50 months in maternal interviews.

Bronson's (1966) research on a number of measures related to distress-proneness also showed stability from 6 to 12 years. These measures included emotional stability, explosiveness, reactivity, anxious-related ratings, fearfulness, and tantrums. Less stability was found from earlier ages to 15 years, although in most cases stability was found across the 12- to 15-year period. In a study by Walker (1967) utilizing self-report, teacher, and peer-nomination ratings, stability of fearfulness was found between the third and fourth and between the fifth and sixth grades.

Summary

All components of temperament observable during late infancy can also be seen during the preschool years and beyond. Now, verbal content comes to direct effortful control, approach, avoidance, and inhibition. In addition, the effortful control that has begun to develop during late infancy continues to develop during this period (see Table 1).

TEMPERAMENT AND PERSONALITY IN ADULTHOOD

Although the argument can be made that theories and studies of adult temperament and personality are irrelevant to a book about temperament in childhood, in fact, dimensions of variability in personality identified for adults show strong similarities with the temperament dimensions discussed in this chapter. We may also wish to consult adult work in order to consider dimensions of childhood variability that may have been missed by the early observers of young infants. Such considerations can prevent the field from too early commitment to, for example, only the nine variables identified by Thomas and Chess (1977) in the young infant.

Negative and Positive Emotionality

In Tellegen's (1985; Watson & Tellegen, 1985) factor analyses of mood scales, he identifies factors corresponding to the primary emotions, and also extracts two higher order orthogonal dimensions which he has labeled Positive and Negative Affect. In this structure, Tellegen identifies a Negative Affect mood dimension with items including calm, placid, and relaxed, at one pole, and distressed, fearful, hostile, and nervous, at the other. Tellegen also identifies a Positive Affect dimension ranging from items such as drowsy, dull, and sluggish to items like active, elated, enthusiastic, and excited. These positive and negative affective factors have been replicated across many investigations (Watson & Clark, 1984; Watson & Tellegen, 1985), and may be related to the experiential aspect of positive and negative emotionality that we are able to observe in young children.

In addition, higher order factors derived from Tellegen's Multidimensional Personality Questionnaire include three orthogonal factors, two of which correspond closely to this mood structure (Tellegen, 1985). The first is labeled Positive Emotionality, and it includes feelings of well-being, social potency, and pleasurable engagement similar to Bandura's (1982) concept of self-efficacy. Scores on Positive Emotionality are correlated with scores on positive mood. The second factor, including feelings of stress, worry, resentment, and negative engagement, is labeled Negative Emotionality, and is positively correlated with scores on negative mood affect. Finally, Tellegen identifies a Constraint factor, including characteristics of cautiousness, restraint, and timidity, as opposed to impulsivity and sensation-seeking.

Tellegen (1985) notes similarities between these three factors and Eysenck's (1967, 1976; Eysenck & Eysenck, 1985) dimensions of Extraversion, Neuroticism, and Psychoticism respectively, and between Tellegen's Positive Emotionality and Gray's Approach (behavioral activation) and Tellegen's Negative Emotionality and Gray's Anxiety (behavioral inhibition) dimensions. Gray's model is discussed in more detail in Chapter 6. Other factor-analytic personality theorists have also put forward frequently replicated higher order factors that Norman (1963) has called the 'big five', and these factors have been widely replicated (McCrae & Costa,

1985). Three of the 'big five' include factors of Activity–Extraversion, Anxiety–Neuroticism, and Conscientiousness–Ego-Control, which are similar to the Positive Emotionality, Negative Emotionality, and Constraint dimensions identified above.

Cloninger's model for personality, described in Chapter 6, specifies the dimension of Harm Avoidance, which he notes is similar to Gray's Behavioral Inhibition System (and also to Kagan et al.'s behavioral inhibition), Novelty Seeking, similar to Gray's Behavioral Activation or Approach system including emotional dependence, sentimentality, sympathy, persistence, and sensitivity to social cues (Cloninger, 1986, 1987a, b), and Reward Dependence. This third dimension has not been generally explored as a temperamental one, although it may specify a cluster of characteristics that could be usefully explored in studies of temperament in childhood.

Activity Level and Constraint

Unlike the other dimensions discussed in this chapter, activity level has not emerged as one of the 'big five' or 'big three' personality factors, except to the extent that it would be represented in the negative pole of a Constraint dimension or as part of the extraverted pole of Extraversion–Introversion. Buss and Plomin (1975) argue, however, that since many of the major personality inventories do not include items assessing activity, such a factor is unlikely to be found. They note that when activity items were added to the Comrey Scale of personality, a general activity factor emerged (Duffy, Jamison, & Comrey, 1969). In addition, Buss and Plomin's temperament scale for adults (the EASI; Buss & Plomin, 1975), as well as the Guilford–Zimmerman Temperament Survey (Guilford & Zimmerman, 1956) have clear activity factors.

In the experimental literature for adults there is good evidence for the individual differences in motor tempo: rate of tapping measures are positively correlated across finger, arm, leg, and foot, yielding an individual tempo measure (Keele, Pokorny, Corcos & Ivry, 1985). These differences may be related to the observations of Gesell and Ames (1937) on individual differences in speed of movement (including grasping and prone progression) described above. In addition, measures devised to assess Type A personality contain activity items (Friedman & Rosenman, 1974), although anger items in Type A assessment scales appear to be more related to proneness to heart attack than are activity measures (Matthews, 1982).

As described above, adult studies of personality frequently identify a factor associated with Constraint or Control. Seen in the light of developmental work, there appear to be at least two possible temperamental developmental contributions to this dimension. One is the relatively passive inhibition of approach seen in behavioral inhibition or fear and the other is effortful impulse control. In a study of adult temperament and personality (Gobeo, 1986) using an adult scale we have developed (Derryberry & Rothbart, 1988), we have found Tellegen's Constraint factor to be positively related to self-reported fear. Constraint was also positively related to our measure of self-reported effortful inhibitory control, although our measures of fear and inhibitory control were not related to each other.

In comparing behavioral inhibition to inhibitory control, it is important to remember that behavioral inhibition of approach can be seen to be exogeneously controlled by stimuli signalling novelty or challenge, whereas effort is under more active cognitive control of the individual. Effort is similar to the temperamental factor or 'will' emerging from early factor analytic work in Britain (Webb, 1915) and overlaps with the Blocks' (Block & Block, 1980) constructs of ego-control and ego-resiliency. If we consider levels of regulation of behavior, inhibition of approach would be seen to operate at the anticipatory level and be conditioned to environmental cues. Effortful control operates as well at the level of verbal self-regulation. The two will be in conflict when fear opposes conscious self-instruction to perform an act.

Temperament and Personality

Personality can be viewed as a more inclusive term than temperament, in that personality includes cognitive structures such as self-concept, in addition to specific expectations and attitudes toward the self and others. It is to be expected that the cognitive aspects of personality, including self-concept, will increasingly influence the expression of an individual's temperament across development. Personality can also be seen to include strategies for adaptation that mediate between the person's biological endowment, cognitive structures, and the possibilities and demands of the environment.

Thus, even persons who are temperamentally not highly prone to negative emotional reactions may, through a set of unfortunate socialization experiences, become generally discouraged and/or highly critical of themselves and others, thereby frequently experiencing distress. On the other hand, individuals temperamentally highly susceptible to distress may structure their lives to avoid distress, developing strategies of avoiding or withdrawing from even mild unpleasantness, thereby rarely experiencing negative emotions. Personality differences thereby contribute greatly to the experience and expression of temperament. Developmental considerations suggest that, for the young infant temperament constitutes almost the whole of personality; for the adult, additional aspects of personality including social cognitions and cognitive self-regulative strategies (e.g. blaming others for negative events) will have strong effects on emotions and behavior.

Developmental Influences upon Temperament Assessment

Although Tellegen's (1985) three dimensions of adult personality appear similar to positive and negative emotionality and inhibitory control identified in childhood, by adulthood the expression of temperament will have been subject to powerful effects of socialization. Thus, as described above, socialization experiences may have created negative emotion where little previously existed. Negative socialization experiences could, of course, interact with high temperamental negative emotionality, and a distress-prone person subjected to high levels of criticism in the family might be especially susceptible to developing negative feelings about the self. The operation of protective self-regulatory strategies may also serve to shelter an individual who is highly subject to negative emotions. It is therefore important that temperament measures for the older child and adult consider not only the individual's temperamental emotionality, but their self-regulatory strategies as well.

To assess temperament in adulthood, then, one approach would be to assess emotionality, activity, and attention in situations that have *not* been subject to strong socialization influences, as in laboratory assessments of attention, or to assess individual's reactions to standardized presentations of potentially distress-producing stimuli, even though subjects may typically avoid such stimuli. Another approach to assessing temperament is to gather information about individuals' usual self-regulative strategies: What kinds of situations do they seek? What kind do they avoid? Items of the latter variety are in fact frequently used in tests of Introversion–Extraversion and Stimulation Seeking in older children and adults (Eysenck, 1965; Eysenck & Eysenck, 1975; Zuckerman, 1983). Again, the presence of self-regulatory behaviors gives researchers evidence allowing inferences about the level of stimulation the person experiences as positive or negative.

Kagan (1974) has put foward five occasions that are likely to elicit distress and/or anxiety states:

(1) anticipation of an undesirable event
(2) unassimilated discrepancy
(3) unpredictability
(4) recognition of inconsistency between belief and behavior
(5) recognition of dissonance between or among beliefs

I would additionally suggest these conditions for distress:

(6) direct experience of high intensities of stimulation (overstimulation)
(7) the removal, loss, or blocking of a desired object or goal
(8) negative self-evaluations

Indeed, the last two of Kagan's categories – (4) and (5) – may be subsumed under category (8), negative self-evaluations, to the extent that lack of consistency or rationality is seen as negative in people's evaluation of their own behavior.

Listing these circumstances for eliciting negative emotions raises an important developmental issue in the assessment of temperament. When we consider negative emotion due to unpredictability, unassimilated discrepancy, and negative self-evaluation, we are talking about cognitive judgments that, so far as we know, the newborn is not capable of making. Thus, for the newborn infant, high intensities of stimulation due to physical discomfort, including hunger, are likely to predominate in the elicitation of negative affect, while such physical discomfort is much less likely to be a common occasion for distress for adults. On the other hand, well-socialized adults may experience their strongest negative affect when they fail to live up to desired standards for themselves, circumstances that do not exist for the young infant. Changes with development in the usual eliciting conditions for negative reactions mean that in order to assess negative emotionality over the life span, we may need to vary the kinds of situations sampled across age. This criterion is met as investigators attempt to develop age-appropriate assessments of temperament (Kagan & Reznick, 1986; Matheny *et al.*, 1984). Alternatively, we need to devise simple methods for getting at temperamental characteristics, such as assays of components of attention or physiological reactivity, that can be applied at many periods during the life span.

DEVELOPMENTAL CHANGES IN LEVELS OF CONTROL

For the newborn, approach, withdrawal, and attentional orienting appear to be driven either by stimuli immediately present in the environment or by endogenous state conditions (Korner, 1972; Wolff, 1966). Throughout development, behavior will be influenced by endogenous state conditions, as when a state of boredom leads the individual to sensation or risk seeking. The relative control of the person by environment versus self will change across the course of development, however. In this discussion, I refer to control by direct environmental or endogenous stimulation (e.g. hunger, thirst sensations) as Level 1 control. (The levels of control discussed here are adapted from those proposed by Schneirla (1959, 1965), Luria (1961), and others.) In Level 1 control, distress is associated with visual avoidance, even in the newborn. Satisfaction of hunger and other needs for physical comfort result in a more positive, less avoidant state. In older children, Level 1 control operates when the hand is quickly removed from a hot stove or a radio is turned off because it is too loud.

Information from the environment that will influence the infants' reaction is immediately present in Level 1 control. Level 2 control, on the other hand, is evidenced when the child reacts to signals indicating that there will be an upcoming event of some importance, e.g. when the infant is activated or soothed by the sight of the mother's preparation of breast or bottle for feeding. At a later time, sight of the bottle may lead to self-regulatory activity such as reaching (Wolff, 1987). Level 2 control involves expectancy and anticipation. Izard (1977) has reported that although younger infants cry when they receive an injection, it is not until 9 months that the child shows anticipatory distress to the sight of the nurse or doctor with the hypodermic needle. Anticipation allows for the avoidance or seeking of stimulation before the stimulation is actually present, allowing us to use terms like 'stimulation-seeking' (Zuckerman, 1979, 1983) to describe this behavior.

Level 3, intentional or effortful control, strongly related to attention, is not seen until later in the first year of life when the child comes to inhibit stimulus-driven reactions, allowing for the pursuit of goal-directed activities in the face of distraction (Diamond, 1981, 1985). When children are able consciously to verbally control their behavior by creating self-instructions, we may speak of Level 4 control. If Luria (1961) is correct, Level 4 control will have been preceded by a period when others can direct the child's behavior through verbal instructions.

As development proceeds, self-regulating acts increasingly *precede* the stimulus events that influence them, and with the onset of verbal self-regulation, individuals gain the power to create their own positive or negative experiences through self-instruction, self-praise, and self-criticism. The latter processes have been widely studied by social-learning theorists (e.g. Bandura, 1986; Mischel, 1983) but they are not present in the infant. It is important to note that at no developmental period is Level 4 the sole means of control, even in the adult, who often operates at lower levels.

It is important to consider levels of control in connection with temperament, because verbally self-regulative acts allow individuals to behave in ways that oppose their temperamental characteristics. This allows for greater flexibility of behavior, but adds a complication to the assessment of temperamental characteristics. At the same time, temperamental characteristics of distractibility, attention span, and effort are basic to the operation of these higher levels of control over behavior, and are of interest in the study of adults as well as children.

TEMPERAMENT AND SOCIAL DEVELOPMENT

Having reviewed research on temperament and development, I will now take a more speculative approach to temperament and development, applying temperamental constructs within the context of Sander's (1962, 1969) model of early social development. Sander's model has proved especially useful in thinking about the role of development in parent–child interaction, and it has previously been employed in a discussion of emotional development by Sroufe (1979) and by me (Rothbart, 1984). Sander describes a set of issues or adaptations faced by caregiver–infant pairs in the course of early development, based on his obervations of 22 mother–child pairs over the first 20 months of life. Sander writes:

> After following ten or fifteen of the pairs we could begin to anticipate the time of appearance of some of the important concerns the mother would express, or, on the other hand, feel relieved about. This gave the impression that we were watching a sequence of adaptations common to all the different mother–infant pairs, although acted out somewhat differently by each. Each advancing level of activity which the child became capable of manifesting demanded a new adjustment in the mother–child relationship. (Sander, 1969, p. 191)

Although Sander applied this approach to infancy and the early toddler period, it can be applied throughout development, whenever changes in environmental demands and/or changes in the individual require adjustments in the social unit in order for adaptation to occur.

In addition to the adaptations described by Sander, I would add two general sources of challenge for the dyad: one is the level of emotionality and self-control expected of the child by the caregiver at each period of development; the second is the parent's set of upper and lower bounds for excitement (Bell, 1974) and the degree to which they match those of the child (both of these constructs are examples of Thomas and Chess's (1977) and Lerner and Lerner's (1983) concept of 'goodness of fit'). The child may not measure up to the parents' expectations for a child of a given age, and the child may exhibit behavior that does not fit between the parents' upper and lower bounds or vice versa (see discussion of Bell's construct

Table 2   Developmental issues identified by Sander (1969, p. 192)

Issue	Title	Span of months	Prominent infant behaviors that became coordinated with maternal activities
1	Initial regulation	1–3	Basic infant activities concerned with biological processes related to feeding, sleeping, elimination, postural maintenance, etc., including stimulus needs for quieting and arousal
2	Reciprocal exchange	4–6	Smiling behavior that extends to full motor and vocal involvement in sequences of affectively spontaneous back and forth exchanges. Activities of spoon feeding, dressing, etc. become reciprocally coordinated
3	Initiative	7–9	Activities initiated by infant to secure a reciprocal social exchange with mother or to manipulate environment on his/her own selection
4	Focalization	10–13	Activities by which infant determines the availability of mother on his/her specific initiative; tends to focalize need-meeting demands on the mother
5	Self-assertion	14–20	Activities in which infant widens the determination of his/her own behavior, often in the face of maternal opposition

above. Sander (1962, 1969) suggests that early problems in adaptation may create lasting difficulties for the dyad, although an alternative position argues that early difficulties may later be overcome. If caregiver and child prove to be better at handling some developmental issues than others, it is possible that earlier issues not adequately dealt with may be outweighed by more favorable outcomes of later developmental issues, including those of middle childhood and beyond (R. Harmon, personal communication, 1981).

Sander's early developmental issues are listed in Table 2. A caveat should be introduced, however: cultural values and traditions will influence whether an item is important enought to become an issue, and also the time at which it becomes an issue. Thus, the stages described here offer a framework that is constrained by our time and our society. Below, each of the stages is discussed in light of individual differences in temperament. Additional stages in childhood could be added to this scheme, especially the periods of school entry, middle childhood interactions with peers, and adolescence, but they will await later, more complete, treatments of temperament and social development.

Initial Regulation

Sander (1962, 1969) suggests that the first major issue faced by caregiver and newborn is regulation of the infant's biological processes in eating, sleeping, and modulating states of excitement or arousal, including distress. Among the aspects of temperament described above, the major dimensions important to this period are the child's susceptibility to distress (negative emotionality) and, probably more important, the child's degree of soothability. Individual differences in susceptibility to distress will influence the frequency of daily crying episodes. In addition, the child's soothability will affect the ease with which the caregiver can assist the child in transitions from active distress to a calm, awake state, and from distressed wakefulness to sleep. As noted above, measures of irritability and unsoothability are positively correlated.

The child's own self-regulatory soothing activities will also be important from the start: some infants will be able to soothe themselves more readily than others and they may employ thumb-sucking or face- and hair-rubbing to do so. Use of a pacifier is an interesting soothing technique in that it is originally introduced by the caregiver, but is accepted and used by some infants but not by others. Some infants appear more at the mercy of extended periods of distress than others, and parents use a variety of techniques to try to 'bring them down'.

In their study of self-calming in 6-month-old infants, West et al. (1986) found no significant relation between infant self-calming in the laboratory and measures of home environment, but high self-calming in the infant was related to independent observer's ratings of mothers as being more emotionally responsive, more involved, and more effective as caregivers. These relationships between child characteristics and mother–child interaction suggest the possibility that a calm and easily calmed infant may contribute to making the mother 'look good' when the mother is being rated for her sensitivity and her caregiving skills in interacting with that infant. Of course, the argument can also be made that the mother's early interaction with the child was the source of the infant's reactivity and soothability; longitudinal research from the newborn period might help address this concern.

A negative relation between activity level and soothing has also been suggested. Brazelton (1985) writes that characteristics of the newborn predictive of later 'intense, unreachable' crying periods are 'high motor activity, poor consolability and rapid change of state' (Brazelton, 1985, pp. 331–332). Brazelton noted that quiet infants appeared to be able to fall asleep more easily, sometimes with the aid of self-regulation such as thumb-sucking. Escalona (1968) observed that quiet infants showed more self-directed activities than more active infants, and that mothers of 1- to 3-month-old infants more often attempted to soothe active infants than inactive infants when they cried. They did so, at least for Escalona's small sample of six active infants because 'they knew their babies were likely to become exceedingly distressed if allowed to remain uncomfortable for any length of time. Inactive babies, on the other hand, very rarely reached high peaks of unpleasurable excitation. They might whimper, fret, or cry for a short time, yet subside even if left unattended' (Escalona, 1968, p. 118).

In spite of frequent attempts to soothe the more active infants, however, only two of them were observed to be soothed. It is interesting that the two active infants who were soothed by their mothers were receiving massive stimulation. This stimulation included vigorous rocking, bouncing, holding the baby very tightly to the mother's body, and 'patting so energetically that observers thought it ought to be called "pounding"' (Escalona, 1968, p. 119). Although Escalona did not approve of this method, she noted that the two active infants with whom it was used did become more quiet, although it may have been due to fatigue rather than soothing.

Schaffer and Emerson (1964) identified activity level as a mediating variable in the behavior of infants they identified as cuddlers and non-cuddlers. They suggest that non-cuddlers (children who resist cuddling) are generally active and restless, demonstrating restlessness at an earlier age than they do resistance. Schaffer and Emerson suggest that for these more active infants, tactile soothing is less comforting. As caregivers discover this, cuddlers and non-cuddlers come to receive differential experience in tactile stimulation, with cuddlers regularly soothed by tactile means and non-cuddlers more likely soothed by rough play, interaction with toys, or being walked and carrried around. Schaffer and Emerson do not see this situation as causing problems for the caregiver and child so long as caregivers are flexible about the soothing techniques they use.

In Escalona's (1968) view of the dyad, in cases where the best efforts of the mother did not make the child comfortable:

> This not only meant recurrent distress for the babies, but also placed their mothers in a situation where they expended loving efforts without the immediate gratification of seeing the babies respond. Maternal feeling and behavior depend heavily on the mother's perception of herself as someone who knows what is best for the baby and who knows herself effective in tending and satisfying his needs ... Thus, women who are inexperienced or plagued by anxiety for reasons unrelated to the baby's behavior can be greatly hindered in acquiring a sense of basic competence if the infant happens to be one who reacts intensely to fatigue and does not respond well to the usual soothing measures. In such circumstances, an intrinsic reaction pattern on the infant's part may have far-reaching consequences for the quality of the subsequent mother–child relationship. Yet our sample, small as it is, also contains examples to document the fact that mothers who bring great confidence to the task of caring for young babies may be nearly immune to the disruptive consequences of having a 'difficult' baby to care for. (Escalona, 1968, p. 108)

Later we consider the relation of temperament to individual differences in children's experience of competence, their strategies for regulating and being regulated by others, and their socialization experiences. Here we see, however, some of the ways in which characteristics of infants may affect caregivers' feelings of competence, and how a general attitude of competence on the caregiver's part may make infant 'difficulty' an irrelevant consideration to the early functioning of the dyad.

Reciprocal Exchange

The second issue or set of adaptations put forward by Sander (1962, 1969) emerges at 4–6 months, although we may wish to place it a little younger, at 2–3 months (Kistiakovskaia, 1965). During this period, which Sander calls reciprocal exchange, we see smiling, vocalizing, and motor activation expressed by infant and caregiver in their face-to-face interaction. Fraiberg (1977) calls it an expression of the language of love.

Here we see evidence of the active expression of infant positive emotionality, although we should note that as expressed, it often includes a good deal of self- and other-regulation. Microanalyses of videotape records of mother–infant reaction demonstrate repeated switches of attention of both caregiver and infant in looking toward and away from the partner (Stern, 1974). The caregiver is also likely to use the infant's looking away as an indication that the infant's upper bound of stimulation is being approximated. When this occurs, the caregiver also looks away, lowering the level of stimulation so that the infant will be able to re-enter the interaction. In the period of reciprocal exchange, the caregiver is active in both providing stimulation and modulating stimulation so as to control the interaction and not allow the infant to be overstimulated.

The expression of positive reactions by the infant has strong effects upon the caregiver. Robson and Moss (1970) interviewed mothers about the time when they felt their child recognized them as a special individual, the moment when they saw their child as an individual, and the time when their own feelings of love for the infant developed. Many mothers did not have these feelings for the infant as a newborn; they developed along with the child's smiling, eye contact, and vocal responsiveness at the 2–3 month period. It has also been suggested that positive and approaching infants may also receive more attention from caregivers under institutional conditions than less outgoing children (Rutter, 1972).

In contrast to the soothing provided to change the state of distressed infants, caregivers appear to attempt to regulate their infants' positive emotional expression by eliciting and maintaining it. Smiling and laughter from the infant is read as, 'I like it', and the caregiver is likely to repeat the previous stimulus event or a variant on it when the child has reacted positively (Rothbart, 1973). Fraiberg (1974) has noted that parents of blind infants may use high levels of physical stimulation in order to elicit more positive affect in their infants. However, this encouragement of positive affect also appears to be culturally influenced, and Caudill and Weinstein (1969) report that American mothers stimulate and arouse their infants to a greater degree than do Japanese mothers. Kistiakovskaia (1965) notes the importance of visual orienting to the 'animation complex' and describes case studies where the rate of occurrence of positive affect is greatly increased by the presentation of stimuli to deprived infants.

Interactions observable during the period of reciprocal exchange provide good illustrations of Escalona's (1968) important construct of 'effective experience'. Child X, who is active, engages in positive interactions with objects in the absence of other people; child Y, who is relatively inactive, engages in positive interactions with objects only when they are presented by a caregiver. The effective experience with objects for child X and child Y are similar when child X is alone and child Y is playing with the caregiver, but the conditions for bringing about a given experience, given temperamental differences between the children, are quite different. This is a basic point for thinking about social development: the presence of toys in the home, used as a measure of home environment may give us some indication about the experience of X, but it means little about Y's experience unless caregiver intervention is also present.

In addition, simply coding what the parent does in interacting with the child will not tell us about the child's effective environment: a parent's interaction with Y that leads to the child's object involvement and learning may be so exciting for X that s/he is unable to maintain object focus. The concept of 'effective experience', or perhaps the 'effective environment', stresses the importance of caregiver flexibility in dealing with children so as to maximize their most promising experiences with the world. Escalona's (1968) concept of 'effective experience' is very similar to the idea of 'organismic specificity' put forward more recently by Wachs and Gandour (1983).

Initiative

The third issue Sander (1962, 1969) identifies is seen as emerging in the period 7–9 months, although again we may wish to place it a little earlier at about 6 months. During this time, infants come to be seen by the caregiver as active agents in getting what they want; organized approach responses emerge as the infant gains control of the arms and hands for reaching and the body and limbs for creeping and crawling. Whereas in earlier periods it is chiefly the caregiver who exercises intention in influencing the infant (even though caregivers may not wholly succeed at this), the child's own goal-related activities now become increasingly evident to the caregiver. Sander notes that some parents who very much enjoyed interacting with their infants when the interactions were guided by the *parents*' desires and goals may come to see the child's expression of intention and initiative as the first skirmish in what will be a long-term battle of wills. In this battle, parents may also take a position like the one Sander observed toward a child in his sample: 'Ned has to learn that *he* doesn't win, that *we* win' (Sander, 1969, p. 208).

The period of initiative also marks the beginning of a set of active interactions between individual and environment that will continue for a lifetime. This set of interactions can result in the development of skills or their lack of development, and it can also result in feelings of effectance or competence or of discouragement (Harter, 1983). Individual differences in strength of approach tendencies and in the controls that inhibit approach (with inhibitory controls developing later than the initial approach tendencies) will be of great importance in these interactions. Individual differences in approach and inhibitory tendencies are likely to influence the degree to which a child desires and pursues a given goal, the child's response to novelty, punishment, or other challenge when approach toward the goal may be inhibited, and the negative affect felt when the goal is blocked (frustration) or lost (sadness), with stronger negative reactions occurring to more highly sought and desired goals.

In discussing these temperament-related effects, however, we must not forget the great importance of feedback from the environment in influencing a child's general attitudes of approach versus withdrawal or inhibition. Children characterized by strong motor approach and low controls for inhibiting approach (that is, low behavioral inhibition and/or effortful inhibitory control) may be especially likely to come into conflict with caregivers. Children who feel keen desire and can show approach tendencies but who are also capable of strong inhibitory controls can channel their approach tendencies toward acceptable objectives, if caregivers provide direction. Children with slow-building approach tendencies, and more particularly children with strong inhibitory tendencies (who tend to react to novelty by closing down and non-approach) will need encouragement in order to develop the skills that allow them to actively cope with the environment.

Let us now consider some examples of the interaction of approach and cognition. In doing so, some of the powerful environmental influences on individual differences in approach should become clear. Joseph Church (1961) has written of young children's approach orientation toward objects:

> There are forms that ask to be grasped, textures that invite palpation, and holes and crevices that invite probing with a forefinger. It is the way the environment feeds back to his actions that forms the baby's schemata: the paper that crackles or tears, the plastic toy that skitters away from his awkward fingers, the chair that refuses to budge, the toy car that rolls backward and forward but not sideways, the food that sticks to hands, the flavors and odors and sounds that come from everywhere, the pliancy and resiliency and heft and intractability of things. (Church, 1961, p. 40)

When Church speaks of the feedback of environmental outcomes on schemata, he is talking about how what an object does influences how it is used and understood, but he is also talking about the development of more general approach schemata, that is, general positive versus negative orientations toward the environment. Taken in their greatest extreme, these tendencies may be characterized in terms of a child who says 'yes' to new experience, a child who says 'no', and a child who says 'maybe, but only a little at a time'. These orientations of approach versus inhibition and avoidance in the child are *also* shaped by the feedback of the child's experience, including caregivers' attending to the child's signalled desires, their playing with and talking to the child, and providing materials for the child to explore freely, with all of these conditions serving to strengthen approach and exploration tendencies in the child. In Chapter 16, van den Boom describes an experimental study where creating some of these conditions increased exploration in infants. General attitudes of approach versus inhibition or withdrawal will also be shaped, however, by the limits the caregiver sets on the actions of the child, and sometimes these limits are severe. The limits may be set by not presenting the opportunities for a child to approach and explore, or by presenting these opportunities while at the same time demanding that the child inhibit approach. Some children will be capable of this inhibition, some will not. Both will be affected by the limits, with the latter group of children likely to experience conflict with the parent as well. In our laboratory one parent noted to us that her 13-month-old infant had learned not to touch things on the table. This child would not approach our laboratory materials without extended encouragement.

Children who are highly approaching but who also have the capacity to inhibit approach may thus adopt relatively non-active attitudes toward physical objects in response to parental restrictions, although their potential for such action may have been present at the start. Other children who are active but cannot inhibit approach may be in frequent conflict with adults when those adults place objects within their reach yet prohibit their exploration. Such interactions between caregiver, child, and environment may lead to attitudes of belligerence or anxiety in the child. Children in custodial institutions may also have so little experience in what objects and human beings are 'good for' that the general attitudes they develop will be ones of apathy. We can see in these early-developing attitudes of the child the beginnings of feelings of competence, effectance, or mastery, and also the beginnings of feelings of discouragement, lack of interest, belligerence, and helplessness.

We have written earlier about possible differences between children who develop behavioral inhibition early versus those who develop it later (Rothbart & Derryberry, 1981). Children developing controls later will have a period of direct interaction with environmental challenges allowing for active sensorimotor adaptations to the environment (skill development). Children with earlier developing controls, on the other hand, may be more prone to passive avoidance in novel or challenging situations. At the same time, they may engage in more watching and thinking about what is going on, allowing facilitation of representational capacities. Thus, although we may speak of a 'catch up' for children who develop controls later, the intervening experience for the two groups of children will differ in important ways, and both groups will be changed by the intervening experience.

Escalona (1968) sees activity level as a mediating variable in the degree to which the caregiver is needed to create an optimal environment for learning and the development of skills in the child. She suggests that caregivers's interaction and presentation of objects may be needed for more quiet children to become actively involved with objects. For the more active child, on the other hand, whose interest in objects while alone may be sufficient for extended periods of learning to occur, the caregiver's interaction may lead the child to such high social interest that it distracts the child from object manipulation. Caregiver involvement also can involve high arousal activities that result in relative non-involvement with environmental objects.

In Fries and Woolf's (1953) discussion of neonatal activity type, they hypothesize that quiet children, especially those prone to withdrawal, will be more likely to be waited upon by family members. In some highly nurturant families, they suggest, less active children might be given little opportunity to act for themselves. This situation is seen as predisposing child and family toward instrumentally dependent relationships, leading to social interactions in which children gain mastery over the environment chiefly through enlisting others to act on their behalf. Fries and Woolf hypothesize that active children, on the other hand, will at an earlier point begin to act independently upon the environment, possibly leading to anger and frustration when that action is thwarted by other family members. Such children would be more likely to gain mastery on the basis of their own activity.

Fries and Woolf (1953) also suggest that more quiet children might predominantly gain experience via visual and auditory (and possibly olfactory) experience rather than through the 'active muscular experimentation' (Fries & Woolf, 1953, p. 52) seen in more active children. In addition, they hypothesize that, given cultural standards for gender, active boys and quiet girls might have an easier time of adjusting to what is expected of them. This hypothesis has found support in Stevenson-Hinde and Hinde's (1986) finding that shyness in girls is associated with positive interactions with parents, and shyness in boys with negative interchanges, and in Buss's (1981) finding that the tone of fathers' interaction with active sons was more positive than the tone of their interaction with quiet sons. Finally, Fries and Woolf suggest that quiet children may be more prone to the defenses of withdrawal and fantasy, and that active children may be more likely to direct aggression outwardly, quiet children inwardly.

Focalization and Attachment

Sander (1962, 1969) identifies the period of focalization as beginning between the ages of about 10 and 13 months. During this period, chidren's locomotor skills allow them to establish and maintain proximity with the caregiver on their own initiative. This is a period when isssues of security may become especially important for the child, perhaps in part because of increased behavioral inhibition to novelty or challenge, resulting in states of uncertainty or anxiety that can be moderated by the parent's presence. In Bowlby's (1969) description of children's development, this period is a time of strong and active proximity seeking to the attachment figure that will extend through the second year of life and into the third.

Secure attachment has been identified by some theorists as critical to later social and intellectual development. The attachment relation, if secure, is seen as constituting the base for later exploration, achievement, and social success (Ainsworth, 1973; Sroufe, 1979; Sroufe & Waters, 1977). Ainsworth and Sroufe argue that the basis of a secure attachment is the primary caregiver's sensitivity to the child and his/her maintenance of regular proximity to the child. This argument places the balance of influence on later social development on the early behavior of the caregiver, and tends to neglect the contributing characteristics of the individual child. These contributions of the child are discussed in more detail in Chapter 16, by van den Boom.

Others have argued that infants may differ in their need for deriving security from the caregiver (Kagan, 1982b; Rothbart & Derryberry, 1981; Thomas, Chess, & Korn, 1982). A child who rarely uses the caregiver as a secure base may do so because the caregiver is not an active source of security, but the child may also be not distressed enough in the situation to require caregiver support (Rothbart & Derryberry, 1981). As noted above, children also differ from each other in the degree to which they can soothe themselves, and the child's self-directed, self-regulatory techniques in addition to the self-regulatory use of others as a source of security will be important in the security balance.

This is not to say that security is of no importance for exploration; it is clearly very important (Bowlby, 1969). It is only to say that any formula identifying the environment as the sole cause of the development of security is not sufficient. Goldsmith and Alansky's (1987) meta-analysis of temperament and attachment studies indicates that there is a low but significant correlation between children's negative emotionality and their diagnosis of having an insecure attachment. A recent temperament–attachment study has also suggested that infants higher in duration of orienting may be identified as insecure–avoidant because they do not shift attention away from the toys readily enough to greet the parent (Bradshaw, Goldsmith, & Campos, 1988). An alternative interpretation is, of course, that these children are comfortable enough in the situation that they do not need to resort to regulation from the caregiver. Finally, it is clear that many more factors than child temperament and maternal sensitivity and availability will influence security of attachment, including family stress and children's illnesses and accidents (Murphy, 1981).

Self-Assertion

The final developmental issue identified by Sander in his 1969 work involves infants 14–20 months of age. During this period, children are developing a sense of self which may include feelings of their own effectiveness (or non-effectiveness). Sander notes that a child's increasing self-assertion during this time may also run the child afoul of continuing parental needs for control. In addition, children may now begin to promote their own feelings of competence by disagreeing with and negating their parents' desires (Spitz, 1957).

Development of self-understanding has important cognitive and social implications (Damon & Hart, 1982). It is likely that our future knowledge of the development of self will include many elements, and the emergence of some of these elements will have begun before the stage of self-assertion described by Sander. Thus, we would expect that the infant's experience of bodily feelings of distress and pleasure might be a component of self-perception from the earliest days.

Another early-developing aspect of self is likely the feeling of intention when an object is desired and the child moves toward it, and the feeling of self as a source of influence upon the world when the object is reached and grasped or otherwise acted upon. With the onset of behavioral inhibition it is also likely that self-related feelings of uncertainty and inability to act are developing. In the communication area, Winnicott (1960) discusses the child's use of signals to direct the parent's actions as an early expression of the developing ego. Altogether, these early components of self might be thought of as constituting a sensorimotor self, and individual differences in temperament such as positive and negative emotionality, approach tendencies, and behavioral inhibition would be among many influences contributing to the sensorimotor self.

Research on development of a cognitive and conceptual sense of self suggests that by age 21–24 months, 75% of infants will recognize themselves in mirror representations. At that time, a spot of red surreptitiously placed on the child's nose will be identified from a mirror representation, and the child will try to rub it off (Lewis & Brooks, 1978). Children at 2 years will also label pictures of themselves and differentiate them from pictures of other children. With the development of the child's conceptions of objects, we would expect that children would come to be able to view themselves as objects and as potential causes of events in the world, including bad events. While such perceptions can be related to self-assertion, that is, to increasingly exercising one's own control of events, they may also be related to feelings of increasing inadequacy and vulnerability.

As the capacity for inhibitory control develops and language can be used for self-instruction, society can also strongly influence the content and action of self-control. Now rules for behavior can be internalized and one part of the self (the interpreting, conscious, and effort-producing part) can act upon other parts of the self to carry them out. The interpreting process can then come to perceive the self as an object among other objects, and to note that it is possible to influence one's own behavior and feelings as one influences the state of other objects, allowing us to speak of self-control or willed action. If rules have not been followed, the interpreting, conscious self can also act to punish itself through self-evaluations leading to distress or through initiating actions that are painful or difficult.

Individual differences in self-regulatory controls such as effort, ego-control, and ego-resiliency would be expected to contribute strongly to these aspects of self. Self-control at the level of verbal self-regulation has been much studied recently by social-learning theorists such as Bandura (1986). It should be noted, however, that Bandura's work on self-efficacy stresses individuals' *cognitive* judgments of self-efficacy. We have considered here the possibility, however, that many feelings of the self as efficacious or uncertain are present at a much earlier time than are verbal judgments of the self's efficacy. They are present in the sensorimotor self. In addition, it is likely that these sensorimotor feelings of effectance or inadequacy *continue* to precede and accompany action when conscious controls are not actively operating. With development, cognitive components of self are added, but the feeling and acting aspects of self will persist, and they can be seen in feelings of helplessness or in experiences of strong self-control that can in turn influence self-related cognitions.

Later important developments in self-perception will come when the child is able to rank the self in comparison with others; this activity takes on added power in a society such as the United States that stresses individual success and competition with others. As the child comes to understand that objects possess qualities over time and across transformations, and that people also possess qualities across time and over situations (personality traits), the child finds further sources of self-evaluation that can lead to positive or negative emotions (Damon & Hart, 1982). At this point, the child will be able to feel negative or positive emotions in ways that are greatly distanced from the early experiences of the sensorimotor self. Again, temperamental individual differences can contribute to the salience of positive or negative rankings and qualities one assigns oneself in self-evaluation.

The qualities persons assign to themselves can of course also include an understanding of their own temperament. Chess and Thomas, in Chapter 19 of this volume, note that knowledge of one's temperament can lead a person to structure situations so as to keep a given temperamental disposition under control. Thus, a person with an intense temper may attempt to avoid situations where expression of anger would be likely. This understanding of one's temperament allows for an increasing flexibility in behavioral control that goes far beyond the newborn infant's reactions, and it

makes stability of the expression of temperament from infancy to adulthood less
likely.

Self-Regulation via Others: Horney's Theory

Let us now consider some of the ways in which children (and adults) can make use
of others for their own self-regulatory purposes, through reviewing a few aspects
of Karen Horney's (1939, 1945, 1950) theory of personality. Negative self-
evaluation is a potent source of distress to the socialized individual, and Horney's
theory speaks to the issue of the person's attempts to avoid negative self-
evaluations. She suggests that children and adults set up for themselves the goal of
achieving and maintaining an ideal self, constructed from images they have received
from their parents and culture, a goal that is actually impossible to attain. Attempts
to meet the goal will thus frequently be seen to be inadequate according to the
person's internalized standards. Because the ideal self is impossible to attain, the
knowledge of failure to achieve it can potentially create great distress for the
person. To circumvent negative feelings associated with this self-evaluation,
individuals may externalize or shift the responsibility for their imperfect and
undesirable actions or thoughts to others. In doing so, sources of bad or possibly
self-incriminatory acts are seen as existing outside the self, so that anxiety resulting
from feelings of failure will be circumvented.

Horney suggests that persons develop strategies of orienting themselves with
respect to others that allow them to avoid anxiety. One of these orientations
involves moving toward others and letting them take care of us. As the other person
provides care, so the other person can also be given the responsibility for decisions
we have let them make (or perceived them as making). In Horney's model, self-
protective needs associated with this orientation include the need for affection and
approval and the need for a dominant partner in living. When satisfaction of these
needs is threatened, the person may be subject to powerful anxiety.

The second orientation involves moving against others, while perceiving
ourselves as the source of right and others frequently as the source of wrong.
Self-protective needs associated with this orientation include needs for power and
prestige, personal admiration by others, and personal achievement. The third
orientation involves our moving away from others, mentally or physically or both,
so as to be free of the pain of inadequate social interaction. The latter orientation
often involves setting narrowly confined limits of life, and is associated with self-
protective needs of self-sufficiency and independence, perfection, and unassail-
ability (Bischof, 1970).

Assuming that any individual may make use of one or a variety of these
orientations, would individual differences in temperament be expected to incline a
person to one or another of these approaches? One possibility is that the child who
is easily soothed may come to view others as sources of support from a very early
age. Fries and Woolf (1953) have also argued that a quiet child might be especially
likely to be cared for by others, predisposing this child toward the use of dependent
strategies. We might also expect that the child who is fearful or easily overwhelmed
by situations might develop a strategy of narrowing the field, thereby keeping

circumstances under control, and avoiding highly stimulating confrontations with others. Individuals with strong approach tendencies, on the other hand, might be especially prone to experiencing frustrations in dealings with others and reacting to those frustrations with impulses toward action against others. Strong behavioral inhibition or ego-control will of course counter these aggressive impulses.

Given that individuals represent a mixture of temperamental dispositions and that the culture (as in the establishment of gender roles) and life situations create pressure for differing adaptations, a typology of individual personality orientations is no more appropriate than is a typology of temperaments. Nevertheless, making connections across the domains of temperament and personality theory may be very useful in our ultimate understanding of social and emotional development.

Mastery Motivation, Temperament, and Effectance

Susan Harter (1978) has developed a framework for thinking about the development of effectance or mastery motivation that is especially well suited to relating temperament and social learning. In her model, Harter describes socialization promoting effectance motivation as including the adult's use of positive reinforcement, approval of independent mastery events in the child, and lack of reinforcement for the child's dependent actions. Other influences on the development of effectance motivation include the availability of optimal challenges and successes, the child's internalization of goals and self-rewards, the experience of intrinsic satisfactions, and self-perceived competence and control. All are likely to affect attitudes of approach toward problems. Bandura and Schunk's (1981) research also suggests that increasing the children's perceived self-efficacy will result in increased activity and approach in a given situation

Socialization detracting from effectance motivation includes adult disapproval or lack of reinforcement for the child's independent attempts at mastery and reinforcement of dependency on adults. Other negative influences include the experience of failure at mastery attempts (and, I would add, lack of available challenges), anxiety in achievement situations, dependence on external goals and approval, and perceived lack of competence and control. Harter takes a componential approach to these influences and effects, allowing her to chart the developmental course of different elements of the model. In her work, she goes beyond the relatively non-developmental approaches of some of the major social-learning theorists (e.g. Bandura, 1974; Mischel, 1973). Harter's model suggests that the experience of children in a situation will influence their tendency to approach or withdraw from it.

We might now briefly consider how constructs of temperament could make a contribution to Harter's model. Individual differences in negative emotionality and behavioral inhibition might predispose some children to feelings of failure and anxiety in connection with achievement; environmental supports for mastery may be especially important for these children. Other more positive and approaching children may be especially predisposed toward the intrinsic pleasures associated with mastery attempts. These latter children may also make their parents 'look good' in their socialization of achievement in that they rarely make dependency overtures or show reliance on adult judgments of successful performance.

It is true that we do not yet understand temperament well enough to allow a detailed understanding of social and emotional development. Nevertheless, research work to date does allow us to grasp the outlines of individual differences among children that need to be considered in such models. It is highly unlikely, given the complexity of temperament and the complexity of environments and environment–temperament interactions, that we will ever be able to make strong predictions of outcomes for individuals in society. Nevertheless, it is not too early to consider the major socialization values associated with the study of temperament since the pioneering work of Chess, Thomas, and Escalona: respect for the individuality and integrity of each child, and flexibility in creating environments that may lead to positive outcomes for them and for us.

ACKNOWLEDGMENTS

This work has been supported in part by NIMH grants 2674 and 43361 and by a grant from the Center for the Study of Women in Society, University of Oregon. The author is very grateful to Susan Green, Dolph Kohnstamm, Adam Matheny, Michael Posner, Myron Rothbart and Alexander Thomas for their critical comments.

REFERENCES

Achenbach, T.M. (1982). *Developmental psychopathology*, 2nd edn. New York: Wiley.

Adamson, L.B. & Bakeman, R. (1985). Affect and attention: Infants observed with mothers and peers. *Child Development*, **56**, 582–593.

Ainsworth, M.D.S. (1973). The development of infant–mother interaction. In B.M. Caldwell & H.N. Ricciuti (Eds), *Review of child development research*, Vol. 3. Chicago: University of Chicago Press.

Ames, E.W., Khazaie, S., Gavel, S. & Farrell, T. (in press). Mother's reports of the effectiveness of soothing techniques. *Cry Newsletter*.

Bakeman, R. & Brown, J.V. (1980). Early interaction: Consequences for social and mental development at three years. *Child Development*, **51**, 437–447.

Bandura, A. (1974). Behavior theory and the models of man. *American Psychologist*, **29**, 859–869.

Bandura, A. (1982). Self-efficacy mechanisms in human agency. *American Psychologist*, **37**, 122–147.

Bandura, A. (1986). *Social foundations of thought and action: A social cognitive theory*. New York: Prentice-Hall.

Bandura, A. & Schunk, D.H. (1981). Cultivating competence, self-efficacy, and intrinsic interest through proximal self-motivation. *Journal of Personality and Social Psychology*, **41**, 586–598.

Bardwick, J. (1971). *Psychology of women*. New York: Harper.

Bates, J.E. (1987). Temperament in infancy. In J.D. Osofsky (Ed.), *Handbook of infant development* (pp. 1101–1149). New York: Wiley.

Bates, J.E., Freeland, C.A.B. & Lounsberry, M.L. (1979). Measurement of infant difficultness. *Child Development*, **50**, 794–803.

Bates, J.E., Maslin, C.A. & Frankel, K.A. (1985). Attachment security, mother–child interaction, and temperament as predictors of behavior problem ratings at age three years.

In I. Bretherton & E. Waters (Eds), *Growing points in attachment theory. Monographs of the Society for Research in Child Development*, Serial No. 209.

Bates, J.E., Olson, S.L., Pettit, G.S. & Bayles, K. (1982). Dimensions of individuality in the mother–infant relationship at 6 months of age. *Child Development*, **53**, 446–461.

Battle, E. & Lacey, B. (1972). A context for hyperactivity in children over time. *Chia Development*, **43**, 757–773.

Bayley, N. & Schaefer, E.S. (1963). Consistency of maternal and child behavior in the Berkeley Growth Study. *American Psychologist*, **18**, No. 7.

Beckwith, L. (1979). Prediction of emotional and social behavior. In J.D. Osofsky (Ed.), *Handbook of infant development* (pp. 671–706). New York: Wiley.

Bell, R.Q. (1974). Contributions of human infants to caregiving and social interaction. In M. Lewis & L.A. Rosenblum (Eds), *The effect of the infant on its caregiver* (pp. 1–20). New York: Wiley.

Bell, R.Q., Weller, G.M. & Waldrop, M. (1971). Newborn and preschooler: Organization of behavior and relations between periods. *Monographs of the Society for Research in Child Development*, **36** (1–2, Whole No. 142).

Bell, S.M. & Ainsworth, M.D.S. (1972). Infant crying and maternal responsiveness. *Child Development*, **43**, 1171–1190.

Berridge, K.C. & Grill, H.J. (1984a). Alternating ingestive and aversive consummatory responses suggest a two-dimensional analysis of palatability in rats. *Behavioral Neuroscience*, **97**, 563–573.

Berridge, K.C. & Grill, H.J. (1984b). Isohedonic tastes support a two-dimensional hypothesis of palatability. *Appetite*, **5**, 221–231.

Birns, B. (1965). Individual differences in human neonates' responses to stimulation. *Child Development*, **36**, 249–256.

Birns, B., Barten, S. & Bridger, W. (1969). Individual differences in temperamental characteristics of infants. *Transactions of the New York Academy of Sciences*, **31**, 1071–1082.

Bischof, L.J. (1970). *Interpreting personality theories*, 2nd edn. New York: Harper & Row.

Block, J.H. & Block, J. (1980). The role of ego-control and ego-resiliency in the organization of behavior. In W.A. Collins (Ed.), *Minnesota symposium on child psychology*, Vol. 13 (pp. 39–101). New York: Erlbaum.

Bloom, L.B., Beckwith, R. & Capatides, J. (1987). Developments in the expression of affect. Manuscript, Columbia University.

Bornstein, M.H., Gaughran, J.M. & Nomel, P. (1986). Infant temperament: Theory, tradition, critique, and new assessments. In C.E. Izard & P.B. Read (Eds), *Measuring emotions in infants and young children*, Vol. II (pp. 172–202). Cambridge: Cambridge University Press.

Bowlby, J. (1969). *Attachment and loss*, Vol. 1, *Attachment*. New York: Basic Books.

Bradley, B.S. (1985). Failure to distinguish between people and things in early infancy. *British Journal of Developmental Psychology*, **3**, 281–291.

Bradshaw, D.L., Goldsmith, H.H. & Campos, J.J. (1988). *Attachment, temperament, and social referencing: Interrelationships among three domains of infant affective behavior*. Center for the Study of Emotion Technical Report No. 88–02, University of Oregon.

Brazelton, T.B. (1973). *Neonatal Behavioral Assessment Scale*. London: Spastics International Medical Publications.

Brazelton, T.B. (1984). *Neonatal Behavioral Assessment Scale*, 2nd edn. London: Spastics International Medical Publications.

Brazelton, T.B. (1985). Application of cry research to clinical perspectives. In B.M. Lester & C.F.Z. Boukydis (Eds), *Infant crying: Theoretical and research perspectives* (pp. 325–340). New York: Plenum.

Brazelton, T.B., Koslowski, B. & Main, M. (1974). The origins of reciprocity: The early mother–infant interaction. In M. Lewis & L.A. Rosenblum (Eds), *The effect of the infant on its caregiver*. New York: Wiley.

Brazelton, T.B., Nugent, J.K. & Lester, B.M. (1987). Neonatal Behavioral Assessment Scale.

In J.D. Osofsky (Ed.), *Handbook of infant development* (pp. 780–817). New York: Wiley.

Brock, S.E., Rothbart, M.K. & Derryberry, D. (1986). Heart rate deceleration and smiling in 3-month-old infants. *Infant Behavior and Development, 9,* 403–414.

Bronson, G. (1974). The postnatal growth of visual capacity. *Child Development, 45,* 873–890.

Bronson, W.C. (1966). Central orientations: A study of behavior organization from childhood to adolescence. *Child Development, 37,* 125–155.

Bronson, W.C. (1967). Adult derivatives of emotional expressiveness and reactivity control: Developmental continuities from childhood to adulthood. *Child Development, 38,* 801–817.

Bronson, W.C. (1972). The role of enduring orientations to the environment in personality development. *Genetic Psychology Monographs, 86,* 3–80.

Buss, A.H. & Plomin, R. (1975). *A temperament theory of personality development.* New York: Wiley.

Buss, A.H. & Plomin, R. (1984). *Temperament: Early developing personality traits.* Hillsdale, NJ: Erlbaum.

Buss, D.M. (1981). Predicting parent–child interactions from children's activity level. *Developmental Psychology, 17,* 598–5.

Buss, D.M., Block, J.H. & Block, J. (1980). Preschool activity level: Personality correlates and developmental implications. *Child Development, 51,* 401–408.

Byrne, J.M., Clark-Touesnard, M.E., Hondas, B.J. & Smith, I.M. (1985). Stability of individual differences in infant visual attention. Poster presented at meetings of the Society for Research in Child Development, Toronto, April 1985.

Cairns, R.B. & Hood, K.E. (1983). Continuity in social development: A comparative perspective on individual difference prediction. In P.B. Baltes & O.G. Brim (Eds), *Life-span development and behavior,* Vol. 5 (pp. 301–358). New York: Academic Press.

Campos, J.J., Barrett, K.C., Lamb, M.E., Goldsmith, H.H., & Stenberg, C. (1983). Socioemotional development. In M. M. Haith & J. J. Campos, Vol. Eds, for P.H. Mussen (Ed.), *Handbook of Child Psychology, Volume II: Infancy and developmental biology.* New York: Wiley, 783–916.

Carey, W.B. & McDevitt, S.C. (1978). Revision of the Infant Temperament Questionnaire. *Pediatrics, 61,* 375–379.

Carr, T.H., Brown, T.L. & Vavrus, L.G. (1985). Using component skills analysis to integrate findings on reading development. In T.H. Carr (Ed.), *The development of reading skills* (pp. 95–108). San Francisco: Jossey-Bass.

Caudill, W.D. & Weinstein, H. (1969). Maternal care and infant behavior in Japan and America. *Psychiatry, 32,* 12–43.

Church, J. (1961). *Language and the discovery of reality.* New York: Vintage Books.

Cloninger, C.R. (1986). A unified biosocial theory of personality and its role in the development of anxiety states. *Psychiatric Developments, 3,* 167–226.

Cloninger, C.R. (1987a). Neurogenetic adaptive mechanisms in alcoholism. *Science, 236,* 410–416.

Cloninger, C.R. (1987b). A systematic method for clinical description and classification of personality variants. *Archives of General Psychiatry, 44,* 573–588.

Cohen, L.B. (1972). Attention-getting and attention-holding processes of infant visual preferences. *Child Development, 43,* 869–879.

Cohen, L.B. (1976). Habituation of infant visual attention. In T.J. Tighe & R.N. Leaton (Eds), *Habituation.* Hillsdale, NJ: Erlbaum.

Coldren, J.T., Colombo, J., O'Brien, M., Martinez, R. & Horowitz, F.D. (1987). The relationship of infant visual attention across social interaction and information processing tasks. Paper presented at meetings of the Society for Research in Child Development, Baltimore, April 1987.

Columbo, J. T., O'Brien, M., Mitchell, D.W. & Horowitz, F.D. (1986). Infant visual habituation: Stability and reliability in the first year. Paper presented at the International Conference of Infant Studies, Los Angeles, April 1986.

Coltheart, M. (1985). Cognitive neurospsychology and the study of reading. In M.I. Posner & O.S.M. Marin (Eds), *Attention and performance XI* (pp. 3–37). Hillsdale, NJ: Erlbaum.

Crockenberg, S. & Smith, P. (1982). Antecedents of mother–infant interaction and infant irritability in the first three months of life. *Infant Behavior and Development*, 5, 105–119.

Damon, W. & Hart, D. (1982). The development of self-understanding from infancy through adolescence. *Child Development*, 53, 841–864.

Derryberry, D. & Rothbart, M.K. (1984). Emotion, attention, and temperament. In C. Izard, J. Kagan & R. Zajonc (Eds), *Emotion, cognition and behavior*. Cambridge: Cambridge University Press.

Derryberry, D., & Rothbart, M.K. (1988). Arousal, affective and attentional components of adult temperament. *Journal of Personality and Social Psychology,* 55, 953–966.

Diamond, A. (1981). Retrieval of an object from an open box. Paper presented at the meetings of the Society for Research in Child Development, Boston.

Diamond, A. (1985). Development of the ability to use recall to guide action, as indicated by infants' performance on AB̄. *Child Development*, 56, 868–883.

Diamond, S. (1974). *The roots of psychology*. New York: Basic Books.

Douglas, V.I. (1980). Treatment and training approaches to hyperactivity: Establishing internal or external control. In C.K. Whalen & B. Henker (Eds), *Hyperactive children*. New York: Academic Press.

Duffy, K.E., Jamison, K. & Comrey, A.L. (1969). Assessment of a proposed expansion of the Comrey Personality Factor System. *Multivariate Behavioral Research*, 4, 295–307.

Eaton, W.A., & Enns, L.R. (1986). Sex differences in human motor activity level. *Psychological Bulletin*, 100, 19–28.

Eckblad, G. (1981). *Schema theory*. New York: Academic Press.

Emde, R.N., Gaensbauer, T.J. & Harmon, R.J. (1976). Emotion expression in infancy. *Psychological Issues*, Monograph No. 37.

Emde, R.N. & Robinson, J. (1978). The first two months: Recent research in developmental psychobiology and the changing view of the newborn. In J. Noshpitz & J. Call (Eds), *American handbook of child psychiatry*. New York: Basic Books.

Emmerich, W. (1964). Continuity and stability in early social development. *Child Development*, 35, 311–322.

Emmerich, W. (1968). Personality development and concepts of structure. *Child Development*, 39, 671–690.

Escalona, S.K. (1968). *The roots of individuality: Normal patterns of development in infancy*. Chicago: Aldine.

Eysenck, H.J. (1967). *The biological basis of personality*. Springfield, IL: Charles C. Thomas.

Eysenck, H.J. (Ed.) (1976). *The measurement of personality*. Baltimore, MD: University Park Press.

Eysenck, H.J. & Eysenck, M.W. (1985). *Personality and individual differences*. New York: Plenum.

Eysenck, H.J. & Eysenck, S.B.G. (1975). *Manual of the Eysenck Personality Questionnaire*. San Diego: Edits.

Eysenck, S.B.G. (1965). *Manual of the Junior Eysenck Personality Inventory*. London: Hodder & Stoughton.

Fraiberg, S. (1974). Blind infants and their mothers: An examination of the sign system. In M. Lewis & L. Rosenblum (Eds), *The effect of the infant on its caregiver*. New York: Wiley.

Fraiberg, S. (1977). *Every child's birthright: In defense of mothering*. New York: Basic Books.

Freedman, D.G. & Freedman, N.A. (1969). Differences in behavior between Chinese-American and European–American newborns. *Nature*, 224, 1227.

Friedman, M. & Rosenman, R.H. (1974). *Type A behavior and your heart*. New York: Knopf.

Friedman, S. (1972). Habituation and recovery of visual response in the alert human newborn. *Journal of Experimental Child Psychology*, **13**, 339–349.

Fries, M.E. (1954). Some hypotheses on the role of congenital activity types in personality development. *International Journal of Psychoanalysis*, **35**, 206–207.

Fries, M.E. & Woolf, P. (1953). Some hypotheses on the role of congenital activity type in personality development. In R. Eissler *et al.* (Eds), *The psychoanalytic study of the child*, Vol. 8. New York: International Universities Press.

Frodi, A.M., Lamb, M.E., Leavitt, L.A. & Donovan, W.L. (1978). Fathers' and mothers' responses to infant smiles and cries. *Infant Behavior and Development*, **1**, 187–198.

Fullard, W., McDevitt, S.C. & Carey, W.B. (1980). Toddler Temperament Scale. Unpublished manuscript, Department of Educational Psychology, Temple University.

Garai, J.E. & Scheinfeld, A. (1968). Sex differences in mental and behavioral traits. *Genetic Psychology Monographs*, **77**, 269–299.

Garcia-Coll, C.T., Kagan, J. & Reznick, J.S. (1984). Behavioral inhibition in young children. *Child Development*, **55**, 1005–1019.

Garcia-Coll, C.T., Sepkoski, C. & Lester, M.B. (1982). Effects of teenage childbearing on neonatal behavior in Puerto Rico. *Infant Behavior and Development*, **5**, 227–236.

Gesell, A. & Ames, L.B. (1937). Early evidence on individuality in the human infant. *Scientific Monthly*, **45**, 217–225.

Gibbons, J.L., Johnson, M.O., McDonough, D.M. & Reznick, J.S. (1986). *Behavioral inhibition in infants and children*. Paper presented at the meetings of the International Conference on Infant Studies, Los Angeles, April 1986.

Gobeo, B. (1986). Correlates of shyness in self-report with emphasis on perceived reactivity. Honors thesis, University of Oregon Psychology Department, Eugene, Oregon.

Goldsmith, H.H. & Alansky, J.A. (1987). Maternal and infant temperamental predictors of attachment: A meta-analytic review. *Journal of Consulting and Clinical Psychology*, **55**.

Goldsmith, H.K., Buss, A. H., Plomin, R., Rothbart, M.K., Thomas, A., Chess, S., Hinde, R.A. & McCall, R.B. (1987). Roundtable: What is temperament? Four approaches. *Child Development*, **58**, 505–529.

Goldsmith, H.H. & Campos, O. (1982). Toward a theory of infant temperament. In R. Emde & R. Harmon (Eds), *Attachment and affiliative systems* (pp. 161–193). New York: Plenum.

Goldsmith, H.H. & Campos, J.J. (1986). Fundamental issues in the study of early temperament: The Denver Twin Temperament Study. In M.H. Lamb & A. Brown (Eds), *Advances in developmental psychology*. Hillsdale, NJ: Erlbaum.

Graham, F.K., Strock, B.D. & Ziegler, B.L. (1981). Excitatory and inhibitory influences on reflex responsiveness. In W.A. Collins (Ed.), *Aspects of the development of competence*. Hillsdale, NJ: Erlbaum.

Gray, J.A. (1971). *The psychology of fear and stress*. New York: McGraw-Hill.

Gray, J.A. (1982). *The neuropsychology of anxiety*. Oxford: Oxford University Press.

Guilford, J.P. & Zimmerman, S. (1956). Fourteen dimensions of temperament. *Psychological Monographs*, **70** (Whole No. 417).

Hagekull, B. & Bohlin, G. (1981). Individual stability in dimensions of infant behavior. *Infant Behavior and Development*, **4**, 97–108.

Halverson, C.F., Moss, H.A. & Jones-Kearns, S.J. (1977). Longitudinal antecedents of preschool social behavior. Paper presented at the meetings of the Society for Research in Child Development, New Orleans, March 1977.

Halverson, C.F. & Waldrop, M.F. (1973). The relations of mechanically recorded activity level to varieties of preschool play behavior. *Child Development*, **44**, 678–681.

Halverson, C.F. & Waldrop, M.F. (1976). Relations between preschool activity and aspects of intellectual and social behavior at age 7½. *Developmental Psychology*, **12**, 107–112.

Harter, S. (1978). Effectance motivation reconsidered: Toward a developmental model. *Human Development*, **21**, 34–64.

Harter, S. (1983). Developmental perspectives on the self-system. In E.M. Hetherington, Vol. Ed. for P.H. Mussen (Ed.), *Handbook of child psychology*, Vol. IV: *Socialization, personality and social development* (pp. 275–386). New York: Wiley.

Hinde, R.A. (1983). Ethology and child development. In M.M. Haith & J.J. Campos, Vol. Eds for P.H. Mussen (Ed.), *Handbook of child psychology*, Vol. II: *Infancy and developmental biology* (pp. 27–94). New York: Wiley.

Hinde, R.A. & Bateson, P. (1984). Discontinuities versus continuities in behavioral development and the neglect of process. *International Journal of Behavioral Development*, 7, 129–143.

Hochschild, A.K. (1979). Emotion work, feeling rules, and social structure. *American Journal of Sociology*, 85, 551–575.

Hoffman, M.L. (1975). Developmental synthesis of affect and cognition and its implications for altruistic motivation. *Developmental Psychology*, 11, 605–622.

Hoffman, M.L. (1981). Development of the motive to help others. In J.P. Rushton & R.M. Sorrentino (Eds), *Altruism and helping behavior: Social, personality and developmental perspectives*. Hillside, NJ: Erlbaum.

Honzik, M.P. (1965). Prediction of behavior from birth to maturity. (Book review.) *Merill-Palmer Quarterly*, 11, 77–88.

Horney, K. (1937). *The neurotic personality of our time*. New York: Norton.

Horney, K. (1945). *Our inner conflicts*. New York: Norton.

Horney, K. (1950). *Neurosis and human growth*. New York: Norton.

Horowitz, F.D. & Zinn, P.L. (1987). The Neonatal Behavioral Assessment Scale. In M. Wolraich & D.K. Routh (Eds), *Advances in behavioral pediatrics*, Vol. 3. Greenwich, CT: JAI.

Hsu, C.C., Soong, W.T., Stigler, J.W., Hong, C.C. & Liang, C.C. (1981). The temperamental characteristics of Chinese babies. *Child Development*, 52, 1337–1340.

Huttenen, M.O. & Nyman, G. (1982). On the continuity, change and clinical value of infant temperament in a prospective epidemiological study. In R. Porter & G.M. Collins (Eds), *Temperamental differences in infants and young children* (pp. 240–247). Ciba Foundation Symposium 89. London: Pitman.

Izard, C.E. (1977). *Human emotions*. New York: Plenum.

Jacklin, C.N. & Maccoby, E.E. (1978). Social behavior at thirty-three months in same-sex and mixed-sex dyads. *Child Development*, 49, 557–569.

Kagan, J. (1971). *Change and continuity in infancy*. New York: Wiley.

Kagan, J. (1974). Discrepancy, temperament and infant distress. In M. Lewis & L. A. Rosenblum (Eds.), *The origins of fear* (pp. 229–248). New York: Wiley.

Kagan, J. (1982a). *Psychological research on the human infant: An evaluative summary*. New York: W.T. Grant Foundation.

Kagan, J. (1982b). The construct of difficult temperament: A reply to Thomas, Chess and Korn. *Merrill-Palmer Quarterly*, 28, 21–24.

Kagan, J. & Moss, H.A. (1962). *Birth to maturity*. New York: Wiley.

Kagan, J. & Reznick, S. (1986). Temperamental inhibition in early childhood. In R. Plomin & J. Dunn (Eds), *The study of temperament: Change, continuities, and challenges* (pp. 53–67). Hillsdale, NJ: Erlbaum.

Kagan, J., Kearsley, R.B. & Zelazo, P.R. (1978). *Infancy: Its place in human development*. Cambridge, MA: Harvard University Press.

Kagan, J., Reznick, S. & Snidman, N. (1987). The physiology and psychology of behavioral inhibition in young children. *Child Development*, 58, 1459–1473.

Kaye, K. (1978). Discriminating among normal infants by multivariate analysis of Brazelton scores: Lumping and smoothing. In A.J. Sameroff (Ed.), *Organization and stability of newborn behavior. A commentary on the Brazelton Neonatal Behavior Assessment Scale. Monographs of the Society for Research in Child Development*, 43 (Serial No. 177), No. 5–6, 60–80.

Keele, S.W. & Hawkins, H.H. (1982). Explorations of individual differences relevant to high level skill. *Journal of Motor Behavior*, 14, 3–23.

Keele, S.W., Pokorny, R.A., Corcos, D.M. & Ivry, R. (1985). Do perception and production share common timing mechanisms?: A correlational analysis. *Acta Psychologia*, 60, 173–191.

Kenofer, B., Rothbart, M.K. & O'Curry, S. (in preparation). Looking and acting: Individual differences in fixation time and activity level during infancy.

Keogh, B., Pullis, M.E. & Caldwell, J. (1982). A short form of the Teacher Temperament Questionnaire. *Journal of Educational Measurement*, **19**, 323–329.

Kinsbourne, M. (1984). Toward a model for the attentional deficit disorder. *Minnesota Symposium on Child Psychology*, **16**, 137–166.

Kistiakovskaia, M.I. (1965). Stimuli evoking positive emotions in infants in the first months of life. *Soviet Psychology and Psychiatry*, **3**, 39–48.

Kopp, C.B. (1982). Antecedents of self-regulation: A developmental perspective. *Developmental Psychology*, **18**, 199–214.

Korner, A.F. (1972). State as a variable, as obstacle and as mediator of stimulation in infant research. *Merrill-Palmer Quarterly*, **18**, 77–94.

Korner, A.F. & Thoman, E.B. (1972). The relative efficacy of contact and vestibular-proprioceptive stimulation in soothing neonates. *Child Development*, **43**, 443–453.

Krakow, J.B. & Johnson, K.L. (1981). The emergence and consolidation of self-control processes from 18 to 30 months of age. Paper presented at the meetings of the Society for Research in Child Development, Boston, April 1981.

Krakow, J.B., Kopp, C.B. & Vaughn, B.E. (1981). Sustained attention during the second year: Age trends, individual differences, and implications for development. Paper presented at the meetings of the Society for Research in Child Development, Boston, April 1981.

Lagrasse, L., Gruber, C. & Lipsitt, L. (in press). The infantile expression of avidity in relation to later assessments of inhibition and attachment. In S. Reznick (Ed.), *Perpectives in behavioral inhibition*. Chicago: University of Chicago Press.

Larson, S.K., DiPietro, J.A. & Porges, S.M. (1987). Neonatal and NBAS performance are related to development across at 15 months. Paper presented at meetings of Society for Research in Child Development, Baltimore, MD, April 1987.

Lawson, K.R. & Turkewitz, G. (1980). Intersensory function in newborns: Effect of sound in visual performance. *Child Development*, **51**, 1295–1298.

Lee, C. & Bates, J. (1985). Mother–child interaction at age two years and perceived difficult temperament. *Child Development*, **56**, 1314–1326.

Lerner, J.V. & Lerner, R.M. (1983). Temperament and adaptation across life: Theoretical and empirical issues. In. P.B. Baltes & O.G. Brim (Eds), *Life-span development and behavior*, Vol. 5 (pp. 197–231). New York: Academic Press.

Lewis, M. & Brooks, J. (1978). Self-knowledge and emotional development. In M. Lewis & L.A. Rosenblum (Eds), *The development of affect*. New York: Plenum.

Lewkowicz, D.J. & Turkewitz, G. (1981). Intersensory interaction in newborns: Modification of visual preferences following exposure to sound. *Child Development*, **52**, 827–832.

Lipton, E.L., Steinschneider, A. & Richmond, J.B. (1961). Autonomic function in the neonate: Individual differences in cardiac reactivity. *Psychosomatic Medicine*, **23**, 472–484.

Lipton, E.L., Steinschneider, A. & Richmond, J.B. (1966). Autonomic function in the neonate: VII. Maturational changes in cardiac control. *Child Development*, **37**, 1–16.

Luria, A.R. (1961). *The role of speech in the regulation of normal and abnormal behavior*. New York: Liveright.

Luria, A.R. (1966). *Higher cortical functions in man*. New York: Basic Books.

Maccoby, E.E. (1980). *Social development*. New York: Harcourt Brace Jovanovich.

Maccoby, E.E. & Jacklin, C.N. (1974). *The psychology of sex differences*. Stanford, CA: Stanford University Press.

MacDonald, K.B. (1989). *Social and personality development*. New York: Plenum.

Malatesta, C.A., Grigoryev, P., Lamb, C., Albin, M. & Culver, C. (1986). Emotion socialization and expressive development in preterm and full-term infants. *Child Development*, **57**, 316–330.

Martin, R. (1984). *The Temperament Assessment Battery Manual*. University of Georgia, unpublished manuscript.

Matheny, A.P., & Dolan, A.B. (1975). Persons, situations and time: A genetic view of behavioral change in children. *Journal of Personality and Social Psychology, 32,* 1106–1110.

Matheny, A.P., Jr, Riese, M.L. & Wilson, R.S. (1985). Rudiments of infant temperament: Newborn to nine months. *Developmental Psychology, 21,* 486–494.

Matheny, A.P., Jr, Wilson, R.S. & Nuss, S.M. (1984). Toddler temperament: Stability across settings and over ages. *Child Development, 55,* 1200–1211.

Matthews, K.A. (1982). Psychological perspectives on the Type A behavior pattern. *Psychological Bulletin, 91,* 293–323.

Maziade, M., Boudreault, M., Thivierge, J., Caperaa, P. & Cote, R. (1984). Infant temperament: SES and gender differences and reliability of measurement in a large Quebec sample. *Merrill-Palmer Quarterly, 30,* 213–216.

McCall, R.B. (1979). Qualitative transitions in behavioral development in the first two years of life. In M.H. Bornstein & W. Kessen (Eds), *Psychological development from infancy: Image to intention* (pp. 183–224). Hillsdale, NJ: Erlbaum.

McCall, R.B. (1981). Nature–nurture and the two realms of development: A proposed integration with respect to mental development. *Child Development, 52,* 1–12.

McCall, R.B. (1986). Issues of stability and continuity in temperament research. In R. Plomin & J. Dunn (Eds), *The study of temperament: Changes, continuities and challenges* (pp. 13–26). Hillsdale, NJ: Erlbaum.

McCrae, R.R. & Costa, P.T., Jr (1985). Updating Norman's 'Adequate Taxonomy': Intelligence and personality dimensions in natural language and in questionnaires. *Journal of Personality and Social Psychology, 49,* 710–721.

McDevitt, S.C. & Carey, W.F. (1981). Stability of ratings vs. perceptions of temperament from early infancy to 1–3 years. *American Journal of Orthopsychiatry, 51,* 342–345.

McGuire, I. & Turkewitz, G. (1979). Approach–withdrawal theory and the study of infant development. In M. Bortner (Ed.), *Cognitive growth and development.* New York: Brunner/Mazel.

Miller, E.M. & Bates, J.E. (1986). Relationships between mother perceptions and observed episodes of infant distress: Components of perceived difficult temperament. Paper presented at the meetings of the International Conference on Infant Studies, Los Angeles, April 1986.

Minton, C., Kagan, J. & Levine, J. (1971). Maternal control and obedience in the two-year-old. *Child Development, 42,* 1873–1894.

Mischel, W. (1973). Toward a cognitive social learning theory reconceptualization of personality. *Psychological Review, 80,* 252–283.

Mischel, W. (1983). Delay of gratification as process and as person variable in development. In D. Magnusson & V.P. Allen (Eds), *Human development: An interactional perspective* (pp. 149–165). New York: Academic Press.

Moss, H.A. (1967). Sex, age and state as determinants of mother–infant interaction. *Merrill-Palmer Quarterly, 13,* 19–36.

Moss, H.A. & Sussman, E.J. (1980). Longitudinal study of personality development. In O.G. Brim & J. Kagan (Eds), *Constancy and change in human development.* Cambridge, MA: Harvard University Press.

Muir, D. & Field, J. (1979). Newborn infants orient to sounds. *Child Development, 50,* 431–436.

Murphy, L.B. (1981). Explorations in child personality. In A.I. Rabin, J. Aronoff, A.M. Barcley & R.A. Zucker (Eds), *Further explorations in personality* (pp. 161–195). New York: Wiley.

Nebylitsyn, V.D. (1950). The relation between sensitivity and strength of the nervous system. In B.M. Teplov (Ed.), *Typological features of higher nervous activity in man,* Vol. I. Moscow: Academy of Pedagogy.

Nebylitsyn, V.D. (1972). *Fundamental properties of the human nervous system.* New York: Plenum.

Norman, W.T. (1963). Toward an adequate taxonomy of personality attributes: Replicated factor structure in peer nomination personality ratings. *Journal of Abnormal and Social Psychology*, **66**, 574–583.

Olson, G.M. & Sherman, T. (1983). Attention, learning and memory in infants. In M.M. Haith & J.J. Campos, Vol. Eds for P.H. Mussen (Ed.), *Handbook of child psychology*, Vol. II, *Infancy and the biology of development* (pp. 1001–1080). New York: Wiley.

Osofsky, J. & Danzger, B. (1974). Relationships between neonatal characteristics and mother–infant interaction. *Developmental Psychology*, **10**, 124–130.

Papousek, H. & Papousek, M. (1978). Interdisciplinary parallels in studies of early human behavior: From physical to congitive needs, from attachment to dyadic education. *International Journal of Behavioral Development*, **1**, 37–49.

Pavlov, I.P. (1927). *Conditioned reflexes* New York: Oxford University Press.

Pavlov, I.P. (1928). *Lectures on conditioned reflexes*. New York: International Publishers.

Pederson, F. & Bell, R. (1970). Sex differences in preschool children without histories of complications of pregnancy and delivery. *Developmental Psychology*, **3**, 10–15.

Persson-Blennow, I. & McNeil, T.F. (1980). Questionnaires for measurement of temperament in one- and two-year-old children: Development and standardization. *Journal of Child Psychology and Psychiatry*, **21**, 37–46.

Peters-Martin, P. & Wachs, T. (1984). A longitudinal study of temperament and its correlates in the first 12 months. *Infant Behavior and Development*, **7**, 285–298.

Pettit, G.S. & Bates, J.E. (1984). Continuity of individual differences in the mother–infant relationship from 6 to 13 months. *Child Development*, **55**, 729–739.

Pien, D. & Rothbart, M.K. (1980). Incongruity, humor, play and self-regulation of arousal in young children. In A. Chapman & P. McGhee (Eds), *Children's humor*. New York: Wiley.

Plomin, R. & DeFries, J.C. (1985). *Origins of individual differences in infancy: The Colorado Adoption Project*. New York: Academic Press.

Posner, M.I. (1978). *Chronometric explorations of mind*. Hillsdale, NJ: Erlbaum.

Posner, M.I. & Presti, D.E. (1987). Selection attention and cognitive control. *Trends in Neuroscience*, **10**, 12–17.

Posner, M.I. & Rothbart, M.K. (1981). The development of attentional mechanisms. In J. Flowers (Ed.), *Nebraska Symposium on Motivation*. Lincoln: University of Nebraska Press.

Prechtl, H. (1977). *The neurological examination of the full-term newborn infant*, 2nd edn. London: Spastics International Medical Publications.

Reed, M.A., Pien, D.P. & Rothbart, M.K. (1984). Inhibitory self-control in preschool children. *Merrill-Palmer Quarterly*, **30**, 131–147.

Reznick, J.S., Kagan, J., Snidman, N., Gersten, M., Baak, K. & Rosenberg, A. (1986). Inhibited and unihibited children: A follow-up study. *Child Development*, **57**, 660–680.

Richards, J.E. (in press). Heart rate response and heart rate rhythms and infant visual sustained attention. To appear in P.K. Ackles, J.R. Jennings & M.G.H. Coles (Eds), *Advances in psychophysiology*, Vol. 3. Greenwich, CT: JAI Press.

Riese, M.L. (1987). Temperamental stability between the neonatal period and 24 months. *Developmental Psychology*, **23**, 216–222.

Robson, K.S. & Moss, H.A. (1970). Patterns and determinants of maternal attachment. *Journal of Pediatrics*, **77**, 976–985.

Rosenblum, L.A. & Moltz, H. (1983). *Symbiosis in parent–offspring relations*. New York: Plenum.

Rothbart, M.K. (1973). Laughter in young children. *Psychological Bulletin*, **80**, 247–256.

Rothbart, M.K. (1981). Measurement of temperament in infancy. *Child Development*, **52**, 569–578.

Rothbart, M.K. (1984). Social development. In M.J. Hanson (Ed.), *Atypical infant development*. Baltimore, MD: University Park Press.

Rothbart, M.K. (1986). Longitudinal observation on infant temperament. *Developmental Psychology*, **22**, 356–365.

Rothbart, M.K. (1987). A psychobiological approach to the study of temperament. In. G. Kohnstamm (Ed.), *Temperament discussed* (pp. 63–72). Amsterdam: Swetz & Zeitlinger.

Rothbart, M.K. (1988). Temperament and the development of inhibited approach. *Child Development*, **59**, 1241–1250.

Rothbart, M.K. (in press). Behavioral approach and inhibition. In S. Reznick (Ed.), *Perspectives on behavioral inhibition*. Chicago: University of Chicago Press.

Rothbart, M.K. & Derryberry, D. (1981). Development of individual differences in temperament. In M.E. Lamb & A.L. Brown (Eds), *Advances in developmental psychology*, Vol. 1. Hillsdale, NJ: Erlbaum.

Rothbart, M.K. & Goldsmith, H.H. (1985). Three approaches to the study of infant temperament. *Developmental Review*, **5**, 237–260.

Rothbart, M.K. & Posner, M.I. (1985). Temperament and the development of self regulation. In L.C. Hartlage & C.F. Telzrow (Eds), *The neuropsychology of individual differences: A developmental perpective*. Plenum.

Ruff, H.A. (1986). Components of attention during infants' manipulative exploration. *Child Development*, **52**, 105–114.

Rutter, M. (1972). *Maternal deprivation reassessed*. Baltimore, MD: Penguin.

Rutter, M. (1983). Statistical and personal interactions: Facets and perspectives. In D. Magnusson & V. Allen (Eds), *Human development: an interactional perspective*. New York: Academic Press.

Rutter, M. (1987). Continuities and discontinuities from infancy. In J.D. Osofsky (Ed.), *Handbook of infant development* (pp. 1150–1198). New York: Wiley.

Rutter, M. & Garmezy, N. (1983). Developmental psychopathology. In E.M. Hetherington, Vol. Ed. for P.H. Mussen (Ed.), *Handbook of child psychology*, 4th edn, Vol. 4 (pp. 775–911). New York: Wiley.

Saarni, C. (1979). Children's understanding of display rules for expressive behavior. *Developmental Psychology*, **15**, 424–429.

Saarni, C. (1982). Social and affective functions of nonverbal behavior: Developmental concerns. In R. Feldman (Ed.), *Development of nonverbal behavior*. New York: Springer Verlag.

Sander, L.W. (1962). Issues in early mother–child interaction. *Journal of the American Academy of Child Psychiatry*, **1**, 141–166.

Sander, L.W. (1969). The longitudinal course of early mother–child interaction: Cross case comparison in a sample of mother–child pairs. In B.M. Foss (Ed.), *Determinants of infant behavior*, Vol. IV. London: Methuen.

Schachter, F.F., Shore, E., Hodapp, R., Chalfin, S. & Bundy, C. (1978). Do girls talk earlier? Mean length of utterance in toddlers. *Developmental Psychology*, **14**, 388–392.

Schaefer, E.S. & Bayley, N. (1963). Maternal behavior, child behavior, and their inter-correlations from infancy through adolescence. *Monographs of the Society for Research in Child Development*, **28**, No. 3.

Schaffer, H.R. (1974). Cognitive components of the infant's response to strangeness. In M. Lewis & L.A. Rosenblum (Eds), *The origins of fear*. New York: Wiley.

Schaffer, H.R. & Emerson, P.E. (1964). Patterns of response to physical contact in early human development. *Journal of Child Psychology and Psychiatry*, **5**, 1–13.

Schneirla, T.C. (1959). An evolutionary and developmental theory of biphasic processes underlying approach and withdrawal. Republished in 1959 in L.R. Aronson, E. Tobach, D.S. Lehrman & J. Rosenblatt (Eds), *Selected writings on T.C. Schneirla*. San Francisco: Freeman.

Schneirla, T.C. (1965). Aspects of stimulation and organization in approach–withdrawal processes underlying vertebrate behavior development. Republished in 1972 in L.R. Aronson, E. Tobach, D.S. Lehrman & J. Rosenblatt (Eds), *Selected writings of T.C. Schneirla*. San Francisco: Freeman.

Selman, R. (1980). *The growth of interpersonal understanding*. New York: Academic Press.

Smith, P. & Dagliesh, L. (1977). Sex differences in parent and infant behavior in the home. *Child Development*, **48**, 1250–1254.

Snow, M.E., Jacklin, C.N. & Maccoby, E.E. (1983). Sex-of-child differences in father–child interaction at one year of age. *Child Development*, **54**, 227–232.

Spitz, R.A. (1957). *No and yes: On the genesis of human communication.* New York: International Universities Press.

Sroufe, L.A. (1979). The coherence of individual development. *American Psychologist*, **34**, 834–841.

Sroufe, L.A. & Waters, E. (1977). Attachment as an organizational construct. *Child Development*, **48**, 1184–1199.

Stechler, G. & Latz, E. (1966). Some observations on attention and arousal in the human infant. *Journal of the American Academy of Child Psychiatry*, **5**, 517–525.

Steinschneider, A. (1973). Determinants of an infant's cardiac response to stimulation. In D.N. Walcher & D.L. Peters (Eds), *The development of self-regulatory mechanisms.* New York: Academic Press.

Stern, D.N. (1974). Mother and infant at play: The dyadic interaction involving facial, vocal, and gaze behaviors. In M. Lewis & L.A. Rosenblum (Eds), *The effect of the infant on its caregiver.* New York: Wiley.

Stevenson-Hinde, J. & Hinde, R.A. (1986). Changes in associations between characteristics and interactions. In R. Plomin & J. Dunn (Eds), *The study of temperament: Changes, continuities and challenges.* Hillsdale, NJ: Erlbaum.

Stevenson-Hinde, J. & Simpson, A.E. (1982). Temperament and relationships. In R. Porter & G.M. Collins (Eds), *Temperamental differences in infants and young children* (pp. 51–61). Ciba Foundation Symposium 89. London: Pitman.

Strauss, M.E. & Rourke, D.L. (1978). A multivariate analysis of the neonatal behavioral assessment scale in several samples. In A.J. Sameroff (Ed.), *Organization and stability of newborn behavior. A commentary on the Brazelton Neonatal Behavior Assessment Scale. Monographs of the Society for Research in Child Development*, **43** (Serial No. 177), Nos 5–6, 81–91.

Suomi, S.J. (1984). The development of affect in rhesus monkeys. In N. Fox & R. Davidson (Eds), *The psychobiology of affective development.* Hillsdale, NJ: Erlbaum.

Suomi, S.J. (1986). Anxiety-like disorders in young nonhuman primates. In R. Gittelman, (Ed.), *Anxiety disorders of childhood* (pp. 1–23). New York: Guilford Press.

Tellegen, A. (1985). Structures of mood and personality and their relevance to assessing anxiety, with an emphasis on self-report. In A.H. Tuma & J.D. Maser (Eds), *Anxiety and the anxiety disorders.* Hillsdale, NJ: Erlbaum.

Tennes, K., Emde, R., Kisley, A. & Metcalf, D. (1972). The stimulus barrier in early infancy: An exploration of some formulations of John Benjamin. In. R.R. Holt & E. Peterfreund (Eds), *Psychoanalysis and contemporary science*, Vol. 1. New York: Macmillan.

Thomas, A. & Chess, S. (1977). *Temperament and development.* New York: Brunner/Mazel.

Thomas, A., Chess, S. & Birch, H.G. (1968). *Temperament and behavior disorders in children.* New York: New York University Press.

Thomas, A., Chess, S., Birch, H.G., Hertzig, M.E. & Korn, S. (1963). *Behavioral individuality in early childhood.* New York: New York University Press.

Thomas, A., Chess, S. & Korn, S.J. (1982). The reality of difficult temperament. *Merrill-Palmer Quarterly*, **28**, 1–20.

Tucker, D.M. & Williamson, P.A. (1984). Asymmetric neural control systems in human self-regulation. *Psychological Review*, **91**, 185–215.

Tuddenham, R.D. (1959). The constancy of personality ratings over two decades. *Genetic Psychology Monographs*, **60**, 3–29.

Vygotsky, L.S. (1966). Development of the higher mental functions. In A. Leontyev, A.R. Luria & A. Smirnov (Eds), *Psychological research in the USSR.* Moscow: Progress.

Wachs, T.D. & Gandour, M.J. (1983). Temperament, environment, and six-month cognitive–intellectual development: A test of the organismic specificity hypothesis. *International Journal of Behavioral Development*, **6**, 135–152.

Walker, R.N. (1967). Some temperament traits in children as viewed by their peers, their teachers, and themselves. *Monographs of the Society for Research in Child Development*, **32** (Whole No. 6).

Watson, D. & Clark, L.A. (1984). Negative affectivity: The disposition to experience aversive emotional states. *Psychological Bulletin*, **96**, 465–490.

Watson, D. & Tellegen, A. (1985). Toward a consensual structure of mood. *Psychological Bulletin*, **98**, 219–235.

Webb, E. (1915). Character and intelligence. *British Journal of Psychology Monographs*, **I**, No. 3.

Werner, E. (1988). A cross-cultural perspective on infancy: Research and social issues. *Journal of Cross-Cultural Psychology*, **19**, 96–113.

West, P.D., McLaughlin, F.J., Rieser, J.J., Brooks, P. & O'Connor, S. (1986). Individual differences in infant temperament: Consistency and covariates of self-calming in six month olds. Paper presented at the meetings of the International Conference on Infant Studies, Los Angeles, April 1986.

Wilson, R.S. (1977). Twins and siblings: Concordance for school-age mental development. *Child Development*, **48**, 211–216.

Wilson, R.S., Brown, A.M. & Matheny, A.P., Jr (1971). Emergence and persistence of behavioral differences in twins. *Child Development*, **42**, 1381–1398.

Winnicott, D.W. (1960). The theory of the parent–infant relationship. Republished in 1965 in *The maturational processes and the facilitatious environment* (pp. 37–55). New York: International Universities Press.

Wohlwill, J.F. (1980). Cognitive development in childhood. In O.G. Brim & J. Kagan (Eds), *Constancy and change in human development*. Cambridge, MA: Harvard University Press.

Wolff, P.H. (1965). The development of attention in young infants. *Annals of the New York Academy of Sciences*, **118**, 8–30.

Wolff, P.H. (1966). The causes, controls, and organization of behavior in the neonate. *Psychological Issues*, **5** (Monograph 17).

Wolff, P.H. (1987). *The development of behavioral states and the expression of emotions in early infancy*. Chicago: University of Chicago Press.

Yang, R.K. & Halverson, C.F. (1976). A study of the 'inversion of intensity' between newborn and preschool-age behavior. *Child Development*, **47**, 350–359.

Zuckerman, M. (1979). *Sensation seeking: Beyond the optimal level of arousal*. Hillsdale, NJ: Erlbaum.

Zuckerman, M. (1983). A biological theory of sensation seeking. In M. Zuckerman (Ed.), *Biological bases of sensation seeking, impulsivity and anxiety*. New York: Erlbaum.

13

Temperament and Personality

ALEXANDER THOMAS AND STELLA CHESS
New York University Medical Center

The past few decades have witnessed a progressively increasing body of knowledge concerning the significance of temperament for both normal and abnormal psychological development. These findings have raised a number of important conceptual and practical issues, which are discussed in the other chapters of this volume, as well as in a number of recent publications (Chess & Thomas, 1984; Goldsmith *et al.*, 1987; Plomin & Dunn, 1986; Porter & Collins, 1982). One basic question concerns the relationship of temperament to that broad psychological generalization we label 'personality'. Are temperament and personality just two different formulations of the same group of psychological phenomena? If they differ, in what way do they differ, and how do they influence each other?

CONCEPTS OF PERSONALITY

A voluminous literature of personality studies exists and keeps growing with each passing year. Clinicians and academic psychologists contribute theories and methods of study, and offer data to support their particular theoretical or methodological biases and to challenge opposite formulations. These efforts have not brought a consensus, to say the least. Rather, as Gardner Murphy put it after decades of highly respected personality research, 'the scientific effort to study personality has proved to be extraordinarily difficult. It is a labor fraught with conflict, frustration, the discovery of one's limitations and mistakes, the endless necessity for backtracking and doing over' (Murphy, 1968, p. 16). This judgment still remains valid, 20 years later. Frustrating and difficult it may be, but any developmental theory must come to grips with a conceptualization of personality, unless one takes the mechanical behaviorist stance that personality is part of the unknowable 'black box' of the mind.

In this regard, the lack of consensus over the definition of personality parallels a

Temperament in Childhood   Edited by G.A. Kohnstamm, J.E. Bates and M.K. Rothbart
© 1989 John Wiley & Sons Ltd

similar inability to agree on a definition of temperament, as reviewed in the preceding chapters of this volume by Bates and Rothbart (see Chapters 1 and 12). Rather than attempt a critical review of the various theories of personality, which would require a volume in itself, we should be content to apply McCall's comment regarding the lack of consensus on a definition of temperament also to personality theory: 'We have no very good definition of intelligence either, but that has not stopped us from studying it ... Neither do I worry which definition is correct. To me, definitions are not valid or invalid, confirmable or refutable. Instead, they are more or less useful' (McCall, in Goldsmith *et al.*, 1987, p. 524).

In our own studies, we have found it useful to consider personality to be the composite of those enduring psychological attributes which constitute the unique individuality of the person, and which are expressed in diverse behaviors in different life situations, both concurrently and over time. We agree with the eminent psychiatrist Judd Marmor's (1983) enumeration of the many variables that have to be considered in a systematic study of personality: parenting; temperament; the diverse personality patterns and culturally acquired value systems of the parents; economic, racial and ethnic realities; dietary adequacy or inadequacy; the nature of relationship with sibs, extended family members, peers, teachers and other influential individuals. He concludes, 'We begin to get a glimpse of how difficult it is to accurately trace the origins of specific personality patterns at all, let alone to try to derive them from just one or two variables' (Marmor, 1983, p. 856). A similar criticism of the attempt to derive personality patterns from one or two variables, whether they be temperament, instinctual drive-reduction models, operant conditioning, or any other single factor, has been made forcefully, by (among others) the developmental psychologist Walter Mischel (1977) and the developmental psychiatrist Michael Rutter (1980).

It is true, as Rothbart points out in Chapter 12, that for the young infant temperament constitutes almost the whole personality. Temperament attributes can be identified and rated early in infancy and encompass the greater part of the infant's psychological functioning. However, other factors, such as the ones enumerated above by Marmor, soon come to be increasingly influential, together with temperament, in shaping the course of any individual's personality development.

As we have reviewed the developmental course of our New York Longitudinal Study (NYLS) subjects, we have been deeply impressed by the diversity of interactional processes and personality outcome which has been so evident from one subject to another, as each matured from infancy to childhood, through adolescence, and into early adult life. To take a few examples, one girl at age 4 years impressed her nursery school teacher as unusually competent, self-confident and responsible, and at age 21 impressed our interviewer as exactly the same kind of person. Another girl, who in early and middle childhood was a friendly, cooperative and openly communicative member of her family, in early adult life became self-centered, impulsive, secretive and irresponsible. A boy, who in childhood played the role of *enfant terrible*, delighted in making embarrassing remarks about adults and peers, and was indifferent to serious activities, became at age 22 a serious, thoughtful and responsible young adult.

Thus, whatever theoretical orientation an investigator may have as to the development and nature of personality, it cannot be equated with temperament. A consensus as to this issue has gradually developed among temperament researchers. One notable exception is the personality scheme formulated by Hans Eysenck, which is based on only two variables: 'At the highest and most inclusive level of personality description, we are apparently dealing with two main dimensions, the one ranging from high degrees of emotionality to very low emotion reactivity, the other ranging from high degrees of introversion to high degrees of extroversion' (Eysenck, 1967, p. 40). This system has two clear faults:

(1) The number of variables are too limited to account for all or even many of the factors that influence personality development;
(2) The items comprising these two categories appear to confound temperamental factors with other aspects of personality structure.

Eysenck's concepts, while they have influenced some European research workers, have found little favor in the United States.

OUR OWN DEFINITION OF TEMPERAMENT

Throughout our own studies of temperament, starting in the 1950s, we have emphasized the concept of temperament as behavioral style, or the *how* of behavior (Thomas, Chess, Birch, Hertzig & Korn, 1963). We have considered temperament to be a biologically determined innate characteristic of the individual, though its expression and even its characteristics can be influenced by environmental experiences. This formulation of temperament has served to highlight its difference from motivations, or the *why* of behavior. The emphasis on this contrast, which we elaborate on more fully in Chapter 19, is important because most mental health practitioners in the past labeled temperament as motivational in origin and many still do.

By 'motivational in origin' we mean those behaviors which are basically determined by the individual's subjective purposes and goals. For example, two children may react to a specific uncomfortable or frustrating situation with intense negative emotional expressiveness – loud crying, angry remarks, etc. In one child this tantrum behavior may be motivational in origin, i.e. derived from a clear-cut desire to pressure her parents to give in to what she, the child, wants and has been refused. The second child may show the same behavior, not because she is using it for a specific goal in that one situation, but because it is an expression of a general temperamental attribute. In both cases the behavior indicates that the child is distressed or frustrated, but if it is assumed that there is always a definite purpose in the youngster's mind that is motivating the behavior, the parent or clinician will focus on trying to identify the youngster's intrapsychic purpose and why it is so important that she is making such a fuss over it. If, on the other hand, the behavior is temperamental and not primarily purposive in origin, then the assumption that it must be motivational in origin can have unfortunate consequences for the strategy of dealing productively with the child's emotional outburst.

Nevertheless, human behavior is goal-directed and motivated. As a result, the expression of an individual's behavior, even if it is basically shaped by temperament, can appear to be motivated. Thus, for example, a child whose temperament involves a negative response to new situations will feel discomfort in such a setting, such as the first entry to nursery school. The child will then be motivated to relieve this discomfort by one behavioral strategy or another. The behavior is motivated but the primary basis for the motivation is the child's temperament. For example, the child may cling to the mother and cry if she attempts to leave the room. If this behavior is interpreted as primarily motivational, the child will be labelled as anxious, insecure, immature and overdependent on her mother. The teacher and the clinician will then focus on what the mother has been doing in the past and currently to create such insecurity in the child. If, however, the behavior is due to the child's temperamental reaction to distress to most if not all new situations, then the focus of management will be entirely different. Instead, of 'blaming the mother', the mother and teacher can work together to give sufficient time to adapt and be comfortable in this first school experience. As the child becomes gradually more and more at ease, she will cling to the mother less and less, and the mother can shorten her stay in the school, until she finally can drop the child off at the school entrance. The child's original clinging behavior was motivated to relieve her discomfort, but the primary basis for this motivation was her temperament.

The more precise definition for temperament should therefore emphasize its *primary* role in determining certain behaviors, in which motivation then enters as a *secondary* consequential factor. On a broader level, we can conceptualize temperament as a mediating variable between the external stimulus and the brain's response to that stimulus.

THE SELF-CONCEPT AND DEFENSE MECHANISMS

Before considering the many ways in which temperament and personality influence each other, it is useful to define briefly two important aspects of personality: the self-concept and defense mechanisms.

Self-Concept

The uniqueness of the human mind is perhaps most exquisitely manifested in the self-concept or sense of personal identity. It is true that a young chimpanzee can recognize and identifiy its reflection in a mirror, indicating at least crude awareness of 'self' (Goodall & Hamburg, 1975). However, there is no evidence that the development and differentiation of the self-concept in the chimpanzee or other non-human species proceed beyond this simple level. Humans, by contrast, have a conscious awareness of self – a sense of identity as separate unique persons. We change over time, as we cope with one sequence of life experience after another, yet always a central core of our psychological being appears to remain intact and to endure. The 60-year-old knows she is vastly different from the young adult she was a 20; at the same time she feels deeply that she is the same person as she was at 20.

Each individual has a sense of autonomy, yet only really knows herself through her social interactions with other human beings.

A number of studies suggest that definite evidence of self-differentiation can be identified in the infant, starting at about 9 months of age (Lewis & Brooks, 1974, 1975). The development of the self-concept then proceeds rapidly through preschool and middle childhood years, through adolescence, and into adult life. Whether the growing child develops a positive or negative self-concept then depends primarily on her success in mastering the social and task demands that society makes on her at successive age-periods. Also important is the feedback she receives from the influential persons in her life. If her successes are ignored or belittled, this will discourage her appreciation of her abilities and foster a negative self-concept. A commitment to an interactionist concept of the developmental process, in which sequential organism–environment interactions may produce significant psychological changes at any age period, implies that major changes in the self-concept can occur at any time in adult life, as well as in childhood or adolescence. A qualitative change in role functioning, a radical change in the social environment, an important success or failure in life, a crisis which is surmounted or fumbled – all these can have important and even profound consequences for the self-concept.

The nature of a person's self-concept, whether as a child or an adult, can deeply affect the nature of her behavioral functioning. Self-fulfilling prophecies are not unlikely. A person with a positive self-concept and confidence in mastering the demands of her environment is likely to cope with assurance and with the mobilization of her assets and life experiences, so that success is likely in most if not all life situations. These successes will enhance her positive self-concept and make her even more ready to meet new challenges with confidence and effectiveness. The person with a negative self-concept, by contrast, is likely to be doubtful or even defeatist as to her ability to utilize her capacities and life experiences to promote her goals, and feels that her behavior will typically result in unfavorable consequences. She will then function inadequately and in a self-defeatist way, often even in routine situations. Repeated failures will then confirm her in her negative self-evaluation, and make subsequent failures even more likely.

Defense Mechanisms

These mechanisms were first identified systematically within the psychoanalytic movement. But over the years different clinical researchers have proposed a number of different conceptualizations of the origins and dynamics of defense mechanisms. We can define defense mechanisms operationally, without recourse to any theoretical bias, as behavioral strategies which attempt to cope with stress or conflict which the individual cannot or will not master directly. This definition, although derived originally from psychoanalytic theory and practice, can be used in the analysis of behavioral dynamics independently of the psychoanalytic framework. The same holds true of the various specific defense mechanisms – *suppression–repression*, *denial*, *avoidance*, *reaction formation*, *rationalization*, *displacement*, *projection* and *sublimination*. *Humor* sometimes appears as a defense mechanism which serves to avoid facing a problem by joking over it. At other times it is a facet of a non-defensive attractive personality and is not used to deny or avoid a problem.

When excessive stress and the impossibility of direct mastery are present, the resort to one or another defense mechanism is likely. This may happen with environmental demands which the individual cannot meet because of her temperament, academic demands which are beyond the individual's intellectual abilities, overwhelming environmental stress, or severe distortions of brain functioning. There are also many occasions in which a person may have the capacity to cope directly and effectively with a new demand, yet fail to do so, and turn instead to some defense mechanism. This may happen for various reasons. Certain past experiences may have created a conditioned response that any stress is dangerous. Or the demand may be presented by parent, teacher or employer in an ambiguous or confusing form. Or, as another example, the kind of effort required to master the demand may appear, rightly or wrongly, to alienate the individual from her peer group.

The use of defense mechanisms is not necessarily always unhealthy. Sometimes a person with a basically self-confident self-image may be faced with an excessively stressful demand or conflict which she cannot master directly. This may evoke the temporary utilization of a defense mechanism which gives her the opportunity to resolve the stress positively. To take a simple example, an adolescent who is initially shy and uncomfortable in a new situation may experience this typical reaction in joining a new peer group. She may rationalize her initial peripheral and outwardly detached involvement with the group in various ways (she is worried about a friend who is ill, she has a severe headache, she has to get home early, etc.) and gain the time necessary to make her typical gradual positive adjustment. It is a different story, however, when someone uses a defense mechanism repeatedly and chronically. She then does not reap the psychological and material rewards of successful direct mastery, and the use of the defense mechanism may unfavorably affect her social life and her work activities.

TEMPERAMENT AND PERSONALITY

Having outlined some of the factors that make the study of personality a complex and multifactorial task, we can turn to the basic questions of this chapter: how does temperament influence personality, and, conversely, how does personality influence temperament? We can consider these questions under a number of subheadings:

(1) Direct influences;
(2) 'Goodness of fit';
(3) Temperament and self-concept;
(4) Temperament and defense mechanisms.

Direct Influence of Temperament on Personality and of Personality on Temperament

This is an extraordinarily difficult issue to study systematically in terms of significant group trends. With regard to temperament, so many environmental variables and perhaps also late-appearing genetic factors can influence the ratings of temperament, that only modest consistency over time has been evident (Chess & Thomas, 1986; McCall, 1986; McDevitt, 1986). As to personality factors, their systematic study has been fraught with widely conflicting concepts and approaches. To quote Gardner Murphy again, 'the scientific effort to study personality has proved to be extraordinarily difficult' (Murphy, 1968, p. 16). It is also true that there are different views as to the theoretical concepts and significant categories of temperament, though these are much less divergent than the conflicts regarding personality formulations.

In Chapter 12, Rothbart has summarized a number of attempts to show the influence of temperament on personality. Unfortunately, these studies involve primarily simple group correlations, which leave a great deal to be desired. Thus, she cites several studies which report that more active children 'were more aggressive and dominant with peers', 'more likely to engage in frenetic play' and 'to be less compliant'. But these reports raise a number of questions. How many of the more active children showed these characteristics and under what circumstances? Were there other specific factors in the 'frenetic' and 'less compliant' children, such as excessive attempts by parents and teachers to curb the motor activity? Were the ratings of 'aggression' and 'dominance' contaminated by the possibility that the high activity of these children led them to be leading figures in their peer play activities?

In our later chapter (Chapter 19) we quote Rutter on the difficulties in making sweeping generalizations about human behavior. He suggests that it may be 'preferable to take an idiographic approach which explicitly focuses on the individuality of human beings ... in terms of the idiosyncracies which make each person uniquely different from all others' (Rutter, 1980, p. 5).

In our own NYLS, for the above reasons, we have not attempted to analyze the group correlations between earlier or concurrent temperament and personality. We have instead focused on the relationship between temperament and the level of functional behavioral adaptation (Chess & Thomas, 1984). However, we have found in individual subjects a number of influences of temperament on personality, and of personality on temperament, and these are of interest but do not justify broad generalizations.

One young man, Edward, was a slow-to-warm-up child temperamentally (negative reactions to new situations with slow adaptability). His shyness with new situations was handled well by his parents, with support, encouragement and lack of excessive pressure to adapt quickly. As a result, Edward never developed a major behavior problem and went through college and professional school successfully, though not brilliantly. When we last interviewed him at age 29 he was functioning in his profession, in an area devoted to community services to the poor. This position was underpaid and offered little opportunity for material advancement. It did require him to act quickly and assertively in all kinds of complicated new situations and with new people. This he accomplished without excessive stress. His shyness with social situations had, however, not only continued, but had grown worse to the point where he was socially isolated, had no close male friends, and was severely sexually inhibited. How do we explain this dichotomy of functioning?

He had high moral and ethical standards which he learned from his parents. These appeared to be the motivating force which overcame his shyness at work. Socially, these standards were not as meaningful and did not serve to counterbalance his temperamental pattern, as they did at work. He talked openly about his problems, and was eager to obtain professional help, which we arranged.

By contrast, there is Ronald, whose slow-to-warm-up temperament as a child was more extreme than Edward's, even resulting in a school phobia in the early grades. His parents also managed his problem well, with our advice, and his difficulties with new situations improved gradually. He went through college with the ambition to make his way up the ladder in the corporate world. This he is doing successfully, and his ambitions outweigh any temptations to withdraw from any new situation which, if he did, might affect his career adversely. He is married and has a number of friends. However, he refuses to discuss any of his discomfort with the new, which still is evident at times, and insists that he never had a school problem as a youngster. He is using the defense mechanism of *denial* successfully so far, though the future is unpredictable.

Here we have two subjects, Edward and Ronald, with similar temperamental patterns and problems as children, which influenced their personality development, yet with dramatically different outcomes in their late twenties.

Then there is Bernice, a girl with high activity, positive mood and quick adaptability as a child. She ran eagerly and cheerfully to perform any errand requested by parent or teacher, and was a favored child at home and at school. Her eagerness to gain the praise her quick compliance brought, turned, however, progressively into the characteristic of impulsivity as she grew into middle childhood. She began to plunge thoughtlessly into a number of actions which were embarrassing and damaging. Her parents set strict rules for her as to what was permissible activity, and she basically complied. At age 13, however, impulsive behavioral difficulties again appeared in relation to increased academic demands, the onset of puberty, and the new complexities of adolescent peer interactions. With a few months, her father, who had been a stabilizing authoritative (but not authoritarian) figure in the family, died suddenly and unexpectedly. We had given the same advice for quiet consistent limit-setting, but this time the mother could not follow our advice. Bereft of her husband and his influence, stretched to her limits physically by having to return full-time to a demanding and difficult job, she was unable emotionally to cope with her daughter's crises and outbursts, in addition to attending to the needs of her other three young children. The girl's problems escalated, her interaction with her mother and sibs became increasingly hostile and disruptive, and she developed a severe sociopathic behavior disorder, including truancy, sexual promiscuity, stealing and lying. Several attempts at psychotherapy were unsuccessful.

Bernice left home at 18, and her behavior, now at age 30, is essentially unchanged. She supports herself at a job much below her potential, admits she behaves impulsively, and at times puts on an air of repentance and determination to change. This lasts only to the next antisocial activity which attracts her, which now includes severe drug abuse. Bernice's impulsivity, which derived from her childhood temperament, and the praise she received for it, has been her downfall. However, her life course might have been different if her father had lived, and the positive aspects of her temperament had been channeled into healthy directions.

We could cite many other cases which would reiterate the same theme. Temperament influences personality development, and personality influences the expression of temperament. But in each case idiosyncratic factors – sometimes explainable, sometimes not – as well as unpredictable life events, played a crucial role in this temperament–personality interaction. The task of the clinician and the clinical researcher is to tease out the multiple factors that are involved, estimate the importance of each one in that particular case – which may be different in another case – and build a strategy of treatment and data analysis based on the findings. This remains one of the most difficult and yet necessary tasks for temperament workers in clinical practice and in research.

'Goodness of Fit'

In the first 3 years of life a sequential series of demands for socialization are made upon the child: the establishment of regular sleep and feeding schedules; cooperation in bathing, clothing, hair and nail cutting; discipline – the 'don'ts' and 'mustn't dos'; toilet training; establishment of positive relations with other family members and peers; and, for many, if not most American children, the adaptation to a day-care center or nursery school. Some families demand in addition compliance to special idiosyncratic values, such as one NYLS mother who insisted that her 3-year-old son learn formalistic manners of speech and behavior, which inevitably made him the scapegoat of his neighborhood peer group.

The management of this progressive process of socialization for the young child is almost always the responsibility of the parents or parent surrogates. Here the child's temperament plays a vital role. If there is a 'goodness of fit' between the parents' attitudes and practices and the child's temperamental ability to master these demands, development will proceed smoothly and the basis will be laid for a healthy personality structure. If, on the contrary, there is a 'poorness of fit' so that the child's temperament cannot cope adequately with these social expectations, excessive stress for the child is likely, and the basis will be laid for unhealthy personality development or even a personality disorder.

There is no single magical recipe for achieving a goodness of fit. Different parents may use different approaches that are effective. Differences in cultural norms may also shape the nature of the parents' expectations and the specific management techniques they use with their children. Also, as important as this child–parent interaction is in the early years, it is only the *beginning* of the child's psychological functioning and personality development. Later life experiences or delayed maturational changes may modify or even change qualitatively the course of an individual's behavioral patterns and personality structure – whether in childhood, adolescence or adult life. We have witnessed such changes, which are often so unpredictable, in a number of our NYLS subjects, as we have followed them from infancy into adult life (Chess & Thomas, 1984). A good start for an infant psychologically is desirable, just as it is with physical health. But a good start or a poor start psychologically or physically does not mean that dramatic change cannot occur at any subsequent age period.

It should be emphasized that the child–caregiver interaction is not a one-sided process, in which the child's functioning and development is shaped primarily by the parents' activities. The child also plays a highly active part in the process, through her temperamental attributes. The success or failure of the parents' management depends on the child's temperament as much as it does on their own specific attitudes and practices.

The child's temperament can also be an important influence on the parents' attitudes and practices. If the infant is an easy child temperamentally, and the process of socialization proceeds smoothly, the parents are all too likely to interpret this result as meaning that they are good, sensitive parents. This success as parents may enhance their self-esteem, which is all to the good, even if the child's temperament has also contributed to this desirable developmental course. This positive effect on the parents' self-image can also enhance their affection for the child and their tolerance for minor misjudgments in handling the infant. If, on the contrary, the infant is a difficult child temperamentally, the process of socialization is likely to proceed with turmoil, stress and one difficulty after another. The parents of such a child, and especially the mother, are then all too likely to judge themselves as incompetent or perhaps even unconsciously become hostile to the child. Guilt reactions are common, which only confuse the parents and aggravate their difficulties in managing the child.

From the beginning of our NYLS project we hypothesized that the child's own characteristics could influence the parents' attitudes and practice. This concept was in sharp contrast to the dominant developmental theories of the 1950s, which assumed that it was only the parent who was the primary agent in the infant's development. As we gathered and analyzed our data, our hypothesis was abundantly confirmed (Chess, Thomas & Birch, 1959). The child is indeed an active agent in her own development, and the various ways in which this occurs were spelled out in our 1968 volume (Thomas, Chess & Birch, 1968).[1]

In short, the infant's temperament is an important factor in the beginnings of her personality development, through its mediating role on the effects on the parents' self-image as parents, which then can influence the parents' management of the child.

Temperament and the Self-Concept

As we have noted above, the nature of a person's self-concept, which is so crucial in shaping her psychological functioning, depends primarily on her success or failure in mastering the social and task demands that society makes upon her at successive age periods. Here the goodness or poorness of fit between the child's temperament and the demands and expectations of parents, teachers and peer group plays a most important role. With goodness of fit, the child will have one experience after another in which she is successful and achieves positive recognition for her achievements. This provides the basis for a healthy self-confident self-image. The opposite is true where there is a poorness of fit and the child's temperament prevents her from meeting the positive expectations of parents, teachers or peers. The crystallization of a negative self-image, with all its unfavorable consequences, then becomes a real danger. (The influence of a goodness or poorness of fit on the development of the self-concept is not restricted to temperament–environment interactions, as important as they are. Success or failure in meeting unrealistic parental expectations for academic, social or athletic achievement can have similar outcomes.)

In the NYLS a number of subjects were exposed to excessive stress and denigration in their childhood years by parents who made demands that the children could not meet because of their temperamental characteristics. In some cases the youngsters suffered a sense of inadequacy and the expectation of failure, and developed a negative self-concept, with seriously damaging consequences for their subsequent psychological development. In some other cases, however, the youngsters showed a surprising resilience in the face of such unfavorable interactions with their parents. They were able to distance themselves emotionally from their parents, develop and concentrate on favorable relationships with peers and teachers, and sometimes even with the parents of their peers. These positive experiences outside the home appeared to counterbalance their unfavorable home environment, and they came to adult life with a positive rather than a negative self-concept (Chess & Thomas, 1984). Our preliminary analysis of this group has as yet not given us a satisfactory answer as to why they were able to escape the unfavorable consequences of their poorness of fit temperamentally with their parents' expectations. We suspect that the answer may be different from one case to another.

These findings highlight the fact that high risk in childhood does not inevitably predict an unfavorable outcome. Werner and Smith, in their large-scale longitudinal study of the children of Kauai, Hawaii, make this same point:

> In this cohort of 698, 204 children developed severe behavior or learning problems at *some time* during the first two decades of their lives ... Yet there were others – also *vulnerable*, exposed to poverty, biological risks, and family instability, and reared by parents with little education or severe mental health problems – who remained *invincible* and developed into competent and autonomous young adults who 'worked well, played well, loved well, and expected well'. (Werner & Smith, 1982, pp. 2–3)

It is a major challenge to developmental psychology and psychiatry to mount serious studies of such stress-resistant, high-risk children. Our own hypothesis would be that temperament will be identified as an important, but by no means the only, factor responsible for such stress resistance.

Self-Insight

It is a valuable personality asset for an individual to have insight into her own personality characteristics. She then has the capacity to control or modify a particular behavioral response in a situation where its spontaneous expression may be undesirable. This self-insight with regard to temperament can be very useful, especially with regard to one or another temperamental attribute which may be near or at the extreme level of ratings. We discuss this issue, together with several case illustrations, in Chapter 19.

Temperament and Defense Mechanisms

Poorness of fit in the temperament–environment interaction, which renders the individual repeatedly incapable of direct mastery of expectations and demands, is likely to evoke one or another defense mechanism. An intriguing question is whether there are significant correlations between temperamental characteristics and the specific defense mechanisms an individual may develop. We have insufficient data from the NYLS to attempt ourselves to pursue this question systematically. Such a study could be valuable for both its theoretical and practical implications.

CONCLUSION

In this chapter we have indicated the complexities and problems involved in the study of personality. We have also tried to show how our increasing knowledge of the functional significance of temperament has served to clarify some of our concepts of personality and the dynamics of its development. We can be hopeful that as temperament research continues, among its contributions will be a further enhancement of our knowledge of the origins and evolution of personality patterns.

NOTE

[1] This concept of the child as an active agent in her own development was also proposed in an influential article by Richard Bell (1968).

REFERENCES

Bell, R.Q. (1968). A reinterpretation of the direction of effects in studies in socialization. *Psychological Review*, **75**, 81–95.

Chess, S. & Thomas, A. (1984). *Origins and evolution of behavior disorders*. New York: Brunner/Mazel. Reprinted by Harvard University Press, 1987.

Chess, S. & Thomas, A. (1986). *Temperament in clinical practice*. New York: Guilford Press.

Chess, S., Thomas, A. & Birch, H. (1959). Characteristics of the individual child's behavioral responses to the environment. *American Journal of Orthopsychiatry*, **29**, 791–802.

Eysenck, H.J. (1967). *The biological basis of personality*. Springfield, IL: Charles C. Thomas.

Goldsmith, H.H., Buss, A.H., Plomin, R., Rothbart, M.K., Thomas, A., Chess, S., Hinde, R.A. & McCall, R.B. (1987). What is temperament? Four approaches. *Child Development*, **58**, 505–529.

Goodall, J.A. & Hamburg, D. A. (1975). Chimpanzee behaviors as a model for the behavior of early man: New evidence on possible origins of human behavior. In S. Arieti (Ed.), *American handbook of psychiatry*, 2nd edn, Vol. 6. New York: Basic Books.

Lewis, M. & Brooks, J. (1974). Self, other and fear: Infants' reactions to people. In M. Lewis & J.A. Rosenblum (Eds), *The origins of fear*. New York: Wiley.

Lewis, M. & Brooks, J. (1975). Infants' social perception: A constructive view. In L.B. Cohen & P. Salapatek (Eds), *Infant perception from sensation to cognition*, Vol. 2. New York: Academic Press.

Marmor, J. (1983). Systems thinking in psychiatry: Some theoretical and clinical applications. *American Journal of Psychiatry*, **140**, 833–838.

McCall, R.B. (1986). Issues of stability and continuity in temperament research. In R. Plomin & J. Dunn (Eds), *The study of temperament: Changes, continuities and challenges* (pp. 13–26). Hillsdale, NJ: Erlbaum.

McDevitt, S.C. (1986). In R. Plomin & J. Dunn (Eds), *The study of temperament: Changes, continuities and challenges*. Hillsdale, NJ: Erlbaum.

Mischel, W. (1977). On the future of personality measurement. *American Psychologist*, **32**, 246–254.

Murphy, G. (1968). Psychological views of personality and contributions to its study. In E. Norbeck, D. Price-Williams & W.M. McCord (Eds), *The study of personality*. New York: Holt, Rinehart & Winston.

Plomin, R. & Dunn, J. (Eds) (1986). *The study of temperament: Changes, continuities and challenges*. Hillsdale, NJ: Erlbaum.

Porter, R. & Collins, G.M. (1982). *Temperament differences in infants and young children*. Ciba Foundation Symposium No. 89. London: Pitman.

Rutter, M. (1980). Introduction. In M. Rutter (Ed.), *Scientific foundations of developmental psychiatry* (pp. 1–7). London: Heinemann.

Thomas, A., Chess, S. & Birch, H.G. (1968). *Temperament and behavior disorders in children*. New York: New York University Press.

Thomas, A., Chess, S., Birch, H.G., Hertzig, M.E. & Korn, S. (1963). *Behavioral individuality in early childhood*. New York: New York University Press.

Werner, E.E. & Smith, R.S. (1982). *Vulnerable but invincible*. New York: McGraw-Hill.

14

Temperament and Cognition: Relations between Temperament and Mental Test Scores

ADAM P. MATHENY, JR
University of Louisville

One aspect of temperament's contribution to developmental themes is the interface between temperament and cognition (e.g. Rothbart & Derryberry, 1981). Our efforts in this direction have been provoked by the ongoing attempts to achieve a synthesis of social–emotional and cognitive development (for a review, see Cairns & Valsiner, 1984), with a view toward integrating cognitive and non-cognitive behaviors within a biologically based developmental model. For the moment, however, our examination of the overlap between temperament and cognition is more empirical, and guided by the following considerations:

(1) Recent reviews of research on the relations between cognition and emotion/affect point to the empirical connections between the two domains (e.g. Campos, Barrett, Lamb, Goldsmith & Stenberg, 1983; Izard, 1984). Furthermore, developmental theories (e.g. Case, Hayward, Lewis & Hurst, 1987; Izard, 1984) have attempted to provide an integration of cognitive and emotional development. Considering that all theories of temperament include aspects of emotional/affective behaviors (Strelau, 1987), it is reasonable to expect empirical connections between temperamental variables and cognitive variables.

(2) Two conceptualizations of temperament include attention span, task persistence, and distractibility as prominent characteristics. (Derryberry & Rothbart, 1984; Rothbart & Derryberry, 1981; Thomas, Chess, Birch, Hertzig & Korn, 1963). In one form or another, these characteristics are referenced by behaviors that others have identified as cognitive characteristics of young children (McCall, Eichorn & Hogarty, 1977; Stott & Ball, 1965) and as a general component of intelligence (Kaufman, 1975; Stankov, 1983). Rothbart (1986) has provided a theoretical distinction between

Temperament in Childhood   Edited by G.A. Kohnstamm, J.E. Bates and M.K. Rothbart
© 1989 John Wiley & Sons Ltd

attention-as-temperament and attention-as-cognition; the distinction is not made so easily at the empirical level, however. For example, the content among items of temperament questionnaires and rating scales often refers to attentiveness to and persistence on commonplace activities (reading, working puzzles, etc.) that involve cognition. As a consequence, we should expect an empirical connection between temperament behaviors referring to attention, persistence, or distractibility, and cognitive measures.

(3) Individual differences in the emergence, persistence, and transitions of some temperament characteristics may have cognitive prerequisites. Approach/withdrawal (Thomas *et al.*, 1963) and sociability (Buss & Plomin, 1975) refer to situations involving novel objects and events, strangers, and absence of familiar persons. Assessments of the child's behaviors in these situations presuppose that the child is capable of discriminating among familiar and unfamiliar persons, social situations, or a variety of stimuli ranging from the known to unknown. Although this presupposition may hold for most children in most instances, individual differences for the development of these discriminative competencies could evoke individual differences for the temperament characteristics.

(4) Haviland (1976) has pointed out that infant affect is intertwined with our judgments of infant intelligence. Mental tests for infants include a wide variety of items that sample sensory awareness, attention, task persistence, simple problem-solving, and responses to verbal and gestural demands. These tests, such as the Bayley Scales of Infant Development (Bayley, 1969), often index the infant's responses to the tasks by using affective responses. In effect, the infant's sensorimotor intelligence is partially assessed by the infant's expressions, such as smiling, interest, surprise, frustration, and playfulness. From a Piagetian perspective, these affective indices of infant intelligence are expected for theoretical reasons; affect and intelligence are two bonded aspects of the same invariant developmental trend (Case *et al.*, 1987; Gouin-Decarie, 1965; Matheny, 1977; Piaget, 1981).

From this list alone, it is evident that there is an implicit overlap between temperament and cognition. The goal of this chapter is to provide an aerial survey of empirical relations between temperament and cognition with a view toward confirming the implicit overlap. For this survey, we draw solely from temperament measures and mental test scores (infancy to adolescence) obtained by a longitudinal project: the Louisville Twin Study.

BACKGROUND

Mental Testing

The Louisville Twin Study began assessments of infant twins during 1958–59 with a focus on the genetic influences on physical and behavioral development. Twins were recruited from birth certificates and a special effort was made to make the families as fully representative of the socioeconomic distribution of the metropolitan Louisville area as possible. In terms of occupational ratings (Reiss, 1961), about

30% of the families are ranked in the lowest two deciles and about 10% in the highest two deciles. The remaining families are distributed in somewhat equal proportions among the six intermediate deciles.

In the longitudinal program, the twins made visits to the research center every 3 months during the first year, every 6 months during the second and third years, and on an annual basis thereafter, with the annual visit scheduled on the twins' birthdays. During each visit, mothers were interviewed about the twins' behaviors and the twins were given tests for assessing mental development. The tests have included the Bayley Scales of Infant Development (Bayley, 1969) for ages 3 through 24 months; the Stanford–Binet Form L–M (Terman & Merrill, 1973) at 30 and 36 months; the McCarthy Scales of Children's Abilities (McCarthy, 1972) at 4 years; the Wechsler Preschool and Primary Scale of Intelligence (WPPSI; Wechsler, 1967) at 5 and 6 years; and the revised Wechsler Intelligence Scale for Children (WISC-R; Wechsler, 1974) at ages 7 through 9 years. The annual visits were terminated at 9 years, but the WISC-R was repeated at 12 and 15 years when the twins returned for adolescent assessments. The tests selected, either in their original or revised forms, were the best standardized psychometric tests of mental development available. (For additional details, see Matheny, in press; Wilson, 1972, 1974, 1975, 1977, 1978, 1981, 1982, 1983; Wilson & Matheny, 1983b, 1986).

Interviews

In 1971 our research on temperament started with analyses of interviews with mothers. During interviews the mother was asked to report if the twins were similar (concordant) or different (discordant) for a wide variety of behaviors. The analyses of these maternal contrasts within twin pairs at every age proceeded to identify behaviors that clustered together – if twin A was reported to be more attentive than twin B, were there other behaviors that were more typical of twin A in comparison with twin B?

The results provided a nuclear temperament cluster that emerged as early as 6 months and remained stably organized up to 3 years. The cluster was made up of frequency and intensity of temperamental outbursts, social responsiveness, irritability, crying, demanding attention, and shorter attention span (Matheny, Wilson, Dolan & Krantz, 1981; Wilson, Brown & Matheny, 1971). When behavioral differences were reported for a twin pair, one twin was seen as being more prone to upset, anger, irritability, and crying, and more demanding during social interactions with members of the family. By contrast, the co-twin was seen as being less prone to upset, easier to soothe when upset, more content during self-sustained play, and more attentive.

At 3 years, a further differentiation in the patterns of discordance emerged. When one twin was reported to be more approachful to strangers, the co-twin was reported to be wary and somber around unfamiliar persons and more dependent on the mother. This cluster of social responsiveness was identified as being largely independent of the negative aspects of the temperamental cluster, but it was linked to positive emotionality. Moreover, twin analyses indicated that this cluster and the earlier-appearing temperamental cluster were influenced genetically.

The cognitive aspects of these behavioral discordances within twin pairs were not examined in detail. One study, however, found that infant twin pairs who were contrasted for attention and self-sustained play showed differences for preschool mental test scores (Matheny & Brown, 1971). The less attentive twin had lower mental test scores on the WPPSI in contrast with the more attentive co-twin.

Test Behaviors

While the interview analyses were informative, the results were dependent on within-pair contrasts, regardless of magnitude. Therefore, we turned to a more direct method. As part of mental testing of the individual infants, examiners completed the Infant Behavior Record (IBR) which is a component of the Bayley Scales of Infant Development. The IBR consists of 30 rating scales that permit an evaluation of test-taking attributes such as social responsiveness, fearfulness, emotional tone, activity, attention span, and goal-directedness. These scores were the source for factor analyses which identified three temperament factors: Task Orientation, as defined by scales such as attention span and goal-directedness; Test Affect–Extraversion, as defined by social responsiveness and emotional tone; and Activity, as defined by activity and energy. These three factors were (a) consistently identified at every age (ages 3–24 months; 300–400 infants at each age), (b) more stable during the 12- to 24-month period, and (c) genetically influenced for both change and continuity (Matheny, 1980, 1983; Matheny, Dolan & Wilson, 1976). Because the IBR represents behaviors during mental testing, our findings (Matheny, Dolan & Wilson, 1974) that mental test scores were related to the IBR ratings was not unexpected. It should be noted, however, that among all of the rated behaviors, those of social responsiveness, emotional tone, goal-directedness, and attention span provided stronger and more consistent positive correlations with Bayley mental test scores at ages 6–24 months.

Laboratory Observations

On-site observations of twins' temperament were initiated by rating the twins' behaviors during unstructured or 'free-play' conditions during the 3- to 4-hour visit to the research center. This approach toward expanding the methods of assessing temperament yielded provocative findings regarding genetic influences on trait–situation interactions (Matheny & Dolan, 1975). It became obvious, however, that the course of the entire visit and especially the format of observations should be structured to provide standardized activities (Matheny, 1981). Pilot studies were conducted to develop these unique procedures, and in 1976, the research program began longitudinal assessments of temperament as determined by two fully calibrated, standardized sets of laboratory procedures: the first set spanning the ages 3–30 months; the second set spanning the ages 3–4 years.

3–30 Months

The procedures for the infants are described elsewhere (Matheny & Wilson, 1981; Wilson & Matheny, 1986); in brief, infants are confronted with a fixed succession of age-related activities – vignettes – that are provided when the twins are together, with and without parent, and when each twin is without co-twin and parent. Some of the vignettes are designed to promote happy, enthusiastic play; sustained play; variations of activity level; reactions to novelty; and responses to goal blocking. Other vignettes involve being responsive to cuddling, lifted, held, and fed.

The laboratory sessions are videotaped and the staff rate each infant's behavior from the videotapes. The primary behaviors rated are emotional tone, activity, attentiveness, social orientation to staff, vocalizing, and reactions to physical restraint. The ratings are made for each 2-minute period of a protocol that covers 60 minutes; then, all ratings are combined to yield a single composite rating for each behavior. Although these procedures were developed for infant twins, they can be adapted for standardized temperament observations of singletons (Gunnar, 1988).

The initial analysis (Wilson & Matheny, 1983a) was performed at 12 months and it showed that the laboratory behavior could be condensed by factor analyses to yield three factors. The first factor was loaded heavily with the ratings of emotional tone, attentiveness, and social orientation. The second factor was defined by activity and the third factor, by variability scores representing the period-to-period change in emotional tone and activity. A subsequent study of laboratory behavior at 18 and 24 months (Matheny, Wilson & Nuss, 1984b) provided the same first factors defined at 12 months. Therefore, the same primary dimension was found at all three ages; congruence coefficients for factor similarity were .95, .99, and .95 for 12–18 months, 18–24 months, and 12–24 months, respectively (also see Matheny, Wilson & Thoben, 1987). The age-to-age stabilities for the infants' scores on this temperament factor – labeled Tractability – were .37 and .66 for 12–18 months and 18–24 months, respectively (also see Matheny, 1984, 1986). Thus, the laboratory observations yielded a temperament factor – Tractability – that was consistently identified at 12–24 months, encompassed many of the same salient features observed during test-taking, and reflected the behaviors clustered on the basis of maternal interviews.

A second factor identified at 18 and 24 months was defined by activity and vocalizing. This factor, representing an infant's active excitement, was similar to the activity factor found at 12 months.

3–4 Years

The parental reports of an emergent social cluster at 3 years led us to consider this developmental trend as part of temperament assessments. From a developmental perspective, this period from 3 to 4 years is suitable for the demonstration of gregarious and prosocial aspects of social behaviors. Moreover, during this period, parents of twins reported a high incidence of competitive behaviors. Therefore, we developed a laboratory-based method that would permit structured observations of twins' cooperative and competitive behaviors.

The laboratory observations and rating scales capitalize on the laboratory procedures developed for infants but vignettes were added to provide opportunities for the twins to compete for the same toys or cooperate on constructive tasks

(Matheny, Wilson & Nuss, 1984a). The number of rating scales was also expanded to include assertive behaviors and surgency (the degree to which the child vigorously engages in an activity). Factor analyses of these rating scales at 3 and 4 years revealed a first factor at both ages that was defined by surgency, emotional tone, and activity. Children with higher scores on this factor would be described as more forceful during interactions within each vignette, more positive in emotional tone, and more active. A second factor was largely defined at 3 years by assertiveness, and at 4 years, by assertiveness and less attentiveness. A complete description of these factor analyses and the genetic analyses for twin pairs can be found in Matheny (1987).

Neonatal Assessments

While 3 months was the first age for twin infants to be brought into the research center for longitudinal assessments, a testing program was initiated to evaluate infants in the hospital within a few days after delivery. The neonatal testing program was designed to permit observations of behaviors expressive of temperament – e.g. irritability, resistance to soothing, activity, and reactivity. During a 3- to 4-hour appraisal, feeding, sleeping, orienting behaviors, and responsiveness to stressful and soothing stimuli were observed and rated (see Riese, 1982, 1983). Single or aggregate newborn temperament variables – irritability, resistance to soothing, activity awake, activity asleep, reactivity (responsivity to visual and auditory stimuli), and reinforcement value – have predicted infant temperament assessments during the first 2 years. For example, newborn irritability predicted negative emotional tone in the laboratory at 9 months (Matheny, Riese & Wilson, 1985) and at 24 months (Riese, 1987). Newborn temperament assessments have not focused on predicting mental development; unpublished data however, indicate that, among the full-term newborns, higher ratings of the newborns' orienting responses are associated with higher Bayley mental test scores at 3–12 months (r values between .29 and .41).

Temperament Questionnaires

As an adjunct to the direct observations and interviews, temperament question-naires have been provided at every visit. Because the interview queries had drawn heavily from the temperament research of the New York Longitudinal Study (NYLS: Thomas et al., 1963), we chose NYLS questionnaires formulated by that conceptualization.

The major impetus for the NYLS approach has been the sequence of question-naires spanning an interval from infancy to adolescence. As these questionnaires became available we chose the Infant Temperament Questionnaire (ITQ; Carey & McDevitt, 1978) to provide to parents when the twins were 6 and 9 months old. For the interval from 12 to 30 months the parents were given the Toddler Temperament Scale (TTS; Fullard, McDevitt & Carey, 1984); for 3–7 years, the Behavioral Style Questionnaire (BSQ; McDevitt & Carey, 1978); and for 8–12 years, the Middle Childhood Temperament Questionnaire (MCTQ; Hegvik, McDevitt & Carey, 1982).

More recently, another NYLS-based, self-report and rating questionnaire has been given to the 12-year-old twins for self-assessment. This instrument, a revised version of the Dimension of Temperament Survey (DOTS-R; Lerner, Palmero, Spiro & Nesselroade, 1982; Windle & Lerner, 1986), provides ratings of the same features of the NYLS temperament characteristics.

At every age, when sample size permitted, factor analysis of the temperament questionniares was conducted for the nine characteristics of temperament. In general, the first factor (unrotated) extracted at each age was largely defined by loadings from approach/withdrawal, adaptability, mood, and attention/persistence. For ages 12, 18, and 24 months, this factor – labelled Tractability – has also been found to correlate with the Tractability factor from laboratory observations: 12 months, .52; 18 months, .38; 24 months, .52 (Matheny, Wilson & Nuss, 1984b).

TEMPERAMENT AND MENTAL TESTS

Infancy

The temperament factors from laboratory observations (12–24 months), mental test behaviors as rated on the IBR (12–24 months), and temperament questionnaires (12–24 months) were examined for their relations with the Bayley mental test score at 12, 18, and 24 months. The correlations are presented in Table 1.

Most of the correlations range between .20 and .30 except for Task Orientation, the temperament measure that most reflects the sustained attention and persistent efforts of the infant during mental testing. It is of interest that, among the

Table 1   Correlations between temperament factors and Bayley mental test scores at 12, 18, and 24 months

Temperament factors, source, and key rating scales	Age at mental test (months)		
	12	18	24
Tractability: lab observations (emotional tone; attentiveness; social orientation)	.28* (n=84)	.28** (n=89)	.27* (n=77)
Tractability: Toddler Temperament Questionnaire (adaptability; mood; approach)	.09 (n=48)	.27* (n=65)	.28* (n=59)
Task orientation: Infant Behavior Record (object orientation; goal-directedness; attention span)	.37**	.54**	.48**
Test affect–extraversion: Infant Behavior Record (social-examiner; cooperativeness; fearfulness; emotional tone)	.30**	.28**	.42**
Activity: Infant Behavior Record (activity; body motion; energy)	.24*	.18**	−.03

n factors from Infant Behavior Record between 291 and 339.
*$P \leq .05$; **$P \leq .01$.

remaining measures, factors from the laboratory and questionnaire ratings were generally comparable for predicting mental test scores. Examination of the individual rating scales from laboratory, questionnaire, and IBR indicated that ratings of emotional tone (laboratory and IBR), approach/withdrawal (questionnaire), social responsiveness (laboratory and IBR), and adaptability (questionnaire) provided almost equivalent correlations with infant mental test scores regardless of age. In effect, the infant with higher mental test scores was likely to receive higher ratings for the following characteristics: sustained attention and persistence; positive emotion or mood; cooperation with and adaptation to ongoing changes; and an approachful stance to unfamiliar persons, events, and objects. More recent analyses indicate that behavioral inhibition (laboratory, IBR, and questionnaire) can be linked throughout infancy and is influenced genetically (Matheny, 1989).

The remaining temperament characteristic – activity – was positively correlated with mental test scores at 12 months but the relation became essentially zero by 24 months. As we will show for later ages, activity becomes negatively correlated with intelligence. This longitudinal trend has been noted among other correlations between infant scores and infant activity (Bayley & Schaefer, 1964).

Childhood

The research on the laboratory observations at 3 and 4 years is still incomplete; therefore, only the factor scores from the laboratory ratings at 3 and 4 years were correlated with concurrent IQ scores. Only the first factor at 3 years, defined by surgency, emotional tone, and activity, was correlated (–.24) with 3-year IQ. All the other factors at 3 and 4 years had no relations with IQ scores. Thus, the preliminary data from the laboratory observations indicated that a 3-year-old who is forceful in acquiring and keeping toys, positive, and active is likely to have a relatively lower IQ score obtained at the same age.

The NYLS-based questionnaires for temperament provide the most extensive data sets during childhood. The correlations between temperament and intelligence test scores obtained at 3, 4, 5, 6, 8, 9, and 12 years are provided in Table 2. Year 7 is not shown because of small sample size for questionnaires. At 3 years, only the full-scale IQ score is available for the Stanford–Binet. At 4 years, the McCarthy Scales of Children's Abilities provides a single score – technically called a General Cognitive Index – which is equivalent to a full-scale IQ score. At 5 through 12 years the intelligence test scores are divided into verbal and performance IQ scores, a division typical of Wechsler tests of intelligence. The temperament factor – Tractability – that was extracted from the questionnaires at each age was also correlated with intelligence test scores. The correlations for this factor are also provided in Table 2.

An overview of the correlations indicates that few relations between temperament and intelligence exceed a correlation of .30. Two trends are evident: adaptability and attention/persistence are more likely to be associated with intelligence measures; when verbal and performance IQ scores are separated, more correlations are found between verbal IQ and temperament.

Table 2 Temperament: relation with IQ scores at 3–12 years

Categories of temperament	Age (years)											
	3	4	5		6		8		9		12	
	FS	FS	V	P	V	P	V	P	V	P	V	P
Activity			−.21	−.24			−.27	−.26		−.28		
Rhythmicity/ predictability							.27	.21	.28	.21		
Approach			.25				.21	.20				−.27
Adaptability	.25	.30	.24		.32	.25			.20			
Intensity							−.28			−.28	−.61	
Mood							.28	.31				
Attention/ persistence	.22		.27	.21	.46	.25	.31	.29			.36	
Distractibility			−.26									
Threshold							.23			.20		
Tractability	.20		.28	.20	.24		.30	.27	.35	.31		

IQ measured by Standford–Binet (L–M) at 3 years; McCarthy Scales of Children's Abilities at 4 years; Wechsler Preschool and Primary Scale of Intelligence at 5 and 6 years; Wechsler Intelligence Scale for Children – Revised at 8, 9, and 12 years. Temperament rated on the Behavioral Style Questionnaire at 3, 4, 5, and 6 years; Middle Childhood Temperament Questionnaire at 8, 9, and 12 years.

FS, full-scale; V, verbal; P, performance.

Only values of $r \geq .20$ are shown.

Number of subjects (n): 3 years, 164; 4 years, 196; 5 years, 197; 6 years, 170; 8 years, 158; 9 years, 198; 12 years, 84.

Despite the tendency for some temperament characteristics to maintain rather consistent associations with IQ scores, the number of characteristics that significantly correlated with IQ varied by age. At ages 3, 4, and 6 years, IQ was related to no more than two of the nine temperament characteristics. By contrast, at ages 5 and 8 years, there were at least five characteristics associated with IQ scores. At 8 years, the increase in IQ–temperament relations could be attributed to the MCTQ being comprised of more temperament items with cognitive features. That is, the parent is being called upon to make judgments about behaviors in the context of cognitive-related pursuits, such as persistence in doing homework, complaining about school, spending time on a project, or ignoring distractions while reading. At 5 years, however, the temperament questionnaire, the BSQ, is the same as that given at 3, 4, and 6 years. The types of IQ tests changed during this period, but year-to-year stabilities of IQ scores from 3 to 6 years are high (correlations from .74 to .87). Moreover, the year-to-year stabilities for the BSQ, while not so high as for IQ scores, are high enough to expect some continuity in

IQ–temperament relations. For example, the average year-to-year stability for approach/withdrawal for the BSQ is .69 (from this sample). Given the stability for approach/withdrawal and the stability for IQ, one might expect that if approach/withdrawal is associated with IQ at one age, a somewhat similar association should be found at other ages. Such was not the case. In effect, the varying numbers of IQ-temperament correlations suggest that there are development changes for the overlap between IQ and temperament.

The temperament factor, Tractability, as generally defined by loadings from approach/withdrawal, adaptability, mood, and attention/persistence, also provided rather consistent correlations with IQ. By and large these correlations were equivalent to the average of the correlations between IQ and the individual characteristics loading on the Tractability factors.

Self-Assessed Temperament

A final analysis determined the relations between NYLS temperament, self-rated by the DOTS-R given to the 12-year-olds, and the WISC-R verbal and performance IQ scores obtained at the same age. These correlations (see Table 3) are interesting in that they tended to demonstrate more clearly the relation betwen temperament and verbal IQ. Moreover, the magnitudes of the correlations tended to be higher than those found when the mother rated the child's temperament. This latter distinction is particularly evident at 12 years when the nine maternal ratings and the

Table 3   Dimensions of temperament: relation with IQ scores at 12 years

	Verbal IQ	Performance IQ
Activity		
General		
Sleep		
Approach	.41	.32
Flexibility	.32	
Mood		
Rhythmicity		
Sleep	.49	.57
Eating	.28	
Daily		
Distractibility	.35	.39
Persistence	–.33	
Task orientation		
Tractability	.44	.39

Temperament assessed by self-rating using the revised version of the Dimension of Temperament Survey.

n = 50; only values of $r > .27$ ($P < .05$) are shown.

Tractability factor provided only four significant correlations with IQ scores. By contrast, the self-ratings and the Tractability factor provided 11 significant correlations with IQ scores.

Developmental Consistencies

An underlying thread among the correlations is the recurrent positive relations between mental test scores and a small set of temperament characteristics. In the NYLS scheme, attention span/persistence, approach/withdrawal, adaptability, and mood – taken as individual characteristics or in combination with the factor Tractability – are the source of overlap. These depict the child with higher mental test scores as being more attentive to and persistent on tasks, more approachful to unfamiliar persons, objects or events, more adaptable when experiential changes occur, and more positive in mood. Moreover, these temperament characteristics tend to be related more to the verbal components of intelligence tests.

Other studies conducted within the temperament framework add to these results. Burk (1980) compared the temperament of 125 gifted (IQ > 130) children in nursery school through second grade with the norms for the BSQ (McDevitt & Carey, 1978). The gifted group was rated as significantly more approachful, adaptable, persistent, and positive in mood. Thomas and Chess (1977) found that achievement test scores of children in grades one through six were correlated with adaptability and approach/withdrawal. Somewhat similar results have been obtained for intelligence measures or achievement test scores for 3- to 4-year-olds (Moller, 1983), children in the first grade (Martin, Nagle & Paget, 1983), and children in grades two through four (Mevarech, 1985). In the main, the range of correlations between temperament and cognitive measures has been between .20 and .40; some correlations with achievement measures, however, have been found to be even higher, between .60 and .80 (e.g. Martin et al., 1983; Pullis & Cadwell, 1982).

Studies in which temperament-like characteristics and mental development have been correlated are even more numerous. Bayley's early studies (Bayley & Schaefer, 1964) of children's cognitive and social behaviors indicated that the emotional correlates of mental growth became evident during infancy and could be traced throughout childhood. Active and emotionally positive infants and then, later, extraverted children tended to have higher mental test scores obtained concurrently.

Bayley (1970) viewed the non-intellective attributes of children as both modifiers of mental growth and determiners of the characteristic manner by which children respond cognitively. An extension of the latter view is that the positive manner of the child during testing will elicit higher evaluations from the examiner (Haviland, 1976; Stevenson & Lamb, 1979). In effect, a child's positive, extraverted style of performance modifies an examiner's determination of the child's competence.

Lamb, Garn, and Keating (1981) in a study of almost 34000 8-month-old infants found low-order (.17 for males, .16 for females) but significant correlations between infant sociability and Bayley mental test scores even when social (playful) mental test items were omitted. With the playful items included, sociability and Bayley test scores correlated .26.

McCall *et al.* (1977) analyzed the components of the Bayley mental test items obtained for Bayley's original longitudinal sample. They found for female infants a subcomponent of test items that were also socially and emotionally related. McCall *et al.* (1977) reasoned that social dispositions marked mental ability because the onset and maintenance of imitative learning and language are fostered in a social milieu. In the main, the evidence was similar to that summarized by Bayley (1970): the mental development of positive, sociable female infants tended to be more advanced than that of shy, reserved female infants. Other studies of similar characteristics have yielded similar results (Beckwith, Cohen, Kopp, Parmalee & Marcy, 1976; Birns & Golden, 1972; Clarke-Stewart, Umweh, Snow & Pederson, 1980; Crano, 1977; Gouin-Decarie, 1965; Emmerich, Cocking & Sigel, 1979). When the focus has been placed on the less approachful, more fearful, or less sociable child, cognitive growth has also been found to be slower (e.g. Field *et al.*, 1978; for reports on infants, see references for the Louisville Twin Study).

Attention/persistence and similar temperament characteristics have been shown to have repeated associations with cognitive growth during childhood. In addition to the reports from the Louisville Twin Study, other studies (Goldsmith & Gottesman, 1981; McCall, Appelbaum & Hogarty, 1973; McCall *et al.*, 1977; Seegmiller & King, 1975; Yarrow & Pedersen, 1976) found that the more attentive, task-persistent, goal-directed infant or child tends to obtain higher mental test scores. Keogh (1982) and Mevarech (1985), among others, indicated that this facet of temperament correlates with academic achievement as well.

Adaptability or flexibility is a temperament characteristic that appears to have consistent relations with cognition, as found in several studies (e.g. Martin *et al.*, 1983; Moller, 1983; Thomas & Chess, 1977). The results provided in this chapter document its pervasive association with intelligence. More generally, the increasing ability of the child to modify behavioral strategies or to be flexible in the face of altered circumstances is a central theme of Piaget's (1981) adaptive links between affect and cognition and a pervasive characteristic of temperament as described in the NYLS. Adaptability has both cognitive and temperamental features; consequently, it is not surprising to see that adaptability or flexibility, as temperament, correlates with cognitive measures obtained throughout childhood.

In view of the associations between the individual temperament characteristics, described above, and intelligence, the repeated correlations between the Tractability factor and intelligence would be expected. Tractability as extracted from the temperament questionnaires is largely comprised, except for mood, of approach/ withdrawal, adaptability, and attention/persistence. Whether one considers Tractability as a phenotypic cluster of individual characteristics of temperament or as a temperament on its own (Kohnstamm, 1988), it is evident that the cognitive-temperament interface can be detected by this one temperament feature alone.

Developmental Inconsistencies

An examination of the correlations in Tables 1–3 reveals several instances of a given temperament providing only sporadic correlations with mental test scores and instances of a given temperament changing from a positive to a negative correlation with mental test scores.

The most notable sporadic correlations are found for mood, which, as an emotional aspect of temperament, enters into the relations with infant test scores, but contributes nothing thereafter except at year 8. Apparently, positive or negative mood of children has little bearing on children's mental abilities past infancy (Bayley & Schaefer, 1964). A happy, contented infant may score higher on infant tests, but a similar demeanor affords no prediction of test scores at later ages – except for age 8 years. Mood's influence, if any, is only through its contribution to the factor Tractability, suggesting that a positive or negative mood has cognitive implications only in combination with other temperament characteristics.

The inversions of correlations between temperament and mental tests, infancy and childhood, are more easily interpreted. For example, activity during infancy has a developmental advantage that is not retained during later childhood. Infants are presented with developmental tasks that are more readily accomplished with active zest (Bayley & Schaefer, 1964). At later ages, cognitive tasks call upon a less active, more reflective attitude (Kagan & Kogan, 1970). As a consequence, one must be mindful that activity as temperament has qualitative and contextual features that qualify associations with cognition. Similar considerations are discussed in the literature on cognitive style (Klein, 1970).

Distractibility provides an inconsistency as well. For the 12-year-olds, self-reports of temperament show that the more distractible child had higher IQ scores. This is a finding contrary to the temperament literature on clinical cases (Thomas, Chess & Birch, 1968); in a normal population, however, relatively higher levels of distractibility may represent an ability to switch attention. Stankov (1983) has reasoned that dual tasks require attention-switching or time-sharing, and such tasks are better measures of adult intelligence than attention or vigilance on single tasks. We speculate that distractibility is a marker for this attention-switching aspect of general intelligence among the 12-year-olds. Further support for this notion is the additional finding that the more attentive/persistent 12-year-olds had lower IQ scores. Although this speculation does not pertain to distractibility as employed clinically, it suggests that the developmental advance of intelligence may place greater importance on sustained attention for younger children (see Table 1 and 2) and distractibility in the form of attention-switching for children reaching adolescence.

As a final note, it is interesting that rhythmicity in general had almost no correlations with mental test scores until 8 years but provided an overlap thereafter. At 12 years, sleep rhythmicity had unexpectedly large correlations with IQ scores. Thus, the latent regularities of basic vegetative processes and especially sleep, as temperament, seem to denote biophysiological mechanisms that underlie cognitive development (Dolan & Matheny, 1974; Weissbluth, 1986). It is beyond the scope of this chapter to examine this connection in greater detail; unpublished data, however, indicate that sleep irregularities in conjunction with the other characteristics at 8 through 12 years may be indicative of subclinical depression not necessarily marked by a persistent negative mood (Weinberg, Rutman, Sullivan,

Penick & Dietz, 1973). For example, in addition to dysphoric mood, children evaluated as more depressed are seen as being difficult to get along with (less adaptable), socially withdrawn, preoccupied with self-deprecatory ideation, and less distracted by external events. Sleeping disturbances, eating problems, and a reduction of cognitive capabilities add to the clinical picture.

Developmental Transitions

Developmental views of the origins of affect/emotion and cognition place the roots of both domains in biological origins (e.g. Izard, 1979; Piaget, 1981). The Piagetian view, in particular, emphasizes the co-determination of affect and cognition by the developmental plan that requires successive adaptations to the inevitable disequilibria that take place in both domains. The steady stream of altered circumstances evokes both affective and cognitive adaptations (Piaget, 1981) that call upon increasing abilities of the child and increasing flexibility to modify behavioral strategies. In general terms, the developing child is called upon to be adaptable.

With the pervasiveness of adaptability as background, our attention is drawn to those ages during which there is a notable lack of relation between mental test scores and temperament characteristics other than adaptability. The comparison is striking; excluding adaptability and the factor Tractability, which adaptability helps define, there is at most one characteristic – attention/persistence – that correlates with IQ scores at 3, 4, and 6 years. This relative paucity of relations is in sharp contrast with years 5 and 8, which provide many highly equivalent correlations between temperament measures and IQ tests. In developmental terms, these ages depict decoupled temperament–cognition relations that may represent periods of stage transitions for temperament, cognition, or both. Approximately similar ages have been found to represent transitions in cognitive skills (Horn, 1970; McCall et al., 1973; White, 1965), and it can be argued that it is the stage transitions in cognition *per se* that account for the apparent change in the patterns of correlations. We believe, however, that the invariantly yoked development of cognition and affect/emotion argues for periods of transition to take place for affect and emotion, as reflected by measures of temperament. Our view, therefore, is that during periods of stage transition, cited among others to be at about 3–4 years and 6–7 years (Case et al., 1987; McCall et al., 1977), the connections between temperament and mental test scores become asynchronized. McCall et al. (1977) advanced a Piagetian view of these developmental transitions of cognition by pointing out that measures become less stable across the ages spanning the stage transitions. Uzgiris (1977), however, points out that it is not the change in age-to-age stabilities but the concurrent disequilibria in the system that represent the Piagetian view. Our results support Uzgiris' interpretation because we find that the age-to-age stabilities of the IQ and temperament measures remain quite similar throughout the stage transitions. Interpretations of a similar kind can also be found in other sources (Case et al., 1987; Gouin-Decarie, 1978).

Although this issue cannot be resolved by the presence or absence of correlations, and especially low-to-moderate levels of correlations, it is highly likely that there are developmental shifts in the overlap between emotion/affect aspects of temperament and cognition. From a developmental perspective, one might expect individual differences in these shifts to follow an orderly sequence, although there is no reason to believe that the sequence should be ordered by chronological age. From Rothbart's views (see Chapter 12) one might order the sequence in part according to maturational age. Case *et al.* (1987) organize the sequence of their affective transitions according to mental age, and Izard's (1984) developmental view of the emergence of specific emotional expressions could be employed to order the sequence according to the onset and elaboration of overt affective displays. Although these views are not mutually exclusive, the developmental phenomena examined by each view differ enough that a single aspect of temperament alone cannot encompass all of the evolving developmental overlaps with cognition.

CODA

An extensive review (Hubert, Wachs, Peters-Martin & Gandour, 1982) of measures of early temperament has pointed out that the validity of dimensions of temperament could be demonstrated by divergent validity – the degree to which temperament is unrelated to other behavior domains including cognition. The substance of this view is that the temperament construct can be clarified by distinguishing the overt behaviors assessed for temperament from the overt behaviors assessed for cognition. If the empirical data presented in this chapter are representative, however, such a clear distinction will be difficult to achieve. In fact, we believe that an ultimate model of temperament development can be realized by including cognition.

Formal theoretical statements permit temperament and cognition to be defined so that investigators within each domain have been isolationists by practice. In the traffic of the ongoing behaviors of the child, however, relations between the two domains are such that developmental commerce between the two domains is inevitable. Authorities (e.g. Strelau, 1986; Thomas & Chess, 1980) have considered that the expression of temperament can be found in all types of behavior, including the cognitive. We can add that the expression of cognition can be found in the temperament behaviors as well. Our task is to trace the developmental interdependencies between the two domains so that the route from infant temperament to adult personality can be understood. To that end, we require longitudinal studies that span the formative years to the adult level and include adequate measures of cognition, temperament, and personality.

ACKNOWLEDGMENTS

This chapter represents the efforts of Ronald S. Wilson who, before his death in 1986, devoted most of his research career to the Louisville Twin Study. The research was supported in part by the Courier-Journal and Louisville Times Foundation, the National Science Foundation (BNS76–17315; P2B3098), the National Institute of Child Health and Human Development (HD03217; HD22637; HD21395), the National Institute of Mental Health (MH23884;

MH39772), the Office of Child Development (90–C–922), the W.T. Grant Foundation and the John D. and Catherine T. MacArthur Foundation.

The professional assistance of R. Arbegust, M. Hinkle, J. Lechleiter, B. Moss, S. Nuss, D. Pildner, D. Sanders, and A. Thoben, and the cooperation of over 500 families with twins are gratefully acknowledged.

REFERENCES

Bayley, N. (1969). *Bayley Scales of Infant Development.* New York: Psychological Corporation.

Bayley, N. (1970). Development of mental abilities. In P.H. Mussen (Ed.), *Carmichael's manual of child psychology*, 3rd edn (pp. 1163–1209). New York: Wiley.

Bayley, N. & Schaefer, E.S. (1964). Correlations of maternal and child behaviors with the development of mental abilities: Data from the Berkeley Growth Study. *Monographs of the Society for Research in Child Development,* **29** (6, Whole No. 97).

Beckwith, L., Cohen, S., Kopp, C., Parmalee, A. & Marcy, T. (1976). Caregiver–infant interaction and early cognitive development in preterm infants. *Child Development*, **47**, 579–587.

Birns, B. & Golden, M. (1972). Prediction of intellectual performance at 3 years from infant tests and personality measures. *Merrill-Palmer Quarterly*, **18**, 53–58.

Burk, E. (1980). Relationship of temperamental traits to achievement and adjustment in gifted children. Doctoral Dissertation, Fordham University. Cited in Martin, R.P. (1983).

Buss, A.H. & Plomin, R. (1975). *A temperament theory of personality.* New York: Wiley.

Cairns, R.B. & Valsiner, J. (1984). Child psychology. *Annual Review of Psychology*, **35**, 553–577.

Campos, J.J., Barrett, K., Lamb, M.E., Goldsmith, H.H., & Stenberg, C. (1983). Socioemotional development. In M.M. Haith & J.J. Campos (Eds.), Infancy and developmental psychobiology, Vol. 2 of P.H. Mussen (Ed.), *Handbook of Child Psychology*, 4th edition (pp. 783–915). New York: Wiley.

Carey, W.B. & McDevitt, S.C. (1978). Revision of the Infant Temperament Questionnaire. *Pediatrics*, **61**, 735–739.

Case, R., Hayward, S., Lewis, M. & Hurst, P. (1987). Toward a neo-Piagetian theory of cognitive and emotional development. *Developmental Review*, 7, 261–312.

Clarke-Stewart, K.A., Umweh, B.I., Snow, M.E. & Pederson, J.A. (1980). Development and predictability of children's sociability from 1 to $2\frac{1}{2}$ years;. *Developmental Psychology*, **16**, 290–302.

Crano, W. (1977). What do infant mental tests test? A cross-lagged panel analysis of selected data from the Berkeley Growth Study. *Child Development*, **48**, 144–151.

Derryberry, D. & Rothbart, M.K. (1984). Emotion, attention and temperament. In C.E. Izard, J. Kagan & R. Zajonc (Eds), *Emotion, cognition and behavior.* New York: Cambridge University Press.

Dolan, A. & Matheny, A.P. (1974). Childhood sleep characteristics and reading achievement. *JSAS Catalog of Selected Documents in Psychology,* **4**, 76 (Manuscript No. 1087).

Emmerich, W., Cocking, R.R. & Sigel, I.E. (1979). Relationships between cognitive and social functioning in preschool children. *Developmental Psychology*, **15**, 495–504.

Field, T., Hallock, N., Ting, G., Dempsey, J., Dabiri, C. & Shuman, H. (1978). A first-year follow-up of high risk infants: Formulating a cumulative risk index. *Child Development*, **49**, 119–131.

Fullard, W., McDevitt, S.C. & Carey, W.B. (1984). Assessing temperament in one- to three-year-old children. *Journal of Pediatric Psychology*, **9**, 205–217.

Goldsmith, H.H. & Gottesman, I.I. (1981). Origins of variation in behavioral style: A longitudinal study of temperament in young twins. *Child Development*, **52**, 91–103.

Gouin-Decarie, T. (1965). *Intelligence and affectivity in early childhood.* New York: International Universities Press.

Gouin-Decarie, T. (1978). Affect development in a Piagetian context. In M. Lewis & L.A. Rosenblum (Eds), *The development of affect*. New York: Plenum.

Gunnar, M. (1988). Salivary cortisol and studies of infant temperament and reactivity. Presented at International Conference on Infant Studies, Washington, DC.

Haviland, J. (1976). Looking smart: The relationship between affect and intelligence in infancy. In M. Lewis (Ed.), *Origins of intelligence: Infancy and early childhood* (pp. 353–378). New York: Plenum.

Hegvik, R.L., McDevitt, S.C. & Carey, W.B. (1982). The Middle Childhood Temperament Questionnaire. *Developmental and Behavioral Pediatrics, 3*, 197–200.

Horn, J.L. (1970). Organization of data on life-span development of human abilities. In L.R. Goulet & P.B. Baltes (Eds), *Life-span developmental psychology: Research and theory*.

Hubert, N.C., Wachs, T.D., Peters-Martin, P. & Gandour, M.J. (1982). The study of early temperament: Measurement and conceptual issues. *Child Development, 53*, 571–600.

Izard, C.E. (1979). Emotions as motivations: An evolutionary–developmental perspective. *Nebraska Symposium on Motivation, 26*, 163–200.

Izard, C.E. (1984). Emotion–cognition relationships and human development. In C.E. Izard, J. Kagan & R.B. Zajonc (Eds), *Emotions, cognitions, and behavior* (pp. 17–37). New York: Cambridge University Press.

Kagan, J. & Kogan, N. (1970). Individuality and cognitive performance. In P.H. Mussen (Ed.), *Carmichael's manual of child psychology*, 3rd edn (pp. 1273–1365). New York: Wiley.

Kaufman, A.S. (1975). Factor analysis of the WISC-R at eleven age levels between $6\frac{1}{2}$ and $16\frac{1}{2}$ years. *Journal of Consulting and Clinical Psychology, 43*, 135–147.

Keogh, B. (1982). Children's temperament and teachers' decisions. In R. Porter & G. Collins (Eds), *Temperamental differences in infants and young children* (pp. 269–279). London: Pitman.

Klein, G.S. (1970). *Perception, motives, and personality*. New York: Knopf.

Kohnstamm, G.A. (1988). Is tractability a neglected aspect of temperament? Paper presented at Temperament Conference, Bellagio, Italy, May 1988.

Lamb, M.E., Garn, S. & Keating, M. (1981). Correlations between sociability and cognitive performance among eight-month-olds. *Child Development, 52*, 711–713.

Lerner, R.M., Palermo, M., Spiro, A. & Nesselroade, J. (1982). Assessing the dimensions of temperamental individuality across the life-span: The Dimensions of Temperament Survey (DOTS). *Child Development, 53*, 149–160.

Martin, R.P. (1983). Temperament: A review of research with implications for the school psychologist. *School Psychology Review, 12*, 266–273.

Martin, R.P., Nagle, R. & Paget, K. (1983). Relationships between temperament and classroom behavior, teacher attitudes, and academic achievement. *Journal of Psychoeducational Assessment, 1*, 377–386.

Matheny, A.P., Jr (1977). Assessment of infant mental development: Tetchy and wayward approaches. In J. Volpe (Ed.), *Clinics in perinatology* (pp. 187–200). Philadelphia: Saunders.

Matheny, A.P., Jr (1980). Bayley's Infant Behavior Record: Behavioral components and twin analysis. *Child Development, 51*, 1157–1167.

Matheny, A.P., Jr (1981). Assessment of temperament in twin children: A reconciliation between structured and naturalistic observations. In L. Gedda, P. Parisi & W. Nance (Eds), *Twin research*, Vol. 3, *Intelligence, personality, and development* (pp. 279–282). New York: Alan Liss.

Matheny, A.P., Jr (1983). A longitudinal study of stabililty of components from Bayley's Infant Behavior Record. *Child Development, 54*, 356–360.

Matheny, A.P., Jr (1984). Twin similarity in the developmental transformation of temperament as measured in a multimethod, longitudinal study. *Acta Geneticae Medicae et Gemellologiae, 33*, 181–190.

Matheny, A.P., Jr (1986). Stability and change in infant temperament: Contributions from the infant, mother, and family environment. In G.A. Kohnstamm (Ed.), *Temperament discussed* (pp. 49–55). Lisse (Neth.): Swetz & Zeitlinger.

Matheny, A.P., Jr (1987). Developmental research of twin's temperament. *Acta Geneticae Medicae et Gemellologiae*, **36**, 135–143.

Matheny, A.P., Jr (1989). Children's behavioral inhibition over age and across situations: Genetic similarity for a trait during change. *Journal of Personality*, **57** (2), 1–21.

Matheny, A.P., Jr (in press). Developmental behavioral genetics. In M. Hahn, J. Hewitt, N. Henderson & R. Benno (Eds), *Genes, development, and behavior*. New York: Oxford University Press.

Matheny, A.P., Jr & Brown, A.M. (1971). Activity, motor coordination and attention: Individual differences in twins. *Perceptual and Motor Skills*, **32**, 151–158.

Matheny, A.P., Jr & Dolan, A.B. (1975). Persons, situations, and time: A genetic view of behavioral change in children. *Journal of Personality and Social Psychology*, **32**, 1106–1110.

Matheny, A.P., Jr, Dolan, A.B. & Wilson, R.S. (1974). Bayley's Infant Behavior Record: Relations between behaviors and mental test scores. *Developmental Psychology*, **10**, 696–702.

Matheny, A.P., Jr, Dolan, A. & Wilson, R.S. (1976). Twins: Within-pair similarity on Bayley's Infant Behavior Record. *Journal of Genetic Psychology*, **28**, 263–270.

Matheny, A.P., Jr, Riese, M.L. & Wilson, R.S. (1985). Rudiments of infant temperament: Newborn to nine months. *Developmental Psychology*, **21**, 486–494.

Matheny, A.P., Jr & Wilson, R.S. (1981). Developmental tasks and rating scales for the laboratory assessment of infant temperament. *JSAS Catalog of Selected Documents in Psychology*, **11**, 81 (Manuscript No. 2367).

Matheny, A.P., Jr, Wilson, R.S., Dolan, A. & Krantz, J. (1981). Behavioral contrasts in twinships: Stability and pattern of differences in childhood. *Child Development*, **52**, 579–588.

Matheny, A.P., Jr, Wilson, R.S. & Nuss, S. (1984a). Developmental tasks and rating scales for the laboratory assessment of social interaction at 3 and 4 years. *JSAS Catalog of Selected Documents in Psychology,* **14**, 22, (Manuscript No. 2643).

Matheny, A.P., Jr, Wilson, R.S. & Nuss, S.N. (1984b). Toddler temperament: Stability over ages and across settings. *Child Development*, **55**, 1200–1211.

Matheny, A.P., Jr, Wilson, R.S. & Thoben, A. (1987). Home and mother: Relations with infant temperament. *Developmental Psychology*, **23**, 323–331.

McCall, R.B., Appelbaum, M.I. & Hogarty, P.S. (1973). Developmental changes in mental performance. *Monographs of the Society for Research in Child Development*, **38** (3, Serial No. 150).

McCall, R.B., Eichorn, D.H. & Hogarty, P.S. (1977). Transitions in early mental development. *Monographs of the Society for Research in Child Development*, **42** (3, Serial No. 171).

McCarthy, D. (1972). *McCarthy Scales of Children's Abilities*. New York: Psychological Corporation.

McDevitt, S.C. & Carey, W.B. (1978). The measurement of temperament in 3- to 7-year old children. *Journal of Child Psychology and Psychiatry*, **19**, 245–253.

Mevarech, Z.R. (1985). The relationships between temperament characteristics, intelligence, task-engagement and mathematics achievement. *British Journal of Educational Psychology*, **55**, 156–163.

Moller, J.S. (1983). Relationships between temperament and development in preschool children. *Research in Nursing and Health*, **6**, 25–32.

Piaget, J. (1981). *Intelligence and affectivity: Their relationship during child development*. Palo Alto, CA: Annual Reviews.

Pullis, M. & Cadwell, J. (1982). The influence of children's temperament characteristics on teacher's decision strategies. *American Educational Research Journal*, **19**, 165–181.

Reiss, A.J. (1961). *Occupations and social status*. New York: Free Press of Glencoe.

Riese, M.L. (1982). Procedures and norms for assessing behavioral patterns in full-term and stable pre-term neonates. *JSAS Catalog of Selected Documents in Psychology*, **12**, 6 (Manuscript No. 2415).

Riese, M.L. (1983). Assessment of behavioral patterns in neonates. *Infant Behavior and Development*, **6**, 241–246.

Riese, M.L. (1987). Temperament stability between the neonatal period and 24 months. *Developmental Psychology*, **23**, 216–222.

Rothbart, M.K. (1986). A psychobiological approach to the study of temperament. In G.A. Kohnstamm (Ed.), *Temperament discussed* (pp. 63–72). Lisse (Neth.): Swets & Zeitlinger.

Rothbart, M.K. & Derryberry, D. (1981). Development of individual differences in temperament. In M.E. Lamb & A.L. Brown (Eds), *Advances in developmental psychology*, Vol. 1. (pp. 37–86). Hillside, NJ: Erlbaum.

Seegmiller, B. & King, W. (1975). Relations between behavioral characteristics of infants, their mothers' behaviors, and performance on the Bayley mental and motor scales. *Journal of Psychology*, **90**, 99–111.

Stankov, L. (1983). Attention and intelligence. *Journal of Educational Psychology*, **75**, 471–490.

Stevenson, M.B. & Lamb, M.E. (1979). Effects of infant sociability and the caretaking environment on infant cognitive performance. *Child Development*, **50**, 340–349.

Stott, L.H. & Ball, R.S. (1965). Infant and preschool mental tests: Review and evaluation. *Monographs of the Society for Research in Child Development*, **30** (3, Serial No. 101).

Strelau, J. (1986). Stability does not mean stability. In G.A. Kohnstamm (Ed.), *Temperament discussed* (pp. 59–62). Lisse (Neth.): Swets & Zeitlinger.

Strelau, J. (1987). Emotion as a key concept in temperament research. *Journal of Research in Personality*, **21**, 510–528.

Terman, L.M. & Merrill, M.A. (1973). *Standford–Binet Intelligence Scale*. Boston: Houghton-Mifflin.

Thomas, A. & Chess, S. (1977). *Temperament and development*. New York: Brunner/Mazel.

Thomas, A. & Chess, S. (1980). *The dynamics of psychological development*. New York: Brunner/Mazel.

Thomas, A., Chess, S. & Birch, H.G. (1968). *Temperament and behavior disorders in children*. New York: New York University Press.

Thomas, A., Chess, S., Birch, H.G., Hertzig, M. & Korn, S. (1963). *Behavioral individuality in early childhood*. New York: New York University Press.

Uzgiris, I.C. (1977). Commentary on McCall, R.B., Eichorn, D.H. & Hogarty, P.S. (1977). Transitions in early mental development. *Monographs of the Society for Research in Child Development*, **42** (3, Serial No. 171).

Wechsler, D. (1967). *Wechsler Preschool and Primary Scale of Intelligence*. New York: Psychological Corporation.

Wechsler, D. (1974). *Wechsler Intelligence Scale for Children – Revised*. New York: Psychological Corporation.

Weinberg, W.A., Rutman, J., Sullivan, L., Penick, E.C. & Dietz, S.G. (1973). Depression in children referred to an educational diagnostic center: Diagnosis and treatment. *Journal of Pediatrics*, **83**, 1065–1072.

Weissbluth, M. (1986). Early sleep problems and temperament. In G.A. Kohnstamm (Ed.), *Temperament discussed* (pp. 147–153). Lisse (Neth.): Swets & Zeitlinger.

White, S.H. (1965). Evidence for a hierarchical arrangement of learning processes. In L.P. Lipsett & C.C. Spiker (Eds), *Advances in child development and behavior*, Vol. 2 (pp. 187–220). New York: Academic Press.

Wilson, R.S. (1972). Twins: Early mental development. *Science*, **175**, 914–917.

Wilson, R.S. (1974). Twins: Mental development in the pre-school years. *Developmental Psychology*, **10**, 580–588.

Wilson, R.S. (1975). Twins: Patterns of cognitive development measured on the Wechsler Preschool and Primary Scale of Intelligence. *Developmental Psychology*, **11**, 126–134.

Wilson, R.S. (1977). Mental development in twins. In A. Oliverio (Ed.), *Genetics, environment, and intelligence* (pp. 305–334). Amsterdam: Elsevier.

Wilson, R.S. (1978). Synchronies in mental development: An epigenetic perspective. *Science*, **202**, 939–948.

Wilson, R.S. (1981). Synchronized developmental pathways for infant twins. In L. Gedda, P. Parisi & W.E. Nance (Eds), *Twin research*, Vol. 3, *Intelligence, personality, and development* (pp. 199–209). New York: Alan Liss.

Wilson, R.S. (1982). Instrinsic determinants of temperament. In CIBA Foundation Symposium 89, *Temperamental differences in infants and young children* (pp. 121–140). London: Pitman.

Wilson, R.S. (1983). The Louisville Twin Study: Developmental synchronies in behavior. *Child Development*, **54**, 298–316.

Wilson, R.S., Brown, A.M. & Matheny, A.P., Jr (1971). Emergence and persistence of behavioral differences in twins. *Child Development*, **42**, 1381–1398.

Wilson, R.S. & Matheny, A.P., Jr (1983a). Assessment of temperament in infant twins. *Developmental Psychology*, **19**, 172–183.

Wilson, R.S. & Matheny, A.P., Jr (1983b). Mental development: Family environment and genetic influences. *Intelligence*, **7**, 195–215.

Wilson, R.S. & Matheny, A.P., Jr (1986). Behavior-genetic research in infant temperament: The Louisville Twin Study. In R. Plomin & J. Dunn (Eds), *The study of temperament: Changes, continuities, and challenges* (pp. 81–97). Hillsdale, NJ: Erlbaum.

Windle, M. & Lerner, R.M. (1986). Reassessing the dimensions of temperamental individuality across the life span: The revised Dimensions of Temperament Survey (DOTS-R). *Journal of Adolescent Research*, **1**, 213–230.

Yarrow, L.J. & Pedersen, F.A. (1976). The interplay between cognition and motivation in infancy. In M. Lewis (Ed.), *Origins of intelligence: Infancy and early childhood* (pp. 379–399). New York: Plenum.

15

Longitudinal Stability of Temperament within a Behavioral Style Framework

BERIT HAGEKULL
University of Uppsala

An overview of different theoretical approaches to the broad field of temperament has been given in a recent roundtable discussion (Goldsmith *et al.*, 1987). In this discussion, criteria for accepting a characteristic as temperamental varied widely, but one of the few points of consensus was the expectation of relative stability of temperament dimensions over time. Based on this presumption, fundamental questions of developmental significance emerge. They concern the existence and developmental course of temperamental characteristics, both in general and within the individual, as outlined by Rothbart in Chapter 12.

The aim of the present chapter is to review methods and results from a project in which three basic questions about stability of temperament have been addressed within a behavioral style framework:

(1) Is there dimensional stability of temperament across age?
(2) Are there age-related changes in temperament dimensional expressions?
(3) Is there individual stability in temperament development?

Phrased in the terminology of Chapter 12, these questions concern stability of structure, invariance in development, and normative stability. The emphasis here will be on the statistical tools and reasoning behind our research on stability. In approaching stability problems, conceptual distinctness of proposed dimensions of temperamental variability seemed to us to be a prerequisite.

CONTENT ANALYSIS EVALUATED

The behavioral style conceptualization of temperament as outlined by Thomas and Chess in the New York Longitudinal Study (NYLS; see, for instance, Thomas &

Temperament in Childhood   Edited by G.A. Kohnstamm, J.E. Bates and M.K. Rothbart
© 1989 John Wiley & Sons Ltd

Chess, 1977, for an overview) can be characterized as a basically non-theoretical approach, where a major objective has been to identify and describe dimensions of individuality that might be of significance for the developmental process. To achieve this aim, a complete description of the infant's or child's behavioral repertoire as expressed in the largest possible range of life situations was sought for developing measurement instruments and, later, more theoretical reasoning. The dimensionality of infant behavior was established by means of a content analysis of parent-report data, where the criteria for a dimension were ubiquitousness (scorable in the parent interview protocols for all 22 of the 3-month-old infants used for the analysis) and variability (Thomas, Chess, Birch, Hertzig & Korn, 1963). In this way, nine categories of temperament were established, and these have been the basis and inspiration for a large amount of research within the area of temperament. The behavioral style conceptualization has continued to rest on these criteria and on the style definition of temperament, which states that the subject of interest is the *how* of behavior (style) rather than the *what* (content) or the *why* (motivation).

A new research area, as child temperament was at the start of the NYLS, has much to gain from an approach geared to the phenomenon itself, in this case the behavioral variability in young children. The most obvious advantage was the possibility of yielding an exhaustive and relatively unbiased description of early individuality. However, when addressing the fundamental question of dimensionality in the observed behavioral variability, employing the method of intuitive content analysis as the sole basis for conclusions has major drawbacks. The subjective nature of the categorization procedure gives no assurance that the behaviors grouped together constitute separate and unidimensional categories. Further, the time-consuming nature of the analysis makes it practically impossible to use a large sample for establishing the dimensions, which leaves open the possibility of unrepresentativeness.

As has been pointed out (Bohlin, Hagekull & Lindhagen, 1981; Buss & Plomin, 1984), questions of dimensionality may best be approached with factor analysis. Not only do factor analytic techniques give an objective grouping of items based on inter-item correlations, but the possibilities for comparing solutions using subjective and theoretical criteria together with more objective statistical guidelines have made factor analysis the method of choice for problems of dimensionality, scale construction, etc. (e.g. Gorsuch, 1974; McKennell, 1970). Recently, the development of Linear Structural Relationships (LISREL) statistical programs (e.g. Jöreskog & Sörbom, 1984), allowing model building and hypothesis testing on the basis of correlational statistics, has made factor analysis even more attractive.

The objective of an initial pilot study (Bohlin, Hagekull & Lindhagen, 1979) was to investigate the dimensionality of infant behaviors as described within the NYLS and also to explore the possibilities of applying factor analytic methodology in this area. The study was designed to constitute a direct test of the dimensional structure established for early infancy by content analysis. As a methodological starting point the Infant Temperament Questionnaire (ITQ; Carey, 1970) was chosen. This instrument was designed to represent the interview material gathered within the NYLS and to yield scores on the nine NYLS dimensions: activity level, rhythmicity, approach–withdrawal, adaptability, threshold of responsiveness, intensity of reaction, quality of mood, distractibility, and attention span and persistence. The ITQ consists of 70 statements intended to cover the total spectrum of behavior of infants aged 3.5–8 months. The items describe specific infant behaviors in specified situations and have three response alternatives. The sample consisted of all infants ($n = 164$) born during a certain month in the district of Uppsala. The infants were 3–5 months of age at the time of questionnaire completion, and the response frequency was 78%, that is, 128 parents filled in the questionnaire.

Before applying factor analytic methods to the data, 11 of the 70 items were discarded because of low absolute response frequencies. The remaining 59 items were still sufficient for a structure of nine dimensions to emerge. Using the method of principal factoring with units in the diagonal (classical factor analysis could not be applied because of skewed distributions due to few response steps), orthogonal and oblique rotations with 5–11 factors were tried in an attempt to find the psychologically most meaningful solution. In interpreting the factors, factor loadings $\geq .35$ were considered. The orthogonal nine-factor solution, accounting for 44.4% of the total variance, was chosen as the most informative and meaningful solution.

In the interpretation of the nine factors it appeared that six (factors 2–7) could be interpreted reasonably well in terms of broad behavioral dimensions. Factor 2 was composed of items describing intensity and activity; factor 3, the regularity of various behaviors. The common aspect of behaviors in factor 4 appeared to be the recognition of novelty in environmental stimulation. Factor 5 contained persistence, distractibility, and threshold items, supposedly mirroring threshold for different external and internal disturbances. Factor 6 concerned general infant mood, and factor 7, the tendency to reject or accept situations that were new to the infant. Three factors were not interpretable in terms of a general behavioral tendency. Thus, factors 1 and 8 each concerned behaviors in a specific situation, namely, reactions to wet and soiled diapers and to various aspects of the feeding situation. Factor 9 contained behaviors in different situations, but a common behavioral tendency was not easily discerned.

A comparison of the content of these factors with the NYLS dimensions indicated that seven of the NYLS categories were represented in five of the obtained factors. Thus, the dimensions of intensity of reaction and activity level were represented in factor 2, rhythmicity and mood dimensions in factors 3 and 6, respectively, and the fifth factor represented the concept of threshold of responsiveness. Factor 7 seemed to tap the adaptability and the approach–withdrawal dimensions. However, in spite of these similarities in conceptualization, the actual allocation of items to specific dimensions showed correspondence between the two studies only for the rhythmicity items. Factors 5, 6, and 7 contained items from NYLS dimensions other than their proposed equivalents. Several items which in the ITQ were scored in the activity, intensity, mood, adaptability, and approach–withdrawal dimensions also did not load in the corresponding factors.

Only two other attempts at replicating the early infancy NYLS structure from the widely used ITQ have been found in the literature (cf. Buss & Plomin, 1984). Rapoport, Pandoni, Renfield, Lake and Ziegler (1977) factor analyzed ITQ data from 185 5-month-old infants, selecting a five-factor principal components solution accounting for 27% of the variance. The five factors dealt with contented adaptable behavior, activity and vigor, negative social responses and crying, mildness, and regularity. Recently, the large-scale Australian Temperament Project (see Chapter 29, by Prior, Sanson & Oberklaid), on the basis of a sample of about 2500 4- to 8-month-old infants (Sanson, Prior, Garino, Oberklaid & Sewell, 1987), has presented a nine-factor solution to the problem of grouping items from the revised ITQ (Carey & McDevitt, 1978). Neither the Australian nor the Rapoport *et al.* study allowed detailed examination of item loading patterns but it seems clear that the only dimension common to all three studies and the original NYLS conceptualization would be that of rhythmicity.

It was concluded that the NYLS-based ITQ provided a usable starting point for factor analytic investigation of behavioral dimensionality in infancy. However, on the basis of the factor analytic groupings of behaviors, the subjective content analysis used in the NYLS to establish dimensions could be seriously questioned. Buss and Plomin (1984), Gibbs, Reeves, and Cunningham (1987), and the Australian group (Prior *et al.*, see Chapter 29) factor analyzed NYLS-based questionnaire data for older children and reached the same conclusion. In our study, less than half the total variance was accounted for in the clusters, pointing to the existence of situation-specific behavioral variance in the items. When the whole behavioral repertoire is expected to fit into broad categories of functioning, overinclusion in intuitive groupings of behaviors would seem to be a risk, and unique behavioral variance in data could thus be overlooked. Also the clustering of specific items in our analyses pointed to problems with intuitive categorizations. The unifying element in a dimension might not be the behavioral disposition intended by the researcher but rather some other common feature in, for instance, the environmental setting.

DIMENSIONALITY OF INFANT BEHAVIOR

The continued work on the description of dimensionality of early behavioral variability was guided by the following ideas and principles:

(1) The measurement instrument should be inclusive of the stylistic aspects of infant emotionality, activity, and attention-related behaviors (cf. Rothbart's definition of temperament, in Chapter 12), and also of the regularity in biologically based behaviors, displayed in a representative range of situations that normal infants encounter.

(2) Because of the rapid behavioral development during infancy, the behavioral descriptions in the measurement instrument must be adapted to specific age periods.

(3) Variability in consecutive age periods should be investigated in separate analyses during a broad age range in infancy.

(4) Response scales must contain more than three steps to avoid skewed distributions.

(5) Cross-validation of dimensional structures should be performed.

In the development of a new questionnaire, only items that had been factor analyzed in the pilot study were considered, and 16 of those were excluded because of loadings < .35 in any of the six factors regarded as broad behavioral dimensions. Another eight items were discarded because of being similar in content to other items. To get a more complete description of behaviors/situations for infants 3 months to 1 year old, information was gathered through interviews with 12 parents of infants of different ages, and item formulations and response scales were tried out. One questionnaire was developed for infants in the age range of 3–10 months (the Baby Behavior Questionnaire; BBQ), and another for the ages 11–15 months (the Toddler Behavior Questionnaire; TBQ). The BBQ contained 54 items and the TBQ 60 items to be answered on five-step response scales with verbal descriptions of the end alternatives. Of the items in the BBQ, about 70% were directly translated or slightly modified ITQ items. In the TBQ, the corresponding proportion was around 60%.

Large samples were needed to perform the analyses described above. The BBQ was sent to a representative sample in Uppsala county consisting of all parents with infants born during four specific months, and the TBQ was mailed 9 months later to the parents with the youngest infants in the BBQ sample. The response frequencies were around 70%, yielding two BBQ age groups (3–6 months, $n = 381$; and 6–10 months, $n = 410$) and a TBQ sample of 357 infants with an age range of 11–15 months. For cross-validational purposes, the samples were randomly split. (Futher details about the questionnaires, samples, and analyses can be found in Bohlin *et al.*, 1981, and in Hagekull, Lindhagen & Bohlin, 1980).

In order to investigate the gradual development of the dimensionality of behavioral variation, the starting point for analyses was the sample of the youngest infants, 3–6 months old. After having found an acceptable solution for this group, our work aimed at establishment of structures in older age groups and comparisons between ages. Solutions with six to nine extracted factors were obliquely and orthogonally rotated and compared in terms of factor stability, structure simplicity, and item specificity. Selected solutions were cross-validated through replication in sample subgroups, involving comparisons of Procrustes rotated solutions by the help of congruence coefficients, distributions of residuals, and salient variable indexes (see Gorsuch, 1974, for a discussion of comparison procedures). A final solution was chosen as the best representative of the dimensional structure in each of the three age groups. These solutions are listed in Table 1 with factor names resulting from the interpretation procedure.

Interpretation of Dimensions

Apart form the statistical tools used for comparing solutions, judgments of the psychological meaningfulness of the different factors were important guides in the decision-making process. In the interpretation phase, only items with factor loadings $\geq$ .30 were considered. Because a temperament trait had been conceptualized as a behavioral disposition likely to influence overt behavior in many situations, one criterion for factor meaningfulness was interpretability in terms of *broad behavioral* dimensions. Thus, the factor should describe behaviors

Table 1　Interpreted factor solutions for different age groups

Factor no.	Younger BBQ sample (3–6 months)	Older BBQ sample (6–10 months)	TBQ sample (11–15 months)	Combined BBQ samples (3–10 months)
1	Intensity/ Activity	Intensity/ Attentiveness	Intensity/ Activity	Intensity/ Activity
2	Regularity	Regularity	Manageability	Regularity
3	Approach–Withdrawal	Manageability	Regularity	Approach–Withdrawal
4	Frustration tolerance	Approach–Withdrawal	Approach–Withdrawal	Sensory sensitivity
5	Sensory sensitivity	Sensory sensitivity	Sensory sensitivity	Attentiveness
6	Attentiveness	Activity	Sensitivity to new food	Manageability
7	Sensitivity to new food	Sensitivity to new food	Attentiveness	Sensitivity to new food
8	–	Mood in routine care situations	Adaptability	–
Hyperplane count	59%	62%	62%	60%
Double loading items	3	2	2	1
Explained proportion of total variance	34.2%	37%	34.3%	33.6%

BBQ, Baby Behavior Questionnaire; TBQ, Toddler Behavior Questionnaire.

in a range of situations and an underlying behavioral disposition should be discernible as the unifying element of the items making up the factor. In all age groups, the majority of factors reflected such broad dispositions (see Table 1). In each age group, however, one situation-specific factor appeared, namely, sensitivity to new food. This dimension was not considered meaningful from the point of view of temperament.

Another factor, which appeared in the older age groups, described behaviors in many different situations. Persistence, mood, activity (in diaper-change and bath situations), and, in the 6- to 10-month age group, adaptability items clustered here, but a unifying behavioral disposition was difficult to find. There was, however, correspondence between this dimension and the factor analytic construct of tractability derived in the Louisville Twin Study (Matheny, Wilson & Nuss, 1984; Wilson & Matheny, 1983) from scale scores for 12- to 24-month-old infants on an NYLS-based questionnaire for toddlers (Fullard, McDevitt & Carey, 1984). The tractability factor obtained at 12 months contained adaptability, attention/ persistence, approach, mood, and distractibility scales. Wilson and Matheny (1983) described this factor as 'the major constellation that mothers perceived as expressive of temperament' (Wilson & Matheny, 1983, p. 179). We interpreted our factor in terms of infant manageability, a child characteristic possibly evolving from the close everyday mother–infant interaction. The factor was retained, leaving future research to elucidate further the conceptual status of the underlying dimension.

The rest of the factors were easily interpreted on the basis of their salient loadings as mirroring relatively broad behavioral dispositions. The NYLS definition of temperament as the *how* of behavior was imposed on the obtained factors in order to reach a better understanding of the conceptual basis of the dimensions (Hagekull, 1982). This was done by trying to extract the unifying element in each factor. It was then asked if the common denominator of these items could be seen as a stylistic aspect of behavior. This was clearly the case for the Intensity/Activity factors, for the factors describing rhythmicity in biologically based functions, for the Approach–Withdrawal categories, describing emotional reactivity to novel persons and situations, and for the factors dealing with sensitivity to sensory stimulation. The two age-specific factors describing reactions in frustrating situations and adaptability of behaviors in new settings also seemed to reflect styles of behavior. The unifying behavioral element in the Attentiveness factors, on the other hand, was more likely to be alertness or cognitive capacity. Most items described whether a reaction occurred or not rather than the how of responding, and these factors were thus seen as reflecting a broad behavioral, but not a behavioral style, dimension. However, as discussed by Rothbart in Chapter 12, attentional processes have been included in several other temperament approaches, and a distinction between attention-getting and attention-holding processes could be made. This distinction was reflected in our dimensional structure, in that attention-getting behaviors had clustered in the Attentiveness factors, while behaviors indicative of attention-holding processes were found in the Manage-ability factors.

A question of great relevance to the conceptualization of the obtained factors concerned the validity of the parent-report methodology. Could parent descriptions be said to reflect infant behavior? This was investigated in a series of empirical studies where directly observed infant behavior was related to maternal BBQ ratings (Hagekull, Bohlin & Lindhagen, 1984). The estimated concurrent validity coefficients showed that a minimum of 28% (Sensory sensitivity) and a maximum of 69% (Attentiveness) of the variance in the dimensional descriptions could be attributed to actual infant behavior.

For the TBQ, several sources of validity evidence could be put together. These included parental agreements, and observer–mother and observer–father agree-ments (Hagekull, 1985; Hagekull & Bohlin, 1986; unpublished data for parental agreement in an ongoing longitudinal study including around 120 families). Adopting a criterion for dimensional validity of at least two significant correlations, it can be concluded that all TBQ scales, except Attentiveness (with one significant correlation) give valid accounts of infant behavior.

Dimensional Stability Across Age

Visual inspection of the factor solutions obtained for different age groups (Table 1) revealed similarities in terms of number of dimensions and in types of dimensions.

There were also, however, dissimilarities, suggesting some instability (cf. Rothbart, Chapter 12). In each period, one age-specific factor appeared. Such clusterings might be representations of a disappearing characteristic (Frustration tolerance), of an emerging dimension, not discernible until certain behaviors have been more fully developed (Mood in routine care situations and Adaptability), or just chance results. The retainment of such disparate factors in a system can be made dependent upon further cross-validation data and on the possibility of making homogeneous scales on the basis of items with salient factor loadings. Another difference between the age periods pertained to the Manageability factor, which did not appear in the youngest age group but explained large amounts of variance in the oldest age group, where it was extracted as the first or the second factor in all solutions tried. The third difference concerned intensity, activity, and attentiveness items, which were combined or split in different ways in the three solutions.

In statistical comparisons of the different age-group solutions, the first step was to explore the possibility of obtaining a single solution accounting for the behavioral variability during the first two periods. This was done in a series of exploratory analyses performed on the combined BBQ sample of 791 infants, aged 3–10 months, followed by a series of confirmatory analyses based on the previously selected solutions for the separate age groups. After cross-validation, a seven-factor solution, accounting for 33.6% of the variance (see Table 1), was found to yield the most meaningful and stable description.

The second step was to investigate the dimensional similarity between the BBQ age group (3–10 months) and the TBQ age group (11–15 months) in a comparison between the structure covering the whole BBQ age range and the eight-factor solution established for the TBQ sample (Hagekull *et al.*, 1980). Visual inspection of factor names indicated great similarity, the only exception being the Adaptability factor in the TBQ solution which had no counterpart in the sample of younger infants. The final evaluation of structural similarity was performed with Cattell's *s*-index according to the procedure described by Gorsuch (1974), where pairs of factors are compared in terms of salient loadings. The results showed close correspondence for six of the dimensions. The Attentiveness factors showed more item dissimilarities, and the Adaptability factor was not related to any factor in the solution for the sample of younger infants.

Thus, about a third of infant behavioral variability from 3 to 15 months could be accounted for by the same set of seven dimensions, although the item descriptions differed in some cases due to developmental level studied. Not all dimensions could be considered as reflecting behavioral style, but in further work they were all retained, except the situationally very specific factor concerning reactions to new food. The conceptually somewhat diverging dimensions of Attentiveness and Manageability seemed interesting as potentially important for the development of cognitive capacities and the parent–infant relationship.

Age-Related Development and Individual Stability

Scales were constructed on the basis of salient loadings in the factors (Hagekull & Bohlin, 1981). To optimize homogeneity and number of items in each scale, the procedure using coefficient alphas outlined by McKennell (1970) was followed. A homogeneous adaptability scale could not be constructed from the salient loadings, and thus two sets of six scales each (one for BBQ ratings and one for TBQ ratings) were developed to measure the same six dimensions. The mean of the scale items, each scored from 1 to 5, were used as scale scores for individuals. Test–retest checks (Hagekull & Bohlin, 1981) showed sufficient reliability for research purposes (*r* range .63 to .93; *Md* = .79).

Age changes in the expression of the different dispositions were investigated with *t*-tests; for comparisons between BBQ and TBQ data, only items indentical in corresponding scales were used (Hagekull, 1985; Hagekull & Bohlin, 1981). In general, group mean changes followed a pattern that could be predicted from general motor, cognitive, and socioemotional development. Infants became more intensive and active, more regular in eating, sleeping, and elimination patterns, and more attentive to minor discrepancies in the environment from the first half-year to the second. During the second half-year of life, as a group they also showed more withdrawing tendencies in new situations (possibly an expression of the stranger-anxiety phenomenon; e.g. Sroufe, 1977), they became less sensitive to strong environmental stimulation, and the parents also described them as less manageable, that is, they showed more negative mood, less persistence in self-amusement, and less concentration in different situations.

Significant developmental changes in the same directions were also found in comparisons between the two older age groups, with two exceptions. The regularity of biologically based functions and the withdrawing tendencies did not increase. Recent data (unpublished) from our ongoing longitudinal study allowed comparisons between TBQ scale values at the mean ages of 10 months and 15 months, that is, slightly higher ages than in the comparison between the two older samples in the original study. Here two significant changes appeared according to both maternal and paternal ratings: sensory sensitivity decreased and manage-ability increased. The manageability change, which is contrary to the previously described trend, might be a reflection of the more advanced motor development in the oldest group, which might decrease infants' need for parental stimulation and negative mood outbursts, and thus be reflected in a higher manageability score.

With these changes in levels of dimensional expression in mind, individual stability in terms of product–moment correlations has been explored both in the original samples described above and in other smaller samples (e.g. Hagekull, 1985; Hagekull & Bohlin, 1981). Stability coefficients from different studies covering different intervals and age periods between 3 and 15 months have been explored. The widest range of values and the lowest median are found for the Manageability dimension, which suggests that this clustering of behaviors could be more dependent than other dimensions upon environmental influences. Its highest stability values are obtained in the oldest age period, 10–15 months. For the other dimensions the stability coefficients range from low to modest (cf. Chapter 12, by Rothbart). In summary, there is a core of common variance over the age periods studied which to a large extent could be attributed to individually stable infant behavioral variability.

Conceptualization of the Manageability Dimension

During the factor analytic and interpretational work described above, the factor that in the beginning was somewhat tentatively named Manageability posed interesting conceptual problems because of its gradually evolving special characteristics: late appearance and relatively low homogeneity in the younger age group ($\alpha = .51$), increasing importance and homogeneity with age, a behavioral disposition not easily discerned as having a unifying item element and thus unclear relationship to temperament constructs, a U-shaped development over the ages studied, and relatively low normative stability. Recently, the similarity of our Manageability dimension to constructs described by researchers working in other theoretical frameworks has been pointed out (Kohnstamm, 1988).

In the Manageability factors, activity and adaptability to new routines were important features in the younger sample, while persistence and mood items were more prominent at the older ages. Low manageability in the younger ages would include an infant with low persistence in self-amusement and with a new toy, showing negative mood and high activity level during diapering, high activity during bathing, and slow adaptability in new places. A 1-year-old of low manageability would show low concentration and persistence in various activities, such as toy play, playful social interaction, book reading, and in feeding situations. This child would also exhibit negative mood in many routine care situations, such as nail-cutting, diapering, dressing, and after feeds. Adhering to the general idea of behavioral variability as being partly of constitutional orgin (cf. Goldsmith *et al.*, 1987), we searched for an early-appearing infant characteristic as a contributor to the evolvement of the Manageability dimension. Our tentative guess was that irritability or negative emotionality as defined by Rothbart (Chapter 12) would be related to manageability (Bohlin *et al.*, 1981).

Some behavioral dimensions described by other researchers had no direct counterparts in our dimensional system, including irritability (e.g. Birns, Barten & Bridger, 1969; Moss, 1967; Riese, 1983; Wilson, Brown & Matheny, 1971), soothability (e.g. Birns *et al.*, 1969; Korner, 1971; Riese, 1983; Rowe & Plomin, 1977), and cuddliness (e.g. Korner, 1971; Schaffer & Emerson, 1964). In a small study ($n = 29$), these dimensions were directly observed by mothers of infants (age range 12–32 weeks, $M = 22.6$ weeks). Soothability and cuddliness were studied in a number of structured observation situations with the type of methodology developed in our validity studies (Hagekull *et al.*, 1984), and each irritability outburst was recorded in a diary during a period of 8 days. The observational data were related to BBQ ratings of the infants made immediately before and after the observations (mean interval = 8.9 weeks). The results showed significant correlations between frequency of irritable outburst and both BBQ Manageability ratings ($r = .45$, $p < .05$ for the combined BBQ scores). No relationship was found for type of irritable outbursts; neither soothability nor cuddliness was significantly related to manageability.

Another approach to the problem of finding the behavioral disposition underlying the Manageability dimension was to search for relationships between newborn behavior as assessed with the Brazelton Neonatal Behavioral Assessment

Scale (Brazelton, 1973; for clustering of the behaviors, see Lester, Als & Brazelton, 1982) and later BBQ/TBQ ratings ($n = 37$) obtained at infant ages 4 and 12 months (Hagekull, 1985). It was hypothesized that the neonatal dimensions of orientation, habituation, and regulation of state would be related to manageability. The results showed regulation of state, which partly can be seen as the child's ability to ease distress and irritability by its own means, to be related to manageability at 4 months ($r=.35$, $p<.05$). Orientation and habituation were associated with TBQ manageability at 12 months ($r=.38$ and $-.36$, respectively, $p<.05$). These results fit in nicely with BBQ/TBQ item content at the different ages. Thus, the more self-regulatory ability (and probably the less irritability) the newborn infant had shown, the more content s/he was as a 4-month-old baby when left to amuse her/himself and in new situations. When concentration, persistence, and mood became more important aspects of manageability around 1 year of age, the neonatal capability of orienting to new stimuli was shown to be of predictive value. Rapid habituation in newborn infants was predictive of low persistence, which might be seen as equivalent to rapid habituation, and negative mood at 12 months.

Finally, the conceptual similarities between the Manageability dimension and the well-known construct of difficultness (a constellation of slow adaptability, negative mood, irregularity, withdrawal in new situations, and intense reactions, developed within the NYLS: see, for instance, Thomas, Chess & Birch, 1968) prompted a statistical test of the correspondence between the two constructs. This was achieved by trying to establish with LISREL model building and second order factor analysis a BBQ and a TBQ construct of difficultness from longitudinal data in the youngest and the oldest age groups ($n = 322$) in the original samples (Hagekull, 1985). It was concluded that no difficult-child construct could be established in the 3- to 6-month age period, which seemed logical, in view of the non-existence of a Manageability dimension in this period. In the 11- to 15-month sample, however, a valid latent factor structure with an acceptable fit to the model was found, comprising the dimension of Manageability as its most important factor, and also the Intensity/Activity, Regularity, and Approach–Withdrawal dimensions. This structure also closely resembled the empirically derived Australian Easy–Difficult Scale (see Chapter 29, by Prior et al.), comprising the dimensions cooperation-manageability and irritability (capturing the essence of our Manageability factor), and approach.

In summary, manageability might well have early-appearing roots in both a self-regulatory capacity to modulate bodily state and in the environmentally directed attentional capacities of orientation and habituation. These capacities have previously been related to irritability or negative emotionality (see Chapter 12, by Rothbart), which thus might be the underlying manageability infant characteristic. Infant distress behaviors are most important contributors to the parent–infant relationship. Isofar as the Manageability dimension reflects the amount of such behaviors, it could be hypothesized that it would exert an influence on both maternal experiences and behavior, which indeed it has been shown to do (Hagekull & Bohlin, 1986, and in press). Furthermore, this child characteristic could also be an important basis for a later-developing dimension of difficultness.

Conceptualization of the Approach–Withdrawal Dimension

Another scale of potential interest for developmental psychology is the Approach–Withdrawal dimension. In contrast to the Manageability dimension, this factor was highly stable across rotations and ages in both position in the factor solutions and in item content. Its normative stability, however, was relatively low (although significant coefficients were obtained for all intervals), showing the same pattern as Manageability, with a stability increase only in the last period studied.

Although the dimension was given the same name as its origin in the NYLS dimensional structure, it differed in an important respect: the BBQ/TBQ Approach–Withdrawal scales were more narrow in the range of situations and behaviors described than the NYLS category. The NYLS categorization suggested that reactions to *all* types of new encounters (food, toys, persons, places, etc) should be referred back to the same behavioral disposition. The factor analytic treatment of our data showed this to be an untenable position (cf. Bates, 1986). In the BBQ/TBQ factors, items concerning emotional reactions to new social encounters clustered together with a more general item asking about adaptability to new situations/places (which of course often entails unfamiliar social aspects as well as a new physical environment). The item content and the relatively low stability during the first year suggested that there might be a link between our social Approach–Withdrawal dimension and the stranger-anxiety phenomenon, known to appear during the second half-year of life. A more precisely phrased question would be: is stranger reactivity towards the end of the first year, including both positive and negative reactions, an age-related phenomenon that normally developing individuals experience, independent of their early-appearing approach–withdrawal dispositions?

From longitudinal observations in our ongoing research, predictive relationships have recently been investigated (unpublished data). Correlations between 4-month data (thus obtained before stranger-anxiety reactions normally occur) and 10- and 12-month sociability (as assessed in a situation designed to elicit positive stranger responses; Stevenson & Lamb, 1979) showed little predictive value for the Approach–Withdrawal dimension ($r=.14$, $n= 107$, $p<.10$ at 10 months; $r=.03$ at 12 months). Negative emotional reactions to strangers were studied in the classical infant–stranger encounter situation (e.g. Sroufe, 1977) at 10 months, and at 12 months with a measure of crying/fussing when the parent left the infant alone with a stranger during a home observation. There was a low significant and discriminative relationship ($r= -.19$, $n= 111$, $p<.05$; no other temperament scale predicted the reactions) between 4-month approach and 10-month negative reactions to the approaching stranger when the mother was not present. The prediction to age 12 months yielded a lower value in the same direction ($r = -.13$, $n= 114$, $p<.10$); high approach predicted low degree of crying.

These low predictive correlations suggested that the stranger reactions emanating during the second half of the first year might be relatively independent of earlier reaction tendencies to new social encounters. This result could be referred back to the development of behavioral inhibition (as discussed by Rothbart in Chapter 12), a self-regulatory control system which might undermine stability in expression of stranger reactions during the first year of life. Insofar as age of onset and behavioral manifestations of this system vary between individuals, high correlations could not be expected. If there is independence between the processes governing early social reactivity and later behavioral inhibition of social behaviors, stranger-reaction stability could not be expected. To address questions of the interdependence and relative significance of early social approach and later-appearing inhibition tendencies as disclosed in social situations, predictive relationships from the first and second half-year of life to future social behaviors should be investigated.

CONCLUSIONS

The work reported illustrates the usefulness of factor analytic approaches to a search for order and structure in the behavioral diversity exhibited by young infants. Several statistical tests and indexes aided us in the search process along with the necessarily more subjective/conceptual criterion of psychological meaningfulness. With this approach we have been able to demonstrate that the same set of dimensions can be used to describe about a third of the variation in behavior during a large part – about 12 months – of the early infancy period. With the relatively homogeneous scales obtained, we have also demonstrated developmentally related changes in levels of behavioral expression of the dispositions as well as modest normative stability across several time intervals. Exciting outcomes of this work were also the questions and problems arising in the interpretation of the constructs obtained. Such questions have formed one of the bases for our ongoing research aimed at achieving a deeper understanding of child individuality. As Rutter (see the discussion section in McNeil & Persson-Blennow, 1982) has pointed out, the final answer as to what constitutes useful temperament variables lies in the predictive relationships researchers can establish between temperament and other important developmental constructs. Temperament researchers have just begun the search.

ACKNOWLEDGMENTS

This research was financed by the Swedish Council for Research in the Humanities and Social Sciences.

REFERENCES

Bates, J.E. (1986). The measurement of temperament. In R. Plomin & J. Dunn (Eds), *The study of temperament: Changes, continuities and challenges*. Hillsdale, NJ: Erlbaum.

Birns, B., Barten, S. & Bridger, W. (1969). Individual differences in temperament characteristics of infants. *Transactions of the New York Academy of Sciences*, **31**, 1071–1082.

Bohlin, G., Hagekull, B. & Lindhagen, K. (1979). *Early individuality: Dimensions in infant behavior*. Uppsala Psychological Reports, No. 248. (ERIC Document Reproduction Service No. ED 176881.)

Bohlin, G., Hagekull, B. & Lindhagen, K. (1981). Dimensions of infant behavior. *Infant Behavior and Development*, **4**, 83–96.

Brazelton, T.B. (1973). *Neonatal Behavioral Assessment Scale*. London: Spastics International Medical Publications.

Buss, A.H. & Plomin, R. (1984). *Temperament: Early developing personality traits.* Hillsdale, NJ: Erlbaum.

Carey, W.B. (1970). A simplified method for measuring infant temperament. *Journal of Pediatrics,* **81**, 188–194.

Carey, W.B. & McDevitt, S. (1978). Revision of the Infant Temperament Questionnaire. *Pediatrics,* **61**, 735–739.

Fullard, W., McDevitt, S.C. & Carey, W.B. (1984). Assessing temperament in one- to three-year-old children. *Journal of Pediatric Psychology,* **9**, 205–217.

Gibbs, M.V., Reeves, D. & Cunningham, C.C. (1987). The application of temperament questionnaires to a British sample: Issues of reliability and validity. *Journal of Child Psychology and Psychiatry,* **28**, 61–77.

Goldsmith, H., Buss, A.H., Plomin, R., Rothbart, M.K., Thomas, A., Chess, S., Hinde, R.A. & McCall, R.B. (1987). What is temperament? Four approaches. *Child Development,* **58**, 505–529.

Gorsuch, R.L. (1974). *Factor analysis.* Philadelphia: W.B. Saunders.

Hagekull, B. (1982). Measurement of behavioral differences in infancy. *Acta Universitatis Upsaliensis. Abstracts of Uppsala Dissertations from the Faculty of Social Science,* No. 26.

Hagekull, B. (1985). The Baby and Toddler Questionnaires: Empirical studies and conceptual considerations. *Scandinavian Journal of Psychology,* **26**, 110–122.

Hagekull, B. & Bohlin, G. (1981). Individual stability in dimensions of infant behavior. *Infant Behavior and Development,* **4**, 97–108.

Hagekull, B. & Bohlin, G. (1986). Mother–infant interaction and perceived infant temperament. *International Journal of Behavioral Development,* **9**, 297–313.

Hagekull, B. & Bohlin, G. (in press). Early infant temperament and maternal expectations related to maternal adaptation. *International Journal of Behavioral Development.*

Hagekull, B., Bohlin, G. & Lindhagen, K. (1984). Validity of parental reports. *Infant Behavior and Development,* **7**, 77–92.

Hagekull, B., Lindhagen, K. & Bohlin, G. (1980). Behavioral dimensions in one-year-olds and dimensional stability in infancy. *International Journal of Behavioral Development,* **3**, 351–364.

Jöreskog, K.G. & Sörbom, D. (1984). *LISREL VI. Analysis of linear structural relationships by maximum likelihood, instrumental variables, and least squares methods,* 3rd edn. Uppsala: University of Uppsala, Department of Statistics.

Kohnstamm, G.A. (1988). Is tractability a neglected aspect of temperament? Paper presented at the Conference of Temperament Risk Factors in Children, Their Identification and Management by Health Services and Educators, Bellagio, Italy, May 1988.

Korner, A.F. (1971). Individual differences at birth: Implications for early experience and later development. In J.C. Westman (Ed.), *Individual differences in children* (pp. 69–82). New York: Wiley.

Lester, B.M., Als, H. & Brazelton, T.B. (1982). Regional obstetric anasthesia and newborn behavior: A reanalysis toward synergistic effects. *Child Development,* **50**, 340–349.

Matheny, A.P., Wilson, R.S. & Nuss, S.M. (1984). Toddler temperament: Stability across settings and over ages. *Child Development,* **55**, 1200–1211.

McKennell, A. (1970). Attitude measurement: Use of coefficient alpha with cluster or factor analysis. *Sociology,* **4**, 227–245.

McNeil, T.F. & Persson-Blennow, I. (1982). Temperament questionnaires in clinical research. In *Temperamental differences in infants and young children.* Ciba Foundation Symposium No. 89. London: Pitman.

Moss, H.A. (1967). Sex, age, and state as determinants of mother–infant interaction. *Merrill-Palmer Quarterly,* **13**, 19–36.

Rapoport, J.L., Pandoni, C., Renfield, M., Lake, C.R. & Ziegler, M.G. (1977). Newborn dopamine-β-hydroxylase, minor physical anomalies, and infant temperament. *American Journal of Psychiatry,* **134**, 676–679.

Riese, M. (1983). Behavioral patterns in full-term and preterm infants. *Acta Geneticae Medicae et Gemellogiae*, **32**, 209–220.

Sanson, A., Prior, M., Garino, E., Oberklaid, F. & Sewell, J. (1987). The structure of infant temperament: Factor anlaysis of the Revised Infant Temperament Questionnaire. *Infant Behavior and Development*, **10**, 97–104.

Schaffer, H.R. & Emerson, P.E. (1964). The development of social attachments in infancy. *Monographs of the Society for Research in Child Development*, **29** (3), Serial No. 94.

Sroufe, L.A. (1977). Wariness of strangers and the study of infant development. *Child Development*, **48**, 731–746.

Stevenson, M.B. & Lamb, M.E. (1979). Effects of infant sociability and the caretaking environment on infant cognitive performance. *Child Development*, **50**, 340–349.

Thomas, A. & Chess, S. (1977). *Temperament and development.* New York: Brunner/Mazel.

Thomas, A., Chess, S. & Birch, H.G. (1968). *Temperament and behavior disorders in children.* New York: New York University Press.

Thomas, A., Chess, S., Birch, H.G., Hertzig, M. & Korn, S. (1963). *Behavioral individuality in early childhood.* New York: New York University Press.

Wilson, R.S., Brown, A.M. & Matheny, A.P. (1971). Emergence and persistence of behavioral differences in twins. *Child Development*, **42**, 1381–1398.

Wilson, R.S. & Matheny, A.P. (1983). Assessment of temperament in infant twins. *Developmental Psychology*, **19**, 172–183.

16

Neonatal Irritability and the Development of Attachment

DYMPHNA C. VAN DEN BOOM
University of Leiden

There is currently some disagreement among attachment and temperament theorists as to both the relation between infant temperament and attachment in general, and the role of temperament in influencing Strange Situation assessments in particular. At one extreme is the view that infant temperament is not related in any causal way to attachment classifications (Sroufe, 1985; Sroufe & Waters, 1982). At the other extreme is the view that the classifications reflect the infant's characteristic temperamental response to a stressful situation rather than attachment quality (Chess & Thomas, 1982; Kagan, 1984). In this paper we shall discuss theoretical links between attachment and irritability, the dimension of infant behavior that is unanimously agreed upon by most temperament theorists as an instance of temperament. In addition, the results of two empirical studies on this relationship, an observational and an intervention study, will be reported.

In the Bowlby/Ainsworth tradition, attachment (in contrast to attachment behavior) is viewed as a relational construct (Sroufe & Fleeson, 1986). Attachment classifications, although based solely on infant behavior, are presumed to reflect the history of caregiver sensitivity (Matas, Arend & Sroufe, 1978). Temperament, on the other hand, is not simply an interactional phenomenon, in that it is seen to exist apart from the interactional process (Campos, Barrett, Lamb, Goldsmith & Stenberg, 1983). Mother–infant interaction, nevertheless, influences the expression of temperament, and an important feature of temperament is its role in regulating social interaction. Because attachment refers to the presence of an affective bond between mother and infant (Ainsworth, Blehar, Waters & Wall, 1978), and temperament is closely related to emotion (Goldsmith & Campos, 1982), investigators have suggested that individual differences in temperament could conceivably affect attachment in any of several ways (Campos *et al.*, 1983; Goldsmith, Bradshaw & Rieser-Danner, 1986; Rothbart & Derryberry, 1981).

Temperament in Childhood   Edited by G.A. Kohnstamm, J.E. Bates and M.K. Rothbart
© 1989 John Wiley & Sons Ltd

Theoretical integration of the concepts of attachment and temperament is still in its infancy, and most research aimed at discerning empirical relationships between temperament and attachment consists of simply correlating parents' perceptions of temperament with assessments of the security of attachment. Goldsmith *et al.* (1986) rightly point out that this is only a crude first approach to the issue. Both temperament and attachment researchers are nevertheless studying variables that influence the quality of mother–infant interaction and both types of variable may be expected to influence the quality of the attachment relationship at the end of the first year.

ATTACHMENT AND TEMPERAMENT AS SOCIAL BEHAVIOR

Attachment theory and temperament theories distinguish the theoretical constructs attachment and temperament from actual instances of behavior (Ainsworth, 1973; Rothbart & Goldsmith, 1985). Both attachment and temperament are inferred from behavior, and most of the behavior with which both kind of theories are concerned is social behavior (Stevenson-Hinde & Hinde, 1986). Social behavior is usually observed in interactions, that is, exchanges that are limited in time, and interactions can be described by specifying the content and their quality or style. Relationships involve a series of interactions in time between individuals known to each other (Hinde, 1976).

Hinde (1979) has specified eight dimensions as a framework for describing relationships and understanding their dynamics, ranging from the properties of specific interactions to more global properties of the relationship. One of the most crucial of these properties is the quality of the interactions within a relationship. In attachment theory maternal sensitivity is an example of an interactional quality that is of crucial importance for the security of the attachment relationship. If attachment is viewed as a relational construct (Sroufe & Fleeson, 1986) which arises from interaction, then individual differences in infant–mother interaction will lead to differences among attachment relationships by the end of the first year. Because interaction is determined by the contributions of each partner in a process of mutual influence, it can be predicted that some aspects of early infant behavior might influence interaction and eventually be associated with outcomes of the attachment process (Waters & Deane, 1982).

Clearly the concept of temperament will be relevant to only some of the properties of interactions and relationships. It may have little relevance, for instance, to the content of interactions (e.g. the kinds of things individuals do together), but be highly relevant to their quality, and indirectly relevant to properties such as intimacy and interpersonal perception (Hinde, 1979; Stevenson-Hinde & Hinde, 1986). As such it will be important to take temperament into consideration when studying the development of attachment relationships in mother–infant dyads. If temperament particularly influences the quality of the interaction, it might be predicted that it would also be associated with attachment outcomes.

IRRITABILITY AS AN ASPECT OF TEMPERAMENT

At present the field of temperament is characterized by divergency in approaches, with theorists disagreeing about the actual dimensions of temperament. Nevertheless, one thing temperament theorists agree about is the inclusion of negative emotions in their multidimensional constructs of temperament. Negative emotionality is accepted by most theorists as an instance of temperament. Besides that it has been shown to influence the quality of mother–infant interaction (Crockenberg & Acredolo, 1983; Linn & Horowitz, 1983).

The most influential recent theory of temperament has come from the New York Longitudinal Study (Thomas & Chess, 1977) which focuses on individual differences in the stylistic aspects of behavior. Thomas and Chess delineated nine dimensions of temperament and negative emotion is captured in two of their dimensions, quality of mood and intensity, both of which are included in their description of the 'difficult' child as exhibiting negative mood and high intensity of responses.

Emotionality is one of the three broad dimensions identified by Buss and Plomin (1984). In terms of temperament, arousal is the crucial component that yields inherited individual differences. Buss and Plomin consider distress, the tendency to become upset easily and intensely, to be primordial emotionality. It is assumed that distress, the most primitive negative emotion, differentiates during infancy into fear and anger.

Negative emotionality is included in Rothbart and Derryberry's (1981) temperament construct of reactivity which refers to the excitability, responsivity, or arousability of the behavioral and physiological systems of the organism. Negative emotionality is approached in terms of the duration or intensity of stimulation which can be endured before a distress threshold is reached. Infants appear to differ in the levels of stimulation or arousal which they can experience before distress is elicited. Once such a threshold is attained, infants also differ in the peak to which their distress reactions rise: some infants seldom move beyond moderate fussiness, while others build all the way to hard, harsh wailing. Some infants also rise gradually toward their peak of distress, while other infants may move rapidly to the level of intense crying. The reactivity and self-regulation approach described by Rothbart and Derryberry (1981) is similar to the theory proposed by Strelau (1983) for adults.

Goldsmith and Campos (1982) identify temperament as individual differences in the probability of experiencing and expressing the primary emotions and arousal. The organization of affect is of special importance to social interaction. Cognitive processes are excluded from the definition of temperament. Goldsmith and Campos (1982) do not propose a particular list of temperament variables. In their review of the variables proposed by each of the major theories they conclude that many of the temperament scales have a component of emotional expression, even though the scales differ according to the degree to which they express discrete affects. In this temperament-as-affect approach anger and fearfulness are among the primary emotions that reflect negative emotionality.

Kagan, Reznick and Snidman (1986) find it too early to list a minimal set of fundamental temperamental dispositions. In their behavioral inhibition approach two related candidates refer to the child's initial behavioral reactions to unfamiliar people, objects, and contexts or challenging situations. The tendency to withdraw or to approach such incentives, which is moderately stable, is seen most clearly during the transition from infancy to early childhood. The underlying predisposition of individual differences in behavioral inhibition and lack of inhibition may be observed before the age of 3 in a different form. Kagan *et al.* suggest that if the biological bases for the differences in inhibition are present during the first months of life, they might be reflected in extreme distress to frustration, extreme irritability, poor quality of sleep, chronic constipation, and other symptoms reflecting high levels of arousal in the central nervous system circuits involving the hypothalamus, pituitary, adrenal, reticular activating system, and the sympathetic arm of the autonomic nervous system.

Bates (1980) has focused his efforts on the identification of the temperamental type called 'difficult'. Bates' (1982) operational definition of difficult temperament is centered around parentally perceived difficultness and originates from his interest in the social impact of temperament. The Infant Characteristics Questionnaire (ICQ) was developed which contains rating items about behavior patterns which Thomas, Chess, Birch, Hertzig and Korn (1963), Thomas, Chess and Birch (1968), Prechtl (1963), and Robson and Moss (1970) had identified as potentially important individual differences in infants and toddlers. The questionnaire also contains the key question of how much difficulty the infant would present the average caregiver. Factor analysis delineated difficultness at 6 months as frequent and intense fussing and crying, with style and adaptation to novelty being relatively independent of difficultness (Bates, Freeland & Lounsbury, 1979). Negative emotionality is the central feature of difficultness at age 13 months, too.

Although the social impact perspective is the starting point for Bates' research, he is also interested in the objective component of perceived difficultness. For this purpose he investigated the meaning of the difficultness factor in terms of the infant's behavior by comparing mother, father, and observer reports. Bates *et al.* (1979) found moderately high correlations between mother and father ICQ factor scores; low but significant correlations between mother and father ICQ scores and the corresponding observer ICQ ratings for the difficultness factor; and low but significant correlations between the mother ICQ factor fussy/difficult and two home-observation factors of fussiness and unsoothability.

Another kind of information on the objective component of difficultness concerns the qualities of the infant's cries, independent of their frequency of occurrence. On the basis of maternally perceived difficultness Lounsbury and Bates (1982) selected four examples each of difficult, average, and easy babies, and recorded samples of their hunger cries. Unrelated mothers of infants listened to the cry tapes and indicated that the cries of the more difficult infants were more irritating and spoiled-sounding than the cries of easier infants. Sound spectrographs of the cries also revealed different features of the cries of different infants. The more difficult infants had longer pauses between their cry sounds and made higher-pitched sounds at volume peaks. Thus, the findings of Bates and his associates (Bates *et al.*, 1979; Bates, Olson, Pettit & Bayles, 1982; Lounsbury & Bates, 1982) suggest that perceived difficultness is determined in large part by frequent and intense fussing and crying of the infant and that this parentally reported difficultness has an objective component.

In sum, the most viable temperament theories to date demonstrate a nearly universal inclusion of irritability (or negative emotionality) as a temperament trait. Bates' (1986) research has shown that this dimension of temperament contributes importantly to perceptions of infant difficultness. Since in the majority of temperament approaches irritability is legitimately referred to as temperament, this supports our decision to investigate the mechanism by which *irritability* influences the quality of the interaction and, hence, the quality of the attachment relationship. This process will be delineated in the next section.

IRRITABILITY AND ATTACHMENT

Irritability as a Potential Influence on Attachment

Proceeding from Bowlby's (1969) attachment theory, Bischof (1975) developed a control model capable of accounting for basic processes of social behavior. The model consists of the integration of a security and an arousal system. Of special interest in Bischof's model is the incorporation of individual differences such as 'dependency' (security system) and 'enterprise' (arousal system) as codeterminants of the action of behavioral systems. The concept of security has a special connotation in Bischof's model. Ainsworth and Wittig (1969) introduced the concept of 'security of attachment' to account for differences in the intensity of attachment behavior. However, this term does not clearly distinguish between an emotional state (feeling more or less secure) and an environmental fact (the degree to which a given mother is capable of influencing this state) (Bischof, 1975). Bischof uses the term in the former sense only, denoting by security a hypothetical intraorganismic variable which increases with the proximity and the quality of the mother. The individual-differences variable that influences this felt security is dependency.

Dependency is conceived of as a variable that is controlled by endogenous factors. It refers to the fact that children differ in the need of wanting to be reassured. Again, as in the case of the concept of security, the term dependency does not refer to the objective fact of actually being dependent on other people but, rather, to the subjective state of feeling so (Bischof, 1975). In brief, the security system specifies that the general level of security felt by the infant is controlled by information about properties of the mother. This security level is matched against the degree of dependency. If dependency exceeds security, attachment behaviors are activated. Bowlby (1969) conceives of the security system as a negative feedback loop. An increasing distance between mother and child, everything else being equal, releases a behavior appropriate to reduce this distance, Bischof (1975), on the other hand, conceives of the control system in question as bidirectional. His model accounts for the possibility that the deviation of security from its reference is in the other direction – that is, if there is an excess of security, security exceeds dependency, resulting in withdrawal from the attachment figure.

The phenomenon of fear has a well-defined place in the arousal system of Bischof's (1975) model. Throughout life an infant is surrounded by objects, live or inanimate, with which it must try to cope. When confronted with novel objects a child might block every behavioral response because, temporarily, she does not know what to do. This behavior, however, is not advisable if the stimuli are relevant, i.e. indicate that something pertinent for the child is likely to happen. To produce the right response eventually, the child has to ascertain information about the objects concerned, and this implies exploration of the objects. In the arousal system Bischof (1975) also introduces an individual-differences variable which is called enterprise. Enterprise, like dependency in the security system, is conceived of as being controlled by endogenous factors. This variable refers to differences in the way individuals resolve the above-mentioned conflict. Generally, the hypothetical construct arousal is conceived of as a homeostatic variable that engenders fear responses when it exceeds a certain optimum level, but instigates exploration when it falls short of that level. This optimum level is controlled by the internal variable 'enterprise' (Bischof, 1975).

The security and arousal systems are distinct from one another, but combined into a compound model. This compound model predicts that fear-evoking stimuli are likely to intensify attachment behavior toward familiar objects, whereas the proximity of attachment figures, conversely, turns the individual more toward exploration of novel objects. The behavioral systems are put into action, according to the model, by a deviation of security or arousal from their reference variables in either direction (Bischof, 1975).

Bischof's (1975) model is an elegant integration of current theories of attachment, fear, and exploration. This model on the attachment–exploration balance incorporates the individual-differences variables 'dependency' in the security system and 'enterprise' in the arousal system. We now consider the possibility that infant irritability is the endogenous factor controlling these variables.

Irritability as a Potential Influence on the Infant's Security System

Bischof's (1975) model on the attachment–exploration balance incorporates the individual-differences variable 'dependency' (security system) to allow for differences in attachment behavior that cannot be fully explained by sensitivity of or physical distance from the mother. In this chapter irritability is proposed as the endogenous factor controlling this variable, and I now argue that irritability (an important aspect of temperament) probably influences a very crucial dimension of the interactional process, namely its quality. The mechanism through which irritability in turn exerts its influence on the security system is the subject of this section.

An irritable infant can be expected to use relatively more distress signals as attachment behaviors than a non-irritable infant. Distress signals, however, have a different type of function in a control model than more positively toned attachment behaviors.

The feedback of positively toned attachment behaviors, like approaching and smiling, is positive. The behaviors increase with the proximity of the mother and produce consequences likely to enhance them (Bischof, 1975). If a child needs security from the mother, using positive signals as a means of correcting disequilibrium is likely to be more effective that using distress signals. Positive signals intensify with reduced distance between child and mother. Therefore, it is more likely that the mother will remain responsive to the signals until the child's need for security is satisfied.

Distress signals, on the other hand, operate throught a negative feedback mechanism. They intensify when distance from the mother becomes larger. Resorting to distress signals as a means of correcting disequilibrium within the system puts a lot of demand on the behavior of the mother. In order to satisfy the child's need for security, reduction of distance has to be brought about completely by the mother. When other means of signalling behavior have developed already in the child the mother may be even less willing to respond promptly to the distress. Or the mother may resort to less effective behaviors to reduce distance, like vocalizing instead of picking the child up. Because intensity of distress also decreases with proximity (Bischof, 1975), the mother may stop responding before the child's need for security is met. Reduction of intensity may convey the message that the need is less urgent. Overall, distress signals seem to be less effective in the correction of disequilibrium within the system than positive attachment signals, because of the negative feedback they provide and the demand they put on the behavior of the mother.

In sum, infant irritability may be a potential influence on the internal variable 'dependency' in a bidirectional model of the attachment–exploration balance. Attachment behavior is elicited by a too distant and too prolonged withdrawal of the mother. Irritable infants will resort more to distress signals as a means of reducing this distance than non-irritable infants do. Distress signals, however, are less effective than more positively toned attachment signals because they operate through negative rather than positive feedback.

Irritability as a Potential Influence on the Infant's Arousal System

Irritability may also control the internal variable 'enterprise'. We have already shown that the emission of distress calls may reduce the likelihood that the child will receive sufficient care from the mother. If the level of felt security provided by the mother is insufficient to meet the child's need for security, the child's arousal level will be elevated, and a high level of arousal will lead to fearful behavior and will therefore reduce the child's exploratory tendencies.

There is some correlational evidence that corroborates this notion. Difficult infants, who have been shown to emit distress signals with a high frequency (Bates et al., 1979), show slower cognitive development (Dunst & Lingerfelt, 1985; Field et al., 1978; Sostek & Anders, 1977; Wachs & Gandour, 1983). In addition, infants who are fearful as assessed in the laboratory tend to score lower on tests of infant development (Lamb, 1982). Fear of exploration of the environment and fear of orienting to interesting features of it can result in behavioral disorganization and may prevent learning in the immediate situation.

Thus, irritability may be expected to exert a negative influence on the arousal system by activating the fear component more often than the exploratory component. This, in turn, may negatively influence the quality of the child's exploratory behaviors since the child will have less opportunities to practice her exploratory capacities.

Irritability as a Potential Influence on the Infant's Internal Working Model

Individual differences in irritability may also influence the internal working model of the infant. According to Bowlby (1969) a child constructs internal working models of important aspects of the world in the course of interacting with the physical and personal world. With the aid of working models, the child perceives and interprets events, forecasts the future, and constructs plans. Of special importance within the working model of the world in the development of attachment are working models of the self and attachment figures. A key feature of the working model of the self is the notion of how acceptable the self is in the eyes of the attachment figure (Bowlby, 1973). Conversely, a crucial feature in the working model of the attachment figure is this figure's accessibility and emotional supportiveness. Because of their origin in actual interpersonal transactions, the internal working models of self and attachment figures develop in close complementarity (Bretherton, 1987).

Infant irritability can be expected to affect the infant's state of felt security by influencing the development of expectations of sensitive responsiveness, especially from social partners (Thompson, 1986). The contingency aspect inherent in maternal sensitive responsiveness, among one of the most important of early expectations concerned, may be influenced by the infant's degree of irritability. Most of the research on the early development of contingency perception has employed experimentally manipulated non-social conditions. Beginning with Watson (1971) researchers have looked at the effects of non-contingent versus contingent stimulation on later learning. These experiments show that infants can respond appropriately to the contingency inherent in learning situations from a relatively early age.

It is a small step from the work of Watson (1971) to the role of contingency in parent–child interactions. In contrast to experimental situations, however, the response contingency in social encounters is highly imperfect and irregular, but this does not necessarily inhibit the development of contingency awareness (Watson, 1979). To explain the extent of the problem of detecting such less-than-perfect contingencies Watson distinguishes two types of conditional probabilities, in one of which a response does not occur after every one of an infant's relevant behaviors. An example would be a mother who goes to her infant's crib sometimes, but not every time the infant begins to cry. The other type is the situation where the behavior of an infant does not always precede the occurrence of the response in question, that is, the infant's behavior is not always necessary for the stimulus event to occur. This would be the case if the mother comes to her infant's crib occasionally when the infant is not crying. The extent of the problem with less than perfect contingencies is in large part a function of the degree to which the two types of probabilities are different from base-rate probabilities for the occurrence of the infant's behavior and the mother's response. If such differences are relatively large, then the infant should have an easy time perceiving a contingency between its behavior and a response.

To use the previous example again, the infant should have relatively little difficulty in detecting a contingency between its crying and the appearance of its mother if the mother's base rate of approaching is quite low but her likelihood of approaching when her infant cries is quite high. The infant should also have little difficulty in detecting a contingency if it seldom cries, but nearly every time crying occurs, the mother suddenly appears. In contrast, the infant should, in theory, have a much more difficult time detecting a contingency if the mother is equally likely to appear when the infant is crying as when it is not crying. Of course if the mother is far more likely to appear following the infant's cries than when the infant is not crying, the contingency again becomes relatively easy to detect. It is the discrepancy between conditional and base-rate probabilities that is most important, according to Watson (1979), not the absolute values of such probabilities.

This does not imply, however, that absolute levels of these probabilities are unimportant in consideration of perception of contingency. On the contrary, perception of contingency becomes increasingly difficult as the absolute value of the base rate of an infant's distress behavior increases. It was argued above that it is unlikely that a mother will show a high rate of responding to distress signals. This implies that the discrepancy between conditional and base-rate probabilities will be high in dyads with irritable infants. This, in turn, will have a negative impact on the infant's perception of contingency and hence on the infant's working model of the attachment figure. Another expectation put forward was the use of more global ways of responding on the part of the mother. If the mother responds to infant distress with behaviors she is also likely to use in response to other infant signals, perception of contingency becomes difficult. For instance, if the mother's base rate of vocalizing is quite high and she also uses vocalizing in response to her infant's distress it will be difficult for the infant to detect the contingency between crying and vocalizing. If, on the other hand, the mother resorts to effective soothing strategies in response to distress, the perception of contingency on the part of the infant will be facilitated, since it is unlikely that the mother will use soothing behaviors in response to other infant signals.

Irritability has been described as the endogenous factor influencing the internal variables of both the security and the arousal systems. It has been shown how this particular infant characteristic may influence both the attachment and exploratory components in a negative way resulting in an over-representation of anxious attachments among irritable infants. Exploratory behavior will also be of a relatively low quality because of reduced opportunities to explore the environment caused by an unusually high amount of activation of the fear component of the arousal system. Hence, irritability can be expected to influence the balance between attachment and exploration. Although irritability directly influences the internal variables of the model, we also delineated the consequences this will have for the ensuing interaction between mother and infant. And this, in turn, will have consequences for the infant's internal working model of the attachment figure and the self.

LONGITUDINAL STUDIES

We have been investigating the relationship between irritability and attachment in two studies. In an observational study we sought to gain insight into the influence of infant irritability on the developing attachment relationship during the first 6 months of life and on the quality of the attachment relationship at the end of the first year. The purpose of the second, intervention, study was to examine the effect of improving maternal sensitive responsiveness on the quality of the interaction, the quality of the infant's exploratory behavior, and the quality of attachment. An intervention study initiated from attachment theory requires the identification of infants at risk for developing an insecure attachment relationship with the mother. The most crucial variables in this regard are those that influence the quality of maternal–infant interaction. Potential determinants of later interactive disharmony have been put foward by both attachment and temperament researchers. From an attachment-theory point of view the crucial variable is maternal sensitive responsiveness, of which lower levels have been found in mothers from lower class families (Brown *et al.*, 1975; Egeland & Sroufe, 1981; Vaughn, Egeland, Sroufe & Waters, 1979). From a temperament-theory point of view infant irritability has been found to be related to the quality of mother–infant interaction. Hence, irritable infants born in lower class families may be expected to be at risk for developing an insecure attachment relationship with the mother.

The Observational Study

The primary purpose of the observational study was to describe in detail developmental change in patterns of interaction in mother–infant dyads with irritable and non-irritable infants during the first 6 months of life. In addition, the quality of attachment was assessed at the age of 1 year, and maternal perception of infant behavior was measured at 6 and 12 months of age. Therefore, the observational study covered the period from shortly after birth up till the age of 1 year. Primary emphasis was placed on objective recording of detailed behavior in an unstructured situation with observations carried out every month. This allowed us to investigate developmental change in patterns of interaction, a neglected aspect in longitudinal studies. Longitudinal studies have tended either to describe the average pattern of change across time, or to examine measures of stability across time, or factors summarizing the interactional behaviors. Only a few investigators have reported how mother–infant interactions change during the infancy period (e.g. Belsky, Taylor & Rovine, 1984; Crockenberg & McCluskey, 1986; Green, Gustafson & West 1980).

Thirty mothers and their infants were followed from birth to 12 months of age. All infants were firstborn children of lower socioeconomic status, intact families. All infants were carried to term and weighed more than 2500 g at birth. All mothers and infants were in good physical health and were not considered at risk. To determine the degree of infant irritability the Neonatal Behavioral Assessment Scale (NBAS; Brazelton, 1973) was administered on the tenth and the fifteenth day of life. It was deemed important to measure infant irritability shortly after birth and independent of the mother's behavior. Though admittedly not a test of temperament, clusters of items derived from the NBAS appear to be congruent with the characteristics of temperament described in the literature (Strauss & Rourke, 1978). Relationships have been established with aspects of functioning associated with the construct of temperament (Worobey, 1986). Therefore, scores from the *peak of excitement*, *rapidity of build-up*, and *irritability* items were combined and averaged across the two administrations. Infants whose irritability scores were 6 or higher were considered irritable. The NBAS had to be administered to 89 infants to find the predetermined number of 15 irritable infants. Thus, 17% met the criterion of irritability. Besides these 15 irritable infants the sample consisted of 15 non-irritable infants. Infants with scores below 6 were considered non-irritable.

During the first 6 months of life, mother–infant interaction was observed at home for 40 minutes on two occasions. One visit was scheduled in the morning; the other one, in the afternoon. Thus, every month 80 minutes of observational data were collected per dyad. Infant categories consisted of positive and negative social signals. For the mothers, looking, affective, stimulating, and soothing behaviors were recorded, that is, behaviorally based measures of maternal sensitivity. The observers were blind to the infant's irritability classification. We also employed ratings to determine maternal sensitivity. The rating scales we used were the scales on maternal sensitivity developed by Ainsworth for the first quarter of the first year. The rating scales pertain to the mother's general attitude towards the baby and her role, the feeding situation, availability and interaction, amount and quality of physical contact, responsiveness to crying, amount and appropriateness of social contact, and facilitation of sensorimotor development.

While the main thrust of the research efforts went into the observation of mother–infant interaction we did not want to lose all information that was not based on direct observation. We therefore used a temperament questionnaire as an additional probe. The ICQ (Bates *et al.*, 1979) was selected because its main factor 'difficulty' consists of items on negative emotionality. Both mothers and observers filled out the ICQ when the infants were 6 months of age and again when they were 12 months of age and came into the laboratory to measure attachment quality.

When the infants were 12 months old, they were brought to our laboratory for a follow-up visit and were videotaped as they experienced the Strange Situation devised by Ainsworth and her associates. These tapes were scored by two trained observers who were blind to the children's previous history.

The results clearly point out differences in the distribution of attachment classifications. We tested whether the distributions in the irritable and the non-irritable samples resembled each other. The two groups were compared using the Mann–Whitney test. The distributions differed significantly ($U=57.5$, $p<.025$) due to an over-representation of anxiously-avoidant attached infants in the irritable group. Of course we are aware of the fact that the sample in this study was small. The result, however, was replicated in the intervention study which included 100 irritable infants.

Differences in interactive style between dyads with irritable and dyads with non-irritable infants, with consequences for the quality of attachment at the end of the first year of life, were also discerned. We found the interaction of dyads with irritable infants to be characterized by maternal unresponsiveness, while the opposite was true for dyads with non-irritable infants (van den Boom, in press). This finding supports the predictions made by the bidirectional model of attachment and exploratory systems. The model gave rise to the expectation that two aspects of interaction would hinder maternal sensitive responsiveness. The first was a high amount of irritable behavior, expected to suppress maternal responsiveness because of the negative feedback provided. The second aspect was the use of less effective soothing strategies, that is, behaviors that are likely to occur in response to different kinds of infant behaviors and not specifically to infant fussing and crying.

In this observational study we were mainly interested in antecedents of the quality of attachment, and sequential analyses were performed on behavioral frequencies summed over individuals having the same attachment classification (A, B, or C) at the age of 12 months. Since the majority of irritable infants proved to be anxiously attached, the A and C attachment groups consisted mainly of irritable infants, while the B group consisted mainly of non-irritable infants. The sequential analyses revealed that mothers of A infants indeed ignored infant crying for part of the time it occurred. And, if the infants were soothed, the soothing strategies were of a distant nature, that is, behavioral strategies were used that are also often used in response to non-distress behaviors of an infant. These soothing behaviors do not always seem to be effective when an infant is fussing and are certainly not effective when an infant is crying. Although mothers of later C infants seemed to use more effective soothing strategies they also used distracting behaviors that even increased infant distress. Hence, mothers of C infants showed highly variable responses to infant distress. They sometimes tried to relieve distress, while at other times they even stimulated distress behavior. Hence, mothers of C infants seemed to be using the most ineffective strategies at times as a response to infant crying.

Although no specific predictions were made with regard to positively toned attachment behaviors, differences between A and C infants were revealed here too. Mothers of A infants showed interactive behaviors with regard to positive attachment signals that were of a distant nature as was the case with their soothing behavior. Mothers of C infants alternated positive reponses with ignoring the infant altogether, again a way of interacting characterized by highly variable responses to infant signals as was the case with soothing.

Our next analyses were canonical correlation analyses between the different measures employed: NBAS scores, observational data, ratings, and ICQ scores by mothers and observers. The analyses were performed for the irritable and the non-irritable groups separately. For babies falling in the non-irritable group it was found that infants who were categorized as high orienters on the NBAS became engaged in effective stimulating and positive social interactions with their mothers. A pattern of interaction characterized in the non-irritable group by an increase in social engagement between mother and infant with age was associated with maternal responsiveness. In such a developmental pattern of interaction infants were also perceived as sociable by observers at 6 months and as sociable by their mothers at 12 months of age. Maternal sensitive responsiveness and observers' perceptions of infant sociability were associated, that is, mothers being judged as sensitive in their interactive behavior had infants perceived as sociable by observers. In addition, observers' and mothers' perceptions of sociability converged both at 6 and 12 months of age. Thus, both mothers and observers perceived non-irritable infants as sociable when they were 6 and 12 months old. Hence, in the non-irritable group a high level of orientation shortly after birth was associated with mutual social engagement in the interaction later on in the first year of life, and with maternal sensitive responsiveness. In addition, non-irritable infants were perceived as sociable by both their mothers and observers.

For the irritable group a different pattern of significant canonical corrrelations emerged. A developmental change pattern of interaction characterized by a gradual retreat from contact with the infant with age was related to maternal unresponsiveness. Irritability as measured with the NBAS was associated with maternal perceptions of difficultness at both 6 and 12 months of age, and maternal perceptions of difficultness at 6 and 12 months were related. In addition, this perception of difficultness was related to a developmental pattern of interacting reflecting increasing maternal non-involvement with age. The above pattern of results suggests that infant irritability measured shortly after birth by the NBAS is a valid indicator of maternal perceptions of difficultness 6 and 12 months later, at least for the group of extremely irritable babies. Also, maternal perceptions of difficultness for this group are relatively stable during the first year of life, and mothers of irritable infants gradually refrain from interacting with them. The nexus of relationships in the irritable group suggests the plausibility of a functional relationship between temperament and attachment which takes the following form. Individual differences in irritability influence the mother's responsiveness to her infant, with consequences for the kind of attachment relationship that the child develops with the mother (van den Boom, 1988).

These findings indicate that an intervention aimed at enhancing maternal sensitive responsiveness in dyads with irritable infants should be aimed at responsiveness to both negative and positive infant signals. Maternal behavior seems to lack effectiveness in dealing with both kinds of signals, at least in dyads with irritable babies from lower class families. Mothers of irritable A infants communicate from a distance, which seems to be a hindrance to both the contingency and the appropriateness aspect of a sensitive response. The majority of dyads with irritable infants shows this pattern of interacting. In mothers of irritable C infants, the consistency aspect is mainly disturbed. Thus, the intervention for dyads with irritable infants from lower class families should be aimed at enhancing three aspects of sensitive responsiveness: contingency, consistency, and appropriateness. More specifically, appropriate responses to positive and negative signals have to be incorporated in the mother's behavioral repertoire, that is, behaviors that are specifically tuned to infant signals. General responses must be avoided because they will hinder contingency awareness in the infant. Distance interaction must be avoided because it will hinder the contingency aspect of sensitive responsiveness as well. Highly variable responses must be avoided because they are a hindrance to the consistency aspect of maternal sensitive responsiveness.

The Intervention Study

In the observational study it was demonstrated that preventive intervention in dyads with irritable infants from lower class families seems to be worth the effort. In the first place, a relatively high proportion of anxiously-attached infants was found in the irritable group, indicating that irritable infants from lower class families are at risk for developing an insecure attachment relationship with the mother. In addition, in maternal interaction behavior, problems were detected relating to disturbances in different aspects of sensitive responsiveness, the key feature of interactive behavior for the development of a secure attachment relationship. Based upon these findings, an intervention program was developed and implemented in a group of dyads with irritable infants from lower class families. The intervention was specifically aimed at improving maternal sensitive responsiveness, and was guided by the stages of this response process, that is, perceiving infant signals, interpreting them correctly, selecting an appropriate response, and implementing it effectively. Intervention began with manipulations to affect maternal attentive behavior. Since attentiveness to signals of an interaction partner is critical for performing sensitive responsive behavior and since an infant's gaze signals provide feedback to the mother on whether she is providing appropriate levels of stimulation, the mother's enhanced attentiveness to infant behavior will affect their interaction in a positive way. Behaviors of mothers used for this purpose were imitation, repetition of vocalizations, and silencing during gaze aversions.

It often happened that the infant fussed or cried during the intervention sessions. These instances were used as behavioral change targets regarding sensitive responsiveness to negative infant signals. When the infant started to cry some mothers spontaneously soothed them. If this was not the case, mothers were asked to soothe their infants. This led to a discussion about the importance of soothing a crying infant and about effective soothing techniques. For mothers with a crying baby it is important to show that interactions with their baby can be positive and rewarding. Therefore, mothers were asked to play with their infant when she was not crying. During these playful interactions attention was devoted to recognizing infant signals, responding appropriately, and observing the infant's subsequent response. Verbal reinforcement was used when interaction proceeded adequately. Intervention during actual interaction gives mothers a sense of effectance. Mothers have the feeling that they can actually bring about positive behavior in their infants themselves.

Most of the studies initiated from an attachment framework have been correlational in nature. To determine conclusively whether changes in maternal behavior result in changes in infant behavior, experimental manipulation of maternal interactive style is necessary. A natural (quasi-) experiment was conducted, in which the effect of enhancement of maternal sensitive responsiveness on the quality of mother–infant interaction, the quality of infant exploratory behavior, and the quality of attachment, was studied. The intervention was deliberately restricted to manipulating this one variable to facilitate evaluation of the intervention's effects. Many infant intervention progams are so multifaceted that it is difficult to ascertain which aspect of the intervention is responsible for which change in a participant's behavior.

The independent variable in this experiment was the intervention aimed at positively influencing maternal sensitive responsiveness to infant signals. The dependent variables were threefold. The quality of mother–infant interaction, and more specifically maternal sensitive responsiveness, was the first dependent variable. Change in maternal behavior was determined through observations of mother–infant interaction. The observational procedure was the same as in the observational study. Secondly, we investigated the effect of the intervention on the quality of infant exploratory behavior, the second dependent variable in this study. The quality of attachment constituted the final dependent variable of the intervention study.

In order to study intervention effects on maternal and infant behavior a four-group design was used (Solomon & Lessac, 1968), consisting of two experimental and two control groups. The sample consisted of 50 experimental dyads with irritable infants and 50 control dyads with irritable infants, for a total of 100 dyads with irritable infants. The infants were selected on the same irritability criterion used in the observational study and sampling followed a similar format as in that study. In order to find the predetermined number of 100 irritable infants the NBAS had to be administered to 588 infants. As was the case in the observational study 17% of infants from lower class families proved to be irritable according to the criterion used in the studies reported in this chapter. The average irritability score of the infants was 6.78. (All the NBAS were administered by the author.)

Observations were conducted at the age of 6 months (pretest) and when the infants were 9 months old (post-test). For both pretest and post-test, two home visits were paid to every family (within one week). One visit was scheduled in the morning; the other visit in the afternoon. On every visit, 40 minutes of mother–infant interaction were recorded. Pre- and post-test observations for the same family were performed by different observers in order to avoid unintentional bias during observations, and across groups observations were conducted by different observers.

The second dependent variable was related to infant exploratory behavior. The quality of exploration was measured in a free-play situation. The choice of behavioral measures to index exploratory quality was suggested by the studies of Sorce and Emde (1981) and Belsky, Garduque, and Hrncir (1984) and by descriptive empirical research on exploration. The third dependent variable was the quality of attachment. Between the ages of 12 and 13 months a follow-up measure was conducted for every mother–child dyad, consisting of observation of the dyads in the Strange Situation procedure.

The results of the intervention study clearly point out the effect of the intervention on maternal interactive behavior. Program mothers were more responsive, more stimulating, and more controlling of their infant's behavior when compared to control mothers. Infants of mothers who participated in the intervention were more sociable, displayed more self-centered behavior, explored more, and cried less than control infants. With regard to the quality of the infants' exploratory behavior experimental infants engaged in cognitively sophisticated exploration more and spend less time exploring in less cognitively sophisticated ways than control infants. In addition, indices of infant attachment behavior and exploration were correlated, as would be expected in the case of the existence of a balance between the two behavioral systems (van den Boom, 1988). These findings indicate that the disturbances in interactive style of dyads with irritable infants predicted by our model can be overcome with an intervention aimed at enhancing sensitive responsiveness.

In addition, the intervention had a positive impact on the quality of attachment at the end of the first year of life, that is, significantly more infants of program mothers were securely attached compared to infants of control mothers. Sixty-eight per cent of intervention dyads were securely attached, while only 28% of control dyads received a secure attachment classification. Seventy-two per cent of control dyads were anxiously attached, with 78% of these in the anxiously-avoidant category. These findings were also confirmed when sequences of interactive behavior were explored. Control mothers mainly attended to very negative infant signals, which also seemed to elicit anger. Both mildly negative behaviors and positively toned attachment behaviors were for the most part ignored. Program mothers, on the contrary, responded positively to both negative and positive infant signals.

DISCUSSION AND CONCLUSION

We undertook the joint study of attachment and temperament-like variation in infant behavior to gain insight into possible theoretical links between the two constructs. Currently there is much debate on the question of whether variation in security of attachment is a product of temperamental differences among babies or whether such temperamental variation is not a major determinant of attachment classification. Proponents of either point of view have tended to cast the discussion in terms of either/or explanations (Belsky & Rovine, 1987). We have found that reconciling these theoretically competing points of view empirically is more fruitful.

The most significant theoretical finding of this work was support for a relationship between negative emotionality (assessed neonatally), quality of mother–infant interaction, and attachment classification. We postulated that negative emotionality influences the developing attachment relationship. The data of our observational study have strengthened that view with the crucial evidence the disproportionately high number of anxiously attached infants among the irritable ones.

In our model on the attachment–exploration balance, 'felt security' is the functional goal of infant attachment behavior. Our results suggest that the temperament dimension of negative emotionality is an important contributor to individual variations in felt security. The results of the experimental manipulation of maternal sensitive responsiveness in dyads with irritable infants lends further support to this notion. Enhancing maternal responsiveness seems to foster the infant's sense of felt security, since it leads to an increase in exploratory behavior which is also of a higher quality compared to that of irritable infants receiving a low level of maternal responsiveness.

Hence, infant irritability is an important condition in the relationship between mother and infant in the first year of life, making it difficult for mothers to adjust their actions to the child's predispositions. That mothers can be taught to do so is reflected by the increase in maternal responsiveness and the amount and quality of infant exploratory behavior after intervention. This intervention was geared to the characteristics of individual mother–infant dyads. However, it is futile for anyone to hope to produce an ideal 'prescription' that is valid for everybody. Not all experimental infants developed a secure attachment relationship with their mothers. Besides this, one must be wary of a new trend or relationship, however intriguing and fascinating, discovered in only a single study. So far, very few studies with irritable infants have been conducted, and the ones that have do not present concordant results (Fish & Crockenberg, 1981). Replications should, for instance, address the question of how easily these techniques might be taught to others, since in this study all the intervention sessions were performed by the same person. Hence, conclusions as to practice are insecure unless some corroboration is forthcoming. One should also be aware of the possibility of disordinal interaction, a phenomenon which has been clearly demonstrated in genetics. Disordinal interaction refers to the situation in which environmental variables affect individuals of different constitutions in opposite ways. Martin, Maccoby, and Jacklin's (1981) observation that maternal responsiveness increased exploration in young boys but decreased it in girls provides an example of a disordinal interaction effect.

This research project has advanced our knowledge of the developing attachment relationship in irritable infants by a firsthand account of their experiences and relationship with mother in the family circle. It has always been postulated that the infant contributes to the mother–infant relationship. This research has been able to clarify one component of infant behavior that clearly has an important impact. The upshot is that negative emotionality in infants seems to be more responsible than maternal behavior for the development of an anxious attachment relationship. However, with appropriate intervention the balance can be shifted. Lytton (1981) once posed the question: 'What difference do parents' practices or their attitude toward their children really make?' His conclusion was that whether the climate in which the child is reared is a caring one or not *does* matter. This clearly seems to be the case for irritable infants reared in lower class families.

REFERENCES

Ainsworth, M.D.S. (1973). The development of infant–mother attachment. In B.M. Caldwell & H.N. Riciutti (Eds), *Review of child development research*, Vol. 3. Chicago: University of Chicago Press.

Ainsworth, M.D.S., Blehar, M.C., Waters, E. & Wall, S. (1978). *Patterns of attachment: A psychological study of the Strange Situation.* Hillsdale, NJ: Erlbaum.

Ainsworth, M.D.S. & Wittig, B.A. (1969). Attachment and exploratory behavior of one year olds in a Strange Situation. In B.M. Foss (Ed.), *Determinants of infant behavior*, Vol. 4. London: Methuen.

Bates, J.E. (1980). The concept of difficult temperament. *Merrill-Palmer Quarterly*, **26**, 299–319.

Bates, J.E. (1982). Temperament as a part of social relationships: Implications of perceived infant difficultness. Paper presented at the International Conference on Infant Studies, Austin, TX.

Bates, J.E. (1986). The measurement of temperament. In R. Plomin & J. Dunn (Eds), *The study of temperament: Changes, continuities and challenges.* Hillsdale, NJ: Erlbaum.

Bates, J.E., Freeland, C.A.B. & Lounsbury, M.L. (1979). Measurement of infant difficultness. *Child Development,* **50**, 794–802.

Bates, J.E., Olson, S., Pettit, G. & Bayles, K. (1982). Dimensions of individuality in the mother–infant relationship at six months of age. *Child Development,* **53**, 446–461.

Belsky, J., Garduque, L. & Hrncir, E. (1984). Assessing performance, competence, and executive capacity in infant play: Relations to home environment and security of attachment. *Developmental Psychology,* **20**, 406–417.

Belsky, J. & Rovine, M. (1987). Temperament and attachment security in the Strange Situation: An empirical rapprochement. *Child Development,* **58**, 787–795

Belsky, J., Taylor, D.G. & Rovine, M. (1984). The Pennsylvania infant and family development project II: The development of reciprocal interaction in the mother–infant dyad. *Child Development,* **55**, 706–717.

Bischof, N. (1975). A systems approach towards the functional connections of fear and attachment. *Child Development,* **46**, 801–817.

Bowlby, J. (1969). *Attachment and loss,* Vol. 1, *Attachment.* New York: Basic Books.

Bowlby, J. (1973). *Attachment and loss,* Vol. 2, *Separation: Anxiety and anger.* New York: Basic Books.

Brazelton, T.B. (1973). Neonatal Behavioral Assessment Scale. Philadelphia: J.B. Lippincott.

Bretherton, I. (1987). New perspectives on attachment relations: Security communication, and internal working models. In J.D. Osofsky (Ed.), *Handbook of infant development.* New York: Wiley.

Brown, J.V., Bakeman, R., Snyder, P.A., Fredrickson, W.T., Morgan, S.T. & Hepler, R. (1975). Interactions of black inner-city mothers with their newborn infants. *Child Development,* **46**, 677–686.

Buss, A.H. & Plomin, R. (1984). *Temperament: Early developing personality traits.* Hillsdale, NJ: Erlbaum.

Campos, J.J., Barrett, K.C., Lamb, M.E., Goldsmith, H.H. & Stenberg, C. (1983). Socioemotional development. In P.H. Mussen (Ed.), *Handbook of child psychology,* Vol. II, *Infancy and developmental psychobiology.* New York: Wiley.

Chess, S. & Thomas, A. (1982). Infant bonding: Mystique and reality. *American Journal of Orthopsychiatry,* **52**, 213–222.

Crockenberg, S.B. & Acredolo, C. (1983). Infant temperament ratings: A function of infants, or mothers, or both? *Infant Behavior and Development,* **6**, 61–72.

Crockenberg, S.B. & McCluskey, K. (1986). Change in maternal behavior during the baby's first year of life. *Child Development,* **57**, 746–753.

Dunst, C. J. & Lingerfelt, B. (1985). Maternal ratings of temperament and operant learning in two- to three-month-old infants. *Child Development,* **56**, 555–563.

Egeland, B. & Sroufe, L.A. (1981). Attachment and early maltreatment. *Child Development,* **52**, 44–52.

Field, T., Hallock, N., Ting, G., Dempsey, J., Dabiri, C. & Shuman, H.H. (1978). A first-year follow-up of high-risk infants: Formulating a cumulative risk index. *Child Development,* **49**, 119–131.

Fish, M. & Crockenberg, S. (1981). Correlates and antecedents of nine-month infant behavior and mother–infant interation. *Infant Behavior and Development,* **4**, 69–81.

Goldsmith, H.H., Bradshaw, D.L. & Rieser-Danner, L.A. (1986). Temperament as a potential influence on attachment. In J.V. Lerner & R.M. Lerner (Eds), *New directions for child development: Temperament and social interaction during infancy and childhood.* San Francisco: Jossey-Bass.

Goldsmith, H.H. & Campos, J.J. (1982). Toward a theory of infant temperament. In R.N. Emde & R.J. Harmon (Eds), *The development of attachment and affiliative systems.* New York: Plenum.

Green, J.A., Gustafson, G.E. & West, M.J. (1980). Effects of infant development on mother–

infant interaction. *Child Development*, **51**, 199–207.

Hinde, R.A. (1976). On describing relationships. *Journal of Child Psychology and Psychiatry*, **117**, 1–19.

Hinde, R.A. (1979). *Towards understanding relationships*. New York: Academic Press.

Kagan, J. (1984). *The nature of the child*. New York: Basic Books.

Kagan, J., Reznick, J.S. & Snidman, N. (1986). Temperamental inhibition in early childhood. In R. Plomin & J. Dunn. (Eds), *The study of temperament: Changes, continuities and challenges*. Hillsdale, NJ: Erlbaum.

Lamb, M.E. (1982). Individual differences in infant sociability: Their origins and implications for cognitive development. In H.W. Reese & L.P. Lipsitt (Eds), *Advances in child development and behavior*, Vol. 16. New York: Academic Press.

Linn, P. & Horowitz, F. (1983). The relationship between infant individual differences and mother–infant interaction during the neonatal period. *Infant Behavior and Development*, **6**, 415–427.

Lounsbury, M.L. & Bates, J.E. (1982). The cries of infants of differing levels of perceived temperamental difficultness: Acoustic properties and effects on listeners. *Child Development*, **53**, 677–686.

Lytton (1981). *Parent–child interaction*. New York: Plenum.

Martin, J.A., Maccoby, E.E. & Jacklin, C.N. (1981). Mothers' responsiveness to interactive bidding and nonbidding in boys and girls. *Child Development*, **52**, 1064–1067.

Matas, L., Arend, R.A. & Sroufe, L.A. (1978). Continuity of adaptation in the second year: The relationship between quality of attachment and later competence. *Child Development*, **49**, 547–556.

Prechtl, H.F.R. (1963). The mother–child interaction in babies with minimal brain damage. In B.M. Foss (Ed.), *Determinants of infant behavior* , Vol. 2. London: Methuen.

Robson, K.L. & Moss, H.A. (1970). Patterns and determinants of maternal attachment. *Journal of Pediatrics*, **77**, 976–985.

Rothbart, M.K. & Derryberry, D. (1981). Development of individual differences in temperament. In M.E. Lamb (Ed.), *Advances in developmental psychology*, Vol. 1. Hillsdale, NJ: Erlbaum.

Rothbart, M.K. & Goldsmith, H.H. (1985). Three approaches to the study of infant temperament. *Developmental Review*, **5**, 237–260.

Solomon, R.L. & Lessac, M.S. (1968). A control group design for experimental studies of developmental processes. *Psychological Bulletin*, **70**, 145–150.

Sorce, J.F. & Emde, R.N. (1981). Mother's presence is not enough: Effects of emotional availability on infant exploration. *Developmental Psychology*, **17**, 737–745.

Sostek, A.M. & Anders, T.F. (1977). Relationships among the Brazelton Neonatal Scale, Bayley Infant Scales, and early temperament. *Child Development*, **48**, 320–323.

Sroufe, L.A. (1985). Attachment classification from the perspective of infant–caregiver relationships and infant temperament. *Child Development*, **56**, 1–14.

Sroufe, L.A. & Fleeson, J. (1986). Attachment and the construction of relationships. In W.W. Hartup & Z. Rubin (Eds), *Relationships and development*. Hillsdale, NJ: Erlbaum.

Sroufe, L.A. & Waters, E. (1982). Issues of temperament and attachment. *American Journal of Orthopsychiatry*, **52**, 743–746.

Stevenson-Hinde, J. & Hinde, R.A. (1986). Changes in associations between characteristics and interactions. In R. Plomin & J. Dunn (Eds), *The study of temperament: Changes, continuities and challenges*. Hillsdale, N.J: Erlbaum.

Strauss, M.E. & Rourke, D.L. (1978). A multivariate analysis of the Neonatal Behavioral Assessment Scale in several samples. In A.J. Sameroff (Ed.), *Organization and stability of newborn behavior: A commentary on the Brazelton Neonatal Behavior Assessment Scale. Monographs of the Society for Research in Child Development*, **43**, 81–91.

Strelau, J. (1983). *Temperament, personality, activity*. New York: Academic Press.

Thomas, A. & Chess, S. (1977). *Temperament and development*. New York: Brunner/Mazel.

Thomas, A., Chess, S. & Birch, H.G. (1968). *Temperament and behavior disorders in children*. New York: New York University Press.

Thomas, A., Chess, S., Birch, H.G., Hertzig, M.E. & Korn, S. (1963). *Behavioral individuality in early childhood*. New York: New York University Press.

Thompson, R.A. (1986). Temperament, emotionality, and infant cognition. In J.V. Lerner & R.M. Lerner (Eds), *New directions for child development: Temperament and social interaction during infancy and childhood*. San Francisco: Jossey-Bass.

van den Boom, D.C. (in press). The influence of infant irritability on the development of the mother–infant relationship in the first six months of life. In J.K. Nugent, B.M. Lester & T.B. Brazelton (Eds), *The cultural context of infancy*, Vol. 2. Norwood NJ: Ablex.

van den Boom, D.C. (1988). Neonatal irritability and the development of attachment: Observation and intervention. Doctoral dissertation. University of Leiden.

Vaughn, B., Egeland, B., Sroufe, L.A. & Waters, E. (1979). Individual differences in infant–mother attachment at twelve and eighteen months: Stability and change in families under stress. *Child Development*, 50, 971–975.

Wachs, T.D. & Gandour, M.J. (1983). Temperament, environment, and six-month cognitive–intellectual development: A test of the organismic specificity hypothesis. *International Journal of Behavioral Development*, 6, 135–152.

Waters, E. & Deane, K.E. (1982). Infant–mother attachment: Theories, models, recent data, and some tasks for comparative analysis. In L.W. Hoffman, R. Gandelman & H.R. Schiffman (Eds), *Parenting: Its causes and consequences*. Hillsdale, NJ: Erlbaum.

Watson, J.S. (1971). Cognitive–perceptual development in infancy: Setting for the seventies. *Merrill-Palmer Quarterly*, 17, 139–152.

Watson, J.S. (1979). Perception of contingency as a determinant of social responsiveness. In E.B. Thoman (Ed.), *The origins of the infant's social responsiveness*. Hillsdale, NJ: Erlbaum.

Worobey, J. (1986). Convergence among assessments of temperament in the first month. *Child Development*, 57, 47–55.

Section Four

Applications of Temperament Concepts

17

Applications of Temperament Concepts

JOHN E. BATES
Indiana University

Most of the fast-growing temperament literature considers social and develop-mental processes that are of interest to clinicians, educators, and parents. Between November 1984 and July 1987, the period of my most recent systematic search of the literature, 62% of the 157 newly abstracted articles focused on temperamental variables' correlations with practice-relevant indexes. Frequent topics in these 98 articles were attachment, behavior problems, developmental handicaps, and school adjustment. Another 28% of the articles focused on conceptual–theoretical issues, such as psychometric properties of questionnaires or the role of genetics in temperament. The final 10% addressed both conceptual and practical issues. It is my impression that this sort of distribution has continued in the literature appearing most recently, too. This chapter considers both theoretical and empirical advances in major issues for clinicians. It also considers direct applications to practice, featuring a relatively extensive description of the author's own uses of temperament concepts in treating childhood behavior problem cases. Further perspectives are offered in the subsequent chapters of this section.

Temperament is usually defined as dimensions of personality that are basic, early appearing, biologically rooted, and fairly continuous. Major examples are activity, negative emotionality, and fearful reactions to novelty. At a more basic level, temperament dimensions most often concern patterns of emotional expression, activity, and attention deployment. (The many issues of definition are detailed in Section One of this volume.) Temperament increasingly gives specific, measurable meaning to the notion that child constitution affects social relations and personality development. The term temperament is becoming a major way to acknowledge children's contributions to the social matrix and their own development.

Practitioners have been intrigued by the possibility that temperament profiles can help predict how different children will react to environmental stresses, normative developmental challenges, and to various medical, psychological, and

Temperament in Childhood   Edited by G.A. Kohnstamm, J.E. Bates and M.K. Rothbart
© 1989 John Wiley & Sons Ltd

educational interventions. There has also been keen interest in understanding how children affect their socializing environments. If research does in fact show that temperament helps predict social development, this would mean that temperament measures could help in selecting intervention and prevention goals, as well as strategies.

Research to develop good temperament measures and to describe the role of temperament in children's development is under way, despite rather limited consensus about temperament definitions. A little research has used temperament in direct clinical applications. For example, there are at least two projects using infant temperament scores as the focus of prevention screening. Perhaps the most orderly sequence would be to settle the issues of definition and predictive validity first, and then try temperament measures in practical situations. However, better practical tools are needed right now, so in actuality, efforts will be made to use temperament in advance of solid, empirical evidence. They may not build upon an ideal base of research, but at least some of the efforts will be instructive in their own right.

The first major part of this chapter will address the issue of how temperament might be involved in the child's social relationships, and hence affect social development. This issue is pivotal in the eventual derivation of clinical applications of temperament concepts, but at the present, conceptual and methodological questions have to be the major focus. In the second major part of the chapter, the more focal question of how temperament variables relate to child psychopathology is addressed. It should be noted at the outset that I use the term psychopathology as a descriptor of emotional and behavioral problems of varying degrees of intensity, and not merely in reference to severe or clinically diagnosed disorders. Concluding the second part of the chapter is a discussion of direct clinical applications.

THE ROLE OF TEMPERAMENT IN SOCIAL INTERACTION

Temperament has some role in social interaction, almost by definition. However, exactly what to look for empirically is not so clear. There are many different qualities of interaction and many different ways that temperament could be involved in the social matrix across the stages of development. This complexity could be daunting to researchers, but hopefully not too daunting, because the ultimate practical value of temperament concepts will rest on empirical findings. Existing data on main effects are considered here first, and then two major kinds of statistical interaction effect.

Direct Child Effects on Parents

Attention has recently turned to how the child may affect the socializing environment. It is now widely recognized that there could be direct, main effects of temperament upon the social system. Bell (1968) and Thomas, Chess, and Birch (1968) placed this kind of hypothesis before the field just 20 years ago. Only a few of the many types of temperament effect have been systematically studied.

Difficultness

Difficultness temperament has been the best studied for its possible impact. Although the various definitions do have a common core of emotionality, there are differences among the operational definitions used by different studies. I have seen fairly similar patterns of results from the different definitions, but other analyses of the literature might someday notice crucial differences. For now it appears useful to stress the commonality of the definitions. I would argue that difficultness primarily concerns *negative emotionality* (Bates, 1980, 1987). We have suggested that a major basis of this elevated emotionality is the child being seen as socially demanding and unable/unwilling to entertain him/herself (Bates, Miller & Bayles, 1984). Many would suppose that difficultness or other adverse temperamental qualities in the child might produce or at least be correlated with adverse qualities of mother behavior. My reading of the data has been that direct, negative effects of temperament on the social environment are *not* typically observed by empirical researchers in infancy (Bates, 1987). Crockenberg (1986) reaches a fairly similar conclusion on the basis of 16 studies, many of which dealt with infants. Of the 16 studies, seven revealed no negative effects, but some positive effects, and nine showed negative effects. When I consider the 16 studies in Crockenberg's review, I am unable to dismiss the seven with non-findings as simply due to methodological weaknesses – many of them are from state-of-the-art studies, with relatively large sample sizes and well designed behavioral assessments. Three recent studies, not in Crockenberg' (1986) review, are supporting examples: Rothbart (1986) found no significant relationships between mother-perceived temperament and mother behavior at 3–9 months; Matheny, Wilson, and Thoben (1987) and Daniels, Plomin, and Greenhalgh (1984) found the same at 12–24 months.

Factors in adverse effects of difficultness. Findings of adverse effects sometimes appear to be associated with a special characteristic of the sample, such as high-risk background or very small number of subjects. This makes it possible that there are actually interacton effects operating rather than main effects that would generalize across the whole population (Bates, 1987; Crockenberg, 1986). Interaction effects will be discussed in a later subsection of the chapter.

Another factor in the nine studies listed by Crockenberg as showing adverse effects is that they often involved toddlers or older infants rather than younger infants. Wachs has pointed to this pattern (e.g. in Wachs & Gruen, 1982), both in his own data and in the literature in general. Our own research provides an example of this: Bates, Olson, Pettit, and Bayles (1982) found only (modest) positive temperament effects on observed interactions at 6 months of age. Pettit and Bates (1984) got similar findings in the longitudinal study at 13 months. However, Lee and Bates (1985) did find some adverse effects of difficult temperament on interactions between now 24-month-old toddlers and their mothers. Mothers of the high-difficult group of children used certain aversive control tactics more frequently than mothers of easier children. This longitudinal study also showed that mother reports of temperament were even predictive from 6 and 13 months, which strengthens any attribution of the results to child effects (as explained below).

Thomas and Chess discovered through a qualitative review of their temperament interviews that most mothers with difficult infants (according to the formal temperament score) described overall impressions of the child in very positive terms, but they became less positive in the second and third years (A. Thomas, personal communication, 8 August 1988). McDevitt and Carey (1981) found, similarly, that during infancy mothers tended to rate their infants as difficult on a global scale less often than the infants were categorized as difficult on the basis of the standard algorithm using the many particular mother-report items of the Infant Temperament Questionnaire; however, during toddlerhood this difference disappeared.

The increasing adverse effect may have to do with the increasing demand on children to be cooperative (Campbell, 1989; Crockenberg, 1986; Wachs & Gruen, 1982), and the increasing salience of social control issues in parent–child relations. Thomas (personal communication, 8 August 1988) suggests that the infant's negative emotionality was not so far from the parent's perception of the norms, but by toddlerhood the mother knew that other children were adapting more smoothly and 'began to feel either victimized or guilty and to act accordingly'. On the basis of discrepancies between a summary rating and composite, Carey (personal communication, 22 July 1988) suggests, in a related vein, that during infancy mothers of difficult infants could be affected by the difficult temperament but be in denial about the difficultness, whereas in toddlerhood they acknowledge it.

I have just reviewed the empirical evidence on the impact of difficult temperament on systematically observed parent–child interaction. It does not preclude the possibility that clinicians might notice adverse effects in particular cases or that parents could report such effects when asked the right questions. It is also possible that empirical research could detect the effects if the observation periods were considerably more frequent and sampled a greater range of situations. From the current evidence, however, it does not appear that the impact of difficultness on parenting behavior is very strong in most cases.

Activity

Activity level is another temperament variable thought to affect parenting. A number of the studies that considered the role of difficult temperament also looked at other temperament variables, including activity level. To my knowledge, none has found significant correlations between infant activity and quality of parenting. One might explain or predict a lack of such correlations, based on the limited mobility of the infant, and thus the limited opportunity for activity level to affect the parent–child relationship. One could also argue that individual differences in activity level do not even become stable until after infancy (Buss & Plomin, 1984; cf. Bates, 1987). However, in toddlerhood and beyond, one would expect some effects due to activity level. This might even extend to the later months of the first year, as some active children become more physically mobile. Parents of highly active children in the New York Longitudinal Study (NYLS) tended to report, according to qualitative analyses, that they were especially vigilant lest the children hurt themselves; some parents were stressed by this need for vigilance (A. Thomas, personal communication, 8 August 1988).

In a recent empirical study, Simpson and Stevenson-Hinde (1985) found little support for a link between active child temperament and adverse parent–preschool child interactions. Campbell and her colleagues, on the other hand, did find a link (Campbell, Breaux, Ewing & Szumowski, 1986), but their study compared preschoolers identified by their parents as 'hyperactive' with a normal control group. In a longitudinal comparison of maternal behavior toward two siblings at the same point in development, Dunn and Plomin (1986) found that the child's activity level at 24 months predicted the relative level of mother verbal behavior toward the child at 36 months. The more active of the siblings was spoken to less by the mother at the later age. As with difficultness/negative emotionality, the effects of the activity variable probably depend in part on the developmental level of the child and special characteristics of the sample.

Sociability

Sociability is a third temperament variable that in theory should have impact on social relations. This refers to a tendency to enjoy meeting and being with people. Relatively few studies have addressed the issue, and few of these have found links between early temperament and parenting behaviors (Bates, 1987). However, Dunn and Plomin's (1986) study of family comparisons of siblings found two correlations between mother ratings of children's sociability at age 2 and observed maternal behavior: as one might expect on the basis of commonsense notions of sociability or extraversion, the more sociable of a pair of siblings received more verbal and more controlling behavior from the mother than the less sociable child got at the same age. These findings suggest that there may be some role for early sociability in the parent–child relationship, but further research is needed.

Effects on Attachment

One of the most widely used indicators of quality of the parent–child relationship in the early phases of development is attachment security. A number of researchers have searched for hypothesized links between temperament and attachment. The evidence generally suggests that attachment security and infant temperament are only very tenuously linked (e.g. Bates, 1987). The typical study (e.g. Bates, Maslin & Frankel, 1985; Meyer & Schölmerich, 1984) finds no significant relationship between temperament and attachment classification. Attachment theorists, e.g. Sroufe (1985), argue that the sensitive nurturance that produces secure attachment would generally adjust appropriately to temperamental differences in infants. While arguing that secure vs insecure attachment should not be affected by temperament, Sroufe (1985) did leave open the possibility that the particular category of insecure attachment, e.g. avoidant vs resistant, could be affected by temperament. And research, including our own (Bates et al., 1985) shows that temperament can predict a variety of qualities of the infant's behavior in the attachment assessment situation. The strongest finding, according to the carefully done meta-analysis of Goldsmith and Alansky (1987), is that infants who are temperamentally prone to fear and distress are slightly more likely to demonstrate resistant behavior in the Strange Situation assessment of attachment (also see Thompson & Connell, 1986). Thus, a tendency toward resistant behavior may influence the classification of infants as 'anxiously attached, resistant', but apparently this would not happen in very many cases. This is because the link between the temperament variable and the attachment behavior variable is quite small, and the major attachment classification is a configural judgment based on more than just the presence of resistant behavior (Ainsworth, Blehar, Waters & Wall, 1978). For further consideration of this issue see Chapter 16, by van den Boom.

Summary and Comment

Do adverse qualities of temperament in a child produce or even simply co-occur with deficiencies in the parent–child relationship? Based on a moderate amount of research, my current conclusion is 'no', in the first year or so, but 'maybe' in later years. Temperament probably plays an important role in the later years too, but it becomes harder for the scientist or clinician to distinguish the basic temperament from the overlays of experience. One can assume with less trepidation that an association between an early measure of temperament and parent behavior reflects the process of a constitutional characteristic shaping the child's environment. One assumes this with greater trepidation as child relationship histories lengthen. The dominant paradigms of social development all suggest that experience plays a major role in shaping the personality of the child, including characteristic emotional and other responses that some might consider to be temperament. One should not, however, make the mistake so often made before the 1960s, of attributing nearly all personality to experience. Children could in part shape the environment that shapes them. For the present I would interpret temperament–environment correlations even in young infant–parent dyads as probably reflecting some confounding between constitution and environment, although not as much as among older children. I would expect that this confounding will ultimately be described as a dynamic system, but at the present this cannot be done, empirically. Although the evidence for negative impact of temperament on parent–infant relations is weak, there are some indications (e.g. Bates *et al.*, 1985; Lee & Bates, 1985) that temperament characteristics perceived in young infants do predict relationship problems in toddlers and preschoolers, when autonomy issues have become more salient.

The present review has not discussed the positive effects that temperament may have, for example the increased amounts of maternal attention directed to difficult infants observed in some studies. The potential practical implications of the modest, positive effects do not seem to be as important to address in the present context as the adverse implications. However, for fuller discussions of what evidence there is on such effects, see Bates (1987) and Crockenberg (1986).

Direct Child Effects on Teachers

The school is another important context for potential main effects of temperament. Keogh (1986) reviews a number of studies where teacher ratings of children's temperament were found to be associated in predictable ways with a variety of indicators of the child's relationship with the teacher and the ultimate benefit derived from schooling. Particularly likely to be linked with the school variables are the temperament variables that cluster in a factor Keogh has named Task Orientation, including task persistence, low distractibility, and low activity. (See Chapter 24, by Martin, for a review of a systematic series of studies on these variables.) Also relevant in some studies are qualities of the child's social adaptability. In the current chapter, only a brief summary of the extensive work will be given (see also Chapter 23, by Keogh, and Chapter 24, by Martin). According to Keogh,

> Children's temperaments may influence teachers' evaluations of pupils' performance, their decisions about grades, and their perceptions of pupils' abilities [relatively independent of a child's IQ]. It may well be that temperamental variations ... also affect the amount and nature of time teachers spend with particular children. We can only speculate about the impact these differences in teachers' attitudes and behaviors have on children's views of their own adequacy and competence in school. (Keogh, 1986, p. 101)

In brief, empirical associations between teacher-perceived temperament and important child–teacher relations appear more solid than the comparable evidence for an effect upon the parent–child relationship. However, as explained below, the evidence should not be regarded as necessarily indicating child effects. The same point applies to correlations between parent behavior and temperament.

Methodological Issues in Child Effects Research

Inherent aspects of the study of naturally occurring social relationships make it difficult to assume that an adult's behavior is caused by a child characteristic. (This is, of course, the inverse of observations made by Bell in 1968.) The ultimate origin of a child behavior or trait thought to affect adult behavior could itself be a product of prior transactions with the adult, as Crockenberg (1986) and others have recognized. A conceivable scenario might involve a teacher who has an idiosyncratic dislike of a child, perhaps associated with some non-temperament characteristic of the child. The teacher's attitude may be transmitted to the child through subtle, non-verbal communications, and the child, in turn, develops a resistant attitude toward the teacher. The teacher then sees adverse temperament qualities in the child, at least on the occasion of filling out a temperament questionnaire.

Similarly, one may observe poor-quality parenting in mothers who report that their infants have difficult temperament. However, in actuality, mother attitudes may have been the earliest cause of the perceived difficultness, whether it is regarded as based on accurately perceived infant behaviors that the mother has experienced, or simply on biased perceptions. There have been a number of studies showing that maternal attitudes measured prenatally can predict the positivity–negativity of perceived temperament measured postnatally, e.g. Vaughn, Bradley, Joffe, Seiffer & Barglow (1987). A study by Field *et al.* (1985) showed that mothers who were highly prone to depression/anxiety and negative about the impending arrival of their child were more likely than comparison-group mothers to perceive their infants at age 3–5 months as high in negative emotionality. They were also likely to be rated as engaging in lower quality face-to-face play with their infants. These outcomes in the risk group were associated at the 3- to 5-month age with self-reported depression and anxiety in the mother and fussy-type behaviors of the infants in the face-to-face play.

The same maternal dispositions could possibly affect measures of temperament other than parent or teacher report. The child behavior from which temperament is inferred, even by an objective observer, could be a product of the adult–child relationship. On the other hand, Crockenberg's (1987) study of adolescent mothers found that an observation index of baby irritability (time to calm after mother intervention at 3 months of age) was not significantly correlated with either the mother's prenatal attitudes about responsiveness or observed latency to intervene when the infant was upset. This shows that, on careful checking, the adult-effect interpretation of correlations between child temperament and adult behavior may itself not always hold. Nevertheless, the basic point is that the child-effects interpretation is only one of at least two plausible interpretations of correlations found between child temperament and adult behavior. As mentioned previously, the future challenge is to define empirically these two influence processes in dynamic relation to one another.

We now turn from the topic of direct, main effects of temperament to interaction effects, considering first the effects of temperament as potentially depending on qualities of the particular environment, and then later effects of the environment as they might depend on the particular child.

Indirect Effects of Child Temperament

Goodness of Fit

From the beginning of the child temperament literature, in the early writings of the Thomas and Chess group (e.g. Thomas *et al.*, 1968), there has been recognition that the implications of a child's temperament profile should to a large extent depend on the fit between the temperament and the social group's pre-existing tendencies (Lerner & Lerner, 1983; and see Chapter 19, by Thomas & Chess). For example, a child with an active, socially excitable temperament in a family that engages in and appreciates intense social and motoric activity is a better fit than a temperamentally similar child in a subdued family. The tension in the latter case between the child and family tendencies could be resolved by the parents learning to give the child adequate stimulation at crucial times, and the child learning to find more stimulation in quiet, symbolic pursuits. In such a case, the family might experience stress, but tolerable, well defined, and effectively handled stress. This family would be unlikely to present itself to a professional practitioner. More likely to be seen professionally would be families where the stress is being resolved in negative ways, e.g. where the parents of a demanding, noisy child are alternately passive–rejecting and hostile–coercive (cf. Patterson, 1982). Conceptualizations such as this one can be quite useful clinically; Thomas and Chess (e.g. Chess & Thomas, 1984; Thomas & Chess, 1977, and see Chapter 19) have provided a number of compelling examples. The clinician who considers the child's temperament will also consider the child's temperament in terms of fit to a specific family, and will not necessarily wait for better empirical definition of the theoretically crucial fit process. Nevertheless, better empirical definition should be sought too.

Empirical demonstrations of fit. The basic concept of goodness of fit has been explored empirically in a variety of ways. However, results so far have provided relatively sparse description. Crockenberg and her associates have been the most diligent in the search for such interaction effects, and have detected a few. For example, Crockenberg (1987) found that the infant irritability measure, observed time-to-calm at 3 months, predicted angry, non-compliant child behavior in a structured task at 2 years, but only when irritable babies had highly punitive mothers. However, there were no direct or interaction effects of temperament upon mother anger–punitive control. (Nor was it found that maternal punitiveness was a product of the interaction of baby irritability and mother social support.) For a description of a few other relevant interactions effects, e.g. involving sex of infant and family social class, see Crockenberg (1986).

Although the exploration for goodness of fit interactions in parent–child data has been far from systematic, it has been more impressive than in school data, according to Keogh (1986). Keogh nevertheless manages to describe one of the most interesting, empirically supported interaction effects in either area of research: handicapped preschoolers with positive temperament characteristics tended to get less attention from their teachers than handicapped children with negative temperaments, whereas positive temperament in non-handicapped preschoolers was associated with more teacher interaction than was negative temperament. Several interesting explanations are plausible. One interpretation is that the preschool teachers of handicapped children were inclined to respond to the children's negative, demanding behaviors more than the pleasant ones. This, in turn, is perhaps due to negative affect in a handicapped pupil creating a greater problem than negative affect in a non-handicapped pupil. Or perhaps the handicapped children's positive social skills were less developed than those of the non-handicapped children's, and thus less likely to elicit teacher involvement. Or perhaps the difference in teacher responses was simply due to differences in teacher–pupil ratios.

Statistics defining fit. Plomin and Daniels (1984) have argued that the most commonly used approaches to assess statistical interactions involving temperament in relation to environment are inadequate. For example, some studies have operationalized goodness of fit by computing the discrepancy between a temperament score and a score based on environmental preference, and correlating this difference with a measure of child outcome. For example, school-children's temperament might be subtracted from a teacher's general expectations for temperament as a way of predicting child behavior problems. One problem with this approach is that environmental expectations may show little variability, as in the case of the tendency for a high degree of similarity across teachers in preferences for child behavior characteristics. More importantly, the difference-score method fails to partial out the main effects of environment and temperament. Therefore, even if there is a correlation between the temperament–environment discrepancy score and the criterion variable, this does not necessarily indicate a true interaction effect, and thus is weak support for the goodness-of-fit model.

To cope with such artifacts, Plomin and Daniels (1984) suggested instead the use of hierarchical multiple regression, in which an interaction term (e.g. the child's temperament score multiplied by the environment score) is added to a multiple regression equation after adding separate terms for temperament and environment. Plomin and Daniels report some systematic searches for interactive effects involving temperament and environment indexes in predicting children's behavioral adjustment. The analysis turned up some main effects but practically no interaction effects. Plomin and Daniels concluded that 'so far, it is consider-ably easier to talk about temperament interactions than it is to find them' (Plomin & Daniels, 1984, p. 161).

While the interactive term technique has statistical advantages over the other methods used for defining goodness of fit, it is far from completely satisfactory. For one thing, there are many ways to define interaction in a statistical sense; multiplication of variables is only one way in which there can be an interactive effect, and multiplication of non-independent variables could produce complica-tions in interpretation (Viken, in preparation). In fact, people talk about statistical interaction in a wide variety of ways, and many of the effects spoken of as interactions could be reduced to artifacts of method (such as unit of scaling or that long-time bugaboo of clinical research, variance due to source of data, e.g. parent report vs direct observation). Viken (in preparation) suggests that the term 'interaction' be generally avoided. The exception would be traditional analyses of variance with truly orthogonal, experimentally controlled factors. Whether or not one chooses to follow this advice, the methodological complexity of the topic must be kept in mind.

Researchers are poised upon an era of increasing use of statistical models with higher order relationships. They are going beyond the bivariate relations measured by the correlation coefficient and its close relatives, t-tests, main effects analysis of variance tests, etc., and increasingly using partial and multiple correlations, analysis of variance interaction tests, analysis of covariance, etc. As Rutter (1983) points out, the search for theoretically meaningful interaction effects could be a long one, since there are so many alternative types of statistical analysis. Rutter's (1983) suggestion, in essence, is to aim research toward empirical discovery of conceptually interesting processes, yet stay aware of how methodology affects interpretation of observations.

The Lerners and their associates have been diligent in bringing the topic of goodness of fit to the literature, and in trying to assess it empirically. And appropriately, they have recently been diligent in pointing out the shortcomings of the attempts to test empirically the notion as a model. Windle and Lerner (1986) take the Plomin and Daniels (1984) critique a step further. First, they describe attempts to use hierarchical multiple regression to show goodness of fit in which they actually found no significant interaction effects after removing the variance associated with the separate temperament and environment variables. They recognize that part of this failure to demonstrate goodness of fit must be due to the lack of variation in their measures of environmental demands. However, more importantly, they criticize their past research as attempting to measure goodness of fit as a static quality rather than as a dynamic, transactional process. This implies that future attempts to assess goodness of fit should be longitudinal. There should be repeated measurements of the child's effect on the environment and vice versa, with the aim of showing how temperament–environment correlations arise over time. This is a good recommendation, but it introduces a further complication into the topic of interaction effects; it involves processes of change in the child and the social environment over repeated transactions (see Rutter, 1983, for discussion of this point).

The notion that an individual's temperament would have different implications for development in different contexts in an appealing one. It should be possible to study the notion empirically. However, as the field begins to turn from simple, main effects models to more complex, interactive models, it is clear that there is an exponential increase in the methodological challenges. This means, I would predict, that the empirical specification of fit processes will proceed more slowly than might be wished, at least in the near future. We next turn to a companion kind of interaction effect, organismic specificity.

Organismic Specificity

Organismic specificity is a term coined to refer to the differential effects of a given environmental feature upon different children (Wachs & Gruen, 1982). The elegant research of Escalona (1968) has for some time made it seem quite sensible, even necessary, to hypothesize individuality of response to environment in human development. There are a great many anecdotal examples of children who have some major feature of environment in common, yet develop differently. However, there is very little empirical evidence. Perhaps the most widely cited example is DeVries' (1984) observation in an African group of better famine survival for difficult babies than for easy ones. Empirically demonstrating an individual response effect is very difficult, just as with the task of demonstrating goodness of fit. Nevertheless, as Wachs and Gruen (1982) have argued, there is sufficient evidence at this time to view organismic specificity as a likely possibility.

The root of an individual response effect could be a non-temperament factor, such as gender, but pertinent to this chapter, some of the evidence concerns the mediational role of temperament.

Specificity in the role of difficultness in cognitive development. Wachs and Grandour (1983) found evidence suggesting that the cognitive development of infants with an easy temperament was more strongly predicted by the amounts of social stimulation they received than was the cognitive development of difficult infants. Easy infants' cognitive development seems to have been relatively inferior in the absence of positive stimulation. There is not yet a clear explanation for why this effect should exist.

The role of difficult temperament as a mediator of the effects of the environment may depend on what kind of environmental feature is considered. Wachs (1987) found difficult infants to be *more* sensitive to a possible stress factor in the home environment: for difficult babies, but not easy ones, when the home had high levels of 'person traffic', the babies tended to show less advanced mastery behavior in a structured test, in the form of more time off task and less mastery manipulation of objects. This finding converges with a finding of Wachs and Gandour (1983): noise and confusion in the home correlated with lower levels of cognitive development in difficult infants, but did not make a difference in the easy group. The Wachs studies suggest, then, that the difficult infant's cognitive development is at risk from negative or stressful features of the environment, such as noise, whereas the easy infant's cognitive development is at risk from deficiencies in positive features of the environment, such as social stimulations.

In partial contrast to Wachs and Gandour (1983), Maziade, Cote, Boutin, Bernier, and Thivierge (1985) found that temperament did interact with environmental qualities in forecasting intellectual development. However, Maziade *et al.* found that, instead of easy infants, difficult infants reared in more intellectually stimulating or middle to upper class families showed better cognitive development at age 4 years than those reared in less stimulating or lower class families. These associations between family class or communication level and child IQ did not hold among the average or easy temperament groups. Maziade *et al.* interpret the data as suggesting that in the higher socioeconomic status (SES) families the difficult infant can elicit extra amounts of stimulation, thereby promoting intellectual development; in lower SES families, difficult temperament does not elicit extra stimulation because it is not available; and easy infants do not elicit development-promoting responses from the environment, even in the higher SES families. This is quite reasonable.

However, there is one aspect of the Maziade *et al.* (1985) data that is more puzzling: in families rated by an interviewer as superior in instrumental and affective communication, the easy infants' IQ outcomes at age 4 were apparently lower (mean = 108) than easy infants' IQs in the families rated as inferior in communication (mean = 119). Consistent with the stimulation-resources interpretation (above), among difficult children the IQ tended to be higher in superior communication families (mean = 126) than in inferior communication families (mean = 117). The IQ of children with average temperament did not differ much according to type of family (superior mean = 115, inferior mean = 120). These data suggest that the link between difficultness and IQ in the superior communication families may be as much due to the lagging IQ development of their easy children as the surging development of their difficult children. If the IQ score is interpreted as a partial reflection of environmental stimulation, why would the easy infant be less well stimulated in a family with superior communication qualities than in one with inferior qualities? It would appear that the index of communication quality is rather different than the index of SES, even if the two indexes may be correlated, as supported by our own research (Olson, Bates & Bayles, 1984); the paradoxical effect of easy temperament is not seen in the relationship between temperament and IQ as mediated by social class. Perhaps there is some sample-specific variation in the Maziade *et al.*, subgroup of easy temperament + superior communication families. In small groups, as in the analyses being discussed, there can sometimes be disproportionate distributions on some theoretically irrelevant variable that affects the correlations under study. For example, there could have been a disproportionate number of easy + superior group children who were anomalously low in IQ for reasons unrelated to temperament, such as constitutional deficits in central nervous system functioning, or the cumulative effects of mothers who were actually understimulating due to chronic depression.

The fact that the Maziade *et al.* (1987) results do not precisely replicate the Wachs and Gandour (1983) results in showing that easy infants are the ones more at risk from lack of positive stimulation is not critical. Wachs and Gandour measured cognitive development in infancy, which is a rather different outcome measure than Maziade *et al.* got from their IQ tests in the preschool era. Nevertheless, it is an intriguing discrepancy, and one should await further research before settling on any particular model of how temperament might mediate between the environment and cognitive development.

In summary, temperamental easiness has been found to potentiate the link between infants' inferior cognitive development and lower environmental stimulation, and temperamental difficultness has been found (twice) to potentiate the link between inferior cognitive development and environmental stresses. However, at least one study has found that the link between environment and eventual cognitive development is stronger in difficult infants.

Specificity in the role of difficultness in emotional development. Temperamental difficultness might be a buffer/risk factor for outcomes in emotional adjustment, too. Rutter and Quinton (1984) found some support for this idea in their study of the children of psychiatric patients. The child subjects were various ages. Rutter and Quinton found that in the relatively rare cases of children who were seen as difficult in the first year of study but not showing behavior problems (as rated by the teacher), there was a higher likelihood (2 of 3 cases) of showing such problems a year later than not showing them. On the other hand, of the cases who did not have difficult temperament at the start, very few showed problems a year later (2 of 13).

Specificity in the role of activity in cognitive development. Another temperament variable, activity, has more consistently shown mediational effects on development, although there is still a paucity of data. It has been observed for some time that highly active infants are less likely to show the negative effects of understimulation on cognitive development than more passive infants, in both family and institutional environments (Escalona, 1968; Rutter, 1981). Two recent studies from Wachs' laboratory support this pattern, while also suggesting that the active infant may actually do better under conditions of lower intensity of stimulation: Gandour

(1987) found that toddlers perceived as high active showed relatively high exploratory competence if they were from families low in intensity of stimulation, and relatively low competence where stimulation was highly intense; the low-active toddlers showed the exact reverse pattern. A very similar kind of pattern of high- vs low-active group effects was observed by Wachs (1987), concerning the link between frequency of parent naming of objects and infants' mastery behavior. The high-active group showed negative correlations between parent object naming and their own mastery behavior, while the low-active group showed positive correlations.

Overall, there is evidence in support of the conceptually appealing hypothesis that individual differences in temperament mediate the effects of environment, especially in the area of cognitive development. However, there is not much evidence, and what evidence there is forms few coherent patterns. There is reason for optimism that the line of research is plausible. Wachs (1985) has suggested that research should focus on a particular list of environmental qualities that have been shown to have only modest correlations with child cognitive development, e.g. crowded home. This would seem to allow greater room for the mediation by child characteristics. Despite this remarkably specific guideline, it cannot be assumed that the research path is clear. I will mention several methodological points relative to both the goodness of fit and organismic specificity types of statistical interaction.

Challenges in the Detection of Interaction Effects

As efforts intensify to understand very complex systems and processes in child social development, increasingly sophisticated questions about interaction effects are addressed. Many researchers feel that the main effects models have not proved compelling. Most would agree that the road to truly efficacious clinical applications must someday pass through well-defined person-by-environment interactions. At the same time, however, I would like to emphasize that the road to well-defined interaction effects probably will need to pass through well-defined models of main effects.

At the current time, the field has only begun the process of determining what the main effects are. There are probably crucial improvements to be made in the basic measurement of the major constructs, such as temperamental and environmental concepts. There are also advances that can be made in linear, additive models, through the application of multivariate techniques such as multiple regression and structural equations. The fact that a single variable, such as temperamental adaptability to novelty, does not explain by itself clinically important portions of the variance in an outcome such as later behavior problems (Bates & Bayles, 1988) does not necessarily imply that the next test of the concept's efficacy must be in the form of interaction tests. It may well be that the simple addition of other variables, such as quality of parenting or other temperament variables, might significantly improve accounts of children's variations in developmental paths (as perhaps suggested by the multiple regression analyses of Bates & Bayles, 1988). Rutter (1983) has given several clinically important, non-temperament examples of this kind of effect.

Another way the general topic of interaction effects has been discussed is in terms of linear (i.e. additive) vs more complex, non-linear models (e.g. with multiplicative terms). The issue has been considered for a long time in the area of personality assessment and prediction of performance. Wiggins' (1973) review suggests that linear models have generally been about as high in predictive power, and much simpler to use than non-linear models. Following the criterion of parsimony, additive models would be the standard of comparison for more complex, interactive models (e.g. Plomin & Daniels, 1984).

Despite the need for further research on main effects models, it does seem highly likely that there are interaction effects involving temperament. If nothing else, there are some elegant, meaningful examples in non-temperament variables, such as the antecedents in childhood and current stress and social support of adulthood depression (Rutter, 1983). However, it still remains to be proved that the compound condition of individuality in response to environmental features dependent on temperament, or vice versa, can be described and quantified in conceptually meaningful ways. Yet to be adequately ruled out, despite preliminary encouragement from the few relevant studies, is the possibility that the individuality components are essentially idiosyncratic – what psychometricians call 'error variance'. The outlines of research programs to rule out this hypothetical randomness are being sketched (e.g. Wachs, 1985; Windle & Lerner, 1986). The results will be of great interest.

In the foregoing discussion, the implicit frame of reference in thinking about the task of describing individual differences has been what Allport (1958) referred to as the nomothetic – i.e. looking for patterns that generalize across individuals. (The 'individual' for me could be a child, a child–parent dyad, or even a whole family system.) The alternative approach is an idiographic approach – an attempt to see whole individuals in all their uniqueness. Allport (1962) renamed the latter approach 'morphogenic' in order to emphasize the search for the organized pattern in the personality of the individual. There can be no argument that each person is unique. However, I believe I am not unique in not having found much lasting enlightenment in others' idiographic descriptions, however much I may have enjoyed them as I read them or however essential they are in clinical practice. Ultimately, science seeks to summarize phenomena in general laws. One special value of the idiographic approach might be that it offers chances to detect in individuals patterns that would be missed in nomothetic approaches, especially complex systems of characteristics. Chess and Thomas have given the example of focusing qualitative analyses on cases that are discrepant from the statistical trends (e.g. Chess & Thomas, 1984). This is valuable for suggesting plausible processes to be evaluated empirically in further work. Another possible use, which is implicit in the idiographic approach, but which I have not seen in the personality development area, would be to analyze large numbers of morphogenic/idiographic descriptions in relationship to one another, with the goal of detecting more general patterns of organic uniqueness. The impetus for this aim is the growing literature on non-linear systems, which shows that there can be beautiful and elegantly modeled patterns even amongst seemingly chaotic diversity of forms in nature, for example in weather patterns or the developing motor system of the human infant (Gleick, 1987; Thelen, 1989).

Endeavors to discover general patterns of interactive effects face methodological complexities and pitfalls, centering on the shortcomings in concepts and measures of both temperament and environment. Researchers probably should navigate by two, equally important stars: (a) theoretically meaningful, specific models of temperament's roles in developmental processes and (b) replication of findings, whether the findings originally come from *a priori* hypotheses, 'fishing expeditions', or even serendipity. With these two guides, research on the notions of organismic specificity and goodness of fit will eventually produce useful tools for the practitioner.

TEMPERAMENT AND CHILD PSYCHOPATHOLOGY

One of the most important questions concerning temperament is its role in child psychopathology. This question could have been addressed in the preceding section on social interaction, because psychopathology is one of the facets of the child's social relations. The question was assigned a separate section, however, because psychopathology connotes so much more than social interaction. Psychopathology is also conceived of in terms of patterns of individual, subjective experience. Furthermore, it can be thought of as patterns of social perception, since it relies on adult views that the child is presenting/having problems. This perception is almost always based on a combination of subjective and objective experiences with the child. Similarly, but at a higher level of the process of defining psychopathology, the psychologist, psychiatrist, clinical social worker, and school counselor partially structure the parent's or teacher's report via their interview or questionnaire. They do this through what they ask, and how they scale and interpret the answers, all based on their knowledge, assumptions, and perceptual biases. In using the term psychopathology, I am referring to emotional or behavioral problems of varying degrees of intensity, not just ones that are severe or clinically diagnosed. The next subsection will consider how temperament helps in understanding the development of child psychopathology. The following one will discuss clinical implications.

Associations Between Temperment and Psychopathology

The main focus of this section will be on the issue of whether parentally perceived temperament variables predict child psychopathology. There have also been studies of how temperament is related to behavior problems at school. These studies give an important new perspective to the definition of school behavior problems, but are well summarized by Keogh (1986, and see Chapter 23) and by Garrison and Earls (1987), so I will mention only a few studies concerning teacher reports of behavior problems. There have also been some studies in which the child temperament measures are themselves predicted by parent psychopathology. For example, mothers with severe psychopathology, including schizophrenia and depression, perceive more difficult and fearful temperament in their infants, either concurrently (Field *et al.*, 1985; Sameroff, Seifer & Barocas, 1983) or retrospectively (Silverton, Finello & Mednick, 1983). However, the special emphasis of this section will be on studies using temperament as an advance, rather than concurrent, predictor. There are also a number of studies in which temperament assessed after toddlerhood is used to predict psychopathology in later childhood. One important example of this kind of study is that by Thomas *et al.* (1968). Maziade (see Chapter 22 this volume) provides another such example. In the current chapter, I will primarily describe research in which temperament has been assessed in the infancy–toddler era.

Theoretical Models

What temperament variables should predict behavior problems vs positive adjustment, and how should they predict them? Thomas, Chess, and Birch (1968) opened the attack on these questions. They asked whether difficult temperament (a combination of tendencies to show negative mood, rejection/fear of novel situations and slow adaptation to change, intense expression of affect, and lack of rhythmicity in such things as hunger and fatigue) would predict risk for behavior problems. Aspects of their difficult temperament concept have been challenged on empirical grounds. In a number of studies, with a variety of questionnaires, it has been found that rhythmicity is not associated with the cluster even within the Thomas *et al.* type of questionniare. It has also been found that the mother's ratings of infant difficultness are more associated with negative mood than unadaptability/fear (Bates, 1987). Nevertheless, studies do find that the mood and unadaptability scales tend to cluster (e.g. see Chapter 22, by Maziade), and the Thomas *et al.*, difficultness dimension, including rhythmicity, has been the most frequently used. This is probably due not only to the conceptual appeal of the concept described by Thomas *et al.* but also the popularity of parent-report questionnaires based on the pathbreaking Thomas *et al.* definitions.

Other variants of the difficultness notion have also been hypothesized to play a role in behavior problems. Olweus (1987) did not measure temperament in infancy, but suggests on the basis of later childhood data that adolescent boys' aggression is partly due to active and irritable temperament. Spivack, Marcus, and Swift (1986) interpreted their longitudinal data as showing that the child in the primary grades who is likely to be delinquent as an adolescent is one who is temperamentally 'overly and disruptively involved socially and who fails to modulate his or her own behavior to accommodate to others'. These are just two examples. Almost all recent models of the development of psychopathology include the notion of enduring temperamental qualities, especially qualities considered difficult for adults to handle. The first empirical issue, then, is whether difficultness variables actually do predict behavior problems.

Findings

The most crucial question, again, is whether *infant* difficultness would predict behavior problems. Thomas *et al.* (1968) are very often cited as having established in their NYLS that difficult infants are at risk for later behavior problems. This is incorrect. Clearly, Thomas *et al.* thought that difficult temperament would be found to be a risk factor, and their very useful, longitudinal clinical impressions indicated that it could play a role. However, their empirical analyses showed that the scales in their difficultness composite did not begin to significantly forecast behavior problems until 3 years of age or later. They concluded that it was probably not the difficult temperament in itself that led to the continuity in these cases, but rather the fit between the child's temperament and the kind of child management response shown by the parents. The mis–citation of Thomas *et al.*, as supporting a direct link between infant temperament and later behavior problems is so widespread that it may be achieving the status of a myth in the literature. Fortunately, this particular flaw in scholarship probably does not have disastrous consequences. There is, in fact, subsequent evidence that supports the original hunch of Thomas *et al.*

Maziade (see Chapter 22) reports that his longitudinal study, like that of Thomas *et al.*, did not find infant temperament to predict behavior problems at age 4 years. Maziade and his colleagues, like Thomas *et al.* (1968), assessed behavior disorders via clinical interviews. Although even extreme temperament scores in infancy did not predict later behavior problems, they did predict temperament at the later age, especially in boys, and temperament at age 4 was concurrently associated with psychopathology. This study essentially replicates the findings of Thomas *et al.* (1988). However, neither Maziade nor others are convinced that temperament in fact plays no early role; the question is how to detect the role. Would the results be the same if different measures of temperament or psychopathology were used?

Several recent studies, including our own, have shown that there are direct links between maternal ratings of infant temperament in the first 2 years and maternal reports of behavior problems at ages 3–6 years. In our own research (e.g. Bates & Bayles, 1988) temperament predicted later behavior problems even after controlling for the potentially confounding variables of observed mother–child interaction and mother personality. Our longitudinal research with the Infant Characteristics Questionnaire (ICQ) has shown that maternally perceived difficult temperament (defined primarily as frequent, intense expressions of negative emotion) predicts both internalizing and externalizing behavior problems at 3–6 years (Bates *et al.*, 1985; Bates & Bayles, 1988). A second ICQ scale, unadaptability to new people and situations, also predicted later behavior problems, making better predictions at all ages to internalizing problems than externalizing problems. This is consistent with an interpretation of unadaptability to new people and situations as anxiety tendencies. Another ICQ variable, appearing in the versions of the questionnaire designed for children in the second year, concerned resistance to management of activity. This variable predicted better to externalizing than to internalizing behaviors, fitting with its content.

Thus, we have observed a differentiated predictiveness in early mother reports of temperament. Difficultness predicted both major dimensions of behavior problems vs positive adjustment, while unadaptability predicted later anxiety problems better than acting-out problems, and resistance to control predicted later acting out better than anxiety. It was particularly striking to see similar kinds of differentiation at both 3 and 6 years, and to consider that the moderately high levels of overlap found between internalizing and externalizing outcome scales could have worked against finding differentiated continuity. This degree of differentiation mitigates the potential criticism that the correlations merely reflect a continuing, global bias in maternal perceptions of the child. It is also consistent with the differentiation that has been observed several times in continuity of mother reports on behavior problem scales from preschool to school age – internalizing-type scales to internalizing, and externalizing to externalizing (e.g. Garrison & Earls, 1987; Richman, Stevenson & Graham, 1982).

Our research has also found that observed parent–child interactions can predict behavior problems. Aggregated variables describing mothers' positive involvement with their infants and toddlers were negative predictors of behavior problems at 6 years of age (Bates & Bayles, 1988), although not at 3 years (Bates *et al.*, 1985). Relatively high levels of positive involvement, including behaviors such as affection, teaching concepts, and making requests predicted the relative absence of behavior problems. (Indexes of the child's behavior have not shown much predictiveness.) Using additive combinations of early temperament scales, age 3-year behavior problem scales, and positive involvement variables, we were able to account for appreciable portions of the variance in internalizing and externalizing problem scores of both girls and boys at age 6 years (Bates & Bayles, 1988).

However, there is still the possibility that what the mother has perceived in infancy is predictive only of qualities that occur in the context of the same, mother–child relationship. This would moderate any conclusions about the link between early temperament reports and later behavior problem reports. It would reflect shortcomings in the operational definition of temperament, or a lack of implications of the abstract concept of temperament for later school behavior, at least as defined by current behavior problem measures. In our own longitudinal study, early temperament scores were generally not predictive of teacher reports at age 6 years (Olson, Bates & Bayles, 1986). We will search at later ages in further follow-ups.

Another important study is that of Cameron (1978), based on the Thomas *et al.* NYLS data. In the past I had interpreted Cameron's findings as support for the goodness-of-fit model. Cameron (personal communication, 28 June, 1988) has indicated, however, that the data are actually more supportive of a linear, additive model, analogous to that of Bates and Bayles (1988). Cameron (1978) used the Thomas *et al.* data to show empirically that a combination index of difficultness (omitting rhythmicity) and persistence in actions at age 1 year (summing withdrawal, low adaptability, negative mood, and high persistence), plus poor parenting at age 3 years, was predictive of later behavior problems. Cameron (1978) also found a direct link between his temperament risk index at 1 year and later behavior problems for girls, although not for boys. The link was not quite statistically significant, but in the expected direction.

Guerin and Gottfried (1986) report a study similar to our own. They found that mother-report, 18-month ICQ scores were modestly to moderately correlated with mother-report behavior problem scores at years 3–6. Temperament scores were not very predictive of teacher reports of behavior problems at 6 years, but the correlations for girls did reach significance. Guerin and Gottfried's results did not show quite as clear a differentiation in predictiveness of the different kinds of ICQ scales as the Bates *et al.* results. Convergent with the Bates *et al.* data, unadaptability predicted somewhat better to internalizing problems than externalizing, but this was clear only for boys, and only at age 5 years. The resistance to management factor predicted externalizing problems slightly better than internalizing at 4 and 5 years, but not at 6 years. Difficultness predicted both internalizing and externalizing, just as in the Bates *et al.* study. Perhaps the replication would have been more complete if Geurin and Gottfried had used ICQ measures from more than one age. Bates *et al.* (1985) and Bates and Bayles (1988) used measures from 6, 13, and 24 months, creating cross-age composites where possible. The aggregation may have reduced a crucial component of psychometric error, and allowed the differentiation to show through more clearly. There does appear to be some differentiation in the continuity of maternal perceptions, but it is not yet adequately established.

There are several other studies that confirm the direct link between mother reports of temperament in the first 2 years and later behavior problems. Wolkind and De Salis (1982) found that their version of difficult temperament (negative mood plus irregular cycles in hunger, sleep, etc.), based on interviews with mothers at age 4 months, predicted internalizing and externalizing behavior problems at age 42 months. Swets-Gronert (1986) used Dutch versions of both a questionnaire based on the Thomas–Chess system (Persson-Blennow & McNeil, 1982) and the ICQ (Kohnstamm, 1984). She found that infant and toddler difficultness predicted behavior problems at 3 and 5 years. She also replicated our finding that unadaptability predicted internalizing problems only, while difficultness predicted both internalizing and externalizing problems. Kohnstamm (1987) extended the pattern even further: he found that mother reports on the Netherlands ICQ in the infancy to toddlerhood period predicted, in differentiated fashion, to preschool teacher ratings of the children. Resistance to control predicted a lack of task orientation and higher levels of hostility, but not boldness–timidity. Unadaptability predicted more timidity, and to a lesser degree, lack of hostility. Kohnstamm used a different composite for difficultness than the previous research, separating parent ratings of negative mood from those of difficulty of caregiving, and failed to find links with the teacher reports. Finally, Torgersen (1984) found that mother-report infancy measures of negative mood, withdrawal, and difficultness as a summary variable were modest-level predictors of anxiety and psychosomatic problems at 6 years of age. She did not find that infancy measures predicted conduct problems at 6 years.

Interpretation

In brief, it does appear that maternal perceptions of infants' and toddlers' characteristics, especially ones pertaining to general negative emotionality, reactions to new people and situations, and manageability, are predictive of later reports of behavior problems, especially ones seen by the mother herself. However, the correlations are of modest size and the patterns of continuity from infancy onward in anxiety-type vs acting-out-type behaviors are not clearly differentiated paths in all of the studies. Potential moderator variables like sex of child and quality of parent–child relationship have not yet been systematically studied.

Nevertheless, the differentiated links that have been found do make theoretical sense (Bates, 1987): anxiety or distress tendencies seem likely to have constitutional components, and this would help account for the continuity between unadaptability and anxiety problems. Children's differences in manageability of activity (e.g. intensity of need for stimulation) could also have a constitutional basis, although the assumption is more speculative than that for anxiety. This would help explain continuity between early resistance to control and later externalizing problems. Clues in recent research make it seem likely that there will be found psychophysiological substrates to the emotional reactions of the child. In school-age children referred for behavior problems, those who are predominantly showing conduct problems are relatively under-reactive autonomically to stimuli, while those with anxiety problems are relatively high in reactivity (Delameter & Lahey, 1983; Raine & Venables, 1984a,b; van Engeland, 1984). These findings converge with those for adults (Hare & Schalling, 1978). The patterns are consistent with an interpretation of temperamental style. However, the style would not have to be inherited, since by middle childhood there has been plenty of time to acquire emotional response tendencies. Kagan and his associates (e.g. Kagan, Reznick & Snidman, 1986) have demonstrated early-appearing, stable characteristics in the autonomic responses of highly fearful vs uninhibited children. These data give a stronger suggestion of a constitutionally based, temperamental quality. However, even if some such characteristics are inherited or otherwise inborn, there is no reason to rule out interest in acquired dispositions, e.g. ones that come about as the result of chronic stress or parental mismanagement. The only question is whether and how to include these under the general rubric of temperament (as discussed in Chapter 1, by Bates).

I have been especially intrigued by the question of how it happens that difficultness, even when defined narrowly, as via the ICQ, predicts later externalizing and internalizing problems. This question is not yet answered, but we have recently suggested (Bates, 1987) one good possibility: difficultness, even when defined primarily by parent reports of frequent fussing and crying, is actually made up of two, correlated components.

(1) *The need by the child for high levels of stimulation.* In fact, the leading attribution of mothers for the difficultness of their young infants seems to be that the infants are bored and demanding attention (Bates *et al.*, 1984). Could this be the root of a coercive pattern in infant–mother interaction? The infant fusses, the parent delivers stimulation, and the infant stops fussing. If such a pattern were to continue, either due to excessive demand for stimulation by the child or insufficient attention by the parents to the infant when not fussing, in a few years it would come to resemble the pattern one sees so often in acting-out children in the clinic. Patterson (1982) has eloquently described the role of the coercive process in aggressive behavior problems, e.g. where the parent tries to modulate the child's disruptive behavior and the child aversively counter-controls the parent, and the parent disengages. Temperament is one of the roots in Patterson's (1988) process model of the origin of aggressive behavior disorders. Another aspect of the coerciveness is that children referred for externalizing problems often seem to be hungry for social reactions from others, and willing to be annoying to get them. I

have seen this in family therapy sessions many times. Spivack *et al.* (1986) have empirically described this in elementary school children.

If stimulation-demanding somehow takes a coercive turn and becomes external-izing behavior problems, what, then, is the source of the need for stimulation? One possibility is an inborn, hereditary predisposition, perhaps related to individual differences in Strelau's (1983) concept of reactivity. It is explained in previous chapters of this volume (see Chapter 1, by Bates, and Chapter 3, by Strelau) that there may be individual differences in how the brain suppresses and augments stimulation, leading to differences in preference for stimulation. There may also be a component of sociability in this pattern of stimulation-demanding. Buss and Plomin (1984) have identified a disposition to seek social stimuli such as attention as an inherited dimension of temperament.

The other possibility is an acquired disposition. Weissbluth (see Chapter 18) makes a strong argument for the importance of sleep deficits in creating neuro-hormonal changes that affect the infant's irritability and stimulation demands. Weissbluth points out that the stress of even relatively minor sleep loss can produce difficult temperament, as defined both on the surface, behavioral level and the underlying, psychophysiological process levels. I have observed the fatigue process Weissbluth describes. The child's attention becomes more and more fragmented, and the child is less able to extract meaningful information from the environment, exploring more and more frantically. In a young infant, this may culminate in crying that can only be terminated by vestibular stimulation, as in walking with the baby. In an older child, the child's actions become disorganized, destructive, or directly attention-demanding. Of course, sleep deficits are not the only stress that can produce such patterns, but they are certainly a leading cause in infancy. Whether the roots are inherited or acquired, a predisposition to demand stimulation seems most likely to be predictive of later externalizing problems, either through its potential for contributing to coercive parent–child interactions (as in the parent responding to a fussy baby), or through its potential for high levels of parent–child management conflict (as in the child exploring too vigorously). This component of difficultness would probably not predict internalizing problems.

(2) *High sensitivity to aversive stimuli* is the second proposed component of difficultness. This is more hypothetical, but has a reasonable basis in theory and folk wisdom. This component may actually be a part of difficultness that overlaps with the unadaptability dimension. Typically, there are modest degrees of overlap between ICQ difficultness and scales of unadaptability or fear (Bates *et al.*, 1984). This sensitivity component is conceptualized in terms related to the construct of anxiety. When one is in an anxious or highly aroused state, one may react to relatively minor aversive stimuli with distress. A baby who is seen to fuss or cry a lot may be expressing distress, e.g. due to fear or minor physical discomfort, rather than a need for stimulation. This seems possible, but so far we have been unable to get a satisfactory index of such an oversensitivity construct (Bates *et al.*, 1984). It appears that the mothers we have worked with are generally unaware of such differences in their infants, perhaps because they are all maintaining such optimal physical environments for their infants. Ultimately, it seems likely that one might be able to detect the postulated component of difficultness via controlled

stimulation and psychophysiological measures of child response. The basic prediction is that this component of difficultness would predict internalizing problems better than externalizing.

If the model is correct, then there should be some difficult infants, probably a minority, who are high on only the second, sensitivity component. There should be others, probably a majority, who are high on only the first, stimulation-demanding component. And there should be others high on both components. Further, knowing the child's position on the two components should improve the prediction of the internalizing and externalizing dimensions in later childhood over prediction from the undifferentiated difficultness dimension.

The above research and suggested further directions represent a start on the question of how temperament might be related to child psychopathology vs positive adjustment. There are some other questions that have barely begun to be addressed. One is whether infant temperament assessed through structured, laboratory procedures would show comparable predictability to later behavior problems. Perhaps the Louisville Twin Study (e.g. Matheny *et al.*, 1987), which is a longitudinal study with an excellent battery of early laboratory and parent-report measures of temperament, will be offering data on this question.

Another issue is whether temperament variables can be found to interact in particular ways with potential moderator variables. There are already some indications that the quality of the parent–child relationship and the sex of the child play a role in how temperament variables predict outcomes. The literature is not well advanced in this area – few direct replications have been done, and there are many possibilities that have not been tried. However, as indicated in the earlier section on moderator effects, the questions are crucial, and the methodological and theoretical problems are an important focus. One especially interesting and plausible formulation is suggested by Rutter and Quinton (1984), as discussed previously: family stresses should affect a difficult child more adversely than an easy one. There is some evidence that this is true of boys in the face of the stresses of divorce (Hetherington, 1987). It will be crucial to extend this to prestress and infancy measures of temperament. Again, however, it is possible that temperament-like behavior traits could be acquired as well as constitutional. Indeed, perhaps one of the problems in tracing the continuity of difficultness is due to the separate nature of acquired and inherited components of the phenotypic behavior pattern. In some instances the two components may augment one another, e.g. when the child creates an environment that provides continual exercise of a predisposition to negative emotionality and ultimately biases the autonomic response system toward high levels of stress response. In other instances, the components may compete with each other, e.g. when the parents prevent excess stress and make it easier for the child to learn how to modulate emotions.

Using Temperament in Solving Behavior Problems

Despite the generally rudimentary state of knowledge about the role temperament plays in developmental process, clincians are using the concepts in their attempts to deal with child behavior problems.

Can Temperament Concepts be Used for Prevention?

It is far too early for a meaningful answer to the prevention question. Very few attempts have been made to use temperament measures as a basis for screening. And the literature suggests that the available instruments are too low in reliability and validity for screening on any basis but an experimental one (e.g. see Hubert, Wachs, Peters-Martin & Gandour, 1982). In an ideal screening program one would know that the construct being assessed is closely linked with risk for the outcome targeted for prevention, and one would know that the screening measure is a good measure of the construct, in the sense of accurately identifying cases that are and are not at risk. As indicated earlier in this chapter and elsewhere (e.g. see Chapter 1, by Bates), these ideals are not currently met in the temperament area. Nevertheless, there have been several attempts to use parent temperament questionnaires as a basis for preventive interventions.

One good example is the study by Cameron and Rice (1986). Cameron and Rice briefly considered and dismissed concerns about the psychometric and theoretical meaningfulness of the questionnaires. They concluded that for clinicians working in pediatric settings and having to deal with issues pertaining to infant or preschool temperament, 'the question is not whether to include considerations of temperament in daily practice but how to do so' (Cameron & Rice, 1986, p. 223). Cameron and Rice developed predictions of issues likely to face parents of children with several temperament types. For example, they expected energetic, fast-adjusting infants to present more problems in the areas of accident risk, assertiveness, and mealtime issues. They assessed temperament in the clientele of large health-maintenance organizations via parent report on the Carey question-naire at age 4 months. They then sent parents the predictions that most closely fit the temperament profile of the infant, along with suggestions about how to deal with the issues. Then, they surveyed the parents again 4 or 8 months later to see whether the predictions had been correct. In the second of their two experiments, Cameron and Rice had a control group of parents given the temperament question-naire at 4 months and followed up concerning the issues presented by the infant, with no predictions intervening. They found that their predictions were correct to a statistically significant degree for those parents followed up at 8 months, but the prediction accuracy did not reach significance for those parents followed up at 12 months, despite extremely large sample sizes. The parents indicated that they appreciated the anticipatory guidance, with slightly greater levels of appreciation coming from parents whose children showed higher levels of temperament-related problems. Cameron and co-workers have continued with the large-scale screening research, most recently evaluating whether personal counseling (as opposed to written advice) was more needed with certain kinds of temperament problems than others. Personal advice was particularly important for the more difficult children, especially around separation issues (J. Cameron, personal communication, 27 June 1988). The Cameron results support the potential usefulness of the general approach of anticipatory guidance based on temperament scores, but further research is needed to evaluate and improve the efficacy of the particular screening and intervention techniques prior to wider application.

Most temperament researchers would probably be uncomfortable with the use of the current generation of temperament questionnaires as the basis for screening and prevention efforts. Nevertheless, the need for such efforts is likely to override the misgivings. Other such programs are under way. For example, there is a new program in a mental health center in LaGrande, Oregon that seeks to identify children from the general population, not just those referred for services, who have behavioral problems that appear related to temperament. After screening, the plan is to counsel parents and teachers on how to deal more effectively with the children, and to evaluate the impact of the program (M. Levno, personal communication, 21 January 1988; B. Smith, personal communication, 22 June 1988).

Individual Case Applications

Temperament concepts are also used in more conventional clinical applications. For example, a psychiatrist in New York has a children's clinic specially devoted to dealing with problems construed in terms of temperament, and has published a book on the topic for parents (Turecki & Tonner, 1985). Other clinicians use temperament concepts in their practice, but in a more incidental fashion. My own applications fall under this latter category. Temperament concepts are directly useful in treating some, but far from a majority of the cases in our clinic. They seem to be more useful when the children are under age 7.

My general approach to using temperament concepts combines principles from several master clinicians. From Brazelton (1969) I take an emphasis on helping parents appreciate individual differences in children as they develop. From Chess and Thomas (e.g. 1984) I take an emphasis on recognizing and escaping from the trap of escalating negative effect, while still gradually exposing the child to new adaptational demands. From Minuchin (e.g. Minuchin & Fishman, 1981) I take an emphasis on reframing the child's behavior in the content of the family environment; this is a means of opening the parents to positive change. From Minuchin and other family therapists I also take an emphasis on maintaining generational boundaries. Child behavior can have effects upon parenting and teaching behaviors (Bates, 1975, 1976; Bell & Harper, 1977), interacting with characteristics of the adult (e.g. Bates & Pettit, 1981). Nevertheless, the parent has primary responsibility for creating positive conditions for the child's growth. Marking this generational boundary while at the same time reframing the child's behavior into temperament terms communicates that the 'diagnosis' of the child's temperament is to be used by the parent for making changes in caregiving rather than as an excuse for the difficulties.

One case example involves a 6-year-old boy whose mother initially complained of frequent tantrums, coerciveness, and inconsiderate and risky behavior. Part of my approach involved recasting the child's behavior in temperament-like terms. I described the child as high in negative emotionality, demanding high levels of social and other kinds of stimulation, and resisting outside control. I described how the mother and the boy's older brother were getting upset by the negative emotionality aspects of the boy's attempts to act in accord with his temperament, and falling into coercion traps. I told the mother that the child needed attention, action, and a sense of control, and that she needed to make sure that the boy got extra doses of these things. However, the boy also needed to learn ways to control himself and to be more aware of others' needs. The mother's defensiveness was reduced by attributing her son's coerciveness to relatively neutral needs for attention and action rather than relatively negative excesses or deficits in the child or her. This made it more possible for her actually to use specific recommendations to change her behavior with the child. She was able to give the child more warmth and positive control and less reactive, negative control. She was also made aware of the likelihood that the basic challenges with her child would probably continue for quite a few years. In order to keep such a child on a positive track, she would probably need to stay alert to the redevelopment of coercive cycles and look for developmentally appropriate ways of channeling energy (cf. Kazdin's (1987) interesting discussion of the chronic nature of conduct problems).

In the case of a fearful, inhibited child, I tend to frame the problem in terms of the child being sensitive and highly aware of environmental changes. I emphasize that this can be good, but the child needs help in managing novel and intense stimuli. I then show the parents how to help the child manage these stresses through standard clinical techniques of redirecting attention, direct coping behaviors and cognitive self-statements, graded exposure exercises, and muscular and mental relaxation. Again, the advantage of a temperament formulation is that it can deflect the parent from attributions based on negatively valenced attributes of the child or themselves.

In both externalizing and internalizing problems, it is sometimes helpful to imply genetic inheritance for the temperamental roots. This allows one or both parents more closely to identify with the child despite the chronic conflicts they have been having with the child. For example, in the case of an active, externalizing child, often one or both parents can recall problems dealing with their own activity levels, and can begin to see that activity is not in itself a problem (in fact, high activity level can be associated with greater adaptive success, e.g. in adult career; Bates, 1987). In the case of one boy, who was so disruptive that he was expelled from first grade, uncovering that the father had as a boy shared the son's activeness was the first step in getting father and son more involved with one another. This was a crucial early objective in the treatment.

In the past few years, as I have become familiar with Marc Weissbluth's work, I have been increasingly using the concept of sleep-loss stress in situations where I had tended to use more elementary temperament concepts previously. In one recent case, a 4-year-old girl began to be resistant and throw tantrums in her preshool. The foster mother reported that the girl had become chronically hard to handle at home, too. The girl was living in an environment that most would consider highly stressful – in a foster family with three other young children, with a foster mother who was separated, and in a small mobile home. Her natural mother had left the state some months earlier, and her father was in prison. The event that apparently precipitated the upswing in negative emotion was that the girl's grandfather announced that he was too busy to continue taking the girl for occasional visits to the father. Other events may have contributed as well, including the marital problems of the foster mother. It could be seen that the girl was anxious and angry, probably about the lack of a stable attachment figure and about the increasing frictions of living in an underendowed environment.

It was easy to see the need for interventions addressing the child's need for emotional security and positive guidance. However, it was not easy to see much inclination in the foster mother for the kinds of commitment called for by conventional approaches to these goals. I expected the first interview to be the last, and it was. I developed a sleep-deficit hypothesis as a supplement to the first one (emotional insecurity plus coercive cycles). In fact the mother had been putting the child to bed at variable times, along with the other, older children, and the child was getting around 10 hours sleep per night. This put her in the lowest 10% of children her age, according to charts produced by Weissbluth (1987). I suggested that the mother create a special bedtime for the girl. The bedtime was to be half an hour or so before the other children's and to be special in an emotional sense, too. It was to be a special time for the mother to enjoy the girl, let her know she cared, and help her wind down, with bathing and story reading. The mother was able to envision this change, and according to the preschool teacher, implemented it. The conflicts in the classroom disappeared in about a week, and the mother reported fewer problems with the girl at home.

A second case involved a 3-year-old boy who, after tearing apart the waiting room of the clinic where he was being assessed, had been recently diagnosed at 'attention-deficit disorder with hyperactivity'. He had been asked to leave several day-care centers, one as recently as a few months before the family moved to our town. The child had never napped well, especially at day-care, had slept only 8 hours a day as an infant, and now slept only about 8–9 hours per night. The parents kept a log for us that showed both sleep and major incidents of problem behavior. The log suggested that the child went through a cycle of cumulating sleep deficits, culminating in a 'horrible' day or two. The parents started putting the child to bed a few minutes earlier each night and making sure he got more naps. After about 2 weeks the child was getting 45–60 minutes more sleep per day. The behavior problems noticeably declined; he less often had times when he went on hyperactive rampages; and these times were usually attributable to sleep deficit.

The sleep-deficit cases illustrate especially well the clinical value of inquiring beneath the surface of the temperamental behavior pattern. One could assume in any given given case that chronic fussiness represented a wired-in temperament pattern in the child. However, if the pattern were in part due to sleep-loss stress, then the treatment would be unlikely to be nearly as efficient as one derived from a more pertinent formulation. Another distinction (discussed earlier) in root causes for difficult temperament that might be clinically important is the distinction between fussing and crying for reasons of needing social stimulation vs the same behavior as an expression of sensitivity to stress. If the parents can be attuned better to the particular needs of their child, they can more efficiently resolve their conflicts with the child.

While it is important to work on the problem presented by the family rather than imposing a wholly different agenda on the clients, it is also crucial to reframe the problem, to state it differently from the family's original formulation. Otherwise, the family will continue to try to solve the problem in ways consistent with their original formulation, and this way has already been proved ineffective, or they would not have consulted a professional in the first place (Fisch, Weakland & Segal, 1982). One of the main values of the temperament concept is just this reframing. Parents are inclined to interpret a child's misbehavior as reflecting something that they are doing wrong (or, more typically, that the spouse is doing wrong), or as a character defect in the child. 'Temperament' is one way of escaping from a framework of blame, thereby reducing resistance to change.

Suppose, however, for the sake of argument, that a parent came in with a ready-made, longstanding 'temperament' formulation for their problem with the child, and suppose that this formulation was relatively sophisticated in terms of current theory. Following the principle of reframing, I would be much less likely to offer temperament factors in my formulation of the problem than if temperament had not been part of the parents' original formulation. I might describe the problem as one in which all the family members had become victims of an abstract but powerful 'system'. Or I might even describe the child's misbehavior as an attempt to be helpful to the family (Madanes, 1984). The problems presented by clients have enough facets that a clinician would not be at a loss for bases for reframing.

Having described some applications of temperament in dealing with children's behavior problems, I would like to emphasize two general cautions. First, I do not believe that temperament concepts are ready for use as screening variables for case-finding or preventive interventions, as described in the beginning of the section on prevention. It is probably worthwhile that there be some experimental programs of this type, but they should be well connected to the evolving literature, and they should have strong evaluation research components. Second, as should be clear from previous sections of this chapter, temperament concepts are not fully validated, so when used in a clinical context, they should be used hypothetically, as a relevant and partly true fiction.

In the future, however, after further research, temperament concepts and measures may play a more direct role in preventing and treating behavioral or emotional problems. It may be possible to identify particular temperament profiles, with known behavioral and emotional patterns, which put certain kinds of family systems at high risk for producing child problems. My best guess, based on current research (above), is that a difficult, stimulation-demanding infant with passive, uninvolved or rejecting parents will be found to be most at risk from problems, especially of the externalizing sort. And this risk would be most fully activated under conditions of family stresses, such as major financial problems or divorce.

Summary

In this section, theory and evidence have been reviewed concerning the role of temperament, especially difficultness, in the development of children's behavior/ emotional problems. It appears that there is indeed a basis for arguing that temperament plays a role in the problems. In some instances, the role may be one of contributing to conflicts between the child's needs and the supports of the environment, as in the case of the difficult infant who is demanding of stimulation. In other instances, the role may be one of predisposing the child to condition anxiety easily. The questions here are many, especially concerning the specifics of the ways in which temperament variables interact with environmental supports and stresses. However, there have been major advances in empirical support for the hypothesis that early temperament predicts later adjustment.

This section has also discussed ways in which temperament concepts can be directly applied in clinical work with children's behavior problems. The concepts have been particularly useful in some cases in reframing the child's behavior and in offering non-threatening, specific recommendations. The clinical importance of looking for the root causes of the surface temperament-like behaviors is illustrated with the sleep-loss stress formulation.

OTHER PROBLEMS POSSIBLY CONNECTED TO TEMPERAMENT

The present chapter has emphasized the links between temperament variables and social relationships and ordinary varieties of child psychopathology. This reflects the relative emphasis given to these issues in the literature. However, it also represents a bias in my own research and clinical interests. There have also been applications of temperament concepts to the understanding and treatment of a number of other child problems that I have not carefully reviewed.

Developmental Disabilities

The last time I wrote a major review of the temperament area (Bates, 1987), I devoted only one paragraph to the burgeoning literature on temperament and developmental disabilities. After seeing a preprint of this chapter, Susan Goldberg (personal communication) rightly criticized the chapter for not addressing this important topic more fully. I am going to pass over developmental disabilities lightly in the current chapter, too. However, this time, the topic is addressed at more adequate length in a companion chapter (Chapter 20, by Goldberg & Marcovitch). Wachs (1988) has pointed out to those interested in developmental disabilities that there are major variations in the developmental patterns and outcomes of children even when they are in the same, supposedly homogeneous category. The ultimate impact of a handicap is determined not just by the nature and severity of the handicap, but also by factors such as the nature of transactions with the social environment. Thus, although developmental disabilities are primarily diagnosed on the basis of cognitive and sensorimotor variables, it is important to assess other kinds of characteristics, too, including temperament. McDevitt (1988) suggests that the major value of temperament assessments in cases of developmental disability will not be in explaining causes or effects of the disabilities, but, rather, predicting how a child will respond to environmental conditions and changes, how the child's handicaps and strengths in cognitive and sensorimotor areas will interact with variations in environment. In cases of difficult temperament, McDevitt recommends more frequent professional monitoring and extra supportive or preventive intervention.

Probably the largest part of the temperament research in the developmental disability area has addressed the question of the temperament of Down's syndrome children. The answer has been somewhat surprising: it appears that Down's syndrome children are not particularly easy as infants, contrary perhaps to popular stereotypes, but that after age 2 years, they begin to show more signs of an easy temperament. Goldberg and Marcovitch thoughtfully review the evidence on this and related matters (see Chapter 20).

Pediatric Concerns

Problems in physical health, function, and growth are another area in which temperament concepts have been used. Carey (1986) has considered conditions besides retardation that might influence temperament, including other congenital conditions, such as minor physical anomalies, perinatal complications, and central nervous system problems caused by a variety of factors. He concludes that there has been insufficient research on the role of such conditions in modifying temperament, but that there is evidence suggesting the possible value of the research. Carey (1986) also has discussed ways in which temperament might predispose a child to clinical conditions involving not only behavioral adjustment, but also general health, accident-proneness, child abuse, colic, and sleep problems. For example, Carey suggests that a temperamentally low threshold for stimulation might predispose an infant to colic. For the current volume Carey has written a chapter (Chapter 21) that addresses not only clinical applications of temperament concepts, but the interface between clinical practice and basic research on temperament.

As another example, Weissbluth (1982) has suggested that difficult temperament might play a role in the prevention of sudden infant death syndrome. Infants with a congenital problem in respiratory control might be disposed to episodes of apnea, i.e. interrupted breathing, but difficult temperament appears to make it less likely that they will have the dangerous elevations of progesterone that would inhibit waking during an apneic episode. There are many other ways in which the concepts of temperament can be useful in pediatric practice. Weissbluth addresses in detail the linkage between sleep disorders and temperament in Chapter 18.

Developmental Psychology Research

A final topic is practical but not clinical in the usual sense of the term. It concerns the possible role of children's temperament in the practice of basic research on developmental psychology. Many important generalizations about early cognitive and sensory development have been based on experimental procedures with infants. Invariably, some percentage of infants become too fussy to finish the laboratory procedure. It has been generally assumed that such data losses were due to random variations in infant state. However, a few recent studies call that conclusion into question. Wachs and Smitherman (1985) found that temperamental difficultness and unadaptability (mother report on the ICQ) predicted a number of the female infants who would not complete a standard habituation procedure. Similarly, Fagen, Ohr, Singer, and Fleckenstein (1987) found duration of orienting and distress to novel stimuli (mother report on the Infant Behavior Questionnaire: Rothbart, 1981) predicted response to a conditioning procedure. The results suggest that infant traits and not just their states can be roots of subject loss in an experiment. In studies where many subjects have been lost, the results may not generalize to all infants. However, the effect sizes have been small enough that the validity of the corpus of experimental data is not in great danger. Nevertheless, as Wachs and Smitherman argue, experiments that consider individual differences, e.g. temperament, might enhance our knowledge about early cognitive and sensory development. Here, then, is a way in which the assessment of individual differences in temperament has practical implications that may ultimately affect our most basic, theoretical understandings of normative developmental processes.

CONCLUSION

The practical implications of temperament concepts are probably a major impetus behind the more basic research on the concepts. One relevant issue is the role of temperament in children's social relations. The data reviewed here suggest that there may be less adverse impact from adverse temperament features on the child's relations with parents than might have been assumed, at least during infancy. In the second and later years, however, there do appear to be stronger links between temperament and parent–child interaction. Another aspect of the role of temperament is its effects in statistical interaction with other variables, such as sex of child or family stress. The evidence and methodological concerns in this area were discussed in detail. This is an area of promise, but also methodological and theoretical complexity.

The chapter also discussed the role of temperament, especially variants in the concept of difficult temperament, in child psychopathology. Recent research has shown that mother perceptions of infant and toddler characteristics of difficultness, unadaptability to novelty, and resistance to control of activity predict later perceptions of the child's behavioral adjustment. There are some interesting differentiations in how the different infancy measures predict to different kinds of outcome adjustment dimensions, e.g. early unadaptability predicting better to later anxiety problems than acting-out problems. Furthermore, the predictive links involving difficultness made it worthwhile to speculate on the possibly diverse roots of difficultness, including stimulation hunger, oversensitivity to aversive stimuli, and sleep-loss stress.

Finally, the chapter considered direct clinical applications of temperament concepts. It was concluded that the concepts do indeed have clinical relevance, e.g. as illustrated by several case examples, but that they are probably not defined well enough at this point for widespread use in preventive intervention, despite some promising forays in this direction.

In subsequent chapters, distinguished clinicians will address further aspects of the important issue of how temperament concepts can be of practical use.

REFERENCES

Ainsworth, M.D.S., Blehar, M.C., Waters, E. & Wall, S. (1978). *Patterns of attachment.* Hillsdale, NJ: Erlbaum.

Allport, G.W. (1958). What units shall we employ? In G. Lindzey (Ed.), *The assessment of human motives* (pp. 239–260). New York: Rinehart.

Allport, G.W. (1962). The general and the unique in psychological science. *Journal of Personality*, **30**, 405–422.

Bates, J.E. (1975). Effects of children's imitation vs. nonimitation on adults' verbal and nonverbal positivity. *Journal of Personality and Social Psychology*, **31**, 840–851.

Bates, J.E. (1976). Effects of children's nonverbal behavior upon adults. *Child Development*, **47**, 1079–1088.

Bates, J.E. (1980). The concept of difficult temperament. *Merrill-Palmer Quarterly*, **26**, 299–319.

Bates, J.E. (1987). Temperament in infancy. In J.D. Osofsky (Ed.), *Handbook of infant development*, 2nd edn (pp. 1101–1149). New York: Wiley.

Bates, J.E. & Bayles, K. (1988). The role of attachment in the development of behavior problems. In J. Belsky & T. Nezworski (Eds), *Clinical implications of attachment* (pp. 253–299). New York: Erlbaum.

Bates, J.E., Maslin, C.A. & Frankel, K.A. (1985). Attachment security, mother–child interaction, and temperament as predictors of behavior problem ratings at age three years. In I. Bretherton & E. Waters (Eds), *Growing points in attachment theory and research. Society for Research in Child Development Monographs*, Serial No. 209, 167–193.

Bates, J.E., Miller, E.M. & Bayles, K. (1984). Understanding the link between difficult temperament and behavior problems: Toward identifying subtypes of difficultness. Paper presented at International Conference on Infant Studies, New York, April 1984.

Bates, J.E., Olson, S.L., Pettit, G.S. & Bayles, K. (1982). Dimensions of individuality in the mother–infant relationship at 6 months of age. *Child Development*, **53**, 446–461.

Bates, J.E. & Pettit, G.S. (1981). Adult individual differences as moderators of child effects. *Journal of Abnormal Child Psychology*, **9**, 329–340.

Bell, R.Q. (1968). A reinterpretation of the direction of effects in studies in socialization. *Psychological Review*, **75**, 81–95.

Bell, R.Q. & Harper, L.V. (1977). *Child effects on adults*. Hillsdale, NJ: Erlbaum.

Brazelton, T.B. (1969). *Infants and mothers: Differences in development*. New York: Dell.

Buss, A.H. & Plomin, R. (1984). *Temperament: Early developing personality traits*. Hillsdale, NJ: Erlbaum.

Cameron, J. (1978). Parental treatment, children's temperament and the risk of childhood behavior problems. 2. Initial temperament, parental attitudes, and the incidence and form of behavioral problems. *American Journal of Orthopsychiatry*, **48**, 140–147.

Cameron, J.R. & Rice, D.C. (1986). Developing anticipatory guidance programs based on early assessment of infant temperament: Two tests of a prevention model. *Journal of Pediatric Psychology*, **11**, 221–234.

Campbell, S.B. (1989). The socialization and social development of hyperactive children. In M. Lewis & S. Miller (Eds), *The handbook of developmental psychopathology*. New York: Plenum.

Campbell, S.B., Breaux, A.M., Ewing, L.J. & Szumowski, E.K. (1986). Correlates and predictors of hyperactivity and aggression: A longitudinal study of parent-referred problem preschoolers. *Journal of Abnormal Child Psychology*, **14**, 217–234.

Carey, W.B. (1986). Clinical interactions of temperament: Transitions from infancy to childhood. In R. Plomin & J. Dunn (Eds), *The study of temperament: Changes, continuities and challenges* (pp. 151–162). Hillsdale, NJ: Erlbaum.

Chess, S. & Thomas, A. (1984). *Origins and evolution of behavior disorders: From infancy to early adult life*. New York: Brunner/Mazel.

Crockenberg, S.B. (1986). Are temperamental differences in babies associated with predictable differences in care giving? In J.V. Lerner and R.M. Lerner (Eds), *Temperament and social interaction during infancy and childhood. New Directions for Child Development*, No. 31, 53–73. San Francisco: Jossey-Bass.

Crockenberg, S. (1987). Predictors and correlations of anger toward and punitive control of toddlers by adolescent mothers. *Child Development*, **58**, 964–975.

Daniels, D., Plomin, R. & Greenhalgh, J. (1984). Correlates of difficult temperament in infancy. *Child Development*, **55**, 1184–1194.

Delameter, A.M. & Lahey, B.B. (1983). Physiological correlates of conduct problems and anxiety in hyperactive and learning-disabled children. *Journal of Abnormal Child Psychology*, **11**, 85–100.

DeVries, M.W. (1984). Temperament and infant mortality among the Masai of East Africa. *American Journal of Psychiatry*, **10**, 141.

Dunn, J. & Plomin, R. (1986). Determinants of maternal behaviour towards 3-year-old siblings. *British Journal of Developmental Psychology*, **4**, 127–137.

Escalona, S. (1968). *The roots of individuality*. Chicago: Aldine.

Fagen, J.W., Ohr, P.S., Singer, J.M. & Fleckenstein, L.K. (1987). Infant temperament and subject loss due to crying during operant conditioning. *Child Development*, **58**, 497–504.

Field, T., Sandberg, D., Garcia, R., Vega-Lahr, N., Goldstein, S. & Guy, L. (1985). Pregnancy problems, postpartum depression, and early mother–infant interactions. *Developmental Psychology*, **21**, 1152–1156.

Fisch, R., Weakland, J.H. & Segal, L. (1982). *The tactics of change: Doing therapy briefly*. San Francisco: Jossey-Bass.

Gandour, M.J. (1987). Activity level as a dimension of temperament in toddlers: The validity of its measurement and its relevance for the organismic specificity hypothesis. Doctoral dissertation, Purdue University.

Garrison, W.T. & Earls, F.J. (1987). *Temperament and child psychopathology*. Newbury Park, CA: Sage.

Gleick, J. (1987). *Chaos: Making a new science*. New York: Viking.

Goldsmith, H.H. & Alansky, J.A. (1987). Maternal and infant temperamental predictors of attachment: A meta-analytic review. *Journal of Consulting and Clinical Psychology*, **55**, 805–816.

Guerin, D. & Gottfried, A.W. (1986). Infant temperament as a predictor of preschool behavior problems. Presented at International Conference on Infant Studies, Los Angeles, April 1986.

Hare, R.D. & Schalling, D. (Eds) (1978). *Psychopathic behaviour: Approaches to research*. London: Wiley.

Hetherington, E.M. (1987). Presidential address. Presented at Society for Research in Child Development, Baltimore, April 1987.

Hubert, N.D., Wachs, T.D., Peters-Martin, P. & Gandour, M.J. (1982). The study of early temperament: Measurement and conceptual issues. *Child Development*, **53**, 571–600.

Kagan, J., Reznick, J.S. & Snidman, N. (1986). Temperamental inhibition in early childhood. In R. Plomin & J. Dunn (Eds), *The study of temperament: Changes, continuities and challenges* (pp. 53–65). Hillsdale, NJ: Erlbaum.

Kazdin, A.E. (1987). Treatment of antisocial behavior in children: Current status and future directions. *Psychological Bulletin*, **102**, 187–203.

Keogh, B.K. (1986). Temperament and schooling: Meaning of 'goodness of fit'? In J.V. Lerner and R.M. Lerner (Eds), *Temperament and social interaction in infants and children* (pp. 89–108). San Francisco, CA: Jossey-Bass.

Kohnstamm, G.A. (1984). Bates' Infant Characteristics Questionnaire (ICQ) in the Netherlands. Presented at International Conference on Infant Studies, New York, April 1984.

Kohnstamm, G.A. (1987). The surplus value of maternal temperamental perceptions in predicting teacher ratings of child behavior. Upublished paper, University of Leiden.

Lee, C. & Bates, J. (1985). Mother–child interaction at age two years and perceived difficult temperament. *Child Development*, **56**, 1314–1326.

Lerner, J.V. & Lerner, R.M. (1983). Temperament and adaptation across life: Theoretical and empirical issues. In P.B. Baltes & O.G. Brim, Jr (Eds), *Life span development and behavior*, Vol. V (pp. 197–231). New York: Academic Press.

Madanes, C. (1984). *Behind the one-way mirror: Advances in the practice of strategic therapy*. San Francisco: Jossey-Bass.

Matheny, A.P., Wilson, R.S. & Thoben, A.S. (1987). Home and mother: Relations with infant temperament. *Developmental Psychology*, **23**, 323–331.

Maziade, M., Cote, R., Boutin, P., Bernier, H. & Thivierge, J. (1987). Temperament and intellectual development: A longitudinal study from infancy to four years. *American Journal of Psychiatry*, **114**, 144–150.

McDevitt, S.C. (1988). Assessment of temperament in developmentally disabled infants and preschoolers. In T. Wachs & R. Sheehan (Eds), *Assessment of young developmentally disabled children*. New York: Plenum.

McDevitt, S.C. & Carey, W.B. (1981). Stability of ratings vs. perceptions of temperament from early infancy to 1–3 years. *American Journal of Orthopsychiatry*, **51**, 342–345.

Meyer, H.-J. & Schölmerich, A. (1984). Similarity in the quality of attachment between first-and second-born siblings and their mothers. Paper presented at International Conference on Infant Studies, New York, April 1984.

Minuchin, S. & Fishman, H.C. (1981). *Family therapy techniques*. Cambridge, MA: Harvard.

Olson, S.L., Bates, J.E. & Bayles, K. (1984). Mother–infant interaction and the development of individual differences in children's cognitive competence. *Developmental Psychology*, **20**, 166–179.

Olson, S.L., Bates, J.E. & Bayles, K. (1986). Predicting social and cognitive competence at age 6 from early mother–child interaction. Presented at International Conference on Infant Studies, Los Angeles, April 1986.

Olweus, D. (1987). Environmental and biological factors in the development of aggressive behavior. In W. Buikhuisen & S. Mednick (Eds), *Explaining crime*. Leiden: Brill.

Patterson, G.R. (1982). *Coercive family process*. Eugene, OR: Castalia.

Patterson, G.R. (1988). Factors relating to stability and changes in children's aggressive behavior over time. Presented at the Earlscourt Symposium on Childhood Aggression, Toronto, June 1988.

Persson-Blennow, I. & McNeil, T.F. (1982). New data on test–retest reliability for three temperament scales. *Journal of Child Psychology and Psychiatry*, **23**(2), 181–183.

Pettit, G.S. & Bates, J.E. (1984). Continuity of individual differences in the mother–infant relationship from 6 to 13 months. *Child Development*, **55**, 729–739.

Plomin, R. & Daniels, D. (1984). The interaction between temperament and environment: Methodological considerations. *Merrill-Palmer Quarterly*, **30**, 149–162.

Raine, A. & Venables, P.H. (1984a). Electrodermal nonresponding, antisocial behavior, and schizoid tendencies in adolescents. *Psychophysiology*, **21**, 424–433.

Raine, A. & Venables, P.H. (1984b). Tonic heart rate level, social class and antisocial behavior in adolescents. *Biological Psychology*, **18**, 123–132.

Richman, N., Stevenson, J. & Graham, P. (1982). *Preschool to school: A behavioural study*. London: Academic Press.

Rothbart, M.K. (1981). Measurement of temperament in infancy. *Child Development*, **52**, 569–578.

Rothbart, M.K. (1986). Longitudinal observation of infant temperament. *Developmental Psychology*, **22**, 356–365.

Rutter, M. (1981). *Maternal deprivation reassessed*, 2nd edn. New York: Penguin.

Rutter, M. (1983). Statistical and personal interactions: Facets and perspectives. In D. Magnusson & V. Allen (Eds), *Human development: An interactional perspective* (pp. 295–319). New York: Academic Press.

Rutter, M. & Quinton, D. (1984). Parental psychiatric disorder: Effects on children. *Psychological Medicine*, **14**, 853–880.

Sameroff, A.J., Seifer, R. & Barocas, R. (1983). Impact of parental psychopathology: Diagnosis, severity, or social status effects? *Infant Mental Health Journal*, **4**, 236–249.

Silverton, L., Finello, K. & Mednick, S. (1983). Children of schizophrenic women: Early factors predictive of schizophrenia. *Infant Mental Health Journal*, **4**, 202–216.

Simpson, A.E. & Stevenson-Hinde, J. (1985). Temperamental characteristics of 3- to 4-year-old boys and girls and child–family interactions. *Journal of Child Psychology and Psychiatry*, **26**, 43–53.

Spivack, G., Marcus, J. & Swift, M. (1986). Early classroom behaviors and later misconduct. *Developmental Psychology*, **22**, 124–131.

Sroufe, L.A. (1985). Attachment classification from the perspective of infant–caregiver relationships and infant temperament. *Child Development*, **56**, 1–14.

Strelau, J. (1983). *Temperament, personality, activity*. New York: Academic Press.

Swets-Gronert, F. (1986). *Temperament, taalcompetentie en gedragsproblem van jonge kinderen (Temperament, language proficiency and behavior problems)*. Lisse (Neth.): Swets & Zeitlinger.

Thelen, E. (1989). Self-organization in developmental processes: Can systems approaches work? In M. Gunnar (Ed.), *Systems in development: The Minnesota Symposium in Child Psychology*, Vol. 22 (pp. 77–117). Hillsdale, NJ: Erlbaum.

Thomas, A. & Chess, S. (1977). *Temperament and development*. New York: Brunner/Mazel.

Thomas, A., Chess, S. & Birch, H.G. (1968). *Temperament and behavior disorders in children*. New York: New York University Press/London: University of London Press.

Thompson, R.A. & Connell, J.P. (1986). Temperament, emotion, and social interaction. Paper presented at International Conference on Infant Studies, Los Angeles, April 1986.

Torgersen, A.M. (1984). Relations between temperament, stress and behavior symptoms in the development from birth to six years. Presented at Advanced Study Institute. Human Assessment: Advances in Measuring Cognition and Motivation. Athens, Greece.

Turecki, S. & Tonner, L. (1985). *The difficult child*. New York: Bantam Books.

van Engeland, H. (1984). The electrodermal orienting response to auditive stimuli in autistic children, normal children, mentally retarded children, and child psychiatric patients. *Journal of Autism and Developmental Disorders*, **14**, 261–279.

Vaughn, B. E., Bradley, C.F., Joffe, L.S., Seifer, R. & Barglow, P. (1987). Maternal personality variables measured prenatally are predictive of ratings of temperamental 'difficulty' on the Carey Infant Temperament Questionnaire. *Developmental Psychology*, **23**, 152–161.

Viken, R. (in preparation). Integrating theory and practice in the analysis of statistical interactions: Conceptual and empirical approaches. Manuscript, Indiana University.

Wachs, T.D. (1988). Issues in the linkage of assessment to intervention. In T.D. Wachs & R. Sheehan (Eds), *Assessment of young developmentally disabled children*. New York: Plenum.

Wachs, T.D. (1985). Measurement of environment in the study of organism–environment interaction. Paper presented at convention of Society for Research in Child Development.

Wachs, T.D. (1987). Specificity of environmental action as manifest in environmental correlates of infants' mastery motivation. *Developmental Psychology*, **23**, 782–790.

Wachs, T.D. & Gandour, M.J. (1983). Temperament, environment, and six-month cognitive–intellectual development: A test of the organismic specificity hypothesis. *International Journal of Behavioural Development*, **6**, 135–152.

Wachs, T.D. & Gruen, G. (1982). *Early experience and human development*. New York: Plenum.

Wachs, T.D. & Smitherman, C.H. (1985). Infant temperament and subject loss in a habituation procedure. *Child Development*, **56**, 861–867.

Weissbluth, M. (1982). Plasma progesterone levels, infant temperament, arousals from sleep, and the sudden infant death syndrome. *Medical Hypotheses*, **9**, 215–222.

Weissbluth, M. (1987). *Healthy sleep habits, happy child*. New York: Ballantine.

Wiggins, J.S. (1973). *Personality and prediction: Principles of personality assessment*. Reading, MA: Addison-Wesley.

Windle, M. & Lerner, R.M. (1986). The 'goodness of fit' model of temperament–context relations: Interaction or correlation? In J.V. Lerner & R.M. Lerner (Eds), *Temperament and social interaction during infancy and childhood*. *New Directions for Child Development*, No. 31, 109–120. San Francisco: Jossey-Bass.

Wolkind, S.N. & De Salis, W. (1982). Infant temperament, maternal mental stage and child behavioral problems. In R. Porter & G.M. Collins (Eds), *Temperamental differences in infants and young children*. Ciba Foundation Symposium. London: Pitman.

18

Sleep-Loss Stress and Temperamental Difficultness: Psychobiological Processes and Practical Considerations

MARC WEISSBLUTH
Northwestern University Medical School

The terms 'difficult temperament' and heightened 'temperamental emotionality' both describe a single psychobiological state which may be modified by sleep-loss stress. This chapter describes how the biochemical response to the stress of sleep deficits may be a unifying mechanism to explain how the behaviors described by the terms 'difficult' or 'emotional' develop and persist.

Thomas, Chess, and Birch (1968) described the statistical clustering of four temperament traits and made an astute clinical, but not statistical, observation associating these four traits with the trait called regularity. That is, infants who were negative in mood, intense, slowly adaptable, and withdrawing were also described as biologically irregular. This chapter explains that the trait of biologic irregularity or regularity in infancy is especially important in the establishing of healthy daytime sleep patterns and also that the trait regularity is less important in older children because the timing of socially learned habits, such as naps, may override endogenous sleep/wake biological rhythms. Previous writers have not appreciated regularity as an important trait because it is not statistically closely associated with the other four traits throughout early childhood. However, regularity in relation to infant sleep is important.

Thomas *et al.* (1968) described behavioral problems developing during the first 3 years of life in eight children. Sleep problems occurred in five of these eight children with early-onset behavioral problems. Surprisingly, two of these eight children had no other behavioral problems except for disturbed sleeping. As will be explained, the biochemical response to persistent sleep deficits causes sustained difficulties in initiating and maintaining sleep, and precisely because of the disturbed sleep, these overtired infants, feeling the discomfort of fatigue, cry and fuss when awake.

Temperament in Childhood   Edited by G.A. Kohnstamm, J.E. Bates and M.K. Rothbart
© 1989 John Wiley & Sons Ltd

Frequent crying and fussiness are central features of the difficult temperament (Bates, 1980). This paper describes how some of these infants become painfully overtired and overaroused so they cannot easily fall asleep or stay asleep. Continuing sleep deficits result in fatigue-driven fussiness, irritability, or heightened emotionality.

Buss and Plomin (1974) are fundamentally correct when they describe infants who fuss and cry as being in distress. They describe how undifferentiated distress is associated with dominance of the sympathetic nervous system and high autonomic neurologic arousal. They call this excessive crying and fussiness 'primordial emotionality'. This chapter explains how the development of primordial emotionality or high sympathetic arousal in some of these infants can be explained by the evolution in the infant of sleep-loss stress. The biochemical stress response associated with this overtired and overaroused state may directly cause the distressed emotionality.

STRESS HORMONES AND STATES OF AROUSAL

Individual differences in states of arousal may be modulated by the interaction and regulation of stress hormones (Axelrod & Reisine, 1984; Gailland, 1985). However, there is no direct or simple relationship between a specific stress hormone, enzyme, or neurotransmitter and a particular state of arousal or behavior. Rather, combinations of these chemicals in different proportions are of clinical importance. For clarity, they will be discussed separately and only the major interactions will be presented.

Stress Hormones

Epinephrine is secreted from the inner areas of the adrenal gland. Measurements of levels of epinephrine have been related to degrees of *alertness* and *anxiety*. For example, elevations of epinephrine levels occur with stresses caused by public speaking or harassment. *Bidirectionality* of effects means that just as the social circumstances of public speaking can cause anxiety, alertness, and elevations of epinephrine, an epinephrine injection can also cause the subjective state of anxiety and alertness. Epinephrine is produced from norepinephrine predominantly under regulation by glucocorticoids such as cortisol.

Norepinephrine is also produced within the inner areas of the adrenal gland. Measurements of levels of norepinephrine have been related to degrees of *wakefulness* and the activity of the *sympathetic* nervous system. For example, elevations of norepinephrine occur with stresses such as changes of posture or performing mental arithmetic. Just as concentration on mental arithmetic forces wakefulness to override sleep, children can force wakefulness to overcome sleep in order to stay up to play with their parents. The ability to override sleep when motivated highlights the *asymmetry* of sleep and wakefulness. Sleep cannot be forced to override wakefulness; rather, the sleep process overcomes wakefulness depending on preceding sleep loss and the temporal phase of circadian rhythms. The enzyme responsible for the production of norepinephrine from dopamine is predominantly regulated by sympathetic nerve activity.

Cortisol and other glucocorticoids are produced in the outer region of the adrenal gland. The secretion of glucocorticoids is regulated by the anterior pituitary gland in the brain. Many types of stress are associated with increased cortisol levels. Glucocorticoids regulate epinephrine secretion and, to a lesser degree, norepinephrine biosynthesis. In turn, these catecholamines stimulate the anterior pituitary to increase the production of glucocorticoids.

Prolonged or chronic stress causes increased activity of the catecholamine biosynthetic enzymes responsible for the conversion of dopamine to norepinephrine to epinephrine. The activity of these enzymes, under stress conditions, is regulated to varying degrees by glucocorticoids such as cortisol, the anterior pituitary, and neuronal activity. However, during periods of chronic stress, target cells in the adrenal gland may become refractory after prolonged exposure to hormones. This process, whereby the persistent presence of these hormones produces less of a response, is called *desensitization*. Desensitization may be overcome in older, chronically sleep-deprived children utilizing stimulant medication. The connection between sleep and attention span will be discussed later.

States of Arousal

Wakefulness and sleep may be thought of as neurologic macrostates which develop distinct differences by 3–4 months of age. However, within each macrostate there are different degrees and types of arousal. During wakefulness, after 4 months of age, there are periodic variations of arousal along the dimension alert/drowsy. Wakefulness may be divided into two different types with partially independent neuronal systems: (a) phasic wakefulness responsible for arousal from sleep and (b) tonic wakefulness responsible for maintaining the aroused wakeful state. Catecholamine biosynthetic pathway activation produces wakefulness or different degrees of alertness or vigilance, and deactivation is necessary for sleep. During sleep, after 4 months of age, there are periodic variations of arousal during the night along the dimension of light sleep/deep sleep. Sleep may also be divided into two different types with partially independent neuronal systems based on the presence or absence of eye movements. Different neurochemical mechanisms, other than catecholamine deactivation, are involved in sleep state regulation. Additionally, night sleep organization develops at about 6 weeks of age whereas day sleep patterns emerge later at 12–16 weeks of age. States of arousal may be affected by sleep deficits.

Sleep deficits include sleep fragmentation, brief sleep durations, and abnormal sleep schedules occurring either during daytime or night-time sleep. Different sleep deficits may produce different effects on daytime sleepiness (Magee, Harsh & Badia, 1987) and different biochemical responses, but the increased cortisol secretion from sleep-loss stress predictably causes an increase in catecholamines. These chemical changes caused by sleep loss are described in the following section.

NEUROCHEMICAL RESPONSES TO SLEEP LOSS

Cortisol Response

Adrenocortical responsiveness in infants has been demonstrated as early as several hours of age, following circumcision (Talbert, Kraybill & Potter, 1976). Prior to circumcision, among 2- to 3-day-old babies, and after circumcision in 3- to 5-day-old infants, quiet sleep or low level arousal states have been observed to be negatively correlated with plasma cortisol levels (Gunnar, Fisch, Kirsvik & Donhowe, 1981; Gunnar, Malone, Vance & Fisch, 1986). Gunnar *et al.* (1986) discussed how, in some babies, the quiet sleep period following circumcision might be a stress-response coping mechanism to re-establish lower baseline adrenocortical levels. Gunnar, Isensee & Fust (1987) also made the important observation among 1- to 5-day-old infants that the Rapidity of Build-up and Irritability arousal items on the Neonatal Behavioral Assessment Scale (Brazelton, 1973) positively correlated with plasma cortisol levels. In general, plasma cortisol levels increased in response to interventions such as heel-stick blood sampling, measuring, or examining. However, cortisol levels were also dependent on the degree of arousal even in the absence of stimulation.

With increasing levels of arousal states (sleep to awake – quiet to fussy-crying) there was observed a graded increase in cortisol levels among infants 3 days old (Tennes & Carter, 1973). Tennes noted that each baby who was followed weekly from 1 to 13 weeks of age 'had a period when the mother claimed that the infant was fussy and had difficulty going to sleep' (Tennes & Carter, 1973, p. 125). One such child had a clear peak of increased cortisol at between 6 and 10 weeks of age. This child also had the single highest measured cortisol level and a .73 correlation between cortisol levels in general and summed ratings of chronic fussiness during the entire 13-week observation period. Other children in this study who had no clear peak elevations of cortisol and lower overall levels of cortisol had no significant correlation between chronic fussiness and cortisol. This interindividual variation of cortisol levels at different ages and over time might reflect endogenous biological or exogenous social factors. However, it is notable that the peak of fussiness, crying, and wakefulness in all babies always occurs at about 6 weeks of age and it is thought that this behavior is caused by heightened arousal (Weissbluth, 1987a).

The observation that successively higher cortisol levels were associated with increasing degrees of arousal was again noted among 7-day-old to 15-week-old infants along the continuum from quiet sleep, to active sleep, to quiet wakefulness, to crying (Anders, Sachar, Kream, Roffwarg & Hellman, 1970). Anders *et al.* (1970) concluded that the adrenocortical response to mild distress (flicking the infant lightly on the foot to establish crying) and a continuum of increasing cortisol responsiveness to increasing physiologic arousal, including sleep states, were well established by 1 week of age.

Among 1-year-old infants, increased cortisol levels were significantly associated with *fear* of novel animated toys and *anxiety* caused by the absence of the mother for only 1 hour (Tennes, Downey & Vernadakis, 1977). In contrast, pleasant excitement to the animated toys was not associated with elevated cortisol levels.

Tennes *et al.* noted that those 'infants who cried and urgently tried to follow the mother when she left, those who ran to the mother when approached by a stranger, and those who cried and were afraid of animated toys were found to have increased levels of cortisol. Not only do these infants have higher levels associated with the stimuli, but they also tend to have *chronically* higher levels than infants who do not respond with fear or anxiety' (Tennes *et al.*, 1977, p. 184). Therefore, chronically elevated cortisol during the first weeks is associated with fussing, crying, and heightened arousal, but by 1 year of life children with chronically elevated cortisol levels appear more fearful and anxious.

Another study among 1-year-old children by the same researchers (Tennes & Vernadakis, 1977) clearly showed that periods of lower cortisol levels were associated with daytime sleep periods or naps. As previously mentioned, daytime sleep periods develop at 12–16 weeks of age. Tennes' work strongly implies that infants who chronically fail to nap well would be expected to have chronically higher cortisol levels and thus higher levels of arousal which would be manifested by increased fussing/crying as infants, and increased fear/anxiety later. Thus, persistent nap deprivation may be viewed as a chronic sleep deficit and elevated cortisol levels would be the expected biochemical stress response. Uncorrected, this sleep loss might modulate the temperament features of fussing/crying or fear/anxiety in an enduring fashion.

Increased cortisol levels were also measured in children between 1 and 5 years of age who were characterized as highly inhibited by Kagan, Reznick, and Snidman (1987). These inhibited children were also noted to have elevated norepinephrine production reflecting greater sympathetic activity. Extreme irritability and sleepessness were present in some of these inhibited children during the first year of life.

Among adults, the level of adrenocortical activity among poor sleepers is positively correlated with the degree of anxiety and psychologic distress (Johns, Gay, Masterton & Bruce, 1971). The relationship between elevated cortisol levels, poor quality sleep, and increased anxiety has been confirmed in other studies (Adams, Tomeny & Oswald, 1986). It appears that adult poor sleepers have a greater degree of activation or arousal of their central nervous system both when awake and when asleep (Monroe, 1967). This increased arousal is consistent with the expected glucocorticoid stimulation of catecholamine biosynthesis. The major product produced is epinephrine which is mainly associated with levels of alertness and anxiety. Among adults, the consistent association between poor sleep and anxiety (Haynes, Follingstad & McGowan, 1974; Hicks & Pellegrini, 1977; Kazarian, Howe, Merskey & Deinum, 1987) has led to the conclusion that the primary cause of insomnia is psychobiological arousal (Kales *et al.*, 1984). Additionally, unlike the studies of adult insomniacs, among graduate students who were not selected on the basis of sleep habits or anxiety levels, increased cortisol levels were associated with increased subjective ratings of mental alertness (Fibiger, Singer, Miller, Armstrong & Datar, 1984).

Summary

Cortisol secretory responsiveness to mild and severe stress is present in the newborn infant. This response may be graded and correlated with sleep state and behavioral arousal, and may be modified by social environmental effects such as napping. Although there are individual differences at specific ages and over time, elevated cortisol levels are associated with crying/fussing in infancy and with fear/anxiety or inhibition, later. Low cortisol levels are associated with quiet sleep and naps. Chronic sleep deficits beginning in early infancy could cause persistent sleep problems extending into adulthood accompanied by elevated cortisol or epinephrine levels.

Catecholamine Response

Epinephrine is the major catecholamine which is elevated during periods of both wakefulness and sleep in response to the stress of sleep loss (Adams *et al.*, 1986; Levi, 1972; Steinberg, Guggenheim, Baer & Snyder, 1969). In contrast, norepine-phrine levels do not show similar elevations. This is consistent with the observation that cortisol is elevated in response to sleep loss and that the conversion from norepinephrine to epinephrine is regulated by glucocorticoids. It is notable that the studies by Adams *et al.* (1986) and Monroe (1967) show that very small differences in total sleep time, amounting to only 30–40 minutes, produced measurable increases in epinephrine levels and increases in indices of central nervous system activation. Despite the increased epinephrine levels associated with prolonged, experimentally induced sleep loss, there develops a chronic mood change of increased self-reported sleepiness and fatigue (Levi, 1972). Even sleep-fragmentation studies of short duration cause increased subjective sleepiness and fatigue (Bonnett, 1985). Also, in the absence of experimental stresses, increased levels of epinephrine were associated with increased self-reported levels of physical fatigue (Fibiger *et al.*, 1984). Not surprisingly, performance impairments including errors in mental arithmetic (Bonnett, 1985; Downey & Bonnett, 1987) and soldiers missing targets (Levi, 1972) occur with fatigue induced by sleep loss.

Dopamine levels have been positively correlated with self-reported ratings of alertness (Fibiger *et al.*, 1984). Dopamine concentrations in the brain may be reduced by progesterone, which is known to have calming, sleep-inducing properties (Gyermenk & Soyka, 1975; Tandon, Gupta & Barthwal, 1983). Progesterone is a hormone which may act as a neuromodulator to 'alter the gain' (Gailland, 1985) or change the output signal power of a cell in response to a neurotransmitter. Progesterone is an especially attractive candidate for being an important behavioral depressor biochemical because levels of progesterone, produced by the placenta, are unusually high in the newborn for the first 5 days. This time period in the newborn is usually associated with characteristic behaviors of sleepiness, drowsiness, and inactivity. After 5 days of life, placentally derived progesterone levels fall and subsequently progesterone is produced at lower levels by the infant's adrenal glands (Ferris & Green, 1986). It is exactly at this time, at the end of the first week of life, when the infant begins to become more wakeful, alert, fussy, and active.

Summary

The predictable biochemical response to brief sleep durations and fragmented sleep is elevated levels of epinephrine, but not of norepinephrine. The stimulating effects of epinephrine producing alertness and anxiety may be masked by the subjective sensations of sleepiness and fatigue resulting from the sleep loss. Despite the biologic response to enhance alertness during periods of sleep loss, the fatigue may cause impairments of performance.

BIOLOGICAL RHYTHMS, ENTRAINMENT, AND TIMING

Sleep processes in the brain are endogenous biological rhythms and the duration and consolidation of a sleep period depend on its circadian phase (Czeisler, Weitzman, Moore-Ede, Zimmerman & Knauer, 1980; Weitzman, Czeisler, Zimmerman & Moore-Ede, 1981). Specifically, when bedtimes occur at or just after the peak of the temperature cycle, sleep quality is better (longer sleep durations and fewer awakenings) than when bedtimes occur at the trough of the temperature cycle.

After 1 month of age, temperature rhythms appear (Abe, Sasake, Takebayashi, Seki & Roth, 1978); by 3 months, there is a diurnal rhythm of progesterone levels (Solyom, 1984), and at 6 months, distinct circadian cortisol rhythms appear (Onishi *et al.*, 1983). One component of the cortisol secretion rhythm is related to sleep–wake patterns and another component is related to the body temperature rhythm (Czeisler *et al.*, 1980). Thus, there are interrelationships between biologic rhythms involving hormones, temperature, and sleep. As will be discussed later regarding naps for children, lifestyles in adults or habitual parenting practices which disrupt naturally occurring activity–sleep cycles may uncouple rhythms that are usually linked in close temporal order; this produces a state called internal desynchronization.

Cortisol and progesterone levels peak in the morning and the trough occurs in the evening when body temperature rises and epinephrine levels are reaching their peak (Fibiger *et al.*, 1984; Solyom, 1984). In contrast to epinephrine, norepinephrine and dopamine do not have distinctive diurnal variations. Norepinephrine levels are lowest during sleep times (Mullen *et al.*, 1981), even when the sleep period is experimentally shifted away from its normal circadian phase. Among adults, it is clear that daily events, lifestyles, or habitual schedules may modulate circadian rhythms (Atcheson & Tyler, 1975; Fibiger *et al.*, 1984). Among young infants, endogenous rhythmic behaviors may be produced by developing circadian rhythms. For example, evening fussiness, which occurs in all infants and peaks at 6 weeks of age, may be caused by the naturally occurring combination of low progesterone and high epinephrine levels in the evening.

The development of sleep rhythms in infancy is under genetic influence (Webb & Campbell, 1983) and follows a predictable pattern. Initially, the longest single sleep period is only a few hours long and it is randomly distributed around clock time until about 46 weeks postconceptual age. After this age, the longest single sleep period lengthens to about 4–6 hours and it then regularly occurs in the evening.

This is called night sleep organization. About 6–10 weeks later, day sleep becomes organized, with regularly occurring periods of day sleep or naps.

Entrainment means synchronizing circadian rhythms to external time cues such as the alternation of light and darkness. Before the light-sensitive, retina-mediated, entrainment process is fully developed in the infant, maternal behaviors may coordinate the timing of the developing biological clock (Reppert, 1985). Maternal entrainment is accomplished by rhythmic aspects of behavior such as periodic feeding, playing, or soothing to sleep.

The timing of these maternal behaviors with regard to sleep is especially important because sleep periods occurring out of phase with the circadian rhythms for sleep, both at night and during the day, tend to be shorter and fragmented. The correct timing of maternal efforts to soothe the baby to sleep during the day for naps is more difficult to accomplish than for night sleep because of the absence of light–darkness cues and the natural tendency for the mother to engage in activities during the day which interfere with the baby sleeping, such as running errands or playing with the baby during a naturally occurring sleep time.

Naps and daytime rest periods improve mood and performance, but the ability of naps to reverse sleepiness or to recover alertness depends on nap duration, nap consolidation, and most importantly, the temporal placement of the nap relative to the circadian rhythm of daytime drowsiness (Daiss, Bertelson & Benjamin, 1986; Dinges, Orne, Whitehouse & Orne, 1987; Lumley, Roehrs, Zorick, Lamphere & Roth, 1986; Wiegand, Berger, Zulley, Lavor & von Zerssen, 1987). In my experience, it is exactly the *irregularity* of biological functions which makes naps problematic among infants with a *difficult* temperament. Evidence that the absence of naps or the poor timing of naps is a stress to the infant is documented by the previously mentioned studies which showed elevated cortisol levels during wakefulness and decreased cortisol levels during naps (Tennes & Vernadakis, 1977). Because of the intimate relationship between infant behaviors and the biologic responses to the stress of sleep loss, the process of napping can be considered a biochemical modulator of temperament, emotionality, or arousal.

It is important for parents to learn to anticipate when a nap will occur so that they can initiate soothing efforts before the child becomes stressed from lack of sleep. When parents overextend the wakeful state, the child becomes overtired and quickly develops into an overaroused state from increased catecholamine secretion. Now, the child has more difficulty in falling asleep and staying asleep. Thus, a cycle is set in motion whereby sleep loss begets sleep loss.

Summary

The early phases of the ontogenesis of sleep-state control are biologically, not socially, determined. The temporal placement of sleep periods during the day and night influences the restorative benefits of sleep. The ability of sleep to reverse drowsiness or sleepiness depends on whether or not the sleep period is in phase with biological circadian sleep rhythms. Interrupted sleep or sleep fragmentation and brief sleep durations interfere with the active restorative function of sleep.

THE SLEEP-LOSS STRESS SYNDROME

Twin studies have shown that sleep patterns have a genetic component (Webb & Campbell, 1983) but maternal prenatal factors may also be important. For example, maternal smoking results in increased secretion of epinephrine and norepinephrine, but not of dopamine, from the fetal adrenal glands (Divers, Wilkes, Babaknia & Yen, 1981) and the salient distinctive behavior of newborns whose mothers smoked during pregnancy was being rated less consolable (Saxton, 1978). Surprisingly, maternal caffeine in breast-fed infants does not have similar effects (Ryu, 1985). Thus, inherited and non-inherited prenatal and postnatal factors contribute to the development of the infant's 'neuroendocrine individuality' (Strelau, 1986). Chemical individuality and the interactive parental effects elicited in early infancy may lead to significant problems.

Either biological factors initially or parental behaviors later may lead to loss of sleep. In particular, the irregularity of biological rhythms regarding sleep and the parents' failure to synchronize their soothing activities with the infant's sleep periods lead to the development of the sleep-loss stress syndrome. Not sleeping well during the night and not napping well during the day are age-specific risks (Weissbluth, 1987b). For example, the parents whose children are sleeping well during the night at 6 weeks of age subsequently fail to establish naps by 12–16 weeks of age, and this eventually leads to an overtired/overaroused state during the day which then destroys sleep continuity at night. Some components of parental behaviors may be reactive to congenital biologic factors and some components may be independent.

The reasons why this sequence often occurs include innocent parental errors involving inconsistency in soothing to sleep routines, irregularity in sleep times, and oversolicitousness regarding crying at sleep times. Among families whose children do not sleep well, it is common to find marital discord, parental depression or insomnia, or a chaotic lifestyle. These parental errors and family stresses are always magnified when the infant has colic (Weissbluth, 1984a).

Colic occurs during the first 3–4 months and the fussiness, crying, and wakefulness is best viewed as a state of extreme arousal (Weissbluth, 1987a). Parents become discouraged because they cannot easily soothe their colicky child to sleep. Their perception that their child is inconsolable, coupled with their own fatigue, may create unhealthy sleep habits for their child after the colic has passed. Evidence that biologic factors initially play an important role is derived from the observation that even when colicky behavior is suppressed with a drug during the first 3–4 months, thus minimizing parental stress, by 5 months of age the infants are still noted to have difficult temperaments and brief sleep durations (Weissbluth, Christoffrel & Davis, 1984a). In this study, 30% of colicky infants developed a difficult temperament in contrast to infants from an unselected population where only 10% became difficult. Postcolic infants have more frequent and longer night wakings (Weissbluth, Davis & Poncher, 1984b), and frequent night wakings have been associated with a *low sensory threshold* (Carey, 1974).

A group of infants who were identified as either colicky, of difficult tempera-ment, or stimulus-sensitive (low sensory threshold) had statistically significantly lower progesterone levels compared to a group of infants with none of these features (Weissbluth, unpublished). When analyzed separately, colicky or difficult infants had lower levels of progesterone but the group differences were not significantly different (Weissbluth & Green, 1984). As mentioned previously, progesterone in the infant is initially derived from the placenta and later is secreted by the adrenal glands. Because progesterone has a neurodepressive effect, infants with lower levels would be expected to be biochemically less inhibited.

After colic has ended at 3–4 months of age, which coincides exactly with the maturation of circadian sleep/wake rhythms, parental behaviors regarding sleep habits may strongly influence the infant's sleep patterns. However, the temperament of the infant during the first few months may have an enduring influence on parental behaviors.

At 5 months of age, difficult infants sleep 9.6 hours at night and 2.7 hours during the day, while easy infants sleep 11.7 and 3.7 hours, respectively (Weissbluth, 1982a). At this age, night sleep ($r = -.4$) and total sleep ($r = -.5$) duration were most highly correlated with mood ratings. In contrast, nap duration was most highly correlated ($r = -.3$) with attention span or persistence. Persistence was not correlated with night or total sleep durations, and pointedly, this trait, persistence, is not used in the diagnosis of easy/difficult temperament. Impersistence was also associated with 5-month-old male infants selected on the basis of gender, difficult temperaments, and a motorically active sleep pattern (Weissbluth & Liu, 1983). Also, at 5 months of age, difficult infants had higher activities of the enzyme which converts dopamine to norepinephrine (Rapoport, Pandoni, Renfield, Lake & Ziegler, 1977). Norepinephrine is the catecholamine most closely associated with wakefulness. Presumably, many of these difficult and wakeful infants developed increasing sleep loss because the enzyme measurements in the newborn period also correlated with the degree of fussiness at 1 year.

Infants between 4 and 7 months of age who do not sleep well are described as highly emotional by their parents, who use terms such as irritable, fussy, highly strung, wired, screaming, or out of control. By 8–12 months of age, parents add descriptive terms of impersistence such as flighty, unfocused, demanding, or not easily satisfied because nothing interests them for long.

In a longitudinal study of 266 infants in my private general pediatric practice (Weissbluth, unpublished) all but seven children were taking two or three naps at age 9 months. These seven children were allowed by their parents to take only one nap because of protest crying at the second nap time. However, for those seven children, whose median nap duration was one and a half hours, behavior gradually but dramatically worsened. The parents' major observation was a loss of ability to play alone for any length of time. In each instance, by shortening the interval of wakefulness preceding the expected time of the second nap, and ignoring protest crying, two naps were re-established by 12 months of age. The median nap duration for these seven children then increased to 3 hours and the short attention span or impersistence was dramatically and rapidly reversed. All 266 children in this study took naps and a single nap naturally evolved in this entire group at between 15 and 21 months. In contrast, most children seen at about 12 months of age who were referred for consultation primarily for poor quality night sleep were children who were then having *no* naps. Upon re-establishing naps, the first observation made by the parents was that of a longer attention span in these children. Subsequently, parents noted decreased emotionality or a more positive mood. The natural history of the sleep-loss syndrome depends substantially on the degree to which parents are able to avoid behavior which reinforce unhealthy sleep patterns and their willingness to accept the inconveniences associated with establishing healthy sleeping habits.

Older children, at age 3 years, who do not sleep well, are described by their parents as hyperactive (Weissbluth, 1984b). At this age, naps seems to be especially important. Nap durations were correlated with adaptability ratings and the only temperament trait which distinguished those who did from those who did not nap was adaptability. Adaptability was also the only trait associated with the frequency of night waking. Thus, children who did not nap well, not only slept less, but they awoke more frequently at night and were described as less adaptable. The same 60 infants were studied at the ages of 5 months and 3 years (Weissbluth, 1982a, 1984b). It is notable that at both these ages, day sleep duration did *not* correlate with night sleep duration. Also, although the group differences were not significant, the changes in temperament classification over time exactly followed the expected shifts in sleep duration. By age 3 years, easy infants who remained easy children slept a total of 12.4 hours, but those who became more difficult children slept 11.8 hours; difficult infants who became easier children slept 12 hours, but those who remained difficult slept 11.4 hours. Remember, differences in total sleep duration as small as 30 minutes have been shown to have dramatic effects among adults.

By age 4 years, short attention span or impersistence is associated with impaired performance on achievement tests (Palisin, 1986). Between 5 and 9 years, poor sleepers appear more worried, fussy, fearful, irritable, or anxious (Clarkson, Williams & Silva, 1986). At 6 to 12 years, children with insomniac symptoms are more likely to have also developed diagnosable psychiatric symptoms (Dixon, Monroe & Jakim, 1981). Boys between 8 and 12 years diagnosed as hyperactive have more motor activity during sleep (Busby, Firestone & Pivitz, 1981), and increased motor activity during sleep was noted in a study of 5-month-old male infants (Weissbluth & Liu, 1983) and 3-year-old children (Weissbluth, 1984b). In all of these studies on older children, the parents noted persistent problems in initiating and maintaining sleep *since infancy*.

Adolescent chronic poor sleepers, representing about 13% of all adolescents, are characterized as tense, worried, and less able to solve personal problems (Price, Coates, Thoresen & Grinstead, 1978). Similarly, decreased proficiency in solving problems created by life-stress situations, decreased ability to think divergently, and the tendency to be chronically more aroused or energized are characteristics of habitual brief sleepers among college-age Type A students (Hicks, Grant & Chancellor, 1986). By age 40 years, compared to adult-onset insomniacs, child-hood-onset insomniac adults had more severe insomnia and more soft neurological signs (Hauri & Olmstead, 1980). None of these problems is inevitable and clinical experience suggests that sleeping well from early infancy is incompatible with all of the problems.

Kagan (1987) is correct that 'biological sources of variation in the young infant's characteristics invite different treatments by family members' (Kagan, 1987,

p. 1158). The outcome of this interactive effect regarding habitual sleep structuring is variable and this variation in sleep habits explains why studies on different populations produce different results regarding prevalence rates and continuities versus discontinuities in measurements of temperament.

For example, regarding prevalence rates, night waking or 'bedtime struggle' was reported by Kataria, Swanson & Trevathan (1987) to occur in 42% of children between 15 and 36 months. A similar population that had had the advantage of early-onset parent coaching regarding sleeping habits (Weissbluth, 1987b) reported identical problems in only 1%. In addition to prevention through education, management of disturbed sleep, such as re-establishing naps, or shifting sleep schedules (Weissbluth, 1982b), dramatically reverses emotionality and the academic problems associated with sleep loss (Guilleminault, Winkle, Korobkin & Simmons, 1982; Weissbluth, Davis, Poncher & Reiff, 1983).

Continuities in resisting sleep, irritability, crying, and demanding behaviors were noted by Matheny, Wilson, Dolan, and Krantz (1981). They also noted that attention span was inversely related to all these variables. Continuities have also been documented in highly inhibited children. Their physiologic measurements (including high cortisol and epinephrine stress responses) suggested to Kagan (1987) that the inhibited children had 'higher arousal in the stress circuits'. Not surprisingly, sleeplessness was noted among the inhibited children during their first year. Continuities of sleeplessness such as increased latency to sleep (bedtime struggles) and fragmented sleep (night wakings) have been well documented in non-selected pediatric populations (Jenkins, Owen, Bax & Hart, 1984; Kataria *et al.*, 1987). Unchecked, the continued sleep loss would be expected to be associated with serious cognitive and psychosocial problems.

However, there is a reason why, even among superior functioning families, professional intervention may fail to succeed and the sleep-loss stress syndrome persists. The explanation for this failure is based on the *trophic* effects of the elevated cortisol and catecholamines on the developing neurons (Mirmiran, 1986; Shimohira *et al.*, 1986). Elevated neurotransmitters or neuromodulators present during the early stages of postnatal brain development might produce a *permanent* alteration in neuron functioning. Mirmiran states that:

> disturbances observed later in life ... are in fact subtle behavioral symptoms such as hyperactivity, emotional lability, attentional distractibility and sleep disturbances.... It is clear that receptors are dynamic molecules, which may increase or decrease in response to the available neurotransmitter to sustain a homeostatic (optimal) response. However, it is very probable that the set point for optimal response is established during the course of development. (Mirmiran, 1986, pp. 382, 385)

As discussed previously, parents influence the development of sleep patterns that influence the chemical environment bathing the maturing brain. These chemicals function as neuromodulators which create the 'set point for optimal response'. These neuromodulators, according to Gailland (1985), modify the reactivity of the cell to incoming signals from neurotransmitters 'for instance by altering the gain of the transducer system which induces intracellular modifications'. Thus, parents, through their efforts to structure sleep, have an opportunity to influence the neurochemical regulation of alertness, arousal, temperament, or emotionality.

Summary

Sleep loss directly causes impaired performance with subjective sensations of fatigue or sleepiness. Nap deprivation seems particularly important for persistence or attention span. Sleep loss directly elicits an adrenal stress response of increased production of cortisol and indirectly epinephrine. Increasing elevations of epinephrine are associated with sensations of increasing anxiety and alertness. Heightened alertness tends to override natural sleep rhythms, and this, when reinforced with parental attention, allows the child to be partially successful in his attempt to maintain an excessively wakeful state. The too-wakeful state is accomplished by activation of norepinephrine biosynthesis. It is the excessive norepinephrine overflow which, in combination with the other biochemical changes, may produce heightened emotionality, autonomic sympathetic dominance, or the difficult temperament. These children are correctly described by some parents as being so tired that, although they desperately want to go to sleep, they are *unable* to

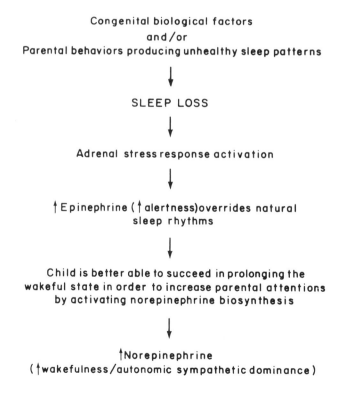

FIGURE 1   Sleep-loss stress biochemically modifies temperaments

do so. Parents, by influencing sleep habits, are able to prevent or modify the severity of sleep-loss stress (Figure 1).

PREVENTION AND TREATMENT: PRACTICAL POINTS

Nurses were able to reduce the behavioral distress response associated with circumcision by using pacifiers (Gunnar *et al.*, 1987). Parents may similarly prevent or reduce the stress caused by sleep loss by establishing healthy sleep habits. The following practical points are explained in greater detail elsewhere (Weissbluth, 1987b).

(1) *Start early*. Educate parents that sleeping well is as important to their child's health as is good nutrition. The advice must be age-specific in terms of sleep duration, sleep schedules, sleep consolidation, and the importance of naps. The advice must be realistic and areas of conflict between your advice and the parents' lifestyle or values must be explicitly discussed. The advice must be tailored to the child's temperament. Early-onset sleep patterning at 6 weeks is appropriate for the easy–regular infant. Parents of difficult–irregular infants might want to wait until 3 or 4 months of age when they know that endogenous sleep rhythms are developed and that now they are able to structure sleep habits in synchrony with these rhythms. Starting too early to shape sleep with these irregular infants usually does not work well because parental fatigue and frustration usually leads to inconsistent handling. However, after about 3–4 months of age, consistency in handling usually produces rapid improvement. Also, some infants are temperamentally stimulus-sensitive and sleep best in quiet and dark rooms. Parents need to understand that once sleep habits are well established, their sensitive infant will be less disrupted by noise and lights, and the temporary inconvenience of keeping the home quiet will produce long-term benefits.

(2) *Avoid the overtired state*. In early infancy, keep the intervals of wakefulness during the day to less than 2 hours, provide less attention at sleep times so the natural sleep process is unopposed. Practice consistency in soothing to sleep behaviors: (a) always holding the child until a deep sleep state develops or (b) always placing the child down at sleep times, after soothing, regardless of sleep state. Practice consistency in presleep rituals, make the sleep environment reasonably dark and quiet, and use the child's natural sleep rhythm as an aid to help him fall asleep.

(3) *Quality of sleep is not the same as sleep durations*. Quality sleep means unbroken sleep occurring at the right times. Parents can learn to distinguish between quality sleep and sleep durations by focusing their attention on their child's behavior following naps. They can contrast their calm, alert, well rested baby following a long, consolidated nap in the crib to their wired, fussy, overtired baby following a nap occurring too late in the afternoon or a fragmented nap in the car or stroller.

(4) *Maintain a sleep log*. Parents should maintain a daily sleep log as a 24-hour bar graph charting sleep periods, wake periods, and mood (calm, fussy,

crying). The parents can become sensitive to their child's natural sleep rhythms and thus synchronize their caretaking activities accordingly. Patterns of sleep that correspond to calm, alert, happy behaviors are compared to patterns of sleep that correspond to opposite behaviors. The display on the sleep log of sleep/wake patterns and changes in mood allows parents to see how they can keep their child well rested. Thus, the sleep log may prevent sleep problems and it may also be therapeutic because interventions may stress the family and they tolerate this stress better when they see on the sleep log that there is some improvement. The failure of the family to cooperate to maintain a sleep log suggests their inability to see disturbed sleep in a problem-solving framework and suggests the presence of significant stress in the family.

(5) *Perfect timing produces no crying.* Do not get sidetracked by overly dwelling on crying. Emphasize *timing* as the means by which you catch that magic moment when the child is tired, but not overtired, and he is then allowed to fall asleep. The sleep log allows parents to fine-tune their sense of timing.

(6) *Nullify the hypothetical connection between 'let cry' and 'feelings of insecurity'.* Explain how different states produce different needs: at sleep times there is the need for sleep; at awake times there is the need for love and attention. But, just as it makes no sense to talk about 'insomnia' during awake times, convince parents that it makes no sense to talk about 'insecurity' at sleep times. Thus, at those exact times when the child needs to sleep but is (a) overtired or (b) wants to play, then it is alright to ignore the child's crying. This is hard for parents to accept and 'let cry' has to be made positive by describing the expected benefits for the child in being well rested. 'Let cry' means that they are allowing sleep to naturally surface unopposed by their interventions.

(7) *Be sympathetic and optimistic.* Acknowledge that while establishing healthy sleep habits is *inconvenient* for parents, it is directly beneficial for the child. Disturbed sleep can always be corrected if families are able to change their behaviors.

(8) *Involve the father.* Changing bedtime or middle of the night routines succeeds only if *both* parents cooperate. Explicitly determine the father's willingness to cooperate: to come home earlier, to allow his wife to put the child to sleep earlier, or respond to some of the middle of the night feedings and awakenings.

These eight points help parents to teach their children healthy sleep habits because they are based on the power of stimulus control. Consistency of sleep-time routines strengthens the cues to sleep, and not reinforcing the child's expectation to be played with at sleep time, even if he cries, weakens cues for behaviors incompatible with sleep. Parents also learn that they are utilizing the age-appropriate endogenous sleep/wake rhythm to assist the child to fall asleep. The education process begins at a few months of age. Parents may be taught, in general terms, that when their child does not sleep well, two responses occur. First, the sleep deficit directly causes impairment of learning, concentration, task-orientation, or maintaining focused attention. Second, the sleep deficit causes fatigue which triggers a chemically stimulating stress response in their child. This stress response is simply the body's way to fight the fatigue with alertness. This stress response adversely affects mood, performance, and temperament. Thus their overtired child also becomes overaroused, more difficult, or more emotional. Additionally, parents may be taught that their own stress interferes with the process of their child falling asleep because the child anticipates bedtime struggles. Conversely, when parents develop a coping attitude and avoid allowing their child to become overtired, they develop a more relaxed attitude at sleep times and their own calmness itself facilitates the process of falling asleep for the child because the child now does not anticipate a bedtime struggle.

REFERENCES

Abe, K., Sasake, H., Takebayashi, K., Seki, F. & Roth, T. (1987). The development of circadian rhythms of human body temperature. *Journal of Interdisciplinary Cycle Research,* **9**, 211–216.

Adams, K., Tomeny, M. & Oswald, I. (1986). Physiological and psychological differences between good and poor sleepers. *Journal of Psychiatric Research,* **20**, 301–316.

Anders, T.F., Sachar, E.J., Kream, J., Roffwarg, H.P. & Hellman, L. (1970). Behavioral state and plasma cortisol response in the human newborn. *Pediatrics,* **46**, 532–537.

Atcheson, J.B. & Tyler, F.H. (1975). Circadian rhythms: man and animals. In R.O. Greep & E.R. Astwood (Eds), *Handbook of Physiology.* Washington, DC: American Physiological Society.

Axelrod, J. & Reisine, T.D. (1984). Stress hormones: their interaction and regulation. *Science,* **224**, 452–459.

Bates, J.E. (1980). The concept of a difficult temperament. *Merrill-Palmer Quarterly,* **26**, 299–319.

Bonnett, M.H. (1985). Effect of sleep disruption on sleep, performance, and mood. *Sleep,* **8**, 11–19.

Brazelton, T.B. (1973). *Neonatal Behavioral Assessment Scale.* London: Statistics International Medical Publications.

Busby, K., Firestone, P. & Pivitz, R.T. (1981). Sleep patterns in hyperkinetic and normal children. *Sleep,* **4**, 366–383.

Buss, A.H. & Plomin, R. (1984). *Temperament: Early developing personality traits.* Hillsdale, NJ: Erlbaum.

Carey, W.B. (1974). Night waking and temperament in infancy. *Journal of Pediatrics,* **84**, 756–758.

Clarkson, S., Williams, S. & Silva, P.A. (1986). Sleep in middle childhood: A longitudinal study of sleep problems in a large sample of Dunedin children aged 5–9 years. *Australian Pediatric Journal,* **22**, 31–35.

Czeisler, C.A., Weitzman, E.D., Moore-Ede, M.C., Zimmerman, J.C. & Knauer, R.S. (1980). Human sleep: Its duration and organization depends on its circadian phase. *Science,* **210**, 1264–1267.

Daiss, S.R., Bertelson, A.D. & Benjamin, L.T. (1986). Napping versus resting: Effects on performance and mood. *Psychophysiology,* **23**, 82–88.

Dinges, D.F., Orne, M.T., Whitehouse, W.G. & Orne, E.C. (1987). Temporal placement of a nap for alertness: Contributions of circadian phase and prior wakefulness. *Sleep,* **10**, 313–329.

Divers, W.A., Wilkes, M.M., Babaknia, A. & Yen, S.S.C. (1981). Maternal smoking and elevation of catecholamines and metabolites in the amniotic fluid. *American Journal of Obstetrics and Gynecology*, **141**, 625–628.

Dixon, K.N., Monroe, L.J. & Jakim, S. (1981). Insomniac children. *Sleep*, **4**, 313–318.

Downey, R. & Bonnett, M.H. (1987). Performance during frequent sleep disruption. *Sleep*, **10**, 354–363.

Ferris, B. & Green, O.C. (1968). Pregnanediol excretion of newly born infants. *American Journal of Diseases of Childhood*, **115**, 693–697.

Fibiger, W., Singer, G., Miller, A.J., Armstrong, S. & Datar, M. (1984). Cortisol and catecholamine changes as functions of time-of-day and self-reported mood. *Neurosciences and Biobehavioral Reviews*, **8**, 523–530.

Gailland, J.M. (1985). Neurochemical regulation of the states of alertness. *Annals of Clinical Research*, **17**, 175–184.

Guilleminault, C., Winkle, R., Korobkin, R. & Simmons, B. (1982). Children and nocturnal snoring: Evaluation of the effects of sleep-related respiratory resistive load and daytime functioning. *European Journal of Pediatrics*, **139**, 165–171.

Gunnar, M.R., Fisch, R.O., Kirsvik, S. & Donhowe, J.M. (1981). The effects of circumcision on serum cortisol and behavior. *Psychoneuroendocrinology*, **6**, 269–275.

Gunnar, M.R., Isensee, J. & Fust, L.S. (1987). Adrenocortical activity and the Brazelton Neonatal Assessment Scale: Moderating effects of the newborn's biomedical status. *Child Development*, **58**, 1448–1458.

Gunnar, M.R., Malone, S., Vance, G. & Fisch, R.O. (1986). Coping with aversive stimulation in the neonatal period: Quiet sleep and plasma cortisol levels during recovery from circumcision. *Child Development*, **56**, 824–834.

Gyermenk, L. & Soyka, L.F. (1975). Steroid anesthetics. *Anesthesiology*, **432**, 331–344.

Hauri, P. & Olmstead, E. (1980). Childhood-onset insomnia. *Sleep*, **3**, 59–65.

Haynes, S.N., Follingstad, D.R. & McGowan, W.T. (1974). Insomnia: Sleep patterns and anxiety level. *Journal of Psychosomatic Research*, **18**, 69–74.

Hicks, R.A., Grant, F. & Chancellor, C. (1986). Type A-B status, habitual sleep duration and perceived level of daily life stress of college students. *Perceptual and Motor Skills*, **63**, 793–794.

Hicks, R.A. & Pellegrini, R.J. (1977). Anxiety levels of short and long sleepers. *Psychological Reports*, **41**, 569–570.

Jenkins, S., Owen, C., Bax, M. & Hart, H. (1984). Continuities of common problems in preschool children. *Journal of Child Psychiatry*, **25**, 75–89.

Johns, M.W., Gay, T.J.A., Masterton, J.P. & Bruce, D.W. (1971). Relationship between sleep habits, adrenocortical activity and personality. *Psychosomatic Medicine*, **33**, 499–508.

Kagan, J. (1987). Perspectives on infancy. In J.D. Osofsky (Ed.), *The handbook of infant development*, 2nd edn. New York: Wiley.

Kagan, J., Reznick, J.S. & Snidman, N. (1987). The physiology and psychology of behavioral inhibition in children. *Child Development*, **58**, 1459–1473.

Kales, A., Bixler, E.O., Vela-Bueno, A., Cadieux, R.J., Soldatos, C.R. & Kales, J.D. (1984). Biopsychobehavioral correlates of insomnia: III. Polygraphic findings of sleep difficulty and their relationship to psychopathology. *International Journal of Neurosciences*, **23**, 43–56.

Kataria, S., Swanson, M.S. & Trevathan, G.E. (1987). Persistence of sleep disturbances in preschool children. *Journal of Pediatrics*, **110**, 642–646.

Kazarian, S.S., Howe, M.G., Merskey, H. & Deinum, E.J. (1987). Insomnia: Anxiety, sleep-incompatible behaviors and depression. *Journal of Clinical Psychology*, **34**, 865–869.

Levi, L. (1972). Psychological and physiologic reactions to and psychomotor performance during prolonged and complex stressor exposure. *Acta Medica Scandinavica*, **528** (Suppl.), 119–142.

Lumley, M., Roehrs, T., Zorick, F., Lamphere, J. & Roth, T. (1986). The alerting effects of naps in sleep-deprived subjects. *Psychophysiology*, **23**, 403–408.

Magee, J., Harsh, J. & Badia, P. (1987). Effects of experimentally-induced sleep fragmentation on sleep and sleepiness. *Psychophysiology,* **24,** 528–534.

Matheny, A.P., Wilson, R.S., Dolan, A.B. & Krantz, J.Z. (1981). Behavioral contrasts in twinships: Stability and patterns of differences in childhood. *Child Development,* **52,** 579–588.

Mirmiran, M. (1986). The role of the central monoaminergic system and rapid eye movement sleep in development. *Brain Development,* **8,** 382–389.

Monroe, L.J. (1967). Psychological and physiological differences between good sleepers and poor sleepers. *Journal of Abnormal Psychology,* **72,** 225–264.

Mullen, P.W., Lightman, S., Linsell, C., McKeon, P., Sever, P.S. & Todd, K. (1981). Rhythms of plasma noradrenaline in man. *Psychoneuroendocrinology,* **6,** 213–222.

Onishi, S., Miyazawa, G., Nishimura, Y., Sugiyama, S., Yamakawa, T., Inagaki, H., Katoh, T., Itoh, S. & Isobe, K. (1983). Postnatal development of circadian rhythm in serum cortisol levels in children. *Pediatrics,* **72,** 399–404.

Palisin, H. (1986). Preschool temperament and performance on achievement tests. *Development Psychology,* **6,** 766–770.

Price, V.A., Coates, T.J., Thoresen, C.E. & Grinstead, O.A. (1987). Prevalence and correlates of poor sleep among adolescents. *American Journal of Diseases of Childhood,* **132,** 583–586.

Rapoport, J.L., Pandoni, C., Renfield, M., Lake, C.R. & Ziegler, M.G. (1977). Newborn dopamine-beta-hydroxylase, minor physical anomalies and infant temperament. *American Journal of Psychiatry,* **134,** 676–679.

Reppert, S.M. (1985). Maternal entrainment of the developing circadian system. *Annals of the New York Academy of Science,* **453,** 162–169.

Ryu, J.E. (1985). Effect of maternal caffeine consumption on heart rate and sleep times of breastfed infants. *Developmental Pharmacologic Therapy,* **8,** 355–363.

Saxton, D.W. (1978). The behavior of infants whose mothers smoke in pregnancy. *Early Human Development,* **2,** 363–369.

Shimohira, M., Kohyama, J., Kawano, T., Suzuki, H., Ogiso, M. & Iwakawa, T. (1986). Effect of alpha-methyldopa administration during pregnancy on the development of a child's sleep. *Brain Development,* **8,** 416–423.

Solyom, J. (1984). Diurnal variation in blood 17-hydroxyprogesterone concentrations in untreated congenital adrenal hyperplasia. *Archives of Diseases of Children,* **59,** 743–747.

Steinberg, H., Guggenheim, F., Baer, L. & Snyder, F. (1969). Catecholamines and their metabolites in various states of 'arousal'. *Journal of Psychosomatic Research,* **13,** 103–108.

Strelau, J. (1986). Do biological mechanisms determine the specificity of temperament? In G.A. Kohnstamm (Ed.), *Temperament discussed.* Lisse (Neth.): Swets & Zeitlinger.

Talbert, C.M., Kraybill, S.N. & Potter, H.D. (1976). Adrenal cortical responses to circumcision in neonates. *Obstetrics and Gynecology,* **48,** 208–210.

Tandon, P., Gupta, M.L. & Barthwal, J.P. (1983). Role of monamine oxidase-B in medroxy progesterone acetate (17-acetoxy-6-methyl-4-pregnene-3,20 dione) induced changes in brain dopamine levels in rats. *Steroids,* **42,** 231–239.

Tennes, K. & Carter, D. (1973). Plasma cortisol levels and behavior states in early infancy. *Psychosomatic Medicine,* **35,** 121–128.

Tennes, K., Downey, K. & Vernadakis, A. (1977). Urinary cortisol excretion rates and anxiety in normal one-year-old infants. *Psychosomatic Medicine,* **39,** 178–187.

Tennes, K. & Vernadakis, A. (1977). Cortisol excretion levels and daytime sleep in one-year old infants. *Clinical and Endocrinology Metabolism,* **44,** 175–179.

Thomas, A., Chess, A. & Birch, H.G. (1968). *Temperament and behavior disorders in children.* New York: New York University.

Webb, W.B. & Campbell, S.S. (1983). Relationship in sleep characteristics of identical and fraternal twins. *Archives of General Psychiatry,* **40,** 1093–1095.

Weissbluth, M. (1982a). Sleep duration and infant temperament. *Journal of Pediatrics,* **99,** 817–819.

Weissbluth, M. (1982b). Modification of sleep schedule with reduction of night waking: A case report. *Sleep,* **5**, 262–266.

Weissbluth, M. (1984a). *Crybabies. Coping with colic: What to do when baby won't stop crying.* New York: Berkley.

Weissbluth, M. (1984b). Sleep duration, temperament and Conner's ratings of three-year-olds. *Developmental and Behavioral Pediatrics,* **5**, 120–123.

Weissbluth, M. (1987a). Sleep and the colicky infant. In C. Guilleminault (Ed.), *Sleep and its disorders in children.* New York: Raven Press.

Weissbluth, M. (1987b). *Healthy sleep habits, happy child.* New York: Fawcett Columbine.

Weissbluth, M., Christoffel, K.K. & Davis, A.T. (1984a). Treatment of infantile colic with dicyclomine hydrochloride. *Journal of Pediatrics,* **104**, 951–955.

Weissbluth, M., Davis, A.T. & Poncher, J. (1984b). Night waking in 4- to 8-month old infants. *Journal of Pediatrics,* **104**, 477–480.

Weissbluth, M., Davis, A.T., Poncher, J. & Reiff, J. (1983). Signs of airway obstruction during sleep and behavioral, developmental, and academic problems. *Developmental and Behavioral Pediatrics,* **4**, 119–121.

Weissbluth, M. & Green, O.C. (1984). Plasma progesterone concentrations and infant temperament. *Developmental and Behavioral Pediatrics,* **5**, 251–253.

Weissbluth, M. & Liu, K. (1983). Sleep patterns, attention span and infant temperament. *Developmental and Behavioral Pediatrics,* **4**, 34–36.

Weitzman, E.D., Czeisler, C.A., Zimmerman, J.C. & Moore-Ede, M.C. (1981). Biological rhythms in man: Relationship of sleep–wake, cortisol, growth hormone, and temperature during temporal isolation. In J.B. Martin, S. Reichlin & K.L. Bick (Eds), *Neuro-secretion and brain peptides.* New York: Raven Press.

Wiegand, M., Berger, M., Zulley, J., Lavor, C. & von Zerssen, D. (1987). The influence of daytime naps on the therapeutic effect of sleep deprivation. *Biological Psychiatry,* **22**, 389–392.

19

Issues in the Clinical Application of Temperament

STELLA CHESS AND ALEXANDER THOMAS
New York University Medical Center

In clarifying the concepts and practices involved in the use of temperament in clinical practice, a short historical introduction appears useful.

When we were young psychiatric clinicians in the 1940s and early 1950s we tried to apply the concepts and therapeutic approaches we had been taught. These formulations, though they varied from one school of psychiatry to another, all agreed that the infant was born a *tabula rasa* and that individual differences in personality resulted *exclusively* from differences in environmental stimuli and life experiences, especially within the family and in the first few years of life. All agreed in rejecting the static, mechanical beliefs of past centuries which conceived of development as the mere unfolding and elaboration of fixed characteristics already present in the newborn infant. And a number of scientific studies, empirical data and various theoretical concepts of the developmental process reinforced the belief that the child's environment had a highly significant influence in shaping his physical and psychological characteristics.

But to say that the child's environment was a significant factor in his development was quite different from saying that this was the *sole determining factor*. And it was this latter concept that we and others were taught as if it were proven beyond doubt. However, as our clinical experience and data accumulated, we were repeatedly impressed by our inability to make a direct correlation between environmental influences, such as parental attitudes and practices, and the child's psychological development. There was no question, of course, that these influences played an important role in the child's life, and we, like other clinicians, devoted much effort to trying to persuade parents and others to provide a healthier environment for children. However, we saw many, many instances in which psychopathology in a child occurred even with good healthy parents completely

Temperament in Childhood   Edited by G.A. Kohnstamm, J.E. Bates and M.K. Rothbart
© 1989 John Wiley & Sons Ltd

committed to their children's welfare. Also, at the opposite extreme, there were children who pursued a consistently healthy developmental course, even into adult life, in the face of severe parental disturbance, family disorganization and social stress.

Furthermore, even in cases where parental dysfunction was obviously responsible for the child's behavior problems, there was no consistent pattern between the parental approach and the specific pathology manifested by the child. For example, some children responded to domineering, authoritative treatment by becoming anxious and submissive, while others became defiant and negativistic. It became increasingly evident to us that these discrepancies between the established theories of developmental psychiatry and psychology of the time as opposed to our own observations could only be due to some additional influential factor which was being overlooked. Perhaps children were born with individual differences in their behavior patterns and in their responses to the environment, so that different infants and older children might react differently to the same demands and expectations. Numerous writers (see Thomas, Chess & Birch, 1968, for citations) had commented upon specific individual differences in young children in specific discrete areas of functioning. However, these reports did not provide systematic rating criteria, nor did they report any long-term investigations on the relationship between the findings in early life and the later course of psychological development. The one outstanding example was in the studies of specific abilities, such as intellectual and perceptual differences.

To investigate this question of individual behavioral differences and their functional significance, a long-term longitudinal study starting in early infancy was necessary. We did not start at birth, because a pilot study showed that neonatal behavior varied greatly from hour to hour, presumably due to the effects of the birth process and the maternal hormones and other chemicals still circulating in the infant's blood. This made it impossible for us to achieve stable baseline behavioral data in the neonatal period.

Any investigation must start with one or more hypotheses. We started the New York Longitudinal Study (NYLS) with the hypotheses that:

(1) Infants are born with individual differences in behavioral patterns which can be identified, categorized and rated. These patterns have a biological basis, but their expression and development can be attenuated, heightened, modified or even changed by postnatal influences. These behavior patterns are best subsumed under the term temperament (the term suggested to us by Dr Michael Rutter). Each temperamental category or constellation will be manifested in a variety of circumstances at any age period.

(2) Temperament influences both the characteristics of the caregiver's attitudes and practices and the impact these attitudes and practices have on the child's psychological functioning. In other words, the relationship between temperament and environment is a two-way street, with a continuous influence of the child on the caregiver, and the caregiver on the child.

(3) Temperament is a normal aspect of the child's psychological structure, even for those with extreme ratings in one or another temperamental structure.

(4) We were clear from the beginning that temperament could not be equated with personality. As we put it in our 1968 volume:

> there is an understandable temptation to make temperament the heart and body of a general theory. To do so would be to repeat a frequent approach to psychiatry which, over the years, has been beset by general theories of behavior based upon fragments rather than the totality of influencing mechanisms.... In our view temperament must at all times be considered in its internal relations with abilities and motives and in its external relations with environmental opportunities and stresses. The central requirement that a concept of temperament makes [of existing theories] is that they come increasingly to focus on the individual and his uniqueness ... the same motive, the same adaptive tactic, or the same structure of objective environment will have different functional meaning in accordance with the temperamental style of the given child. (Thomas *et al.*, 1968, pp. 182–183)

VALIDATION OF OUR HYPOTHESES

Our methods and findings have been detailed in a number of publications in the past 30 years (Chess & Thomas, 1984; Thomas & Chess, 1977), including the definitions and criteria for the scoring of the nine temperamental categories and the three temperamental constellations we have identified. Confirmation of these findings has come from a number of research workers in this country and various other countries (Chess & Thomas, 1984; Porter & Collins, 1982; Thomas & Chess, in Goldsmith *et al.*, 1987). In our data collection and analyses special attention has been given at all times to the comprehensive clinical evaluation of all subjects presenting any evidence of behavior disorder. This emphasis arose in the first place because of our concern with the inadequacies of the prevalent clinical theories and practices which was a major factor in our decision to embark on the systematic longitudinal study of the functional significance of temperament. Also, we felt that the identification of the manner in which temperament influences pathological development might give useful clues as to the mechanisms through which temperament affects normal development as well. Such a sequence in scientific studies by which the normal is illuminated by the pathologic is a well-known phenomenon in medical research. Thus, to take two examples, the roles of vitamins and hormones in normal physiology were determined after the identification of various pathological states caused by insufficient or excessive amounts of these substances in the body.

GOODNESS OF FIT

In our research on the behavior disorders that developed in our study population we found that the pathological development in each case could not be explained by temperament alone, or the influence of the environment alone, but required in all cases a consideration of the natural interplay of temperament and environment. This is not surprising, inasmuch as we are all committed to the view that development results from the continuously evolving process of interaction (or transaction, the term some authors prefer) between the organism and the environment at all age–stage levels of functioning. But this broad concept leaves open the question of the specific dynamic processes involved in this interactional model. As Rutter (1980) has pointed out, interactionist views indicate that:

> it is difficult to make valid, broad, sweeping generalizations about human behavior. Attention must be paid to the specificities of person–situation interactions . . . it may be suggested that it is preferable to take an idiographic approach which explicitly focuses on the individuality of human beings – not just in the degree to which they show particular traits or even in terms of the traits which are relevant to them, but more generally in terms of the idiosyncrasies which make each person uniquely different from all others. (Rutter, 1980, p. 5)

And indeed that has been our finding. There was no sweeping generalization that could be applied to each child – or adolescent or adult for that matter. The data on each youngster had to 'take an idiographic approach'.

At the same time, scientific progress does require the development of a general principle or principles which can encompass the findings derived from individual case studies or experiments. As we pondered this issue and reviewed the findings from individual cases, we came to the formulation of the *goodness of fit* concept. This idea was implicit in the hypotheses with which we started our longitudinal study, and gradually crystallized into a formal generalization which was spelled out in our 1968 volume (Thomas *et al.*, 1968), and in our subsequent publications. It has given us the key strategy for the analysis of the ontogenesis and evolution of a behavior disorder, and has also provided the theoretical framework for treatment and prevention.

Simply defined, goodness of fit results when the child's capacities, motivations and temperament are adequate to master the demands, expectations and opportunities of the environment. Such consonance between child and environment promotes optimal positive development. Poorness of fit, on the other hand, results when the child's characteristics are inadequate to master the challenges of the environment, and this leads to maladaptive functioning and distorted development. Goodness or poorness of fit are never abstractions. They have meaning only in terms of the values and demands of a given socioeconomic group or culture.

The goodness of fit concept has provided an effective framework within which to identify the specific dynamics of the organism–environment interaction in each individual case and to trace the evolution of the disorder over time without recourse to speculative, untestable hypotheses (such as conflict over the repression of presumed instinctual drives) or to simplistic unidimensional explanations (such as the pathogenic consequences of maladaptive conditioned reflexes). Goodness of fit involves not only temperament but other characteristics of the child as well. Thus, for example, a child with unrecognized subnormal intellectual capacities may be unable to meet the academic expectations of the teacher; a child with highly superior intellect may be underestimated and frustrated in a routine, mediocre class setting. In either case, there will be a poorness of fit, with unfavorable consequences for the child's school functioning. Or a child with serious interests and ability in one of the creative arts may be the victim of criticism and derogation by parents and peers because he is not the 'All-American athlete'.

The identification of the pattern of poorness of fit in any single instance of behavior disorder therefore requires a multifactorial and multidimensional approach, in which all the possible relevant biological, psychological and social influences, as well as their mutually interactional effects on each other, are identified and analyzed. In one individual, one particular characteristic and one particular environmental demand may be the prime interactional determinant in the development of a behavior disorder, while in another case the significant pathogenic factors may be different, and in a third instance may vary, and so on. In some instances, the biological deviation, such as in infantile autism, schizophrenia, severe brain damage or a major affective disorder, may be so extreme as to constitute the prime determinant of a pathological developmental course. Even in such cases, environmental influences may play a part in exacerbating or mitigating the symptomatology.

At the other extreme, extraordinary stress created by a special environment may be sufficient to produce even severe or protracted behavioral disturbances in most, if not all, individuals subjected to such an event (Erikson, 1976; Terr, 1981).

It is of interest that a number of investigators have also begun to use the goodness of fit model, though some may use other terms, such as 'match and mismatch' (see Chess & Thomas, 1984, p. 22).

The goodness of fit model can be compared to that of natural selection in evolutionary theory. Neither concept specifies that only one or two mechanisms can determine favorable or unfavorable adaptation; instead, they include the possibility that multiple, varied, unpredictable (but nevertheless determined) types of interaction between species or organism and environment can be adaptive or maladaptive. Thus, the concept of goodness of fit emphasizes that multiple, varied and unpredictable types of interactional patterns may lead to either positive or unhealthy psychological development.

CONCEPT OF TEMPERAMENT AND CLINICAL PRACTICE

Aside from the extreme instances of psychopathological characteristics of the child, most young children who show deviant behavior will reflect a poorness of fit produced by environmental demands and expectations which are inappropriate for the child's temperament. In such cases, it is the responsibility of the mental health professional, pediatrician, educator or nurse to identify in the individual child those aspects of temperament and environmental demands which are interacting to produce a poorness of fit. This diagnostic task is similar to that of the physician confronted with a child with symptoms which may have a number of possible causes. The physician must also explore the various possibilities if he or she is to arrive at a correct diagnosis.

Similarly, the clinician who takes the responsibility for diagnosing and treating a child's behavioral difficulties will prove insufficient to this task if he or she ignores the possibility of a temperamental factor in the youngster's difficulties. There may be some cases in which temperament will not be a significant factor in the development of the child's disorder. But in many other cases, in which temperament is an important factor, overlooking this issue can only lead the clinician, the child and the family to a therapeutic approach which is bound to be inadequate and even harmful.

It is also true that if the concept of temperament is to be used effectively the clinician must be able to identify pertinent temperamental characteristics clearly and definitively. Here there arises the opposite danger to that of ignoring temperament. If the criteria of temperament are made all too inconclusive, or if they are limited too strictly, again the clinician may misinterpret the dynamics of the child behavior, with unfortunate therapeutic consequences. For example, Buss and Plomin (in Goldsmith *et al.*, 1987) identify 'sociability' as a distinct temperamental trait. It is true that in many cases sociability may be primarily temperamental – a combination, perhaps, of positive responses to new situations and people and easy adaptability to change. But in other instances sociability may have a non-temperamental basis. A youngster with poor muscular coordination due to athetosis or other organic factors may find himself isolated from his peer group because of his athletic ineptness. He may then respond by judging himself to be fated to be unpopular and give up the attempt to participate actively in his peer group's social activity. To label this behavior as an inborn temperamental trait of poor sociability will not be helpful. What such a youngster needs is training in physical skills so that his athletic ineptness can be minimized, as well as the encouragement of his special talents and interests in which his motor clumsiness will not be a handicap.

At the other extreme, Goldsmith and Campos (1986) would restrict temperament to individual differences in expression of primary emotions. But characteristics such as persistence and distractibility, which would seem clearly to fit under the rubric of temperament, are related more to issues of task performance, such as in academic settings (Keogh, 1982; Martin, Nagle & Paget, 1983; Pullis and Caldwell, 1982), than they are to emotional patterns. To try to fit persistence and distractibility within an emotionality framework would seem to us to be a Procrustean-bed endeavor.

Buss and Plomin go further in restricting their definition of emotionality to a dimension which 'varies from an almost stoic lack of reaction to intense emotional reactions that are out of control' (Buss & Plomin, in Goldsmith *et al.*, 1987, p. 152). But all their examples of intense emotionality are negative ones, such as crying and tantrums. Where does this leave positive emotionality – such as zest, lustiness, pleasure, etc? This is not an academic question. In our recent NYLS follow-up we have seen a young man with intense initial withdrawal reactions to the new, and slow adaptability to change. Once he adapted, however, his initial negative responses became positive, with the same high intensity level. Now, as a young man, he had insight into the nature of his initial reactions of discomfort and a confidence, born of many life experiences, that if he persisted with the activity the distressing feelings would disappear and he would begin to enjoy the activity. But this success brought a new problem. He had many interests and talents and friendships. To all of these he brought a high level of intense pleasure, tried to continue all of them, and inevitably became extremely overinvolved and over-committed. He sought our advice because he had developed many facial and body tics, felt tense, and suffered also from insufficient sleep. The remedy was clear. He had to establish priorities for his various activities, and consciously apportion his time commitments according to these priorities. He accepted this evaluation; it made sense with what he knew about himself. He carried through on our advice, and within a few months his tics had disappeared, he was relaxed, and was sleeping well. In his case, the correct evaluation and guidance would have been missed if the intense *positive* features of his emotionality had been ignored or misinterpreted.

McCall has made the pertinent comment that:

> Temperament researchers have been troubled by their apparent inability to consent to a common definition of temperament. I do not believe they are far away from a reasonably uniform definition and, even if they were, I would not be disturbed by this situation. We have no very good definition of intelligence either, but that has not stopped us from studying it ... Neither do I worry about which definition is correct. To me, definitions are not valid or invalid, confirmable or refutable. Instead, they are more or less useful. (McCall, in Goldsmith *et al.*, 1987, p. 524).

McCall's comments are particularly pertinent for the clinician, who has the immediate responsibility both for the remediation of a child's behavior disorder and also for the guidance of caregivers and others to prevent potential or incipient problems from mushrooming into serious behavior problems. Different investigators, using different hypotheses, may very well sharpen our criteria of temperament, begin to define the biological factors that shape individual differences in temperament, and identify new aspects of temperament that we are presently overlooking. We can confidently predict that this expansion of knowledge will result from the active research work of many investigators and research centers now in progress, and will have important consequences for conceptualizations in developmental psychology and psychiatry.

For the clinician, whether it be the mental health professional, pediatrician, educator or nurse, new findings in temperament research offer the possibility of enhancing effectiveness in treatment and prevention of behavior disorders, as well as of promoting the child's social and academic functioning in school. A definition is useful when it enables the clinician to identify accurately the temperamental trait or traits that are playing a significant role in goodness or poorness of fit in the child–environment interaction and when the definition is precise enough so that temperament is not confused with other characteristics of the child, such as abilities, motivations, value systems or defense mechanisms.

A developmental approach is also important. Sleep irregularity in infancy may be a cause of severe stress for both child and parent, but becomes increasingly less important as the youngster grows older. An easily distractible baby may in early childhood be an asset to the caregiver, who can easily divert the child from poking at electric outlets or attempting other potentially harmful activities. But in later childhood this same distractibility may make it difficult for the youngster to stick to an academic task or domestic responsibility without being drawn away by some transient interesting diversion.

SELF-INSIGHT

Finally, the clinician and the caregiver are in key positions to help the growing child achieve insight into her own temperament. Such insight can give the individual the potential for controlling her temperamental reactions when they could be detrimental, as well as using them forcefully when they can be helpful. There are many opportunities that arise in a child's life which can be used to help her gain such self-understanding. A prominent developmental psychologist recently told us about his daughter's development. As a young child she had the typical pattern of what we call difficult temperament – irregularity in biological functions, withdrawal from the new, slow adaptability, and frequent negative moods and high intensity of expressiveness. Though such children are at high risk for behavior disorder development because they make special demands on the caregivers for handling, this did not occur in this case. The parents were aware of the temperamental basis of the child's difficult behavior and did not blame either themselves or the child. Instead, they maintained a quiet, patient and consistent approach to each new episode of discomfort, turmoil and negative behavior, and gave the child the time she needed to adapt to new demands and expectations. Entry into school, with its many new situations and expectations all coming at once evoked a period of several months of turmoil, loud expressions of dislike for everything about the school, and frequent assertions that she would stay home. The parents calmly but persistently explained to their daughter that they understood her distress, but that she had no choice, she had to go to school, and that she would find it easier as time went on. Gradually the girl adapted, as predicted, and after several months began to enjoy her school day. She was intellectually bright, became interested in learning, and her temperamental intensity now showed itself progressively in enthusiasm and delight over her academic achievement. She sailed through grammar school, and now was faced with the necessity of going on to junior high school, in a new neighborhood and building, with new classmates, and a different curriculum. She began again to show distress, became tense over this transition, and worried that she would not make a positive adjustment. Her parents gave the best reassurance: 'It will be the first grade over again.' The girl got the message that she would be upset at first over this new situation, but, as in first grade, this would gradually disappear and she would again find school a pleasurable and stimulating experience. The parents had, in fact, given her an important lesson in understanding her own temperament and how to master its difficult aspects.

Another girl, a subject in our NYLS, was also a child with difficult temperament. Her parents did not understand her behavior, reacted with inconsistency and impatience and the girl developed a mild behavior problem. The parents came to us for advice, we explained the temperamental issue, and counseled them as to how to handle the difficult situations as they arose. The parents followed our advice – after all, most parents do want to do what is best for their children – and the child's disordered behavior disappeared quickly and she went on to a healthy developmental course. When interviewed recently, in her late twenties, she was launched successfully on a professional career and had an active social life. When asked how often she got angry she replied 'rarely'. She then explained that she knew that once she became angry it was likely to be explosive and she would lose control of herself and the situation. So she had developed techniques of dealing with issues and people where anger could easily be provoked in such a way that she did not have to become angry. She emphasized that she did not avoid such situations and always worked them out without retreat or avoidance, but without anger. In essence this young woman had developed insight, with her parents' help, into her temperamental potential for intense outbursts of anger which were not to her benefit, and had learned alternative strategies of coping with challenging or frustrating situations.[1]

TEMPERAMENT AND CAREER CHOICE

Another question of practical interest is whether the individual's temperament helps to shape the direction of career choice. Does a highly active person choose a career, if the options are available, where there will be the opportunity for a substantial amount of motor activity? Does the person who warms up slowly to new situations prefer, if given the choice, to remain within a familiar job setting rather than to explore something new? This question has been raised indirectly by Super and Harkness (1986) and should comprise a most intriguing and significant aspect of future temperament research.

CONCLUSION

We started our studies of temperament with both practical and theoretical considerations in mind. As the field of temperament research has expanded in the past few decades, our knowledge regarding the practical significance of temperament and our conceptualizations regarding the nature of temperament and the dynamics of its influence on the process of development have flourished. But the more we advance, the more we are challenged by new questions and issues. Judith Dunn has put it well:

> There are, on the one hand, urgent practical questions toward which temperament research can be directed – child abuse, the response of children to stressful change, traumatic experiences or family discord – all of which require research which includes the assessment of temperament. On the other hand, some of the major issues in developmental psychology – the elucidation of the processes involved in developmental change, the different forms of individual–environment correlation, the origins of differences in children's relationships with their family and friends – may well be illuminated by studies which include careful assessments of temperamental differences in children. If we address such questions, we cannot fail to learn more about the nature and developmental implications of the variations among children which we call temperamental differences. (Dunn, 1986, p. 170)

NOTE

[1]Within the context of this single chapter we have been necessarily limited to a brief discussion of the many issues involved in the practical application of temperament concepts – whether by the mental

health professional, the pediatrician, the educator or the nurse. For a detailed discussion of these questions the reader is referred to our volume *Temperament in clinical practice* (Chess & Thomas, 1986).

REFERENCES

Chess, S. & Thomas, A. (1984). *Origins and evolution of behavior disorders.* New York: Brunner/Mazel. (Reprinted in paperback in 1987, Harvard University Press.)

Chess, S. & Thomas, A. (1986). *Temperament in clinical practice.* New York: Guilford Press.

Dunn, J. (1986). Commentary: Issues for future research. In R. Plomin & J. Dunn (Eds), *The study of temperament: Changes, continuities and challenges* (pp. 163–171). Hillsdale, NJ: Erlbaum.

Erikson, K. (1976). *Everything in its path.* New York: Simon & Schuster.

Goldsmith, H.H., Buss, A.H., Plomin, R., Rothbart, M.K., Thomas, A., Chess, S., Hinde R.A. & McCall, R.B. (1987). What is temperament? Four approaches. *Child Development,* **58**, 505–529.

Goldsmith, H.H. & Campos, J.J. (1986). Fundamental issues in the study of early temperament: The Denver Twin Temperament Study. In M.E. Lamb, A. Brown & B. Rogoff (Eds), *Advances in developmental psychology* (pp. 231–283). Hillsdale, NJ: Erlbaum.

Keogh, B.K. (1982). Children's temperament and teachers' decisions. In R. Porter & G.M. Collins (Eds), *Temperamental differences in infants and young children.* Ciba Foundation Symposium No. 89. London: Pitman.

Martin, R.P., Nagle, R. & Paget, K. (1983). Relationships between temperament and classroom behavior, teacher attitudes and academic achievement. *Journal of Psycho-educational Assessment,* **1**(4), 379–386.

Porter, R. & Collins, G.M. (1982). *Temperament differences in infants and young children.* Ciba Foundation Symposium No. 89. London: Pitman.

Pullis, M.E. & Caldwell, J. (1982). The influence of children's temperament characteristics on teachers' decision strategies. *American Educational Research Journal,* **19**(2), 165–181.

Rutter, M. (1980). Introduction. In M. Rutter (Ed.), *Scientific foundations of developmental psychiatry* (pp. 1–7). London: Heinemann.

Super, C.M. & Harkness, S. (1986). Temperament, development and culture. In R. Plomin and J. Dunn (Eds), *The study of temperament: Changes, continuities and challenges* (pp. 131–149). Hillsdale, NJ: Erlbaum.

Terr, L.C. (1981). Psychic trauma in children: Observations following the Chowchilla school-bus kidnapping. *American Journal of Psychiatry,* **138**, 14–19.

Thomas, A. & Chess, S. (1977). *Temperament and development.* New York: Brunner/Mazel.

Thomas, A., Chess, S. & Birch, H.G. (1968). *Temperament and behavior disorders in children.* New York: New York University Press.

20

Temperament in Developmentally Disabled Children

SUSAN GOLDBERG AND SHARON MARCOVITCH
The Hospital for Sick Children, Toronto

Although Carey (1985) has suggested that temperament information may be useful in work with a variety of clinically identified populations (e.g. physically ill, abused, or accident-prone children), temperament instruments have not been widely used with such groups and temperament research has focused largely on normally developing children. Consequently there is little published literature that can guide the clinician towards appropriate use of temperament constructs or instruments. One domain where a literature on temperament in clinically identified populations has begun to accumulate is that of developmentally handicapped children. In this group we include those with delayed development, and sensory and motor impairment, but most of the published data pertain to children with Down's syndrome. Nevertheless, even with these limitations, it provides an opportunity to examine some of the general issues that clinicians and researchers will encounter in work with developmentally handicapped populations. This chapter will review this growing literature which includes several studies of our own.

QUESTIONS AND ISSUES

We began our own research with guidance from clinical experiences. As co-director of a team conducting multidisciplinary assessments of developmentally delayed children, it was evident to one of us (SM) that consideration of child temperament was useful in both assessment and formulation of treatment plans. For example, it seemed that parents' feelings and attitudes concerning their success in caring for the delayed child were related to the child's temperament. In a small pilot study (Marcovitch, 1983) this was demonstrated to be the case: difficult temperament in a child (as rated on the Toddler Temperament Survey) was associated with increased

Temperament in Childhood   Edited by G.A. Kohnstamm, J.E. Bates and M.K. Rothbart
© 1989 John Wiley & Sons Ltd

feelings of maternal frustration. Furthermore, clinical decisions concerning programme referrals for children and parents often included discussions concerning the child's ability to adapt to new settings, how easy or difficult s/he was to manage, his/her activity level, etc., all of these being temperamental variables. Thus, there was a demonstrable place for the use of temperament instruments in such team assessments.

We were also aware of a literature suggesting that children with developmental problems are at greater risk for behaviour disorders than normally developing peers. In pioneering work from the New York Longitudinal Study (Thomas, Chess & Birch, 1968), Chess and Korn (1970) noted that among mentally retarded children, many behaviours characteristic of behaviour disorders appeared as part of the children's syndromes. In a recent Ontario survey (Offord et al., 1987), children with delays in walking and talking were two and a half times more likely to have a behaviour disorder than normally developing peers. Since difficult temperament has consistently been associated with later behaviour problems (Bates, Maslin & Frankel, 1985; Minde et al., submitted; Rutter, Birch, Thomas & Chess, 1964), and indeed among some researchers is defined on that basis (Thomas et al., 1968), identification of developmentally handicapped children with difficult temperament may be an important part of preventive service programmes.

Finally, there is some evidence that difficult temperament in a child who has other problems that increase the caregiving burden is more stressful to parents than difficult temperament in healthy normally developing children (Thomas & Chess, 1977). Thus, identification of difficult temperament may be a useful marker for assessment of parental as well as child needs.

As we considered how temperament evaluation might best be used in assessment of developmentally handicapped children, many questions arose. Available temperament questionnaires are standardized for specific age groups. Should the temperament of a child with delayed development be assessed with the use of instruments appropriate to chronological age or developmental stage? Many developmentally delayed children reveal vastly discrepant developmental stages in different skill areas. If one were to rely on developmental stage for assessing temperament, which developmental domains should be given priority? In a recent study, Gunn and Berry (1985b) compared temperament in a group of children with Down's syndrome to that in controls of the same chronological age (CA), same mental age (MA), and of their siblings. While there were some significant differences in each set of comparisons, the pattern of differences varied with the comparison group. The children with Down's syndrome were more rhythmic, less intense, and more positive in mood than both MA- and CA-matched norms. They were more approachable, adaptable, and lower in threshold for stimulation than the MA-matched norms, but had a higher threshold and were less persistent than the CA-matched norms. They were less persistent than their siblings. Thus, in clinical use, evaluation of temperament may lead to differing conclusions if different sets of norms are used as the reference point.

A second question is whether some syndromes are characterized by particular temperament features. Much of the research that we review here is a common exemplar of this question as there has been great interest in ascertaining whether there is any basis for the stereotype of children with Down's syndrome as temperamentally easy. If there are temperamental features associated with specific syndromes, this may be useful to researchers in elucidating biological contributions to temperament. It may also indicate that for clinical purposes temperament norms for children with specific syndromes might be of use.

Use of temperament instruments in clinical populations also raises questions about temperament constructs. Two approaches have been taken in defining difficult temperament. The first, identified with Thomas *et al.* (1968), defines difficult temperament as a constellation of behaviour characteristics associated with subsequent behaviour problems. An alternative approach, taken by Bates, Freeland, and Lounsbury (1979), was to ask mothers of infants to identify behaviours that would present difficulties to the 'average mother'. These two approaches have led to different but overlapping characterizations of difficult temperament. Thomas *et al.* (1968) included among the signs of difficult temperament low rhythmicity, withdrawal from new situations, poor adaptability, high intensity of moods, and predominance of negative moods. Bates *et al.* (1979) found that fussiness, inability to be soothed, and high intensity of moods were the elements that mothers considered to constitute difficulty. These appeared to be similar to the mood and intensity dimensions of Thomas and his colleagues.

In subsequent studies, Bates and his colleagues did find an association between their measure of difficult temperament in infancy and later behaviour problems reported by mothers (Bates *et al.*, 1985). On the temperament instruments designed by Carey and his colleagues (Carey & McDevitt, 1978; Fullard, McDevitt & Carey, 1984; McDevitt & Carey, 1978), in addition to reporting frequency of specific behaviours that are used in arriving at a rating for each of nine dimensions of temperament, parents are asked to give their global impressions of their child as easy, difficult, or average. Assuming that the parents' responses on this three-point scale reflect their judgments as to what is difficult, Carey and McDevitt's (1978) report that these parental impressions on the Infant Temperament Questionnaire are related to scored ratings on the dimensions of temperament identified by Thomas *et al.* (1968) suggests that characteristics that parents find difficult overlap with those selected by Thomas *et al.* (1968) as markers for later behaviour problems.

Since these concepts and instruments were largely developed with normally developing children, when we consider developmentally delayed and handicapped children, we may ask whether it is appropriate that temperament and behaviour problems should be defined in relation to normative data. Both temperament and behaviour problems can have different significance in the context of a developmental handicap. For example, high intensity of mood is considered a sign of difficult temperament in both of the approaches described above, yet it is possible that extremely low intensity of emotional expression may be problematic for parents of delayed or handicapped children and may also be a feature of some behaviour problems (e.g. in social interactions) or psychiatric disorders (e.g. depression). The absence of facial expression in blind infants (Fraiberg, 1977) and the subdued emotional expressions of infants with Down's syndrome (Cicchetti & Sroufe, 1978; Emde, Katz & Thorpe, 1978) have been described as frustrating

Table 1 Studies in temperament in developmentally handicapped children

Study	Diagnostic group*	Sample n	X CA	X MA	Other†	Instrument‡	Findings	Comment
Baron (1972)	DS	18	11.3 m	?		ITQ	Means were above Carey norms on all nine dimensions, not tested statistically	Concluded that temperament in DS infants is most like that of Carey's 'average' group
Gunn, Berry, and Andrews (1981)	DS younger older	28 (15) (13)	14 m 30 m	10 m 17 m	Mixed SES, predominantly middle class, in support programmes	ITQ	Majority fell into middle range on the nine dimensions, five children showed two or more signs of 'difficult' temperament	Mothers' impressions on interview were of 'easier' child than the Carey rating
Gunn, Berry, and Andrews (1983)	DS	15	35 m	14 m	2-year follow-up of above sample	TTS	Infants who were 'difficult' 2 years earlier had moved towards 'easier' ratings on TTS	Extremely small sample
Gunn and Berry (1985a)	DS	23	57 m	31 m	14 M, 9 F; mixed SES – predominantly middle class	BSQ	DS had higher scores than norms on activity, persistence, and distractibility; lower scores on rhythmicity, and mood; 'easy-difficult' distribution no different from norms	Same sample as above at older age
Gunn and Berry (1985b)	DS Normal siblings	37 13	30 m 30.5 m	17.9 m		TTS	DS more rhythmic, less intense, more positive mood than norms for matched MA, less rhythmic, less persistent than siblings	
Bridges and Cicchetti (1982)	DS Time 1 Time 2	74 (28)	4-22 m 10.6 m 16.9 m	6-18 m	41 M, 33 F, 29 first born 45 later born, Caucasian, no other sensory or neurological deficits	ITQ	DS group rated more 'difficult' than Carey norms, mothers' impressions were 'easier' than ratings; DS group – lower scores on approach, threshold, and persistence than norms	
Rothbart and Hanson (1983)	DS	8 10 9	6 m 9 m 12 m	?	Intervention programme, mixed SES	IBQ	DS – lower scores on motor activity, vocal activity, and smiling and laughter at all ages; DS had higher fear and orienting scores at 6 and 9 m, and higher startle at 6 and 12 m; no differences in activity level, distress to limitations, or soothability	Very small DS group; substantial normal sample which was part of standardization process for the IBQ
	Normal	115 149 106	6 m 9 m 12 m		Solicited from birth announcements, 59% return, mixed SES			

Study	Groups	N	Age	Age (DQ)	Sample	Measure	Findings	Comments
Greenberg and Field (1982)	Mixed handicaps: DS, CP, deaf, blind, delayed / Normal	43 / 12	20 m / 9 m	10 m / 10 m	All in nursery school	ITQ – mothers and teachers (observations by research staff)	Normal and DS infants less 'difficult' than delayed < CP < deaf and blind infants	Not clear how many in each handicap group
Heffernan, Black, and Poche (1982)	DS / Mixed other neurological problems	17 / 40	21.4 m	?	63% M lower middle class, 25% black	ITQ and TTS both parents rated	No difference between DS and others; no difference between total sample and norms on overall categories, but lower activity level, persistence, approach, and higher threshold than norms	
Van Tassel (1984)	Mildly delayed / Normal	15 / 25	9.8 m / 8 m		22 M, 18 F, Caucasian, 92% intact families 11 first born, 29 later born	Parent Perception of Baby Temperament	Delayed infants lower in positive mood, less approaching than normal	No measure of persistence
Marcovitch (1983)	DS / N / UD	20 / 20 / 22	2–5 yrs	?		TTS	Full range of temperament types in all of the diagnostic subgroups: 'difficult' temperament associated with mother report of difficulty in coping	
Marcovitch, Goldberg, MacGregor, and Lojkasek (1986)	DS / N / UD	32 / 29 / 35	39 m	(DQ) 57.0 m / 58.2 m / 66.8 m	Middle class	TTS, mother and father ratings	Total sample – more approaching, less intense, less persistent, higher threshold than norms; UD group – lower activity level than norms; diagnostic group differences on activity level, approach, distractibility	

Total 96

Study	Groups	N	Age	Age	Sample	Measure	Findings	Comments
Marcovitch, Goldberg, Lojkasek, and MacGregor (1987)	DS / N / UD	41 / 30 / 39	39 m	57.0 m / 58.2 m / 66.8 m	Same sample as above with addition of 14 children who had only mother ratings	TTS	Total sample ratings 'easier' than norms; maternal impressions of children somewhat more 'difficult' than norms; related to ratings differently in three groups	Some indication that what mothers find 'difficult' is different from mothers of normal children

Total 110

*DS, Down's syndrome; CP, cerebral palsy; N, neurological problems; UD, unexplained delay.
†SES, socioeconomic status.
‡ITQ, Infant Temperament Questionnaire; TTS, Toddler Temperament Survey; BSQ, Behavioural Style Questionnaire.

and/or disappointing to parents. A child in either of these groups might be rated as easy on traditional temperament measures yet be difficult for parents to manage and also be at risk for behaviour problems because the inability of adults to read his/her behaviour cues could lead to disorganized and disorganizing social experiences. Greenberg and Field (1982) studied temperament of children with a variety of developmental handicaps including Down's syndrome, cerebral palsy, and visual and hearing impairments, and found that important characteristics of these children were not captured by traditional temperament instruments. This included features such as passivity, absence of active play, flat affect, and neutral responses.

Little of the available research explicitly addresses these issues. We outline these questions because this is a potentially fertile field of research that will be invaluable to clinicians and deserves further attention.

OVERVIEW OF STUDIES

Table 1 summarizes the studies that we have included in this review. With only a few exceptions (Rothbart & Hanson, 1983; Van Tassel, 1984) all have used the temperament instruments designed by Carey and his colleagues for infants (Carey & McDevitt, 1978), toddlers (Fullard, McDevitt & Carey, 1984), or 3- to 7-year-olds (McDevitt & Carey, 1978). It is also clear that infants, toddlers, and preschoolers with Down's syndrome are the most extensively studied group, appearing in all but one study (Van Tassel, 1984) either as the sole study group (Baron, 1972; Bridges & Cicchetti, 1982; Gunn & Berry 1985a,b; Gunn, Berry, & Andrews, 1981, 1983) or as a major diagnostic group among others (Greenberg & Field, 1982; Hefferman, Black & Poche, 1982; Marcovitch, 1983; Marcovitch, Goldberg, Lojkasek & MacGregor, 1987; Marcovitch, Goldberg, MacGregor & Lojkasek, 1986).

The focus on children with Down's syndrome reflects the fact that they represent the largest *homogeneous* group of developmentally delayed children that are diagnosed soon after birth and are therefore available for studies in the infancy period where interest in temperament is high. However, the majority of developmentally delayed children have delays that are unexplained. In our own research (Goldberg, Marcovitch, MacGregor & Lojkasek, 1986; Marcovitch *et al.*, 1986, 1987) we have found that the latter group, which is large but *heterogeneous*, differs markedly from the group with Down's syndrome in a number of child and family characteristics. Therefore, the extent to which one can generalize to other populations must be considered with caution. Some evidence on this point will be presented in the section on comparisons among delayed populations. Only a small proportion of studies included assessment of a normal comparison group (Greenberg & Field, 1982; Gunn & Berry, 1985b; Rothbart & Hanson, 1983; Van Tassel, 1984) with the remainder relying on normative data for comparisons.

In addition, most of these studies rely on very small samples. In part this reflects the small size of the population and limited access to large numbers of developmentally handicapped infants and children. However, it is for this very reason that it is useful to review these studies systematically. Consistency in findings across studies may indicate better reliability than can be inferred from the original individual studies. Inconsistency in findings can indicate where statistically significant findings in a small sample may be chance occurrences.

Temperament and Developmental Delay (Down's Syndrome)

Since most of the studies rely on instruments used by Carey and his colleagues, we will try to be consistent with their terminology in the following discussion. Temperament *ratings* refer to cumulated scores on the questionnaires that are based on the nine specific temperamental features or dimensions (e.g. activity level, persistence) in accordance with the Thomas *et al.* (1968) definitions and descriptions. Temperament *categories* refer to an overall characterization of temperament in one of five groups ranging from easy to difficult based on *algorithms* for combining ratings on the features relevant to difficult temperament. Temperament *impressions* refer to direct answers to the question 'How would you describe your child's temperament? Easy, average, or difficult?' In spite of this terminology, it should be clear that all of these measures are based on rating schemes that reflect parent perceptions of a child's temperament.

Table 1 shows that all but one study included a group with Down's syndrome. Several of these studies were designed explicitly to ask whether the stereotype of the child with Down's syndrome as being temperamentally easy has any empirical basis (Baron, 1972; Bridges & Cicchetti, 1982; Gunn *et al.*, 1981). Others which included a Down's syndrome group as part of a larger study also addressed this question (Marcovitch, 1983; Marcovitch *et al.*, 1986). These studies concur that there is a wide range of temperament variation among children with Down's syndrome, not substantially different from that in normally developing children. At the same time, some children with Down's syndrome are, in fact, categorized as difficult. Bridges and Cicchetti (1982) found that, in their sample of 74 infants with Down's syndrome, maternal *ratings* on the Infant Temperament Questionnaire indicated more difficult temperament than the normative sample, although mothers' *impressions* showed that they considered their children to be easier than the *ratings* they gave. By way of contrast, in one of our own studies with three groups of developmentally delayed preschoolers (Marcovitch *et al.*, 1987), children in all three groups (Down's syndrome, neurological problems, unexplained delays) were rated as easier than the normative sample on the Toddler Temperament Survey, while mothers' *impressions* showed that they considered their children to be more difficult than their *ratings* indicated.

One obvious difference between these two studies is the differing age groups sampled. We therefore organized all the studies which provided *ratings* on specific temperament features in Table 2 and ordered the data by age. For studies which did not use the instruments of Carey and his colleagues, we included data where it appeared that a similar or related measure could be obtained. Table 2 shows that persistence and approach/withdrawal are the dimensions where differences between children with Down's syndrome and a normal comparison group (or norms) have been most consistently reported. For persistence, regardless of the age of the sample, those with Down's syndrome are rated as less persistent than

Table 2 Comparison between children with Down's syndrome and normally developing children on temperament dimensions

Study	Age of Sample ($\overline{X}$)	Temperament dimensions								
		Persistence	Approach	Threshold	Positive mood	Activity level	Rhythmicity	Intensity	Distractibility	Adaptability
Rothbart and Hanson (1983)	6 m 9 m 12 m	NA	Less*	NA	Less†	NA	NA	NA	NA	NA
Bridges and Cicchetti (1982)	10 m 16 m	Less	Less	Lower						
Heffernan, Black, and Poche (1982)‡	21 m	Less	Less	Higher		Lower				
Gunn and Berry (1985b)	30 m vs CA match	Less	Less	Higher				Less		
	30 m vs MA match	Less	More	Lower	More		More	Less		More
Marcovitch, Goldberg, MacGregor, and Lojkasek (1986)	39 m	Less	More	Higher						
Gunn and Berry (1985a)	57 m	Less			More	Higher	More		More	

*Inferred from measures of fearfulness.
†Inferred from measures of smiling and laughter.
‡This study included children with other delays, not separated from the Down's syndrome group in these analyses.

normally developing children. Although some of the samples in Table 2 are very small and therefore probably not representative, the consistency across studies is striking and therefore probably represents a reliable finding. However, persistence is not traditionally part of the constellation of features comprising difficult temperament.

Approach/withdrawal does form part of the difficult temperament constellation and Table 2 indicates that among children with Down's syndrome, those with an average chronological age up to 30 months were less approaching (or more withdrawing), while those who were older were more approaching. This shift is in the direction of easier temperament with increasing age. The tabled data for positive mood, and rhythmicity also suggest a possible shift with increasing age in the direction of easier temperament.

Though most studies have reported differences on the threshold dimension, there is no obvious developmental trend in the pattern of findings. As noted earlier, these findings should properly be viewed with respect to the specific comparison group used. In particular, as the Gunn and Berry (1985b) data indicate, whether norms or control subjects were matched for chronological or mental age is important. In most studies using norms (Bridges & Cicchetti, 1982; Gunn & Berry, 1985a; Marcovitch et al., 1986) the delayed children were compared to the closest mental age norms available. However, these 'matches' are relatively crude and the existence of developmental trends in both normative data and data for delayed children raises questions about the accuracy of such matches.

For example, the two studies with longitudinal data, those of Gunn et al. (1983) and Gunn and Berry (1985b) also report data consistent with this pattern. Infants who had been *categorized* as difficult at their first assessment were found on second assessment to have *ratings* shifted in the direction of easier temperament. In addition, the overall distribution of temperament *categories* shifted towards the easier end of the continuum at the second assessment. Bridges and Cicchetti (1982) also had longitudinal data in their study, but did not report differences between older and younger groups. Additionally, Carey and McDevitt (1978) have described similar shifts in normally developing children.

Thus, it appears that in children with Down's syndrome, as in prior samples of normally developing children, there is a shift towards reports of easier temperament with increasing age. Furthermore, in comparison studies, older children with Down's syndrome are rated as temperamentally easier than normally developing peers, although as infants they have often been rated more difficult.

Comparisons Among Different Delayed Populations

Four studies in Table 1 have made comparisons of temperament among groups of children with different disabilities (Greenberg and Field, 1982; Heffernan et al., 1982; Marcovitch, 1983; Marcovitch et al., 1986). Only one of these studies (Heffernan et al., 1982) reported no temperament differences between a group of 17 children with Down's syndrome and 40 children with a variety of disabilities. Further analyses in this study therefore combined these two subgroups for subsequent comparisons with norms. However, the remaining studies all reported diagnostic group differences. Greenberg and Field (1982) found that normal and Down's syndrome infants were rated less difficult than three other groups of handi-capped infants: delayed, cerebral palsied, and sensory-impaired. With a total sample of 43 children and five diagnostic groups, it is not clear how many infants were in each group nor how representative each group could be of its population. Differences among diagnostic groups were found in two of our own studies of preschoolers with Down's syndrome, neurological problems, and unexplained delays (Marcovitch, 1983; Marcovitch *et al.*, 1986). However, children with Down's syndrome were not always rated easier than the others.

In the first study, with 20 children in each diagnostic group, children in the neurologically handicapped group were *rated* less persistent than the others. In the second study, there were 32 children with Down's syndrome, 29 with neurological problems, and 35 with unexplained delays, rated by both mothers and fathers. There were significant group differences in activity level and distractibility. For activity level, children with Down's syndrome were *rated* most active (and closest to the norms) followed by the group with neurological problems and then those with unexplained delays. For distractibility, the group with neurological problems received the highest *ratings* (and was closest to the norms) followed by the Down's syndrome group and then those with unexplained delays. In a similar analysis of only maternal *ratings* (Marcovitch *et al.*, 1987) the groups also differed on approach/withdrawal, with the neurological group scored as most approaching followed by the Down's syndrome group and then the unexplained delay group, which was rated closest to the normative mean.

In this case, though there were differences between groups in activity level, approach/withdrawal, and distractibility, the Down's syndrome group was not always at the easy end of the continuum (Marcovitch *et al.*, 1986). However, when we considered maternal *impressions*, more of the preschoolers with Down's syndrome were considered easy or average than those in either of the other two diagnostic groups (Marcovitch *et al.*, 1987). In general, maternal *impressions*, being global judgements have not been considered reliable indicators of temperament on their own. Nevertheless, these *impressions* provide some evidence that parents may consider children with Down's syndrome easier in temperament or easier to manage than children with other developmental handicaps. It is conceivable that one source of evidence contributing to the 'Down's syndrome stereotype' arose in the period when most children with Down's syndrome were institutionalized and institutional caregivers found them easy to manage relative to the other children in their care.

The data reviewed thus far do indicate that there is some basis for the stereotype of the older child with Down's syndrome as being temperamentally easy. In contrast, infants with Down's syndrome are, if anything, temperamentally more difficult than the average child. However, a generalization or stereotype is of limited use in understanding individual children and the data indicate sufficient temperamental variation among delayed children (and those with Down's syndrome in particular) that generalizations cannot be substituted for first-hand evaluation.

Relation Between Impressions and Ratings

Carey (1985) has suggested that it may be clinically useful to note the agreement or disagreement between *ratings* and *impressions*. In particular, a mother's *ratings* which lead to *categorization* of a child as easy, combined with an *impression* of difficulty, may be a clue to psychosocial difficulties of the mother, or interactive difficulties between the pair. Carey and McDevitt (1978) have reported that among normally developing infants there is generally a good agreement between categorizations based on *ratings* and *impressions*, with discrepancies generally in the direction of maternal *impressions* describing an easier child than the obtained *categorization*. Bridges and Cicchetti (1982) reported that in their group of infants with Down's syndrome this was also the case. However, in our own (older) sample of pre-schoolers, discrepancies between *categorizations* and *impressions* were common, and mothers' *impressions* were generally in the direction of considering children to be more difficult than the obtained *categorization*. This discrepancy was most marked in the group of children with unexplained delays (where only 28% of children were categorized similarly), followed by the group with neurological problems (43% similar), and least evident in the group with Down's syndrome (49% similar) (Marcovitch *et al.*, 1987). However, even in the Down's syndrome group, a large proportion of children who had been *categorized* as easy were described by their mothers as average or difficult.

Rather than conclude that the majority of our mothers were experiencing psycho-social problems or interactive difficulties with the child, we considered the possibility that perception of difficulty by mothers of developmentally handicapped children may rely on behavioural features other than those traditionally considered to mark difficult temperament. Since we considered higher *ratings* on each of the nine dimensions of temperament to be in the direction of difficult temperament, we tested the prediction that the more difficult the mother considered the child to be, the higher the child would be rated on each of the nine temperament characteristics. Among mothers whose children had Down's syndrome and those whose children had neurological problems, this was the case for several temperament character-istics (intensity of moods, adaptability, and activity level in the Down's syndrome group, and these three plus persistence and mood quality in the neurological problem group). It was also of interest that children who were described as more difficult were rated as *more* approaching than those described as easy. In the traditional definition of difficult temperament, difficulty is associated with *less* approaching (or more withdrawing) behaviour. However, in the group with unexplained delays, there was no relationship between *ratings* on any temperament characteristic and maternal *impressions*.

To interpret these findings it is necessary to return to the possible meaning of *ratings*, *categorizations*, and *impressions* of temperament. We feel that *ratings* are most closely based on parent attempts to describe the child's behaviour without any attention on the parent's part to naive theories of temperament or judgments about those behaviours. By aggregating some individual items as a *rating* of persistence. others as a *rating* of activity, etc., we impose some theoretical constructs on these descriptions. We impose further constructs, entailing a definition of difficult temperament, by entering *ratings* into an algorithm to obtain a temperament *categorization*. Parent *impressions* presumably reflect each individual's judgment about what is easy, average, or difficult. We therefore assume that discrepancies between *impressions* and *categorizations* or between *impressions* and *ratings* indicate that parents' judgments or implicit theories about what makes a child difficult are at variance with definitions used by temperament researchers.

The finding that there were diagnostic group differences in the relationship between *ratings* and *impressions* suggests that parents in these three groups consider their children's temperament differently. In particular, we suggest that in the absence of an explanation for a child's unusual or frustrating behaviour, mothers attribute these behaviours to the child's difficult temperament. Differences between mothers in the Down's syndrome and neurological groups, both instances where a diagnosis is available, suggest to us that different histories in each diagnostic group have led to different expectations of child behaviour on the part of mothers. In each of these groups the 'difficulty' has a different meaning to mothers. Furthermore, the finding that mothers of delayed children associate more approaching behaviour with difficulty contrasts with the normative expectation that withdrawal rather than approach is related to difficult temperament. All three groups in our study were more approaching (i.e. less withdrawn) than the average in the normative sample. Possibly in a child with limited cognitive skills, the lack of caution in approaching new situations is more worrisome to parents than the same trait in a more competent child. These data suggest that it is clinically useful to explore the relationship between *ratings* and *impressions* in individual families with a view towards enabling parents to distinguish features of child behaviour that are disability-related and those that are temperamental, and to identify those which are problematic for parents without regard to whether or not they are theoretically related to 'difficult' temperament. It also indicates that attention to specific features of temperament is probably more valuable than the global *categorization* of easy–difficult temperament.

Relation Between Ratings of Mothers and Others

Thus far, we have discussed findings based primarily upon maternal responses to temperament questionnaires. The vast majority of studies in the literature and all of the normative data are based upon maternal *ratings* and *impressions* of children. However, several studies listed in Table 1 have obtained *ratings* from individuals other than mothers, either fathers (Heffernan *et al.*, 1982; Marcovitch *et al.*, 1986) or teachers and research staff (Greenberg and Field, 1982). In the latter study, although correlations between raters were moderate, mothers tended to rate their infants' temperaments on the Infant Temperament Questionnaire as less difficult than did research staff, who in turn rated them as less difficult than did teachers. Heffernan *et al.* (1982) compared mother and father *ratings* for a subgroup of 26 in their sample. The only reported difference was that mothers rated their children as less adaptable than did fathers. Both of these samples included children with a variety of disabilities.

In our own study (Marcovitch *et al.*, 1986), which included preschoolers from three diagnostic groups, mothers and fathers differed in their *ratings* of activity level, distractibility, and approach/withdrawal. Mothers rated their children as more active, more distractible, and more approaching than did the fathers. There were no significant group differences in this pattern. We interpreted all of these differences as being in the direction of mothers' reporting increased difficulty, since prior analysis had shown that increased approach, although traditionally considered to be in the direction of easier temperament, was associated with mothers' *impressions* of increased difficulty in our sample. It also seemed to confirm our intuition that mothers, who bear most of the responsibility for the care of the handicapped child, would be more likely to describe their children as difficult than fathers.

Discrepancies among raters of temperament have been discussed in depth in the literature on normal children from the perspective of the limitations of parent-report measures of temperament and the difficulties of establishing a gold standard against which to measure different methods of assessing temperament. When observers or raters show high agreement in rating a child's behavioural character-istics, we can assume that they are all responding to characteristics that reside in the child. When there is disagreement, it is difficult to ascertain whether the discrepancies reflect inconsistency in the child's behaviour, different samples of the child's behaviour that are available to different observers, or perceptions that are influenced by the characteristics of the observer. While this determination is important in the development of temperament instruments and temperament theory, for the purposes of clinical assessment, such discrepancies are probably best used as an opportunity for exploration. For example, discrepancies between fathers and mothers in describing a child's temperament may reflect different expectations of the child from each parent or more general parental conflicts that might be relevant to treatment planning. Unusually high agreement might reflect lack of independence in reporting: the father may rely on the mother's reports for his impressions of temperament; parents may have discussed the questionnaires while completing them. On the other hand, high agreement between parents on a child's temperament may facilitate agreement between parents on appropriate behaviour management strategies. Thus, similarities and differences in parent reports of temperament can be used in clinical assessments to explore aspects of family functioning that are relevant to the child's care.

Temperament and Social Interactions

Unlike the extensive studies in the normally developing population on the relations between temperament and concurrent or subsequent social interactions or relation-ships, such data for developmentally delayed children are rare. Greenberg and Field (1982) compared responses of mothers to the Infant Temperament Questionnaire with observer impressions of temperament (using the direct questions at the end of the maternal form) based upon videotaped mother–infant and teacher–infant inter-actions, and observations during classroom free play. While there was some concordance across interaction situations and between observers of the inter-actions, no direct comparisons between observers on ratings were made.

Marcovitch (1983) found that mothers whose children were temperamentally difficult on the basis of mothers' ratings on the Toddler Temperament Scale were likely to be less animated, less appropriate in vocal behaviour, and to exhibit more negative behaviours in interactions with their child than mothers whose children were temperamentally easy. Additionally, in both this study and our larger follow-up (Marcovitch *et al.*, 1987), temperament, whether based on maternal *impressions* or *ratings*, was related to the degree of satisfaction or frustration mothers expressed in caring for their developmentally disabled child. Difficult temperament was associated with increased frustration (Marcovitch *et al.*, 1987).

Thus, while there is some evidence of expected relations between temperament and social interactions and relationships for the developmentally delayed child, it is noticeably sparse. In part, the clinical utility of temperament assessment depends on a demonstrable relationship between scores or ratings on temperament instruments and child and/or caregiver behaviours in a variety of situations. Clearly this is an area in need of expanded research.

Clinical Utility of Temperament Measures with Exceptional Populations

The discussion thus far has focused on research on temperament in a subgroup of exceptional populations. However, as Carey (1985) has stated, temperament is 'not just an interesting concept worthy of research'. Understanding a child's temperament can aid both clinician and parent understanding of particular children and guide interventions to foster positive parent–child interaction. Carey discusses the utility of temperament data in pediatric practice with parents of normally developing children. However, a good understanding of a developmentally delayed child's temperament constellation is also clinically useful in many of the same ways. Earlier, Carey and McDevitt (1980) discussed diagnostic and therapeutic approaches to hyperactivity, and proposed that problems in behaviour and learning be diagnosed in terms of a broad profile which included the child's temperament or behavioural style.

The same approach could be of use for other developmental and behavioural problems. To our knowledge, there has been little published that addresses the clinical utility of temperament data in intervention with developmentally delayed children. However, there is a body of data associated with a measure of parental stress that appears to include a temperament component, the Parenting Stress Index (PSI; Abidin, 1986). The PSI was developed to examine stressors that affect parenting behaviour. Since stress factors are multidimensional, the PSI contains several subscales, one of which has much in common with traditional temperament measures.

The PSI is a 120-item clinical and research questionnaire designed to assess factors influencing stress in the parental role. In addition to an overall score, it provides scores for three domains: child, parent, and life events. Subscales in the child domain include adaptability, acceptability, demandingness, mood, distractibility/hyperactivity, and reinforcement of parent.

Several of these subscales draw upon items developed by Thomas *et al.* (1968) to assess adaptability, intensity, approach/withdrawal (adaptability subscale), mood

(mood subscale), activity level, and persistence (distractibility/hyperactivity subscale). The development of the PSI included studies with a variety of clinically identified populations including children with Down's syndrome, other forms of mental retardation, autism, hyperactivity, spina bifida, hearing impairment, neurological impairment, and a variety of medical problems. The manual lists over 50 studies, of which 15 are concerned with children who had medical, developmental, or emotional problems and six are concerned with the effects of intervention or services on child and/or family. Thus, this is potentially a valuable source of information about temperament assessment in clinical programmes. Unfortunately, the majority of these studies are unpublished. Although brief summaries are provided in the PSI manual, the information is too limited for thorough evaluation. However, the summary indicates that relative to populations of normally developing children, those with developmental handicaps are perceived by parents as a greater source of stress as indicated by elevated child-domain scores. Without further details, the extent to which the 'temperament subscales' account for these parental reports of increased stress is not evident. A valuable research project would be to test the extent of overlap between the PSI child domain and its subscale scores and more traditional measures of temperament. Since the PSI now seems to be gaining wide use in both clinical and research settings, it may be a valuable source of information about temperament and its role in assessment and treatment of clinically identified populations.

CONCLUSION

In the opening section we discussed questions and issues concerning the use of temperament measures in clinical settings with developmentally disabled children. Our review indicates that published information is extremely sparse and, for the most part, does not address the salient questions. We have identified a number of areas worthy of further research. These include possible development of a normative data base for specific handicapped populations, better documentation of developmental changes in temperament of developmentally disabled children, the relationship of temperament to social interactions in these populations, and investigation of non-traditional instruments such as the PSI, which may provide clinicians with temperament data in other forms. Perhaps most important for the use of clinicians is the need for more formal reports on the utility of temperament data in assessment and treatment of children with specific developmental problems. While individual clinicians will undoubtedly continue to use temperament instruments effectively in their care of developmentally disabled children and we have suggested some of these uses, such practice will be greatly enhanced as a shared literature on the topic emerges.

REFERENCES

Abidin, R. (1986). *The Parenting Stress Index manual*, 2nd edn. Pediatric Psychology Press.
Baron, J. (1972). Temperament profile of children with Down's syndrome. *Developmental Medicine and Child Neurology*, **14**, 640–643.

Bates, J.E., Freeland, C.A.B. & Lounsbury, M.L. (1979). Measurement of infant difficultness. *Child Development*, **50**, 794–803.

Bates, J.R., Maslin, C.A. & Frankel, K.A. (1985). Attachment security, mother–child interaction and temperament as predictors of behaviour problem ratings at age three years. In I. Bretherton & E. Waters (Eds), *Growing points of attachment theory and research. Monographs of the Society for Research in Child Development*, **50** (1–2), Serial No. 209.

Bridges, F.A. & Cicchetti, D. (1982). Mother's ratings of the temperament characteristics of Down's syndrome infants. *Developmental Psychology*, **18**, 238–244.

Carey, W.B. (1985). Clinical use of temperament data in pediatrics. *Journal of Developmental and Behavioral Pediatrics*, **6**, 137–142.

Carey, W.B. & McDevitt, S.C. (1978). Revision of the Infant Temperament Questionnaire. *Pediatrics*, **61**, 735–739.

Carey, W.B. & McDevitt, S.C. (1980). Minimal brain damage and hyperkinesis: A clinical viewpoint. *American Journal of Diseases of Childhood*, **134**, 926–929.

Chess, S. & Korn, S. (1970). Temperament and behaviour disorders in mentally retarded children. *Archives of General Psychiatry*, **23**, 122.

Cicchetti, D. & Sroufe, L.A. (1978). An organizational view of affect: Illustration from the study of Down's syndrome infants. In M. Lewis & L. Rosenblum (Eds), *The development of affect*. New York: Plenum.

Emde, R., Katz, E. & Thorpe, J. (1978). Emotional expression in infancy: 2. Early deviations in Down's syndrome. In M. Lewis & L. Rosenblum (Eds), *The development of affect*. New York: Plenum.

Fraiberg, S. (1974). Blind infants and their mothers: An examination of the sign system. In M. Lewis & L. Rosenblum (Eds), *The effect of the infant on its caregiver*. New York: Wiley.

Fullard, W., McDevitt, S.C. & Carey, W.B. (1984). Assessing temperament in one- to three-year-olds. *Journal of Pediatric Psychology*, **9**, 205–217.

Greenberg, R. & Field, T. (1982). Temperament ratings of handicapped infants during classroom, mother, and teacher interactions. *Journal of Pediatric Psychology*, **7**, 387–405.

Gunn, P. & Berry, P. (1985a). The temperament of Down's syndrome toddlers and their siblings. *Journal of Child Psychology and Psychiatry*, **6**, 973–979.

Gunn, P. & Berry, P. (1985b). Down's syndrome temperament and maternal response to descriptions of child behaviour. *Developmental Psychology*, **21**, 842–847.

Gunn, P., Berry, P. & Andrews, R.J. (1981). The temperament of Down's syndrome infants: A research note. *Journal of Child Psychology and Psychiatry*, **22**, 189–194.

Gunn, P., Berry, P. & Andrews, R.J. (1983). The temperament of Down's syndrome infants: A research note. *Journal of Child Psychology and Psychiatry*, **24**, 601–605.

Heffernan, L., Black, F.W. & Poche, P. (1982). Temperament patterns in young neurologically impaired children. *Journal of Pediatric Psychology*, **22**, 189–194.

Marcovitch, S. (1983). Maternal stress and mother–child interaction with developmentally delayed preschoolers. Unpublished doctoral dissertation, York University Toronto, Ontario.

Marcovitch, S., Goldberg, S., Lojasek, M. & MacGregor, D. (1987). The concept of difficult temperament in the developmentally disabled preschool child. *Journal of Applied Developmental Psychology*, **8**, 151–164.

Marcovitch, S., Goldberg, S., MacGregor, D. & Lojkasek, M. (1986). Patterns of temperament variation in three groups of developmentally delayed preschool children: Mother and father ratings. *Developmental and Behavioral Pediatrics*, **7**(4), 247–252.

McDevitt, S.C. & Carey, W.B. (1978). The measurement of temperament in 3- to 7-year-old children. *Journal of Child Psychology and Psychiatry*, **19**, 245–253.

Minde, K., Goldberg, S., Perrotta, M., Washington, J., Lojkasek, M., Corter, C. & Parkes, K. (submitted). Continuities and discontinuities in the development of 64 very small premature infants to four years of age.

Offord, D., Boyle, M.H., Szatmari, P., Rae-Grant, N., Links, P., Cadman, D.T., Byles, J.A., Crawford, J.W., Munroe Blum, H., Bynne, C., Thomas, H. & Woodward, C.A. (1987).

The Ontario Child Health Study: Prevalence of disorder and rates of service utilization. *Archives of General Psychiatry,* **44**, 832–836.

Rothbart, M.K. & Hanson, M.J. (1983). A caregiver report comparison of temperament characteristics of Down's syndrome and normal infants. *Developmental Psychology,* **19**, 766–769.

Rutter, M., Birch, H., Thomas, A. & Chess, S. (1964). Temperament characteristics in infancy and the later development of behaviour disorders. *British Journal of Psychiatry,* **110**, 651–661.

Thomas, A. & Chess, S. (1977). *Temperament and development.* New York: Brunner/ Mazel.

Thomas, A., Chess, S. & Birch, H. (1968). *Temperament and behavior disorders in children.* New York: New York University Press.

Van Tassel, E. (1984). Temperament characteristics of mildly developmentally delayed infants. *Developmental and Behavioral Pediatrics,* **5**, 11–14.

21

Practical Applications in Pediatrics

WILLIAM B. CAREY
Private Practice of Pediatrics, and Children's Hospital of Philadelphia[1]

TEMPERAMENT: AN IMPORTANT CLINICAL REALITY

Most of the recent research and writing in the field of children's temperament has treated the subject as representing a significant change in the way parent–child interactions are conceptualized. Children can no longer be viewed as just passively receiving the imprint of the environment. However, most of these recent expositions have not progressed much beyond viewing temperament as an interesting theory or 'construct'. One prominent researcher has even gone as far as to say that investigation in the field has little to offer the clinician (Plomin, 1982) and that the notion of the difficult child should be abandoned (Daniels, Plomin & Greenhalgh, 1983).

Experienced clinicians and clinical temperament researchers have no doubts that temperament is a significant clinical reality and not just an interesting theory. We know that it is a real phenomenon, that it matters considerably in the lives of parents and children, and that it can be measured well enough for clinical use (Rutter, 1982).

Since few of the contributors to this volume are full-time clinicians, it is appropriate for a pediatrician in private practice to stress practical applications of temperament differences in a primary medical care setting. Theoretical issues are intriguing but their discussion is better left to other contributors who have them as their principal interest. This chapter is concerned with a variety of practical issues, as the reader will note by scanning the headings.

UNIQUE RELATIONSHIP BETWEEN CLINICIANS AND TEMPERAMENT RESEARCH

Many academicians in temperament research seem not to appreciate fully the unique relationship we clinicians have with this subject. Clinicians have been the

Temperament in Childhood   Edited by G.A. Kohnstamm, J.E. Bates and M.K. Rothbart
© 1989 John Wiley & Sons Ltd

primary instigators of research in the field and are the principal professional consumers of research findings.

Although some psychologists can be mentioned as having had an important role in our unfolding knowledge of temperament differences, it has been physicians who have supplied most of the initial impetus. The impressive list from the ancient and modern world includes: Hippocrates, Galen, Pavlov, Gesell, Brazelton, Thomas and Chess. This relationship did not happen by chance. Physicians are required by the nature of their profession to immerse themselves in the real world and all its confusing complexity and to do the best they can with what they have available to help their patients. By contrast, academic psychologists and their spiritual ancestors in natural philosophy have been freer to speculate about the nature of things relatively unencumbered by the annoying inconsistencies of the practical world and the cries for help from patients.

As academic interests (theory building) have overtaken clinical interests (problem solving) in temperament research, much effort has gone into elaboration of the theories and technologies of the field. Not only has the largely medical origin of the field been forgotten but also the practical utility of the research is only occasionally considered. Practical clinical applications are generally ignored or considered only as an afterthought. Yet, is it not the ultimate social value of behavioral science research to solve human problems? Are not clinicians in medicine, psychology and education the principal professional consumers of research in this field?

SPECIAL REQUIREMENTS OF CLINICAL MEASUREMENT

While academic psychologists rightly put strong emphasis on the need for psycho-metrically sound instruments and all users of these scales should be concerned with accuracy, we clinicians have special additional priorities. The two most important of these are: the clinical relevance of the theories on which they are based and the practicality of the techniques. Several other points will be added to these. (These thoughts on measurement problems have been presented in greater detail elsewhere – see Carey, 1987.)

Clinical Relevance

For temperament theories to be of maximum value they should include characteristics pertinent to clinical problems. The vast variety of behaviors in the domain of behavioral style can be subdivided and arranged according to a variety of conceptual schemes, and no one can fairly claim to be definitive. Given the nature of the material, that may never be possible. It is inevitable that the theoretical orientation of the observer will exert a powerful influence on the way that person organizes the phenomena. For a clinician it is hard to imagine a more compelling influence than clinical relevance.

Thomas and Chess began their investigation with observations and parental descriptions of behavior. From these they extracted a set of characteristics that they believed would make children hard to manage. Their longitudinal study demonstrated with which of these characteristics and under what circumstances behavior problems arose (Thomas, Chess & Birch, 1968). McDevitt and I (with associates) have attempted in our four questionnaires to measure these same characteristics as faithfully as possible. We believe we have achieved our goal with a reasonable degree of success (Carey, 1983a).

By contrast, academic researchers (theory builders) have generally drawn their ideas for the conceptualization and subdivision of temperament from various theoretical sources rather than from direct observations of children. The clinical value of the characteristics and their possible therapeutic relevance have seemed to matter less. Also, many academic researchers have not tried to identify temperament risk factors, such as the difficult child syndrome, and some have clearly been perplexed as to what to do about this useful concept (Daniels *et al.*, 1983).

An example will illustrate how academic researchers have diminished the value of their research and writing by forgetting about clinical relevance. In April 1985, Goldsmith organized a roundtable on temperament theories at a meeting of the Society for Research in Child Development. Four points of view were represented: those of Thomas and Chess; Buss and Plomin; Rothbart; and Goldsmith. In the published version of this excellent exchange of ideas (Goldsmith *et al.*, 1987) comments were offered by two non-participating observers. One of them, McCall (a well-informed developmental psychologist but not a temperament researcher himself), concluded that the evidence supported four temperament characteristics: activity, reactivity, emotionality and sociability. He gave no reason for omitting the separate dimensions of adaptability and rhythmicity/predictability. Yet, none of the nine Thomas and Chess dimensions is more important clinically than adaptability. It repeatedly emerges as one of the traits making the greatest difference in social adjustment (Carey, 1985). The Pavlovian typology also includes an equivalent of it under the term 'mobility of the nervous system', and it has been shown to be related to anxiety and neuroticism (Strelau, 1983). However, some theories do not include a characteristic of adaptability, flexibility, malleability or manageability. My point here is that rational speculation is not enough to decide which characteristics to include in a theory and in measurements of temperament. One must be guided by observations of real children and by a concern for what is clinically relevant, not by data reduction, majority rule or devotion to an authority.

Practicality of Measurement Techniques

My other major point as a clinician advising research scientists about the design and evaluation of temperament questionnaires would be that these scales must be practical. To be sure, any instrument we use must be reliable and valid and must have a sufficient number of items appropriately worded and randomly arranged. Yet, such a technique must also be sufficiently brief and simple to be clinically useful.

Let me illustrate this point with the stories of two measures of the neurophysiological status of newborn infants: the Apgar test (Apgar, 1953) and the Brazelton Newborn Behavior Assessment Scale (NBAS; Brazelton, 1973). The Apgar score evaluates the newborn as to five criteria (color, heart rate, irritability, respiratory effort and muscle tone), each with a 0–2 rating and a total score of 0–10. The infant's status can be evaluated and recorded within a minute. Values under 7 at 5 minutes have considerable power of prediction of problems with the central nervous system. Virtually all newborn infants are now routinely rated by these criteria, at least in the USA. The NBAS, on the other hand, appraises the infant according to 27 neurobehavioral tests. The results do have some predictive power for the newborn period but the test takes at least 20 minutes to perform correctly, about twice the length of time for a complete routine newborn physical examination. The NBAS is frequently used by researchers but virtually not at all by clinicians. Unfortunately it is too long to be practical.

However, the requirement for simplicity does not give license for oversimplification. Examples of this are: (a) design of a scale that is too simple in the first place, such as the Conners (1969) scale; (b) making an abbreviation of an existing scale by an arbitrary discarding of many of the carefully selected items, as Milliones (1978) did; and (c) attempting to shorten an established scale by an inappropriate use of factor analysis. A recent example of this was the report (Sanson, Prior, Garino, Oberklaid & Sewell, 1987) of an effort to use an item factor analysis to abbreviate the Infant Temperament Questionnaire (ITQ). This process unfortunately deprived the scale of a third of its properly functioning items and totally removed three of its clinically relevant categories.

Thus, for a temperament scale to be useful to clinicians it must be brief and simple but not excessively so. Factor analysis can be a great help in finding out which characteristics cluster together, as several researchers have noted (for example, Keogh, 1986; Wilson & Matheny, 1986). I would like to suggest that any data reduction accomplished by means of factor analysis should be automatically distrusted until the findings are shown to be clinically plausible or can be otherwise empirically verified.

Other Concerns in Clinical Measurement

Besides the two important principles of clinical relevance of theories and practicality of techniques, there are several additional points that should be stressed by a pediatric practitioner trying to help academic researchers achieve maximum practical value from their efforts.

(1) The necessity for clinicians of relying heavily on parental reports of children's behavior. The physician learns in his training that up to 80–90% of the diagnostic process depends on the history, the report of the patient or the parents of the child about what has been happening. Of course, one does not have to believe everything one is told but it is quite impossible to function as a physician only on the basis of what one observes directly. Results of the history, the physical examination and indicated laboratory tests are fused into a diagnostic impression, which is the basis for management. Even in this age of high technology the history remains the basis of the diagnosis. By contrast, psychology gained respectability as it split off from philosophy

about a hundred years ago by making observations in laboratories. Much progress has been achieved through this form of scientific experimentation. Nevertheless, it is a very different approach from that needed by clinicians.

(2) In view of clinicians' reliance on parental reports, the need for academic researchers to provide clinicians with the best possible techniques to use. Parent-report questionnaires intended for clinical use should be designed for that purpose, standardized in that setting, and their usefulness determined there. This has been one of the guiding principles in the design of our four scales (Carey, 1983a) but it has not been for most others.

(3) The primary need now for more sophisticated testing of the existing scales, especially as to validity, and the design of improvements where needed. Our four questionnaires have all achieved reasonable degrees of proficiency in retest and internal consistency reliabilities, total figures all being in the 0.85 range (Carey, 1983a). Validity has been very hard to test because there exists no comprehensive, standardized observation technique against which to check the maternal reports. Almost all the studies using brief observations (3 hours or less) have demonstrated a moderate degree of validity (Carey, 1982b).

Three frequently cited studies claim to show that maternal reports of infant temperament resemble the mothers' prenatal attitudes more closely than they do the actual temperament of the infant. In fact, they do no such thing (Carey, 1983b; Carey & McDevitt, 1985). The relationships between prenatal attitudes and postnatal infant behavior were few, weak and inconsistent. The infant behaviors very briefly observed were not the same ones mothers reported in the ITQ. In other words, the mothers were asked to count apples, the outside observers counted oranges, and the inevitable disagreement was interpreted as a failure of the scale or the mothers. Subjective factors do enter into all observations of behavior but probably not to the extreme degree claimed by these reports.

(4) The need for a greater appreciation of the difference between specific ratings and general impressions of temperament. Some researchers in this field have had considerable problems with the basic terminology. According to the Thomas and Chess (1977) view, the child's temperament is the largely innate behavioral style characteristics of the child. Various caretakers and professional observers may witness different samples of behavior in the child and report them with dissimilar emphases. The child's temperament may be conceived of as an abstraction or summary of many examples of behavior in the mind of the observer, but the behavioral style itself is in the child. In our view, specific 'ratings' of temperament, whether by parents or professional persons, are descriptions of more or less what the child actually does, recorded in multiple scored judgments as to the frequency of various reactions in a wide range of situations (McDevitt & Carey, 1981). On the other hand, general 'perceptions' should indicate hastily or casually formed global impressions, whether by parents or professional persons, which may be valid but are more likely than specific ratings to be influenced by factors in the observer or the observer's situation. It is appropriate for temperament

questionnaires to seek both specific ratings and general perceptions but one must make clear which is which and try not to blend the two (McDevitt & Carey, 1981).

The failure to keep these distinctions clear has led to a number of problems in the measurement of temperament and in reports in professional journals. (a) The mixture of specific ratings and general impressions in the same questionnaire leaves the user uncertain about the specific or general nature of the data produced. Similarly confusing is the effort to measure difficult temperament directly rather than first determining the temperament itself, and then finding out whether it is perceived as difficult in this particular setting. (b) Another problem has arisen when clinicians interested in intervention have offered elaborate advice to parents based only on the infant's temperament rating without any consideration for how the parents are perceiving or reacting to it (Cameron & Rice, 1986). (c) The most frequent problem, however, is the habit of some of referring to specific ratings as perceptions. If a parent rates a child in a way that makes him/her be scored as difficult but the parent does not regard the child as difficult, it is obviously absurd to say that the parent perceives the child as having difficult temperament. This is one of the most common errors by inexperienced researchers.

(5) Better identification of distortions in parental reporting and finding ways to minimize them in specific ratings and understand them in general perceptions. Any human observations of events, whether in the natural, biological or behavioral spheres, will contain errors. If physicists can make misjudgments of natural phenomena, it should not alarm us that mothers may make mistakes in reporting their children's behavior. We need to know what kind of mothers make what kind of errors under which circumstances. Studies so far have not been very helpful.

(6) The questionable validity of brief professional observations. As a medical clinician, I should like to challenge the common assumption by behavioral scientists that, just because the behavior is observed by a trained person, it is automatically valid. Physicians know that childrens' behavior in their offices can be very unrepresentative. One nursing researcher found that her conclusions about an infant's temperament did not agree well with the mother's report until she (the researcher) had been watching the infant for at least 15 hours (G. Millor, personal communication, March 1984) and yet some researchers consider sufficient their observations of temperament for only minutes. Brief observations of behavior have not been compared with longer ones to see whether the shorter ones are truly representative. Furthermore, inter-rater reliability is no substitute for validity.

(7) The need for a comprehensive, standardized professional observation technique. With the possible exception of the modification of Bayley's Infant Behavior Record by Wilson and Matheny (1986), there is no comprehensive, standardized observation technique. There is no adequate way to validate brief professional observations or maternal reports. It will be a major challenge to develop such a technique. Many hours of detailed observations

by trained persons will be necessary to come anywhere near to the vast experience the mother has had with the child. For example, verification of her reports on regularity of waking or rejection of new foods will require observations of several examples of these specific behaviors.

Until such a standard of measurement has been evolved and used, criticisms of the validity of parental reports should be more restrained.

EXTENSIVE CLINICAL INTERACTIONS OF TEMPERAMENT

The range of clinical interactions of temperament is far greater than is generally recognized in most reviews of the subject. If clinical interactions are discussed at all in the current psychological literature, they are limited to the impact of the child's temperament on ordinary parent–child interactions or in the production of behavior problems. However, recent clinical reviews (Carey, 1981, 1985, 1986a) recognize that temperament should be studied both as an outcome of various clinical conditions and as a factor predisposing to them.

Temperament as an Outcome of Clinical Conditions

Referring the reader for a fuller treatment of the subject to the clinical reviews mentioned above, I shall just make a few summary statements here. As research in the field has progressed over the last two decades, it has become clear that the traditional model of genetic processes interacting with the psychosocial environment is an oversimplification. The model must be expanded to include as participants in the interaction the child's general physical, neurological and developmental status and the non-human environment.

Two levels of clinical conditions potentially influence the child's temperament. The first is biological insults or 'risk factors', such as prematurity or toxemia, in which organic pathology may or may not be documented in the child. The other is established organic diseases such as malnutrition or cerebral palsy. The specific examples of these two categories include:

(1) prenatal conditions – genetic, chromosomal and other congenital anomalies;
(2) pregnancy and perinatal stresses – both obstetrical and medical complications;
(3) postnatal insults to the central nervous system such as malnutrition and toxins;
(4) handicapping conditions of the central nervous system such as cerebral palsy and information-processing deficits;
(5) general medical illness such as anemia and hypothyroidism.

Conclusions about clinical conditions affecting temperament must be tentative at present because of the paucity of the data. However, the most convincing evidence to date seems to indicate that chronic conditions affecting the nervous system such as malnutrition or toxins are more likely to affect temperament than the more transient ones such as abnormal delivery or head trauma. An example is the possible effect of chronic lead intoxication in decreasing the child's attention.

Temperament as a Factor Predisposing to Clinical Conditions

The original interest of the New York Longitudinal Study of Thomas *et al.* (1968) was with behavior problems, but the field has moved considerably beyond that relatively narrow focus. A possible or probable relationship with temperament has been demonstrated with all major areas of children: their physical health, development and behavior. Just as physicians were the leaders in pointing out the importance of temperament to the behavior sciences, so also should it be our role to enlarge the awareness of academic researchers as to the full extent of clinical interactions.

In the area of physical health certain temperament characteristics have been found or suspected to predispose to: (a) organic problems such as accidents and child abuse, (b) functional disorders such as colic, functional abdominal pain, sleep problems and enuresis, and (c) disorders of nutrition and growth – as in failure to thrive, obesity, and death in famine conditions. The confusing relationship between temperament and the putative neurological syndrome of 'attention-deficit disorder' will be discussed later in the chapter. The child's temperament appears to influence the developmental rate through differences in selection and utilization of various elements in the environment. The work of Thomas *et al.* (1968) and about ten other studies leaves no doubt that certain temperament characteristics such as the difficult child syndrome predispose children to problems in behavioral adjustment. Finally, children's academic and social performance at school has been shown in several reports to be related to such characteristics as adaptability and persistence/attention span (see especially Keogh, 1986).

Even this deliberately superficial review of clinical interaction of temperament should challenge the researcher looking for fascinating and valuable areas to investigate.

CLINICAL USE OF TEMPERAMENT IN PEDIATRIC CARE

Let us turn now from considerations of measurement problems and the extent of clinical interactions to a discussion of the actual use of temperament data in clinical practice. First, we review the three general levels on which temperament data can aid the clinician in fostering parent–child relationships. Then we shall examine the specific diagnostic situations in which these data are most useful, in particular with the difficult child.

In a paper published elsewhere (Carey, 1982a) I have described in some detail the three major ways in which temperament data are useful to the clinician, especially the practising pediatrician. The most superficial level of involvement is *general educational discussions* between the clinician and the parent. In this process the concept of normal individual differences is presented in general terms or in relation to instructions about feeding, sleeping, crying or other normal child-care situations. In this way parents should develop a greater awareness and understanding of normal individual differences in behavior. Parents can then appreciate that some behavioral predispositions are present at birth, are not their fault, and may change with time. Nevertheless, general discussions may not be enough to meet the parents' needs.

The second level is the *identification of the particular child's temperament profile*, which provides parents with a more organized picture of the child's behavioral style and of possible distortions in their perceptions of it. This is primarily useful to the clinician when the child is rather difficult, has one of the other temperament risk factors, or when the mother's general perceptions of the child are quite different from her own specific ratings. This clarification process may provide the parents with enough insight for them to make their own healthy shifts in interactions with the child.

Third, the clinician may attempt to *influence the temperament–environment interaction* when a 'poor fit' and resulting stress are leading to reactive symptoms, by suggesting alternative methods of parental management. With successful handling the stress of the interaction should diminish and the reactive symptoms disappear. Meanwhile the parents and teachers must learn to live in a more tolerant and flexible manner with the child's relatively less changeable temperament.

Where is the exact point in the developmental–behavioral diagnostic process at which a knowledge of the child's temperament makes a contribution? A recent paper (Carey, in press) describes in some detail a pediatric algorithm for handling parental concern about children's behavior (see Figure 1). A summary of that procedure is presented here.

Assuming that the parents have expressed concern, asked for help, and agreed to work on the problem, the first diagnostic decision is whether there is a behavior problem present (physical and developmental problems are considered simultaneously). If, using the suggested criteria, the clinician determines that there is a behavior problem present, the severity is estimated. In serious ones, such as major depression or antisocial behavior, temperament probably plays little or no role in causation or in diagnosis. In moderate behavior problems, when symptoms are significant but not severe, temperament data may clarify the diagnosis and affect management. An example is the situation of the difficult child with an inflexible teacher. The friction between the two and the resulting behavior problem would not have happened with an easier child or a more patient, resourceful teacher. Knowing the reaction pattern of the child, helps to explain why the behavior problem arose and sets limits on how much of the behavior will change with more skilful management. The reactive problem will lessen and probably disappear with the right shifts of the environment but the temperament pattern will continue.

If the clinician has determined that the criteria for a behavior problem do not exist (or it is only a minor one such as nail-biting or bed-wetting) but the parents are still concerned, then two possible explanations remain. On the one hand, there may be stress from a temperament–environment interaction such as when the parents are coping with a difficult child but there is no secondary behavior problem. On the other hand, there may be a parental misperception of the child's behavior. If there is no behavior problem and no temperament risk factor, the parental concern may have been aroused because of their own problems. It may be

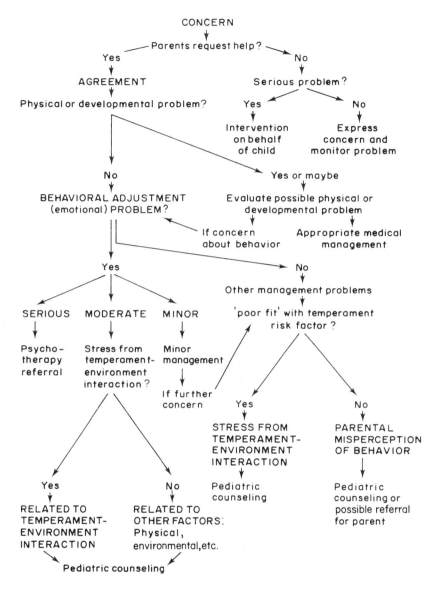

FIGURE 1   Pediatric algorithm for behavior management problems

simply parental misinformation or inexperience, or it may be more complicated issues such as parental depression, hostility or marital discord. For example, the parent undergoing marital break-up may project some of her discontent onto the child.

Thus, there are two common specific uses of temperament data in the diagnostic process. If a behavior adjustment problem exists, these data may clarify the diagnosis and affect the management. If there is parental concern but no behavioral adjustment problem, the child's temperament may be the source of the concern.

The *management of the difficult child* has been described in three separate publications (Carey, 1986b; Chess & Thomas, 1986; Turecki & Tonner, 1985) within the last few years. Although the recommendations were arrived at independently in different clinical settings, they are quite similar. All three describe the steps of:

(1) recognizing the problem of difficult temperament by the clinician;
(2) revision of parental understanding and management;
(3) other techniques to provide relief for the parents.

The pediatric plan (Carey, 1986b) further subdivides the second step of revision of parental management into: (a) general counseling of the parents for information, perspective and confidence, (b) specific counseling of them as to coping techniques for concerned but detached handling, and (c) direct counseling of the older child. The pediatric plan adds a fourth step of referral to a mental health specialist but only for severe reactive problems, not for the temperament itself.

MODIFYING THE CONCEPTS OF THE 'DIFFICULT CHILD' AND 'GOODNESS OF FIT' TO MEET CLINICAL NEEDS

The concepts of the 'difficult child' and 'goodness of fit' were both introduced by Thomas and Chess (1977; Thomas *et al.*, 1968). They are major contributions and indispensable to the clinical use of the concept of temperament. However, as the years have passed and more experience has accumulated, it has become evident that they need to be modified in order to maximize their practical utility.

The Difficult Child

In their New York Longitudinal Study Thomas *et al.* (1968) found that a set of five temperament characteristics predisposed children to reactive behavior problems. These were: low rhythmicity, low approach, low adaptability, high intensity and negative mood. This useful clinical concept was readily accepted by many child-care professional persons but was rapidly generalized by different investigators far beyond the original scope to other ages, settings and outcomes. Consequently various problems have arisen in both practical and clinical areas. Further evidence has shown that the stress-producing characteristics vary somewhat in different age groups, that the same characteristics may be involved in rather different interactions in other cultures or subcultures, and that other characteristics may be more important for other unfavorable outcomes.

A solution suggested to resolve these problems is the restriction of 'difficult temperament' to its original usage (characteristics, age, setting and outcome) and the introduction of a more general term that will cover any temperament characteristics likely to be troublesome in certain settings (Carey, 1986b). 'Temperament risk factors' for poor fit are defined as any temperament characteristics predisposing a child to a poor fit (incompatible relationship) with his or her environment, to excessive interactional stress and conflict with the caretakers, and to secondary clinical problems in the child's physical health, development or behavior. These risk factors are usually perceived and experienced by caretakers as hard to manage, but may not be. The outcome depends on the strength and durability of the characteristics and on the environmental stresses and supports.

Thus, the difficult and slow-to-warm-up child would have temperament risk factors for reactive behavior problems in populations such as those studied by Thomas and Chess. A low sensory threshold may be a temperament risk factor for 'colic' or night waking in an infant in an excessively stimulating environment. 'Low task orientation' (low persistence/attention span, high distractibility and high activity) places most urban elementary schoolchildren at risk for problems in school performance.

This sharpening of terminology should clarify further explorations of clinical interactions of temperament.

Goodness of Fit

According to the originators of this valuable concept,

> goodness of fit results when the properties of the environment and its expectations and demands are in accord with the organism's own capacities, motivations and style of behavior ... Conversely, poorness of fit involves discrepancies and dissonances between environmental opportunities and demands and the capacities and characteristics of the organism so that distorted development and maladaptive function occur. (Chess & Thomas, 1983)

This point of view implies that if the environment is sufficiently responsive to the child's needs, he or she will do well. There seems to be an assumption that almost any temperament characteristics can be accommodated successfully by some reasonably available environmental alterations.

There are two principal problems in applying this theory in clinical practice. One is that some temperament risk factors may be so strong, pervasive and durable that most caretakers may be overwhelmed in their efforts to manage them. For example, some children may be so difficult or so active as to overtax the normal adaptive capacities of the available environmental resources. The other problem is that many persons in the environment have limited willingness or ability to adapt to the characteristics of the child. For example, the average elementary school teacher probably has only a moderate tolerance and flexibility in dealing with an in-attentive or active child. In these situations the concept of goodness of fit may have diminished value. The temperament characteristics themselves may thus become the clinical problem rather than by generating a secondary condition through the interaction.

This argument should not be misconstrued as support for the popular concept of 'attention deficit disorder'. This presumed syndrome of behaviors, assumed by some to be due to brain malfunction, is believed to be directly responsible for much of the problems in learning and behavior in American elementary schools. However, the behaviors have not been demonstrated to constitute a syndrome, have not been differentiated from normal temperament variations, and have various origins and outcomes depending on the circumstances (Carey, 1986c).

The goodness of fit model remains extremely valuable and should be retained. The important point to remember is that some temperament risk factors are so strong and durable that they can be well handled only by a very narrow range of environmental settings. No caretaker or other individual in the environment has unlimited capacities to adapt to the needs of the child. It appears, therefore, that in some situations a poor fit is almost inevitable.

WHERE DO WE GO FROM HERE?

The best way to assess the current status of temperament risk factors and their clinical utility is to ask three questions:

(1) What do we know that is useful?
(2) How is that being used or how could it be used clinically?
(3) What further do we need to know?

These questions were deliberated at a recent international conference by a small group of clinical researchers and a report of their conclusions has been published (Carey & McDevitt, 1989).

What do we know that has been shown to be useful? Children's temperament risk factors have a considerable effect on their relationships with people, especially with caretakers. They also affect the child's performance of tasks such as school work and relations with the non-human environment. They have a significant impact on the caretakers themselves, affecting their self-esteem, mood, etc. A 'poor fit' can lead to excessive stress in the relationship and to a variety of secondary problems in the child's physical health, development and behavior. Various clinical conditions, such as malnutrition and toxins, may affect the child's temperament.

What has been done or should be done with these findings? The general concept of temperament risk factors is helpful to medical clinicians and parents but routine specific determinations are of uncertain value in pediatric well-child care. The use of the concept is definitely helpful in parent education, in stressful parent–child relations, and in behavioral interventions encountered in pediatric or mental health settings. Routine screening for temperament risk factors in educational settings or psychological evaluation has been attempted very little, if at all, despite their potential value. However, routine temperament screening in schools cannot be recommended at this time. Determinations of temperament risk factors have been helpful in evaluating school performance problems but have not been widely used yet.

What steps for the future to enhance knowledge and practice? Better testing, especially as to validity, is needed for existing questionnaires and improvements must be made where indicated. A comprehensive, standardized observation technique for temperament determinations would facilitate the validation of parental reports and of brief observations by clinicians and researchers but would be hard to achieve. Certainly indicated are further investigations of the value of temperament determinations in screening, diagnosis and management of problems in medicine, psychology and education. The education of the health service and education professions should incorporate to a greater extent these useful concepts and practices. Miscellaneous other issues deserving investigation include: a further clarification of the dynamics of 'poor fit', a resolution of the overlap of temperament and 'attention deficit disorder', and such questions as whether temperament can be changed.

SUMMARY

Temperament is a significant clinical reality. A unique relationship exists between clinicians and temperament research. Clinical measurements of temperament have special requirements. Temperament interacts extensively with clinical conditions. Temperament data are useful clinically in educational discussions, individual counseling and behavioral interventions. Suggestions are made for clarifying concepts and increasing the practical value of research.

NOTE

[1]Address for correspondence: 319 West Front Street Media, PA 19063-2399, USA.

REFERENCES

Apgar, V. (1953). A proposal for a new method of evaluation of the newborn infant. *Anesthesia and Analgesia,* **32,** 260.

Brazelton, T.B. (1973). *Neonatal Behavioral Assessment Scale.* Philadelphia: J.B. Lippincott.

Cameron, J.R. & Rice, D.C. (1986). Developing anticipatory guidance programs based on early assessment of infant temperament: Two tests of a prevention model. *Journal of Pediatric Psychology,* **11,** 221–234.

Carey, W.B. (1981). The importance of temperament–environment interaction for child health and development. In M. Lewis & L. Rosenblum (Eds), *The uncommon child.* New York: Plenum.

Carey, W.B. (1982a). Clinical use of temperament data in pediatrics. In R. Porter & G. Collins (Eds), *Temperamental differences in infants and young children.* London: Pitman.

Carey, W.B. (1982b). Validity of parental assessments of development and behavior. *American Journal of the Diseases of Children,* **136,** 97–99.

Carey, W.B. (1983a). Clinical assessment of behavioral style or temperament. In M.D. Levine, W.B. Carey, A.C. Crocker & R.T. Gross (Eds), *Developmental–behavioral pediatrics* (pp. 922–926). Philadelphia: W.B. Saunders.

Carey, W.B. (1983b). Some pitfalls in infant temperament research. *Infant Behavior and Development,* **6,** 247–254.

Carey, W.B. (1985). Interactions of temperament and clinical conditions. In M. Wolraich & D. Routh (Eds), *Advances in developmental and behavioral pediatrics,* Vol. 6 (pp. 83–115). Greenwich, CT: JAI Press.

Carey, W.B. (1986a). Clinical interactions of temperament: Transitions from infancy to childhood. In R. Plomin & J. Dunn (Eds), *The study of temperament: Changes, continuities and challenges* (pp. 151–162). Hillsdale, NJ: Erlbaum.

Carey, W.B. (1986b). The difficult child. *Pediatrics in Review,* **8,** 39–45.

Carey, W.B. (1986c). Practitioner commentary. In E.K. Sleator & W.E. Pelham, Jr (Eds), *Attention deficit disorder* (pp. 191–200). E. Norwalk, CT: Appleton-Century-Crofts.

Carey, W.B. (1987). Temperament diagnosis in pediatrics. Paper presented at Workshop on the Diagnosis of Temperament, University of Bielefeld, West Germany, September 1987.

Carey, W.B. (in press). Temperament and its role in developmental-behavioral diagnosis. In M. Gottlieb & J. Williams (Eds) *Developmental-behavioral disorders* Vol. 2 (pp. 49–65). New York: Plenum.

Carey, W.B. & McDevitt, S.C. (1985). Letter to the Editor about Zeanah *et al.*: Prenatal perception of infant personality: A preliminary investigation. *Journal of the American Academy of Child Psychiatry,* **24**, 502–503.

Carey, W.B. & McDevitt, S.C. (Eds) (1989) *Clinical and educational applications of temperament research.* Amsterdam: Swets & Zeitlinger; Berwyn, PA: Swets North America.

Chess, S. & Thomas, A. (1983). Dynamics of individual behavioral development. In M.D. Levine, W.B. Carey, A.C. Crocker & R.T. Gross (Eds), *Developmental–behavioral pediatrics* (pp. 158–175). Philadelphia: W.B. Saunders.

Chess, S. & Thomas, A. (1986). *Temperament in clinical practice.* New York: Guilford Press.

Conners, C. (1969). A teacher rating scale for use in drug studies with children. *American Journal of Psychiatry,* **126**, 884–888.

Daniels, D., Plomin, R. & Greenhalgh, J. (1983). Correlates of difficult temperament in infancy. *Child Development,* **55**, 1184–1194.

Goldsmith, H.H., Buss, A.H., Plomin, R., Rothbart, M.K., Thomas, A., Chess, S., Hinde, R.A. & McCall, R.B. (1987). Roundtable: What is temperament? Four approaches. *Child Development,* **58**, 505–529.

Keogh, B.K. (1986). Temperament and schooling: Meaning of 'goodness of fit'? In J.V. Lerner & R.M. Lerner (Eds), *Temperament and social interaction in infants and children* (pp. 89–108). San Francisco, CA: Jossey-Bass.

McDevitt, S.C. & Carey, W.B. (1981). Stability of ratings vs. perceptions of temperament from early infancy to 1–3 years. *American Journal of Orthopsychiatry,* **51**, 342–345.

Milliones, J. (1978). Relationship between perceived child temperament and maternal behaviors. *Child Development,* **49**, 1255–1257.

Plomin, R. (1982). Childhood temperament. In B. Lahey & A. Kazdin (Eds), *Advances in clinical child psychology* (pp. 1–80). New York: Plenum.

Rutter, M. (1982). Chairman's closing remarks. In R. Porter & G. Collins (Eds), *Temperamental differences in infants and young children* (pp. 294–297). London: Pitman.

Sanson, A., Prior, M., Garino, E., Oberklaid, F. & Sewell, J. (1987). The structure of infant temperament: Factor analysis of the Revised Infant Temperament Questionnaire. *Infant Behavior and Development,* **10**, 97–104.

Strelau, J. (1983). *Temperament, personality, activity.* New York: Academic Press.

Thomas, A. & Chess, S. (1977). *Temperament and development.* New York: Brunner/Mazel.

Thomas, A., Chess, S. & Birch, H.G. (1968). *Temperament and behavior disorders in children.* New York: New York University Press.

Turecki, S. & Tonner, L. (1985). *The difficult child.* New York: Bantam Books.

Wilson, R.S. & Matheny, A.P. Jr (1986). Behavior genetics research in infant temperament: The Louisville Twin Study. In R. Plomin & J. Dunn (Eds), *The study of temperament: Changes, continuities and challenges.* Hillsdale, NJ: Erlbaum.

22

Should Adverse Temperament Matter to the Clinician? An Empirically Based Answer

MICHEL MAZIADE
Centre de Recherche Laval Robert-Giffard, Hôtel-Dieu du Sacré-Coeur, Québec

Scientific work on child temperament constitutes a unique field that allows creative encounters among developmentalists, psychophysiologists, clinical researchers and epidemiologists. But in spite of much excellent research, clinicians are still waiting for many crucial practical answers about temperament.

Researchers, especially in child psychiatry and psychology, have addressed many questions about child temperament during the past years. Hundreds of scientific reports on temperament have been published. We know more than we did 10 or 15 years ago about basic issues like different ways of conceptualizing temperament and the mutual relationships between these temperament models; the genetic influence on temperament; the patterns of change and continuity in temperament over the years; and the relationship of temperament with developmental characteristics in infants and young children. Considering the number of papers published, much less research has focused on the clinical significance of child temperament when a clinician is faced with seriously deviant children or families in need of practical counseling. Hence large numbers of practitioners still wonder about the real importance of temperament, probably because they have not succeeded in drawing from the current literature clear sets of tools that can be used for assessment and treatment of specific clinical syndromes.

The pioneering work of Thomas and Chess (1977), which inspired a worldwide interest in temperament research, was originally designed to attain better understanding of the development of behavior disorders in children (Thomas, Chess & Birch, 1968). By the meticulous observation of children in their longitudinal cohort, these authors derived inductively a number of temperament traits which they originally defined as the 'how of behavior', or the 'behavioral style'. On the basis of their research, Chess and Thomas (1984, 1986) suggested some practical interven-

Temperament in Childhood   Edited by G.A. Kohnstamm, J.E. Bates and M.K. Rothbart
© 1989 John Wiley & Sons Ltd

tions. Carey (1985) has also drawn attention to many clinical implications of child temperament. Most clinical recommendations are still based on inductive discoveries.

Clinical researchers must now proceed more deductively in investigating the types of association between temperamental features, family attitudes and disorders in children. One important issue for clinicians is at what time in life the child's temperament and the family interactions have stabilized enough to have meaningful significance for prediction of later adjustment. Another question is which particular aspects of family functioning enter into noxious interactions with particular temperamental attributes in the child. And finally, how can we assess temperament as a parameter separate from other clinical variables like behavior deviancies listed in standard nosologies, or family dysfunctions or cognitive abnormalities? These questions and many others call for more clinical and fundamental research on temperament.

Epidemiologists and clinical researchers are interested in temperament as a potential risk and a clinical parameter. We looked at temperamentally extreme infants and older children in the hope that this could bring out meaningful relationships which could be used more rapidly in clinical and in preventive settings. It is now more accepted that the study of extremes can also offer a vision complementary to that coming from the existing studies of subjects distributed along the whole continuum (Kagan, Reznick & Snidman, 1987). The current chapter, using our own clinical data on temperament as well as those of others, will try to separate what is known empirically from what is not known of temperament applications: which clinical inferences have definite empirical basis and which are still hypothetical?

Clinicians are used to approaching problems or situations in a very pragmatic way. Their first question usually is: does temperament exist in the first place? Researchers can tackle this question only indirectly and they (Maziade, Boutin, Côté & Thivierge, 1986a; Rutter, 1987; and see Chapter 1, by Bates) recently made the point clearly that, from a scientific point of view, the temperament models we use are an abstraction. There are various models of this hypothetical construct (Goldsmith *et al.*, 1987). Each model, according to its empirical qualities, will probably prove useful in different practical situations. By bringing together the findings from the different models of temperament, further changes in these models will be made possible, and so on.

VALIDITY OF THE TEMPERAMENT MEASURE

The first question to be considered here is how temperament is to be measured. Many clinicians are particularly interested in the 'easy–difficult' typology. A clustering of the New York Longitudinal Study (NYLS) traits of adaptability, reaction of approach or withdrawal from new stimuli, general quality of mood and intensity has now been replicated many times through second order factor analyses in culture- and age-different samples. This cluster, as the first factor coming out of principal component analysis (PCA), has been identified through parental questionnaires in many American samples (see Matheny, Wilson & Nuss, 1984) in addition to within the NYLS itself (Thomas *et al.*, 1968), in our French-speaking general population of Quebec at different age levels from infancy to 7 years (Maziade, Boudreault, Thivierge, Capéraà & Côté, 1984a; Maziade, Côté, Boudreault, Capéraà & Thivierge, 1984b), in Swedish samples (McNeil and Persson-Blennow, 1982) and even in a child psychiatric sample (Maziade, Caron, Côté, Boutin & Thivierge, in press). A consistent difference from the NYLS original cluster is that rhythmicity does not load strongly on the first factor in the studies. This temperamental cluster differentiates children in the general population and it has been shown to be independent of socioeconomic status in different random samples (Maziade *et al.*, 1986a) (but not in samples intentionally biased for other specific research purposes; Sameroff, Seifer & Elias, 1982). This cluster also shows at least as strong an association with objective laboratory measurements as with maternal or environmental characteristics (Matheny, Wilson & Thoben, 1987). Finally, it displays as a cluster a significant degree of continuity over the years but more so from 3 to 4 years on (Maziade, Côté, Thivierge, Boutin & Bernier, 1989b; McDevitt, 1986; Rutter, 1982), and also displays change under some environmental influences such as the family level of communication or stressful circumstances (Maziade *et al.*, 1989b). But all this will really influence clinicians' practice only insofar as it demonstrates strong relevance to the assessment and treatment of children's behavior deviancies.

ASSOCIATIONS WITH BEHAVIOR DISORDERS

Once empirical evidence exists that a temperamental typology such as the one derived from the NYLS model is replicable and has differentiating value in different Western cultures, being able to distinguish children who are less adaptable, prone to withdrawal from new situations, emotionally intense and having a negative mood from those presenting average or opposite qualities of these traits, four other questions immediately arise:

(1) Most importantly, do we have sufficient replicated evidence that this aggregate of temperament traits is associated with or predisposes to the appearance of clinical behavior disorders of noticeable severity?

(2) Furthermore, what is the difference between an extremely difficult temperament in a child and a clinical behavior disorder; do we have evidence that the two are not confounded?

(3) If it predisposes toward but is not confounded with a clinical behavior disorder, does a very adverse or difficult temperament predispose to a wide variety of disorders in children, or have we some evidence of a specificity in the relationship involved between difficult temperament and the clinical nosology?

(4) Finally, can we obtain clinically useful information about aspects of family functioning that contribute to a mismatch with very difficult temperament in children?

We will examine some of the existing empirical data that could provide tentative answers to these questions.

The clinicians' first question as to whether difficult temperament predisposes to disorders can certainly be answered affirmatively. We have ourselves reported (Figure 1) that 7-year-old children presenting an extremely difficult temperament according to NYLS Factor 1 (subjects placed in the 9–10 extreme centiles as selected from a large random sample (n = 980) of the general population; Maziade et al., 1984b) displayed at age 12 significantly more clinical disorders as assessed blindly by two independent psychiatrists (Maziade et al., 1985). This represents a consistent transcultural replication of the Chess and Thomas (1984) longitudinal findings. Before going further, we must explain that our studies adopted a definition of clinical disorders that resembles that of other epidemiologists (Richman, Stevenson & Graham, 1982; Rutter, 1970), i.e. moderate to severe behavior abnormalities that are sufficiently marked and prolonged to cause distress and disturbance in the child, the family or the community. The clinical judgment was made after a structured interview by a psychiatrist; the taped interview was rated independently by another psychiatrist who was also blind to the temperament scores. Other studies have used, as an outcome variable, the number of symptoms in the child (Bates, Maslin & Frankel, 1985; Wolkind & De Salis, 1982) instead of a judgment on the presence or absence of clinical disorder; this methodological difference must be considered in comparing the results from studies.

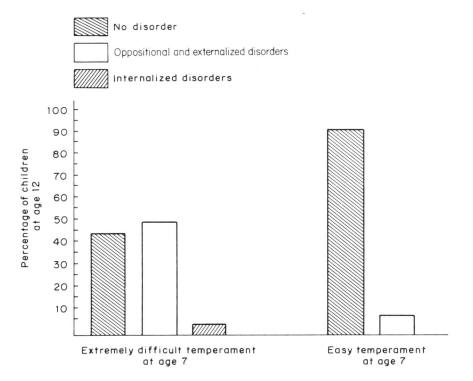

FIGURE 1   Proportions of clinical disorders and types of disorder at age 12 according to types of extreme temperament (Factor 1) at age 7 in the general population.

Other epidemiological studies, using different samplings, have also found an association between adverse traits of temperament and the appearance of behavior disorders (Earls & Jung, 1987; Graham, Rutter & George, 1973) in early or middle childhood. Thus there is evidence that an association between difficult temperament (especially on a cluster resembling the NYLS difficult temperament) and clinical disorders exists from age 3 to 4 years on. However, the existence of such a relationship before age 3 is still controversial. For instance, when we selected infants from the general population as presenting extreme characteristics of difficult temperament on the NYLS model and reassessed them clinically at 4.7 years, we observed that temperament assessed in infancy, even extreme, was not by itself strongly associated with disorders in preschool years, that difficult temperament assessed at 4.5 years was significantly associated with disorders (Figure 2) and that extreme temperament presented a significant degree of continuity from infancy to 4 years especially in boys (Maziade, Côté, Thivierge, Boutin & Bernier, 1989a; Maziade *et al.*, 1988b). These findings are congruent with those of Thomas and Chess (1982) in that temperament assessed before 4 years in their longitudinal study was not predictive of long-term adjustment, whereas temperament assessed from 4 years on was.

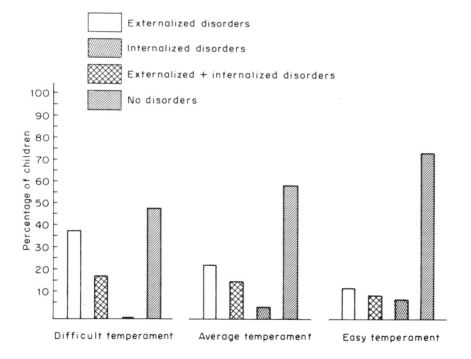

FIGURE 2 Proportions of disorders and distribution of types of disorder at age 4.5 years according to types of temperament at same age (Factor 1) in the general population. *Note*: One temperamentally average and one temperamentally easy child exhibited a moderate language delay associated with their externalized disorder and another temperamentally easy child presented a mild mental retardation.

Lee and Bates (1985) and Bates *et al.* (1985), using a different definition of difficult temperament (mainly composed of negative reactions like fussing and crying) in infants and toddlers, succeeded in detecting a statistically significant but slight correlation between difficult temperament in infancy and the number of symptoms, both externalized and internalized, at age 3–5 years. These researchers also observed an interesting specificity between the type of temperament and the type of symptoms predicted in preschool years: difficult temperament (fussing, crying) at 6 months and early management problems predicted externalized symptoms at age 3–5 years, whereas difficult temperament at 6 months and early fearfulness or unadaptability correlated with later internalizing symptoms.

As we have discussed elsewhere (Maziade *et al.*, 1989a), we are inclined to believe that the slight direct prediction coming from temperament, even extreme, in the first years of life does not necessarily mean that difficult temperament before age 4 years has little relevance to the development of serious clinical disorders. Our findings would be compatible with indirect relationships between temperament in infancy and later outcome. For instance, extreme temperament in infancy was found to be significantly associated with temperament at 4 years, which was itself associated with disorders (Maziade *et al.*, 1989a). Also there is a possibility of a temporary internal cancellation of risk and protective factors early in life in the temperamentally difficult children (Maziade *et al.*, 1989b). For instance, we have found that extremely difficult infants living with better educated parents, or with parents presenting higher abilities of communication, displayed a strikingly higher IQ in preschool years (Maziade, Côté, Boutin, Bernier & Thivierge, 1987b). Then a higher IQ (already known as a possible protective factor; Rutter, 1983) could to some extent cancel out the risk effect associated with difficult temperament in the years preceding school. Further research must address this issue. This absence of a strong association between temperament and disorders in the early years might also be due to:

(1) the inherent nosological difficulties in demarcating precursors of clinical disorders in preschool years;
(2) the radical developmental changes in children during this period which make it methodologically difficult to follow up age-appropriate correspondents of the same personality or environmental concepts from year to year;
(3) the probable instability of early reinforcements and feedbacks from the family toward a child with a difficult temperament, a fixed and mutually reinforcing dysfunctional child–family transactional pattern possibly becoming more apparent or measurable only later in childhood;
(4) methodological limitations in measuring the temperament construct and clinical disorders.

If difficult temperament predisposes to clinical disorders in childhood, we should see a disproportionate number of children displaying a difficult temperament in those referred to child psychiatry. This is exactly what we observed when we systematically assessed temperament in a consecutive sample of 814 children at the intake of the Hôtel-Dieu du Sacré-Coeur, the only child psychiatric center providing outpatient and inpatient services to the urban and suburban areas of Quebec City (around 800 000 population). With a variety of cutting points (based on the norms obtained in the general population) to define a difficult temperament, Maziade *et al.* (in press) found that there were 2.5 children with a difficult temperament in the clinical population for each one in the general population. For example, when 9% of the general population are called difficult with a specific cutting point, 24% of the referred children would be defined as difficult with the same cutting point. This overproportion was seen in boys and in girls. This 2.5 : 1 ratio clearly indicates that children referred to a child guidance clinic are more likely to present an extremely difficult temperament but also that not all clinical children present a difficult temperament, an important point that will be discussed later. Clearly, clinicians are likely to find themselves in the presence of problem children presenting an extremely difficult temperament relating in some degree to the NYLS definition.

Now the third question: is there enough evidence that an extremely difficult temperament cannot be confounded with a clinical disorder? Do the two not just overlap to such a large extent that an extremely difficult temperament amounts to the same thing as a clinical disorder? Data suggest that they do not. As Figures 1 and 2 show, extremely difficult temperaments in the general population are significantly but partially associated with disorders as judged blind by two independent child psychiatrists (Maziade *et al.*, 1985; 1989a). As we have reported for our longitudinal cohort from ages 7 to 12 (Maziade, Côté, Boudreault, Thivierge & Boutin, 1986b), and for that from infancy to 4.5 years (Maziade *et al.* 1989a), a large number of our subjects presenting even an extreme temperament that persisted over the years of the follow-ups did not develop a clinical disorder in the final analysis. Conversely, not all the children attending the clinic (only about one-fourth) presented an extremely difficult temperament. Obviously, no total overlapping between clinical disorders and difficult temperament exists, contrary to what has been advocated by some (Ferguson & Rapoport, 1983; Graham & Stevenson, 1987; Stevenson & Graham, 1982). Research is just beginning to un-cover aspects of the complicated relationship between these two entities. In our own effort better to understand this complex association, we, like other researchers, have focused on some necessarily restricted characteristics of family functioning that possibly interact with an extremely difficult temperament in children. But before going into the family–temperament interaction issue, we shall try to respond to the fourth question that is of interest to clinicians.

Does difficult temperament lead to a wide range of disorders in children or is there some kind of specificity in the relationship? Research has not as yet gone far toward answering the question, partly because of still existing imperfections in the measurements of temperament and in the child psychiatric and psychological nosology. Nevertheless, there are cues pointing to some kind of specificity. Children presenting an extremely difficult temperament in our longitudinal cohorts drawn from the general population (Maziade *et al.*, 1985; 1989a) were more prone, as shown in Figures 1 and 2, to develop externalized disorders in contrast for instance to internalized disorders or developmental delays. For instance, from age 7 to age 12, most children with an extremely difficult temperament developed moderate to severe oppositional disorders (see *Diagnostic and statistical manual of mental disorders*, 3rd edn, revised; American Psychiatric Association, 1987). Their resistance to demands and other externalized symptoms were prevalent at home.

We observed that the type of disorder found in these children was specific to the environment: while at age 12 there was a good concordance between the presence of disorder as diagnosed blind and independently by two psychiatrists and a deviant score on the Rutter behavior scale (Rutter, 1967) filled in by teachers, the teachers surprisingly reported a preponderance of internalized symptoms in school even though externalized symptoms were also present (Maziade *et al.*, 1985). Congruently, as shown in Figure 3, in a random sample of 7-year-olds in the general population, the children with an extremely difficult temperament on Factor 1 on the Thomas & Chess (1977) Parent Temperament Questionnaire (Maziade *et al.*, 1984b) displayed extremely internalized rather than externalized symptoms as described in school by the teacher on the Conners Teacher Questionnaire (CTQ) (Thivierge, Capéraà, Boudreault, Côté & Maziade, 1988). Also converging with the previous analysis at the extremes, we found in this sample a significant association between temperament Factor 1 and the second factor (internalized behaviors) of

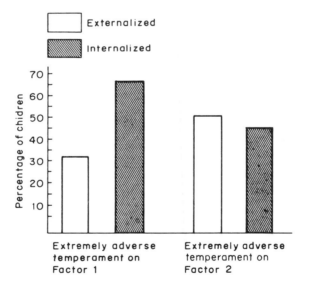

FIGURE 3   Proportions of externalized or internalized extreme behaviors in school according to extreme temperament at 7 years in the general population.
Externalized: Subjects above 80th centile on factor scores distribution on Factor 1 (principal component analysis; PCA) of Conners Teacher Questionnaire
Internalized: Subjects above 80th centile on factor scores distribution on Factor 2 (PCA) of Conners Teacher Questionnaire.
Extremely adverse on Factor 1: Subjects as defined below 20th centile on factor scores distribution on temperament Factor 1 (very low adaptability, withdrawal from new stimuli, negative mood, very intense, low distractibility).
Extremely adverse on Factor 2: Subjects as defined above 80th centile on factor scores distribution on temperament Factor 2 (high activity level, low persistence, high threshold).

the CTQ (Analysis of Variance: $F = 3.98$, $P = .003$, $n = 715$) but no association between temperament Factor 1 and the Factor 1 on the CTQ (externalized behaviors). The CTQ second factor (PCA) contains items such as 'shy', 'fearful', 'appears to be easily led', 'isolates himself from other children', 'sad', while CTQ Factor 1 contains items such as 'quarrelsome', 'excitable', 'impulsive', 'fidgeting', 'disturbs other children', 'teases other children', 'defiant' (Thivierge *et al.*, 1988). This environment specificity of the symptomatology associated with a difficult temperament needs further study.

Moreover, at age 4 years, the extremely difficult children in the general population also presented externalized disorders rather than internalized ones or developmental delays (Figure 2) as measured by the standardized parent interview of Richman *et al.* (1982). We also had some preliminary evidence that extremely difficult infants later displayed more externalized symptoms in the presence of adversity, whereas the temperamentally easiest under stress developed more internalized behaviors (Maziade *et al.*, 1989a). Using a somewhat different definition of difficult temperament, the data of Lee and Bates (1985) also showed that difficult infants were prone to display externalized symptoms at age 2 years, especially problem behaviors in situations necessitating control by the mother.

Data coming from a consecutive sample of children referred to a regional child psychiatric center are congruent with this same trend toward specificity. With this large clinical sample ($n = 814$), we were in a favored position to evaluate a possible specificity between the type of extreme temperament and the type of clinical disorders in referred children. In our previous random samples of the general population, we had selected extreme subjects on Factor 1 (drawn from a PCA) to make two longitudinal cohorts. So when our results showed that extremes on Factor 1 predicted later externalized behavior disorders, we could not eliminate the possibility that it was just a general extremeness in temperament that predicted disorders instead of a specific extremeness on Factor 1. But we had also detected a second orthogonal factor at the PCA at age 7 years in the general population (Maziade *et al.*, 1984b) that was characterized mainly by the traits of sensory threshold, persistence and activity. Also, we had replicated through the same procedure a very similar second factor in the child psychiatric population (Maziade *et al.*, in press). Thus, we could see whether a specific extremeness on each of these temperamental factors would predict different disorders in children referred to a child psychiatric clinic. As shown in Figure 4, we observed that a statistically significant disproportion of externalized disorders was found in the temperamental extremes on the difficult pole of Factor 1 in the clinical population, and a disproportion of developmental delays in the extremes on the adverse pole of Factor 2 (very active, less persistent, high threshold) (Maziade *et al.*, in press). A similar proportion of combined disorders (externalized plus developmental delay) was found in both groups of temperament. In summary, the evidence accumulated so far indicates that extreme temperament on a profile composed of low adaptability, withdrawal from new stimuli, emotional intensity and negative mood is to a greater degree associated with externalized disorders, especially oppositional, at home, in the general population and in a child psychiatric population. However, symptoms seem specific to the environment, at least in middle childhood and in the general population; in school, children with an extremely difficult temperament display a preponderance of internalized over externalized symptoms.

Why do the extremely difficult children of our samples, in middle childhood, in dysfunctional families in terms of discipline develop externalized disorders at home, whereas they are clinically internalized in school? We could speculate that their extreme level of withdrawal and unadaptability are predominantly apparent in school where they must deal with new people and situations; at home, where they are in contact with familiar persons and circumstances, they react through externalized disorders when parental discipline is dysfunctional. In the latter situation, their high intensity and very negative mood would predispose them to defiance and opposition. This and the previously mentioned observation by Bates *et al.* (1985), that difficult temperament predicts externalized or internalized symptoms according to the presence of other associated features in the child or the mother, give encouragement that the future will bring the elucidation of the specific mechanisms in which difficult temperament is involved in the creation of clinical disorders.

Interplay Between Family Functioning and Extreme Temperament

The final question is whether there is evidence that particular aspects of family functioning negatively interact with difficult temperament so as to favor the

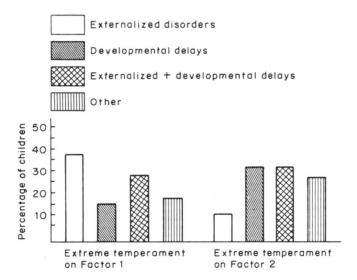

FIGURE 4   Distribution of types of disorders according to types of extreme temperament in a child psychiatric population aged 3–7 years.
   Extreme temperament on Factor 1: Withdrawal, low adaptability, high intensity, negative mood.
   Extreme temperament on Factor 2: High intensity, low persistence, high sensory threshold.

appearance of clinical disorders. Our own clinical experience at the Hôtel-Dieu du Sacré-Coeur over many years suggests that nearly one-half of the problems for which children are referred to a child psychiatric clinic involve externalized problem behaviors (overactivity, opposition or conduct problems), whether alone or in combination with other clinical problems. This was indirectly confirmed recently by our study of a consecutive large sample referred to a child psychiatric clinic (Maziade *et al.*, in press). We also had the clinical impression that a very large proportion of these referred externalized children lived in families showing dysfunctional discipline (in terms of lack of parental consensus about family rules, lack of rule clarity and inconsistency in rule enforcement), be this dysfunction primary or secondary to the clinical child's behaviors. The findings of Bank, Patterson & Reid (1987) seem to some extent compatible with this: most of their children showing aggressivity, conduct or delinquent problems lived in families lacking supervision. These reasons led us, in our epidemiological studies, to look at the way parents control their children's behavior, in addition to family level of communication and other well-replicated psychosocial risk factors such as marital discord, maternal depression, low socioeconomic status (SES), stressful events and so on.

Interestingly, we observed that dysfunctional parental behavior control, as assessed by the McMaster scale (Epstein, Bishop & Levin, 1978; Maziade, Bernier, Thivierge & Côté, 1987a), was associated both in preschool years and in middle childhood with externalized and oppositional disorders in the general population, even when the effects of the other risk factors that we assessed were taken into account (Maziade *et al.*, 1985; 1989a). Moreover, most of the children with an extremely difficult temperament (Factor 1) at age 7, who were living in a dysfunctional family in terms of behavior control, presented oppositional disorders at age 12. Conversely, almost none of the extremely difficult children living in a family with superior functioning in terms of behavior control developed disorders.

Thus, the data suggested that, across middle childhood, extremely difficult temperament on Factor 1 together with dysfunctional discipline was a better predictor than temperament alone. We will have to wait until our follow-up at age 16 years to look further at this temperament–family interplay. At age 4.5 years, in the general population, a difficult temperament (Factor 1) and dysfunctional discipline seem to have separate effects on disorders (Maziade *et al.*, 1989a): the data suggest, in preschool years, only an additivity of the risk associated with difficult temperament and that associated with dysfunctional discipline; we have in preschool years no evidence of a synergy as was observed from age 7 to 12.

On the basis of the data generated from our two longitudinal cohorts, we argued that a noxious and abrasive interaction between difficult temperament on Factor 1 and dysfunctional discipline in the family develops only progressively from early childhood so that it is only in middle childhood that synergy between the two factors can be observed. In other words, as we discussed more fully in a previous report (Maziade *et al.*, 1989a), even though young children with an extremely difficult temperament are predisposed to develop externalized and oppositional clinical behaviors, it is only slowly over the years, as the child acquires more autonomy and is confronted with more complex rules and demands, that his behavior comes to exceed the insufficient disciplinary abilities of some families. These hypotheses are to some degree supported by the findings of Lee and Bates (1985) that difficult temperament was already associated with slight problems at age 2 years in terms of control by the mother. We found that family communication, as opposed to problems in family behavior control, was not related to the appearance of disorders in difficult children in preschool years; rather, family communication seems to interact with extreme temperament to influence cognitive development: infant temperament and IQ at 4 years were associated only in families with superior level of communication and higher SES. Extremely difficult infants developed higher IQ in such families (Maziade *et al.*, 1987b). To summarize, the family attitudes of discipline (rule clarity, consistency in rules enforcement and parental consensus about rules) seem to be a family category that interplays with extremely difficult temperament (Factor 1) in children to create externalized and oppositional disorders in middle or late childhood. At the minimum this is a clear and promising issue for future clinical research.

To sum up, researchers have made modest but definite progress in responding to some of the clinicians' practical questions about difficult temperament. Other clinical questions urgently need answers. For instance, in the children referred to child psychiatry, what differences exist between those presenting an externalized disorder associated with an extremely difficult temperament versus those presenting an externalized disorder without such a temperament? Are these two clinical groups different in terms of the developmental history of the disorders (age of appearance, type of family dysfunction, causative chains of reactions, etc.) that led the child and family to the clinic? If dysfunctional family discipline is a real causal factor involved in the development of disorders in temperamentally difficult children, will these two clinical groups show up as different in terms of family functioning? Are these two groups different in terms of prognosis? Does the adjunction of a difficult temperament to the presence of an externalized disorder influence the course and the outcome of treatment? All these questions matter to the clinician and future clinical research will devote efforts in that direction. Such clinical research might also help in further distinguishing an extremely difficult temperament, which so far has been limited to phenomenological measurements, from a decompensated clinical disorder. This distinction might be clarified for instance by combining, in the same research design, the use of physiological parameters along with that of family, temperament and clinical parameters. In other words, studies should try to identify a physiological marker that would be associated with extreme temperament but not with the externalized (or internalized) disorders to which this temperament predisposes. Our group is just undertaking such an investigation and other researchers will certainly also take that direction. Recent research has succeeded in relating extreme temperamental reactions to physiological variables such as cardiac reactivity (Kagan, Reznick & Snidman, 1986), whereas other workers are beginning to relate child behaviors to biological markers (Tennes, Kreye, Avitable & Wells, 1986). Such future endeavors will help clinicians to make better diagnoses, sounder clinical assessments and hopefully provide more efficient treatment.

REFERENCES

American Psychiatric Association (1987). *Diagnostic and statistical manual of mental disorders*, 3rd edn, revised. Washington, DC: American Psychiatric Association.

Bank, L., Patterson, G.R. & Reid, J.B. (1987). Delinquency prevention through training parents in family management. *Behavior Analyst*, **10**, 75–82.

Bates, J.E., Maslin, C.A. & Frankel, K.A. (1985). Attachment security, mother–child interaction, and temperament as predictors of behavior-problem ratings at age three years. *Monographs of the Society for Research in Child Development*, **50** (1–2, Serial No. 209), 167–193.

Carey, W.B. (1985). Interactions of temperament and clinical conditions. *Advances in Developmental and Behavioral Pediatrics*, **6**, 83–115.

Chess, S. & Thomas, T. (1984). *Origins and evolution of behavior disorders from infancy to early adult life*. New York: Brunner/Mazel.

Chess, S. & Thomas, T. (1986). *Temperament in clinical practice*. New York: Guilford Press.

Earls, F. & Jung, K.G. (1987). Temperament and home environment characteristics as causal factors in the early development of child psychopathology. *Journal of the American Academy of Child and Adolescent Psychiatry*, **26**, 491–498.

Epstein, N.B., Bishop, D.S. & Levin, S. (1978). The McMaster model of family functioning. *Journal of Marriage and Family Counseling*, **4**, 19–31.

Ferguson, H.B. & Rapoport, J.L. (1983). Nosological issues and biological validation. In M. Rutter (Ed.), *Developmental neuropsychiatry* (pp. 369–384). New York: Guilford Press.

Goldsmith, H.H., Buss, A.H., Plomin, R., Rothbart, M.K., Thomas, A., Chess, S., Hinde, R.A. & McCall, R.B. (1987). Roundtable: What is temperament? Four approaches. *Child Development*, **58**, 505–529.

Graham, P., Rutter, M. & George, S. (1973). Temperamental characteristics as predictors of behavior disorders in children. *American Journal of Orthopsychiatry*, **43**, 328–339.

Graham, P. & Stevenson, J. (1987). Temperament and psychiatric disorder: The genetic contribution to behaviour in childhood. *Australian and New Zealand Journal of Psychiatry*, **21**, 267–274.

Kagan, J., Reznick, J.S. & Snidman, N. (1986). Temperamental inhibition in early childhood. In R. Plomin & J. Dunn (Eds), *The study of temperament: Changes, continuities and challenges* (pp. 53–65). Hillsdale, NJ: Erlbaum.

Kagan, J., Reznick, J.S. & Snidman, N. (1987). The physiology and psychology of behavioral inhibition in children. *Child Development*, **58**, 1459–1473.

Lee, C.L. & Bates, J.E. (1985). Mother–child interaction at age two years and perceived difficult temperament. *Child Development*, **56**, 1314–1325.

Matheny, A.P. Jr, Wilson, R.S. & Nuss, S.M. (1984). Toddler temperament: Stability across settings and over ages. *Child Development*, **55**, 1200–1211.

Matheny, A.P. Jr, Wilson, R.S. & Thoben, A.S. (1987). Home and mother: Relations with infant temperament. *Developmental Psychology*, **23**, 323–331.

Maziade, M., Bernier, H., Thivierge, J. & Côté, R. (1987a). The relationship between family functioning and demographic characteristics in an epidemiological study. *Canadian Journal of Psychiatry*, **32**, 526–533.

Maziade, M., Boudreault, M., Thivierge, J., Capéraà, P. & Côté, R. (1984a). Infant temperament: SES and gender differences and reliability of measurement in a large Quebec sample. *Merrill-Palmer Quarterly*, **30**, 213–216.

Maziade, M., Boutin, P., Côté, R. & Thivierge, J. (in press). Extreme temperament and diagnosis: Study in a consecutive child psychiatric sample. *Archive of General Psychiatry*.

Maziade, M., Capéraà, P., Laplante, B., Boudreault, M., Thivierge, J., Côté, R. & Boutin, P. (1985). Value of difficult temperament among 7-year-olds in the general population for predicting psychiatric diagnosis at age 12. *American Journal of Psychiatry*, **142**, 943–946.

Maziade, M., Caron, C., Côté, R., Boutin, P. & Thivierge, J. (in press). Extreme temperament and diagnosis: Study in a consecutive child psychiatric sample. *Archives of*

General Psychiatry.

Maziade, M., Côté, R., Boudreault, M., Capéraà, P. & Thivierge, J. (1984b). The NYLS model of temperament: Gender differences and demographic correlates in a French-speaking population. *Journal of the American Academy of Child Psychiatry,* **23**, 582–587.

Maziade, M., Côté, R., Boudreault, M., Thivierge, J. & Boutin, P. (1986b). Family correlates of temperament continuity and change across middle childhood. *American Journal of Orthopsychiatry,* **56**, 195–203.

Maziade, M., Côté, R., Boutin, P., Bernier, H. & Thivierge, J. (1987b). Temperament and intellectual development: A longitudinal study from infancy to four years. *American Journal of Psychiatry,* **144**, 144–150.

Maziade, M., Côté, R., Thivierge, J., Boutin, P. & Bernier, H. (1989a). Significance of extreme temperament in infancy for clinical status in preschool years. I: Value of extreme temperament at 4–8 months for predicting diagnosis at 4.7 years. *British Journal of Psychiatry,* **154**, 535–543.

Maziade, M., Côté, R., Thivierge, J., Boutin, P. & Bernier, H. (1989b). Significance of extreme temperament in infancy for clinical status in preschool years. II: Patterns of temperament change and implications for the appearance of disorders. *British Journal of Psychiatry,* **154**, 544–551.

McDevitt, S.C. (1986). Continuity and discontinuity of temperament in infancy and early childhood: A psychometric perspective. In R. Plomin & J. Dunn (Eds), *The study of temperament: Changes, continuities and challenges* (pp. 27–38). Hillsdale, NJ: Erlbaum.

McNeil, T.F. & Persson-Blennow, I. (1982). Temperament questionnaires in clinical research. In *Temperamental differences in infants and young children* (pp. 20–35). Ciba Foundation Symposium No. 89. London: Pitman.

Richman, N., Stevenson, J. & Graham, P.J. (1982). *Pre-school to school: A behavioral study.* New York: Academic Press.

Rutter, M. (1967). A children's behaviour questionnaire for completion by teachers: Preliminary findings. *Journal of Child Psychology and Psychiatry,* **8**, 1–11.

Rutter, M. (1970). Epidemiology of psychiatric disorder. In M. Rutter (Ed.), *Education, health and behavior.* London: Longman.

Rutter, M. (1982). Temperament: Concepts, issues and problems. In *Temperamental differences in infants and young children* (pp. 1–19). Ciba Foundation Symposium No. 89. London: Pitman.

Rutter, M. (1983). Stress, coping, and development: Some issues and some questions. In N. Garmezy & M. Rutter (Eds), *Stress, coping, and development in children* (pp. 1–41). New York: McGraw-Hill.

Rutter, M. (1987). Temperament, personality and personality disorder. *British Journal of Psychiatry,* **150**, 443–458.

Sameroff, A.J., Seifer, R. & Elias, P.K. (1982). Sociocultural variability in infant temperament ratings. *Child Development,* **53**, 164–173.

Stevenson, J. & Graham, P. (1982). Temperament: A consideration of concepts and methods. In *Temperamental differences in infants and young children* (pp. 36–50). Ciba Foundation Symposium No. 89. London: Pitman.

Tennes, K., Kreye, M., Avitable, N. & Wells, R. (1986). Behavioral correlates of excreted catecholamines and cortisol in second-grade children. *Journal of the American Academy of Child Psychiatry,* **25**, 764–770.

Thivierge, J., Capéraà, P., Boudreault, M., Côté, R. & Maziade, M. (1988). Reliability and principal component analysis (PCA) of the Conners Teacher Questionnaire (CTQ). In L. M. Bloomingdale (Ed.), *Attention deficit disorder,* Vol. 3. *New Research in Attention, Treatment, and Psychopharmacology* (pp. 161–173). New York: Pergamon.

Thomas, A. & Chess, S. (1977). *Temperament and development.* New York: Brunner/Mazel.

Thomas, A. & Chess, S. (1982). Temperament and follow-up to adulthood. In *Temperamental differences in infants and young children* (pp. 168–175). Ciba Foundation Symposium No. 89. London: Pitman.

Thomas, A., Chess, S. & Birch, H.G. (1968). *Temperament and behavior disorders in children*. New York: New York University Press.

Wolkind, S.N. & De Salis, W. (1982). Infant temperament, maternal mental state and child behavior problems. In *Temperamental differences in infants and young children* (pp. 221–239). Ciba Foundation Symposium No. 89. London: Pitman.

23

Applying Temperament Research to School

BARBARA K. KEOGH
University of California, Los Angeles

Adaptive or maladjustive outcomes are clearly not the products of single variables, but rather are consequences of the interplay of a range of individual and contextual influences. Bell's (1968) seminal paper on bidirectional, reciprocal effects in parent–child relationships, Sameroff and Chandler's (1975) analysis of the continuum of caregiving casualties, and R.M. Lerner's (1982) discussion of children as producers of their own environments are but three examples of a converging literature which argues for multivariate contributions to behavior and which challenges a static model of development. While adopting somewhat different perspectives, these authors have underscored the importance of both individual and contextual contributions to development and behavior, and have emphasized the interactive nature of relations between children and adults. Interest in temperament as an individual difference of importance in education is in part based on recognition of these interactional processes.

Other authors in this volume have addressed definitional and measurement aspects of temperament and have identified important conceptual and methodological issues. Despite continuing ambiguities and inconsistencies, there is considerable evidence to argue for the reality of temperamental differences and for an association between temperament and behavior and adjustment problems. Barron and Earls (1984), Bates, Maslin and Frankel (1985), Graham, Rutter and George (1973), Kolvin, Nichol, Garside, Day and Tweedle (1982), Mauer, Cadoret and Cain (1980), Maziade *et al.* (1985), Olweus (1980), Rutter, Birch, Thomas and Chess (1964), Scholom, Zucker and Stollak, (1979), Swets-Gronert (1985), Terestman (1980), Thomas and Chess (1977), Thomas, Chess and Birch (1968), and Wertleib, Weigel, Springer and Feldstein (1987), working with subjects in different countries, have all identified relationships between children's temperamental attributes and behavior problems. This work as a whole suggests that temperamental characteristics, particularly those making up the 'difficult child'

Temperament in Childhood   Edited by G.A. Kohnstamm, J.E. Bates and M.K. Rothbart
© 1989 John Wiley & Sons Ltd

constellation, may be predisposing for behavioral and psychiatric problems (see Rutter, 1977, for review).

The relationship between temperament and behavior problems has also been corroborated in studies of children identified as 'at risk' or handicapped (Keogh, Bernheimer, Pelland & Daley, 1989, in press; Marcovitch, Goldberg, MacGregor & Lojkasek, 1985; Van Tassel, 1984; Werner & Smith, 1982). Several investigators of temperament in Down's syndrome children have identified a higher proportion of 'difficult' temperament children compared to non-referred samples, thus contradicting the stereotypic picture of Down's children as placid, docile, and of 'easy' temperaments (Bridges & Cicchetti, 1982; Gunn, Berry & Andrews, 1981). A reasonable inference supported by clinical evidence (see Chess, 1974) is that handicapped and risk groups have a higher prevalence of negative or difficult temperament patterns than do non-problem peers. Hefferman, Black and Poche (1982), however, caution that the generalization may not apply across all handicapped groups, as prevalence may vary according to the particular temperament dimensions studied. (See also Chapter 20, by Goldberg & Marcovitch.)

TEMPERAMENT AND SCHOOLING

To date, the bulk of research on temperament has been conducted within the context of home and family, and mothers' reports have been a primary source of data about children. The present chapter contains a discussion of some applications of temperament research to education. Rather than a comprehensive review of research on the topic, the discussion is focused on (a) possible influences of individual differences in children's temperament on their behavior and adjustment in school, and (b) teachers' decisions and interactions with children.

Temperament and Achievement

A number of investigators have described relationships between children's temperamental characteristics and their achievement in school subjects. Martin and his associates (Martin, Nagle & Paget, 1983) found that teachers rated good achievers better than poor achievers on temperament dimensions of persistence, distractibility, approach/withdrawal, and adaptability. D'Agostino (1987) reported that retained kindergarten children were more distractible and less persistent than promoted children. These findings are consistent with those from studies by Chess, Thomas and Cameron (1976), Hegvik (1984), Keogh (1983), J.V. Lerner (1983), Lerner, Lerner and Zabski (1985), Pullis and Cadwell (1982), and Sewell, Thurman and Hutchins (1981) with American samples, and with results of work by Skuy, Snell and Westaway (1985) with black South African children, and Maziade et al. (1985) with French-Canadian children. The reported relationships between temperament and IQ have been mostly moderate to non-significant, although Halverson and Waldrop (1976) reported negative correlations between ratings of high-active and fast-moving behavior styles and IQ. In sum, substantial evidence from a number of research groups documents associations between individual variations in temperament and children's achievement in school. This topic is well reviewed in Chapter 24 by Martin, and so will not be discussed in detail here.

Behavior and Adjustment Problems

There is also evidence from studies across a wide age range of children that temperament plays a part in personal–social adjustment and competence, and that temperamental patterns may be related to behavior problems identified in school (Chess *et al.*, 1976; Krakow, Maguire & Kopp, 1986; Rutter, 1977, 1982; Thomas & Chess, 1977). The particular temperament dimensions or patterns vary somewhat across studies, but adaptability and activity level are implicated with some consistency. For example, Carey, Fox and McDevitt (1977) found that children who had extreme temperament patterns (both difficult and easy) in infancy had more adjustment problems in the early school years than did those with more moderate temperaments. These investigators identified associations between concurrent ratings of temperament and adjustment, pinpointing specificially the temperament dimension of adaptability. Feuerstein and Martin (1981) also found relationships between adaptability and teachers' ratings of preschool children's social competence and adjustment. Billman and McDevitt (1980) observed that preschool children with 'difficult' temperament patterns engaged in more aggressive activities than did their temperamentally 'easy' peers. J.V. Lerner (1983), working with eighth grade pupils, documented that temperament was related to peer-determined sociometric status, such that positive nominations were associated with adaptability and negative nominations were associated with negative mood. Using the factor structure proposed by Keogh, Pullis and Cadwell (1982), Bender (1985) found that Reactivity (intensity of response and response threshold) was associated with behavior problems in a sample of learning-disabled pupils; his learning-disabled sample was also significantly different from the comparison sample of children without learning disability on the Task Orientation factor composed of persistence, distractibility, and activity level.

Although associations between individual differences in children's temperament and their achievement and personal–social adjustment in school have been established, what is yet unclear is the nature of the functional interactions which underlie the relationships. That is, how and in what ways does temperament contribute to children's school experiences? Given the importance of teachers in the day to day school management of educational programs, it is reasonable to hypothesize that teachers are key influences on pupils' experiences. A further hypothesis is that teachers' decisions and their instructional and management behaviors vary in relation to their perceptions of the attributes of pupils, in specific, to individual differences in children's temperament (see Keogh, 1982a for discussion).

TEMPERAMENT AND TEACHER–PUPIL INTERACTIONS

Several recent studies of temperament in schools provide preliminary evidence describing systematic variations in teacher's behaviors which are related to children's temperament. The first examined instructional strategies used by teachers, the second addressed both instructional and management decisions by teachers, and the third focused on the frequency of teacher–pupil interactions. These studies deserve brief review.

Working in schools in the Netherlands, van de Werfhorst (1985, 1986) videotaped children (chronological age 4–7 years) and teachers in an instructional setting while the children worked on a classification task. Teachers' perceptions of children's temperament were gathered with a short form of the Thomas and Chess questionnaire (Keogh *et al.*, 1982), and teachers' instructional behaviors were classified according to categories of: instructions, giving orders and restrictions, asking questions, giving help, and positive and negative reinforcements. Four of eight temperament dimensions were significantly related to teachers' instructional behaviors. Activity, persistence, and distractibility (temperament dimensions making up the Task Orientation factor identified by Keogh *et al.*, 1982) were negatively and significantly correlated with the teaching category of asking questions (values of *r* were −.64, −.50, −.53, respectively). Activity was associated with the category of giving instructions (*r* =.42), and persistence was positively related to teacher behaviors categorized as orders/restrictions (*r* =.47). In contrast, the approach/withdrawal temperament dimension was negatively associated with giving instructions (*r* =−.81) and orders (*r* =−.59), and positively associated with teaching behaviors such as question asking (*r* =.62) and feedback or reinforcement (*r* =.50). van der Werfhorst's observational findings support the interpretation that teachers' instructional and management interactions with pupils vary in relation to children's temperamental attributes, and that teachers' interactions with children low in Task Orientation are characteristically controlling and directing.

Compatible findings were also reported by Pullis (1985) in a study of teachers' decision-making. His sample included 412 learning-disabled pupils and 183 teachers in ten elementary schools in Texas. Approximately 10% of the pupils were in special education resource rooms; the others were in regular classes. Pupils were rated by their teachers on competence (general intellectual ability, classroom motivation, social interaction skills, and academic performance) and on a short form of the Thomas and Chess (1977) Teacher Temperament Questionnaire (Keogh *et al.*, 1982). Teachers were also asked to indicate how much individual children needed monitoring and supervision in various classroom settings, e.g. group instruction, individual seat work, transitions, etc. The results of the multiple-regression analyses, using ratings of competence and temperament as predictors and teachers' decisions as dependent variables, are relevant to the present discussion. The temperament factor of Task Orientation (composed of persistence, distractibility, and activity) was consistently the most powerful contributor to teachers' monitoring decisions in all situations. Reactivity, a temperament factor tapping intensity and over-responsiveness, was also a major contributor, especially in transitions and free-time situations, and especially for regular class teachers. It should be emphasized that the substantial temperament contributions to teachers' decisions emerged over and above the contributions of cognitive and achievement variables which were also included as predictors. Although limited to pupils identified as learning disabled, Pullis's findings provide further support for the importance of pupils' stylistic characteristics in teachers' management and instructional decisions.

The contributions of temperament to teacher–pupil interactions were also reported in a study of handicapped and non-handicapped preschoolers by Keogh and Burstein (1988). Teacher–child interactions were recorded through systematic observations in children's schools in three settings: whole-group instruction, small-group activities, and on the playground (Burstein, 1986). Teachers' perceptions of children's temperament were assessed with a short form of the Thomas and Chess questionnaire (Keogh *et al.*, 1982). Analsyses were based on a three-factor structure of temperament: Task Orientation, Personal–Social Flexibility and Reactivity. Of particular interest was the finding that the pattern of correlations between temperament and the frequency of teacher–pupil interaction varied for the two groups of children. Teachers interacted more with non-handicapped children who had positive temperament profiles (i.e. were high in Task Orientation and Flexibility and moderate in Reactivity) than those with less positive profiles. The pattern was reversed for handicapped children, however, for whom interactions were more frequent with children with more difficult temperament characteristics. It is reasonable that the higher number of interactions with the handicapped children with less positive temperaments was an indication of the teachers' efforts to direct and modify disruptive or inappropriate behaviors and to elicit adaptive behaviors. This interpretation is consistent with the finding of Paget, Nagle and Martin (1984) that high numbers of contacts with teachers were characteristic of children described as withdrawing and low in adaptability and attentiveness.

In sum, although there are still only a limited number of empirical studies assessing temperament or behavioral style within schools, the findings to date suggest that this is a variable of importance, especially in terms of the interactions between teachers and pupils. Findings in the studies reviewed above suggest that pupils' temperament is associated with the frequency of their interactions with teachers, with teachers' decisions about management within the classroom, and with teachers' instructional strategies.

TEMPERAMENT, TEACHERS, AND TEACHING

Classroom observation studies document the many teacher–pupil interactions within any school day (Brophy & Evertson, 1981; Jackson & Lahaderne, 1967) and confirm that teachers' time and attention are not spread evenly among all pupils (Wilcoxen, 1984). Further, the nature of interactions has been shown to vary, some contacts between teachers and pupils being primarily social in nature, others being exclusively instructional or managerial (Silberman, 1969). It is difficult to account for these differences by looking exclusively at teacher characteristics or at child characteristics. Rather, a number of investigators have proposed 'goodness of fit' as a model to explain the observed differences in teacher–pupil interactions (Keogh, 1986; J.V. Lerner, 1983, 1984; Lerner *et al.*, 1985, 1986; Thomas & Chess, 1977).

Goodness of Fit

In their work on goodness of fit, Lerner and Lerner (1983; Lerner *et al.*, 1986) emphasize that just as individuals bring unique sets of characteristics to situations, so settings vary, presenting different demands and providing different feedback in response to individual attributes. Lerner *et al.* (1985, 1986) note that contextual demands in schools may be both social and/or physical. Thus, in a given classroom, demands may be primarily related to teachers' expectations, values, and attitudes or to the pressures which follow from conditions of the physical environment. Examples of the first might be teachers' views about the goals of instruction or about 'appropriate' and acceptable behaviors; examples of the second might be overcrowded classrooms or the structured or unstructured organization of the instructional program.

A lack of fit is obvious when pupils are asked to do tasks which they are physically or cognitively unable to perform, or when the curriculum or instructional program is too difficult or too easy for their ability or skill levels. A lack of fit may also be evident if teachers' values and expectations for pupils' behavior and decorum differ from the cultural and familial values and behavior patterns which the child brings to school. Still another possible contribution to goodness of fit relates to temperament, as children's stylistic characteristics may or may not be compatible with teachers' expectancies for school-appropriate behavior and/or with the instructional program employed. Klein's (1980, 1982) research with young children in different school or day-care settings is relevant to this point, as she found the impact of particular temperament attributes varied by settings. Activity level was correlated with adjustment in a structured day-care center; for kindergarten children the salient temperament dimensions were withdrawal, persistence, and threshold of responsiveness. Based on results of several studies, Klein suggests that the temperament–adjustment interaction is influenced by 'program structure, goal specificity, and instructional expectations' (Klein, 1982, p. 259). Similar interpretations were made by J.V. Lerner (1983) in her research with eighth grade pupils.

Barclay (1983) included temperament data in a meta-analysis of a series of studies in which effectiveness of various instructional and counseling approaches were compared. Temperament was conceptualized as emotionality, sociability, activity, and impulsivity. Temperament–treatment interactions were identified, such that differences in classroom organization (e.g. 'structured' or 'open') were found to lead to different learning outcomes depending on the temperament attributes of learners. Burstein (1986) also documented major differences in preschool children's interactions with peers and teachers depending on whether the children were in highly structured or free environments; temperamental variables were particularly important in the less structured settings (Keogh & Burstein, 1988). Wilcoxen (1984) described differences in instructional time as a function of the organization of the physical environment (e.g. placement of desks, etc.) in the room. Hall and Cadwell (1984) found temperament attributes particularly influential in school tasks which were repetitive and required sustained performance. A reasonable inference from these studies is that some temperamental attributes are highly compatible with the demands of schools, whereas others lead to dissonance and disrupted interactions with teachers and/or peers. In order to understand goodness of fit in schools, then, it is necessary to consider several components of possible influence in addition to children's characteristics. These include: the nature of the tasks to be learned, the characteristics of the physical environment, and the attitudes, expectancies, and values of the teachers.

Teachers as Decision-Makers

Teachers' roles in the goodness of fit model are best understood if teaching is viewed as decision-making. Shavelson (1976; Shavelson & Stern, 1981) argues that teachers are active information processors who select and integrate information about individual pupils. Information is screened through the teachers' individual attitudes, beliefs, and values, as well as being weighed relative to the instructional tasks to be accomplished and the materials available to accomplish them. Teachers obviously respond to individual differences among pupils in terms of cognitive competence and educational skills, modifying the level of difficulty of tasks and/or manipulating time demands. Perhaps not so obviously, teachers are also sensitive to a number of other individual differences among pupils, including temperament. It is not only *what* children do but *how* they do it that influences teachers' decisions. Thus, children's temperaments, along with their other cognitive and physical attributes, become potential ingredients in 'goodness of fit'. However, if teaching is viewed as decision-making, then children's characteristics are but one part of the interactive equation. To understand goodness of fit it is necessary to consider the characteristics of teachers as well, especially their attitudes and beliefs about pupils and schooling.

Teachers' Views of Teachability

While we should expect some specific variations in teachers' attitudes and expectancies, there is apparently considerable consensus among teachers about desirable attributes of pupils. Lerner *et al.* (1985) gathered teachers' 'demands/expectancies' for school behavior using a modified form of the Dimensions of Temperament Scale. These investigators found that temperament attributes of high attention, approach, and adaptability, along with relatively low activity and low reactivity were especially valued by teachers. These findings are consistent with the notion of 'teachability' proposed by Keogh (1982a) and Kornblau and Keogh (1980). Kornblau and Keogh suggested that teachability is a construct which synthesizes or summarizes teachers' *a priori* views about important school-related characteristics of pupils. Based on self-generated responses from large samples of teachers, Kornblau (1982) identified 33 attributes which were highly agreed upon as characteristics of 'model' or 'ideal' pupils. The characteristics clustered in three major dimensions: cognitive–motivational attributes, school-appropriate behaviors, and personal–social skills. Considering teachers as decision-makers, a reasonable hypothesis is that teachers' views of teachability mediate their instructional and managerial interactions with individual children. In the Kornblau study cognitive characteristics were included in teachers' perceptions of teachability, but personal characteristics reminiscent of temperament or behavioral style were also major contributors.

The possible link between temperamental characteristics and teachers' perceptions of children's teachability was tested in several studies of preschool and elementary school pupils in regular and special education programs (see Keogh, 1982a,b, 1983, for reviews). In general, pupils who were rated low on teachability were found to have teacher-rated temperament patterns similar to those of 'difficult' children described by Thomas and Chess (1977). That is, they were described as low in persistence and high in distractibility and activity low in adaptability, and highly reactive. Their characteristics were, indeed, discrepant from the teachers' ideas about the attributes of model, teachable pupils. As in the Lerner *et al.* (1985) study where pupils' self-reports of their attributes were analyzed relative to teachers' expectations/demands, temperamental variations were associated with teachers' perceptions. These findings argue for the inclusion of temperament variables when considering goodness of fit between teachers and pupils. It should be noted, however, that despite the appeal of the idea of goodness of fit, there is only limited evidence to document the power of the construct when applied to school. This is clearly a challenge for future research.

SOME APPLICATIONS OF TEMPERAMENT TO SCHOOL

From an applied perspective we must ask how insight into the interactions of temperament and schooling can improve the quality of instruction and of children's experiences in school. Understanding the functional nature of temperament–school interactions is of special importance, as school is one of the 'real worlds' where real decisions are made about real children. A number of consistencies have emerged from recent work on temperament in schools. These include the salience of particular temperament dimensions or constellations of dimensions, the need to consider context and setting when interpreting temperament attributes, and the potential usefulness of the goodness of fit model as a way of integrating and interpreting individual and contextual variables. Several implications for educational practice follow from these generalizations. Few have had direct test, but all seem reasonable nominations for future work. The first has to do with psychological assessments of pupils.

Psychoeducational Assessment

School psychologists play an active role in assessment and intervention with problem pupils. Traditionally, however, the scope of assessment has been limited, and the emphasis has been on cognitive and/or motivational variables. While important educationally, those domains do not capture the individual variability expressed in temperament. Thus, it is reasonable that temperament be included in psychologists' evaluations. Martin (1983) suggested that assessment of temperament might be particularly useful in the preschool and early elementary school years. However, he also warned clinicians about the psychometric limitations of many of the assessment techniques, and the danger in oversimplified interpretations. While some assessment systems have credible technical properties, the interpretation and the application of findings vary with the skill and sensitivity of the assessor. In addition, the psychologist's ideas about the definition and organization of temperament will likely influence the nature of the inferences about applications. Assessment using the Thomas and Chess (1977) nine dimensions might yield different results from assessment based on an arousal/inhibition formulation. Different conceptualizations (see Goldsmith *et al.*,

1987) may lead to somewhat different inferences about how temperament might be used within schools – indeed, may lead to different conclusions about its usefulness at all within an educational context.

A second point relative to assessment broadens the question of what should be assessed. Psychological and educational assessments have for the most part focused exclusively on the individual, a focus well grounded in the mental health tradition. Inherent in the goodness of fit model, however, is acknowledgement that both individual and contextual influences are important. Thus, to understand 'goodness' and 'badness' of fit in schools, it is necessary to assess situational as well as individual characteristics. The question is, which contextual variables? Following the Lerner and Lerner (1983; Lerner *et al.*, 1986) argument, both social and physical aspects of the context must be included.

Considering first the physical demands, it is logical that assessment must take into account a range of variables which describes the physical organization of the instructional setting and which also addresses the instructional content and program. Both have been shown to influence the nature of teacher–pupil interactions. The physical environment is only part of the educational context, however. As the Lerners have emphasized, there are demands/expectations which relate to teachers' beliefs, attitudes, and values. Keogh and Kornblau (1980) have shown that teachers have firm views about the pupil attributes which constitute 'teachability'. Feuerstein and Martin (1981) found that teachers value children's behaviors which contribute to 'manageability' and sociability. Thus, adequate assessment of goodness of fit requires collection of data which describe the screens or filters through which teachers' view pupils. It is not just behavior but the significance of the behavior within the context which gives meaning.

Implications for Teachers

The previous suggestions for applications had to do primarily with psycho-educational assessment. There are, however, some implications from temperament research which have more direct relevance for teachers. One has to do with the interaction between pupils, temperament, and classroom management. A number of investigators have documented the impact of classroom organization on instructional effectiveness and on pupils' behavior (see Doyle, 1986, for a comprehensive review). Within the goodness of fit model we would expect that individual differences in pupils' temperament would lead to different behavioral responses to classroom routines. Thus, sensitivity to pupils' temperament may provide teachers with useful management information. Awareness of temperamental characteristics may allow teachers to anticipate and prevent disruption and disturbance. For example, characteristically highly active, distractible, and impersistent children may be particularly prone to behavior problems during transitions in the school day; characteristically withdrawing and slow to adapt children may need extra time to prepare for changes in routines. The old adage, 'forewarned is forearmed', may be appropriate here.

Closely related, pupils' temperamental variations may influence teachers' attributions about the causes of behavior, these attributions in turn affecting teachers' instructional and management decisions (Keogh, 1982a). Pupils who fit the Thomas and Chess (1977) description of 'slow to warm up' are typically negative or withdrawing to newness and slow to adapt. Their slow adaptability and seeming lack of enthusiasm for change may be attributed to laziness, to lack of motivation, even to negativism; teachers' responses to these attributions are apt to be negative, even punitive. Similarly, persistent high activity and distractibility may be attributed to purposeful misbehavior, this, too, leading to punitive responses by teachers. Awareness of the temperamental basis of differences in pupils' behavior may provide teachers with insight into their reactions to pupils, and may lower the level of negative affect which specific behaviors elicit.

In this regard, one of the most important applications of temperament research may be to increase teachers' understanding of the basis of their affective responses to individual children. In general, teachers find pupils who fit the 'easy child' pattern described by Thomas and Chess (1977) and the 'teachable pupil' pattern described by Kornblau and Keogh (1982) to be enjoyable and rewarding to teach. Their interactions with them are typically positive and frequently social, not exclusively instructional. In contrast, children fitting the 'difficult child' pattern of Thomas and Chess are often less enjoyable to teach; teachers' affective responses may be negative and their interactions limited to instruction and to behavior management. These differences in affective responses are understandable, yet may carry important messages to children. Bates (see Chapter 17) suggests that sensitivity to temperament as a contributor to parent–child interactions helps 'reframe' or reformulate problems within families. The use of temperament to reframe problems in schools is also promising, and may provide teachers with insight into children's behavior as well as increasing understanding of their own responses.

QUESTIONS AND CAUTIONS

Several questions require attention if we are to understand the implications of temperament variations for behavior and adjustment problems in schools. The first addresses the question of whether temperament is merely a semantically different way of describing behavior. In such case, evoking temperament does not provide new information or insight into behavior problems. A second question has to do with antecedents and outcomes. It is sometimes inferred that difficult temperament underlies or is a precursor to problem behavior, that temperament contributes to the development of problems. Yet, there has been relatively little work assessing the proposed causal link; only a few direct tests of the relationships between early temperament and subsequent behavior problems were found in preparation for this chapter (see Bates, Chapter 17). Finally, the functional paths through which temperament mediates problem development require specification. The goodness of fit construct is a potentially useful but still imprecisely delineated model for getting at the link between temperament and problem behavior. Given the current state of our knowledge, it seems fair to conclude that temperament is a provocative and promising aspect of individual differences which has potential consequences for children's experiences in school. Necessary next steps include specification of the processes which explain temperament–school interactions.

ACKNOWLEDGMENTS

Preparation of this chapter was supported in part by the National Institute of Child Health and Human Development under a grant to the UCLA Socio-Behavioral Group of the Mental Retardation Research Center.

I thank Cynthia Ratekin-Bess for consultation and help in preparation of this manuscript.

REFERENCES

Barclay, J.P. (1983). A meta-analysis of temperament–treatment interactions with alternative learning and counseling treatments. *Developmental Review, 3*, 410–443.

Barron, A.P. & Earls, F. (1984). The relation of temperament and social factors to behavior problems in three-year-old children. *Journal of Child Psychology and Psychiatry, 25*, 23–33.

Bates, J.E., Maslin, C.A. & Frankel, K.A. (1985). Attachment security, mother–child interaction, and temperament as predictors of behavior problem ratings at age three years. In I. Bretheron & E. Waters (Eds), *Growing points of attachment: Theory and research. Monographs of the Society for Research in Child Development, 209* (50, No. 1–2).

Bell, R.Q. (1968). A reinterpretation of the direction of effects in studies of socialization. *Psychological Review, 75*, 81–95.

Bender, W.N. (1985). Differences between learning disabled and non-learning disabled children in temperament and behavior. *Learning Disability Quarterly, 8*, 11–18.

Billman, J. & McDevitt, S.C. (1980). Convergence of parent and observer ratings of temperament with observations of peer interaction in nursery school. *Child Development, 51*, 395–400.

Bridges, F.A. & Cicchetti, D. (1982). Mothers' ratings of the temperament characteristics of Down syndrome infants. *Developmental Psychology, 18*, 238–244.

Brophy, J.E. & Evertson, C.M. (1981). *Student characteristics and teaching.* New York: Longman.

Burstein, N.D. (1986). The effects of classroom organization on mainstreamed preschool children. *Exceptional Children, 52*, 425–434.

Carey, W.B., Fox, M. & McDevitt, S.C. (1977). Temperament as a factor in early school adjustment. *Pediatrics, 60*, 621–624.

Chess, S. (1974). The influence of defect on development in children with congenital rubella. *Merrill-Palmer Quarterly, 20*, 255–274.

Chess, S., Thomas, A. & Cameron, M. (1976). Temperament: Its significance for early schooling. *New York University Education Quarterly, 7*, 24–29.

D'Agostino, I. (1987). Children's characteristics related to promotion and nonpromotion in kindergarten. Unpublished doctoral dissertation, University of Southern California.

Doyle, W. (1986). Classroom organization and management. In M.C. Wittrock (Ed.), *Handbook of research on teaching*, 3rd edn. (pp. 392–431). New York: Macmillan.

Feuerstein, P. & Martin, R.P. (1981). The relationship between temperament and school adjustment in four-year-old children. Paper presented at the annual meeting of the American Educational Research Association, Los Angeles, April 1981.

Goldsmith, H.H., Buss, A.H., Plomin, R., Rothbart, M.K., Thomas, A., Chess, S., Hinde, R.A. & McCall, R.B. (1987). Roundtable: What is temperament?: Four approaches. *Child Development, 58*, 505–529.

Graham, P., Rutter, M. & George, S. (1973). Temperamental characteristics as predictors of behavior disorders in children. *American Journal of Orthopsychiatry, 43*, 328–339.

Gunn, P., Berry, P. & Andrews, R.J. (1981). The temperament of Down's syndrome infants: A research note. *Journal of Child Psychology and Psychiatry, 22*, 189–194.

Hall, R.J. & Cadwell, J. (1982). Temperament influences on cognition and achievement in children with learning problems. Paper presented at the annual conference of the American Educational Research Association, New Orleans, LA, April 1982.

Halverson, C.F. & Waldrop, M.F. (1976). Relations between preschool activity and aspects of intellectual and social behavior at age 7½. *Developmental Psychology,* **12**, 107–112.

Hefferman, L., Black, F.W. & Poche, P. (1982). Temperament patterns in young neurologically impaired children. *Journal of Pediatric Psychology,* **7**, 415–423.

Hegvik, R.L. (1984). Three year longitudinal study of temperament variables, academic achievement and sex differences. Paper presented at the St Louis Conference on Temperament in the Educational Process, St Louis, MO, October 1984.

Jackson, P.W. & Lahaderne, H.M. (1967). Inequalities of teacher–pupil contacts. *Psychology in the Schools,* **4**, 204–211.

Keogh, B.K. (1982a). Children's temperament and teachers' decisions. In R. Porter & G.M. Collins (Eds), *Temperamental differences in infants and young children* (pp. 269–279). Ciba Foundation Symposium No. 89. London: Pitman.

Keogh, B.K. (1982b). Temperament: An individual difference of importance in intervention programs. *Topics in Early Childhood Special Education,* **2**, 25–31.

Keogh, B.K. (1983). Individual differences in temperament: A contribution to the personal-social and educational competence of learning disabled children. In J.D. McKinney & L. Feagens (Eds), *Current topics in learning disabilities* (pp. 33–55). Norwood, NJ: Ablex.

Keogh, B.K. (1986). Temperament and schooling: What is the meaning of goodness of fit? In J.V. Lerner & R.M. Lerner (Eds), *New directions for child development: Temperament and social interaction in infants and children* (pp. 89–108). San Francisco: Jossey-Bass.

Keogh, B.K., Bernheimer, L., Pelland, M. & Daley, S. (1989, in press). Behavioral and adjustment problems of children with developmental delays. *European Journal of Special Needs Education.*

Keogh, B.K. & Burstein, N.D. (1988). Relationship of temperament to preschoolers' interaction with peers and teachers. *Exceptional Children,* **54**, 69–74.

Keogh, B.K. & Kornblau, B.W. (1980). Temperament characteristics of children differing in perceived teachability. Unpublished manuscript, University of California, Project REACH, Los Angeles.

Keogh, B.K., Pullis, M. & Cadwell, J. (1982). A short form of the Teacher Temperament Questionnaire. *Journal of Educational Measurement,* **29**, 323–329.

Klein, H.A. (1980). Early childhood group care: Predicting adjustment from individual temperament. *Journal of Genetic Psychology,* **137**, 125–131.

Klein, H.A. (1982). The relationship between children's temperament and adjustment to kindergarten and Head Start settings. *Journal of Psychology,* **112**, 259–268.

Kolvin, I., Nicol, A.R., Garside, R.F., Day, K.A. & Tweedle, E.G. (1982). Temperamental patterns in aggressive boys. In R. Porter & G.M. Collins (Eds), *Temperamental differences in infants and young children* (pp. 252–268). Ciba Foundation Symposium No. 89. London: Pitman.

Kornblau, B. (1982). The Teachable Pupil Survey: A technique for assessing teachers' perceptions of pupil attributes. *Psychology in the Schools,* **19**, 170–174.

Kornblau, B.W. & Keogh, B.K. (1980). Teachers' perceptions and educational decisions. In J.J. Gallagher (Ed.), *New directions for exceptional children*, No. 1, The ecology of exceptional children (pp. 87–101). San Francisco: Jossey-Bass.

Krakow, J.B., Maguire, S.R. & Kopp, C. (1986). Sustained attention and self-control: A longitudinal follow-up. Paper presented at the annual meeting of the Western Psychological Association, Seattle, WA, May 1986.

Lerner, J.V. (1983). The role of temperament in psychosocial adaptation in early adolescents: A test of a 'goodness of fit' model. *Journal of Genetic Psychology,* **143**, 149–157.

Lerner, J.V. (1984). The import of temperament for psychosocial functioning: Tests of a goodness of fit model. *Merrill-Palmer Quarterly,* **30**, 177–188.

Lerner, J.V. & Lerner, R.M. (1983). Temperament and adaptation across life: Theoretical and empirical issues. In P.B. Baltes & O.G. Brim, Jr (Eds), *Life-span development and behavior,* Vol. 5 (pp. 197–231). New York: Academic Press.

Lerner, J.V., Lerner, R.M. & Zabski, S. (1985). Temperament and elementary school children's actual and rated academic performance: A test of a 'goodness of fit' model. *Journal of Child Psychology and Psychiatry*, **26**, 125–136.

Lerner, R.M. (1982). Children and adolescents as producers of their own development. *Developmental Review*, **2**, 342–370.

Lerner, R.M., Lerner, J.V., Windle, M., Hooker, K., Lenerz, K. & East, P.L. (1986). Children and adolescents in their contexts: Tests of a Goodness of Fit model. In R. Plomin & J. Dunn (Eds), *The study of temperament: Changes, continuities, and challenges*. Hillsdale, NJ: Erlbaum.

Marcovitch, S., Goldberg, S., MacGregor, D.L. & Lojkasek, M. (1985). Individual differences in maternal stress, child temperament and mother–child interaction with developmentally delayed preschoolers. Paper presented at The Council for Exceptional Children's 63rd Conference, Anaheim, CA, April 1985.

Martin, R.P. (1983). Temperament: A review of research with implications for the school psychologist. *School Psychology Review*, **12**, 266–273.

Martin, R.P., Nagle, R. & Paget, K. (1983). Relationships between temperament and classroom behavior, teacher attitudes, and academic achievement. *Journal of Psychoeducational Assessment*, **1**, 377–386.

Mauer, R., Cadoret, R.J. & Cain, C. (1980). Cluster analysis of childhood temperament data on adoptees. *American Journal of Orthopsychiatry*, **50**, 522–534.

Maziade, M., Capéraà, P., Laplante, B., Boudreault, M., Thivierge, J., Côté, R. & Boutin, P. (1985). Value of difficult temperament among seven-year-olds in the general population for predicting psychiatric diagnosis at age 12. *American Journal of Psychiatry*, **142**, 943–946.

Olweus, D. (1980). Familial and temperamental determinants of aggressive behavior in adolescent boys: A causal analysis. *Developmental Psychology*, **16**, 644–660.

Pullis, M. (1985). LD students' temperament characteristics and their impact on decisions by resource and mainstream teachers. *Learning Disabilities Quarterly*, **8**, 109–122.

Pullis, M. & Cadwell, J. (1982). The influence of children's temperament characteristics on teachers' decision strategies. *American Educational Research Journal*, **19**, 165–181.

Rutter, M. (1976). Individual differences. In M. Rutter & L. Hersov (Eds), *Child psychiatry: Modern approaches* (pp. 3–21). Oxford: Blackwell Scientific.

Rutter, M. (1982). Temperament: Concepts, issues and problems. In R. Porter & G.M. Collins (Eds), *Temperamental differences in infants and young children* (pp. 1–19). Ciba Foundation Symposium No. 89. London: Pitman.

Rutter, M., Birch, H.G., Thomas, A. & Chess, S. (1964). Temperamental characteristics in infancy and the later development of behavioral disorders. *British Journal of Psychiatry*, **110**, 651–661.

Sameroff, A.J. & Chandler, M.J. (1975). Reproductive risk and the continuum of caretaking causality. In F.D. Horowitz, S. Scarr-Salapatek & G. Siegel (Eds), *Review of child development research*, Vol. 4 (pp. 187–244). Chicago: University of Chicago Press.

Scholom, A., Zucker, R.A. & Stollak, G.E. (1979). Relating early child adjustment of infant and parent temperament. *Journal of Abnormal Child Psychology*, **7**, 297–308.

Sewell, T.E., Thurman, S.K. & Hutchins, D. (1981). Temperament and cognitive styles in academic achievement of low-income black preschool children. Paper presented at the annual meeting of the American Educational Research Association, Los Angeles, CA, April 1981.

Shavelson, R.J. (1976). Teachers' decision making. In N.L. Gage (Ed.), *The psychology of teaching methods. Yearbook of the National Society for the Study of Education*, **75**, 372–414.

Shavelson, R.J. & Stern, P. (1981). Research on teachers' pedagogical thoughts, judgments, decisions, and behavior. *Review of Educational Research*, **51**, 455–498.

Silberman, M.L. (1969). Behavioral expression of teachers' attitudes toward elementary school students. *Journal of Educational Psychology*, **60**, 402–407.

Skuy, M., Snell, D. & Westaway, M. (1985). Temperament and the scholastic achievement and adjustment of black South African children. *South African Journal of Education*, **5**,

197–202.

Swets-Gronert, F.A. (1985). Temperament and behavioural problems in young children. Paper presented at the Workshop on Temperament and Development in Childhood, Leiden, The Netherlands, July 1985.

Terestman, N. (1980). Mood quality and intensity in nursery school children as predictors of behavior disorder. *American Journal of Orthopsychiatry,* **50**, 125–138.

Thomas, A. & Chess, S. (1977). *Temperament and development.* New York: Brunner/Mazel.

Thomas, A., Chess, S. & Birch, H.G. (1968). *Temperament and behavior disorders in children.* New York: New York University Press.

van der Werfhorst, F.H. (1985). Temperament and teacher–child interaction. Paper presented at the Workshop on Temperament and Development in Childhood, Leiden, The Netherlands, July 1985.

van der Werfhorst, H. (1986). Temperament and teacher–child interaction. In G.A. Kohnstamm (Ed.), *Temperament discussed: Temperament and development in infancy and childhood* (pp. 141–147). University of Leiden, The Netherlands.

Werner, E.E. & Smith, R.S. (1982). *Vulnerable, but invincible: A longitudinal study of resilient children and youth.* New York: McGraw-Hill.

Wertleib, D., Weigel, C., Springer, T. & Feldstein, M. (1987). Temperament as a moderator of children's stressful experiences. *American Journal of Orthopsychiatry,* **57**, 234–245.

Wilcoxen, A.G. (1984). Relationships among teacher attitudes and teacher–pupil interactions in special education classes. Unpublished doctoral dissertation, University of California, Los Angeles.

24

Activity Level, Distractibility, and Persistence: Critical Characteristics in Early Schooling

Roy P. Martin
University of Georgia

Instruction, as practised in most elementary schools, requires a child to sit in a designated seat (most of the time), and attend to learning materials presented by the teacher. Further, this instruction typically takes place in a room in which the learning of 20–40 children is aided by one or perhaps two adult supervisors (a teacher and sometimes an aide). Because of this characteristic of the instructional setting, the teacher is unable to spend extended periods of time directing the attention of any one child to the learning materials presented.

Given this kind of instructional environment, it can be hypothesized that the child who has the ability independently to sustain attention to learning materials, and to persist in task performance even if the task is difficult (is being initially learned) or boring (has been learned and can be performed readily), has a distinct advantage over a peer who does not have this ability. Further, it can be hypothesized that this environment rewards the child who is able to remain as physically immobile as is possible, since gross motor movement may impede the attention to learning materials of the child who is moving, and/or it may create environmental stimulation (e.g. noise) that disturbs the attention of other students.

From another perspective, this environment could place at risk those children who, for whatever reason, are less able to focus and sustain their attention and those children who are more active. Those for whom the fit between the demands of this environment and their characteristics is especially bad may be educationally or psychiatrically diagnosed as being hyperactive or as having an attentional deficit. It is noteworthy that in the current version of the *Diagnostic and statistical manual of mental disorders* (DSM-III-R) of the American Psychiatric Association (1987), a child can fit the category of Attention-Deficit Hyperactivity Disorder primarily on the basis of behavior in school.

Temperament in Childhood   Edited by G.A. Kohnstamm, J.E. Bates and M.K. Rothbart
© 1989 John Wiley & Sons Ltd

> The essential features of this disorder are developmentally inappropriate degrees of inattention, impulsivity, and hyperactivity ... Manifestations of the disorder usually appear in most situations, including at home, in school, ... and in social situations, but to varying degrees. Some people, however, show signs of the disorder in only one setting, such as ... at school. Symptoms worsen in situations requiring sustained attention, such as listening to a teacher in a classroom ... or doing class assignments. (DSM-III-R, p. 50)

While there is some recognition that genetic or constitutional factors may predispose a child toward heightened activity level, distractibility, and poorer attentional abilities, little research has addressed the educational correlates and sequelae of these characteristics. What literature does exist is predominantly focused on the extreme manifestations of these behaviors in the context of hyperkinesis or attention-deficit disorder research. In this research the characteristics of activity, distractability, and persistence (and sometimes impulsivity and aggression) are viewed as a disease syndrome. Thus, there is a large volume of research comparing 'normals' and children with the syndrome (see Barkley, 1981).

There appears to be a need for research which studies the educational impact of activity level, distractibility, and persistence when these characteristics are considered from a temperament point of view; that is, they are considered as traits that may be genetic or constitutional in etiology, and are normally distributed in the general population. Such research might begin to point out how these characteristics affect classroom behavior, teacher attitudes and behavior, and achievement.

Towards this end, the purpose of the present chapter is to review research carried out by me and my students which looks at educational correlates of activity level, distractibility, and persistence. The original purpose of the research was to study the impact on schooling of six characteristics of children 3–7 years of age. The characteristics studied included adaptability to changing environments, the initial response to novel environments, and emotional intensity, as well as activity level, distractibility, and persistence. However, this review will be limited to the research on the last three characteristics.

The review is limited in three other important ways. First, all studies reviewed used the same temperament measure (Temperament Assessment Battery for Children; Martin, 1988). Second, only temperament measurement in the form of teacher ratings will be reported. Finally, all studies (with one exception) involved temperament measurement of kindergarten and first grade children.

INSTRUMENT

Assessment of activity level and attentional processes was obtained from the Teacher Form of the Temperament Assessment Battery for Children (TABC; Martin, 1988). This questionnaire is a modification of the Teacher Temperament Questionnaire originally published by Thomas and Chess (1977). This rating scale consists of 48 items describing behaviors of children as they occur in school. The rater responds to each item on a seven-point scale on the basis of the frequency with which the behavior described in the item occurs (hardly ever, infrequently, once in a while, sometimes, often, very often, or almost always). The Teacher Form of the

TABC was designed to measure six of the nine temperamental constructs operationalized by Thomas and Chess (1977).

One of the scales considered is the Activity scale, designed to measure the motoric vigor of the child. Examples of items include: 'Child seems to have difficulty sitting still, may wiggle a lot or get out of seat.' 'Child runs rather than walks.' 'Child is able to sit quietly for a reasonable amount of time (as compared to classmates).' (This item is scored in reverse direction.) The internal consistency of this scale has been studied in several samples and tends to be in the .82 to .86 range across samples (Martin, 1988). The test–retest reliability over 6 months using the same teacher as a rater was .79 and .85 in two samples. Over 12 months using different teachers for the assessments at time 1 and 2, the stability was .57 and .67 with two samples (Martin et al., 1986).

The Distractibility scale was designed to measure the ease with which the child's attention can be interrupted by environmental stimuli, particularly low-level stimuli that interrupt ongoing task-related school behavior. A high score is indicative of a tendency to be easily distracted. Examples of items include: 'Child is easily drawn away from his/her work by noises, something outside the window, another child's whispering, etc.' 'Child cannot be distracted when he/she is working (seems able to concentrate in the midst of bedlam).' 'Child is among the first to notice if a messenger, parent, or another teacher comes into the room.' Across several samples, the internal consistency reliability of this scale in the form of the alpha coefficient has been determined to be in the .85 to .88 range (Martin, 1988). Across a 6-month retest interval, the stability coefficient for this scale was .70 and .80 for two samples. For a 12-month retest interval using different raters at time 1 and 2, the figures were .53 and .49 (Martin et al., 1986) for the two samples.

The Persistence scale was designed to measure two related sets of behaviors, attention span and the tendency to continue attempting the solution of difficult learning or performance problems. A high score is indicative of longer attention and a tendency toward continuation of attention on difficult tasks. Examples of items are: 'If child's activity is interrupted, he/she tries to go back to the activity.' 'Child quickly becomes impatient with a task he/she cannot grasp, and goes on to something else.' 'Child can continue at the same activity for an hour.' Across several samples the internal consistency reliability of this scale (alpha coefficient) has been found to be in the .87 to .92 range (Martin, 1988). The temporal stability across a 6-month retest interval using the same rater was determined to be .78 and .79 in two samples. The stability across a 12-month interval using different raters was determined to be .47 and .43 for two different samples (Martin et al., 1986).

RESEARCH FINDINGS: QUESTIONS ANSWERED

How are Activity, Distractibility, and Persistence Related?

The Activity, Distractibility, and Persistence scales of the TABC tend to be moderately correlated. Across five samples (approximate n of 100 each), the correlations between activity and distractibility ranged from .48 to .72. Correlations between activity and persistence for the same samples ranged from −.20 to −.56. The correlations between distractibility and persistence ranged from −.56 to −.76. Martin, 1988; Paget, Nagle & Martin, 1984).

Factor analyses (principal components analysis with varimax rotation) of the TABC at the scale level tend to produce a two-factor solution with activity, distractibility, and persistence loading above .50 on the first factor (Martin, 1988).

Many factor analyses of temperament scales at the item level have produced an attention-span factor on which distractibility and persistence items load heavily whether utilizing as raters parents (Hinde, Easton, Meller & Tamplin, 1982; Lerner, Palermo, Spiro & Nesselroade, 1982; Matheny, 1986), clinicians (Matheny, 1980), or teachers (Keogh, 1982). In parent and clinician ratings, activity items are typically found in a different factor than distractibility and persistence items (Hinde *et al.*, 1982; Lerner *et al.*, 1982; Matheny, 1980) but utilizing teacher ratings they tend to be in the same factor (Keogh, 1982). In elementary school classrooms, attention and activity are probably linked because of the demand characteristics of the situation (a crowded place requiring sustained attention on learning materials). The same may not be true in the home, where stationary task performance is not the dominant activity.

What is the Relationship Between Teacher-Rated Activity, Distractibility, and Persistence, and Classroom Behavior?

Martin, Nagle and Paget (1983) report on a study in which the classroom behavior of 42 children in two first grade classrooms was observed. Each child was observed on 3 days with a total observation for each child of 60 5-second observation intervals. Observations were obtained using the Schedule of Classroom Activity Norms observation system (McKinney, Mason, Perkerson & Clifford, 1975). Temperament ratings from teachers were obtained approximately 1 month prior to the initiation of classroom observation.

In order to check on the validity of the teacher ratings, a correlation was obtained between observed distractibility and the teacher rating of distractibility. The resulting correlation was .40. Activity and persistence were not significantly correlated with the observed distractibility. Considering the brief observation period and thus the unreliability of these data, this result was considered substantial evidence for the discriminant validity of ratings on this variable.

The issue most directly addressed in this research was the relationship between constructive and non-constructive classroom behavior, and activity, distractibility, and persistence ratings of teachers. It was found that all three child characteristics were significantly correlated with observed 'constructive self-directed activity' (−.50, −.55, .46, respectively), and with observed 'gross-motor inappropriate behavior' (.55, .50, −.60, respectively). Distractibility and persistence were also significantly related to 'non-constructive self-directed activity' (e.g. child taps the desk with his/her pencil; child plays with his/her shoe strings) (.35, −.38, respectively), and with 'non-constructive peer interaction' (.46, −.35, respectively).

These data indicate that active, distractible, and non-persistent children engage in a variety of behaviors which are detrimental to classroom performance and learning. If such behaviors continue over the first few years of schooling, it would be expected that grades and achievement scores would suffer. It might also be assumed that teachers find such students disruptive and difficult to deal with.

What is the Relationship Between Temperament and Teacher Attitudes?

Martin *et al.* (1983) obtained teacher ratings of activity, distractibility, and persistence for 113 children in six first grade classrooms. Approximately 6 months later, these teachers were asked four questions developed by Silberman (1969) related to their attitudes about the children. The two questions that most directly related to the acceptance–rejection dimension were as follows:

(1) Name three children in your class you would like to have in class again for the sheer joy of it. (This question was thought to isolate those children for whom the teacher had an attachment attitude.)
(2) If you could reduce your class by three children, which three would it be? (This question was thought to isolate those children for whom the teacher had an attitude of rejection.)

A series of analyses was performed to determine whether or not children nominated by a particular question differed from children not nominated for that group. Children nominated for the attachment group (question 1) were significantly more persistent than those not nominated for that group. Children in the rejection group (question 2) were rated as significantly more active and more distractible than other children, but not less persistent.

In a similar study by Conner (1983) in which temperament ratings were obtained in kindergarten and the Silberman attitude questions asked of different teachers in the first grade, those children nominated for the attachment group were found to be more persistent, less active, and less distractible. The rejection group was rated as more active by teachers.

These studies indicate that teachers find less active, less distractible, and more persistent children more enjoyable to work with, and would like to remove children who are more active and more distractible from their classrooms. Assuming these attitudes relate to teacher behavior in some way, it might be hypothethesized that teachers respond to more active, more distractible, and less persistent children in a less warm and helpful manner (perhaps being more critical), which would further add to the burden these children face in the classroom.

What is the Relationship Between Temperament and Student–Teacher Interaction?

Paget *et al.* (1984) have studied the relationship of teacher-rated temperament to the dyadic interactions between students and teachers. The Teacher Form of the TABC was completed by ten first grade teachers. Children in these classes (total of 105 students) were observed using the Brophy and Good (1969) observation system. The temperament ratings preceded the classroom observation by about 1 month.

The scale scores from the TABC were factor analyzed (principle components analysis with varimax rotation) and three factors were isolated. One of the factors had loadings above .50 for activity, distractibility, and persistence, and the factor loading for distractibility was $-.94$. Therefore this factor was labeled Task Attention. Factor scores for all three factors were calculated and used to predict observed categories of behavior. Using a criterion of P less than .01 for all predictions, it was determined that the number of Response Opportunities observed, and the number of Child-Initiated Contacts observed were not significantly predicted by temperament ratings. However, significant predictions were obtained for the category labeled Behavior Contacts. These were observed interactions

Table 1   Relationship between activity, distractibility, and persistence, and academic achievement

		Achievement			
		Grades		Standardized tests	
Temperament	Time span* (years)	Reading	Math.	Reading	Math.
Activity					
Study 1	½	$-.43$	$-.42$	$-.45$	$-.24$
Study 2	½	$-.29$	NS		
Study 3	1	$-.58$	$-.49$	$-.25$	$-.36$
				$-.51$	$-.34$
Study 4	2	$-.40$	$-.42$	NS	NS
Study 5	4	$-.39$	$-.30$	$-.42$	$-.26$
Distractibility					
Study 1	½	$-.56$	$-.52$	$-.45$	$-.39$
Study 2	½	$-.63$	$-.52$		
Study 3	1	$-.41$	$-.43$	$-.55$	$-.59$
				$-.49$	$-.45$
Study 4	2	$-.61$	$-.59$	NS	NS
Study 5	4	$-.30$	$-.35$	$-.48$	$-.48$
Persistence					
Study 1	½	.65	.60	.49	.48
Study 2	½	.69	.61		
Study 3	1	.48	.60	.63	.50
				.62	.60
Study 4	2	.64	.72	NS	NS
Study 5	4	NS	.37	.45	.43

*Time between measurement of temperament and measurement of achievement.

Study 1: Martin and Holbrook (1985); $n = 104$; temperament and achievement measured in first grade.
Study 2: Martin, Nagle, and Paget (1983); $n = 80$; temperament and achievement measured in first grade.
Study 3: Martin, Gaddis, Drew, and Moseley (1988); $n = 117$; temperment measured in kindergarten.
Study 4: Martin et al. (1988); $n = 22$; temperament measured in preschool.
Study 5: Martin et al. (1988); $n = 63$; temperament measured in first grade.

between teacher and child that did not focus on learning of teacher or self-presented materials, but focused on the management of behavior, such as getting out of ones set without permission, talking to a peer at an inappropriate time, making inappropriate noises, etc.

Two types of behavior contacts were isolated, behavior contacts praised and behavior contacts criticized. The Task Attention factor made a significant contribution to the prediction of both of these types of behavior contacts, although the direction of the contribution was different (positively related to behavior contacts praised, and negatively related to behavior contacts criticized). Task attention played the largest role in predicting behavior contacts criticized although the correlation for this factor alone was low ($r = .10$).

These results tentatively demonstrate that teachers' interactions directly related to instruction, including questions and other academic interactions, are not directly influenced by characteristics of children. However, teachers do respond with behavioral criticism more to low-attention, distractible children. This kind of interaction probably makes life in the classroom less positive for the criticized child and the teacher who must manage this behavior.

What is the Relationship Between Temperament, and Academic Achievement?

Table 1 lists five studies in which the correlation between activity level as rated by the teacher and achievement was calculated. In these studies, the achievement scores were obtained from 5 months to 4 years after the temperament scores were obtained. As can be seen, correlations were generally in the .20 to .50 range for reading and mathematics grades, and for standardized test performance in reading and mathematics. The mean correlations (using appropriate r to z transformations) were about .10 lower for the standardized test performance than for grades.

A similar pattern is observed in Table 1 for the relationship between distractibility and achievement, and for persistence and achievement. However, the correlations for these two variables are about .10 higher on average than for activity; that is, they range from about .30 to .60. The validity of teachers' ratings of activity, distractibility, and persistence in prediction of achievement over a 4-year interval is particularly impressive. Table 1 reveals that in study 5, first grade ratings of activity, distractibility, and persistence predicted standardized achievement scores in fifth grade at .41 on average (range of .25 to .48). This indicates considerable continuity in the effects of these characteristics over the early elementary school years.

These studies clearly show that higher activity level, greater distractibility, and less persistence are associated with lowered achievement. However, many questions remain about the meaning of this relationship. First, is this relationship simply a reflection of the relationship between scholastic ability and these variables? Second, do these variables affect achievement because they affect classroom and out-of-classroom learning? Third, do these variables primarily affect performance on learned material (as in completing classroom homework and in attending to standardized tests) rather than on the actual learning of that material? In all likelihood, all three factors operate, but the relative effect of each is still a matter of conjecture.

What is the Relationship Between Temperament and Scholastic Ability?

Table 2 lists four studies in which the relationship between activity, distractibility, and persistence, and scholastic ability was calculated. The results of these studies reveal that the relationship is affected by (a) the sample and/or the measure of ability that is used (i.e. there is considerable variability in the relationship from study to study), (b) the temperamental variable studied (i.e. the relationships with persistence were stronger than those with distractibility and activity level), and (c) the gender of the child. With regard to the last point, in the one study in which correlations were calculated separately for each gender, the relationship between these characteristics and achievement was stronger for males than for females.

The relationship between temperament and academic ability is so strong that it raises the issue as to whether or not temperament ratings by teachers are influenced by the teachers' perception of the child's academic ability. As a part of his dissertation research, Holbrook (1983) found that teachers' estimates of IQ were correlated .58 with assessed IQ. Thus, only about 36% of the variance in estimated IQ can be attributed to measured IQ; this sets a cap of about 36% of the shared variance between IQ and temperament ratings that could be attributable to measured IQ. Teachers probably are biased by a general knowledge of the child ability level, but this biasing effect is in all likelihood modest.

Three other factors probably operate to create this rather high correlation. First, children who are less distractible and more persistent will do better on the measure of scholastic aptitude (particularly if it is assessed in a group setting), since such measurement devices require active attention manifested over a considerable length of time. Second, brighter students are probably less active, less distractible, and more persistent in the classroom because they can deal with the learning materials more comfortably than can their peers: they require less effort and thus can maintain that effort over longer periods of time. Further, they probably enjoy demonstrating their competence through appropriate classroom activities. In contrast, performing for the less competent child means having a greater likelihood

Table 2   Relationship of teacher-rated activity, distractibility, and persistence to cognitive ability

| | Ability measure | n | Correlation | | |
			Activity	Distractibility	Persistence
Martin and Holbrook (1985)	Otis–Lennon Mental Abilities Test	104	−.15	−.29	.41
Moseley (1986)	Boehm Test of Basic Concepts	117	−.52	−.57	.72
Martin (unpub.)	Stanford–Binet or McCarthy	67M 38F	−.47 −.24	−.40 −.35	.59 .38
Martin (unpub.)	Stanford–Binet or McCarthy	53	−.56	−.48	.64

of demonstrating incompetence, so performance is less likely to be as positive an experience. This might result in inappropriate classroom activity, and easily diverted attention.

The third link between activity level, distractibility, and persistence, and cognitive ability is that attention is in all probability a part of general intellectual ability. In infancy, attention has been found to be one of the strongest predictors of cognitive ability measured during the preschool years (see Caron, Caron & Glass, 1983; Fagan, 1984, 1985; Fagan & McGarth, 1981; Fagan & Singer, 1982; Lewis & Brooks-Gunn, 1981; Rose & Wallace, 1985a,b). In a review of this literature, Bornstein and Sigman (1986) reported that the median correlation between these types of measures and later measured cognitive ability was .46.

There is not enough data presently available to help us determine the relative weight that should be given to each of these factors in 'explaining' the relationship between activity level, distractibility, and persistence, and cognitive ability. It seems likely it is a mix of all three factors, however.

GENERAL DISCUSSION AND CONCLUSION

The research reviewed in this chapter adds considerable support to the notion that activity level, distractability, and persistence play important roles in education processes and products in early elementary school, particularly in the first grade. These characteristics are related in important ways to the behavior of the child in the classroom, the interaction of the teacher and the child, the attitudes held about children by teachers, and academic achievement. Correlations with achievement, both in the form of grades assigned and standardized test scores, are particularly impressive, approximating the correlations between measures of scholastic aptitude and achievement.

These kind of data seem to indicate that teacher ratings of activity, distractibility, and persistence during the preschool or kindergarten year could be used as a screening device for specialized instructional procedures during the first grade year. The use of the Teacher Form of the TABC for this purpose would require a substantial development effort to establish optimal cut-off scores for the various screening purposes for which the instrument might be used. Screening, of course, is not an end in itself, but a step toward some type of specialized treatment. Without the availability of appropriate differential learning environments screening has little utility. Toward this end, perhaps temperamental conceptions of readiness for specific types of instruction might play a role in the future.

The data reported in this chapter provide indirect support for the hypothesis that temperament may play a role in predisposing children toward attention-deficit disorders. If the place of temperament in attention-deficit disorders is to be more clearly established, there must be large-scale longitudinal research efforts that follow very young children at risk of such disorders. One further question suggested by the current review is whether distractibility and persistence are best considered as temperaments or as aspects of the cognitive domain. Several temperament theories explicitly include these attributes in their list of temperaments (e.g. Thomas & Chess, 1977), while others (e.g. Buss & Plomin, 1984) do not. Goldsmith and Campos (1982) include only some aspects of attentional processes in their list of temperaments. The critical issue here is not simply one of the breadth of inclusiveness of the theory, which is a rather arbitrary decision, but one of model building in which the relationship of attention and related processes to general '*G*', and to temperamental characteristics is delineated.

REFERENCES

American Psychiatric Association (1987). *Diagnostic and statistical manual of mental disorders*, 3rd edn, revised. Washington, DC: American Psychiatric Association.

Barkley, R.A. (1981). *Hyperactive children: A handbook for diagnosis and treatment*. New York: Guilford Press.

Bornstein, M.H. & Sigman, M.D. (1986). Continuity in mental development from infancy. *Child Development*, **57**, 251–274.

Brophy, J.E. & Good, T.L. (1969). *Analyzing classroom interaction: A more powerful alternative*. Report No. 26. Austin: Research and Development Center for Teacher Education, University of Texas.

Buss, A.H. & Plomin, R. (1984). *Temperament: Early developing personality traits*. Hillsdale, NJ: Erlbaum.

Caron, A.J., Caron, R.F. & Glass, P. (1983). Responsiveness to relational information as a measure of cognitive functioning in nonsuspect infants. In T. Field & A. Sostek (Eds), *Infant born at risk: Psychological, perceptual, and cognitive processes* (pp. 181–209). New York: Grune & Stratton.

Conner, R.E. (1983). The relationship between student temperament and behavioral characteristics and teacher attitudes of attachment, concern, indifference, and rejection. Unpublished Doctoral Dissertation, University of Georgia.

Fagan, J.F. (1984). The intelligent infant: Theoretical implications. *Intelligence*, **8**, 1–9.

Fagan, J.F. (1985). A new look at infant intelligence. In D.K. Determan (Ed.), *Current topics in human intelligence*, Vol. 1, *Research methodology* (pp. 223–246). Norwood, NJ: Ablex.

Fagan, J.F. & McGarth, S.K. (1981). Infant recognition memory and later intelligence. *Intelligence*, **5**, 121–130.

Fagan, J.F. & Singer, L.T. (1982). Infant recognition memory as a measure of intelligence. In L.P. Lipsitt (Ed.), *Advances in infant research*, Vol. 2 (pp. 31–78). Norwood, NJ: Ablex.

Goldsmith, H.H. & Campos, J.J. (1982). Toward a theory of infant temperament. In R.N. Emde & R.J. Harmon (Eds), *The development of attachment and affiliative systems* (pp. 161–193). New York: Plenum.

Hinde, R.A., Easton, D.F., Meller, R.E. & Tamplin, A.M. (1982). Temperamental characteristics of 3–4 year-olds and mother–child interaction. In *Temperamental differences in infants and young children* (pp. 66–86). Ciba Foundation Symposium No. 89. London: Pitman.

Holbrook, J. (1983). Pupil temperament characteristics, the teacher's appraisal of their intelligence and assignment of grades. Unpublished doctoral dissertation, University of Georgia.

Keogh, B.K. (1982). Children's temperament and teachers' decisions. In *Temperamental differences in infants and young children* (pp. 269–285). Ciba Foundation Symposium No. 89. London: Pitman.

Lerner, R., Palermo, M., Spiro, A. & Nesselroade, J. (1982). Assessing the dimensions of temperamental individuality across the life-span: The Dimensions of Temperament Survey (DOTS). *Child Development*, **53**, 149–160.

Lewis, M. & Brooks-Gunn, J. (1981). Visual attention at three months as a predictor of cognitive functioning at two years of age. *Intelligence*, **5**, 141–147.

Martin, R.P. (1988). The Temperament Assessment Battery for Children: Manual. Brandon, VT: Clinical Psychology.

Martin, R.P., Gaddis, L., Drew, D. & Moseley, M. (1988). Prediction of elementary school achievement from preschool temperament: Three studies. *School Psychology Review*, **17**, 125–137.

Martin, R.P. & Holbrook, J. (1985). Relationship of temperament characteristics to the academic achievement of first-grade children. *Journal of Psychoeducational Assessment*, **3**, 131–140.

Martin, R.P., Nagle, R. & Paget, K. (1983). Relationships between temperament and classroom behavior, teacher attitudes, and academic achievement. *Journal of Clinical Psychology*, **39**, 1013–1020.

Martin, R.P., Wisenbaker, J., Matthews-Morgan, J., Holbrook, J., Hooper, S. & Spalding, J. (1986). Stability of teacher temperament ratings over six and twelve months. *Journal of Abnormal Child Psychology*, **14**, 216–232.

Matheny, A.P. (1980). Bayley's Infant Behavior Record: Behavioral components and twin analysis. *Child Development*, **51**, 1157–1167.

Matheny, A.P. (1986). Stability and change in infant temperament: Contributions from the infant, mother, and family environment. In G.A. Kohnstamm (Ed.), *Temperament discussed: Temperament and development in infancy and childhood* (pp. 49–58). Berwyn, PA: Swets.

McKinney, J.D., Mason, J., Perkerson, K. & Clifford, M. (1975). Relationship between classroom behavior and academic achievement. *Journal of Educational Psychology*, **67**, 198–203.

Moseley, M. (1986). Effects of temperament on achievement in early childhood. Unpublished Doctoral Dissertation, University of Georgia.

Paget, K.D., Nagle, R.J. & Martin, R.P. (1984). Interrelationships between temperament characteristics and first-grade teacher–student interaction. *Journal of Abnormal Child Psychology*, **12**, 547–560.

Rose, S.A. & Wallace, (1985a). Cross-modal and intramodal transfer as predictors of mental development in full-term and preterm infants. *Developmental Psychology*, **21**, 949–962.

Rose, S.A. & Wallace, I.F. (1985b). Visual recognition memory: A predictor of later cognitive functioning in preterms. *Child Development*, **56**, 843–852.

Silberman, M. (1969). Behavioral expression of teachers' attitudes toward elementary school students. *Journal of Educational Psychology*, **60**, 402–407.

Thomas, A. & Chess, S. (1977). *Temperament and development*. New York: Brunner/Mazel.

25

Temperament: Conceptual Issues and Clinical Implications

MICHAEL RUTTER
Institute of Psychiatry, London

CONCEPTUAL ISSUES

As earlier chapters of this volume have made clear, numerous controversies surround scientific concepts of temperament (see also Bates, 1987; Garrison & Earls, 1987; Goldsmith *et al.*, 1987; Kohnstamm, 1986; Plomin & Dunn, 1986; Porter & Collins, 1982; Rutter, 1987a). Yet the lay public has long accepted that people differ in their characteristic styles of behaviour and that, to some extent, these styles have a constitutional origin. Indeed, the notion that human beings are constitutionally different in ways that shape their personality style goes back over 2000 years to the time of Hippocrates (Mora, 1980). It is striking that the concept of four vital body 'humours' provided some of the key words still used today to describe personality styles in lay parlance – melancholic, sanguine, choleric and phlegmatic. Physiologically determined behavioural attributes also apply to Chinese notions of human nature being composed of a balance between the forces of *Yin* and *Yang*, and to the constructs used by the ancient Hindus (Garrison & Earls, 1987). Of course, the particular physiological hypotheses put forward to explain individual differences in temperament now seem primitive and misguided. Nevertheless, it is pertinent that there was general acceptance of a biological basis for temperamental propensities.

In modern times, advances in physiological understanding led to a shift of site of the focus of interest from the liver and bodily fluids to the nervous system. Thus, Pavlov (1927) proposed a typology of nervous systems to account for individual differences in responses to conditioning procedures. Also, the behavioural typologies in vogue today among adult personality theorists such as Eysenck (1953, 1967, 1983) and Gray (1983) in the United Kingdom and Tellegen (1985) and

Temperament in Childhood   Edited by G.A. Kohnstamm, J.E. Bates and M.K. Rothbart

Cloninger (1986) in the United States are conceptualized in terms of their supposed neurobiological origins.

The present-day study of child temperament, although it has led to rather similar concepts, had somewhat different origins. Gesell (1937) pioneered the study of behavioural individuality in human infants, and Diamond's (1957) book on *Personality and temperament* noted the importance of individual differences. However, temperament research was first firmly put on the map by the New York Longitudinal Study initiated in the 1950s by Alexander Thomas and Stella Chess together with Herbert Birch (Chess & Thomas, 1984; Thomas & Chess, 1977; Thomas, Chess, Birch, Hertzig & Korn, 1963). They emphasized that individual differences in behavioural reaction patterns were evident in infancy and argued that these differences were a reflection of the make-up of the child rather than of the environments encountered. It was recognized that children differed in numerous respects, such as body build and intelligence; temperament was differentiated in terms of its concern with variations in *behavioural* propensities. Within the behavioural domain, temperament was set apart on the basis that it referred to a person's preponderant *style* (that is to 'how' characteristics), rather than the content of what was done (the 'what') or to motivational features (the 'why') or to capacities or skills. There was also the requirement that the characteristics be present in all individuals to varying degrees – that is they were dimensional features. The particular temperamental dimensions that were identified were not chosen on any theoretical basis; rather, there was an inductive analysis of detailed behavioural descriptions of infants in order to pick out the features that seemed best to differentiate individuals. The result was nine dimensions that spanned motoric functions (activity level), task involvement (persistence), emotions (intensity and valence or quality) and social engagement (approach/withdrawal to new situations and adaptability).

As Bates brings out well in Chapter 1 of this volume, the 30 years or so since the first reports by Thomas and his associates have seen much argument over both the conceptualization and measurement of temperamental features. Although many writers have come to agree that temperament should be applied only to characteristics that are evident in infancy, strongly heritable, and stable over time, these restrictions are mistaken in my view. The first specification (present in the initial papers of Thomas and his colleagues) was introduced in order to focus attention on constitutional qualities and to exclude learned patterns of behaviour. The intention is appropriate but there are several rather different reasons why the requirement is problematic (Rutter, 1970). To begin with, there are many examples of constitutional qualities that are not evident in infancy and which take time to manifest; language is an obvious example. Also, it is not correct to suppose that genetic determination is strongest in infancy before learning has had time to take place. To the contrary, for most characteristics, heritability *increases* as children grow older (Plomin, 1986). This is partly because intra-uterine and perinatal environmental influences have a major impact in the infancy period and partly because maturational differences (biologically determined, but not by the same genetic factors that influence temperamental variation) are strongly influential in early life (see McCall, 1981). Moreover, it is a fact that for all characteristics, measures in early infancy do not show strong correlations with adult qualities. That is especially the case with all behavioural characteristics that have been regarded as temperamental (Bates, 1987).

The requirement of high heritability sounds reasonable if the intention is to focus on constitutionally determined qualities but nevertheless, it too presents some difficulties (Hinde, in Goldsmith *et al.*, 1987). For a start, there is the practical problem that most studies of heritability have been based on highly fallible measures (see below); accordingly, the data for this requirement are inadequate. Also, most human qualities have a strong genetic component so that the requirement does not exclude much. Moreover, the empirical evidence does not indicate that qualities thought to be temperamental have an obviously stronger genetic component than those thought not to be so (e.g. psychiatric disorders) (see Plomin, 1986; Rutter *et al.*, in press; Vandenberg, Singer & Pauls, 1986). But, in addition, it is incorrect to equate 'constitutional' with 'heritable'. As Hinde (in Goldsmith *et al.*, 1987) emphasized, constitutional features may be environmentally induced. For example, this has been shown with respect to the influence of prenatal androgens on both neural organization (Arnold & Gorski, 1984) and behavioural qualities (Mayer-Bahlberg, Ehrhardt & Feldman, 1986). Similarly, early stress experiences have been shown to bring about lasting changes in the neuroendocrine system and in emotional responses (Hennessy & Levine, 1979; Hunt, 1979). While the concept of temperament does indeed require a constitutional basis for the qualities, this has to be seen in terms that extend beyond high heritability, in spite of the fact that high heritability may often be found.

The third specification of stability over time would seem to follow from the requirement of constitutional origin. However, the process of development is intrinsically one of change and patterns of change are genetically influenced (Plomin, 1986). Biologically determined characteristics will not necessarily be manifest in the same way throughout the course of development, even though strong continuities and coherence are to be expected (Hinde & Bateson, 1984; Rutter, 1987a; Sroufe, 1979). Also, even characteristics with a strong biological basis are likely to be influenced by environmental forces – as shown by the findings on height (Tizard, 1975) and intelligence (Rutter, 1985; Schiff & Lewontin, 1986).

During recent years there has been increasing attention paid to the issues involved in the measurement of temperamental characteristics (see Bates, 1986a,b, 1987; Campos, Barrett, Lamb, Goldsmith & Stenberg, 1983; Hubert, Wachs, Peters-Martin & Gandour, 1982; Plomin, 1983; Rothbart & Goldsmith, 1985; Rutter, 1982). At one time, the main emphasis was on the psychometric qualities of individual instruments (and most research has relied on single-instrument assessment of temperament). However, although these are important (as they are for any instrument), there has been an increasing realization that no single instrument can possibly provide an unbiased measure. Temperamental qualities are abstractions and not directly observable discrete behaviours (Rutter, Birch, Thomas & Chess, 1964). The latent variable of temperament (Rutter, 1987a) is conceptualized as that aspect of behaviour that reflects the person contribution (as distinct from relationship or situational aspects) and which refers to biologically based individual differences in behavioural style (rather than to the content of behaviour or to motivational components). Parental reports aim to get nearest to this through tapping parental observations of the child's behaviour in a range of different situations over time. Nevertheless, even the very best of parent measures will necessarily include components reflecting error, perceptual bias, relationship qualities (because many of the situations observed will involve the parent as a participant) and situation specificities (because parents have few opportunities to observe their children at school or in other people's homes or playing and talking with other children). Also, all behaviour will include cognitive and motivational components. The intensity of a person's emotional reactions, or activity level, or reaction to new situations will be influenced by their cognitive processing of the situation and by their self-concept, as well as by stylistic temperamental features. In other words, temperament constitutes just one aspect of personality (Rutter, 1987a). There is no ready solution to the problem of how to get closest to the abstraction or latent concept. Clearly, multiple measuring devices and multiple situations help to overcome measurement biases and error (Epstein, 1979, 1983). However, statistical procedures, such as structural equation modelling, can take measurement further by partitioning and measuring the different elements of the bias and error and not just reducing their influence (Rutter & Pickles, in press). There may also be advantages in including physiological features in the triangulation of measurement, as done by Kagan, Reznick and Snidman (1987) in their assessment of behavioural inhibition (see Chapter 8).

Whatever the combination of measures used, and whatever statistical technique is used to put measures together, there has to be consideration of which kinds of situations should be used to tap temperamental qualities. At first sight, one might think that the concept of a 'trait' means that it should manifest in all situations, that is, it is defined by its pervasiveness. However, that is not necessarily the case. Thus, Suomi's research (1983, 1987; see also Chapter 10, by Higley & Suomi) suggests that emotionality features are best shown in stressful situations; individual differences in emotionality are much less evident in everyday non-stressful circumstances. Similarly, it may be that certain temperamental qualities need to be assessed in terms of responses to novel situations. For example, this is explicit in the Thomas *et al.* (1963) dimensions of approach/withdrawal and adaptability and in the Kagan *et al.* (1987) quality of behavioural inhibition.

The last conceptual issue to mention is that involved in the choice of dimensions of temperament. Clearly, there is a need to reduce the almost infinite list of adjectives that could be applied to behavioural styles to a more manageable small number of *meaningful* dimensions. The question is how best to do so. Psychometricians have tended to favour using factor analysis as a means of deriving dimensions on the basis of patterns of intercorrelations between different behavioural features. However, although one set of data to be considered along with others, factor analysis findings do not seem to me to constitute a satisfactory criterion (Rutter, 1982). The more important issue in my view is the *functional* grouping of behaviours. That is, the choice of dimensions and their groupings needs to be decided on whether they are useful and whether they share the same qualities. Thus, usefulness might be considered in terms of strength and distinctiveness of effects on interpersonal interactions, or on associations with the later development of particular types of psychiatric disorder, or on developmental consistency. Functional equivalence between temperamental features would be decided on similar grounds and on the basis of comparable correlations with neurobiological measures, or of evidence that they reflect the same genotype. Of course, it could well turn out that different answers are given with different measures of functional equivalence. If so, there needs to be study of why that is the case in order that one may gain a greater understanding of the meaning and biological basis of the temperamental qualities.

In this discussion of the concept of temperamental characteristics, attention has been drawn to a variety of problems and it is all too evident that we lack the empirical data to enable rational decisions to be taken on many of the questions raised. It is necessary, therefore, to ask how a clinician can use the concept now? If temperament is a theoretical abstraction rather than a directly observable quality, does it have any practical utility at the moment? I think that it does, because there is evidence in support of the key elements involved in the construct (Bates, 1987; Rutter, 1982). That is, it is clear that there is behavioural individuality, that to an important extent this reflects person characteristics, that there is a significant constitutional component, that there is moderate consistency in individual differences after infancy and that individual differences in behavioural style do predict in clinically relevant ways. In other words, it seems to me reasonable to accept the proposition that there is a person component to styles of behaviour and that this is constitutionally based, although (like all human characteristics) it is affected by environmental influences.

TEMPERAMENTAL DIMENSIONS

Half a dozen years ago, Plomin (1983) argued that 'all that the field of temperament can offer with confidence to the clinician is its emphasis on individuality' (Plomin, 1983, p. 82). I accept that that is indeed the most basic message but it doesn't seem much to build on if that is all. Plomin went on to argue for the need to separate off behavioural characteristics that met the criteria for temperament in order to avoid the concept of temperament becoming lost through excessive diffusion. The attempt to narrow down the list of temperamental variables is part of that endeavour. The problem is that there is no universal agreement on what should be included and excluded. Plomin urged restriction to just three features – emotionality, activity and sociability; Bates (Chapter 1) suggested seven characteristics and others have argued for a variety of different permutations (see Goldsmith et al., 1987).

I think that one should not be put off by the differences, as there is considerable overlap between the approaches. Moreover, they do provide quite useful ways of thinking about how people may differ in their behavioural styles. Thus, there is general agreement that it is useful to consider temperament in terms of emotional responses to novelty or to situations involving stress or challenge or adaption; of sociability or a propensity to engage in interactions with others; and of task involvement or response to non-social stimuli. There is, perhaps, most uncertainty on how to conceptualize the last of these domains. Buss and Plomin (1986) have focused on activity level in terms of tempo and energy expenditure but those investigators who have been most influenced by clinical implications have been more inclined to use concepts of impulsivity and of sensation-seeking or novelty-seeking (Cloninger, 1986; Gray, 1983; Quay, 1977). Aggressiveness, too, might be put forward on the basis of its temporal stability and heritability (Olweus, 1979; Rushton, Fulker, Neale, Nias & Eysenck, 1986). However, it has been argued that behavioural tendencies such as impulsivity or aggressiveness are derivative of combinations of more basic, simple temperamental dimensions and/or arise from the interaction between temperamental features and social constraints (Buss & Plomin, 1975). It is of some theoretical and practical importance to decide between alternatives but the evidence that would enable one to do so is not yet available.

Somewhat similar problems attend the temperamental 'difficultness' concept. It seems to be unacceptable to define a person construct in terms of other people's reactions to the behaviour. On the other hand, it is reasonable to suppose that certain aggregations of temperamental characteristics may involve an increased probability of engendering negative interpersonal interactions or behavioural disturbance. There is some evidence that this may be so (see Chapter 22, by Maziade; also reviews by Bates, 1987; Carey, 1985; Garrison & Earls, 1987). In other words, the behavioural style appears to have substantial predictive validity. What remains problematic is that different investigators have used somewhat different (although markedly overlapping) constellations or mixtures of temper-amental features, and there has not emerged a satisfactory unifying concept of just what characterizes the personal style that gives rise to the difficulties. However, Bates' suggestion (Chapter 17) that it may involve two separate components, sensation-seeking and high sensitivity to aversive stimuli, is a good one. If so, rather different consequences would be expected for the two components.

It would be helpful if the research findings provided a clear structure or classi-fication that told one how to conceptualize different dimensions of temperament and which aspects of behavioural style most meaningfully differentiated individuals in terms of constitutionally based features. It has to be admitted that such a structure is not available. There are important leads that serve to guide research and which also aid clinical thinking but that is as much as can be claimed.

CLINICAL IMPLICATIONS

Because that appears to be the current state of the art, I do not myself find it most useful clinically to start thinking about child characteristics from a temperamental perspective. Rather, I prefer to begin with a more general person construct and then, only secondarily, ask myself which aspects of that construct can be construed in temperamental terms. Nevertheless, I assume the clinical utility of the tempera-mental concept on the basis of the fairly consistent evidence that temperamental qualities are statistically associated with an increased risk of psychiatric disorder (see Garrison & Earls, 1987; Rutter, 1987a; also Chapter 17, by Bates). However, for that statistical association to be useful in dealing with individual patients, it is necessary to consider what mechanisms might be involved (Rutter, 1977).

Direct Vulnerability to Psychopathological Disorders

The first alternative is that certain temperamental attributes directly create an increased vulnerability to certain psychopathological disorders. Kagan *et al.* (1987) have suggested that this may be the case with the characteristic of behavioural inhibition when encountering strange situations or unfamiliar persons, especially when associated with high physiological arousal (see also Chapter 8). These features as measured at 21 months have been shown to predict both inhibited behaviour and physiological indices at $5\frac{1}{2}$ and $7\frac{1}{2}$ years. It was also noted that inhibited behaviour at $7\frac{1}{2}$ years was often associated with fears and that behavioural inhibition was particularly common in the offspring of parents with anxiety and affective disorders (Rosenbaum *et al.*, 1988). Conversely, unusually *low* autonomic reactivity has been associated with recidivist delinquency in adolescence and early adult life (see Magnusson, 1988; Rutter & Giller, 1983). The evidence with respect to both sets of psychopathological associations (i.e. with anxiety disorders and with delinquency) leaves many questions unanswered. Thus, the nature of the behavioural–physiological connections remains uncertain and the mechanisms involved in the association with disorder are not known. The same applies to the links between the characteristic of 'difficultness' and conduct ('externalized') disorders (see Chapter 22, by Maziade). Several possibilities need to be considered. Graham and Stevenson (1987a; Stevenson & Graham, 1982) have suggested that in some cases the supposed temperamental trait is actually *synonymous* with a mild manifestation of disorder – i.e. the temperamental feature and psychiatric disorder represent different degrees of the *same* phenomenon. This may apply when disorder is diagnosed solely on the basis of an extreme of some general characteristic such as anxiety or oppositional behaviour but it seems unlikely when the disorder is diagnosed on the presence of behaviours that are *qualitatively* different from the temperamental feature, as is usually the case (Rutter, 1987a; but see Graham & Stevenson, 1987b; Rutter 1987b). However, an adequate test of the hypothesis requires evidence on whether or not the correlates (genetic, physiological and psychosocial) of temperament and of psychiatric disorder are different; such evidence is so far lacking. Nevertheless, it is already clear that individuals with the *same* degree of temperamental feature may *differ* on the presence of disorder, so that some additional mechanism must be postulated.

Alternatively, it could be that the temperamental feature predisposes to disorder because the individual is extreme on some continuously distributed trait that makes the person's interactions with the environment more liable to create problems. This is the proposition put forward, for example, by Eysenck (1977) with respect to the role of 'conditionability' in predisposition to criminality. There are two main problems with this type of suggestion: the lack of evidence on the role of the hypothesized mediating variable (such as 'conditionability') and the uncertainty on the dimensionality of the attribute. Thus, both Kagan *et al.* (1987), with respect to behavioural inhibition, and Magnusson (1988), with respect to low physiological reactivity and inattention/overactivity/aggressivity, noted that the strongest associations arose with particular behaviour–physiology constellations rather than with any single continuous variable. It may be that the psychopathological risk arises from a *qualitatively* distinct person variable and not from a *quantitative* variation on a dimensional temperamental variable. In the same way, we may ask whether sensation-seeking is a temperamental variable or a psychopathological risk factor associated with hyperkinetic disorder and delinquency (Quay, 1988).

It seems reasonable to accept that personological features are associated with an increased vulnerability to psychopathological disorders but it remains uncertain whether this is best conceptualized in temperamental or risk-factor terms, and little is known on the processes involved in the vulnerability.

Increased Susceptibility to Psychosocial Adversities

One possible mechanism is that the temperamental quality renders the individual more susceptible to psychosocial adversities. The general notion of organism–environment or gene–environment interactions is well accepted. Thus, there are two genetically distinct varieties of the plant golden rod (Thoday, 1969); one responds to strong sunlight by *in*creased growth and the other by *de*creased growth. In the human psychopathological arena there is some limited evidence that to some extent the genetic factors associated with antisocial behaviour may operate through an increased susceptibility to psychosocial hazards (Cadoret, 1982, 1985). However, although statistical techniques to study gene–environment interactions are available (Kendler & Eaves, 1986), there are few well-substantiated examples of their occurrence (Plomin, De Fries & Fulker, 1988). It is very reasonable to suppose that temperamental qualities *could* operate through the creation of an increased susceptibility to negative environmental influences; thus, behavioural inhibition and low physiological reactivity might operate in this fashion. However, although there are suggestions that temperament 'difficultness' may have this effect in middle childhood (see Chapter 22, Maziade), few clinical studies have tested for this mechanism.

'Goodness of Fit'

A related, but somewhat different, suggestion is that children of different temperamental qualities have different needs, and that the consequences therefore depend on whether or not there is a good 'fit' with the environments encountered (Lerner & Lerner, 1983; see Chapter 19, by Thomas & Chess). The suggestion is conceptually appealing because it gets away from the unbiological notion that certain traits are adaptive in all circumstances (see Hinde, 1982), and because it is in keeping with findings outside the arena of temperament. For example, deaf children obviously differ from hearing children in their responsiveness to the spoken voice. They have the same basic need for communicative interchange but this has to be met via gesture and sign rather than speech. Probably because of that difference, it appears that deaf children reared by deaf parents may fare better in some respects than deaf children reared by hearing parents (Meadow, 1975; Meadow, Greenberg & Erting, 1983; Meadow, Greenberg, Erting & Carmichael, 1981). Similarly, because of their handicaps, autistic children require more structure in their social environment than do normal children (Howlin & Rutter, 1987). In the field of temperament, too, it is noteworthy that (albeit on a very small sample), De Vries (1984) found that during famine conditions in Africa a 'difficult' temperament was protective in leading to survival – presumably because infants with such characteristics demanded and received more attention and food. Similarly, Schaffer (1966) found that high activity was protective (in relation to developmental retardation) for infants raised in a poor institution. In other circumstances, of course, such temperamental characteristics are associated with risk rather than protection.

The general proposition that temperamental features do not have the same effects in all conditions is also supported by the findings on sex differences. Thus, Buss (1981) found that high activity was associated with positive interactions between fathers and sons but with negative interactions between fathers and daughters; Maccoby, Snow and Jacklin (1984) found that mothers tended to back away from difficult sons whereas the reverse applied with girls; and Stevenson-Hinde and Hinde (1986) found that shyness in boys was associated with largely negative interpersonal interactions whereas in girls the correlates were largely positive.

Clearly, whether or not a particular temperamental style predisposes to psychiatric disorder is likely to be influenced by other people's reactions and responses. Extreme shyness may elicit either supportive comforting responses or irritated angry reactions from parents. Similarly, what is seen as 'difficultness' in one child may be viewed as 'manliness' or 'independence' in another. Moreover, it should not be assumed that accepting responses are always the most helpful. Dweck and Elliot (1983) have pointed out that the tendency to blame low achievement in boys on their not trying hard enough or on their 'bad' behaviour may serve as a spur to improved performance because the critical reaction carries the implicit positive message that they are capable of better. Conversely, a supportive 'never mind, you did your best' response to girls' task failure may take away self-confidence and striving. The hope that knowledge about a child's particular temperamental make-up should lead to an understanding of what would be the optimal parental style of handling remains unfulfilled. We simply do not know how to translate measurement of a child's temperament into a prescription for parental practice (or for teacher actions). Nevertheless, that does not mean that we know nothing or that parental counselling on the basis of temperamental concepts is useless. It is often helpful for parents to appreciate that a child's behaviour may reflect a temperamental style, at least in part, and that inhibited or difficult behaviour does not necessarily stem from either a failure in upbringing by the parents or motivational problems in the child ('lack of trying' in the inhibited child or 'deliberate naughtiness' in the difficult child). It may also be helpful for parents to understand how the child's characteristics are leading to patterns of family interactions that are maladaptive in their effects. Bates (Chapter 17) gives good examples of what this may mean in actual clinical practice.

Child Effects on Other People

One aspect of considering the implications of temperament in interactional terms is appreciation that children's characteristics may shape other people's responses to them. Bell (1968) and Thomas, Chess and Birch (1968) forced a rethink on socialization research by pointing out that many of the findings might reflect the effect of a child on its parents rather than the other way around. During the 21 years since that suggestion was made, there have been advances in the research strategies that may be used to separate child and parent effects (Bell & Chapman, 1986) and research findings that demonstrate child effects have slowly accumulated (Bell & Chapman, 1986; Bell & Harper, 1977; Houts, Shutty & Emery, 1985; Lerner & Spanier, 1978). Yet Bates (1987; see also Chapter 17) has concluded that there is no evidence of child effects (with respect to temperamental qualities) in infancy and only weak evidence for effects in later years. Also, Plomin and Daniels (1987) have shown that most of the variations in parental treatment of different siblings in the same family are not genetically determined in infancy.

While I accept their summaries of the evidence, I doubt whether the conclusions can be extended to extremes of temperament during the post-infancy years. That is because the evidence for child effects with respect to other child characteristics is stronger. For example, it has been shown that the language ability of children is a powerful determinant of variations in parental conversational style (Cross, Nienhuys & Kirkman, 1985); that people's physical appearance influences other people's reactions to them (Goodman, Richardson, Dornbusch & Hastorf, 1963; Lerner, 1982); and that mothers interact differently with preterm infants than with full-term babies (Goldberg & Di Vitto 1983). Brunk and Heinggeler (1984) showed experimentally that children's compliance and oppositional behaviour elicited different parental behaviours. Also, if hyperactive children's behaviour is made more normal through the use of stimulant medication, this is often accompanied by changes in parental behaviour (Barkley, 1981; Schachar, Taylor, Wieselberg, Thorley & Rutter, 1987). Furthermore, in our own study of temperamental features in the children of mentally ill parents we found that those with adverse temperamental characteristics were more likely to be the target of parental criticism (Rutter, 1978). In addition, as reviewed by Keogh (1986), there is evidence of associations between temperamental qualities of children and teachers' behaviour towards them.

Many of these studies concern school-age children, and Bates (Chapter 17) has argued that in the post-infancy years it is more difficult to distinguish the basic temperament from the overlays of experience. That argument is based on the questionable assumption that environmental effects increase with age. In fact, the empirical evidence suggests that the reverse is the case – genetic effects are stronger in the post-infancy years (Plomin, 1986). However, that is a separate issue from the question of whether the effect is from child to parent or the converse. The experimental data indicate the reality of child effects.

Why, then, is this not more apparent in the temperamental studies? Probably, part of the explanation is that the effects are greater with extremes of temperament than with variations in the middle of the range (Bates, Maslin & Frankel, 1985; Lee & Bates, 1985). Also, perhaps, the temperamental qualities that have been measured have not been the most salient ones for effects on personal interactions. In addition, too, it is quite possible that child effects in infancy are not as great as in middle childhood. However, it should be added that the negative evidence on child effects for temperamental attributes is weak. The studies are relatively few in number; they rely on single, mostly questionnaire, measures of temperament; they focus on a limited range of parental behaviours; and most concern small babies in situations where the mothers are more in control than is the case with older children in less structured situations. Be that as it may, the evidence suggests that the qualities of children *do* influence other peoples' reactions to them. While the evidence is limited that this applies to temperament as well as other qualities, I think that it is likely that it does – at least with extremes. The possibility that to some extent people shape their own environments, that nature helps to shape nurture (Scarr & McCartney, 1983), needs to be considered in parental counselling.

Range of Experiences

Another way in which temperamental attributes may operate is in children's *choice* of activities and environments (Rutter, 1975). The friendly approaching child will seek more social encounters than will a timid inhibited child and, as a result, will gain more experience in coping with social situations and with meeting and getting to know unfamiliar people. Also, impulsive, active, temperamentally difficult children may be more likely to put themselves in risky situations (climbing trees or getting on the garage roof), and so have more accidents (see Carey, 1985; also Matheny, 1987; Nyman, 1987; Rutter, Chadwick & Shaffer, 1983). Thus, temperamental features may predispose to or protect against risky environmental experiences. But, also, the experiences in part brought about by temperamental characteristics may serve to strengthen or attenuate the characteristics themselves. Suppose that behavioural inhibition is activated by novel, challenging or stressful social situations. The child whose inhibition has lead to an avoidance of new situations will find more later circumstances strange and stressful than the child with similar initial inhibition who has been encouraged to mix socially and who has been supported in learning to cope with social encounters, while being allowed time to get used to new situations before being pressed to interact. Empirical data make clear that to an important extent children *do* change in their behavioural styles as they grow older, even though substantial consistency is maintained. Parents need to be helped both to accept the reality of individual differences among their children and to appreciate how the ways in which children are dealt with may serve to make such differences more or less adaptive in their consequences. It is true that we lack adequate data on which styles of parenting have which effects on which characteristics, but it is evident that patterns of upbringing *do* make a difference.

Temperament and Personality Development

The last issue to consider is the role of temperamental differences in personality development (Rutter, 1987a). The distinction between temperament and personality is not a matter of age in spite of the fact that the former term has been primarily used in childhood and the latter in adult life (Berger, 1982; Prior, Crook, Stripp, Power & Joseph, 1986). Rather, it is that personality involves much more than constitutionally based stylist behavioural tendencies. Personality reflects the patterning that each person, as a thinking being, develops as a way of dealing with traits with which he is endowed, the social contexts that he encounters and the experiences he has received (Rutter, 1987c). Thus, it involves a set of cognitions about ourselves, our relationships and our interactions with the environment (Rutter, 1987a). These constitute the self-system that is made up of such qualities as self-esteem, self-efficacy and social problem-solving skills (Harter, 1983). That this is so would be accepted by most people. What is uncertain is just *how* temperamental characteristics interact with cognitive sets to make up personality. To what extent, for example, does behavioural inhibition or neuroticism or introversion predispose to learned helplessness? Insofar as the temperamental features and cognitive set are associated with one another, do the temperamental features predispose directly to emotional disorder with the cognitive features no more than epiphenomena, or is the psychiatric risk mediated by the cognitive set to which the temperamental trait gives rise, or are the trait and the cognitive set independently influential? We do not know. The different approaches to personality have remained regrettably separate from one another (Rutter, 1987a).

Recognizing that we lack key data, there are nevertheless two implications for current clinical practice. First, it is necessary to accept that, at least after infancy and especially in later childhood and adult life, it is not possible unambiguously to separate temperamental features from motivational and cognitive features on the basis of observation or interview measures alone, however well they are devised. Of course, careful study of the person's behaviour over time and across different situations can take one a long way in sorting out which aspects are which and it is the inferences based on such study that constitute the basis for clinical decisions. Secondly, how people behave will be in part determined by the ways in which they *view* their own temperamental characteristics. One important clinical goal is to help individuals see the positive side of the traits they possess and to assist them to use these traits in adaptive ways.

CONCLUSIONS

Research on temperament over the last 30 years, as reviewed in other chapters, has provided us with a substantial corpus of knowledge. As emphasized by the pioneers of temperamental research, the concepts and findings have very important implications for clinical practice. However, in spite of all we know, there is no straightforward fashion in which measurement of a person's temperamental qualities can lead directly to particular clinical interventions. It is essential to recognize the statistical associations between temperamental characteristics and psychiatric risk but, if that recognition is to be made use of in therapy, it is also necessary to understand the mechanisms underlying the association. There are only limited empirical data on the study of mechanisms but it appears that they are likely to include: direct vulnerability to psychopathological disorders; increased susceptibility to psychosocial adversities; 'goodness of fit' with the environment; child effects on other people; temperamental influences on choice of experiences; and temperamental contributions to personality development.

REFERENCES

Arnold, A.P. & Gorski, R.A. (1984). Gonadal steroid induction of structural sex differences in the central nervous system. *Annual Review of Neuroscience*, **7**, 413–442.

Barkley, R.A. (1981). The use of psychopharmacology to study reciprocal influences in parent–child interaction. *Journal of Abnormal Child Psychology*, **9**, 303–310.

Bates, J. (1986a). On the relationship between temperament and behavior problems. In G.A. Kohnstamm (Ed.), *Temperament discussed: Temperament and development in infancy and childhood* (pp. 181–189). Lisse (Neth.): Swets & Zeitlinger.

Bates, J. (1986b). The measurement of temperament. In R. Plomin & J. Dunn (Eds), *The study of temperament: Changes, continuities and challenges* (pp. 1–11). Hillsdale, NJ: Erlbaum.

Bates, J.E. (1987). Temperament in infancy. In J.D. Osofsky (Ed.), *Handbook of infant development*, 2nd edn (pp. 1101–1149). New York: Wiley.

Bates, J.E., Maslin, C.A. & Frankel, K.A. (1985). Attachment security, mother–child interaction and temperament as predictors of behaviour-problem ratings at age three years. In I. Bretherton & E. Waters (Eds), *Growing points of attachment and research. Monographs of the Society of Research in Child Development*, Series 209, 50, Nos. 1–2.

Bell, R.Q. (1968). A reinterpretation of the direction of effects in studies of socialization. *Psychological Review*, **75**, 81–95.

Bell, R.Q. & Chapman, M. (1986). Child effects in studies using experimental or brief longitudinal approaches to socialization. *Developmental Psychology*, **22**, 595–603.

Bell, R.Q. & Harper, L.V. (1977). *Child effects on adults*. Hillsdale, NJ: Erlbaum.

Berger, M. (1982). Personality development and temperament. In R. Porter & G. Collins (Eds), *Temperamental differences in infants and young children*. Ciba Foundation Symposium No. 89. London: Pitman.

Buss, D.M. (1981). Predicting parent–child interactions from children's activity level. *Developmental psychology*, **17**, 59–65.

Brunk, M.A. & Henggeler, S.W. (1984). Child influences on adult controls: An experimental investigation. *Developmental Psychology*, **20**, 1074–1081.

Buss, A.H. & Plomin, R. (1975). *A temperament theory of personality development*. New York: Wiley.

Buss, A.H. & Plomin, R. (1986). The EAS approach to temperament. In R. Plomin & J. Dunn (Eds), *The study of temperament: Changes, continuities and challenges*. Hillsdale, NJ: Erlbaum.

Cadoret, R.J. (1982). Genotype–environmental interaction in antisocial behaviour. *Psychological Medicine*, **12**, 235–239.

Cadoret, R.J. (1985). Genes, environment and their interaction in the development of psychopathology. In T. Sakai & T. Tsuboi (Eds), *Genetic aspects of human behavior* (pp. 165–175). Tokyo: Igaku-Shoin.

Campos, J.J., Barrett, K., Lamb, M.E., Goldsmith, H.H. & Stenberg, C. (1983). Socioemotional development. In M.M. Haith & J.J. Campos, Vol. Eds for P.H. Mussen (Ed.), *Infancy and developmental psychobiology*, Vol. 2, *Handbook of child psychology*, 4th edn (pp. 783–915). New York: Wiley.

Carey, W.B. (1985). Interactions of temperament and clinical conditions. *Advances in Developmental and Behavioral Pediatrics*, **6**, 83–115.

Chess, S. & Thomas, A. (1984). *Origins and evolution of behavior disorders*. New York: Brunner/Mazel.

Cloninger, C.R. (1986). A unified biosocial theory of personality and its role in the development of anxiety states. *Psychiatric Developments*, **3**, 167–226.

Cross, T.G., Nienhuys, T.G. & Kirkman, M. (1985). Parent–child interaction with receptively disabled children: Some determinants of maternal speech style. In K.E. Nelson (Ed.), *Children's language*. Hillsdale, NJ: Erlbaum.

De Vries, M.W. (1984). Temperament and infant mortality among the Masai of East Africa. *American Journal of Psychiatry*, **141**, 1189–1194.

Diamond, S. (1957). *Personality and temperament*. New York: Harper.

Dweck, C.S. & Elliot, E.S. (1983). Achievement motivation. In E.M. Hetherington (Ed.), *Handbook of child psychology*, Vol. 4, *Socialization, personality and social development* (pp. 643–692). New York: Wiley.

Epstein, S. (1979). The stability of behavior: I: On predicting most of the people much of the time. *Journal of Personality and Social Psychology*, **37**, 1097–1126.

Epstein, S. (1983). Aggregation and beyond: Some basic issues of the prediction of behavior. *Journal of Personality*, **51**, 360–392.

Eysenck, H.J. (1953). *The structure of human personality*. London: Methuen. New York: Wiley.

Eysenck, H.J. (1967). *The biological basis of personality*. Springfield, IL: C.C. Thomas.

Eysenck, H.J. (1977). *Crime and personality*. London: Paladin.

Eysenck, H.J. (1983). Aggregation and beyond: Some basic issues of the prediction of behavior. *Journal of Personality*, **51**, 360–392.

Garrison, W. & Earls, F. (1987). *Temperament and child psychopathology*. Newbury Park: Sage.

Gesell, A. (1937). Early evidence of individuality in human infants. *Scientific Monthly*, **45**, 217–255.

Goldberg, S. & Di Vitto, B.A. (1983). *Born too soon: Preterm birth and early development*. San Francisco: W.C. Freeman.

Goldsmith, H.H., Buss, A.H., Plomin, R., Rothbart, M.K., Thomas, A., Chess, S., Hinde, R.A. & McCall, R.B. (1987). Roundtable: What is temperament? Four approaches. *Child Development*, **58**, 505–529.

Goodman, N., Richardson, S.A., Dornbusch, S.M. & Hastorf, A.H. (1963). Variant reactions to physical disabilities. *American Sociological Review*, **28**, 429–435.

Graham, P. & Stevenson, J. (1987a). Temperament and psychiatric disorder: The genetic contribution to behaviour in childhood. *Australian and New Zealand Journal of Psychiatry*, **21**, 267–274.

Graham, P. & Stevenson, J. (1987b). Letter: Temperament, personality and personality disorder. *British Journal of Psychiatry*, **150**, 872–873.

Gray, J.A. (1983). Anxiety, personality and the brain. In A. Gale & J.A. Edwards (Eds), *Physiological correlates of human behaviour*, Vol. III, *Individual differences and psychopathology*. New York: Academic Press.

Harter, S. (1983). Developmental perspectives on self-system. In E. Hetherington (Ed.), *Socialization, personality and social development*, Vol. 4, *Handbook of child psychology*, 4th edn. New York: Wiley.

Hennessy, J. & Levine, S. (1979). Stress, arousal and the pituitary–adrenal system: A psychoendocrine hypothesis. In J.M. Sprague & A.N. Epstein (Eds), *Progress in psychobiology and physiological psychology* (pp. 133–178). New York: Academic Press.

Hinde, R.A. (1982). Attachment: Some conceptual and biological issues. In C.A. Parkes & J. Stevenson-Hinde (Eds), *The place of attachment in human behavior* (pp. 60–76). London and New York: Tavistock.

Hinde, R.A. & Bateson, P.P.G. (1984). Discontinuities versus continuities in behavioural development and the neglect of process. *International Journal of Behavioral Development*, **7**, 129–143.

Houts, A.C., Shutty, M.S. & Emery, R. (1985). The impact of children on adults. In B.B. Lahey & A.E. Kazdin (Eds), *Advances in clinical child psychology*, Vol. 8 (pp. 267–307). New York: Plenum.

Howlin, P. & Rutter, M. with Berger, M., Hemsley, R., Hersov, L. & Yule, W. (1987). *Treatment of autistic children*. Chichester: Wiley.

Hubert, N.C., Wachs, T.D., Peters-Martin, P. & Gandour, M.J. (1982). The study of early temperament: Measurement and conceptual issues. *Child Development*, **53**, 571–600.

Hunt, J.McV. (1979). Psychological development: Early experience. *Annual Review of Psychology*, **30**, 103–143.

Kagan, J., Reznick, J.S. & Snidman, N. (1987). The physiology and psychology of behavioral inhibition in children. *Child Development,* **58**, 1459–1473.

Kendler, K.S. & Eaves, L.J. (1986). Models for the joint effect of genotype and environment on liability of psychiatric illness. *American Journal of Psychiatry,* **143**, 279–289.

Keogh, B.K. (1986). Temperament and schooling: Meaning of 'goodness of fit'? In J.V. Lerner & R.M. Lerner (Eds), *Temperament and social interaction in infants and children* (pp. 89–108). San Francisco, CA: Jossey-Bass.

Kohnstamm, G.A. (Ed.) (1986). *Temperament discussed: Temperament and development in infancy and childhood.* Lisse (Neth.): Swets & Zeitlinger.

Lee, C. & Bates, J. (1985). Mother–child interaction at age two years and perceived difficult temperament. *Child Development,* **56**, 1314–1325.

Lerner, J.V. & Lerner, R.M. (1983). Temperament and adaptation across life: Theoretical and empirical issues. In P.B. Baltes & O.G. Brim, Jr (Eds), *Life span development and behaviour,* Vol. V (pp. 197–231). New York: Academic Press.

Lerner, R.M. (1982). Children and adolescents as producers of their own development. *Developmental Review,* **2**, 342–370.

Lerner, R.M. & Spanier, G.B. (Eds) (1978). *Child influences on marital and family interaction: A life-span perspective.* New York: Academic Press.

Maccoby, E.E., Snow, M.E. & Jacklin, C.N. (1984). Children's dispositions and mother–child interaction at 12 and 18 months: A short-term longitudinal study. *Developmental Psychology,* **20**, 459–472.

Magnusson, D. (1988). *Individual development from an interactional perspective: A longitudinal study.* Hillsdale, NJ: Erlbaum.

Matheny, A.P. (1987). Psychological characteristics of childhood accidents. *Journal of Social Issues,* **43**, 45–60.

Mayer-Bahlberg, H.F.L., Ehrhardt, A.A. & Feldman, J.F. (1986). Long-term implications of the prenatal endocrine milieu for sex-dimorphic behavior. In L. Erlenmeyer-Kimling & N.E. Miller (Eds), *Life-span research on the prediction of psychopathology* (pp. 17–30). Hillsdale, NJ: Erlbaum.

McCall, R.B. (1981). Nature–nurture and the two realms of development: A proposed integration with respect to mental development. *Child Development,* **52**, 1–12.

Meadow, K.P. (1975). The development of deaf children. In E.M. Hetherington (Ed.), *Review of child development research,* Vol. 5 (pp. 441–508). Chicago, IL: University of Chicago Press.

Meadow, K., Greenberg, M. & Erting, C. (1983). Attachment behaviour of deaf children with deaf parents. *Journal of American Academy of Child Psychiatry,* **22**, 23–28.

Meadow, K.P., Greenberg, M., Erting, C. & Carmichael, M. (1981). Interaction of deaf mothers and deaf pre-school children: Comparisons with three other groups of deaf and hearing dyads. *American Annals of the Deaf,* **126**, 454–468.

Mora, G. (1980). Historical and theoretical trends in psychiatry. In H.I. Kaplan, A.M. Freedman & B.J. Sadock (Eds), *Comprehensive textbook of psychiatry,* Vol. 1, 3rd edn. Baltimore: Williams & Wilkins.

Nyman, G. (1987). Infant temperament, childhood accidents, and hospitalization. *Clinical Pediatrics,* **26**, 398–404.

Olweus, D. (1979). Stability of aggressive reaction patterns in males: A review. *Psychological Bulletin,* **86**, 852–875.

Pavlov, I.P. (1927). *Conditioned reflexes* (trans. G.V. Anrep). London: Oxford University Press.

Plomin, R. (1983). Childhood temperament. In B.B. Lahey & A.E. Kazdin (Eds), *Advances in clinical child psychology,* Vol. 6 (pp. 45–92). New York: Plenum.

Plomin, R. (1986). *Development, genetics and psychology.* Hillsdale, NJ: Erlbaum.

Plomin, R. & Daniels, D. (1987). Why are children in the same family so different from one another? *Behavioral and Brain Sciences,* **10**, 1–15.

Plomin, R., De Fries, J.C. & Fulker, D.W. (1988). *Nature and nurture during infancy and childhood.* Cambridge: Cambridge University Press.

Plomin, R. & Dunn, J. (Eds) (1986). *The study of temperament: Changes, continuities and challenges*. Hillsdale, NJ: Erlbaum.

Porter, R & Collins, C.G. (Eds) (1982). *Temperament differences in infants and young children*. Ciba Foundation Symposium No. 89. London: Pitman.

Prior, M., Crook, G., Stripp, A., Power, M. & Joseph, M. (1986). The relationship between temperament and personality: An exploratory study. *Personality and Individual Differences*, **7**, 875–881.

Quay, H.C. (1977). Psychopathic behavior: Reflections on its nature, origins and treatment. In I.C. Uzgiris & F. Weizmann (Eds), *The structuring of experiences*. New York: Plenum.

Quay, H.C. (1988). Childhood behaviour disorders and the reward and inhibition systems of J.A. Gray. In L. Bloomingdale & J. Swanson (Eds), *Attention deficit and hyperactivity: Third Annual High Point Hospital Symposium*. Oxford: Pergamon.

Rosenbaum, J.F., Biederman, J., Gersten, M., Hirschfield, D.R., Menninger, S.R., Herman, J.B., Kagan, J., Reznick, S. & Snidman, N. (1988). Behavioral inhibition in children of parents with panic disorder and agoraphobia: A controlled study. *Archives of General Psychiatry*, **45**, 463–470.

Rothbart, M.K. & Goldsmith, H.H. (1985). Three approaches to the study of infant temperament. *Developmental Review*, **5**, 237–260.

Rushton, J.P., Fulker, D.W., Neale, M.C., Nias, D.K.B. & Eysenck, H.J. (1986). Altruism and aggression: The heritability of individual differences. *Journal of Personality and Social Psychology*, **50**, 1192–1198.

Rutter, M. (1970). Psychological development: Predictions from infancy. *Journal of Child Psychology and Psychiatry*, **15**, 49–62.

Rutter, M. (1975). *Helping troubled children*. Harmondsworth, Middx: Penguin.

Rutter, M. (1977). Individual differences. In M. Rutter & L. Hersov (Eds), *Child psychiatry: Modern approaches*, 1st edn (pp. 3–21). Oxford: Blackwell Scientific.

Rutter, M. (1978). Family area and school influences on the genesis of conduct disorders. In L.A. Hersov & M. Berger with D. Shaffer (Eds), *Aggression and antisocial behaviour in childhood and adolescence. Journal of Child Psychology and Psychiatry*, Book Suppl. 1. Oxford: Pergamon.

Rutter, M. (1982). Temperament: Concepts, issues and problems. In R. Porter & C.G. Collins (Eds), *Temperamental differences in infants and young children* (pp. 1–19). Ciba Foundation Symposium No. 89. London: Pitman.

Rutter, M. (1985). Family and school influences on cognitive development. *Journal of Child Psychology and Psychiatry*, **26**, 683–704.

Rutter, M. (1987a). Temperament, personality and personality disorder. *British Journal of Psychiatry*, **150**, 443–458.

Rutter, M. (1987b). Letter: Concepts of temperament and child psychiatric disorder. *British Journal of Psychiatry*, **150**, 873–874.

Rutter, M. (1987c). The role of cognition in child development and disorder. *British Journal of Medical Psychology*, **60**, 1–16.

Rutter, M., Birch, H., Thomas, A. & Chess, S. (1964). Temperamental characteristics in infancy and the later development of behavioural disorders. *British Journal of Psychiatry*, **110**, 651–661.

Rutter, M., Chadwick, O. & Shaffer, D. (1983). The behavioural and cognitive sequelae of head injury. In M. Rutter (Ed.) *Developmental neuropsychiatry* (pp. 83–111). New York: Guilford Press.

Rutter, M. & Giller, H. (1983). *Juvenile delinquency: Trends and perspectives*. Harmondsworth, Middx: Penguin.

Rutter, M., Macdonald, H., Le Couteur, A., Harrington, R., Bolton, P. & Bailey, A. (in press). Genetic factors in child psychiatric disorders: II. Empirical findings. *Journal of Child Psychology and Psychiatry*.

Rutter, M. & Pickles, A. (in press). Improving the quality of psychiatric data: Classification, cause and course. In D. Magnusson & L. Bergman (Eds), *Methodological issues in longitudinal research*. Cambridge: Cambridge University Press.

Scarr, S. & McCartney, K. (1983). How people make their own environments: A theory of genotype–environmental effects. *Child Development,* **54**, 424–435.

Schachar, R., Taylor, E., Wieselberg, M., Thorley, G. & Rutter, M. (1987). Changes in family function and relationships in children who respond to methylphenidate. *Journal of American Academy of Child Psychiatry,* **26**, 728–732.

Schaffer, H. R. (1966). Activity level as a constitutional determinant of infantile reaction to deprivation. *Child Development,* **37**, 595–602.

Schiff, M. & Lewontin, R. (1986). *Education and class: The irrelevance of IQ genetic studies.* Oxford: Clarendon Press.

Sroufe, L.A. (1979). The coherence of individual development. *American Psychologist,* **34**, 834–841.

Stevenson, J. & Graham, P. (1982). Temperament: A consideration of concepts and methods. In R. Porter & G. Collins (Eds), *Temperamental differences in infants and young children.* Ciba Foundation Symposium No. 89. London: Pitman.

Stevenson-Hinde, J. & Hinde, R.A. (1986). Changes in associations between characteristics. In R. Plomin & J. Dunn (Eds), *The study of temperament: Changes, continuities and challenges* (pp. 115–129). Hillsdale: NJ: Erlbaum.

Suomi, S.J. (1983). Social development in rhesus monkeys: Considerations of individual differences. In A. Oliverio & M. Zappella (Eds), *The behavior of human infants.* New York and London: Plenum.

Suomi, S.J. (1987). Anxiety-like disorders in young nonhuman primates. In R. Gittelman (Ed.), *Anxiety disorders of childhood* (pp. 1–22). New York: Guilford Press.

Tellegen, A. (1985). Structures of mood and personality and their relevance to assessing anxiety, with an emphasis on self-report. In A. Tuma & J. Maser (Eds), *Anxiety and the anxiety disorders.* Hillsdale, NJ: Erlbaum.

Thoday, J.M. (1969). Limitations to genetic comparison of populations. In G.A. Harrison & J. Peel (Eds), *Biosocial aspects of race. Journal of Biological Science,* Suppl. 1 (pp. 3–14). Oxford: Blackwell Scientific.

Thomas, A. & Chess, S. (1977). *Temperament and development.* New York: Brunner/Mazel.

Thomas, A., Chess, S. & Birch, H. (1968). *Temperament and behavioral disorders in childhood.* New York: New York University Press.

Thomas, A., Chess, S., Birch, H., Hertzig, M. & Korn, S. (1963). *Behavioural individuality in early childhood.* New York: New York University Press.

Tizard, J. (1975). Three dysfunctional environmental influences in development: Malnutrition, non-accidental injury and child minding. In D. Baldrop (Ed.), *Pediatrics and the environment* (pp. 19–27). Unigate Pediatric Workshops No. 2, 1974. London: Fellowship of Postgraduate Medicine.

Vandenberg, S.G., Singer, S.M. & Pauls, D.L. (1986). *The heredity of behavior disorders in adults and children.* New York: Plenum Medical.

Section Five
Cross-Cultural, Socioeconomic Status, Sex and Other Group Differences

26

Temperament in Childhood: Cross-Cultural and Sex Differences

GELDOLPH A. KOHNSTAMM
University of Leiden

Cultures and subcultures are relatively stable in their patterns of child rearing. Important changes take many decades and follow major changes in society, such as an increase in economic prosperity and an increase in the general level of education. Subcultures differ, among other things in their values, interests and patterns of child rearing. Groups of families are consciously or unconsciously directed at reproducing behavioral characteristics in their children which are consistent with their value hierarchies. Individual children, born with specific temperamental dispositions, are socialized into phenotypical behavior patterns that are appropriate, desirable or at least tolerable within subcultural norms.

It seems to be a general tendency of families to avoid the development of extremes in behavior, to strive toward a balance and the avoidance of conflict. As Hinde once remarked: 'There is no clear advantage to rearing children who are extreme in extraversion or introversion, extremely high or low in activity, mechanical or social interests' (R.A. Hinde, personal communication, 1985). Families exert influence to socialize children away from those extreme behavior patterns which the subculture considers undesirable and inappropriate. The general tendency is to shape individual expressions of temperament into socially approved and desired directions. That such processes can lead to conflicts between (sub)cultural values and individual temperamental dispositions is self-evident and has been common knowledge since Hippocrates. Buss and Plomin (1984) have suggested that those in the middle range of any temperament dimension are more likely to be influenced by the environment, while those at the high extreme are likely to alter the environment.

Of course there are large individual differences within any group of families. Individual parents differ in their own temperamental characteristics and in all other

Temperament in Childhood   Edited by G.A. Kohnstamm, J.E. Bates and M.K. Rothbart

aspects of personality. They also differ in their histories. The interaction between the newborn child and its one, two or more daily caregivers is from the very first day an interaction between *individuals*, and not between clones of the statistical construction of the average individual typical for a particular age group within a particular subculture.

This chapter has three parts. The first part reviews studies at the global level yielding comparative results from samples of children living in different nations. In the second part some studies done with children differing in ethnicity but living in the same nation are reviewed. The last and largest part takes a look at one other distinction: that between boys and girls.

The whole of Section Five of this volume has a thoughtful precursor in an article by Super and Harkness (1986) which is to be recommended to the interested reader. We have tried to avoid redundancy by selecting issues and facts that were not mentioned in that article or were mentioned but could not be detailed in the limited number of pages.

CROSS-NATIONAL COMPARISONS: ARE THERE DIFFERENCES IN TEMPERAMENT?

Cross-national and cross-cultural comparative data on temperament in childhood may come from several sources. Two main groups of sources are to be distinguished: (a) observations by trained observers of behavior in real-life daily situations or standardized laboratory observations of children; (b) interviews and questionnaires with parents, day-care workers or teachers as informants, and for older children, self-report questionnaires.

Observations of Children in Their Natural Environment, Standardized Tests and Laboratory Observations

Anthropologists have long reported on temperamental aspects of children's behavior in so-called primitive societies. Classic examples were given by Mead (1948) in *Sex and temperament in three primitive societies*. Influential as this book has been in diminishing Western stereotypical thinking about the universal necessity of certain sex-specific behavioral styles, this sort of anthropological observation is no longer regarded as sufficiently objective and specific.

A new line of research opened when child psychiatrists and psychologists began to make cross-national comparative observations of temperament in infancy and early childhood. For instance, Caudill and Weinstein (1969) observed Japanese and European-American (Caucasian) mothers and their infants and recorded that the Japanese infants cried and vocalized much less than the American babies, whereas the American infants were so much more motorically active than the Japanese that virtually all of the American babies were above the common median and all the Japanese cases below it (Freedman, 1974). Caudill and Weinstein themselves attributed these differences to differential handling by the mothers and not to differences in temperament, whereas Freedman preferred a gene-pool difference hypothesis because of the early appearance of these differences. Super and Harkness (1986) have warned that the seeming coherence of the literature on Oriental–Caucasian differences in temperament 'draws to some degree on the Western stereotype of the reserved, serene, even inscrutable Easterner, an image that is reinforced by anecdotal reports of quiet, attentive school children' (Super & Harkness, 1986, p. 141). Freedman had argued earlier, against such an objection, that 'the stereotypes one people have of another rarely miss the mark altogether, and (that) often the picture is agreed to by those being stereotyped' (Freedman, 1974, p. 156) and that 'while it must be true that mothers of different cultures differentially reinforce their babies' behavior, we must again point out that cultural norms and biological predispositions appear frequently to act in concert' (p. 163). Here we have in a nutshell the seeming insolubility of the nature–nurture debate, in this case with respect to temperamental differences between infants from two different nations and cultures. It will be the same when we discuss sex differences in activity and emotionality. The same data, indicating significant differences, can be interpreted either way, depending on the preferences of the authors.

The number of cross-cultural temperament studies using standardized tests and laboratory observations is still very small. The Neonatal Behavioral Assessment Scale (NBAS) by Brazelton has been used now on a worldwide scale; some of the information this testing procedure gives may be considered temperamental (see Chapter 12, by Rothbart), although as yet little long-term stability of individual differences in NBAS scores has been found. Brazelton, Nugent and Lester (1987) gave an overview of all cross-cultural studies done with the NBAS. The authors recommend that in cross-cultural studies other kinds of assessments be added instead of drawing conclusions from NBAS comparisons only. 'An estimate of gestational age, ... of neurological adequacy ..., of intrauterine conditions of nutrition ..., as well as correct length and weight measurements and Apgar scores, should be added to any behavioral assessment that attempts to evaluate cross-cultural differences in behavior at birth' (Brazelton *et al.*, 1987, p. 799).

Many studies using the NBAS in different nations are in progress. Provided the above-mentioned recommendations can be met and the samples are much larger than those in the pioneer studies, comparative *structural* analyses will become possible. Once the cross-national similarity or difference of structures has been established, comparative longitudinal studies are possible of groups of newborns who are similar in their positions on temperament-like dimensions such as NBAS irritability. The value of the NBAS assessment for the nature–nurture argument is its very early application: a few days after birth differential reinforcement cannot yet have had any influence of real importance on the behavioral characteristics of the newborn. On the other hand, this early moment of assessment is also its weakness, from a temperamental point of view, because one may doubt if the newborn is mature enough and has sufficiently recovered from the recent total change in *Umwelt* to show its 'real' temperament. Would it not be equally doubtful to try to observe 'typical' family interaction patterns a few days after the family has moved into a new house?

Questionnaires and Rating Scales, Either With or Without Interviewing the Informants

The advantage of data obtained with questionnaires instead of with interviews and behavioral observations is that they are inexpensive to collect and thus can easily result in large enough quantities to make statistical analysis meaningful. For group comparisons in the field of temperament and personality two kinds of analysis are mostly done: (a) comparison of means and variances of the distributions, and (b) factor analysis (usually principal component analysis (PCA) with varimax rotation) to see if the underlying structure of the questionnaire is similar enough in the groups compared to assert that the structure of temperament dimensions is the same in both groups.

The first task is hampered by the fact that the samples used for the comparisons are often (a) not representative of a well-defined segment of the population and (b) not large enough for reliable cross-national or cross-cultural comparisons. This is also true for many of the North American instruments which serve as the standards in this sort of research. Next, there is the problem of interpreting the significant differences, if there are any. Personally, I feel much more comfortable with a difference indicator such as Cohen's 'd' (Cohen, 1977) than with the P value of a difference between two means or of the outcome of an analysis of variance. This is mainly because with the large samples in questionnaire research even minuscule differences become statistically significant, which is not the same as psychologically relevant. If one takes the difference between the two means of the two groups one wishes to compare and divides this difference by the pooled standard deviation (which often must be estimated), one obtains d (Cohen, 1977), a scale-independent index of effect size. For example, as we shall see below, the average difference (d) for boys and girls on measures of *motor activity* is now estimated to be .49, which corresponds with half a standard deviation. In evaluating differences in mean ratings on specific scales found between groups responding to scales written in two different languages, my rule of thumb is that I do not get excited about these differences unless they are at least one-third the size of the pooled standard deviation. This relatively high threshold saves me a lot of unnecessary excitement by significant but minuscule differences and is therefore to be recommended to colleagues with a similar temperament.

Comparison of underlying factor structures, even when done rather intuitively at a global inspection level, has been hampered first, by the same deficiencies as mentioned above: too small and non-representative samples, also in the North American 'standard' groups used for the comparisons; and second, by the fact that the original factor analyses on the instruments most often used in cross-cultural comparisons, the Thomas–Chess and Carey–McDevitt questionnaires, were never done according to the psychometric standards desirable for something as tricky as cross-cultural comparisons. The fact that these original analyses never included the individual item scores but only the nine dimension scores has caused a lot of trouble. Psychologists elsewhere first want to know how well the presupposed nine dimensions are replicated in *their* samples, because the translation of the items may have changed their meanings. The usual result is that the nine dimensions are not replicated. Mostly a first factor emerges which has some resemblance with a factor 'difficult' resulting from factor analyzing the nine dimension scores in the original studies. But actually one is comparing apples and oranges and thus can infer very little about the comparability of the underlying factor structures in both groups.

The following short overview of selected studies begins with a large-scale study not hampered by psychometric deficiencies. In Chapter 30 I raise the question of why childhood temperament researchers thus far have negated the work of the authors of this study.

Results Obtained with the Eysenck Personality Questionnaire

The junior version of the Eysenck Personality Questionnaire (J-EPQ) has been used for large-scale cross-national comparisons (Eysenck & Eysenck, 1983, 1985). The Eysencks claim that their 'super' factors Introversion–Extraversion (E), Neuroticism (N), and, more recently, Psychoticism (P) are (a) temperamental and (b) universal. To test the latter claim they had the EPQ answered by large samples of adults in 24 different countries and the J-EPQ by equally large samples of children in ten different countries. Only one of these ten samples (Japan) had as 'few' as 489 subjects. The other nine samples were all over 1000. The factors E, N and P were replicated in all samples of children in Hungary, Spain, Japan, New Zealand, Hong Kong, Singapore, Canada, Denmark, Greece and Yugoslavia.

Apart from showing the replicability of their super factors, the Eysencks compared the mean scores and standard deviations on these factors. They found exceptionally high scores in the Japanese on Introversion and Neuroticism, a finding which seems in harmony with the results of studies on infants and young children mentioned above. A remarkable association the Eysencks have investigated is that between blood-typing and E and N scores. The Japanese have a much higher percentage of blood group AB, and in worldwide comparisons AB tended to be associated with higher average scores on self-reported Neuroticism (Eysenck, 1982; Eysenck & Eysenck, 1985).

Results Obtained with the Revised Dimensions of Temperament Survey (Lerner)

Windle, Iwawaki and Lerner (1987) compared self-report data from early- and late-adolescents in America and Japan. Using highly sophisticated techniques for comparing factor structures, they found very similar dimension patterns underlying the 54-item revised Dimensions of Temperament Survey (DOTS-R). This questionnaire may be particularly well suited for cross-cultural comparisons because of the simple wording of the items, selected to be understood by schoolchildren. Much care was given to the translation into Japanese of the items. Although the sample sizes, particularly of the Japanese adolescent samples, were much smaller than those of the Eysencks mentioned above, the results of the comparison in factor means were strikingly similar to what the Eysencks found. Both the early and the late Japanese adolescents rated themselves significantly lower on Approach (= Introversion), Mood quality (= Neuroticism) and Flexibility. On the other hand, the Japanese 12-year-olds rated themselves higher on two of the three Rhythmicity factors of the DOTS-R. In a parallel study (Windle *et al.*, 1988) the DOTS-R was given to primary caretakers to rate 234 Japanese children of preschool age. Once again the Japanese children were rated as lower in Approach, Mood quality and Flexibility. More information on the cross-cultural Japanese-American comparisons using the DOTS-R is given in Chapter 27.

Some of the Results Obtained with the Original and Revised Infant Temperament Questionnaire (Carey)

In 1973 DeVries used the Carey Infant Temperament Questionnaire (ITQ) in three East African tribes living in Kenya – the Kikuyu, the Digo and the Masai – by interviewing the mothers with the help of interpreters (DeVries & Sameroff, 1984; see also Thomas & Chess, 1977, p. 151). Given the circumstances, the samples, ranging in size from 48 to 77, were fairly large, but not large enough for structural comparative analyses. The means DeVries obtained were very different from Carey's ITQ means, except for Threshold. In fact they were so different – also *among* the three tribes – that many became convinced of the uselessness of comparisons of questionnaire scale-means between groups so different in cultural background.

Hsu, Soong, Stigler, Hong and Liang (1981) translated into Chinese the New York Longitudinal Study (NYLS) questionnaire and the R-ITQ and used them on a sample of 349 mothers of 4- to 8-month-old babies in Taiwan. No factor analysis has yet been reported and thus no Philadelphia–Taiwan factor structure comparison has been made, but that must still be possible if the data have not been lost. The same applies to a study done by Hsu on much larger samples of 3- to 7-year-old children (Hsu, 1982), using the Thomas–Chess questionnaire.

The differences found on the R-ITQ between the Carey–McDevitt means and the Taiwan means exceeded my threshold of excitation on eight of nine dimensions, the only exception being Persistence. The largest differences (about one standard deviation) were obtained for Rhythmicity and Mood, the Taiwanese babies being rated as less regular, and more negative in mood. On all other scales the Taiwanese mothers gave mean ratings that were more on the 'negative' side except for Activity, on which they rated their babies lower than the American mothers did.

Since (a) the social class distribution in both groups was positively skewed to the higher strata, (b) the majority of babies in both groups were first born and (c) the study seems to have been done with great care, the conclusion of the authors that either these Taiwanese middle class babies are on the average more 'difficult' or their mothers perceive them so, or both are true, seems warranted. However, I will have to return to this issue of more 'positive' item and scale means in American samples, when discussing some results obtained with the Infant Characteristics Questionnaire (ICQ: Bates) and the Child Behavior Checklist (CBCL; Achenbach) in American–Dutch comparisons.

Another fairly large study using a French translation of the R-ITQ was done in Quebec City by Maziade and his associates with 336 4-month-old children and 356 8-month-old children (Maziade, Boudreault, Thivierge, Capéraà & Côté 1984; see Chapter 22). When roughly comparing the means and standard deviations on the nine scales, with the same indices from the original American and the Taiwan study, I noticed that the French-Canadian mothers rated their infants on most scales somewhere in between the Taiwanese and American mothers.

A PCA on the nine scale scores revealed a first factor that loaded highest on the scales Approach and Adaptability (>.70) for both age groups. Next came Mood and Distractibility, whereas the first and second factor loaded equally high on Intensity. The first three of these scales, Approach, Adaptability and Mood, together with Intensity, were also found to have highest loadings on a first factor resulting from analyses of NYLS data, with relative consistency over the first 5 years of childhood (Thomas & Chess, 1977). Results like this support the cross-cultural validity of what Thomas and Chess named factor A. Because of Carey's scepticism regarding factor analysis (see Chapter 21), a similar comparison with the original R-ITQ data cannot be made.

Results Obtained with the Infant Characteristics Questionnaire (Bates)

Some cross-national results were also obtained with the ICQ and with the Child Characteristics Questionnaire (CCQ) by Bates (Bates, Freeland & Lounsbury, 1979), and these questionnaires were translated into Dutch, German and Turkish, and served as research instruments in a longitudinal study in The Netherlands. The factor structure obtained by Bates for children from Bloomington, Indiana, was replicated for most of the age groups between 6 months and 4 years in the Dutch study. The original factor analyses were based on the mother ratings of about 7000 children, 1000 of whom were, in fact, from the Dutch-speaking parts of Belgium (Kohnstamm, 1984).

One of the methodological findings of this study was that in the Dutch sample many more mothers only used the scale points that had explicit verbal meanings attached to them. Since in the ICQ/CCQ only the midpoint and the two extremes on the seven-point scales have verbal meanings, about a third of the Dutch mothers did not use the scale values 2, 3, 5 and 6. We think this difference is caused by the greater experience of American young adults with rating scales. In high school, American children are confronted with tests or questionnaires that use line scales, with either verbal meanings or numbers to indicate positions of more or less. Americans have thus become more accustomed than the Dutch, and probably other nationalities as well, to the conventions of rating scales. Using only the midpoint and the extremes of a scale may have the effect of increasing variance, as was indeed the case on most of the items of the Dutch ICQ. At the age of 6 months the variance on 22 of the 28 ICQ items was higher for Dutch children (1780 American and 670 Dutch children) and at the ages of 13 months ($n = 392/907$) and 24 months ($n = 129/383$) the variances on *all* 32 CCQ items were higher for Dutch children. Thus, with all the problems we have already encountered in comparing cross-national results with translated questionnaires, we also have to look at the degrees to which the respondents are accustomed to something as simple – to researchers – as rating scales. That scale-sophistication and degree of education are related can be illustrated with data from this Dutch sample: 42% of the mothers with a lower degree of education did not use the non-labeled scale points, against

26% of the mothers with an intermediate and 11% of the mothers with a higher degree of education. Each group consisted of about 2000 respondents. In a follow-up study of smaller selections from these large groups, it turned out that one particular ICQ scale predicted (.50) later (4 years) Achenbach Teacher's Rating Form teacher ratings on externalizing classroom behaviors, but only when the earlier maternal ratings were made by mothers with at least 12 years of schooling (Kohnstamm, in preparation). In their contribution to this section of the volume (see Chapter 28) Fullard, Simeonsson and Huntington give an overview of North American and Canadian temperamental data related to socioeconomic status (SES). One study which is particularly relevant to the point made here is MacPhee's (1983), in which lower-SES mothers displayed a preference for the extreme points on the R-ITQ scales and avoided the points in the middle.

The American–Dutch comparison of ICQ ratings revealed another kind of cross-cultural difference. In both cultures mothers tended to rate their children as more positive than 'the average child'. But in the American group this tendency was more marked. To give an example: the ICQ has a final question on general difficultness (how difficult would your child be for the average parent?). In a group of 389 mothers of 13-month-old children in Bloomington, Indiana, 25% chose the midpoint ('just about normal') and only 9% chose scale points on the difficult side of the midpoint; thus, about two-thirds of this sample, 66%, rated their children as easier than average. In a Dutch subsample of 903 children of about the same age (12–14 months) a slightly differently worded question resulted in the following percentages: 48 for the midpoint, 12 for the difficult side and only 39 for the easy side of the midpoint. Thus 66% of the respondents in Bloomington against 39% in Holland judged their children as easier than average.

If such a result reflects a real cultural difference, one should find similar results in other American–Dutch comparative studies. Coincidentally there is another large-scale American–Dutch comparative study in which parents scaled their children using the CBCL by Achenbach. I quote from Achenbach, Verhulst, Edelbrock, Baron and Akkerhuis (1987):

> Still other items, such as how well the child does things and gets along with others, may reflect different national biases, as the mean American scores indicate higher proportions of parents rating their children 'above average' on these items. Although it may be true that children like to participate in activities that they excel in, the mean American ratings for how well the child gets along with others and plays/works alone ranged from 1.30 to 1.48, where a score of 1 = 'about the same as other children of his/her age' and 2 = 'better than other children of his/her age'. The Dutch scores on these items ranged from 1.14 to 1.24. Although parents in both countries thus tended to see their children as better than average on these items, American parents appear to have a stronger favorable bias. (Achenbach *et al.*, 1987, p. 323)

In this case the groups consisted of 1300 American and 2033 Dutch children of varying ages between 4 and 16. The CBCL has a group of so-called problem items and a group of competence items. On the problem items the average scores and variances in both samples were very similar, but on the competence items there was a strong tendency for American parents to rate their children higher than Dutch parents did.

In general it is probably so that mothers take on a rosy view when comparing their young children with an abstract 'average' child. One can interpret this as a sign of love and pride. The existence of this bias is a very good thing. Mothers (and fathers?) are probably programmed to fall in love with their babies. This results in an average positively skewed perception of their characteristics, the effect of which is strongest in the first months after birth and thence begins to diminish.

Why would American mothers express this tendency more strongly than Dutch mothers? Do they love their children more, on the average? That is not likely. My hypothesis is that this is the result of a more general difference between the two cultures. In America, knowing how to sell things, including oneself, is a major cultural value. It is apparent not only in advertising and business, but also in academia, education and politics. In Holland this is not (yet?) such a predominant cultural trait. In America, mothers rating their children on a questionnaire (the answers to which are going to be seen by the testers and by who knows who else) will be influenced by this cultural value more because it is a stronger force. Thus, the general tendency towards a rosy view of one's child is in the United States *expressed* more strongly than in Holland. This explains the larger proportion of favorable child temperament ratings in America.

This somewhat daring hypothesis receives support from a different field. Uttal, Lummis and Stevenson (1988) compared American (Minneapolis) with Taiwanese (Taipei) and Japanese (Sendai) children for their ability in mathematics. The mothers of these children were also interviewed on a broad range of subjects. One of the results of this interesting study was that:

> American mothers gave their children higher ratings on intellectual, motivational, and academic characteristics than did Japanese or Chinese mothers, and American mothers were more satisfied with their children's performance. In fact, the levels of satisfaction of mothers of low-achieving American children were nearly as high as those of mothers of high-achieving Japanese children. Similarly, American mothers were less likely to acknowledge the presence of their children's problems in mathematics than were Chinese and Japanese mothers. (Uttal *et al.*, 1988, p. 342)

Thus, temperament researchers doing cross-cultural studies using interviews and rating scales should be wary of the possibility of such cultural differences before interpreting differences between sample means as signs of real temperamental differences.

INTRA-NATIONAL COMPARISONS OF GROUPS DIFFERING IN ETHNICITY

If anything, inter-ethnic differences in studies across nations should be larger than in studies within a nation, where environmental similarities should diminish the original ethnic (or constitutional) differences – that is, if environmental influences have such power. Particularly in studies relying on parental information, in which the average parent's judgment is most certainly biased in the culturally valued direction, such an adaptive power is likely to operate.

Observations of Children in Their Natural Environments

Most of the intra-national natural environment observations of temperamental expressions in groups differing in ethnicity have been done in the United States. Freedman (1974) mentioned comparative observational studies done by his students Green and Kuchner with Chinese-American and European-American preschoolers in the nursery. No precise temperamental information was given, however, nor was it clear from Freedman's account how many children were observed. Freedman reported from Green's study that the Chinese-American preschoolers as compared with European-American preschoolers were less approaching and interacting, less intense and aggressive. He adds to this from his own experience:

> It is common observation in public schools of San Francisco's Chinatown that the Chinese children there are similarly restrained and rarely fight over toys; we have made similar observations in nursery schools in Hong Kong and Shanghai. Further, my wife has spent considerable time observing in San Francisco schools and has noted much the same differentiation there throughout the public school years. (Freedman, 1974, p. 156).

More of this type of comparative observational study, done with Indian-Mexican and Afro-American children, would be useful. A confounding variable is social class, since the European-American comparison groups tend to be middle class and the other groups lower class. This confounding factor was avoided in the Freedman studies because his Chinese-American families were middle class.

Standardized Tests and Laboratory Observations

Kagan, Kearsley and Zelazo (1978) compared 53 Chinese-American children with 63 European-American children across the period from 4 to 29 months. The most significant result was that the Chinese children, whether raised at home or in a day-care center, were consistently more inhibited than the European-Americans during infancy and the transition to childhood (Kagan, 1987; Kagan, Reznick & Snidman, 1986). On most of the testing procedures the Chinese-American children vocalized less often than did the European-American children. In a Strange Situation procedure they were more upset when left with a stranger and stayed close to their mothers for a longer period after reunion. Kagan et al. (see Chapter 8) found a correlation between inhibition and stability of heart rates with the inhibited Chinese-Americans showing more stable heart rates while processing unfamiliar visual and auditory information.

Questionnaires and Rating Scales, Either With or Without Interviewing the Informants

Results Obtained with the Thomas–Chess Interview and Carey Scales

The first study in this category was, most probably, the comparative longitudinal study, begun in 1961 as a supplement to the NYLS, of 95 children of lower class

Puerto-Rican parents. In this case ethnicity and social class were heavily confounded, since the European-American children in the NYLS, most of them of Jewish descent, came from middle and upper-middle class families. The comparison was mainly used for a study of the development of behavior problems, but some information was gathered regarding temperamental differences at the age of 2 or 3 months (Thomas & Chess, 1977). The differences between the two groups were markedly significant for Rhythmicity and Intensity, with Puerto-Rican children being rated as lower in both.

Sameroff and Kelly (in Thomas & Chess, 1977) used the Carey ITQ for a comparison of 54 4-month-old white lower class American infants with 70 black lower class American infants of the same age. Both groups were from Rochester, New York. The black infants were rated as significantly less rhythmic, less adaptable, less approaching and more negative in mood.

Laosa (1982) reported on the use of the Behavioral Style Questionnaire (BSQ; McDevitt & Carey, 1978) with a Chicano, largely working class sample of 95 3- to 4-year-old children. A statistical comparison of means and standard deviations on the nine scales with the original BSQ samples was not reported but on global inspection I saw no exceptional values. As to the structural comparison made in this study, Super and Harkness (1986) report a four-factor analysis with varimax rotation on the dimension intercorrelations of the $3\frac{1}{2}$- and 4-year data. The results were comparable to McDevitt's (1976) factor analysis results from a middle class Anglo-American sample collected in Carey's private practice. At $3\frac{1}{2}$ years the first factor combined Mood, Activity and Persistence; the second Distractibility and Threshold; the third Intensity and Rhythmicity; and the fourth Approach and Adaptability.

To find a similar factor structure in two samples of such diverse cultural backgrounds is a strong argument for the cross-cultural validity of the clusters of particular temperament dimensions.

Weissbluth (1982) used the R-ITQ by Carey and McDevitt to compare a group of 23 Chinese-American infants with a group of 60 non-Chinese infants, 55 of whom were white. Both groups had a mean age of 5 months and no infant was younger than 4 months. In both groups 30% of the fathers were in the highest occupational level as defined by Hollingshead. The other factors in both groups were predominantly skilled manual workers or semi-skilled employees.

The Chinese-American children were rated as significantly less approaching, less adaptable, more negative in mood, less distractible and less persistent than the other infants. In all but the last the means differed one (common) standard deviation or more. With Persistence the difference was half a standard deviation. To quote Weissbluth (1982):

> Responses to specific questions on the Infant Temperament Questionnaire showed that Chinese infants were shyer (i.e., turned away or clung to mother) on meeting another child for the first time ($p < .05$), initially rejected a new babysitter with crying and clinging to mother ($p < .05$), were more fretful initially in a new place or situation ($p < .01$), and cried more when left to play alone ($p < .01$). However, the Chinese-American infants' initial reaction at home to approach by strangers was more often rated as acceptance than was the reaction of the other infants ($p < .01$). (Weissbluth, 1982, p. 101)

Weissbluth notes a striking similarity between the typical slow-to-warm-up infant and the average Chinese-American infant. He points at the similarity to the observational findings by Kagan *et al.* (1978; see above). For the less positive rating on Mood he sees a possible cause in the shorter average night-sleep duration of the Chinese-American infants; this relationship was also seen in the non-Chinese sample and has been reported by him before (Weissbluth, 1981; see Chapter 18).

Beller, Eckert and Kuckartz (1986) made a German and Turkish translation of the ICQ by Bates and used it to get ratings of 28 German and 20 Turkish infants aged 6–21 months. The ratings were made both by the mothers of the infants and their day-care caregivers. Notwithstanding the small numbers in this study, a factor analysis on the items replicated the factor structure of the ICQ as obtained by Bates in Indiana and by Kohnstamm in Holland. Turkish mothers rated their children significantly higher on Inadaptability whereas German mothers perceived their infants as making more excessive dependency demands. The numbers of children in this study have since been expanded considerably (E.K. Beller, personal communication, June 1988) but the results have remained as they were reported.

Finally, one should include in this category of studies the Australian Temperament Project, which is described by Prior, Sanson and Oberklaid in Chapter 29. These authors obtained ratings on the Australian version of the R-ITQ for a large representative sample of infants born in the state of Victoria: a large group of infants with two Australian parents (n = 1593) and smaller groups of infants with one or two parents from a score of other countries. All infants were between 4 and 8 months old. The authors stress the fact that many of the immigrant groups differing in ethnicity maintain close cultural ties, tend to cluster in particular suburban and country areas, and are concerned to promote their own language and culture as far as possible. This unusual and also – for Australia – new tendency makes that country an ideal place for this kind of inter-nation ethnic comparison.

SEX DIFFERENCES IN TEMPERAMENT: ACTIVITY AND EMOTIONALITY AS EXAMPLES

In this chapter the word 'sex' is used instead of 'gender'. The latter word is nowadays preferred by many because it sounds more civilized, has no association with sexuality and does not imply a biological origin. However, dictionaries still reserve 'gender' for a distinction in grammar and not in human beings. The use of 'gender differences' seems to imply that the differences in question are manmade cultural phenomena, as linguistic rules of gender are. To choose either word seems to indicate a preference for one explanation: the observed differences in behavior are inborn or learned. Thus, feminists prefer 'gender' over 'sex' when discussing behavioral differences between males and females. I prefer 'sex' over 'gender' because I want to keep the possibility open that the behavioral differences are, at least partly, caused or facilitated by constitutional factors.

The sex distinction creates two naturally occurring groups in all cultures. In spite of its utmost psychological and sociological importance, it has not been a well-studied subject in the temperament literature. For many centuries adult temperament typology seemed only appropriate for males: practically no examples of temperamental differences in females were given by writers on this subject. When modern twentieth century anthropology, psychiatry and psychology began to collect data on temperament in childhood and adolescence, it was a matter of course to include both sexes in the samples studied without paying much attention to the variable, however. In overviews of the early studies it is remarkable how little attention is paid to sex differences. Diamond (1957), for instance, mentions them for the first time on page 188, in a discussion of Neilon's (1948) follow-up study of Shirley's (1933) babies: 'One cannot dismiss the possibility that within our culture the temperamental characteristics of boys are in general less firmly set at the age of 2, than is the case with girls' (Diamond, 1957, p. 188). In the remainder of his book he rarely mentions the topic of sex differences in the development of temperament. The possibility he did not want to exclude refers to more stability, at an early age, of temperamental characteristics in girls. I will return to this important topic at the end of this chapter.

The first American book to treat the subject at length, though not under the label 'temperament', was Maccoby's (1966) edited volume, later followed more explicitly by Maccoby and Jacklin (1974), notably in chapter 5: 'Temperament: Activity level and emotionality'. The annotated bibliographies in both volumes – the first one compiled by Oetzel – are goldmines for those interested in the early studies. The earliest study relevant to the subject was on resistive reactions during mental testing of 110 children between 6 and 53 months of age (Levy & Tulchin, 1925). This study concluded that boys clung to their mothers more than girls whereas girls attempted to hide more. The most intense resistive reactions, such as struggling and screaming, reached their peak at 18 months for girls and at 30 months for boys. A similar study on an amazingly larger scale was published 4 years later by Goodenough (1929). To quote Oetzel's annotation in Maccoby (1966):

Measures: Testers rated children on shyness, negativism, and distractibility during standard mental tests. Lack of shyness meant leaving mother and coming willingly to be tested.
Subjects: 990 children, 13 months to 6 years, from various social classes.
Results: No sex differences for the group as a whole. However, the trend of improvement with age in all variables started at a later age in boys than it did in girls. Girls started improving at 18 months, boys not until 30 months. Lower-class boys were the least shy of all. (Oetzel, in Maccoby, 1966, p. 254).

These studies were thus the first to find sex × age interactions in behavior patterns which we can now label as temperamental, in the context of this book. A key question concerns the onset and change over age of sex differences in temperamental phenotype. Rothbart (1986) in a study of 46 infants at 3, 6 and 9 months of age could find no differences at all on any of the measures she used:

Neither IBQ's, home observations measures, nor composite measures yielded significant sex differences or Sex × Age interactions. The finding is in keeping with our previous findings of no temperamental sex differences on three cohorts of infants whose parents filled out the IBQ (Rothbart *et al.*, 1977). We had expected possible biases in mothers' perceptions of sex differences (Condry & Condry, 1976) to influence their questionnaire responses even if no differences were to be found in our home observations. However, no sex differences were found using either home observation or parent reports. An important question for future longitudinal temperament research will be determining the age at which sex differences in temperament variables such as activity level, reactions to frustration and fear (Maccoby & Jacklin, 1974) first appear and when and if they become stable. The differences do not seem to be built on differences observable in the first year, at least as we have been able to measure them. (Rothbart, 1986, p. 364)

Evidently, a sample of 46 is too small to make small differences significant; it still is possible that in larger samples small sex differences will be shown to be highly significant, even during the first year and using Rothbart's measures. On the other hand, the finding of no sex differences, as in so many other studies, is reassuring indeed as regards the influence of sociocultural stereotypes on parental ratings. I will return to this issue shortly.

Above we have met two ways of looking at sex differences: as *main* effects, and as effects which only show in *interaction* with other variables, such as age. For developmentalists it all starts with this second category of questions. We simply cannot look at sex × temperament interactions without considering age or the stage of development of the subjects. But there is more than that.

A third, more complicated possibility, already indicated by Diamond's (1957) remark quoted above, is that at specific stages in development the *stability* of specific variables is sex-dependent.

There is also a fourth: that at specific stages in development the predictive power of specific temperamental variables, predicting specific behaviors of the child or specific reactions from parents, teachers or other children, is sex-dependent.

Space does not permit me to do more than give a selection of research relevant to the second category of questions only, the relatively simple question of sex × age effects on temperamental expressions. First the temperamental dimension of activity is used as an illustrative case and second the dimension of emotionality. The choice of these two dimensions, following Maccoby and Jacklin (1974), is motivated by the general consensus among temperament theorists with regard to their temperamental status (Goldsmith *et al.*, 1987).

Motor Activity Level

In this section the expression 'activity level' is used throughout as a shorthand for 'motor activity level' since that is what is actually measured in most of the studies reported here. It is quite important to make this distinction. The word 'active' is a very positively valued attribute, whereas 'motorically active' is not. To find sex differences in motor activity, with males being on the average somewhat more active, says nothing about mental activity or social activity. A child may score low on motor activity and at the same time be always actively reading books. An example of the negative aspects of a higher motor activity level of males (probably in combination with some other factors) is the indisputable fact that boys of all ages have more accidents requiring emergency medical treatment (Block, 1983).

Maccoby and Jacklin (1974) concluded that there was no evidence for sex differences in activity level in children under 12 months, but that the data for older children were more consistent in portraying boys as more active, at least during the preschool years. When categorizing different types of characteristics in three classes – (a) sex differences that are fairly well established; (b) open questions; too little evidence, or findings ambiguous; and (c) unfounded beliefs – activity level was put in the middle category.

Buss and Plomin (1975) concluded from their overview of studies that 'below four years no gender differences in activity emerge from virtually all the studies; above four years a number of studies report that males are more active' (Buss & Plomin, 1975, p. 150). They argued that this rather late appearance proved that sex difference in activity is the result of socialization in culturally shaped sex roles. In their 1984 book *Temperament: Early developing personality traits* they saw no reason to change their views with regard to activity. See also Chapter 4.

Eaton and Enns (1986) in the most complete overview thus far came to a different conclusion. Reviewing 127 different studies, they found an average sex difference of one-half a standard deviation (.49) with males being more active in a large majority of the 127 studies reviewed. The effect was age-dependent. Before birth the average was .33, during infancy .29 during preschool age .44 and at older ages .64.

Quite unexpectedly, the authors found no differences among three types of studies: objective measurement using instruments such as actometers; observation studies using professional observers; and rating scales, including ratings by parents and teachers, and self-ratings. The average differences found for these three groups of methods were .53, .47 and .50.

This latter finding seems to be very important for the whole field of temperament. Activity level is certainly subject to social sex stereotyping as Buss and Plomin (1975) stressed in their explanation of sex differences found only after the fourth year. The Eaton and Enns (1986) study indicates that this social stereotype does not cause the subjective methods, on the average, to *overrate* the difference as measured by objective methods.

On the size of the average difference found in their study these authors write:

> Translated into correlational terms, the obtained effect size represents a point-biserial correlation between sex and activity level of .24, and the proportion of total activity level variance associated with sex is about 5%. Expressed in yet another way, the average male subject (at the 50th percentile) is more active than 69% of the female subjects. (Eaton & Enns, 1986, p. 22)

and

> In the context of other sex difference meta-analyses, a difference of one-half a standard deviation is large for a behavioral variable. Indeed, Deaux (1984) has surmised that 5% of explained variance in a specific social or cognitive variable is an upper boundary for sex differences. Differences of this boundary magnitude and their mean effect sizes include: Spatial ability, .45 (Hyde, 1981); aggression, .50 (Hyde, 1984); mathematical reasoning, .44 (Rossi, 1983); and proportional reasoning, .48 (Meehan, 1984). Within this context, it can be concluded that sex differences in activity level, $d = .49$, are well established, and Maccoby and Jacklin's (1974) equivocal conclusion about activity level sex differences can be set aside. (Eaton & Enns, 1986, p. 25)

Eaton and Enns (1986) also note that such relatively small differences in group means may have dramatic effects on the proportions of males and females at the *extremes* of the distributions. They mention the differential proportions in the case of hyperactivity as an illustration.

Of course these authors could not include all temperament studies done in their meta-analysis. I picked three quite recent questionnaire studies that were *not* included.

(1) A Taiwanese study by Hsu (in Porter & Collins, 1982) on close to 2000 3- to 7-year-old children used a translated version of the Thomas–Chess question- naire for parents. In this study I noted a *d*-value of .37 for activity level, which was the largest sex difference found in that study.

(2) Martin (1988) had teachers rate 257 boys and 222 girls, most of whom were between 5 and 7 years of age, on his Temperament Assessment Battery. On an eight-item activity scale he obtained a *d* of .69, also the largest sex difference found in that study. The items with the highest item-scale correlations were: 'Child seems to have difficulty sitting still, may wiggle a lot or get out of seat' and 'Child is able to sit quietly for a reasonable amount of time (as compared to classmates)'.

(3) In a Dutch longitudinal study (Kohnstamm, in preparation) mothers rated 155 6- and 7-year-old daughters and 168 same-aged sons on the nine items of a scale called Unrest, a PCA combination of items measuring distractibility, motor (un)rest and preference for quiet games as opposed to 'running games' (alpha = .83). For this scale *d* was .43 and for the four motor-activity items separately, *d* was .44, the same value as the average for the preschool age studies (12–72 months) analyzed by Eaton and Enns (1986). For reasons of comparison only, I mention the fact that on our six-item scale called Aggression (alpha = .82) the *d*-value in this study was .58. This is exactly the same value as the average *d* found by Hyde (1984) in a meta-analysis of sex differences in aggression for studies with mean subject age 6 years or less.

Of course, one could easily find more studies which Eaton and Enns (1986) had no chance to include, both with and without significant differences. However, I do not think that the enlargement of the sample of studies reviewed by these authors would change their conclusions.

A very interesting publication is in preparation on the measurement and corre- lates of open-field activity in young children. Halverson, of the University of Georgia, has extensively studied motor activity level across different settings, using actometers, standardized observations and rating scales (Halverson, in prepara- tion). He shows how one needs repeated observations in order to come to reliable estimates. In his studies (C.F. Halverson, Jr, personal communication, 4 November 1988) boys appear in every setting much more active than girls and the sex differences are very large when aggregated data are used. For boys, activity level is correlated with negatively valued variables whereas for girls the opposite is true: as girls become more active they become more likeable and more enjoyable in the eyes of parents and teachers. For boys, repeated actometer scores at age 3 can be predicted from the newborn period (40% of the variance explained) but not for girls. Little girls become more active when in the company of active boys. Halverson sees in activity level a sort of 'G' for childhood personality structure and development.

Teacher-Rated Hyperactivity and Inattentiveness

As noted above, the high end of the motor activity scale is associated with the behavioral disorder called hyperactivity. The preponderance of boys over girls in hyperactivity is a well-documented fact from many studies. Ratios vary from 2 : 1 to 8 : 1. Recently, Luk, Leung and Lee (1988) collected teacher ratings on the Conners scale for a sample of 914 Chinese children, aged 6–12 and living in Hong Kong. Comparing the means and standard deviations on the Conners hyperactivity scale I noted a high d-value of .99. Earlier studies with the same scale by Werry, Sprague and Cohen (1975) in the USA and by Werry and Hawthorne (1976) in New Zealand yielded ds of 1.00 and .71.

In a huge longitudinal British study (Osborn & Milbank, 1987) 7000 10-year-olds from all over Britain were rated by their teachers on several behavioral scales that combined items from the Rutter B-scale and the Conners scale. On the six-item scale called hyperactivity (highest loading item at age 10: 'shows restless or over-active behaviour') d was .47 and sex 'explained 5.6% of the variance compared with 1.6% for the Social Index score' (Osborn & Milbank, 1987, p. 120).

In the Dutch longitudinal study mentioned above (Kohnstamm, in preparation) teachers rated 265 children aged 6–8 years on two different scales for inattentiveness, distractibility and hyperactivity. The d-values for the two scales (intercorrelation .88) were .66 and .73. On two other scales for intro- and extraversion these teachers rated girls on the average slightly more extravert than boys. This means that a role-stereotype explanation for their differential rating behavior does not seem very plausible: if they had acted according to stereotypes, they would have also rated boys higher on extraversion. The same was true for the very large British study mentioned above: no sex differences in teacher-rated extraversion.

Twin Studies

Another sort of data seems relevant for the question of sex × age interactions in activity. Matheny (1980) reported twin correlations for several factors of the Infant Behavior Record (IBR) of the Bayley scales. For the factor called activity, the correlations between identical (monozygotic, MZ) twins, but not between fraternal (dizygotic, DZ) twins, steadily rose with age. For the ages of 6, 12, 18 and 24 months the MZ and DZ correlations were respectively: .24 and .11; .33 and .28; .43 and .14; .58 and .14. The numbers of the MZ twin pairs in this study ranged from 72 to 91; of the DZ twins from 35 to 50.

A comparable increase with age in identical twin correlations was reported by Matheny, Dolan and Wilson (1976) for two separate IBR items: activity and energy. Buss and Plomin (1984), who extracted these data from the original publications, interpreted them as supporting their theory of the heritability of activity and the two other EAS temperaments (emotionality and sociability), because the MZ correlations at all ages were substantially higher than the DZ correlations. They stressed the fact that each member of the twin pairs was rated by a different examiner. However, they did not comment on the increase with age of the similarity of the activity levels of the MZ twins. Could it be that this increase with age and the increase in sex differences with age as reported for the first years of life have the same cause: that motor activity is a trait which only gradually develops into a more or less stable characteristics?

Buss and Plomin (1984) seem as confident about the genetic base of individual differences in activity level as they are about the cultural base of average sex differences in activity level. True, for the small increase in sex differences in activity level during childhood, cultural values and expectations might be responsible. But why would MZ twins (as opposed to DZ twins) gradually come to be rated as more similar in activity, using independent laboratory behavior measurements? A better explanation for both developmental phenomena seems to be that the first year of life is not the best stage to measure genotypical activity level, just as it is not the best stage to measure other later-developing temperamental characteristics (see the above quotation by Rothbart, 1986).

There is an analogy to the measurable genetic influence on the Bayley Mental Development Index. According to Plomin (1987), 'about 15% of the variance in Bayley scores is due to genetic differences among infants; later in childhood, estimates of genetic influence on IQ scores are closer to 50%' (Plomin, 1987, p. 408).

Conclusion

The conclusion with regard to motor activity level must be that boys on the average show somewhat higher levels than girls. This difference increases with age until the early school years. At the high extreme of the scale the proportion of boys is at least twice the proportion of girls. Hyperactive motor behavior is an important component of the behavioral disorder called hyperactivity that also includes inattentiveness and distractibility. With respect to a causal explanation for this sex difference; some believe in worldwide role-stereotyping; others, including myself, believe in worldwide constitutional factors. I think that the cross-cultural universality and the regularity of the differences found make a biological rather than a cultural explanation the most plausible.

Emotionality

To return to Maccoby and Jacklin's (1974) famous overview: what about emotionality? Immediately the problem of differentiation in several kinds of emotion arises.

Crying

In infancy the frequency of crying is used as an index of, as yet, undifferentiated distress. Most of the studies in which crying was measured in Maccoby and

Jacklin's (1974) overview showed no significant sex differences. In four studies boys cried more and in three, girls. But all of these 26 studies were on less than 100 subjects; this is too small to discover small differences.

Kohnstamm (1984) asked large groups of Dutch parents to answer the question 'In general how much does your baby cry or get worked up?' on a seven-point rating scale. Boys were rated somewhat higher in all of eight age groups between 3 and 30 months but significantly so only between 5 and 22 months, with a maximum difference of $d = .23$ between 15 and 18 months. At that particular age level the groups consisted of 462 girls and 479 boys. These sex differences, however small, may well have been caused by the 'worked up' tail of the question. This would be in accordance with the somewhat higher tendency in the average male to respond with intense resistive reactions. Not immediately after birth, because NBAS irritability measures generally show no sex differences, but at the end of the first year, after month 8 or 9 on the average, the two sexes begin to differ in their complacency and in their resistance to control. And since crying and getting worked up at that age is one way of airing irritation and resistance, this is probably the reason why Dutch mothers rated boys on the average somewhat higher.

Maccoby and Jacklin (1974) summarized an early study by Landreth (1941) on factors associated with crying in young children:

> The report included 32 children, ranging in age from just under 3 to 5 years of age, and involved observations in the home as well as at school. Boys cried more frequently at home, and the author suggested that this might reflect a greater tendency on the part of boys to become irked with routines and parental restrictions on their activities. The frequency of crying at nursery school was similar for the two sexes in this sample, but the situations that led to crying were different: girls were more likely to cry because of accidental injury, boys from frustration over dealing with a recalcitrant inanimate object or during conflict with an adult. In other words, when boys cried, this was usually part of a frustration reaction, but for girls this was less likely to be the case. (Maccoby & Jacklin, 1974, p. 179)

Despite the small number of children in this study Landreth's interpretation is intuitively very appealing, at least to me.

Negative Emotional Responses to Frustration

Maccoby and Jacklin (1974) continued their review with evidence from other studies, notably by Goodenough (1931) based on diaries kept by parents of 45 young children and by Van Lieshout (1975) based on laboratory observations of frustration reactions in 64 Dutch children at 18 and again at 24 months.

In the first study the frequency of anger outburst was quite similar for the two sexes up to age 18 months. Thereafter this frequency declined to a low level among girls, but only slightly so among boys, 'so that during the age range 2½ to 5 years, boys became angry at least twice as frequently as girls' (Maccoby & Jacklin, 1974, p. 180).

In the second study children were observed in an observation room, both during free play and after an attractive toy was taken from the child and placed in a plastic box where it could be seen but not obtained without considerable effort. At age 18 months both sexes cried or showed other signs of being emotionally upset in about equal percentages. At age 24 months, however, the number of girls becoming upset at this frustration had declined considerably, 'while boys continued to be upset with about the same frequency that had prevailed among them at age 18 months' (Maccoby & Jacklin, 1974, p. 180).

After reviewing several other studies, 'in which boys have shown more negative reactions (including crying) in a situation where they were frustrated' (p. 180), Maccoby and Jacklin (1974) concluded that 'the frequency of negative emotional response to frustration declines faster in girls than in boys' (p. 182). They rejected the idea that the somewhat greater verbal skills of girls can explain this difference.

In Figure 1 I give an illustration of this sex difference from a totally different source (Kohnstamm, 1984). In a large cross-sectional questionnaire study we posed the question 'How does your child react when you are dressing him/her?', which was an exact translation of one of the items of Bates' ICQ/CCQ. The seven-point scale ranged from 'very well – likes it' to 'doesn't like it at all'. The midpoint was labeled as 'about average – doesn't mind it'. The largest d was found around the second birthday: .40. At the peak of negative reactions to being dressed d was .31.

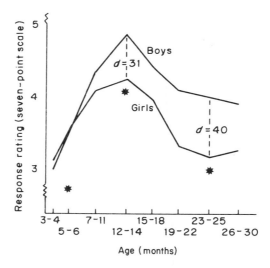

FIGURE 1   Developmental functions for Dutch boys and girls of mean answers given by their mothers to the Infant/Child Characteristics Questionnaire (ICQ/CCQ) question 'How does your baby react when you are dressing him/her?' Possible answers ranged from 1 'very well, likes it' to 7 'doesn't like it at all'. The midpoint, 4 (see the vertical axis) was labeled 'about average, doesn't mind it'. In the ICQ/CCQ the intermediate scale points 2, 3, 5 and 6 have no labels attached. On the vertical axis, scale points 3, 4 and 5 are indicated.

In the graph the means for eight successive age groups are shown, separately for the two sexes. Total sample sizes for the eight groups were: 528, 675, 2082, 907, 938, 704, 385 and 550 subjects. Sex differences are highly significant from age group 12–14 months onwards.

Only two of the d-values are shown.

The asterisks indicate the means of combined scores for boys and girls, originally obtained by Bates et al. (1979) in a longitudinal study in Bloomington, Indiana, USA, with children at ages 6, 13 and 24 months. Sample sizes in that study were 1786, 393 and 129, respectively.

The rise in boys' negative reactions between 3 and 13 months is a little less than one standard deviation; the rise for girls is a little more than one-half a standard deviation. Around their second birthday girls are back to the level they started from, whereas boys are still rated as one-half a standard deviation less positive (or more negative) in their reactions to being dressed.

In passing, it is interesting to see how the averages for Bates' longitudinal American sample (see the asterisks in the graph) show the same developmental function as the Dutch cross-sectional samples. This cross-cultural replication of a developmental function supports its reality.

Fear, Timidity, Anxiety and Neuroticism

Maccoby and Jacklin (1974) reached the following conclusions with regard to fear, timidity and anxiety:

1. Observational studies do not usually show a sex difference in timidity.
2. Teacher ratings and self-reports show girls to be more timid and anxious than boys.
3. Since boys are less willing to admit to fears or anxious feelings (have higher scores on lie and defensiveness scales), the sex difference on anxiety scales may be due to this factor.
4. Physiological measures of fear states have not yet clarified differences on physiological measures within and between sexes (Maccoby & Jacklin, 1974, p. 189).

In their overview of studies, these authors did not include the data collected by the Eysencks in Great Britain with self-reports by children and adolescents on the Eysenck scales for Neuroticism, the Eysenck Personality Inventory (Eysenck, 1965; Eysenck & Eysenck, 1969) and the EPQ (Eysenck & Eysenck, 1975). In Figure 2 their cross-sectional data for EPQ Neuroticism are shown. The sample sizes ranged from 140 of each sex at age 7 to above 200 at ages 8–14; at age 15 the numbers were lower: 148 for boys and 118 for girls. The differences between the means for both sexes were small before age 10 but increased thereafter. At age 14 the d-value for the two true sample means (not between the corresponding points on the regression line in Figure 2) was .48, and at age 15, .50. On the adult version of the EPQ the sex difference in the age group 16–19 (540 boys and 590 girls) was also .50. Thus, girls rated themselves on the average somewhat higher on Neuroticism, in particular after age 10. This is in accordance with the conclusion reached by Maccoby and Jacklin (1974) quoted above but it adds the developmental aspect.

Another example of this age trend is given by a combination of two recent European studies. In the very large-scale British study mentioned in the section on motor activity level (Osborn & Milbank, 1987) also no important sex differences were found for parent and teacher ratings on neuroticism and anxiety at ages 5 and 10. But again after puberty, in a standardization sample of over 1000 Dutch adolescents aged 13–18, girls on the average gave higher self-ratings on the Emotionality scale of a temperament assessment battery for adolescents, the Adolescent Temperament List (Fey & Kuiper, 1984). The d-values obtained with this scale showed an increase over the years of adolescence as depicted in Figure 2 for the EPQ. At the ages of 13, 14, 15 and 16–18 years the ds were .37, .43, .75 and .75, respectively (J.A. Fey & C.M. Kuiper, personal communication, 1988).

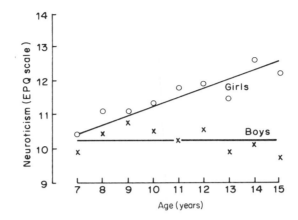

FIGURE 2   Developmental functions for boys and girls on the Neuroticism scale of the
Junior version of the Eysenck Personality Questionnaire. (Reproduced with permission of
the authors from Eysenck & Eysenck, 1975.)

Thus, before puberty, the data regarding neuroticism and anxiety show no
consistent sex differences but in postpuberty the self-report of females still indicate
higher averages of instability. This seems true for the US and for some European
countries.

    With regard to early anger, non-compliance and resistance – all externalizing
forms of negative reactions to frustration – it is impossible not to think about a
relation with the development of sex differences in aggression. The facts about this
development in the North American studies have been summarized in the
thoughtful meta-analysis by Hyde (1984). With regard to the explanation of these
differences I believe with Maccoby and Jacklin (1974) that the male is, for
biological reasons, in a greater state of readiness to learn and display aggressive
behavior, basing the argument in part on studies of the relationship between sex
hormones and aggression. This position *combines* a biologically greater state of
readiness with cultural sex-role transmission. This leads to the viewpoint that
biology and culture are related, in the sense that one can think about cultural
aspects – such as sex roles – partly shaped by the biology of mankind. In this case,
little boys in general can be in a more ready state to resist and to attack, without
being socialized to do so, and without having inherited their individual position on
a resistance dimension from their individual parents or grandparents.

    It can be inferred from the discussion above that the concept 'emotionality' is far
too comprehensive: anxiety, fear, negative reactivity, positive reactivity, anger and
joy are probably not just different manifestations of one underlying basic
dimension. The question about sex differences in emotionality cannot be answered
without first specifying what kind of emotionality.

Beyond the Sex × Age Effects

As stated in the introduction to this chapter section, for developmentalists the small
sex differences in some temperamental characteristics are only interesting in

combination with age and with developmental stage. Two other, more complicated questions were mentioned, one pertaining to differences in stability of specific temperaments, and the other pertaining to sex dependent differences in reactions of parents, teachers, etc. to a specific temperament.

With regard to the former question, more and more longitudinal data suggest very interesting sex differences in *stability* of specific temperamental traits. For instance, in the Australian Temperament Project (see Chapter 29) it was found that in infancy and early childhood parental easy–difficult ratings were more stable for girls. In the majority of studies, however, stability measures are not yet reported for the two sexes separately, so that a meta-analysis is not yet possible. Rutter (1987) observed that 'The finding that the patterns of associations for boys and girls may be quite different has led to a universal acceptance that associations must be studied separately in the two sexes' (Rutter, 1987, pp. 1262–1263). I wish this were also true for the field of temperament in childhood.

The complexities of the latter question always require multivariate statistical techniques, and since there is little uniformity in the use of these techniques, the comparison of research outcomes is not an easy task.

The basic sex differences in temperament, at whatever age, may be small, but culture reacts differently to males and females occupying the same position on specific dimensions. School-age boys and girls in the seventh decile of the common distribution of inhibition or of externalizing reactivity following frustration elicit quite different reactions, dependent upon the culture in general and on social class. The more rigid the sex roles are fixed in a culture or social class, the more different the reactions will be.

Further, the reactions are different according to the situation in which the behavior is exhibited and observed. The fact that in some of the studies, teacher ratings produced larger sex differences than parent ratings probably has several reasons. But one reason certainly is that the school environment with its limited space, its many behavioral restrictions and its intensive social interactions of the two sexes elicits behavior patterns which parents may not always see at home. So rather than thinking that teachers in general are more sex-stereotyped in their perceptions than parents are, we think school life elicits more sex-stereotyped behaviors than life at home.

ACKNOWLEDGMENTS

The corrections and suggestions made by Margot Prior and Mary Rothbart are gratefully acknowledged.

REFERENCES

Achenbach, T.M., Verhulst, F.C., Edelbrock, C., Dana Baron, G. & Akkerhuis, M.S. (1987). Epidemiological comparisons of American and Dutch children: II. Behavioral/emotional problems reported by teachers for ages 6 to 11. *American Academy of Child and Adolescent Psychiatry*, **26**, 326–332.

Bates, J.E., Freeland, C.A.B. & Lounsbury, M.L. (1979). Measurement of infant difficultness. *Child Development*, **50**, 794–803.

Beller, E.K., Eckert, A. & Kuckartz, U. (1986). Some cultural and situational correlates to infant temperament as assessed by German and Turkish mothers living in Berlin. In G.A. Kohnstamm (Ed.), *Temperament discussed*. Lisse (Neth.): Swets & Zeitlinger.

Block, J.H. (1983). Differential premises arising from different socialization of the sexes: Some conjectures. *Child Development,* **54**, 1335–1354.

Brazelton, T.B., Nugent, J.K. & Lester, B.M. (1987). Neonatal Behavioral Assessment Scale. In J.D. Osofsky (Ed.), *Handbook of infant development*. New York: Wiley.

Buss, A.H. & Plomin, R. (1975). *A temperament theory of personality development*. New York: Wiley.

Buss, A.H. & Plomin, R. (1984). *Temperament: Early developing personality traits*. Hillsdale, NJ: Erlbaum.

Caudill, W. & Weinstein, H. (1969). Maternal care and infant behavior in Japan and America. *Psychiatry,* **32**, 12–43.

Cohen, J. (1977). *Statistical power analysis for the behavior sciences*, revised edn (first edn 1969). New York: Academic Press.

Condry, J. & Condry, S. (1976). Sex differences: A study of the eye of the beholder. *Child Development,* **47**, 812–819.

Deux, K. (1984). Analysis of a decade's research on gender. *American Psychologist,* **39**, 105–116.

DeVries, M.W. & Sameroff, A.J. (1984). Culture and temperament: Influences on infant temperament in three East African cultures. *American Journal of Orthopsychiatry,* **54**, 83–96.

Diamond, S. (1957). *Personality and temperament*. New York: Harper.

Eaton, W.O. & Enns, R. (1986). Sex differences in human motor activity level. *Psychological Bulletin,* **100**, 19–28.

Eysenck, H.J. (1982). The biological basis of cross-cultural differences in personality: Blood group antigens. *Psychological Reports,* **51**, 531–540.

Eysenck, H.J. & Eysenck, M.W. (1985). *Personality and individual differences*. New York/London: Plenum.

Eysenck, H.J. & Eysenck, S.B.G. (1964). *Manual of the Eysenck Personality Inventory*. London: University of London Press.

Eysenck, H.J. & Eysenck, S.B.G. (1969). *Personality structure and measurement*. London: Routledge & Kegan Paul.

Eysenck, H.J. & Eysenck, S.B.G. (1975). *Manual of the Eysenck Personality Questionnaire (junior & adult)*. Loughton, Essex: Hodder & Stoughton.

Eysenck, H.J. & Eysenck, S.B.G. (1983). Recent advances: The cross-cultural study of personality. In C.D. Spielberger & J.N. Butcher (Eds), *Advances in personality assessment*, Vol. 2. Hillsdale, NJ: Erlbaum.

Eysenck, S.B.G. (1965). *Manual of the Junior Eysenck Personality Inventory*. London: Hodder & Stoughton.

Fey, J.A. & Kuiper, C.M. (1984). *Adolescenten Temperament Lijst*, Lisse (Neth.): Swets & Zeitlinger.

Freedman, D.G. (1974). *Human infancy: An evolutionary perspective*. Hillsdale, NJ: Erlbaum.

Goldsmith, H.H., Buss, A.H., Plomin, R., Rothbart, M.K., Thomas, A., Chess, S., Hinde, R.A. & McCall, R.B. (1987). Roundtable: What is temperament? Four approaches. *Child Development,* **58**, 505–529.

Goodenough, F.L. (1929). The emotional behavior of young children during mental tests. *Journal of Investigative Research,* **13**, 204–219.

Goodenough, F.L. (1931). *Anger in young children*. Minneapolis: University of Minnesota Press.

Halverson, C.F., Jr (in preparation). The measurement of open-field activity in young children: a critical analysis.

Hsu, C. (1982). Cross-cultural studies. In R. Porter & G.M. Collins (Eds), *Temperament differences in infants and young children*. Ciba Foundation Symposium No. 89. London: Pitman.

Hsu, C., Soong, W., Stigler, J.W., Hong, C. & Liang, C. (1981). The temperamental characteristics of Chinese babies. *Child Development,* **52**, 1337–1340.

Hyde, J.S. (1981). How large are cognitive gender differences? *American Psychologist*, **36**, 892–901.

Hyde, J.S. (1984). How large are gender differences in aggression? A developmental meta-analysis. *Developmental Psychology*, **20**, 722–736.

Kagan, J. (1987). Perspectives on infancy. In Osofsky, J. (Ed.), *Handbook of infant development*. Chichester/New York: Wiley.

Kagan, J., Kearsley, R.B. & Zelazo, P.R. (1978). *Infancy: Its place in human development*. Cambridge, MA: Harvard University Press.

Kagan, J., Reznick, S.J. & Snidman, N. (1986). Temperamental inhibition in early childhood. In R. Plomin & J. Dunn (Eds), *The study of temperament: Changes, continuities and challenges* (pp. 53–65). Hillsdale, NJ: Erlbaum.

Kohnstamm, G.A. (1984). *Bates' Infants Characteristics Questionnaire (ICQ) in the Netherlands*. ERIC reports, ED, 251, 179.

Kohnstamm, G.A. (in preparation). Early temperament and later teacher ratings.

Landreth, C. (1941). Factors associated with crying in young children in the nursery school and at home. *Child Development*, **12**, 81–97.

Laosa, L.M. (1982). Temperament in childhood: Its construct validity and population generalizability. Paper presented at the Fourth Occasional Temperament Conference, Salem, MA.

Levy, D.M & Tulchin, S.H. (1925). The resistant behavior of infants and children. *Journal of Experimental Psychology*, **8**, 209–224.

Luk, S.L., Leung, P.W.L. & Lee, P.L.M. (1988). Conner's teacher rating scale in Chinese children in Hong Kong. *Journal of Child Psychology and Psychiatry*, **29**, 165–174.

Maccoby, E.E. (1966). *The development of sex differences*. Stanford, CA: Stanford University Press.

Maccoby, E.E. & Jacklin, C.N. (1974). *The psychology of sex differences*. Stanford, CA: Stanford University Press.

MacPhee, D. (1983). What do ratings of infant temperament really measure? Paper presented at the biennial meeting of the SRCD, Detroit, MI, April 1983.

Martin, R.P. (1988). *The Temperament Assessment Battery for Children*. Brandon, VT: Clinical Psychology.

Matheny, A.P. (1980). Bayley's Infant Behavior Record: Behavioral components and twin analysis. *Child Development*, **51**, 1157–1167.

Matheny, A.P., Dolan, A.B. & Wilson, R.S. (1976). Within pair-similarity on Bayley's Infant Behavior Record. *Journal of Genetic Psychology*, **128**, 263–270.

Maziade, M., Boudreault, M., Thivierge, J., Capéraà, P. & Côté, R. (1984) Infant temperament: SES and gender differences and reliability of measurement in a large Quebec sample. *Merrill-Palmer Quarterly*, **30**, 213–216.

McDevitt, S.C. (1976). A longitudinal assessment of continuity and stability in temperamental characteristics from infancy to early childhood. Unpublished doctoral dissertation. Temple University.

McDevitt, S.C. & Carey, W.B. (1978). The measurement of temperament in 3- to 7-year-old children. *Journal of Child Psychology and Psychiatry*, **19**, 245–253.

Mead, M. (1948). *Sex and temperament in three primitive societies*. New York: William Morrow.

Meehan, A.M. (1984). A meta-analysis of sex differences in formal operational thought. *Child Development*, **55**, 1110–1124.

Neilon, P. (1948). Shirley's babies after 15 years. *Journal of Genetic Psychology*, **73**, 175–186.

Osborn, A.F. & Milbank, J.E. (1987). *The effects of early education: A report from the Child Health and Education Study*. Oxford: Clarendon Press.

Plomin, R. (1987). Developmental behavioral genetics and infancy. In J.D. Osofsky (Ed.), *Handbook of infant development*. New York: Wiley.

Porter, R. & Collins, G.M. (1982). *Temperament differences in infants and young children*. Ciba Foundation Symposium No. 89. London: Pitman.

Rossi, J.S. (1983). Ratios exaggerate gender differences in mathematical ability. *American Psychologist*, **38**, 348.

Rothbart, M.K. (1986). Longitudinal observation of infant temperament. *Developmental Psychology*, **22**, 356–365.

Rutter, M. (1987). Continuities and discontinuities from infancy. In J.D. Osofsky (Ed.), *Handbook of infant development* (pp. 1150–1198). New York: Wiley.

Shirley, M. (1933). *The first two years*, Vol. III, *Personality manifestations*. Minneapolis: University of Minnesota Press.

Super, C.M. & Harkness, S. (1986). Temperament, development and culture. In R. Plomin & J. Dunn (Eds), *The study of temperament: Changes, continuities and challenges.* (pp. 131–149). Hillsdale: Erlbaum.

Thomas, A. & Chess, S. (1977). *Temperament and development*. New York: Brunner/Mazel.

Uttal, D., Lummis, M. & Stevenson, H.W. (1988). Low and high mathematics achievement in Japanese, Chinese, and American elementary-school children, *Developmental Psychology*, **24**, 335–342.

Van Lieshout, C.F.M. (1975). Children's reactions to barriers placed by their mothers. *Child Development*, **46**, 879–886.

Weissbluth, M. (1981). Sleep duration and infant temperament. *Journal of Pediatrics*, **99**, 817–819.

Weissbluth, M. (1982). Chinese-American infant temperament and sleep duration: An ethnic comparison. *Developmental and Behavioral Pediatrics*, **3**, 99–102.

Werry, J.S. & Hawthorne, D. (1976). Conners' teacher questionnaire: Norms and validity. *Australia and New Zealand Journal of Psychiatry*, **10**, 257–262.

Werry, J.S., Sprague, R.L. & Cohen, M.N. (1975). Conners' teacher ratings scale for use in drug studies with children. *Journal of Abnormal Child Psychology*, **3**, 217–229.

Windle, M., Iwawaki, S. & Lerner, R.M. (1987). Cross-cultural comparability of temperament among Japanese and American early- and late-adolescents. *Journal of Adolescent Research* **2**, 423–446.

Windle, M., Iwawaki, S. & Lerner, R.M. (1988). Cross-cultural comparability of temperament among Japanese and American preschool children. *International Journal of Psychology*, **23**, 547–567.

27

On the Functional Significance of Temperamental Individuality: A Developmental Contextual View of the Concept of Goodness of Fit

Jacqueline V. Lerner, Katherine Nitz, Rachna Talwar and Richard M. Lerner
The Pennsylvania State University

In contemporary psychology, most approaches to the study of temperament view this aspect of personality as pertaining to the stylistic component of an individual's mental or behavioral repertoire (Buss & Plomin, 1984; Windle, 1988). That is, temperament refers to *how* the person does whatever is done. Thus, neither the content of, nor the motivation underlying, behavior is of primary concern in the study of temperament. Instead, individual differences in the style in which a person manifests otherwise identical behaviors are of prime interest. For example, since all children eat and sleep, focus on these contents of the behavioral repertoire would not readily differentiate among them. However, children may differ in the rhythmicity of their eating or sleeping behaviors and/or in the vigor, activity level, or mood associated with these behaviors; such characteristics of individuality are temperamental attributes by our definition.

Over the course of the past decade a significant increase has occurred in the study of temperament, especially during infancy and childhood (Lerner & Lerner, 1986). One reason for this growth in scientific attention is the theoretical role of individual differences in temperament in person–social context relations (Lerner & Lerner, 1986). Interindividual differences in temperament are seen as important moderators of children's success at coping with the stressors or demands encountered in the key settings of life (e.g. the family, the school, the peer group).

Our interest is in the importance of interindividual differences in temperament for the quality of person–context relations. We focus on temperamental individuality because it provides a means for us to test ideas associated with a

Temperament in Childhood   Edited by G.A. Kohnstamm, J.E. Bates and M.K. Rothbart

developmental contextual view of human development (Lerner, 1986, in press; Lerner & Kauffman, 1985). This perspective involves the idea that development occurs through reciprocal relations, or 'dynamic interactions' (Lerner, 1978), between organisms and their contexts. A notion of integrated, or 'fused', levels of organization is used to account for these dynamic interactions (Novikoff, 1945a,b; Schneirla, 1957; Tobach, 1981). Variables from levels of analysis ranging from the inner biological, through the psychological, to the sociocultural, all change interdependently across time (history); as such, variables from one level are both products and producers of variables from the other integrated levels (Lerner, 1982; Lerner & Busch-Rossnagel, 1981). Accordingly, models where one represents the *relations* among levels, and not any level in isolation, are needed to study these dynamic interactions and their functional significance.

One such model is found in the goodness of fit concept we have been testing in the research in our laboratory (e.g. Lerner & Lerner, 1983, 1987, 1989). The goodness of fit concept derives from the view that the person–context interactions depicted within developmental contextualism involve 'circular functions' (Schneirla, 1957), that is, person–context relations predicated on others' reactions to a person's characteristics of individuality: as a consequence of their characteristics of physical and behavioral individuality people evoke differential reactions in their significant others; these reactions constitute feedback to people and influence their further interactions (and thus their ensuing development). The 'goodness of fit' concept allows the valence of the feedback involved in these circular functions to be understood (Lerner & Lerner, 1983, 1987; Thomas & Chess, 1977).

The goodness of fit concept emphasizes the need to consider both the characteristics of individuality of the person and the demands of the social environment, as indexed for instance by expectations or attitudes of key significant others with whom the person interacts (e.g. parents, peers, or teachers). If a person's characteristics of individuality match, or fit, the demands of a particular social context then positive interactions and adjustment are expected. In contrast, negative adjustment is expected to occur when there is a poor fit between the demands of a particular social context and the person's characteristics of individuality.

To illustrate, if a particular characteristic of temperament (e.g. regular sleeping habits) is expected within a given social context (e.g. the family) by a significant other (e.g. the mother), then a child who possesses or develops that behavior will have a good fit with his or her environment. In such cases these children are expected to show positive behavioral interactions in regard to this characteristic, and ensuing developments are predicted to be favorable. If a child does not possess or develop behavior which matches or fits the demands of the context, then negative interactions and unfavorable outcomes are predicted.

In sum, then, within the framework of a developmental contextual perspective, we see temperament as a key instance of behavioral individuality. Through testing the goodness of fit concept, we seek to determine whether the functional significance of temperamental individuality for concurrent person–context relations and for subsequent development lies in the nature of the fit between: (a) the person's characteristics of temperamental individuality (i.e. his/her temperamental style); and (b) the demands (e.g. the expectations or attitudes) regarding temperamental style which are maintained by the significant others in the person's key contexts (e.g. the home, the peer group, the school). It is our view, then, that temperamental individuality, as an instance of organismic individuality, derives its significance for adaptive functioning through its link with the social context. This link is structured on the basis of circular functions between characteristics of temperamental distinctiveness and the reactions and feedback of significant others; the link is given its valence for developmental change by virtue of exchanges textured by the goodness of fit between temperament and the demands of the social context.

Our laboratory has been engaged over the course of about a decade with research testing this developmental contextual model of the functional significance of temperamental individuality for adaptive development. Much of this work has been reviewed elsewhere (e.g. J.V. Lerner, 1984; Lerner & Lerner, 1983, 1987, 1989). Here, then, it may be of most use to present some of our more recent findings devoted to appraising the functional significance of individual temperament–context relations.

Our current work may be divided into four general areas. First, we have developed questionnaire measures of temperament and of the attitudinal component of contextual demands, a component which we have operationalized through the assessment of 'ethnotheories of temperamental difficulty'. Second, we have utilized these measures in a longitudinal study of early adolescence, the Pennsylvania Early Adolescent Transitions Study (PEATS), an investigation wherein temperament–context fit has been related to psychosocial adjustment during the transition from elementary school to junior high school. Third, since the school context is not the only context in which to test the functional significance of temperament–context relations, we have tested the use of the goodness of fit concept model in another key context for development, that is, the home. Here, specifically, we have studied the relation between child's temperament and maternal employment. Fourth, in order more fully to understand temperament–context relations from a developmental contextual perspective it is important to examine these links in as broad a context as possible. To provide such a perspective we have initiated a series of cross-cultural studies involving Japanese and American samples.

MEASURING THE DIMENSIONS OF TEMPERAMENT AND OF ETHNOTHEORIES OF TEMPERAMENTAL DIFFICULTY

Our first current area of research involves developing and testing the empirical utility of a measure of temperament and of contextual demands regarding temperament. It is useful to describe first our temperament measure.

The Revised Dimensions of Temperament Survey

We have developed a questionnaire termed the Revised Dimensions of Temperament Survey (DOTS-R; Windle & Lerner, 1986; Windle et al., 1986). The DOTS-R is a

54-item questionnaire which assesses the temperamental attributes of young children, early adolescents, and young adults. For the first two age groups the DOTS-R assesses nine orthogonal dimensions: Activity Level–General; Activity Level–Sleep; Approach–Withdrawal; Flexibility–Rigidity; Quality of Mood; Rhythmicity–Sleep; Rhythmicity–Eating; Rhythmicity–Daily Habits; and Task Orientation. For the last age group the Task Orientation attribute is differentiated into the attributes of Distractibility and Persistence. For each of the 54 DOTS-R items, the rater (usually a parent in the case of the form of the DOTS-R designed for young children, and the person himself or herself in the case of the forms of the DOTS-R designed for early adolescents and young adults, respectively) is asked to respond to the item, e.g. 'I can't stay still for long' on a four-point scale ranging from 'usually false' to 'usually true'. Scoring the DOTS-R involves forming attribute scores by summing the scores on individual items. Higher DOTS-R scores indicate higher levels of activity level in general and activity level in sleep, a tendency to approach, higher flexibility, a positive mood, higher levels of rhythmicity in sleep, in eating, and in daily habits, and a higher level of task orientation.

Contextual Demands Regarding Temperament

To assess contextual demands regarding temperament we have relied on the concepts of 'developmental niche' and of 'ethnotheory', as formulated by Super and Harkness (1981, 1982, 1988). To explain the role these concepts play in our work, it is useful to recall that Thomas and Chess (1977), in their New York Longitudinal Study (NYLS), have found that particular attributes of a child's or an adolescent's temperament were desired, wanted, or preferred by his or her parents or teachers. Positive mood and rhythmicity of behavior are instances of such desired attributes. In turn, other attributes were found to be unwanted, e.g. withdrawal and high intensity reactions (Thomas & Chess, 1977). When a child possessed desired attributes he or she was easy for the parent or teacher to interact with; when a child possessed undesired attributes then others found it difficult to interact with him or her (Thomas & Chess, 1977). In short, in the NYLS, possession of particular, i.e. wanted, temperamental attributes afforded easy interactions, while possession of other, unwanted, attributes afforded difficult interactions.

Given the existence of easy and difficult temperament attributes, one may ask what influences whether a given attribute is regarded as easy or difficult by a parent, teacher, or peer. What gives a given temperament attribute its particular meaning?

One answer is provided by Super and Harkness (1982, 1988). They point out that the developing person's context is structured by three kinds of influences: the physical and social setting; culturally regulated customs involved in socialization; and the 'psychology' of the caregivers or the other significant people with whom the developing person interacts. This psychology is termed an 'ethnotheory' (Super & Harkness, 1980, 1981, 1989), that is, significant others' preferences, aversions, beliefs, or expectations regarding the meaning or significance of particular behaviors. Together, the three types of influence comprise the *developmental niche* of a person, that is, the set (or sets) of structured demands on the developing person (Super & Harkness, 1981).

Super and Harkness indicate that not all groups have the same preferences or aversions regarding temperament. Across cultures, and even *within* different sub-populations within a culture (e.g. the peers versus the parents of adolescents), differences in expectations, attitudes, and values regarding temperament may exist. These psychological differences are a product of the particular cultural or sub-cultural niche within which the people holding these attitudes, values, and expectations exist. These psychological differences in the meaning of temperament produce, then, differences in what is regarded as a wanted or as an unwanted attribute. Thus, contextual or group differences might exist in how easy or difficult it would be to interact positively with an adolescent because differences may exist in different niches within the adolescent's general ecological milieu in the meaning of (the degree of preference for) a given temperament attribute. In other words, then, because specific cultural, subpopulational, or ecological groups may differ in how much they want particular temperamental attributes, they may differ therefore as well in their ethnotheories (i.e. their attitudes, values, and expectations) regarding the difficulty the possession of a particular temperamental attribute presents for interaction. For instance, an adolescent's peers may differ from his or her parents in their respective 'ethnotheory of temperamental difficulty', i.e. their preferences for temperament and thus their beliefs about whether a particular temperamental attribute affords difficulty (or of course, conversely, ease) of interaction.

Based on this conception of the meaning of preferences about temperament for difficulty of social interaction, the DOTS-R items have been used to assess the ethnotheories regarding temperamental difficulty maintained by the parents, or in some cases, the peers of young children, of early adolescents, and of young adults. For example, in regard to early adolescents the DOTS-R is used in order to produce ethnotheory scores for the same nine temperament attributes as measured by the DOTS-R. For instance, with respect to parents, an item such as 'My child gets sleepy at different times every night' was presented to parents who were told to consider the item in terms of how they *wanted their child to behave*. If the item described the way the parent wanted the child to behave, then the behavior would not make it difficult for the parent to interact with the child, even if the child *always* showed that behavior. However, if the item described behavior the parent did not want quite as much, then more difficult interactions would exist if the child always showed this behavior. Similarly, if the parent wanted the behavior still less, then even greater difficulty would exist in this case. Finally, if the parent did not want to see the behavior at all, then if the child always showed this behavior, the most difficulty for interaction would exist. Thus, based on the degree to which the parent wanted the behavior described in the item, he or she rated the item in regard to the level of difficulty for interaction which would be associated with the behavior. This preference-based rating reflects an ethnotheory component of the demands imposed on the adolescent in his or her developmental niche.

As with the original DOTS-R questionnaire each 'DOTS-R: Ethnotheory' questionnaire uses a four -choice format with high scores indicating greater difficulty of interaction. The response alternatives are '1' = most wanted and therefore *not difficult*, '2' = want somewhat and therefore only a *little difficult*, '3' = want only a little and therefore *somewhat difficult*, and '4' = do not want at all and therefore *very difficult*. If an item is considered not to be important or relevant to the parent then the corresponding response would be 'not difficult'. The scoring procedures for all DOTS-R: Ethnotheory questionnaires (for parents, teachers, or peers) are identical to those used for the DOTS-R (Windle & Lerner, 1986).

Internal consistency coefficients (Cronbach alphas), short-term stability coefficients, and validity data regarding the DOTS-R and the DOTS-R: Ethnotheory forms have been reported by Windle and Lerner (1986), Windle *et al.* (1986), and Windle (1985, 1988). Across all age-level and rater forms of the DOTS-R and DOTS-R: Ethnotheory measures reliability estimates average no lower than .7 and interrelational data provide convergent and discriminant substantiation for the validity of the measures. As such, we have concluded that the measures are appropriate to employ in our tests of the use of the goodness of fit concept in understanding early adolescents' adjustments to the stressors they confront across the transition to junior high school. These tests relate to the second area of research focus within our laboratory.

THE PENNSYLVANIA EARLY ADOLESCENT TRANSITIONS STUDY

Our current tests of the goodness of fit concept have occurred within our conducting the PEATS, a short-term longitudinal study of approximately 150 northwestern Pennyslvania early adolescents, from the beginning of sixth grade across the transition to junior high school and to the end of the seventh grade.

To illustrate our work here, we may note that East, Lerner, and Lerner (1988) determined the overall fit between adolescents' temperament and the demands of their peers regarding desired levels of temperament. Based on the circular functions notion involved in the goodness of fit concept, East *et al.* (1988) predicted that, while no significant direct paths would exist between adjustment and either temperament, measured alone, or temperament–demands fit, fit would influence adolescent–peer social relations which, in turn, would influence adjustment. In short, significant mediated paths, but insignificant direct paths, were expected. These expectations were supported. For 9 of the 12 measures of adjustment employed (involving parents' ratings of behavior problems; teachers' ratings of scholastic competence, social acceptance, athletic competence, conduct adequacy, and physical appearance; and students' self-ratings of scholastic competence, social acceptance, athletic competence, conduct adequacy, physical appearance, and self-worth), both of the two mediated paths (between adolescent–peer group fit and peer relations, and then between peer relations and adjustment) were significant. In no case, however, was a significant direct path found.

Nitz, Lerner, Lerner, and Talwar (1988) found similar results regarding temperamental fit with parental demands and adolescent adjustment. At the beginning of sixth grade the number of significant relations between the adjustment measures and temperament-demands fit did not exceed the number of significant relations between temperament alone and adjustment. However, at both the middle and the end of sixth grade the percentage of significant relations involving adolescent temperament–parent ethnotheory fit scores and adjustment scores was significantly greater than the corresponding percentages involving adolescent temperament alone. Moreover, and underscoring the interconnections among the child–family relations and the other key contexts comprising the ecology of human development, such as the school context, Nitz *et al.* (1988) found almost interchangeable results when fit scores with the peer demands were considered.

In a related study, Talwar, Nitz, and Lerner (1988) found that poor fit with parental demands (especially in regard to the attributes of Mood and Approach–Withdrawal) at the end of sixth grade was associated in seventh grade with low teacher-related academic and social competence and negative peer relations. Corresponding relations were found in regard to fit with peer demands. Moreover, and again underscoring the importance of considering the context within which organismic characteristics are expressed, goodness of fit scores (between temperament and demands) were more often associated with adjustment than were temperament scores alone; this was true in regard to both peer and parent contexts at the end of the sixth grade, and for the peer context after the transition to junior high school (at the beginning of seventh grade). Finally, Talwar *et al.* (1988) grouped the PEATS subjects into high vs low overall fit groups (by summing fit scores across all temperament dimensions). Adolescents in the low-fit group in regard to peer demands received lower teacher ratings of scholastic competence, and more parent ratings for conduct and school problems, than did the adolescents in the high-fit group in regard to peer demands. Comparable findings were found in regard to low vs high fit in regard to parent demands.

Given, then, that the nature of the links among temperamental fit –with peer and with parent demands – and adjustment underscores the connections among two key contexts for the adolescent's development, our research has sought to explore the importance of temperamental individuality and fit by varying context in another manner. Children are not the only people who function in multiple contexts. Parents do so as well. Thus our research has considered also parents as both parents in the home *and* as workers outside of it. This focus pertains to our third area of current research.

TEMPERAMENT AND MATERNAL EMPLOYMENT

The circular functions and 'goodness of fit' concepts have been most often examined in the context of assessing temperamental features of child individuality (Lerner *et al.*, 1986). Our research on the relations between child temperament and maternal employment extends this literature not only by appraising a most significant other in the child's world – the mother – but also by assessing the impact of potential differences among mothers that accrue as a consequence of whether they are employed outside the home. Our assumption is that mothers who work outside the home exist actively in a broader ecological system (Bronfenbrenner, 1979), and they have demands imposed on them by virtue of their being embedded in this system. This embeddedness makes specific features of their child's temperament potentially very significant for the mother–child relationship, for feedback to the child, and for resulting child developments.

Specifically, children who have the temperament characteristics of arrhythmicity, negative mood, slow adaptability, high intensity of responses, and withdrawal are difficult to manage and to interact with easily; they do not respond efficiently to maternal caregiving attempts (Thomas, Chess & Birch, 1968). In fact, we have noted above that Thomas and Chess labeled children possessing these temperament attributes as 'difficult children'. Contrasted with 'easy children', who possess the temperament characteristics of high rhythmicity, positive mood, high adaptability, approach behaviors, and low to moderate intensity of responses, difficult children present management demands on any mother. These demands may be complicated when the mother exists within an extrafamilial (employment) system, which imposes its own demands, such as scheduled attendance, commitment, good performance, and efficiency. Simply, if a mother cannot get her child fed and to bed easily, and if the child does not regularly sleep through the night, the child will evoke reactions in the mother that will differ from those evoked by an easily fed child who goes to sleep readily and sleeps through the night. If a mother comes home from a day of work to face a difficult child, her relationship with the child will probably differ from the mother of a difficult child who is not strained by the additional extrafamilial role of worker.

Of course, another scenario is possible. It may be that the difficult child drives a mother out of the house; a mother might seek outside employment in order to escape from the strain of dealing with a temperamentally difficult child. In other words, then, either of two types of circular functions may exist by virtue of a child's fitting or not fitting demands imposed on him or her as a consequence of the mother's employment outside the home. Can evidence be found for either of these two scenarios?

Research from our laboratory using the New York Longitudinal Study (NYLS) (Thomas & Chess, 1977) data set, an over 30-year, still ongoing longitudinal study of the development of 133 largely white, middle- to upper-middle class children, has made it possible to investigate the relationship between maternal employment and temperament (Lerner & Galambos, 1985) and to test this question. In the results of an initial study focusing on the influences of child characteristics on maternal employment, Lerner and Galambos (1985) interrelated temperament scores derived from codings of NYLS parental interview data (Thomas, Chess, Birch, Hertzig & Korn, 1963) with scores pertinent to maternal employment history. Lerner and Galambos found that, among infants and toddlers, the temperamental characteristics associated with the 'difficult' child (for example, irregularity of biological functions, withdrawal responses, high intensity of reactions, negative mood, and slow adaptability) were related to lower levels of maternal employment during this period of the child's life. In turn, infants and toddlers who possessed 'easy' temperamental characteristics (regularity of biological functions, positive mood and approach behaviors, high adaptability, and low or moderate intensity of reactions) were more likely to have mothers who were employed.

However, the direction of causality in this study was not determined; for instance, it could be that the child of the mother who is employed becomes less demanding, or 'easy'. Our further research will address the issue of causal relations and, we hope elucidate better the child's potentially reciprocal influence on the mother's occupational development.

At this point, however, we can conclude that links exist among temperament, fit, and multiple child and significant others' contexts. Thus, our research suggests the use of a broad, multi-tiered view of the context within which temperament is expressed. This broad approach to context is the emphasis in the fourth of our current research foci.

THE STRUCTURE OF TEMPERAMENT AMONG JAPANESE

The fourth area within which we are currently working involves our interest in testing how the broadest level of analysis within the developmental contextual perspective which guides our work (Lerner & Lerner, 1989) – that is, the sociocultural level – may moderate the link between temperamental individuality and contextual demands. All of our research described to this point has been intracultural, testing in various ways the import for adjustment within American schools, families, and peer groups of having characteristics of temperamental individuality fitting or not fitting with the demands (e.g. ethnotheories) for temperament existing within these settings. However, given that our interest in temperament and in the goodness of fit model derives from our superordinate concern with appraising the utility of the developmental contextual perspective for organizing and extending knowledge of human development, we have begun a line of research which is aimed at assessing whether the implications of temperament for adjustment, as depicted by the goodness of fit model, are moderated by sociocultural context.

To perform this test we selected Japan as a sociocultural setting to contrast with the American ones we have employed. This choice was predicted on the existence of a large number of already-existing cross-national studies of socioemotional development in Japan and the United States, for instance pertaining to attachment (e.g. see Lamb, Hwang, Frodi & Frodi, 1982; Lerner & Ryff, 1978, for reviews), and more specifically, to other developmental contextually-based tests of components of the goodness of fit model (e.g. Lerner, Iwawaki, Chihara & Sorell, 1980). Thus, for both theoretical and empirical reasons we have initiated a program of research involving the assessment of temperament–context relations in Japan.

At this writing, this line of research has advanced sufficiently for us to conclude that temperament is comparably structured within American and Japanese samples. This conclusion represents an important first step in our cultural comparative research; that is, as Eckensberger (1973) has noted, one must be certain that one is measuring the same construct across cultures before one evaluates any differential implications for adjustment of the construct.

In an initial attempt to establish measurement equivalence across cultures, Iwawaki, Hertzog, Hooker, and Lerner (1985) used the DOTS (Lerner, Palermo, Spiro & Nesselrode, 1982) to assess the generalizability of the structure of temperament, identified among American young adult samples on the DOTS, to similarly aged Japanese. The responses of 304 Japanese college students (59.5% males) were studied. The Japanese responses to the DOTS were compared to those of the American sample studied by Lerner *et al.* (1982) through the use of confirmatory factor analysis procedures. The major findings were that: evidence for the five factors present on the DOTS in the American sample was identified also among the Japanese, but large cultural differences existed in factor loadings for the DOTS attribute of Adaptability/Approach–Withdrawal; the loadings were smaller for the Japanese.

Despite these differences in factor loadings, the comparability of DOTS structures in the Japanese and American young adult samples encouraged us to appraise such generalizability in regard to the temperament measure of current use in our research, the DOTS-R (Windle & Lerner, 1986). In a first study, Windle, Iwawaki, and Lerner (1987) investigated this generalizability by studying metric equivalent relations between samples of Japanese and American early adolescents, and between samples of Japanese and American late adolescents. Similar to findings for the American adolescent samples (Windle & Lerner, 1986), nine- and ten-factor models were found adequate to represent the inter-item covariance matrix of the DOTS-R for the Japanese early- and late-adolescent samples, respectively. Metric equivalence between the early- and late-adolescent samples, respectively, was supported via congruence coefficients and restricted (confirmatory), simultaneous group models for each of the separate temperament dimensions. However, statistical tests of differences in factor means were conducted and indicated that American early- and late-adolescents rated themselves higher in approach behavior, mood quality (positive affect), and task orientation. In turn, the Japanese early adolescents rated themselves higher with respect to features of behavioral rhythmicity. Finally, no statistically significant differences were found for almost one-half of the factor mean comparisons.

In the last study we have completed to date of the generalizability of temperament structure in Japan and the United States (Windle, Iwawaki & Lerner, 1988), we compared the item responses on the DOTS-R of Japanese and American preschool children. Consistent with the results of an American preschool sample (Windle & Lerner, 1986), a nine-factor model emerged for the sample of Japanese preschool children. Configurational similarity of salient and non-salient factor loadings for the nine temperament constructs across the two cultural groups was supported via congruence coefficients, which ranged from .73 to .98 (median = .91). Restricted (confirmatory) simultaneous group models for each of the nine temperament constructs indicated that the factor loading patterns were invariant across the two preschool samples, thus supporting the equality of scale metrics or units of measurement across groups. Statistical tests of differences in factor means between the two cultural samples suggested that the primary caregivers of Japanese preschoolers, relative to the primary caregivers of American preschoolers, rated their children as higher in Activity Level – Sleep; and lower in Approach–Withdrawal; Flexibility–Rigidity; Quality of Mood; and Rhythmicity – Sleep. However, no statistically significant differences in mean levels were reported for Activity Level – General; Task Orientation; Rhythmicity – Eating; and Rhythmicity – Daily Habits.

In sum, our research to date in Japan has supported the existence of comparable temperament structures in the two cultures, as measured by the DOTS and by the DOTS-R. Given this evidence for measurement equivalence our research may proceed with our tests of the goodness of fit model and, as such, with our appraisal of whether sociocultural context moderates the relation between temperamental individuality and adjustment. As our research on this topic continues, it will provide – along with our future work in the other empirical areas we have discussed – a richer data base than has existed previously to evaluate the utility of the developmental contextual view of human development. This goal for our research may be usefully discussed in relation to some concluding observations about our approach to the study of the functional significance of temperament.

CONCLUSIONS AND FUTURE DIRECTIONS

Together the concepts of organismic individuality, of context, and of the relations between the two, found in a developmental contextual perspective are quite complex. The simultaneous consideration of these concepts imposes formidable challenges on those who seek to derive feasible research from this perspective. As we have argued, this developmental contextual perspective leads to an integrated, multi-level concept of development, one in which the focus of inquiry is the organism–environment dynamic interaction. Furthermore, such an orientation places an emphasis on the potential for intraindividual change in structure and function – for plasticity – across the life span.

The data we have reviewed here, as well as those derived from other laboratories (e.g. see Baltes, 1987; Hetherington, Lerner & Perlmutter, 1988; Sorenson, Weinert & Sherrod, 1986, for reviews) underscore the current use – across the life span – of a developmental contextual orientation for the study of temperament. Nevertheless, for the future the major challenge for this perspective is, as we have noted, the further derivation and empirical testing of models reflecting the nature of dynamic, interlevel interactions across time. Such tests will profit by triangulation of the constructs within each of the levels of analysis thought to dynamically interact within a given model.

For instance, in regard to the organism–context interactions assessed within the goodness of fit model, temperament could be simultaneously indexed both by more molecular, biological measures (e.g. heart rate; see Kagan, Reznick & Snidman, 1986, and Chapter 8) and by more molar, behavioral measures. Similarly, demands (e.g. of parents) could be simultaneously appraised by assessing both attitudes/ expectations about behavior and actual behavioral exchanges. In addition, temperament and demands could be assessed by both questionnaire and observational measures. Such triangulation would not only provide better convergent and discriminant validation information than currently exists. In addition, better insight would be gained about whether all modalities of functioning within a level of analysis are of similar import for adaptive functioning in particular person–context interactions. Moreover, the standard incorporation of multiple measures into future research is important not only because of the new information it would provide about the developmental contextual model, but also because this information would provide insight into the most useful targets of interventions aimed at enhancing the social behavior of the developing person.

As we have indicated, one reasonably successful path we have taken for exploring the usefulness of a developmental contextual perspective involves the testing of the goodness of fit model of person–context relations. Nevertheless, our own work would profit from the sort of triangulation for which we call. In addition, of course, the goodness of fit model is not the only conception of person–context relations that may be derived from a developmental contextual orientation. There are perhaps an infinity of possible interlevel relations that may occur and a potentially similarly large array of ways to model them. In the future, those testing these perspectives should consider incorporation of multiple measures within each of the levels modeled. Indeed, since current tests of other models derived from a developmental contextual or life-span perspective also have found considerable empirical support (e.g. Baltes, 1987), we can expect that such extensions will be important additions to an already significant foundation.

In sum, the relative plasticity of human development across the life span – a plasticity deriving from the dynamic interactions between organism and context which characterize human functioning – is already well documented (Baltes, 1987; Brim & Kagan, 1980; Featherman, 1983; Hetherington *et al.*, 1988; Lerner, 1984; Sorensen *et al.*, 1986). Thus a future research program including the sorts of directions we suggest should enrich greatly our understanding of the precise conditions promoting and constraining human plasticity and development. Given, then, the present literature, and the promise we see for tomorrow, we believe there is reason for great optimism about the future scientific use of the developmental contextual view of the biological and social bases of development.

ACKNOWLEDGMENTS

The writing of this chapter was supported in part by a grant to Richard M. Lerner and Jacqueline V. Lerner from the William T. Grant Foundation and by NIMH Grant MH39957.

REFERENCES

Baltes, P.B. (1987). Theoretical propositions of life-span developmental psychology: On the dynamics between growth and decline. *Developmental Psychology,* **23**, 611–626.

Brim, O.G., Jr & Kagan, J. (1980). Constancy and change: A view of the issues. In O.G. Brim, Jr & J. Kagan (Eds), *Constancy and change in human development.* Cambridge, MA: Harvard University Press.

Bronfenbrenner, U. (1979). *The ecology of human development.* Cambridge, MA: Harvard University Press.

Buss, A.H. & Plomin, R. (1984). *Temperament: Early developing personality traits.* Hillsdale, NJ: Erlbaum.

East, P.L., Lerner, R.M. & Lerner, J.V. (1988). Early adolescent-peer group fit, peer relations, and adjustment. Unpublished manuscript, The Pennsylvania State University, University Park.

Eckensberger, L.H. (1973). Methodological issues of cross-cultural research in developmental psychology. In J.R. Nesselroade & H.W. Reese (Eds), *Life-span developmental psychology.* New York: Academic Press.

Featherman, D.L. (1983). Life-span perspectives in social science research. In P.B. Baltes & O.G. Brim, Jr (Eds), *Life-span development and behavior,* Vol. 5. New York: Academic Press.

Hetherington, E.M., Lerner, R.M. & Perlmutter, M. (Eds) (1988). *Child development in life span perspective.* Hillsdale, NJ: Erlbaum.

Iwawaki, S., Hertzog, C., Hooker, K. & Lerner, R.M. (1985). The structure of temperament among Japanese and American young adults. *International Journal of Behavioral Development*, **8**, 217–237.

Kagan, J., Reznick, S.J. & Snidman, N. (1986). Temperamental inhibition in early childhood. In R. Plomin & J. Dunn (Eds), *The study of temperament: Changes, continuities and challenges*. Hillsdale, NJ: Erlbaum.

Lamb, M.E., Hwang, C.-P., Frodi, A.M. & Frodi, M. (1982). Security of mother- and father–infant attachment and its relation to sociability with strangers in traditional and nontraditional Swedish families. *Infant Behavior and Development*, **5**, 355–367.

Lerner, J.V. (1984). The import of temperament for psychosocial functioning: Tests of a 'goodness of fit' model. *Merrill-Palmer Quarterly*, **30**, 177–188.

Lerner, J.V. & Galambos, N.L. (1985). Maternal role satisfaction, mother–child interaction, and child temperament. *Developmental Psychology*, **21**, 1157–1164.

Lerner, J.V. & Lerner, R.M. (1983). Temperament and adaptation across life: Theoretical and empirical issues. In P.B. Baltes & O.G. Brim, Jr (Eds), *Life-span development and behavior*, vol. 5 (pp. 197–231). New York: Academic Press.

Lerner, J.V. & Lerner, R.M. (Eds) (1986). Temperament and psychosocial interaction in infancy and childhood. *New directions for child development*. San Francisco: Jossey-Bass.

Lerner, R.M. (1978). Nature, nurture and dynamic interactionism. *Human Development*, **21**, 1–20.

Lerner, R.M. (1982). Children and adolescents as producers of their own development. *Developmental Review*, **2**, 342–370.

Lerner, R.M. (1986). *Concepts and theories of human development*, 2nd edn. New York: Random House.

Lerner, R.M. (in press). Developmental contextualism and the life-span view of person-context interactions. In M. Bornstein & J.S. Bruner (Eds), *Interaction in human development*. Hillsdale, NJ: Erlbaum.

Lerner, R.M. & Busch-Rossnagel, N. (1981). Individuals as producers of their development: Conceptual and empirical bases. In R.M. Lerner & N.A. Busch-Rossnagel (Eds), *Individuals as producers of their development: A life-span perspective*. New York: Academic Press.

Lerner, R.M., Iwawaki, S., Chihara, T. & Sorell, G.T. (1980). Self-concept, self-esteem, and body attitudes among Japanese male and female adolescents. *Child Development*, **51**, 847–855.

Lerner, R.M. & Kauffman, M.B. (1985). The concept of development in contextualism. *Developmental Review*, **5**, 309–333.

Lerner, R.M. & Lerner, J.V. (1987). Children in their contexts: A goodness of fit model. In J.B. Lancaster, J. Altmann, A.S. Rossi & L.R. Sherrod (Eds), *Parenting across the life span: Biosocial dimensions*. Chicago: Aldine.

Lerner, R.M. & Lerner, J.V. (1989). Organismic and social contextual bases of development: The sample case of adolescence. In W. Damon (Ed.), *Child development today and tomorrow*. San Francisco: Jossey-Bass.

Lerner, R.M., Lerner, J.V., Windle, M., Hooker, K., Lenerz, K. & East, P.L. (1986). Children and adolescents in their contexts: Tests of a goodness of fit model. In R. Plomin & J. Dunn (Eds), *The study of temperament: Changes, continuities, and challenges*. Hillsdale, NJ: Erlbaum.

Lerner, R.M., Palermo, M., Spiro, A., III & Nesselroade, J.R. (1982). Assessing the dimensions of temperamental individuality across the life-span: The Dimensions of Temperament Survey (DOTS). *Child Development*, **53**, 149–159.

Lerner, R.M. & Ryff, C.D. (1978). Implementation of the life-span view of human development: The sample case of attachment. In P.B. Baltes (Ed.), *Life-span development and behavior*, Vol. 1). New York: Academic Press.

Nitz, K.A., Lerner, R.M., Lerner, J.V. & Talwar, R. (1988). Parental and peer demands, temperament, and early adolescent development. *Journal of Early Adolescence*, **8**, 243–263.

Novikoff, A.B. (1945a). The concept of integrating levels of biology. *Science,* **101**, 405–406.

Novikoff, A.B. (1945b). Continuity and discontinuity in evolution. *Science,* **101**, 405–406.

Schneirla, T.C. (1957). The concept of development in comparative psychology. In D.B. Harris (Ed.), *The concept of development.* Minneapolis: University of Minnesota Press.

Sorensen, A.B., Weinert, F.E. & Sherrod, L.R. (Eds) (1986). *Human development and the life course: Multidisciplinary perspectives.* Hillsdale, NJ: Erlbaum.

Super, C.M. & Harkness, S. (1981). Figure, ground, and gestalt: The cultural context of the active individual. In R.M. Lerner & N.A. Busch-Rossnagel (Eds), *Individuals as producers of their development: A life-span perspective.* New York: Academic Press.

Super, C. & Harkness, S. (1982). Constitutional amendments. Presentation at the Occasional Temperament Conference, Salem, MA, October 1982.

Super, C.M. & Harkness, S. (1988). The development niche: Culture and the expressions of human growth. Unpublished manuscript, Harvard University, Cambridge.

Talwar, R., Nitz, K. & Lerner, R.M. (1988). Relations among early adolescent temperament, parent and peer ethnotheories, and adjustment: A test of the goodness of fit model. Unpublished manuscript, The Pennsylvania State University, University Park.

Thomas, A. & Chess, S. (1977). *Temperament and development.* New York: Brunner/Mazel.

Thomas, A., Chess, S. & Birch, H. (1968). *Temperament and behavioral disorders in childhood.* New York: New York University Press.

Thomas, A., Chess, S., Birch, H.G., Hertzig, M.E. & Korn, S. (1963). *Behavioral individuality in early childhood.* New York: New York University Press.

Tobach, E. (1981). Evolutionary aspects of the activity of the organism and its development. In R.M. Lerner & N.A. Busch-Rossnagel (Eds), *Individuals as producers of their development: a life-span perspective.* New York: Academic Press.

Windle, M. (1985). Inter-inventory relations among the DOTS-R, EASI-II, and EPI. Unpublished manuscript, Johnson O'Connor Research Foundation, Chicago.

Windle, M. (1988). Psychometric strategies of measures of temperament: A methodological critique. *International Journal of Behavioral Development,* **11**, 171–201.

Windle, M., Hooker, K., Lenerz, K., East, P.L., Lerner, J.V. & Lerner, R.M. (1986). Temperament, perceived competence, and depression in early- and late-adolescents. *Developmental Psychology,* **22**, 384–392.

Windle, M., Iwawaki, S. & Lerner, R.M. (1987). Cross-cultural comparability of temperament among Japanese and American early- and late-adolescents. *Journal of Adolescent Research,* **2**, 423–446.

Windle, M., Iwawaki, S. & Lerner, R.M. (1988). Cross-cultural comparability of temperament among Japanese and American preschool children. *International Journal of Psychology,* **23**, 547–567.

Windle, M. & Lerner, R.M. (1986). Reassessing the dimensions of temperamental individuality across the life-span: The Revised Dimensions of Temperament Survey (DOTS-R). *Journal of Adolescent Research,* **1**, 213–230.

28

Sociocultural Factors and Temperament

WILLIAM FULLARD, RUNE J. SIMEONSSON AND GAIL S. HUNTINGTON
Temple University and University of North Carolina at Chapel Hill

As has been true in other domains of interest in child development, such as intelligence, significant controversy has centered on the role of environmental variables as sources of variation in the conceptualization and measurement of temperament. Among these variables are socioeconomic status (SES), race and ethnicity.

Socioeconomic status is a variable that is often invoked in psychological research to qualify or, in some instances, question findings on the development or functioning of children and families. While there appears to be fairly universal agreement that SES contributes to significant variation in the behavior and functioning of individuals, there is substantially less agreement on how it should be incorporated into psychological research. As Mueller and Parcel (1981) have pointed out in an extensive review of the topic, the inclusion of SES in the developmental literature has largely served two purposes: (a) as a descriptor of the subject population; and (b) as a variable to control or explain data analysis. Mueller and Parcel emphasize that the use of SES in the developmental literature has primarily been for the former purpose.

While there are a number of issues that bear on the controversy in reference to the examination of temperament in children, a fundamental issue reduces to the question, to what extent is temperamental variation in children a function of socioeconomic variables? There are at least two positions from which this question has been addressed. One argues for a minimal SES role, whereas the other assumes that SES may account for significant variation in children's temperament differences. The research of the New York Longitudinal Study (NYLS) group (e.g. Thomas & Chess, 1977) and the work of both Plomin (Plomin & Dunn, 1986) and Rothbart (Rothbart & Derryberry, 1981) have had a strong biological orientation and support a conceptualization of temperament as an individual difference variable, relatively independent of SES. Other researchers, however, have posited a

Temperament in Childhood   Edited by G.A. Kohnstamm, J.E. Bates and M.K. Rothbart
© 1989 John Wiley & Sons Ltd

stronger role for SES in the expressed temperament variation of children. While the source of such variation is not readily defined, research by Vaughn and his colleagues (Vaughn, Bradley, Joffee, Seifer & Barglow, 1987; Vaughn, Taraldson, Crichton & Egeland, 1981), Sameroff and his colleagues (Sameroff, Seifer & Barocas, 1983; Sameroff, Seifer & Elias, 1982a; Sameroff, Seifer & Zax, 1982b) and by others has largely attributed the variation to rater characteristics and measurement error. Based on the review of literature presented in this chapter, it would appear that the evidence to support the latter conclusion is meager. While some studies have reported a relationship between measures of SES and selected temperament characteristics, the overall conclusion is that, at the present time, there is no evidence for a strong and systematic relationship between temperament and SES.

How should the SES variable be examined in research on temperament development in children? As Mueller and Parcel (1981) point out, the researcher first needs to determine whether SES is a variable of interest. If the answer to this question is yes, then the manner in which SES is to be measured must be determined. The measurement technique employed should reflect the most current and relevant conceptualizations of this variable. Based on an extensive review of sociological research and theory appearing in *Child Development* and *Developmental Psychology* for a 2-year period, Mueller and Parcel describe the Hollingshead two-factor index as outdated and advocate the use of occupation-based measures as the best single index of SES. Of these, Mueller and Parcel (1981) identify the Duncan Socioeconomic Index (SEI) and the Siegal Prestige Scale as indices appropriate for North American child-development research.

The need for contemporary SES measures has also been endorsed by Gottfried (1985). However, he found substantial overlap in the Duncan and Siegal indices with the four-factor Hollingshead index. A major difference between the Hollingshead four-factor index and the two occupational measures is that the latter are derived on the basis of a hierarchical ranking of occupations, whereas the former has a multidimensional basis of occupation, education, marital status and gender. Furthermore, while all three SES measures correlated with children's developmental status, the Hollingshead four-factor index showed the strongest associations. Given these findings, Gottfried feels that the Hollingshead four-factor index should be given serious consideration over the occupational indices in developmental research because it 'is suitable for estimating SES of unmarried individuals and heads-of-household of both genders as well as for families' (Gottfried, 1985, p. 85).

The purpose of this chapter is to examine the SES issue in research on the development of temperament in children. To this end, a review of the literature was made, and relevant research was examined to answer two questions: (a) to what extent is SES information included in current research on temperament, and how has it been measured; and (b) what evidence is there for SES effects in studies which have incorporated it into analyses and interpretations. In addition, implications for future research are identified.

REVIEW OF STUDIES

To answer the first question, a computer-assisted search was conducted of *Psychological Abstracts, ERIC* and *Index Medicus* for the subject temperament, covering the years 1985–1987. A second search, covering the same sources, was carried out for the subjects temperament, education, race and SES for the 10 years from 1977 to 1987. The studies reported were conducted predominantly with samples from the United States, although there were some notable exceptions conducted with samples from other countries (e.g. Canada: Maziade, Boudreault, Thivierge, Capéraà & Côté, 1984a; Maziade, Boutin, Côté & Thivierge, 1986a; Maziade, Côté, Boudreault, Thiverge & Boutin, 1986b; Maziade, Côté, Boudreault, Thivierge & Capéraà, 1984b; Maziade, Côté, Boutin, Bernier & Thivierge, 1987; Australia: Oberklaid, Sanson & Prior, 1986; Prior, Kyrios & Oberklaid, 1987; Sewell & Oberklaid, 1986; Sweden; Persson-Blennow & McNeil, 1981). All research articles from the search were reviewed to determine whether SES was mentioned in the report and, if so, how it was measured, and whether the variable was used only for descriptive purposes or was included as an experimental or analytic variable. This review revealed several interesting findings which are summarized in Table 1.

First, of 162 studies reviewed, only 107, or 66%, had any reference to SES in the methodology section. An examination of the manner in which SES has been defined in the 107 studies showed that 71% incorporated SES information only in an impressionistic or generic manner. Illustrative of this form of entry were descriptions of the sample as being primarily middle class (e.g. Brody, Stoneman & Burke, 1987), or studies in which some SES information was provided, but it was non-formal in nature, being a simple description of educational status and/or occupation of subjects (e.g. Bates & Bayles, 1984). In only a small number of studies (29%) was a formal method of SES documentation employed. The most frequent of these was the use of either the two- or four-factor Hollingshead index (68%). In the remaining studies, the Duncan index (16%) or one of a number of other indices were employed.

Table 1   Summary of temperament research: 1977–1987

	Number	Percentage
Number of articles reviewed	162	
Articles with no mention of SES	55	34
Articles that mentioned SES	107	66
Use of SES information (total *n* = 107):		
Impressionistic/descriptive	76	71
Descriptive – formal	31	29
SES measures used (total *n* = 31):		
Hollingshead two-factor	19	61
Hollingshead four-factor	2	7
Duncan	5	16
Other	5	16

Table 2 Summary of SES findings

Study	SES index	SES effect General	SES effect Subscale	Diagnostic clusters Easy	Diagnostic clusters Slow to warm up	Diagnostic clusters Difficult	Qualifiers
Affleck et al. (1984)	Myr./Fr.	Ms – educ. & + depressed Infants less optimal temp.	+ Educ Ms Infants + Active + Approach				
Bates et al. (1982)	Oth.	NR Temp./SES					
Bates and Bayles (1984)	Oth.		L – Adpt.				Author: no substantive relationship
Hsu et al. (1981)	Oth.		L – Rhy. – Persis. + Dist.				Taiwanese subjects
Korn and Gannon (1983)	Imp.					Interac. Eth./SES/Symp.	Confound of SES/Eth.
Luster (1986)	Sieg.	NR Temp./SES					
MacPhee (1983)	Dun.	L + Phlegmatic	L – Persis.			L + BL +	
Maziade et al. (1984a)	H-2		U ++ Rhy.	U + 4 mths		L + 4 mths	Dx diff. disappear at 8 mths
Maziade et al. (1984b)	H-2		U Fem. + Rhy.				
Maziade et al. (1986b)	H-2		U Fem. + Rhy.				
Maziade et al. (1986a)	H-2					L + ?	
Maziade et al. (1987)	H-2					Interaction SES and IQ	

Study	Measure	Findings		Author's note
Persson-Blennow and McNeil (1981)	Oth.	U – Thresh.		random effect
Sameroff et al. (1983)	H-2	At 48 mths children of neurotic Ms – 1 subscale		
Sameroff et al. (1982a)	H-2	LB & LW +Int. – Thresh. LB – Rhy. – Adpt. – Mood – Approach	L BL males +	HW, LW, LB Old ITQ, Race
Sameroff et al. (1982b)	H-2	LB & LW +Int. – Thresh. LB – Rhy. – Adpt. – Mood – Approach	L BL males +	Same study as above, same confounds
Simonds and Simonds (1981)	H-2	U + U +		
Vaughn et al. (1987)	Non-form.		L + BL +	Old ITQ, 1 of 4 studies
Ventura and Stevenson (1986)	H-4	L + optimal		

U = upper SES; L = lower SES; L = less, lower; B = black; W = white; M = mothers; Fem. = female; NR = no relationship; H-2 = Hollingshead two-factor; H-4 = Hollingshead four-factor; Dun. = Duncan; Myr./Fr. = Myrianthopolous/French; Sieg. = Siegal; Oth. = other; Non-form. = non-formal measure; Imp. = impression; Adpt. = Adaptability; Rhy. = Rhythmicity; Persis. = Persistence; Dist. = Distractibility; Thresh. = Threshold; Int. = Intensity. Eth. = Ethnicity; Symp. = Symptomatology.

The second question pertaining to the role of SES in temperament variation in children was approached by examining a set of studies that employed a standard instrument to assess temperament and a specified measure of SES (Table 2). Studies reviewed in this more detailed manner had the following characteristics:

(1) a standard measure of temperament (e.g. Infant Temperament Questionnaire (ITQ), Infant Behavior Questionnaire, etc.);
(2) a formal description of SES (e.g. Hollingshead two- or four-factor index, Duncan index, etc.);
(3) utilization of (1) and (2) in the data analysis.

There were some exceptions to these criteria. For example, a study was included in this survey if SES was described in less formal ways but used in the analysis with temperament. Although not part of the inclusion criteria, parent-report scales were generally used to gather temperament information.

A review of Table 2 indicates that some SES-related differences were found for 17 of the 19 studies. These effects were mostly specific to particular subscales and/or diagnostic categories rather than reflecting general SES differences in temperamental style. In regard to subscale variability, it appears that the nature of findings may differ as a function of the samples studied. Maziade *et al.* (1984a,b, 1986b), for example, have found a relationship between increased rhythmicity and upper class status, at least for girls. On the other hand, Sameroff *et al.* (1982a,b) have reported reduced rhythmicity as a characteristic of both boys and girls from families with lower class status. In the Sameroff findings, however, the relationship is confounded by race in that, in three of four studies, the relationship obtained only for black infants. A summary of the remaining subscale findings would suggest that reduced persistence, greater distractibility and lower adaptability may also be associated with lower SES status (Hsu, Wei-tsuen, Stigler, Hong & Liang, 1981; MacPhee, 1983; Persson-Blennow & McNeil, 1981).

The evidence for a relationship between SES and temperament is not much clearer when an analysis is made of findings pertaining to the diagnostic categories of easy, difficult, and slow to warm up. In two instances, upperclass status was found to be associated with the designation of an easy temperament style (Maziade *et al.*, 1984a; Simonds & Simonds, 1981). In six studies, a difficult temperament was found to be associated with low social class, while in the same studies, an easy temperament was associated with higher SES in only one case. In three of those six studies, however, race was confounded with social class. In two additional studies (Korn & Gannon, 1983; Maziade *et al.*, 1987) the designation of difficult involved an interaction with social class and IQ or ethnicity. These findings, as well as the specific caveats listed in the table, illustrate the fact that no definitive conclusions can be drawn about the role of SES in the expression of behavioral style among children. Given this state of affairs, it may be useful to examine some of the studies in more detail in order to clarify possible confounding issues.

In two of the earliest studies of temperament and SES, Thomas and Chess (1977) reported finding SES effects on rated childhood temperament. The NYLS comprised two principal groups: the well-known middle/upper-middle class sample, which served as the initial longitudinal sample, and a working-class Puerto Rican sample. Thus, the two groups were different in both their sociocultural background and their economic status. Thomas and Chess reported significantly more Puerto Rican infants to be rated as arrhythmic and of low intensity. In a follow-up study of males in the two groups, important differences in both symptomatology and its relationship to difficultness were reported (Korn & Gannon, 1983). These results are suggestive of an interaction between environmental circumstances and temperament in contributing to behavioral difficulties. However, because SES and ethnicity were confounded in the Puerto Rican sample, conclusions regarding SES effects are to be approached with caution (Korn & Gannon, 1983).

The second study cited by Thomas and Chess (1977) referred to an unpublished manuscript by Sameroff and Kelly (undated). Because these data served as the basis for the widely cited Sameroff et al. (1982a, 1983) articles, the results will be summarized together. The sample consisted of two groups. One group was made up of 136 mothers of 4-month-old infants. These mothers were either participants or non-participants in a childbirth education class, and were described as 'white and middle class'. The second group consisted of the mothers of 227 infants who were participants in the Rochester Longitudinal Study. The mothers were classified as having symptoms of mental illness (approximately two-thirds of the sample) or having no symptoms of mental illness. The sample was described as 'heterogeneous on both SES and race variables'. Socioeconomic status was assessed by a 'modified' (undefined) Hollingshead two-factor index.

Because there were few blacks of high SES ($n = 4$) in the study, the data were analyzed using three groups: higher and lower class white and lower class blacks. Temperament was assessed with the original ITQ (Carey, 1970) which was developed as a clinical screening measure and was standardized on a small, middle class sample. Its psychometric and conceptual limitations have been discussed by Carey and McDevitt (1978) and Campos, Barrett, Lamb, Goldsmith and Stenberg (1983). We agree with their conclusions that the original ITQ (Carey, 1970) was not satisfactory for research purposes. Temperament differences were reported as a function of SES, but the results were confounded by the interaction of SES with race.

Vaughn et al. (1981) reported similar findings with a young, black, apparently lower SES sample, also using the original unrevised ITQ. In response to criticism by Carey and others, Vaughn et al. (1987) reanalyzed their 1981 data. They found no SES differences within the population for Sameroff's sample when analyzed separately by race. No trait differences for the lower class, black sample were reported, and they apparently were not considered. The finding that black mothers reported their infants as more difficult was replicated. Because ethnicity and SES were confounded in this group, no conclusions about SES effects can be drawn.

MacPhee (1983), using the revised ITQ (Carey & McDevitt, 1978) with a large sample representative of SES and ethnicity, found that lower SES mothers reported their infants as less persistent. Lower SES mothers, and black mothers regardless of SES, rated more of their infants as difficult. MacPhee examined the mothers' response patterns and found SES effects, with middle class mothers showing a significant tendency to choose middle options (e.g. 'usually does') while lower SES mothers displayed a preference for the extreme options (e.g. 'almost always', 'almost never') and tended not to use middle options. MacPhee interpreted these results as indicating that variance in temperament ratings is attributable to the reading skills, biases and expectations of the rater. MacPhee further suggested the need for attention to instrument characteristics as well as maternal attitudes toward completion of questionnaires. A closer look at the way in which the concept of temperament is viewed by lower SES and black respondents may also be warranted.

ETHNICITY AND TEMPERAMENT

The issue of ethnic influences on the expression of temperamental characteristics is difficult to separate from those of cultural and SES effects. Psychology, with its emphasis on the individual, has only recently come to recognize the importance of the organized environment as an influence on behavior and development (Super & Harkness, 1986a,b) and to examine the set of variables that define cultural diversity. As many have argued, particularly Kessen (1979), it is not the child who is the object of study, but rather the child-in-context. All that the child learns and does takes place within the confines of the cultural and ethnic group of the primary caregivers (Gordon, 1983). The overlap between the definitions of culture and ethnicity makes it clear that it is an exercise in futility to attempt to separate the influence of one from the other, or from the whole. However, for purposes of this chapter, the interplay of temperament and ethnicity will be examined by summarizing studies that involved two or more ethnic or subcultural groups within the same larger culture.

Temperament questionnaires have been constructed or translated for use in North American, European, African and Eastern cultures. While identical results have not always been found with translated measures, the pancultural utility of the concept has been demonstrated. Second, although the majority of studies comparing two or more ethnic/cultural groups have found group differences on temperament dimensions, the question of whether these measured differences result from inborn diversity, variations in child-rearing practices, or differential cultural expectations is, as yet, unanswered (Gordon, 1983; Super & Harkness, 1986a).

Difficulties in determining the source of variation may stem from methodological problems of sample characteristics and item equivalence. For example, studies comparing two or more ethnic groups within the United States (e.g. Korn & Gannon, 1983; Sameroff et al., 1982a) have reported differences on temperament subscales and/or on the composition of the diagnostic clusters. However, in each case, race, culture, ethnicity and SES have been so confounded within the sample as to preclude any conclusions about the relative influence of any one dimension on measured temperament. Another group of within-country studies are those comparing Chinese-American infants with non-Chinese-American infants. Despite the original suggestion that Oriental infants are characterized by lower levels of activity and responsiveness, more recent studies have reached such a variety of conclusions that, if true ethnic differences exist between the two groups, it is as yet not clear where those differences lie (e.g. Caudill & Weinstein, 1969; Freedman & Freedman, 1969; Miyake, Campos & Svejda, 1985; Rosenblith & Anderson-Huntington, 1975; Shand, Lin & Kosawa, 1984; Super & Harkness, 1986a,b).

Another source of methodological difficulty is that of the use of translated measures. It is difficult to be sure that items have the same meaning across cultures, despite care in translation and back translation. If there are questions about the comparability of meaning across subcultures speaking the same language (MacPhee, 1983), there is a strong likelihood of similar problems in translated measures. For example, in a large sample of Australian infants (Sewell & Oberklaid, 1986; and see Chapter 29, by Prior, Sanson & Oberklaid), 'major differences' were found between the temperaments of infants of parents born in Australia versus those of immigrant parents from other countries. In particular, infants of Greek immigrant parents had significantly different scores on five of the nine temperament dimensions and were rated as having a predominantly negative profile (Prior et al., 1986), compared to the infants of native-born Australians. A major confounding variable that can be identified in this study was the general problem of equivalence between original and translated measures, particularly in respect to validity and issues of culturally related differences in response bias (MacPhee, 1983; Prior et al., 1986).

Another study examined environmental influences on the temperaments of infants from three distinct East African societies (DeVries & Sameroff, 1984). Significant differences were found among the groups on all temperament dimensions, except threshold. Other environmental influences, such as modernization, and infant health and family factors had less impact on infant temperament. No main effect was found for the sex of infant on temperament, but a significant interaction of sex with tribal membership was found for selected dimensions. The authors' conclusion that 'a full analysis of the developmental context is imperative whenever individual characteristics are the focus of research' (DeVries & Sameroff, 1984, p. 95) should be heeded in any future research in order to deal with issues of translation and response bias related to cultural and ethnic expectations.

SYNTHESIS

While some relationships between temperament and sociocultural factors have been demonstrated in this chapter, most findings are qualified by confounding factors thereby obscuring the nature of that relationship. Thus, while differences in temperament scores related to SES were found in 17 of 19 reported studies, in a substantial number the authors specifically commented on the lack of generalizability of their findings. For example, in two studies with relatively large samples, the authors concluded that temperament variability was either unrelated to SES or attributable to chance variation. Maziade and his colleagues maintained that temperament was 'essentially independent of values proper to one specific culture' (Maziade et al., 1984a), and that 'a very slight or absent association (exists) between SES and temperament' (Maziade et al., 1986a).

Other researchers have concluded that since only 'one significant difference was found among 27 comparisons ... we are prone to consider this difference as likely reflecting chance variation' (Persson–Blennow & McNeil, 1981). Similar conclusions were reported in two recent reviews. Plomin (1982), in a general review of temperament studies in childhood, concluded that SES is but one of many factors that have not been found to correlate with temperament. Bates (1987) examined the infant temperament literature and indicated that the preponderance of data does not show SES effects. He does, however, report unpublished data by himself and others which suggest there are different interpretations of the rating scales between higher SES and lower SES mothers.

Despite the lack of evidence for a clear relationship, it would be unthinkable to postulate an absence of a relationship between culture and temperament. As Super and Harkness (1986a) have suggested, 'the interface of individual and environment is already central to the temperament literature' (Super & Harkness, 1986a, p. 132). In a broad overview of the influences of culture on temperament, these authors point out that the organization and conceptualization of the environment will influence the manifestations and interpretations of temperament. More narrowly, it may be assumed that subcultural differences will have similar influences. Thus, the variety of factors which contribute to the composite comprising SES and ethnicity may likewise affect how the qualities of an individual's temperament are expressed and how the cultural or subcultural group interprets this expression.

It is important to acknowledge that measurement techniques used to assess temperament may be variously affected by SES correlates and may be regarded in different ways by individuals from separate SES groups. These differences may be attributable to a number of factors:

(1) presuppositions made about the meaning of particular items on the scale;
(2) response biases specific to the measurement technique itself;
(3) cultural differences in the interpretation of behavioral anchor points;
(4) literacy levels associated with SES status.

It might be worthwhile for the community of temperament researchers to be reminded of the similarity of issues faced by IQ researchers during their long history (cf. Haller, 1984; Kamin, 1974; McCall, 1986). As in the case of research on intelligence, much of the interpretation of temperament 'data' has proceeded as if confounding factors had long ago been controlled and understood. Some researchers may have been too quick to reach conclusions using incomplete data sets, inappropriately standardized instruments, or samples confounded by small numbers, thus fueling the controversy.

IMPLICATIONS

The complexity of environmental factors impinging on child-rearing practices and expectations are, of necessity, going to influence both the concept of temperament and its measurement, within and across ethnic and/or cultural groups. Considerably more research is needed in order to disentangle the various factors to determine what, if any, effects are attributable to SES or ethnicity *per se*.

To this end, what specific implications can be identified for research? There are at least three conditions that should be met in any future studies seeking to clarify the sociocultural–temperament relationship. The first of these is to employ comprehensive and appropriate indices of SES status. It is noteworthy that of the 19 studies reviewed in Table 2, only three utilized indices recommended by critics of the SES literature in child development. As indicated earlier in this chapter, Gottfried (1985) has endorsed the Hollingshead four-factor index as one measure that is appropriate for research addressing SES issues. The use of this, and other more relevant and precise SES indices, may help to clarify the role of sociocultural variation in temperament differences in children. A second conclusion is that sociocultural variables, notably race and ethnicity, need to be controlled in order that valid generalizations about SES can be drawn. A third and final issue is that the assessment instruments themselves need to be selected and used in such a manner as to diminish potential confounding. Specifically, the readability level needs to be appropriate for respondents, and the content and format must be free of potential cultural or ethnic biases.

Given the history as well as the growing interest in the clinical applications of temperament assessment, what are the implications of the above findings for practice? Temperament has been implicated in the development of behavioral problems by a number of researchers and clinicians (Carey, 1974; Dunn, Kendrick & McNamee, 1981; Webster-Stratton & Eyberg, 1982; and see Section Four of this volume). These findings have lead to efforts to circumvent later problems by providing temperament counseling for parents to help them cope with the child's present behavior or to avoid future problem behavior (e.g. Cameron & Rice, 1986). Findings of the NYLS data have indicated that it is the child deemed to be 'difficult' who is at greatest risk for the development of behavior problems. Unfortunately, some clinicians and behavioral psychologists have jumped to the conclusion that all children rated as difficult are at risk for later behavioral difficulty. This unwarranted assumption, in combination with the research findings that lower SES children and black children have more often been rated as difficult than higher SES or white children could well lead to automatic stereotyping of those children as potential behavior problems.

A related issue is that using norms and expectations from one culture to describe the behavioral style of children in other, quite diverse cultures is liable to lead to the conclusion that children in other cultures are aberrant. It is likely that cultural expectations influence the socialization of behaviors. For that reason it is essential to look within the culture for normal levels of expression. As Carey (1985) and others (e.g. Thomas, Chess & Korn, 1982) have pointed out, it is the particular characteristics of the child in her/his particular environment that may or may not predispose the child to stressful interactions and behavior problems.

In summary, to reach valid conclusions about the functional utility of temperament for children requires a deeper awareness and appreciation of the impact of the environment than is apparent in much current research. Specifically, the implications of temperament variation for clinical practice focus on the understanding of preventive and habilitative interventions for the child in context. Thus, whether the sources of temperament variation are biological or environmental in nature, or are a complex transaction of the two, it is the nature of the goodness of fit between the child characteristics and the demands of the environment that accounts for developmental outcome. To that end, consideration of the effects of sociocultural factors on temperament variation constitutes important clinical and research practice.

ACKNOWLEDGMENTS

Support for the preparation of this chapter was provided, in part, by the Temple University Center for Research in Human Development and Education. We would like to thank Anders Alfelt, Margaret O'Grady, Lenore Porembo and Lorraine Rittico for their assistance.

REFERENCES

Affleck, G., Allen, D.A., McGrade, B.J. & McQueeney, M. (1984). Factors associated with parents' and professionals' perceptions of infants in an early intervention program. *Applied Research in Mental Retardation, 5*, 305–316.

Bates, J.E. (1987). Temperament in infancy. In J.D. Osofsky (Ed.), *Handbook of infant development*, 2nd edn (pp. 1101–1149). New York: Wiley.

Bates, J.E. & Bayles, K. (1984). Objective and subjective components in mothers' perceptions of their children from age 6 months to 3 years. *Merrill-Palmer Quarterly, 30*, 111–130.

Bates, J.E., Olson, S.L., Pettit, G.S. & Bayles, K. (1982). Dimensions of individuality in the mother–infant relationship at 6 months of age. *Child Development, 53*, 446–461.

Brody, G.H., Stoneman, Z. & Burke, M. (1987). Temperaments, maternal differential behavior, and sibling relationships. *Developmental Psychology, 23*, 354–362.

Cameron, J.R. & Rice, D.C. (1986). Developing anticipatory guidance programs based on early assessment of infant temperament: Two tests of a prevention model. *Journal of Pediatric Psychology, 11*, 221–234.

Campos, J.J., Barrett, K., Lamb, M.E., Goldsmith, H.H. & Stenberg, C. (1983). Socioemotional development. In M.M. Haith & J.J. Campos Vol. Eds for P.H. Mussen (Ed.), *Infancy and developmental psychobiology*, Vol. 2, *Handbook of child psychology*, 4th edn (pp. 783–915). New York: Wiley.

Carey, W.B. (1970). A simplified method for measuring infant temperament. *Journal of Pediatrics, 77*, 188–194.

Carey, W.B. (1974). Night waking and temperament in infancy. *Journal of Pediatrics, 84*, 756–758.

Carey, W.B. (1985). Temperament and increased weight gain in infants. *Journal of Developmental and Behavioral Pediatrics, 6*, 128–131.

Carey, W.B. & McDevitt, S.C. (1978). Revision of the Infant Temperament Questionnaire. *Pediatrics, 61*, 735–739.

Caudill, W. & Weinstein, H. (1969). Maternal care and infant behavior in Japan and America. *Psychiatry, 32*, 12–43.

DeVries, M.W. & Sameroff, A.J. (1984). Culture and temperament: Influences on infant temperament in three East African societies. *American Journal of Orthopsychiatry, 54*, 83–96.

Dunn, J., Kendrick, C. & McNamee, R. (1981). The reaction of first born children to the birth of a sibling: Mothers' report. *Journal of Child Psychology and Psychiatry, 22*, 1–18.

Freedman, D.E. & Freedman, N.C. (1969). Behavioral differences between Chinese-American and European-American newborns. *Nature, 224*, 1227.

Gordon, E.W. (1983). Culture and ethnicity. In M.D. Levine, W.B. Carey, A.C. Crocker & R.T. Gross (Eds), *Developmental–behavioral pediatrics*. Philadelphia: W.B. Saunders.

Gottfried, A.W. (1985). Measures of socioeconomic status in child development research: Data and recommendations. *Merrill-Palmer Quarterly, 31*, 85–92.

Haller, M.H. (1984). *Eugenics: Hereditarian attitudes in American thought*. New Brunswick,

NJ: Rutgers University Press.

Hsu, C., Wei-tsuen, S., Stigler, J.W., Hong, C. & Liang, C. (1981). The temperamental characteristics of Chinese babies. *Child Development,* **52**, 1337–1340.

Kamin, L.J. (1974). *The science and politics of IQ.* Hillsdale, NJ: Erlbaum.

Kessen, W. (1979). The American child and other cultural inventions. *American Psychologist,* **34**, 815–820.

Korn, S.J. & Gannon, S. (1983). Temperament, cultural variation and behavior disorder in preschool children. *Child Psychiatry and Human Development,* **13**, 203–212.

Luster, T. (1986). Influences on maternal behavior: Childbearing support and infant temperament. Paper presented at the International Conference on Infant Studies, Los Angeles, CA.

MacPhee, D. (1983). What do ratings of infant temperament really measure? Paper presented at the biennial meeting of the Society for Research in Child Development, Detroit, MI, April 1983.

Maziade, M., Boudreault, M., Thiverge, J., Capéraà, P. & Côté, R. (1984a). Infant temperament: SES and gender differences and reliability of measurement in a large Quebec sample. *Merrill-Palmer Quarterly,* **30**, 213–226.

Maziade, M., Boutin, P., Côté, R. & Thivierge, J. (1986a). Empirical characteristics of the NYLS temperament in middle childhood: Congruities and incongruities with other studies. *Child Psychiatry and Human Development,* **17**, 38–52.

Maziade, M., Côté, R., Boudreault, M., Thivierge, J. & Boutin, P. (1986b). Family correlates of temperament continuity and change across middle childhood. *American Journal of Orthopsychiatry,* **56**, 195–203.

Maziade, M., Côté, R., Boudreault, M., Thivierge, J. & Capéraà, P. (1984b). The New York Longitudinal Studies model of temperament: Gender differences and demographic correlates in a French-speaking population. *Journal of the American Academy of Child Psychiatry,* **23**, 582–587.

Maziade, M., Côté, R., Boutin, M., Bernier, H. & Thivierge, J. (1987). Temperament and intellectual development: A longitudinal study from infancy to four years. *American Journal of Psychiatry,* **144**, 144–150.

McCall, R.B. (1986). Issues of stability and continuity in temperament research. In R. Plomin & J. Dunn (Eds), *The study of temperament: Changes, continuities and challenges* (pp. 13–26). Hillsdale, NJ: Erlbaum.

Miyake, K., Campos, J. & Svejda, M. (1985). Maternal emotional expression as a determinant of social reactivity in Japanese and American infants. Paper presented at the biennial meetings of the Society for Research in Child Development, Toronto, April 1985.

Mueller, C.W. & Parcel, T.L. (1981). Measures of socioeconomic status: Alternatives and recommendations. *Child Development,* **52**, 13–30.

Oberklaid, F., Sanson, A.V. & Prior, M. (1986). The development of Australian normative data for infant temperament. *Australian Pediatric Journal,* **22**, 185–187.

Persson-Blennow, I. & McNeil, T.F. (1981). Temperament characteristics of children in reaction to gender, birth order, and social class. *American Journal of Orthopsychiatry,* **51**, 710–714.

Plomin, R. (1982). Childhood temperament. In B. Lahey & A. Kazdin (Eds), *Advances in clinical child psychology,* Vol. 6. New York: Plenum.

Plomin, R. & Dunn, J. (Eds) (1986). *The study of temperament: Changes, continuities and challenges.* Hillsdale, NJ: Erlbaum.

Prior, M., Kyrios, M. & Oberklaid, F. (1986). Temperament in Australian, American, Chinese, and Greek infants. *Journal of Cross-Cultural Psychology,* **17**, 455–474.

Rosenblith, J.F. & Anderson-Huntington, R.B. (1975). Defensive reactions to stimulation of the nasal and oral regions in newborns: Relations to state. In J.F. Bosma & J. Showacre (Eds), *Development of upper respiratory anatomy and function: Implications for sudden infant death syndrome.* Department of Health, Education and Welfare Publication, 75–941. Bethesda, MA: NIH.

Rothbart, M.K. & Derryberry, D. (1981). Development of individual differences in temperament. In M.E. Lamb & A.L. Brown (Eds), *Advances in developmental psychology*, Vol. 1. Hillsdale, NJ: Erlbaum.

Sameroff, A.J., Seifer, R. & Barocas, R. (1983). Impact of parental psychopathology: Diagnosis, severity, or social status effects? *Infant Mental Health Journal,* **4**, 236–249.

Sameroff, A.J., Seifer, R. & Elias, P.K. (1982a). Sociocultural variability in infant temperament ratings. *Child Development,* **53**, 164–173.

Sameroff, A., Seifer, R. & Zax, M. (1982b). Early development of children at risk for emotional disorder. *Monographs of the Society for Research in Child Development,* **47** (7), 1–66.

Sameroff, A.J. & Kelly, P. Socioeconomic status, racial and mental health factors in infant temperament. Unpublished manuscript.

Sewell, J. & Oberklaid, F. (1986). Annotation: Temperament in infants and young children. *Australian Pediatric Journal,* **22**, 91–94.

Shand, N., Lin, P. & Kowasa, Y. (1984). Asian and Caucasian differences in spontaneous motor activity from birth through three months. Unpublished manuscript.

Simonds, M.P. & Simonds, J.F. (1981). Relationship of maternal parenting behaviors to preschool children's temperament. *Child Psychiatry and Human Development,* **12**, 19–31.

Super, C.M. & Harkness, S. (1986a). The developmental niche: A conceptualization at the interface of child and culture. *International Journal of Behavioral Development,* **9**, 545–569.

Super, C.M. & Harkness, S. (1986b). Temperament, development and culture. In R. Plomin & J. Dunn (Eds), *The study of temperament: Changes, continuities and challenges* (pp. 131–149). Hillsdale, NJ: Erlbaum.

Thomas, A. & Chess, S. (1977). *Temperament and development.* New York: Brunner/Mazel.

Thomas, A., Chess, S. & Korn, S.J. (1982). The reality of difficult temperament. *Merrill-Palmer Quarterly,* **28**, 1–20.

Vaughn, B.E., Taraldson, B.J., Crichton, L. & Egeland, B. (1981). The assessment of infant temperament: A critique of the Carey Infant Temperament Questionnaire. *Infant Behavior and Development,* **4**, 1–17.

Vaughn, B.E., Bradley, C.F., Joffee, L.S., Seifer, R. & Barglow, T. (1987). Maternal characteristics measured prenatally are predictive of ratings of temperamental 'difficulty' on the Carey Infant Temperament Questionnaire. *Developmental Psychology,* **23**, 152–161.

Ventura, J.N. & Stevenson, M.B. (1986). Relations of mothers' and fathers' reports of infant temperament, parents' psychological functioning and family characteristics. *Merrill-Palmer Quarterly,* **32**, 275–289.

Webster-Stratton, C. & Eyberg, S. (1982). Child temperament: Relationship with child behavior problems and parent–child interaction. *Journal of Clinical Child Psychology,* **11**, 123–129.

29

The Australian Temperament Project

MARGOT R. PRIOR, ANN V. SANSON AND FRANK OBERKLAID
La Trobe University, University of Melbourne and Royal Children's Hospital, Melbourne

The Australian Temperament Project (ATP) is a large-scale prospective longitudinal study of temperament and development in Australian children from infancy to school age. It began with some preliminary work on sampling and measurement problems in 1980 and then in 1983 enrolled a cohort of 2443 infants aged 4–8 months who were closely representative of the infant population of the State of Victoria. The theoretical and methodological background to the project in its initial stages was influenced by the pioneering work of Thomas and Chess (1977) and by the questionnaire methods and clinical emphases of Carey and his colleagues (Carey, 1981; Carey & McDevitt, 1978a,b).

The aims of the project encompassed the issues of delineation, measurement and stability of temperament in an Australian child population; the relationships between indices of temperament and concurrent and later behavioural adjustment; the significance of social class, ethnic and family influences in such relationships; sex differences in both temperament and behavioural adjustment; and the identification of 'at risk' groups of various kinds in early childhood whose development could be followed through to the early years of school. In addition to the large-scale projects whose major findings will be reported here, a number of smaller scale, in-depth investigations of family and child development and behaviour are in progress. The strengths of the project include the exceptional size and representativeness of the sample, the methodological advances in delineating continuity and stability across the age ranges, and the opportunity to explore a variety of social and familial influences in a normative framework as well as the investigation of significant clinical questions. The results of our work suggest strongly that child development in general and temperament in particular are very much context-dependent. Notwithstanding this assertion, many of our findings are broadly convergent with those of North American and European groups.

Temperament in Childhood   Edited by G.A. Kohnstamm, J.E. Bates and M.K. Rothbart
© 1989 John Wiley & Sons Ltd

We were conscious from the outset of the project of the measurement difficulties encountered by anyone who chooses to investigate temperament. Because of the very large sample to be investigated we had to depend on questionnaire/survey methods in the first phases of the study. For our purposes the temperament questionnaires developed by Carey and his colleagues, and based on the nine-dimensional model of temperament proposed by Thomas and Chess appeared initially to be the most useful measures. A major outcome of our research has been the development of these measures into forms which would permit us more easily to investigate both continuity and stability of temperament in a reasonably parsimonious way. However let us first describe the sample of Australian children making up the ATP.

In the State of Victoria, Maternal and Child Health (MCH) nurses, operating from a network of MCH centres across the State, provide support and counselling

Table 1   Background characteristics of the sample

Child characteristics
Age	X = 25 weeks (SD = 5.3 weeks)
Sex	52% male; 48% female
Birth order	47% first-born
	29% second-born
	15% third-born
	9% fourth-born or later
Birth weight	X = 3.4 kg (SD = 0.6 kg)
Gestational age	X = 39 weeks (SD = 2 weeks)
Current weight	X = 7.5 kg (SD = 1.1 kg)
Type of feeding	43% breast
	29% bottle
	23% breast first, now bottle
	5% both

Parental characteristics		Mother	Father
Age:	X	27.9 years	30.5 years
	SD	4.3	5.2
Occupation	Rating 1–2	27%	40%
	Rating 3–4	52%	41%
	Rating 5–6	22%	18%
Education:	Rating 1–3	24%	39%
	Rating 4–5	42%	44%
	Rating 6–8	34%	26%
Country of birth:	Australia	80%	73%
	UK	6%	7%
	Other	14%	20%

Rating of mothers' understanding of questionnaire

68%   No difficulties
24%   Minimal difficulties
 6%   Some difficulties or limited understanding
 2%   Other

to mothers, achieving contact with 94% of all live births. Each local government area (LGA) has one or more such centres. Infants were recruited via MCH centres across the State. The sampling framework was developed for us by the Australian Bureau of Statistics who selected 67 LGAs, 47 rural (839 infants) and 20 urban (1604 infants), to provide a representative sample of infants.

The mother of every 4- to 8-month-old child who attended an MCH centre in a selected LGA in a 2-week period in the autumn of 1983 was given a questionnaire by the MCH nurse, who at the same time also completed a questionnaire on the health and development of the infant. Approximately 3000 questionnaires were distributed with a pool of 2443 usable questionnaires finally being available. Background characteristics of the sample are presented in Table 1.

The Australian revision of Carey and McDevitt's (1978a) 95-item Revised Infant Temperament Questionnaire (R-ITQ) (Oberklaid, Prior, Golvan, Clements & Williamson 1984) was completed by parents (usually the mother), along with an information sheet which requested information on the child's age, sex and birth order; parental ages, country of birth, occupation and educational status; ratings of the child in three areas of behaviour relevant to the age group – colic, sleep problems and excessive crying; and a global rating of how easy or difficult the child was, in comparison to the 'average' child. Maternal and Child Health nurses completed a brief questionnaire which included data on the child's perinatal and developmental history, a rating of the adjustment of the mother–baby pair, a global rating of the child's perceived temperament; and an assessment of the mother's ability to understand and complete the questionnaire. (This last item was necessary as some mothers did not have English as their first language.) Extensive analyses of this large data set were then undertaken (Sanson, Prior, Garino, Oberklaid & Sewell, 1987; Sanson, Prior & Oberklaid, 1985).

In 1984 approximately two-thirds of the original sample were surveyed again, this time using a validated Australian version of the Toddler Temperament Scale (TTS) (Fullard, McDevitt & Carey, 1984). One-third were not followed up to allow us to assess the effects of repeated measurement on responses to temperament questionnaires; they were included in the 1985 follow-up. Families were contacted by mail and asked to complete the TTS. In addition they were asked to provide ratings (severe, moderate, mild or none) of their child's behaviour in eight areas: sleep problems, excessive crying, temper tantrums, excessive shyness, overactivity, mood swings, dependency and accident-proneness. The ages of the children at this survey point ranged between 18 and 24 months, mean 21 months, and the final number of usable questionnaires was 1279.

An identical procedure was followed in 1985 when two-thirds of the children were again followed up, now aged between 30 and 46 months, mean 35.4 months, (n usable = 1360). At this stage parents also completed the Richman and Graham (1971) Behaviour Checklist, as a screening device for current behavioural difficulties.

In 1986 the third follow-up took place via mail-out of questionnaires as in the two toddler surveys. The children were now aged between 44 and 52 months, mean 47.5 months. The instruments used in this follow-up were: (a) Thomas and Chess's Child Temperament Questionnaire (CTQ), with minor revisions for Australian usage; (b) the Preschool Behaviour Questionnaire (Behar & Stringfield, 1974), a well-validated measure of behaviour problems for this age group, which was completed by mothers; (c) the same questionnaire completed by preschool teachers or day-care centre workers for the 300 children attending these facilities. Usable responses were available for 1641 subjects.

Thus, over four consecutive samplings we had temperament and behavioural problem data from the first through to the fourth year of life. The guiding aims for the first part of the project were to establish the soundness of temperament measurement, to assess the continuity of structure across the age range in order to examine stability of temperament (Sanson, Prior & Oberklaid, submitted) and to develop an

Table 2 Factors found at each age level in the Australian Temperament Project (factor numbers in brackets)

Sample Age n	Infant 4–8 months 2443	Toddler 1 18–22 months 1279	Toddler 2 32–36 months 1360	Preschool 44–52 months 1641
	*†Approach (1)	*†Approach (1)	*†Approach (1)	*†Sociability (1)
	*†Irritability (8)	*†Irritability (7)	*†Irritability (2)	
				*†Inflexibility (3)
	*†Cooperation– Manageability (5)	*†Cooperation– Manageability (2)	*†Cooperation– Manageability (3)	
	*Activity– Reactivity (2)	*†Activity– Intensity (4)	*†Activity (7)	*Activity– Mood (5)
	*Rhythmicity (4)	*Rhythmicity (5)	*Rhythmicity (6)	*Rhythmicity (4)
	Persistence (9)	*Persistence (3)	*Persistence (5)	*†Persistence (2)
	Threshold (7)	Threshold (8)	Threshold (8)	Threshold (6)
	–	*Distractibility (6)	*Distractibility (4)	–
	Food Fussiness (3)	–	–	Food Fussiness (7)
	Placidity (6)	–	–	–

*Factors included in short temperament questionnaires.
†Factors included in Easy–Difficult Scales.

Easy–Difficult temperament scale which would be useful clinically and allow us to assess relationships between temperament and other factors in a psychometrically sound way.

Data Structure and Data Reduction in Infancy

A number of problems with respect to the use of the R-ITQ were apparent from the results of the infant study. First, the nine dimensions were found to be considerably intercorrelated, with Approach, Mood and Adaptability being especially strongly related (r values between .52 and .67). Secondly, internal consistency as measured via alpha coefficients was moderate (median .62), with two dimensions, Intensity and Threshold, being barely adequate (.42 and .43). Thirdly, the dimensions varied considerably in their relationships to current behavioural indices; thus although Approach, Adaptability and Mood were consistently related to severity of colic, excessive crying and sleep problems, Persistence, Intensity and Threshold showed minimal relationships.

Our factor analyses of the item-intercorrelations elicited a nine-factor solution accounting for 32% of the variance – a similar percentage to that reported by other workers (e.g. Persson-Blennow & McNeil, 1979; Rowe & Plomin, 1977), which according to the Scree test (Gorsuch, 1974) was the best solution (see Sanson *et al.*, 1987). Table 2 shows the nine infancy factors (left-hand column).

This factor analysis indicated that the original nine dimensions were not empirically the best descriptions of questionnaire content since only Rhythmicity and Persistence re-emerged as reasonably pure factors. Approach and Adaptability combined to form Factor 1 (Approach), whilst Activity and Intensity were combined into either the Activity/Reactivity or the Placidity factor. The Distractibility factor which has attracted considerable critical questioning in many other studies (Earls, 1981) appeared to contain two aspects, perceptual distractibility which loaded on the Activity/Reactivity factor, and a soothability aspect which loaded on the Cooperation/Manageability factor.

Our factors appear similar to those reported by Bohlin, Hagekull and Lindhagen (1981) and to be related to conceptualizations of other researchers (Bates, Freeland & Lounsbury, 1979; Rothbart, 1981). Concurrent functional relationships of the nine factors with the ratings of developmental problems listed above were all significant (r values from .16 to .30; p < 001).

The amount of redundancy demonstrated for the R-ITQ, the discontinuity of some factors with toddler dimensions (see next section) and the variability in functional significance, along with the need for greater parsimony in questionnaire-based research and practice of this type, suggested the desirability of deriving a short form of the scale. Using 30 items from the five main factors of Approach, Cooperation/Manageability, Rhythmicity, Activity/Reactivity and Irritability, we tested a short form temperament questionnaire. Factor analyses of this short form, the 'Short Temperament Scale for Infants' (STSI), confirmed its five-factor structure. For scoring, factor scale scores rather than factor scores were to be used because of their consonance with the scoring techniques used for the original dimensions and their ease of usage for clinical purposes. The alpha coefficients of these scales compared favourably with those of the original nine dimensions, and test–retest correlations were satisfactory. Thus the STSI has the advantages of parsimony, a clear empirical basis and good psychometric properties (Sanson *et al.*, 1987).

We developed a continuous Easy–Difficult Scale (EDS) by combining the STSI Approach, Cooperation/Manageability and Irritability scales, i.e. those with the strongest relationships to behaviour-problem ratings. This scale circumvents the problems of classification into discrete categories resulting in information loss, as exemplified by the Thomas–Chess and Carey system of using an algorithm to classify children as Difficult, Easy, Slow to Warm Up or Intermediate, but clearly is closely related to it. Using one-half of a standard deviation above the mean on this scale as a cut-off, 85.5% of children classified as Difficult via the Carey and McDevitt algorithm are at or above this point. Similarly 95.5% of children classified as Easy by the algorithm were below the cut-off. This infant EDS also has clear parallels in the work of others (Bates *et al.*, 1979; Persson-Blennow & McNeil, 1982; Thomas, Chess & Birch, 1968) and should lend itself to longitudinal studies of the stability of temperament profiles over time.

Data Structure and Data Reduction After Infancy

A similar procedure was followed with data from the three subsequent years of data collection, i.e. factor analysis, development of short forms and development of a continuous EDS for each age level. The results are summarized in Table 2 for each age level, and are very briefly outlined below.

Factor analyses of the toddler data from the first follow-up produced an optimal solution (via the Scree test) containing eight factors accounting for 33.5% of the variance. Separate factor analyses for males and females indicated similar factor structures (Sanson *et al.*, submitted). Six of the factors are parallel to those obtained in the infant factor analyses. The functional significance of the factors varied, with Intensity/Activity and Irritability showing strong relationships to behaviour problems but Distractibility and Threshold showing minimal relationships with any behaviour ratings.

Factor analyses of the second toddler follow-up data produced a very similar pattern of factors (Table 2) indicating good continuity of temperament from 18 months to 3½ years. Functional relationships were again assessed by correlating temperament dimensions with behaviour problem scores. Correlations were strong especially for Irritability and Cooperation/Manageability.

On the basis of these functional relationships in the two toddler follow-ups as well as the parallels to the infant factors, the six factors of Approach, Cooperation/Manageability, Irritability, Rhythmicity, Persistence and Intensity/Activity were chosen for inclusion in a short toddler scale (Short Temperament Scale for Toddlers; STST). Distractibility was also included despite its lack of the aforementioned relationships since it appeared to be a factor of increasing relevance at this stage of the child's development. From the items loading on these seven factors, 30 items were selected for inclusion in the STST (Sanson *et al.*, submitted). Because of shared loadings of the two intensity questions on the

Irritability and Intensity/Activity factors, it was decided to form one composite factor scale from these two factors. Alpha coefficients for the resulting six scales were acceptable, ranging between .85 (Approach) and .56 (Distractibility). The factor scales of Approach, Cooperation/Manageability and Irritability were those most strongly related to behaviour problems. Consequently these three factor scales provided us with an index of easiness to difficultness of temperament and formed our EDS for toddlers, analogous to the EDS for infants.

For the CTQ data collected in 1986, the Scree test indicated that seven factors accounting for 34.2% of the variance (Table 2) were optimal. Of these, only Persistence and Rhythmicity relatively clearly paralleled the original New York Longitudinal Study dimensions. Once again, there was a clear factor reflecting the cooperativeness of the child, here labelled Inflexibility, and paralleling the Cooperation/Manageability factors in all three preceding analyses. However, this factor also included some aspects of negative mood or irritability, which did not appear as a separate factor in this analysis. There was also a factor assessing response to new people and places, here labelled Sociability rather than Approach. Persistence, which was a weak but emergent factor in the TTS, was a more significant factor in this age group. Factors 5, 6 and 7 were conceptually less clear-cut; Factor 5 included items assessing activity level and some aspects of mood, while Factor 6 primarily assessed responsiveness to environmental stimulation, including items from the distractibility, intensity and threshold dimensions. Factor 7 consisted of only three items, all referring to reactions to food and had minimal relationships to behaviour problems. Alpha coefficients ranged from .69 to .84.

Correlations between factors and behaviour problems indicated that the first four factors had highly significant relationships with concurrent problems. This again parallels previous years' data, except that for the first time Persistence is an important predictor. This factor is similar in content to Keogh's (1982) Task Orientation factor, which she has shown is important in school adjustment; it thus appears to be of increasing functional significance as a child grows towards school age.

Using the same selection criteria for items as in earlier years, a short form of the CTQ (Short Temperament Scale for Children; STSC) was developed, consisting of 30 items. Factor analysis confirmed its four-factor structure, consisting of Inflexibility, Persistence, Sociability and Rhythmicity. The combination of Sociability, Inflexibility and Persistence factors resulted in the strongest relationship with our behaviour-problem measures, and paralleled the previous years' EDS scales in structure, except for the inclusion of Persistence. These results are of course a function of the limited item pool emanating from the original Thomas and Chess temperament conceptualization and we would not wish to claim any universality of coverage.

In summary, these 4 years of data have indicated the continuity of several important aspects of temperament, namely the Sociability, Rhythmicity and Cooperation-Manageability/Inflexibility factors. These appear to be salient aspects of temperament at all of the four age levels, although there is some variability in their relative significance at different age levels. Irritability has clear continuity over the first 3 years, but is not a distinct aspect of temperament at 4 years of age.

Persistence, on the other hand, is not a significant aspect of infant temperament, but grows in importance with age; while Distractibility appears salient only in the toddler years. On some factors, then, there is evidence for some homotypic continuity (cf. Kagan, 1971). However, our data have also shown that it is invalid to assume homotypic continuity of all factors or dimensions. Studies which have based estimates of individual stability of temperament upon an assumption that same-named dimensions in different questionnaires are functionally similar, without empirical validation of this, are therefore likely to have derived biased and inaccurate results. (The issue of heterotypic continuity is important and as yet unaddressed in temperament research.)

Stability of Temperament from Infancy to Preschool Age

For the concept of temperament to be meaningful, there must be some stability over time in individuals' temperament profiles. As indicated above, it seems that much of the early investigation of this topic failed to separate the issue of structural continuity clearly from the assessment of individual stability. Through the development of our short questionnaires and EDS measures with demonstrated

Table 3   Correlations between Easy–Difficult Scale, Approach, Rhythmicity, Cooperation/Manageability and Irritability scales at four ages

| | Easy–Difficult Scale | | | Approach/Sociability | | |
	Infancy	Toddler 1	Toddler 2	Infancy	Toddler 1	Toddler 2
Toddler 1–2	.43	–	–	.30	–	–
Toddler 2–3	.39	.69	–	.23	.62	–
Preschool 4–5	.28	.48	.63	.18	.43	.64

| | Rhythmicity | | | Cooperation/Manageability | | |
	Infancy	Toddler 1	Toddler 2	Infancy	Toddler 1	Toddler 2
Toddler 1–2	.39	–	–	.27	–	–
Toddler 2–3	.36	.55	–	.25	.57	–
Preschool 4–5	.32	.42	.64	.17	.36	.45

| | Irritability | | | Persistence | | |
	Infancy	Toddler 1	Toddler 2	Infancy	Toddler 1	Toddler 2
Toddler 1–2	.32	–	–	.56	–	
Toddler 2–3	.28	.65	–	.35	.40	
Preschool 4–5	.20	.43	.52			

| | Distractibility | |
	Toddler 1	
Toddler 2–3	.43	

Irritability in 1983, 1984 and 1985 is correlated with Inflexibility in 1986, since the latter incorporates this factor; Persistence does not appear on the Short Temperament Scale for Infants, i.e. for 1983 data. Distractibility occurs only on the Short Temperament Scale for Toddlers, i.e. for 1984 and 1985 data; $P < .01$ for all correlations.

continuity, we were able to avoid some of these difficulties. We are currently addressing the issue of stability through structural equation modelling. However, we have also conducted preliminary analyses using more traditional methods, and these we will report here.

The most common method used for assessing stability has been correlations between factors at different points in time. This does give some indication of general trends, although it does not give information on the direction of change, nor whether a little change in the majority, or large change in a minority, is the norm. Typically, correlation coefficients have been in the range of .3 to .4 and decreasing as the interval between measurements increases (e.g. Thomas & Chess, 1977). The correlation coefficients over our four age levels for the EDS and the six factors showing some continuity are given in Table 3. It can be seen that the correlations tend to be higher than is usual, especially at the older age levels; this is presumably accounted for by the decontamination of our measures from structural discontinuity. While these correlations, which are between the parallel factors, are generally between .3 and .6 ($X = .38$), the correlations between non-parallel factors (e.g. between Approach in 1983 and Rhythmicity in 1984) are much lower, generally between .00 and .2 ($X = .10$). This is a further indication of both the continuity and conceptual distinctness of these factors.

Another approach to the investigation of stability provided more information on the *patterns* of change evidenced by children over time. Our strategy was to divide children into quartiles, on the basis of their EDS scores, at each of the four data points, and then to trace children's membership of these quartiles over time. Chi-square analyses showed that there was significant stability for each comparison but clearly the extent of this varied as is shown in Table 4 where some of these data are summarized.

It is clear from these data that moderate change is the norm. While in general one-half to two-thirds of children changed quartiles between any two time points, a relatively small number changed from one extreme to another, and very few made such extreme shifts over 1 year (e.g. 3.3% changed from Difficult in 1985 to Easy in 1986, and an identical percentage changed from Easy to Difficult). However, absolute stability is almost equally rare: only 7.3% of children remained in Easy quartiles over all four data points, 6.9% remained in Difficult quartiles at all times, and in both the middle quartiles only one child was similarly placed at all times. Thus for the majority of children some moderate variation in temperament profiles, relative to their age group, is to be expected.

There are two other interesting points which emerge from Table 4. First, as might be expected, the degree of stability decreases as the time interval between measures increases, but in comparison to previous findings (Thomas & Chess, 1977), this trend is surprisingly slight, especially in the two middle quartiles. Once again, this is likely to be due to our attempts to control for structural discontinuity. Secondly, there is considerably more stability at the extremes (the Easy and Difficult quartiles) than in the middle two groups where stability is only a little above chance levels. This suggests that children with more moderate temperament profiles may be more influenced by their environmental context than those with extreme temperaments.

Table 4   Position of children on Easy–Difficult Scale quartiles over 4 years: placement of children from each 1986 quartile in each of three previous years' quartiles (in percentages)

(a) 1986 Easy quartile

Quartile	1985	1984	1983
Easy	58.1*	51.2	44.6
Easy–Average	33.0	27.8	27.6
Average–Difficult	14.0	20.2	21.6
Difficult	3.3	12.4	16.4

In Easy quartile at all four times: 7.3%; at three times: 26.5%; at two times: 36.5%; only in 1986: 29.7%.

(b) Easy–Average quartile

Quartile	1985	1984	1983
Easy	33.0	27.8	27.6
Easy–Average	30.8	27.0	30.5
Average–Difficult	24.3	30.5	25.2
Difficult	12.0	14.7	16.7

In Easy–Average quartile at all four times: 0.2%; at three times: 11.5%; at two times: 39.8%; only in 1986: 48.5%.

(c) 1986 Average–Difficult quartile

Quartile	1985	1984	1983
Easy	14.0	20.2	21.6
Easy–Average	28.2	19.8	26.6
Average–Difficult	37.3	31.6	26.1
Difficult	20.5	28.5	25.6

In Average–Difficult quartile at all four times: 0.2%; at three times: 9.2%; at two times: 40.9%; only in 1986: 49.7%.

(d) 1986 Difficult quartile

Quartile	1985	1984	1983
Easy	3.3	12.4	16.4
Easy–Average	13.0	14.4	29.8
Average–Difficult	31.9	27.6	23.5
Difficult	51.8	45.6	30.3

In Difficult quartile at all four times: 6.9%; at three times: 21.1%; at two times: 31.3%; only in 1986: 40.8%.

*Italic figures indicate the extent of stability across two data points.

RELATIONSHIPS WITH OTHER VARIABLES

On the basis of this extensive psychometric background we were able to consider relationships between temperament and other developmental variables with more confidence.

Sex Differences

In the infant sample data, sex differences were apparent only on the factors of Approach, with males rated as more approaching, and Irritability, with boys more irritable. These differences were quantitatively very slight. There were no sex differences in temperamental difficultness/easiness. In the first toddler follow-up of 18- to 24-month-old children, sex differences emerged for Approach, Cooperation/Manageability, Rhythmicity and Intensity, with boys on the negative ends of these scales except for Approach. For the second toddler follow-up there were significant sex differences on Approach, Cooperation/Manageability and Activity. Boys were more approaching, less cooperative and more active. In the 1986 follow-up of 3- to 4-year-olds, boys were significantly less persistent, more inflexible and more difficult on the EDS. Thus overall, sex differences in temperament were minimal in the first year of life but emerged quite strongly in the second, third and fourth year. Notably, we did not find higher scores on the early activity factors for boys, although they were in evidence when the original TTS *dimension* of activity was used. This perhaps adds to the inconsistency of the data in this area (see Chapter 26, by Kohnstamm). By preschool age, boys were clearly more likely to be at the difficult end of the EDS. Sex differences emerged also in the stability analyses, with girls showing greater stability within the easy to difficult quartiles.

Preschool boys showed significantly more problem behaviours across a range of measures including aggression/hostility, hyperactivity/distractibility and overall problem scores. Again it needs to be noted that with such a large sample, differences may be quantitatively small but still significant.

Prematurity

It has been commonly held that infants born prematurely are more difficult in terms of their temperament and behaviour than full-term infants. Reasons for this include the diminished capacity of the infant to initiate and sustain meaningful social interactions with caregivers (Brazelton, 1979; Goldberg, 1978), the disturbing ambience of the premature nursery (Lawson, Daum & Turkewitz, 1977) and the altered perceptions of the mother towards her premature infant (Di Vitto & Goldberg, 1980). Of the original cohort of 2443 infants enrolled in the ATP, 126 were born prematurely ($<$37 weeks). The only temperament difference found was that premature infants were less 'active–reactive' ($P<.001$); no differences were found on developmental problems for this group (Oberklaid, Prior & Sanson, 1986). Follow-up data on the premature group showed no differences between preterm infants and full-term controls in individual temperament factors, parental ratings of behaviour or on the EDS. Preterms were more likely to be rated on the

Behavioural Checklist as having temper tantrums and daytime wetting and to have higher overall problem scores. For all other Behavioural Checklist items there were no differences. There were no differences on any measure of temperament or behaviour in the preschool period. All of these results were independent of sex, birth order, gestational age and socioeconomic status. We concluded from this series of studies that prematurity is not a risk factor for subsequent problems of temperament and behaviour. Where problems do arise they are likely to be the result of intrinsic or environmental factors in the transaction that are independent of prematurity *per se*, such as severe prenatal stress or difficulties in the caretaking milieu.

Social Class Influences on Ratings of Child Temperament

The index of social class employed in the ATP was a composite one, combining scores on education and occupational level for both parents (Sanson *et al.*, 1987). Since our sampling was representative, these factors were normally distributed in the original infant sample although there has been a slight tendency for lower SES families to drop out in later stages of the study.

At each age of sampling, social class has exerted some influence on temperament ratings. We found quantitatively small but significant associations between SES of parents and: temperamental difficulty, age of infant, reported developmental problems, mothers' and nurses' overall ratings, and mothers' ability to understand and complete the questionnaire. Families at the lower ends of the SES distribution were more likely to have more difficult infants and a higher level of adjustment problems. For the toddler and the preschool age periods, children from the lowest SES quartile generally scored at the more problematic ends of temperament factors, with significant differences consistently emerging across all years on Rhythmicity and on the EDS. This group also showed more behaviour problems overall. However, this effect was not shown when teacher ratings of behaviour problems were used for the preschool sample.

The overall trends for more negative temperament profiles in the lower SES range may perhaps be a consequence of differing conceptions of positive and negative behaviours, or of differing child-rearing values and practices, or perhaps of a combination of factors (Prior, Samson, Carroll & Oberklaid, 1989). We would not wish to claim on the basis of our data that lower SES children are actually more difficult; it may be that current conceptualizations of difficultness are specific to the middle class samples from which so much data have traditionally been drawn. Our findings on this variable are consistent with those of other workers who have explored the effects of rater and family characteristics (e.g. Sameroff, Seifer & Elias 1982; Thomas & Chess, 1977; and see Chapter 26, by Kohnstamm).

Ethnic Factors

From a cross-cultural perspective our findings with regard to ethnic status are of particular interest for this section (Prior, Kyrios & Oberklaid, 1986; Prior, Sanson,

Garino & Oberklaid, 1987). In an earlier comparative study of American, Chinese, Australian and Greek-Australian infants using data from the R-ITQ (Prior *et al.*, 1986). we reported notable cultural differences, with Australian and American infants being relatively similar and generally more positive in temperament than the other two groups. Greek and Chinese infants were very different from the other groups and the Greek-Australians in particular showed a predominantly negative temperament profile. American infants were more active and more rhythmic than all other groups. High reactivity or sensitivity characterized the Chinese group, a finding similar to those reported by Freedman and Freedman (1969) and Kagan. Kearsley and Zelazo (1978).

In the ATP we were able to compare the various ethnic subgroups which make up the population since we had a representative sample of the whole State. Whilst approximately three-quarters of the sample had Australian-born parents, the remaining quarter included families where one or both parents were born in another country. The largest single group (12%) was from the UK, Ireland or New Zealand (combined for analyses because of perceived similarity in cultural background and origins). Infants with parents born in Italy, Greece, Yugoslavia, Asia (excluding the Indian subcontinent) and Lebanon showed differences on a number of temperament dimensions, most consistently on Approach, Adaptability and Distractibility. Factor-based analyses produced similar results. These ethnic groups' scores were consistently towards the more 'difficult' end of these dimensions and similarly these same groups showed a higher number of infants in the Difficult temperament category using the algorithm of Carey and McDevitt (1978a), although not on our EDS (Prior *et al.*, 1987). Developmental problems of colic, sleep difficulties and excessive crying were more commonly reported by some of the ethnic groups. Notably also, the overall ratings given by mothers and by MCH nurses were in the direction of greater difficulties in adjustment amongst all ethnic groups except those from Northern and Western Europe. UK, New Zealand and the Indian subcontinent.

Concerns that language difficulties in some groups may have distorted results were somewhat allayed by the fact that we had excluded from analyses all families where there was a clear indication of language problems. In addition, partial correlations between ethnic status and temperament categorization controlling for level of understanding of the questionnaire and for occupational and educational status showed minimal reduction of the relationships. Similarly, the hypothesis that ethnic status was confounded with SES was also rejected via analyses of covariance controlling for SES. Vulnerability to infant problems as a function of immigrant status does not seem to be a viable hypothesis since some ethnic groups showed no raised incidence of difficulties. In addition, parallel data collected on Greek infants living in Greece had shown a similarly raised incidence of difficult temperament, suggesting a consistent ethnic effect (Kyrios, Prior, Oberklaid & Demetriou, in press). The hypothesis of genetic influences is a difficult one to test since such influences would be hard to disentangle from cultural and family factors which would be important in the interactions between rater and infant (Kyrios *et al.*, in press).

Our follow-up studies of this sample have confirmed, at each year of measurement, an excess of children with difficult temperament, especially in groups with parents from countries of the Mediterranean and Middle Eastern region. In the toddler groups significantly more children with such backgrounds showed developmental problems such as excessive crying, temper tantrums and overactivity, and had higher overall behaviour-problem ratings. Again it needs to be noted that in this large sample such differences may be quantitatively small but still significant.

In the preschool age follow-up, numbers in some of the ethnic subgroups became too small for analysis. However, by comparison with children with two Australian parents, greater temperamental difficulty and more problem behaviours were still reported for Middle Eastern, Southern European and Asian families. The persistence of temperament and behaviour difficulties in the Southern European and Middle Eastern groups across four times of measurement is notable.

Further studies have been carried out, aimed at in-depth investigation of the findings relating to ethnic factors. Results of one of these studies suggest that mothers from non-Australian backgrounds may have different conceptions of those behaviours constituting difficulty in their children. For example, they are more influenced by biological functions and problems in their concepts of easy and difficult characteristics, by comparison with Australian mothers who are more likely to emphasize temperament or personality characteristics (Lusnats, 1988). Child-rearing differences probably also contribute to these findings. Thus the middle class North American conceptualization of difficulty may have much less relevance in other cultures for the 'goodness of fit' (Lerner & Lerner, 1983; Thomas & Chess, 1977) between child and family, and for maternal perceptions of problem behaviour in the child.

Temperament and Behaviour Problems

From the outset of the ATP, our group has been concerned to investigate clinical implications of particular temperament characteristics in examining concurrent and predictive relationships between temperament and behavioural adjustment. At the infancy stage, difficult temperament was significantly related to sleeping problems, colic, excessive crying, mother's and nurse's overall ratings of the infant's difficulty of temperament, and to the nurse's rating of the adjustment of the mother–baby pair (Sanson *et al.*, 1985). For both toddler follow-up studies, as well as for the most recent follow-up of preschoolers, there were significant relationships between the EDS and all behaviour problems: sleep, crying, shyness, dependency, mood swings, accident-proneness, temper tantrums, overactivity, aggression, mother's overall rating of difficulty, the toddler behaviour-problem composite score derived from the Richman and Graham (1971) Behaviour Checklist, and the Behar PBQ behaviour-problems score at preschool age. Greater problems are reported in temperamentally more difficult children.

Not only were these correlations significant for concurrent measures but they persisted with little diminution across the years of measurement; that is, the EDS calculated at each year was related to past behavioural difficulties and it predicted future ones. However, temperamental difficulty was not related to Behar behaviour-problem score as rated by teachers of a subsample of 300 children attending preschool.

In another group of preschoolers in the ATP assessed in greater depth with measures of family functioning included, Kyrios (1988) found that temperamental 'reactivity–manageability' was the best predictor of behavioural adjustment, both concurrently and predictively 1 year later. Since this study included *clinical* assessment of behavioural adjustment and used path-analytic techniques, these results complement our findings using more sophisticated forms of analysis.

A common criticism levelled against the association between difficult temperament and behavioural maladjustment is that measures are confounded, i.e. in rating temperament and behaviour problems, parents (or teachers) are in effect rating the same behaviours. Sanson, Prior and Kyrios (in press) have reported a study in which this potential confounding was explored by having expert raters judge measures of temperament and of behaviour problem for their 'goodness' as measures of each concept. Considerable overlap or contamination was found although this was largely confined to 'internalizing' types of behaviour problems. We have argued that this may suggest the need for better measures of internalized problems rather than for abandonment of traditional temperament measures. We do concur with other researchers who have noted the need for caution in interpreting temperament and behaviour-problem relationships using existing measures.

SUMMARY

A number of issues in the conceptualization and practical implementation of temperament measures continue to be the subject of lively debate in the literature. How reliable are the measures of temperament currently being used? Are we measuring actual attributes of children, or rather perceptions and expectations of parents? The argument that temperament questionnaires measure attributes of the rater as much as the child is given some added credence by our findings of significant and persistent SES and cross-cultural differences in temperament. Rater and/or situational effects were also apparent in our study of differences between mothers and day-caretakers in their ratings of temperament of the same children (Northam, Prior, Sanson & Oberklaid, 1987).

In order for us to look at stability of temperament over time, we have had to address the measurement issues. While previously reported moderate correlations of temperament over time, and the diminished correlation with increasing time, have face validity, we do not know to what extent these results are contaminated by the small, selected samples used or by problems with the temperament questionnaires. Most studies of stability have used questionnaires based on the original Thomas and Chess nine dimensions of temperament. These are intuitively rather than empirically derived and there is little evidence that the behavioural dimensions are strictly comparable across different ages. This makes it difficult to interpret results confidently because we cannot be certain that modest stability is a function of the inherent instability of temperament (individual instability) or of the questionnaires themselves (structural instability), or because of discontinuity in temperament structure itself across time. Our development of psychometrically robust and shorter questionnaires not only has the advantage of parsimony, but has allowed us to be more confident that measures are comparable from one time period to the next. Items on the STSI and STST are empirically based and there is a parallel factor structure over different age periods.

The size and representativeness of the ATP cohort overcomes some of the problem of sample size and selection inherent in other studies. It has also provided us with data that pose additional theoretical and practical questions. The practice of deriving individual temperament profiles by comparison with established 'norms', for example, must now be seriously questioned. If the measurement of temperament is to be a widely used clinical tool, then there may need to be developed comparison data which are age, sex, SES and culture specific.

As the ATP-cohort children become older and enter school, new and important directions and research possibilities arise. As well as continuing to look at issues such as stability and prediction of behavioural adjustment, the influence of temperament on school adjustment and dysfunction will become a focus. There are data suggesting that temperament significantly affects adjustment at school entry (Carey, Fox & McDevitt, 1977), that temperament is an important factor in teachers' perception of a child's classroom functioning (Keogh, 1982) and that temperament in school-age children moderates the untoward effects of stress (Wertleib, Weigel, Springer & Fieldstein, 1987).

The ATP is a very large project and in a short summary chapter it is possible to present only major highlights and perhaps identify salient issues. We have presented our data on the measurement advances we believe we have made, a step which is essential if continuity and stability of temperament are to be taken seriously. We have also highlighted context and rater influences on temperament ratings.

Whilst we would not argue against the psychological, constitutional, or intrinsic basis of temperament (Rothbart & Derryberry, 1981; Strelau, 1983); our work is consistent with contemporary, mainstream developmental psychology in which temperament may be most usefully viewed as a moderator or mediating influence in individual responses to experience in particular contexts.

ACKNOWLEDGMENTS

This work is supported by a grant from the National Health and Medical Research Council of Australia.

REFERENCES

Bates, J.E., Freeland, C.A.B. & Lounsbury, M.L. (1979). Measurement of infant difficultness. *Child Development*, **50**, 794–803.

Behar, L. & Stringfield, S. (1974). A behavior rating scale for the preschool child. *Developmental Psychology*, **10**, 601–610.

Bohlin, G., Hagekull, B. & Lindhagen, K. (1981). Dimensions of infant behavior. *Infant Behavior and Development*, **4**, 83–96.

Brazelton, T.B. (1979). Behavioral competence of the newborn infant. *Seminars in Perinatology*, **3**, 35–44.

Carey, W.B. (1981). The importance of temperament–environment interactions for child health and development. In M. Lewis & L.A. Rosenblum (Eds), *The uncommon child* (pp. 31–55). New York: Plenum.

Carey, W.B., Fox, M. & McDevitt, S. (1977). Temperament as a factor in early school adjustment. *Pediatrics*, **60**, 621–624.

Carey, W.B. & McDevitt, S.C. (1978a). Revision of the Infant Temperament Questionnaire. *Pediatrics*, **61**, 735–739.

Carey, W.B. & McDevitt, S.C. (1978b). Stability and change in individual temperament diagnoses from infancy to early childhood. *Journal of the American Academy of Child Psychiatry*, **17**, 331–337.

Di Vitto, B. & Goldberg, S. (1980). The development of early parent–infant interaction as a function of newborn medical status. In T. Field *et al.* (Eds), *Infants born at risk* (pp. 311–312). Hollingswood, NY: Spectrum.

Earls, F. (1981). Temperament characteristics and behaviour problems in three-year-old children. *Journal of Nervous and Mental Disease*, **169**, 367–373.

Freedman, D.G. & Freedman, N.A. (1969). Differences in behavior between Chinese-American and European-American newborns. *Nature*, **224**, 1227.

Fullard, W., McDevitt, S.C. & Carey, W.B. (1984). Assessing temperament in one- to three-year-old children. *Journal of Pediatric Psychology*, **9**, 205–216.

Goldberg, S. (1978). Prematurity: Effects on parent–infant interaction. *Journal of Pediatric Psychology*, **3**, 137–144.

Gorsuch, R.L. (1974). *Factor analysis*. Hillsdale, NJ: Erlbaum.

Kagan, J. (1971). *Change and continuity in infancy*. New York: Wiley.

Kagan, J., Kearsley, R.B. & Zelazo, P.R. (1978). *Infancy: Its place in human development*. Cambridge, MA: Harvard University Press.

Keogh, B.K. (1982). Children's temperament and teachers' decisions. In R. Collins & R. Porter (Eds), *Temperamental differences in infants and young children* (pp. 269–279). Ciba Foundation. London: Pitman.

Kyrios, M. (1988). Temperament, stress, and family factors in the behavioural adjustment of 3–5 year old children. Unpublished Doctoral Dissertation, La Trobe University.

Kyrios, M., Prior, M., Oberklaid, F. & Demetriou, A. (in press). Cross-cultural studies of temperament: Temperament in Greek infants. *Journal of Cross-Cultural Psychology*.

Lawson, K., Daum, C. & Turkewitz, G. (1977). Environmental characteristics of a neonatal care-unit. *Child Development*, **48**, 1633–1639.

Lerner, J.V. & Lerner, R.M. (1983). Temperament and adaptation across life: Theoretical and empirical issues. In P.B. Bates & O.G. Brim Jr (Eds), *Life span development and behaviour*, Vol. V (pp. 197–231). New York: Academic Press.

Lusnats, G. (1988). Ethnic differences in mother's concepts of easiness and difficultness of temperament. Unpublished Master of Psychology Thesis, La Trobe University, Australia.

Northam, E., Prior, M., Sanson, A. & Oberklaid, F. (1987). Toddler temperament as perceived by mothers versus day-care givers. *Merrill-Palmer Quarterly*, **33**, 213–229.

Oberklaid, F., Prior, M., Golvan, D., Clements, A. & Williamson, A. (1984). Temperament in Australian infants. *Australian Pediatric Journal*, **20**, 181–184.

Oberklaid, F., Prior, M. & Sanson, A. (1986). Temperament of preterm versus fullterm infants. *Journal of Developmental Behavioural Pediatrics*, **7**, 159–162.

Persson-Blennow, I. & McNeil, T.F. (1979). A questionnaire for measurement of temperament in six-month old infants: Development and standardization. *Journal of Child Psychology and Psychiatry*, **20**, 1–13.

Persson-Blennow, I. & McNeil, T.F. (1982). Factor analysis of temperament characteristics in children at 6 months, 1 year and 2 years of age. *British Journal of Educational Psychology*, **52**, 51–57.

Prior, M., Kyrios, M. & Oberklaid, F. (1986). Temperament in Australian, American, Chinese, and Greek infants. *Journal of Cross-Cultural Psychology*, **17**, 455–474.

Prior, M., Sanson, A., Garino, E. & Oberklaid, F. (1987). Ethnic influences on 'difficult' temperament and behavioural problems in infants. *Australian Journal of Psychology*, **39**, 163–171.

Prior, M., Sanson, A., Carroll, R. & Oberklaid, F. (1989). Social class differences in temperament ratings of pre-school children. *Merrill-Palmer Quarterly*, **35**, 239–248.

Richman, N. & Graham, P.J. (1971). A behavioural screening questionnaire for use with three year old children: Preliminary findings. *Journal of Child Psychology and Psychiatry*, **12**, 5–33.

Rothbart, M.K. (1981). Measurement of temperament in infancy. *Child Development*, **52**, 569–578.

Rothbart, M.K. & Derryberry, D. (1981). Development of individual differences in temperament. In M.E. Lamb & A.L. Brown (Eds), *Advances in developmental psychology*, Vol. 1. Hillsdale, NJ: Erlbaum.

Rowe, D.C. & Plomin, R. (1977). Temperament in early childhood. *Journal of Personality Assessment*, **41**, 150–156.

Sameroff, A.J., Seifer, R. & Elias, P.K. (1982). Sociocultural variability in infant temperament ratings. *Child Development*, **53**, 164–173.

Sanson, A., Prior, M., Garino, E., Oberklaid, F. & Sewell, J. (1987). The structure of infant temperament: Factor analysis of the Revised Infant Temperament Questionnaire. *Infant Behavior and Development*, **10**, 97–104.

Sanson, A., Prior, M. & Kyrios, M. (in press). The contamination of temperament and behavioural measures. *Merrill-Palmer Quarterly*.

Sanson, A., Prior, M. & Oberklaid, F. (1985). Normative data on temperament in Australian infants. *Australian Journal of Psychology*, **37**, 185–195.

Sanson, A., Prior, M. & Oberklaid, F. (submitted). Continuity and stability of temperament from infancy to pre-school age.

Strelau, J. (1983). *Temperament, personality, activity*. New York: Academic Press.

Thomas, A. & Chess, S. (1977). *Temperament and development*. New York: Brunner/Mazel.

Thomas, A., Chess, S. & Birch, H.G. (1968). *Temperament and behaviour disorders in children*. New York: New York University Press/London: University of London Press.

Wertleib, D., Weigel, C., Springer, T. & Feldstein, M. (1987). Temperament as a moderator of children's stressful experience. *American Journal of Orthopsychiatry*, **57**, 234–245.

Section Six
Historical and International Perspectives

30

Historical and International Perspectives

GELDOLPH A. KOHNSTAMM
Leiden University

THE LONG HISTORY OF THE FOUR CLASSICAL TEMPERAMENTS APPLIED TO HUMAN MALES

In the history of Greco-Roman and Christian medical and psychological thought the four temperamental types originally discerned by Hippocrates (460 BC) and, much later, elaborated upon by the Roman physician Galen (129–201 AD) were used descriptively for a remarkably long period. This system of classification was only used for male adults; very few writers ever tried to apply the system to women and children.

The history of these four temperaments has been described by many authors, some of whom have done a splendid job. I will mention only two of them. The first is Roback, whose book *The psychology of character* (1927, third edn 1952) was praised by Allport (1937) and Eysenck (1953) for its completeness. Reading Roback is a great pleasure because of his international and multilingual orientation, and his amazingly wide range of reading. Although his own contribution to characterology never seems to have impressed anyone, his historical overview of the literature on temperament, personality and character remains an example of great scholarship. Despite the remarkable first-hand knowledge this American psychologist had of the French, German, Italian, English and Hebrew literature, he regretted that he was unable to cover the Russian and other Eastern European literature as well:

> The omission of references to Russian investigators is apt to give the impression that characterology has made no advance in Russia. The truth is that studies on character have been undertaken there as well as in Poland for some time, but unfortunately the works and reports are for obvious reasons inaccessible (Roback, 1927, third edn 1952, p. 248)

The second, more recent example is Eysenck (1953; see also Eysenck & Eysenck, 1985), who gave a learned and very readable account of the main roads leading

Temperament in Childhood   Edited by G.A. Kohnstamm, J.E. Bates and M.K. Rothbart
© 1989 John Wiley & Sons Ltd

from Kant via Wundt, Gross and Heymans on the one side, and via Jung and Freud on the other, to his own superdimensions: extraversion–introversion and stable–unstable (neuroticism); the modern heirs of this long history of search for the smallest number of basic dimensions of the affective side of personality.

THE SHORT HISTORY OF THE FOUR CLASSICAL TEMPERAMENTS APPLIED TO CHILDREN

Whereas the study of temperament in adulthood has a long and international history (see also Chapter 12, by Rothbart), the study of temperament in childhood is rather young and now only beginning to be internationally oriented. The developmental approach to temperamental differences seems also a rather new phenomenon in the history of thought about temperament, although Rothbart (see Chapter 12) points at Galen's early interest in temperamental differences among children, and Meyer (see Chapter 31) reveals sources from the first half of the nineteenth century. From a popular nineteenth-century book for parents and teachers (Hellwig, 1889, 4th edn; see Chapter 31, by Meyer) I quote the first lines of the description of the sanguine child (my translation):

> This is the lighthearted [literally: lightblooded], gay and nervous child. Cheerful [*frohsinnig*] would perhaps be the best single word we would have to characterize this child. The sanguine child is extraordinarily easily excited. His eyes, mouth, hands and feet are constantly moving. He cannot remain in one position, either sitting or standing. Not to talk for half an hour is close to impossible for him. The sanguine child cannot just walk, he must frolic and run. When he laughs – and he enjoys doing so – he laughs loudly; his whole body, hands and feet help him laugh; but when he cries – which he also enjoys doing – he also cries loudly. (Hellwig, 1889, 4th edn, p. 7)

A different and much later approach to the classical four temperaments was taken by Krasnagorsky (1958; see Chapter 3, by Strelau) from the Leningrad school of Pavlov. He developed his ideas in the 1930s but did not publish the final version of his work until 1958, when, coincidentally, a new school of temperament in childhood was coming to life in New York.

According to Strelau (1984), this was Krasnagorsky's view of the sanguine child (my translation from Strelau):

> Conditioned responses are quickly formed and are durable. The strength of the response is in accordance with the strength of the stimulus. The conditioned inhibition reactions are also quickly formed, strong and lasting. Strong nerve cells of the cortex and a normally excitable, subcortex region warrant good adaptation to the demands of the environment. The activity of the cortex is characterized by its high mobility. This is a lively temperament, easy for parents and teachers to handle and educate. The verbal reactions are quickly formed and in agreement with age norms. Sanguine children ordinarily speak clearly and fast. Their speech is articulated, melodic, well intonated and fluent. Speech is accompanied by lively gestures, facial expressions and emotional excitement. (Strelau, 1984)

A third example of the vitality of Greek and Roman classical ideas is still more recent. The Finnish psychologist Pulkkinen (see Chapter 34, by Torgersen) has done a study using the classical four temperaments for constructing a 52-item temperament scale for children. The items for this scale, called SACHOMEPH (*sa*nguine, *cho*leric, *me*lancholic, *ph*legmatic) were derived from a mixture of (a) European interpreters of the classical four: Kant, Pavlov, Eysenck and Steiner, (b) factor analytic studies by Mischel and Mischel, and (c) Pulkkinen's own work on aggression.

MODERN TEMPERAMENT RESEARCH: THE ADVANCEMENT OF INTERNATIONAL COMMUNICATION

To the present day, temperament research has been done in separate communities with very little exchange of information, overlap and cross-referencing. There are at least five reasons for this lack of communication.

The first is, of course, that different languages, spoken in the different parts of the world, result in different languages being used for publication. The second is the political and financial restrictions on travelling which handicap in particular our colleagues from Eastern Europe. The third is the financial restriction on buying books and subscribing to journals, which handicaps many from everywhere. The fourth is the difference in interests between those who are studying adults (and animals) and those who are studying children. The fifth is the difference in background and interests between the clinically oriented psychiatrists, pediatricians and psychologists and the theory- and research-oriented students of personality and behavior.

Commenting on divisions among researchers in the field of adult temperament, Eysenck wrote in a foreword to a book by Strelau (1985):

> It is a platitude to say that science is international, but certainly as far as psychology is concerned this is more a hope than a reality. There is little communication between English-speaking and non-English-speaking authors, and in particular there has been a true Iron Curtain between authors on the two sides of that dividing line. Little mention is made of European and American authors in the Russian literature and conversely only a few authors on this side of the Iron Curtain have taken the time and trouble to look at the contribution made by Russian, Polish, Hungarian and other authors on the other side of the Curtain. (Eysenck, in Strelau, 1985, p. i)

In the 1960s several British and Russian authors did cross this dividing line: notably, Gray (1964) and Mangan (1967) from the one side and Nebylitsyn (1972) from the other. This resulted in a widely quoted cooperative publication (Nebylitsyn & Gray, 1972).

In the 1970s and 1980s these East–West communications were advanced by the activities of Strelau from the University of Warsaw. Strelau was also one of the first to cross the borders separating the three kinds of subjects: animals, human adults and children. It is interesting to see how the communications developed between Strelau and the Warsaw school on the one side and Thomas and Chess and their school on the other. How did these schools, so differently located and oriented, come to meet? We believe that one major reason was the decision of both schools to adopt the same 'outdated' label as a heading for their research programs: temperament.

In 1963 a young English psychiatrist, Rutter, advised Thomas, Chess and their colleagues in New York to adopt the old word 'temperament' for what they had originally called 'initial or primary reaction patterns' (Porter & Collins, 1982, p. 168, footnote). In the 1950s they had come to discern these patterns for the first 3 months after birth, in cooperation with Herbert Birch. As the subjects of their longitudinal study grew older, they needed a different name for designating the patterns of evolving and changing personality. Still, in their first book, published in 1963 (Thomas, Chess, Birch, Hertzig & Korn, 1963), the authors explicitly avoided the word temperament, which they thought to be too much associated with a 'simplistic typologic position'. As they explained in their second book (Thomas, Chess & Birch, 1968):

> It was our repeated experience in the early and mid-1950's to find most of our colleagues reproaching us for returning to an outdated and discredited constitutionalist position when we expressed the idea that individual organismic behavioral differences important for development might exist in young children. In a period when behavioral disturbance was most generally considered to be produced by the environment, to pay attention to the intrinsic characteristics of the reactor was viewed as a return to a static and almost Lombrosian constitutional typology. (Thomas *et al.*, 1968, p. 6)

It is my opinion that the choice of this label 'temperament' has in a certain sense been a lucky one because it has helped to attract the attention of so many people internationally, including Strelau and his Warsaw school. Thomas and Chess and their colleagues in the New York Longitudinal Study (NYLS) are now generally credited for the wave of interest in temperament in infancy and childhood which became manifest in the 1970s and 1980s. The choice of this label has also been very good for the proliferation of temperament research in childhood, the sheer increase in the number of studies.

There were other reasons for the new interest in the phenomena collected under the label 'temperament' in infancy and childhood. In the United States the book *Personality and temperament* by the psychologist Diamond had appeared in 1957. He gave evidence for the view that individuation of temperament takes place very early in life, so that within the first year of life it is possible to identify behavioral characteristics which the individual is likely to retain into adolescence.

This book, although not widely read and quoted, led to the seminal book by Buss and Plomin (1975): *A temperament theory of personality development*.

Now the train was really moving. An informal international communication network developed of researchers and clinicians interested in children and their problems. In 1974 and 1979 Strelau organized international conferences on temperament and personality in Warsaw. Thomas and Chess attended the second one. During a meeting of the International Society of the Study of Behavioral Development in Lund in 1979 the initiative was taken for the first of a series of 'occasional temperament conferences' in the United States to which a steadily growing number of international researchers was invited. Among those taking this initiative was the late Ronald Wilson, to whom this volume is dedicated. In 1988 the seventh occasional temperament conference was held in Athens, Georgia.

In 1981 Rothbart and Derryberry published their temperament theory (Rothbart, 1981; Rothbart & Derryberry, 1981). The first truly 'cross-cultural' theory in the scientific sense, it sought

> to integrate the views of adult temperament represented by Gray (1972), Eysenck (1967), and Zuckerman (1979), and related Eastern European concepts of the reactivity of the nervous system (Nebylitsyn, 1972; Pavlov, 1935; Strelau, 1975; Teplov, 1964) with [Western, K.] research on social and emotional development during infancy. (Goldsmith & Campos, 1982, p. 169)

A succession of international conferences on temperament in infancy and childhood also took place in Europe (London, 1981, see Porter & Collins, 1982; Leiden, 1985, see Kohnstamm, 1986; Bellagio, 1988, see Carey & McDevitt, 1989). They demonstrated the steadily growing interest for this train with its old flag and mixed bag of new cargo. Many new passengers were attracted by a very practical aspect which had been developed in the 1970s by Carey and by Thomas and Chess: the questionnaires for parents and teachers. With these questionnaires a tradition begun by Hartmann in 1896 (see Chapter 31, by Meyer) was carried on, and with great success. They served as an inexpensive alternative to the lengthy interviews developed by Chess and Thomas for the NYLS. Until then, the only questionnaires to assess personality dimensions in children were self-report inventories, which for obvious reasons could not be used for infants and young children. The youngest age at which these inventories were used was 6 and 7, by Cattell and his co-workers in England (Cattell & Coan, 1958). For younger age groups the researchers had no other possibilities than costly and time-consuming behavioral response measures and observation schemes or the equally time-consuming interview technique by Thomas and Chess. For pediatric practice the advantage of the Carey multiple-choice questionnaire over the Thomas/Chess interview was soon recognized and its use was recommended by medical authorities (e.g. by Gregg, 1973). Thomas and Chess followed Carey's example – though not his scaling technique, which Carey himself abandoned in the 1978 revision of the Infant Temperament Questionnaire – and published in 1977 their Parent and Teacher Questionnaire for children 3–7 years of age as an appendix to their influential 1977 book.

Reviewing this book, Yarrow (1978) wrote:

> Temperament is a concept in the history of psychology and psychiatry that has had a cyclical course, with brief moments in the limelight and longer periods in the shadows. Currently there is a renewed interest in the temperamental roots of behavior. This revitalization is in no small part a result of the studies initiated almost 25 years ago by these authors and their colleagues. (Yarrow, 1978, p. 359)

True as this statement was, it also bears witness to some Americocentrism, because it does not refer to two vital schools of temperament research and thought which sprang from totally different wells: the London school and the Warsaw school. The latter is represented in this volume (Strelau, Chapter 3), but not the former.

THE LONDON SCHOOL OF PERSONALITY

There has been an apparent lack of communication between the American and British students of temperament in childhood. Not infancy, because we have no evidence that the London school was ever interested in temperamental differences in infants. It is even remarkable how little mention the Eysencks make of American research on temperament in infants, right up to their latest publications (e.g. Eysenck & Eysenck, 1985).

On the other hand, it is equally remarkable how American childhood temperament researchers have ignored almost completely the work done by the Eysencks, with notable exceptions in the writings by Rothbart and Derryberry and by Buss and Plomin. The last authors have suggested close resemblances between two of Eysenck's three factors and two of their own:

> We suggest that in childhood, emotionality is the core of neuroticism without conditioned anxiety, and sociability is the core of extraversion stripped of its liveliness component. (Buss & Plomin, 1986, p. 70; see also Buss & Plomin, 1975, 1984)

The 1969 book by Eysenck and Eysenck *Personality structure and measurement* includes a section entitled 'Personality in children'. This section consists of two chapters, one by Rachman on 'Extraversion and neuroticism in childhood', which gives an overview of American and British studies which were considered relevant for testing the hypothesis of the early appearance of those two basic dimensions in childhood. The other chapter, 'Personality dimensions in children' by Sybil B.G. Eysenck, reports the results of administering the junior version of the Eysenck Personality Inventory to 6760 English schoolchildren between the ages of 7 and 16. We have checked nearly all major American temperament in childhood publications since 1975 and have found not a single reference to these two chapters, nor to the great majority of references (both American and British) which they contain. How can this be explained?

One reason might be that the Eysencks, contrary to two other famous English researchers in their prewar publications (Burt, 1937; Cattell, 1933), did not use the word temperament in the titles of their publications. It is my guess that if the Eysencks had chosen the word 'temperament' instead of 'personality' for this part of their 1969 book, the nearly total negation of their work by students of 'temperament' would not have occurred.

Another reason may lie in Hans Eysenck's own personality; he is not particularly known for his appreciation of the work of his colleagues. This has kept him at a certain distance from others. A third reason, somewhat related to the former, is that many of his colleagues in psychology and psychiatry, notably in the United States, are sceptical of his methods of data collection and his ways of drawing conclusions from these data. I have found this to be a very controversial issue among today's leading researchers and something which is not possible to discuss in the open without raising adrenaline levels in the discussants. Briggs (1987) has written an illuminating review of the Eysenck and Eysenck (1985) volume. He remarks that the 'continued exclusion of Eysenck's work from current texts on personality is particularly reprehensible in that few other theories have been stated with as much precision or have produced as many testable hypotheses across as diverse a range of behaviors' (Briggs, 1987, p. 855). On the other hand, Briggs notes that the book 'suffers from an egocentricity that is every bit as disconcerting as the ethnocentricity that has excluded Eysenck from many popular personality texts' (p. 856).

In his 1937 paper 'The analysis of temperament', Burt presented the results of a factor analysis on data from 124 neurotic and delinquent children. He discerned two 'specific' factors which seem identical to the later factors E and N. In *unselected* groups of children and adults Burt saw 'general emotionality' as the most potent factor which obscured the effect of the specific factors.

With regard to the first of a group of specific factors Burt wrote:

> the first factor must be a general trait or tendency which, when positive, predisposes people towards assertive, angry, sociable, and inquisitive behaviour, in short, towards active or aggressive conduct, and, when negative, towards submissiveness, fear, sorrow, tenderness and disgust, in a word, towards repressive or inhibitive emotions. Now a factor of almost exactly the same bipolar kind emerged in the earlier research on correlating emotional assessments for large and random groups of normal children and adults. Moreover, a similar antithesis appears and reappears in the writings of numerous psychologists who have followed very different lines of approach. James' 'explosive' and 'obstructed' types, Guthrie's 'restrained' and 'unrestrained' types, Ostwald's 'romantic' and 'classical' types, Binet's 'objective' and 'subjective' types, the 'extravert' and 'introvert' of Jung, the 'cyclic' and 'schizoid' personalities of Kretschmer and Kraepelin are all variations on the same double theme.
>
> With the present data, this factor contributes, as we have seen, well over half the total variance and is thus responsible for most of the conspicuous differences between the personalities here represented. With unselected groups its effect is somewhat obscured by the more potent factor of 'general emotionality'; but it still remains more easily discernible than that of any other specific factor. (Burt, 1937, p. 182)

And discussing his second specific factor, Burt wrote:

> Here again we have a contrast which is as old as it is familiar. And together the two factors yield a cross-division which corresponds to the most frequent interpretation of the traditional classification of temperaments handed down from Hippocrates and Galen, Hoffding, Ebbinghaus, Külpe, Meumann, Kreibig, Stern, Davenport, Peters, Jung . . . Hitherto, however, such classifications have for the most part been based, not on quantitative assessments or statistical analysis, but on casual impression and armchair speculation; and the types have generally been conceived as neatly opposed and mutually exclusive categories, instead of as elastic and empirical groupings. (Burt, 1937)

These quotations may help to remind us that Burt – notwithstanding his later fraudulent behavior – was a scholar of wide reading in the history of temperament and that his research was probably seminal for the later development of Eysenck's two superdimensions. Having reviewed the work by Guilford and Cattell, Eysenck wrote about himself: 'The third writer to be mentioned in this connection is the present author, who may be said to have continued the work of Spearman and Burt and to have carried on the spirit of the London school' (Eysenck, 1969, p. 36).

THE RETURN OF AN INTERNATIONAL PERSPECTIVE

This book shows how the old name 'temperament' has come into use again, after several decades of disuse and even distrust. The common label seems to give unity to works and interests as different in scope and method as those presented in this book. The adoption of this common label may also have a negative effect: the publications of those who study the same problems but do not elect to call them 'temperamental' seem to belong to a different field.

The chapters in this last section may help us to overcome our natural egocentric disposition, by showing the past and the present of thinking about individual differences in temperament in some of the Western European countries. A chapter from Eastern Europe, contributed by Strelau in the first section, has a similar purpose, as well as presenting a specific and vital conceptual framework.

Many countries, languages and cultures are not represented in this section, although some of the studies done in Australia, Canada, Great Britain, Holland, Japan and Poland have been mentioned in foregoing chapters. For the near future an increase of Asian temperament research is to be expected, notably from India and Japan. In India the psychiatrist Malhotra and her associates have published several studies on temperamental differences in normal and emotionally disturbed children (Malhotra, Malhotra & Randhawa, 1983a,b; Malhotra & Randhawa, 1982). In several European countries not covered in this section the study of temperamental differences in children and youth is also on the increase.

The selection of countries made for this section of the book is thus somewhat arbitrary. This selection does not mean that we see Germany, France, Italy and the Scandinavian countries as the most important for present-day non-US research in the field of temperament in childhood. For a good insight into the *roots* of temperament research, however, the following chapters on the German, Italian and French contributions certainly are indispensable.

ACKNOWLEDGMENTS

The corrections and suggestions made by Harry Beilin and Mary Rothbart are gratefully acknowledged.

REFERENCES

Allport, G.W. (1937). *Personality: A psychological interpretation*. New York: Holt.
Briggs, S.R. (1987). Hawking a good theory. Review of H.J. Eysenck & M.W. Eysenck: Personality and individual differences. *Contemporary Psychology*, **32** (10), 854–856.
Burt, C. (1937). The analysis of temperament. *British Journal of Medical Psychology*, **17**, 158–188.
Buss, A.H. & Plomin, R. (1975). *A temperament theory of personality development*. New York: Wiley.
Buss, A.H. & Plomin, R. (1984). *Temperament: Early developing personality traits*. Hillsdale, NJ: Erlbaum.
Buss, A.H. & Plomin, R. (1986). The EAS approach to temperament. In R. Plomin & J. Dunn (Eds), *The study of temperament: Changes, continuities and challenges*. Hillsdale, NJ: Erlbaum.

Carey, W.B. & McDevitt, S.C. (1989). *Clinical and educational applications of temperament research*. Amsterdam: Swets & Zeitlinger.

Cattell, R.B. (1933). Temperament tests: I. Temperament. *British Journal of Psychology, 23,* 308–329.

Cattell, R.B. & Coan, R.W. (1958). Personality dimensions in the questionnaire responses of six- and seven-year olds. *British Journal of Educational Psychology, 28,* 232–242.

Diamond, S. (1957). *Personality and temperament*. New York: Harper.

Eysenck, H.J. (1953). *The structure of human personality*. London: Methuen; New York: Wiley.

Eysenck, H.J. (1967). *The biological basis of personality*. Springfield, IL: Charles C. Thomas.

Eysenck, H.J. & Eysenck, M.W. (1985). *Personality and individual differences*. New York/London: Plenum.

Eysenck, H.J. & Eysenck, S.B.G. (1969). *Personality structure and measurement*. London: Routledge & Kegan Paul.

Goldsmith, H.H. & Campos, J.J. (1982). Toward a theory of infant temperament. In R.N. Emde & R.J. Harmon (Eds), *The development of attachment and affiliative systems* (pp. 161–193). New York: Plenum.

Gray, J.A. (1964). *Pavlov's typology*. Oxford: Pergamon.

Gray, J.A. (1972). The psychophysiological nature of introversion–extraversion: A modification of Eysenck's theory. In V.D. Nebylitsyn & J.A. Gray (Eds), *Biological basis of individual behavior*. New York: Academic Press.

Gregg, G. (1973). Clinical experience with efforts to define individual differences in children. In J. Westman (Ed.), *Individual differences in children*. New York: Wiley.

Hellwig, B. (1889). *Die vier Temperamente bei Kindern; ihre Aeusserung und ihre Behandlung in Erziehung und Schule*, 4th edn. Paderborn: Esser.

Kohnstamm, G.A. (Ed.) (1986). *Temperament discussed: Temperament and development in infancy and childhood*. Lisse (Neth.): Swets & Zeitlinger.

Krasnagorsky, N.I. (1958). *Vyssaja nervnaja dejatel'nost' rebenka* [Higher nervous activity in children]. Leningrad: Medgiz.

Malhotra, S., Malhotra, A. & Randhawa, A. (1983a). Temperament as a discriminating variable between emotionally disturbed and normal children. *Indian Journal of Clinical Psychology, 10,* 79–83.

Malhotra, S., Malhotra, A. & Randhawa, A. (1983b). Children's temperament: Factorial validity. *Indian Journal of Psychology, 10,* 399–406.

Malhotra, S. & Randhawa, A. (1982). A schedule for measuring temperament in children: preliminary data on development and standardization. *Indian Journal of Clinical Psychology, 9,* 203–210.

Mangan, G.L. (1967). Studies of the relationship between neo-Pavlovian properties of higher nervous activity and Western personality dimensions. *Journal of Experimental Research of Personality, 2,* 124–127.

Nebylitsyn, V.D. (1972). *Fundamental properties of the human nervous system*. New York: Plenum.

Nebylitsyn, V.D. & Gray, J.A. (1972). *Biological bases of individual behavior*. New York: Academic Press.

Pavlov, I.P. (1935). *General types of animal and human higher nervous activity: Selected works*. Republished in 1955. Moscow: Foreign Language Publishing House.

Porter, R. & Collins, G.M. (1982). *Temperament differences in infants and young children*. Ciba Foundation Symposium No. 89. London: Pitman.

Roback, A.A. (1927). *The psychology of character*. 3rd edn, 1952. London: Routledge & Kegan Paul; Cambridge, MA: Sci-art.

Rothbart, M.K. (1981). Measurement of temperament in infancy. *Child Development, 52,* 569–578.

Rothbart, M.K. & Derryberry, D. (1981). Development of individual differences in temperament. In M.E. Lamb & A.L. Brown (Eds), *Advances in developmental psychology*, Vol. 1. Hillsdale, NJ: Erlbaum.

Strelau, J. (1975). Reactivity and activity style in selected occupations. *Polish Psychological Bulletin,* **6**, 199–206.

Strelau, J. (1984). *Das Temperament in der psychischen Entwicklung.* Berlin: Volk und Wissen, Volkseigener Verlag.

Strelau, J. (1985). *Temperamental bases of behavior: Warsaw studies on individual differences.* Lisse (Neth.): Swets & Zeitlinger.

Teplov, B.M. (1964). Problems in the study of general types of higher nervous activity in man and animals. In J.A. Gray (Ed.), *Pavlov's typology.* Oxford: Pergamon.

Thomas, A. & Chess, S. (1977). *Temperament and development.* New York: Brunner/Mazel.

Thomas, A., Chess, S. & Birch, H.G. (1968). *Temperament and behavior disorders in children.* New York: New York University Press; London: University of London Press.

Thomas, A., Chess, S., Birch, H.G., Hertzig, M. & Korn, S. (1963). *Behavioral individuality in early childhood.* New York: New York University Press.

Yarrow, L.J. (1978). Review of Thomas and Chess: Temperament and development. *American Journal of Orthopsychiatry,* **48**, 359.

Zuckerman, M. (1979). *Sensation seeking: Beyond the optimal level of arousal.* Hillsdale, NJ: Erlbaum.

31

Temperament in Childhood: The German Contribution

HANS-JÜRGEN MEYER
Institut für Psychologie der Technischen Hochschule Darmstadt

Research on interindividual differences in such a basic aspect of personality as is called temperament has an especially long tradition in Germany. The first part of this chapter tries to answer the question of whether this general statement is also true for the study of temperament in childhood. In the following part, modern history and the current state of temperament research in German-speaking countries, particularly in the Federal Republic of Germany, is discussed.

HISTORICAL ROOTS

The following presentation about the history of temperament research in Germany is organized around issues that are prominent in modern temperament research and were rooted in the German research tradition of the last century. Included among these themes are:

(1) the problem of defining the term temperament;
(2) the problem of temperament with respect to normative developmental functions;
(3) the problem of change in temperament;
(4) the problem of measuring temperament.

A special section is devoted to (5) the constitutional approach to temperament, which dominated the first half of the twentieth century.

The Problem of Defining the Term Temperament

One of the recurrent themes in temperament research is the question of how to define the term temperament. Already in the beginning of the nineteenth century,

Temperament in Childhood   Edited by G.A. Kohnstamm, J.E. Bates and M.K. Rothbart
© 1989 John Wiley & Sons Ltd

physiological- and psychological-based theories of temperament can be distinguished (Henle, 1876; Sigwart, 1887). With respect to their scientific orientation the two groups of theorists were confronted with different problems. Whereas the physiologically oriented temperament theorists aimed at identifying the constitutional basis of what they called temperament, the psychologically oriented theorists attempted to discuss what aspects of psychological functioning should be called temperament.

In addition to the prevailing humoral theories of those times, new approaches favored solid aspects of the bodily constitution such as characteristics of the blood vessels (Haller, 1757) and the nervous system (Wrisberg, 1780) as the determining factor of temperament. On the other side, theorists interested in psychological phenomena referred to principles of what they called 'soul' (Seele), such as principles of sensation and movement (Platner, 1793) or tension and relaxation of life energy (*Lebenskraft*) (Kant, 1798).

Temperament as a Normative Developmental Function

An outstanding advocate of a psychological-based theory of temperament was Carus (1808), who called upon the psychologist not to characterize temperament on a physiological basis but 'to relate his observations with purely psychological conditions' (Carus, 1808, p. 92). Carus was probably not only the first to formulate a psychological-based theory of life-span development, but also provided an early example of the German tradition in developmental psychology that was prominent until the 1960s (see below). This tradition consists of describing periods of human development in terms of temperamental types. According to Carus, and later Lotze (1881), the classical types of temperament reflect natural periods of human development. The sanguine (French) temperament (low excitability threshold, low intensity, low endurance of sensations and affects, easy-mindedness) characterizes childhood; the choleric (Italian) temperament (low excitability threshold, high intensity, low endurance, impatient-mindedness) characterizes adolescence; the melancholic (British) temperament (high excitability threshold, high intensity, high endurance and innermost serious-mindedness) characterizes adulthood; and the phlegmatic (German) temperament (high excitability threshold, low intensity, high endurance, dull- and calm-mindedness) characterizes old age. This tradition of describing normative developmental functions in terms of temperament has been criticized by those who claimed that individual temperament remains stable throughout the life-span (e.g. Sigwart, 1887).

Temperament and Developmental Change

Questions of stability in temperament were the focus of those theorists of the second half of the nineteenth century who were particularly interested in questions of education and schooling. The philosopher and educationist Herbart (1850, 1884) was probably the first to apply a temperament typology to children. Herbart, influenced by Haller's physiology, postulated three systems or factors of the animal or vegetative basis of what he called individuality: the nutritive system, irritability and sensibility. Defects in any of these systems would result in one of the seven temperaments that he postulated, extending the classical four temperaments. For example, a dominance of the sensibility system and a suboptimal functioning of the other two systems was supposed to be the cause of the melancholic child. Herbart's typological approach has been further elaborated by his pupil Strümpell (1844, 1869), who was particularly interested in the role of temperament with respect to education.

In his two-volume *Beiträge zur Charakterologie. Mit besonderer Berücksichtigung pädagogischer Fragen* ('Contribution to characterology. With particular consideration of educational questions'), Bahnsen (1867) addressed problems of conceptualization, defining temperament as 'pure formal–quantitative differences according to the various degrees of spontaneity, receptivity, impressionability and reactivity' (rein formal–quantitative Unterschiede nach den Graden der Spontaneität, Receptivität, Impressionabilität und Reagibilität) (Bahnsen, 1867, p. 20). He also suggested how temperamentally determined characteristics of the child, such as obstinacy, could best be treated.

In the following years a number of books and articles on the relation between temperament and education appeared. However, contrary to the work of Strümpell and Bahnsen, these were less sophisticated, not only as far as the conceptualization of temperament was concerned, but also in the ideas about the relation between temperament or individuality and educational processes.

An example of the educational literature of those days is Hellwig's (1872) book entitled *Die vier Temperamente bei Kindern. Als Anhang: Das Temperament der Eltern, Lehrer und Erzieher* ('The four temperaments with children. As appendix: The temperament of parents, teachers and educationists'). In this widely circulated book (first edition in 1872, thirteenth edition in 1920) Hellwig dealt with ways to optimize education. According to Hellwig, the knowledge of a child's temperament is particularly important because each child reacts differently to the same treatment according to his temperament. Because of his interest in the application of temperament theory he did not care about a scientific clarification of the term. Accordingly, some of his ideas, particularly those concerning the bodily constitution of temperament, which he identified in the warmth of the blood, was already outdated at that time. Although he defined temperament in psychological terms such as quality of receptivity, impressionability and reactivity, his description of the four types of temperament combines formal, content and body aspects such as body structure, physiognomy, colour of skin, motor movement and facial expression.

In summarizing the characteristics of the choleric child for example Hellwig writes that its body can be characterized by: a stout, muscular structure; by keen expressive features; an intense look; a steadfast bearing; a powerful walk; etc. Psychologically, the choleric child is characterized by traits such as stubbornness, pride and pretension.

Hellwig's suggestions for treatment, in the second section of each chapter about a specific temperament type, aims to foster a balance of all four temperaments that will allow the child to react adequately to specific situational demands. According to Hellwig the best way of reaching this goal is diet, contact with other children, the right choice of games and, above all, religion because 'religion dominates the caprices of temperament' (Hellwig, 1889, p. 61).

As a means of identifying a particular type, Hellwig recommended the observation of the child's physiognomic features and his behavior during play. In addition, Hellwig offered data concerning the distribution of the four temperament types among German children: according to his 'subjective impression' 20% of the children were sanguinic, 10% choleric, 5% melancholic and 5% phlegmatic. The rest of the children showed features of two, three or even four of these types. The proportions, however, varied depending upon the climate in which a child developed, his sex, age, nationality and cultural background.

In addition to a temperament type that remains stable throughout the life-span Hellwig also recognized that temperament is subject to modification during development. For example a 'choleric–sanguinic' adolescent is someone who is sanguinic by nature but choleric according to his developmental stage, e.g. adolescence. An example of the relation between a specific type of temperament and education is Salzsieder's (1920) book entitled *Wie habe ich mich bemüht in die Eigenart der Kinder melancholischen Temperaments einzudringen und welche Folgerungen aus diesem Studium für die Behandlung solcher Kinder gezogen?* ('How did I try to fathom the characteristics of melancholic children and what consequences did I derive from these studies for the treatment of these children?'). Since he believed the melancholic temperament to be innate or acquired, he suggested differential education and therapy.

Like most of their contemporaries Hellwig and Salzsieder were not particularly interested in conceptual issues. Aside from the assumption that temperament can be changed through environmental influences, particularly through education, Hellwig, Salzsieder and others shared the same goal of education derived from the ethics of Kant (1803) and Herbart (1851) as well as Christian ethics: a strong character based on morality. It is likely that because of the conceptual weakness and highly ideological character of the suggestions, these early educational studies on temperament in childhood were not particular influential among child psychologists who may have been afraid that their new science would be dominated by those interested in practical questions (see Bühler & Hetzer, 1929).

The Problems of Measuring Temperament

Because of the influence of the experimental psychologists such as Wundt and Fechner and the developmental contributions of physiologists such as Kussmaul and Preyer, measurement considerations became increasingly important for the new discipline of developmental psychology and its neighbouring discipline called experimental education. This discussion also influenced research on temperament in childhood.

Contrary to those who relied on anecdotal illustrations (Niemeyer, 1799; Ziller, 1856) or who, like Hellwig, believed in subjective impressions as a source of data, a number of child psychologists and educationists attempted to improve the measurement of child temperament. For example, Hartmann (1896) discussed the advantages and disadvantages of three methods of studying temperament or, as he himself preferred to say, individuality in the emotional and volitional area. For practical reasons he rejected observations in experimental settings or, in his words, 'to bring children into situations, in which they are forced to express their emotions' (Hartmann, 1896, p. 142). Instead, he propagated longitudinal, systematic observations of the children, because this method was more objective than parent's reports. 'Doting love, lack of confidence in the school, blindness with regard to one's own flesh and blood will be impeding factors' (p. 149). Nevertheless, he developed a parent questionnaire called the 'Annaberger Eltern-Fragebogen' (Annaberger Parents Questionnaire), the parts of which entitled 'affect and volitional life' probably formed the first parent temperament questionnaire in history. The items referred to aspects such as mood (is your child predominantly happy or sad?), excitability (is your child easily upset?), obedience (does he obey easily?) sociability (does he prefer playing alone or with others?) persistence (does he play with one thing for a long time or does he frequently demand new things?) patience (does he show patience when waiting for something?), etc. Hartmann insisted however that such data should only be used in combination with data derived from direct observation.

The Constitutional Approach to Temperament

In the beginning of the twentieth century, the child's temperament or individuality remained in the focus of those interested in questions of education and schooling, whereas most of the child psychologists were interested in the description of general normative developmental functions, particularly in the field of cognition. This was also true for Stern (1928), the founder of differential psychology. He defined temperament as individual differences in the intensity and durability of energies, that manifest themselves in emotions and volition. Because of the formal nature of these differences, Stern argued that they cannot be modified largely by experiences and therefore are of a particular prognostic relevance. In addition, Stern stated that temperamental dispositions not only affect the dynamic of striving, but also influence body structure.

Some years later the idea about a correspondence between temperament and body structure became central in the constitutional concept of temperament that in one way or another was still prominent in Germany after the Second World War. The most famous constitutional typology was that of the German psychiatrist Kretschmer, who published his ideas in a book entitled *Körperbau und Charakter* ('Body structure and character') (Kretschmer, 1931). Putting it simply, Kretschmer found that a *leptosom* body type (slight) is predominant among schizophrenics whereas a *pycnic* body type (plump) is predominant among patients with a cyclical psychosis. Starting from this pathology, Kretschmer postulated that a correspondence between body structure and character also exists in ordinary individuals. Although Kretschmer spoke of character, his primary focus was on temperament: inherited characteristics of an individual's emotional nature (*Affektivität*) including the susceptibility to emotional stimulation, the prevailing mood and aspects of reactivity or dynamic as reflected in speed and rhythm of intellectual as well as motor functioning. Parallel to the two main types of mental illness Kretschmer differentiated between the *schizothymic* and *cyclothymic* temperament. The characteristics of both types of temperament were thought to be the same as for the two mental illnesses but less extreme and obvious. According to Kretschmer, body structure and certain psychological characteristics, in the extreme case, mental diseases, are related because both have the same biological origin: the endocrine–humoral systems.

The constitutional approach, originally conceptualized for adults, was applied to children mainly in three different ways. Some researchers such as Rothe (1927) simply transferred Kretschmer's ideas to childhood although there were warnings because of the dramatic changes of body structure during and after puberty (Homburger, 1926). Another group of researchers, interested in applying typological thinking to children, not only accepted this critique, but also were sceptical of the clear-cut relation between body structure and temperament (Kroh, 1929; Pfahler, 1929). Therefore they concentrated more on psychological functions: in particular styles of cognition that they thought were not explored enough by Kretschmer, such as basic cognitive styles of stimulus perception and information-processing. According to Pfahler, a number of experiments (e.g. simultaneous work, form–color experiments, interpretation of Rorschach blots, association and memory experiments) with 10- to 11-year-old children demonstrated typical ways of 'schizothymic' and 'cyclothymic' information-processing, resulting from individual differences in perseveration (weak–strong) and attention (narrow, focused vs broad, wandering). Together with susceptibility of emotions and prevailing mood, as well as vital energy or activity, perseveration and attention were thought to be inborn or inherited basic functions of personality, supposed to remain stable throughout development.

Finally a third group of researchers combined the constitutional and the developmental approach, thus taking up the thread of the nineteenth-century child-psychology tradition (Conrad, 1941; Zeller, 1952). Particularly the approach of the neurologist Conrad was still prominent in the 1960s. Greatly simplified, Conrad stated in his genetic approach that types of body structure and related temperament traits of the adult can be compared to the physical and psychological characteristics of stages in human development. In terms of Kretschmer's typology the pyknic-cyclothymic type corresponds to a child's and the leptosom–schizothymic type to an adolescent's body structure and character. According to Conrad, these differences between both types were dependent on genetically determined differences in speed of development, a pyknic–cyclothymic type being the result of the so-called conservative development, and the leptosom–schizothymic type being the result of the propulsive or progressive development. The developmental tempo that finally causes the different types was supposed to be present at birth and to exert its influence throughout development.

THE MODERN HISTORY AND CURRENT STATE OF TEMPERAMENT RESEARCH IN CHILDHOOD

The Beginnings of Modern Temperament Research

Despite the abuse of constitutional typology as a 'scientific' justification of racist ideology during the Third Reich and for the liquidation of millions of people with so-called genetically inferior constitutions, this typology was still referred to after the Second World War, as the second edition (1963) of Conrad's book demonstrates. It is therefore not surprising that the beginning of postwar temperament research in German-speaking countries did not take place in Germany, but in Switzerland where Meili and his co-workers started the Bernese longitudinal study in 1952 (Meili & Meili-Dworetzki, 1972). Their research interest was to identify the fundamental, inborn traits that form 'character'. Inborn traits are those that become manifest at a very early age, are relatively stable and appear in very different aspects of behavior. According to Meili (1951) these criteria are met by the traits of temperament – dynamic, stylistic traits that characterize the 'how' of psychological processes and can therefore be addressed as 'process traits'. Meili and his co-workers assumed that the following traits are temperamental in nature:

(1) vitality, the total amount of available energy, already mentioned by Kant (*Lebenskraft*);
(2) intensity, the strength of psychological processes, already mentioned by Wundt (1903) as a main aspect of temperament;
(3) level of communication, the quality of interrelation between subsystems of the personality, a term introduced by Lewin (1946);
(4) level of differentiation, the level of homogeneity of personality.

According to Meili, the list of dynamic traits can be supplemented by other features such as personal tempo, speed and duration of excitation. These are supposed to influence behavioral traits such as persistence and perseveration, latency, susceptibility to stimulation, facility of expression of emotion and, finally, sociability.

The Bernese longitudinal research project was started in 1952 with a sample of 12 1- to 3-month-old infants. Within the following 3 years this sample was enlarged to up to 26 children. Eight years later a second group of 41 10-day-old babies were enrolled in the study. These groups were observed until the children were 16 and 8 years old, respectively. The measures used were maternal interviews, questionnaires and filmed observations in natural (home, kindergarten, school) as well as in laboratory settings. However, the results of the observations during the first year of life must have been disappointing for Meili and his co-workers. Instead of identifying a number of basic dimensions of behavior as he had hoped, Meili realized that these could not be assessed with any validity because of the infants' strong interindividual differences in reaction to the observer and the film situation. However, these observations led the project into a new direction, the search for a general personality variable called 'basic attitude towards objects'. This was first defined as 'difficulty versus easiness of assimilation of new stimuli' (Lang, 1962), and later differentiated into (a) a cognitive factor called 'ability of structuring' and (b) a temperament factor called 'activation' (Meili & Meili-Dworetzki, 1972). It was hypothesized that the increase of activation when confronted with unfamiliar situations is a constant factor of personality that accounts for the observed relation between irritability in the first year, timidity at 6 and inhibition by the experimental situation at 8 and 15.

As far as temperament research in Germany after the Second World War is concerned, there are obvious reasons why in both parts of Germany, psychology in general, and developmental psychology in particular, followed different roads.

In the German Democratic Republic (GDR) Pavlovian nervous system typology (see Chapter 3, by Strelau) was referred to when temperament was discussed. This was also true for Schmidt-Kolmer (1970) and her co-workers, who outlined a program for nursery education. They differed, however, from Pavlov in stating that the characteristics of the higher nervous system are supposed to change during the course of the first 3 years, not only through maturation but also through the influence of education. The strong, balanced and mobile type, the sanguine in Hippocratic terms, was given the highest credit and hence the aim of nursery education. In addition to this application of Pavlovian typology to nursery education almost no research on temperament in childhood has been carried out by developmental psychologists in the GDR, at least as far as I know. To compensate for this a book by Strelau was translated and published in 1984.

As far as the Federal Republic of Germany (FRG) is concerned, there was also little research on temperament in childhood in the postwar years until the 1970s, as various content analyses of journal publications reveal (for instance, Nickel, 1980). As in other countries the term temperament had disappeared almost completely from psychological textbooks, in particular from those dealing with developmental psychology. As Nickel (1980) pointed out, postwar child psychology in Germany took as a point of departure the research of the 1920s, when little attention was paid to non-cognitive development. In addition, the orientation during the 1950s towards depth psychology did not favor research in this area. Only some practically oriented researchers who were interested in the psychological consequences for children living in postwar Germany referred to some specific temperament concepts (Coerper, Hagen & Thomae, 1954; Harnack, 1958). These studies concentrated mainly on school-age children.

One study, which appeared in the second half of the 1960s, will be presented in some detail, not only because it deals with temperament in infancy, but also because it is an early German example of postwar temperament research that approached international research standards. Although he did not use the word temperament, Schmidt (1966) focused on a prominent problem of current research, namely the validity of caregiver questionnaire ratings of infant personality. A total of 175 infants (6, 16 and 26 weeks old) were rated by their nurses on 31 characteristics, 28 of which were temperamental in nature. Independent of the infant's age, four dimensions resulted from factor analysis which Schmidt interpreted as (a) lively activity, (b) tension vs relaxation, (c) excitability and (d) social orientation. For the resulting secondary factors he used Eysenck's terms, extraversion and emotionality. The fact that the infants' behavioral repertoire developed and differentiated considerably during that age period, whereas the adults' rating patterns in this study did not, made Schmidt suggest that his results said more about the reality of dimensions in adults' rating patterns than about the reality of dimensions in infant personality. Although this particular argument is not convincing because Schmidt limited his observations mainly to sensorimotor behavior, his way of questioning the true meaning of data obtained from raters is very relevant for today's methodological discussions on the value of parental and teacher ratings.

In the same year that Schmidt published his article, a number of German researchers demonstrated their interest in questions of family socialization processes, in particular in the effects of parental styles of child-rearing (e.g. Herrmann, 1966). Like most of their colleagues working in other areas of psychology these researchers increasingly adopted North American ideas, in particular those new and basic assumptions of developmental psychology that became crucial for temperament research: the idea of the transactional character of parent–child relation (Bell, 1968; Harper, 1971) and the idea of early existing interindividual differences (Escalona, 1968; Thomas, Chess, Birch, Hertzig & Korn 1963). However, even these authors were very reluctant to use the word temperament, particularly so because they were not interested in questions of temperament *per se* but in parental concepts of child personality that also included aspects such as motivation and social skills (e.g. Engfer & Schneewind, 1975). Aside from family socialization, the growing interest of German developmental psychologists in the biological determinants of childhood development directed their attention to the role of infant individuality or temperament.

Current Research on Temperament in Childhood

In doing a computer search of German-language literature on temperament in childhood between 1977 and 1987, only 12 articles and books could be identified, including translations of American and English books such as Thomas and Chess's (1977) *Temperament and development* and Rutter's (1975) book *Helping troubled children*. On the other hand, English-language publications by German authors as well as a number of unpublished studies were not (yet) included. However, presently there is a growing interest in this area, as some indicators reveal. First, the number of publications including temperament concepts is increasing rapidly. Secondly, the word temperament is reappearing in handbooks of psychology and in subject indexes of textbooks on developmental psychology. Thirdly, meetings and working groups dealing with problems of temperament have been organized. There was an interdisciplinary workshop on the diagnosis of temperament at the Center For Interdisciplinary Research in Bielefeld in 1987 and a working group of German developmental psychologists discussed the role of temperament in child development at their Eighth National Meeting at Bern.

As to the main content areas of temperament research in the FRG, most studies focus on temperament with respect to maternal responsiveness (Engfer & Gavranidou, 1987; Meyer, 1985; Rennen-Allhoff & Reinhard, 1988), and the development of relationships within families, such as mother–child relationships (Grossmann, Grossmann, Spangler, Suess & Unzner, 1985; Meyer, 1985, 1988a) and marital relationships (Engfer, 1988; Meyer, 1988a). Another area addressed by a number of researchers is the influence of temperament on the development of action and mastery motivation (Lütkenhaus, 1987; Lütkenhaus, Grossmann & Grossmann, 1985; Spangler, 1987; Unzner, 1987; Spangler, Bräutigam & Stadler, 1984). A third topic of current temperament research is the problem of parentally defined difficultness, its antecedents and age-related changes (Engfer & Gavranidou, 1986; Engfer, Gavranidou & Heinig, 1986). The rest of the publications address cultural correlations of infant temperament (Beller, Eckert & Kuckartz, 1986), its relation to psychic stress in children in hospital (Saile, 1989) and differences in temperament between first- and second-born siblings as perceived by their mothers (Meyer, 1986).

Evaluation of Current Research and Future Direction

Although there is growing interest in including temperament variables in developmental studies, none of the researchers is interested in questions of temperament as such. In addition, some authors mentioned above are still reserved in the use of the term temperament because of its history-laden connotations, and instead prefer to speak of individuality or emotional dispositions. In sum, the psychology of temperament has not yet become a distinct field of German developmental psychology.

Partly because of the lack of interest in conceptual issues, German developmentalists rely exclusively on concepts developed by North American researchers (see Meyer, 1988b). The two related concepts of negative emotionality and difficultness as formulated by Thomas and Chess and by Bates are the specific concepts most widely used in the studies mentioned above.

In addition to the adoption of modern American temperament concepts, German researchers rely almost entirely on methods developed by their American colleagues. As in the USA, temperament concepts are mainly measured through parent questionnaires either by Thomas/Chess and Carey or by Bates (Infant Characteristics Questionnaire). However, there are almost as many German versions of these questionnaires as there are researchers involved in temperament studies. Obviously, this complicates comparisons of results not only within the German community of developmentalists, but also with respect to findings reported by North American researchers.

Although one might regret the current exclusive orientation of temperament research in the FRG on ideas and methods developed in the USA, it should also be realized that exactly these ideas and methods revitalized the interest of German developmentalists in childrens' individuality. However, it seems the time has come to study also the ideas and methods developed by Eastern theorists in order to see if an integration is possible and to remember the great German history of thought and research in psychology and psychiatry which reveals the roots of many of our present concepts, methods and fundamental questions. Finally, temperament research in Germany on children is almost exclusively the field of developmental psychology. Experience from other countries suggests that it would be fruitful if colleagues from other fields such as pediatrics, behavioral genetics and education would participate in this area of research.

REFERENCES

Bahnsen, J. (1867). *Beiträge zur Charakterologie*. Leipzig: Brockhaus.
Bell, R.Q. (1968). A reinterpretation of the direction of effects in studies of socialization.

Psychological Review, **75**, 81–95.

Beller, E.K., Eckert, A. & Kuckartz, U. (1986). Some cultural and situational correlates of infant temperament as assessed by German and Turkish mothers living in Berlin. In G.A. Kohnstamm (Ed.), *Temperament discussed* (pp. 133–139). Lisse (Neth.): Swets & Zeitlinger.

Bühler, C. & Hertzer, H. (1929). Zur Geschichte der Kinderpsychologie. In E. Brunswik, C. Bühler, H. Hetzer, L. Kardos, E. Köhler, J. Krug & A. Willwoll (Eds), *Beiträge zur Problemgeschichte der Psychologie: Festschrift zu Karl Bühler* (pp. 204–224). Jena: Fischer.

Carus, F.A. (1808). *Psychologie: Zweiter Band.* Leipzig: Barth & Kummer.

Coerper, C., Hagen, W. & Thomae, H. (1954). *Deutsche Nachkriegskinder.* Stuttgart: Thieme.

Conrad, K. (1941). *Der Konstitutionstypus als genetisches Problem.* Berlin: Springer.

Engfer, A. (1986). Antecedents of behaviour problems in infancy. In G.A. Kohnstamm (Ed.), *Temperament discussed* (pp. 165–180). Lisse (Neth.): Swets & Zeitlinger.

Engfer, A. (1988). The interrelatedness of marriage and the mother–child relationship. In R.A. Hinde & J. Stevenson-Hinde (Eds), *Relationships within families* (pp. 104–118). Oxford: Oxford University Press.

Engfer, A. & Gavranidou, M. (1987). Antecedents and consequences of maternal sensitivity: A longitudinal study. In H. Rauh & H.C. Steinhausen (Eds), *Psychobiology and early development* (pp. 71–99). Amsterdam: North Holland.

Engfer, A., Gavranidou, M. & Heinig, L. (1986). Stability and change in perceived characteristics of children 4 to 43 months of age. Paper presented at the Second European Conference on Developmental Psychology, Rome, Italy.

Engfer, A. & Schneewind, K.A. (1975). Elterliches Erziehungsverhalten und kindliche Persönlichkeit. In H. Lukesch (Ed.), *Auswirkungen elterlicher Erziehungsstile* (pp. 72–95). Göttingen: Hogrefe.

Escalona, S.K. (1968). *Roots of individuality.* Chicago: Aldine.

Grossmann, K., Grossmann, K.E., Spangler, G., Suess, G. & Unzner, L. (1985). Maternal sensitivity and newborn's orientation responses as related to quality of attachment in northern Germany. In I. Bretherton & E. Waters (Eds), *Growing points in attachment theory and research. Society for Research in Child Development Monographs,* Special issue. Serial No. 209, **50**(1–2), 233–256.

Haller, A.V. (1757). *Elementa psychologiae corporis humani.* Lausanne: Bousquet.

Harnack, G.A.v. (1958), *Nervöse Verhaltensstörungen beim Schulkind.* Stuttgart: Thieme.

Harper, L.V. (1971). The young as a stimulus controlling caretaker behavior. *Developmental Psychology,* **4**, 74–88.

Hartmann, B. (1896). *Die Analyse des kindlichen Gedankenkreises als die naturgemässe Grundlage des ersten Schulunterrichts.* Leipzig: Kesselringsche Hofbuchhandlung, (E.v. Mayer) Verlag.

Henle, J. (1876). *Anthropologische Vorträge: Ertes Heft.* Braunschweig: Vieweg & Sohn.

Herbart, J.F. (1850). *Lehrbuch zur Psychologie.* Leipzig: Voss.

Herbart, J.F. (1851). *Schriften zur Pädagogik.* Leipzig: Voss.

Herbart, J.F. (1884). (Ed. K. Richter) *Briefe über Anwendung der Psychologie auf die Pädagogik.* Leipzig: Sigismund & Volkening.

Hellwig, B. (1872). *Die vier Temperamente bei Kindern.* Paderborn: Esser.

Herrmann, T. (Ed.) (1966). *Psychologie der Erziehungsstile.* Göttingen: Hogrefe.

Homburger, A. (1926). *Psychopathologie des Kindesalters.* Berlin.

Kant, J. (1798). *Anthropologie in pragmatischer Hinsicht.* Königsberg: Fr. Nicolovius.

Kant, J. (1803). *Über Pädagogik.* Königsberg: Fr. Nicolovius.

Kretschmer, E. (1921). *Körperbau und Charakter.* Berlin: Springer.

Kroh, O. (1929). Experimentelle Beiträge zur Typenkunde. *Zeitschrift für Psychologie und Physiologie der Sinnesorgane, Ergänzungsband 14.*

Lang, A. (1962). Von der 'Störbarkeit' zur 'Schüchternheit' in der Entwicklung des Kindes: II. Konstanz vom ersten ins achte Jahr. *Schweizer Zeitschrift für Psychologie,* **21**, 113–125.

Lewin, K. (1946). Behavior and development as a function of the total situation. In L. Carmichael (Ed.), *Manual of child psychology* (pp. 918–970). New York: Wiley.

Lotze, R.H. (1881). *Grundzüge der Psychologie*. Leipzig: Hirzel.

Lütkenhaus, P. (1987). Konstitutionelle Faktoren des Leistungshandelns. Paper presented at the 8. Tagung Entwicklungspsychologie, Bern.

Lütkenhaus, P., Grossmann, K. & Grossmann, K.E. (1985). Transactional influences of infants' orienting ability and maternal cooperation on competition in three-year-old children. *International Journal of Behavioral Development, 8*, 257–272.

Meili, R. (1951). *Lehrbuch der psychologischen Diagnostik*. Bern: Huber.

Meili, R. & Meili-Dworetzki, G. (1972). *Grundlagen individueller Persönlichkeitsunterschiede*. Bern: Huber.

Meyer, H.-J. (1985). *Zur emotionalen Beziehung zwischen Müttern und ihren erst- und zweitgeborenen Kindern*. Regensburg: Roderer.

Meyer, H.-J. (1986). Mothers perception of their first- and secondborn's temperament. In G.A. Kohnstamm (Ed.), *Temperament discussed* (pp. 107–114). Lisse (Neth.): Swets & Zeitlinger.

Meyer, H.-J. (1988a). Marital and mother–child relationship: Developmental history, parent personality, and child difficultness. In R.A. Hinde & J. Stevenson-Hinde (Eds), *Relationships within families* (pp. 119–139). Oxford: Oxford University Press.

Meyer, H.-J. (1988b). Temperament. In R. Asanger & G. Wenninger (Eds). *Handwörterbuch Psychologie* (pp. 777–782). München: Psychologie Verlags Union.

Nickel, H. (1980). Child psychology: A review of 30 years of research in the Federal Republic of Germany. *German Journal of Psychology, 4*, 313–334.

Niemeyer, A.H. (1799). *Grundsätze der Erziehung und des Unterrichts für Eltern, Hauslehrer und Schulmänner*. Halle: Waisenhaus.

Pfahler, G. (1929). *System der Typenlehre*. Leipzig: Ambrosius Barth.

Platner, E. (1793). *Philosophische Aphorismen*. Leipzig: Schwichert.

Rennen-Allhoff, B. & Reinhard, H.G. (1988). Temperament von Säuglingen, mütterliches Verhalten und spätere Entwicklung. *Acta Paedopsychiatrica, 51*, 56–59.

Rothe, K.C. (1927). Beobachtungen über Körperbau und Charakter bei Knaben. *Zeitschrift für Kinderforschung, 33*, 223–248.

Rutter, M. (1975). *Helping troubled children*. Harmondsworth: Penguin.

Saile, H. (1989). Zur Erfassung des Temperaments bei Kindern. *Praxis der Kinderpsychologie und Kinderpsychiatrie*.

Salzsieder, P. (1920). Wie habe ich mich bemüht in die Eigenart der Kinder melancholischen Temperaments einzudringen und welche Folgerungen aus diesem Studium für die Behandlung solcher Kinder gezogen? *Zeitschrift für Kinderforschung, 25*, 293–324.

Schmidt, G. (1966). Untersuchungen über Eigenschaftsbeurteilungen von Säuglingen durch Erwachsene. *Archiv für die gesamte Psychologie, 118*, 195–228.

Schmidt-Kolmer, E. (Ed.) (1970). *Pädagogische Aufgaben und Arbeitsweise der Krippen*. Berlin: VEB Verlag Volk und Gesundheit.

Sigwart, C. (1887). Temperament. In K.A. Schmid (Ed.), *Encyclopädie des gesamten Erziehungs- und Unterrichtswesens*, Bd 9 (pp. 399–420). Leipzig: Wunderlich.

Spangler, G. (1987). Zusammenhänge zwischen emotionaler Disposition, alltäglicher Interaktionserfahrungen und kindliche Kompetenzentwicklung im zweiten Lebensjahr: Die Bedeutung von emotional belastenden Situationen. Paper presented at the 8. Tagung Entwicklungspsychologie, Bern.

Spangler, G., Bräutigam, I. & Stadler, R. (1984). Handlungsentwicklung in der frühen Kindheit und ihre Abhängigkeit von der kognitiven Entwicklung und der emotionalen Erregbarkeit des Kindes. *Zeitschrift für Entwicklungspsychologie und Pädagogische Psychologie, 16*, 181–193.

Stern, W. (1928). *Psychologie der frühen Kindheit*. Leipzig: Barth.

Strelau, J. (1984). *Das Temperament in der psychischen Entwicklung*. Berlin: Volk und Wissen Volkseigener Verlag.

Strümpell, L.H. (1844). *Die Verschiedenheit der Kindernaturen*. Dorpat: Severin B.

Strümpell, L.H. (1869). Erziehungsfragen gemeinverständlich erörtert. Leipzig: Verlag für erz. Unterricht.

Thomas, A. & Chess, S. (1977). *Temperament and development*. New York: Brunner/Mazel.

Thomas, A., Chess, S., Birch, H.G., Hertzig, M.E. & Korn, S. (1963). *Behavioral individuality in early childhood*. New York: University Press.

Unzner, L. (1987). Handlungsentwicklung im zweiten Lebensjahr: Der Einfluss des Kindlichen Temperaments und der mütterlichen Feinfühligkeit. Paper presented at the 8. Tagung Entwicklungspsychologie, Bern.

Wrisberg, H.A. (1780). *Primae lineae physiologiae in usum praelectionum academicarum*. Goettingae: Joan Christian Dieterich.

Wundt, W. (1903). *Grundzüge der physiologischen Psychologie*, Bd 3. Leipzig: Barth.

Zeller, W. (1952). *Konstitution und Entwicklung*. Göttingen: Hogrefe.

Ziller, T. (1856). *Einleitung in die allgemeine Pädagogik*. Leipzig: Teubner.

32

The Psychology of Character and Temperament in Italy: A Historical Review and Recent Trends

GRAZIA ATTILI
Consiglio Nazionale delle Ricerche, Rome

The study of temperament in Italy partly mirrors the history of psychology in this country. According to whether temperament was studied or not at the time, scientific contribution reflects the influences on it of approaches coming from disciplines other than psychology; the influences of foreign cultural and scientific tradition on Italian psychology; and more than for any other topic of research, influences of the political and ideological milieu which have always greatly affected the choice of research topics in Italy and the way they are conceptualized and studied.

In the past, studies on temperament in infants and children were very rare and usually were not based on original conceptualizations. Interesting and successful theories were formulated in the field of adult characterology and even though this handbook is about temperament in childhood it is worth reviewing them, first because they often found an application in child psychology and, second, because they greatly affected general scientific attitudes towards this field. Within a chronological framework, it is possible to review studies on and conceptualizations of temperament according to four broad periods which parallel those characterizing Italian psychology:

(1) The period before 1870, greatly affected by philosophical and psychiatric contributions.
(2) The time between 1870 and 1905, when German psychology started to influence Italian psychology and to give it a scientific connotation but with psychological thought (and the psychology of temperament) still strongly under the umbrella of philosophy, anthropology, physiology, psychiatry.

Temperament in Childhood   Edited by G.A. Kohnstamm, J.E. Bates and M.K. Rothbart
© 1989 John Wiley & Sons Ltd

(3) The time between 1905 and 1945: psychological research was carried out using scientific methods and under laboratory conditions, at the beginning under the influence of French and German psychology and then, according to the requirements of fascism (between 1930 and 1945), with the emphasis on national traditions and out of touch with the psychological work carried out in other countries. Original psychological interest in temperament (and character) was mainly in terms of conceptualizing it with interesting research work on temperament coming from physiology.

(4) The time after the Second World War till very recently: this period is characterized by the end of idealistic philosophical tradition – which had influenced psychology in the past – and by the increasing influence of Marxist thought and democratic ideas. The latter led to the neglect and even rejection of psychological research topics that emphasized man's hereditary and genetic factors such as temperament, because these theoretical positions had been used, immediately before and during the war, to support racist doctrines. For this reason and because of the increasing influence of North American psychology (mainly American behaviourism), Italian psychology's conceptualizations have been characterized by a strong emphasis on the influence of environmental factors. Just very recently interest in temperament is again appearing, mainly because of Thomas and Chess's work.

THE CONSTITUTIONAL APPROACH

The Hippocratic Theory of Humours

Until 1870 both in Italy, and in other countries, there was no psychology which might be considered scientific. Nevertheless by the end of the last century psychological phenomena were being studied. Around that time, contributions to psychology came from other disciplines such as philosophy and psychiatry. Temperament was conceptualized within theories reflecting philosophical and medical perspectives. The typology was that described by Hippocrates (460 BC), and by Galen (129–201 AD), influenced by the theory of Hempedocles. According to them, there are four temperaments, each related to a bodily humour and to a cosmic element: a melancholic temperament, associated with black bile, and with cold and dry earth; a sanguine temperament, associated with blood, and with dry and humid air; a choleric temperament, associated with yellow bile, and with dry and hot fire; a phlegmatic temperament, associated with phlegm, and with humid and cold water. It should be said that these Hippocratic types were in vogue for a long time and were acknowledged as valid even by Pavlov and Eysenck. This system – based on focusing on the relations between physical constitution, disposition to illnesses and behaviour, and on the assumption that common elements are shared by body and character – was used, and not only in Italy, precisely in classifying adults, and non-human primates (see Figure 1). Further-more, the term temperament was, at that time and long afterwards, interchangeable with character. In fact since ancient times till the 1930s (when personality started to

FIGURE 1 The four temperaments of anthropoid primates. Clockwise, from top left: the sanguine orang-utan; the melancholic gibbon; the choleric gorilla; the phlegmatic chimpanzee. (From N. Pende (1947) *La scienza moderna della persona umana*. Milano: Garzanti)

be studied systematically), temperament and character were very distinct concepts, the first one referring to constitutional and hereditary dispositions, the second to the result of environmental influences leading constitutional factors to develop as well as to change. But although the two terms had a different meaning, temperament and character were used by theorists as synonyms.

The Morphological Phase

By the end of the last century (around 1870) the fame of the new scientific German psychology – based on experimental research work carried out in psychological laboratories – started to spread through Europe and the United States. In Italy too, scientifically oriented psychological thought started to develop. Nevertheless psychological contributions continued to be made under the umbrella of philosophy, anthropology, physiology and psychiatry. Contributions to the psychology of character were given at that time (and even up to 1945) by physicians. Typology of character or of temperament (morphological, physio-logical, morpho-physio-psychological typologies) was based on observation, sometimes of normal individuals, but often of individuals affected by pathological disturbances. The choice of these subjects was based on the hypothesis that pathology caricatures normal typology and makes observation easier.

Notable scientific work was carried out under the leadership of De Giovanni (1891) and Pilo (1892) and a new term was adopted to replace the word 'temperament', i.e. 'constitution'. In fact, according to these scholars (whose approach was very similar to that of Sigaud in France around 1900), human morphology, i.e. the body's constitution, is responsible for psychological types. As De Giovanni (1891) wrote, the cause of *morbilita*, the pathology of temperaments, is the morphology of the organism. He held that the organization and anatomical distribution of the nervous system affect the way individuals feel and react to stimuli, leading to individual differences in temperament. The nervous system affects other systems such as the general alimentary system but the extent of this influence is modulated by an individual's organic dispositions due to her/his morphology.

The Physiognomical Approach

At the very end of the last century and the beginning of this one (1870–1905) studies on psychological types were still being carried out mainly under the umbrella of disciplines other than psychology. A great, although very questionable and often questioned, contribution was made by a psychiatrist, Cesare Lombroso, who somehow 'invented' a new scientific field, Criminal Anthropology. In 1905 Lombroso even founded a Journal, *Archivio di Psichiatria, Antropologia Criminale e Scienze Penali per servire allo studio dell'uomo alienato e delinquente*, the aim of which was – according to the positivistic ideology of the time – to contribute to the utilization of scientific knowledge. It was mainly aimed at giving support to legislative reforms involving asylums and prisons. Lombroso's concepts had a great success not only in Italy but also in many European countries. His importance nowadays is mainly related to the fact that it was partly his concepts which caused the longlasting rejection of approaches devoted to studying anything linked to hereditary and genetic dispositions.

Lombroso (1876, 1893), held that criminals have an inherited, constitutional morphological habitus which differs from normal men's and that insanity is found in such people. His view was that this sort of people's perverse instincts are hereditary and impossible to change. Size and shape of the skull, and of the face and other parts of the body, produced a typology which included: the born vagabond (*vagabondo nato*), the wandering imbecile (*imbecille vagabondo*), the womanly type (*tipo femmineo*), the born spy (*spia nata*), the born criminal genius (*genio reo nato*), and the normal or criminal madman (*pazzo normale e reo*). Criminals and madmen were characterized by prognathism and by a spheroid, pentagonoid and rhomboid skull (in normal men the skull is helixoidal). Lombroso described the criminal morphology thus: the ears, upper jaw, crest of the forehead and eye-sockets are bigger than in normal men; the nose is long and crooked; the lips are protruding and thick; the hair is dark; there is no beard; the eyes are two-coloured or blue, or green. These physical traits are associated with insensitivity to physical and psychological pain; absence of moral sense; impulsiveness; courage; morbid, intense and inconsistent emotions; propensity to take revenge; and cruelty towards others. There is an interesting description of a young girl 9 years of age, Luisa C.:

> She has weak intelligence, bad instincts, high level of distractibility, tantrums, propensity to steal since the age of three; she wanders around and screams without any reason, throws away dolls and socks; is highly excitable ... Her father is mad.... Her type is the born criminal: Down's syndrome physiognomy, enormous jaw and cheekbones, prognathism, flat nose. (Lombroso, 1893)

The ideology underlying these concepts is clearly racist and classist. Nevertheless Lombroso had the merit of promoting a psychological interest in the problem of madness and criminality. In fact his empirical approach to the study of 'criminals' as individuals with psychological and psychopathological problems took the place of the traditional approach of studying 'the crime' solely as an action and only on theoretical grounds. Many psychiatrists and neurologists of his time were asked by the court to give an expert opinion and psychological classification of criminals. The opinion delivered to the court by a neurologist, Colucci (1907) about a Neapolitan sculptor who murdered his wife out of jealousy is well known. Lombroso himself was asked by the court to give an expert opinion on a man, Alberto Olivo, who in Milan in 1903, in a state of epileptic unconsciousness, murdered his wife. This case became a famous one, both for the murderer being discharged by the court due to a procedural error and for the autobiography later written by Olivo in which he accused his deceased wife of having ruined his life by her difficult and violent temperament. Lombroso, in a book written together with Olivo's lawyer (Lombroso & Bianchi, 1905) stated that Olivo had to be considered innocent, because he was an irresponsible madman who had inherited his epilepsy and madness from his parents. The authors advised putting Olivo in an asylum and not in prison, neither of which actually happened. After Lombroso, 'criminal psychology' became a new research field in psychology, even though subsequently criminal psychologists, particularly Gemelli (1946), were definitively anti-Lombrosian. The link between criminality and pathological disturbances of the character was also analyzed in studies concerning childhood and adolescence by Lombroso himself (1894) and by Ferrari (1914). The latter stressed the contribution of innate predisposition and alterations to the character to the formation of a criminal personality in adolescence.

Functionalism and Biotypology

In the first half of this century (until the end of the Second World War), psychologists in Italy were 'scientifically' oriented, that is they based their research work on experiments carried out in laboratory situations. Temperament and character were viewed as too complex topics to be studied by means of experiments. Works on temperament by psychologists were for this reason mainly theoretical and reflect, as we will see later, the idealistic philosophy of that time. Nevertheless some interesting empirical work on the character of infants and children was carried out by child psychologists and psychiatrists (Bonaventura, 1930, 1936; De Sanctis, 1925) in order to demonstrate the applicability of experimental methods in characterology. The acknowledged influence on these works was European, Latin American and Anglo-Saxon tradition: the aim was to focus on the functions through which character can be traced (attention, imitation, influenceability) rather than to identify extreme types, as was popular in German psychology.

Attention and imitation, for example, were studied by means of experiments in 7- to 12-month-olds. Attention was studied in terms of initial reaction to stimuli and its changes during human development: two groups were identified, one initially interrupting their action, being slow in adapting, and having fixed attention, and the other quickly adapting and having mobile attention. Differences were considered constitutional and it was stressed that, even though in the course of life character is transformed by living conditions and socializing factors such as family and school, some original constitutional 'nucleus' is retained all life long (Bonaventura, 1936). According to this model, attentional inconsistency in adolescents is explained in terms of an encephalopathy based on hereditary predisposition (Bonaventura, 1936).

Contribution to the study of adult temperament was still being made by scholars coming from those disciplines which could also base their theories on empirical evidence. Notable work was done by a physiologist, Nicola Pende, who focused on the relationship between the endocrines and the conditions of the mind and body. He labelled his theory 'human bio-typology' (Pende, 1939). He held that all aspects of the human being, that is constitution, temperament, character and intelligence, are not separate, independent parts and should thus be studied as a whole. His typology was based on the morphological typology of Viola (1906), although he stressed psychological characteristics. As he said, at the basis of human morphological biotypes are two pillars, one functional and one psychological. Temperament is the dynamic aspect of a person. According to Pende, endocrine

FIGURE 2 The four human morphological–dynamic biotypes in the art of Albrecht Dürer. From left to right: St John (*asthenic longilineous*); St Peter (*sthenic brevilineous*); St Marc (*asthenic brevilineous*); St Paul (*sthenic longilineous*). (From N. Pende (1947). *La scienza moderna della persona umana*. Milano: Garzanti.)

variations are linked to morphological and functional characters: each type is based on one endocrine gland prevailing over another one and morphologically on the ratio between skull and face, and between the upper part of the body and the legs. His classification comprised four types (see Figure 2):

(1) *Sthenic longilineous (longilinei stenici)*: They have a hyperthyroid constitution, 'longitudinal diameters of the body in excess over the horizontal
diameters,... thinness hardly overcome by hypernutrition,... diminished
carbohydrate tolerance,... accelerated metabolism, irritability of the
vegetative nervous system,... marked psychic irritability, hypermotivity,
cerebral restlessness,... prococious and pronounced development of intelligence'.

(2) *Asthenic longilineous (longilinei astenici)*: They have hyposurrenal or hypo-
genital constitution; they are tachypsychics and heretistics.

(3) *Sthenic brevilineous (brevilinei stenici)*: They have hypersurrenal and hyper-
genital constitution; they are slow and consistent, sociable, warm and
euphoric.

(4) *Asthenic brevilineous (brevilinei astenici)*: They have hypothyroid constitution; they are stable, slow and depressive.

Pende's typology has much in common with German psychiatrists' classifications
such as that of Kretschmer (1951) – which was to influence much of Italian
psychiatry – and with Hippocrates' typology: the *longilineous* type is similar to
Kretschmer's *leptosomeous–schyzothymic* and to Hippocrates' *habitus phtisicus;*
brevilineous is similar to Kretschmer's *pycnic–cyclothymic* and to Hippocrates'
habitus apoplecticus. Pende's typology had a great success but was very soon
criticized because of the difficulty of making objective physiological measures in
this field.

IDEALISM AND THE CRISIS OF TYPOLOGY

In about the 1930s Italian psychologists, under the influence of idealism in
philosophy and of Gestalt theory in psychology, started to criticize constitutionalist
typologies. No empirical work was done by them, but their critical approach to
temperament and character led to some original conceptualizations.

Gemelli (1930, 1931, 1947, 1948), one of the fathers of Italian psychology, followed
a functional-dynamic approach, concluding that man should be studied as a whole.
He claimed that typologies cannot be taken too seriously given that similar
characteristics can be found in different types. Psychology should not aim to
describe a character's structure. Instead it should provide evidence of the psychological processes underlying behaviour. According to Gemelli it is not necessary to
know the causes of character (constitution, inheritance, biochemistry). The psychological factors causing individuals to react and to adapt to the environment should
be studied. Character is shaped by an individual's reactions to the social environment. It is plastic and modifiable. It is a psychological process unifying every
psychological activity which is the result of reacting to the environment.

Gemelli's approach can be considered clinical and led him within criminology to
promote a 'clinic of criminal acts' based on the rejection of temperament classifications and personality typologies (Gemelli, 1948).

Temperament typologies came under criticism from many other psychologists. It
was said that typologies were too many and contradictory (German typologies of

temperament had been imported into Italy); empirical measures were hard to find; on the basis of available classifications individual diagnoses were impossible to trace: clear-cut types were found only in pathological patients, not in normal people (Metelli, 1950). According to Iacono (G. Iacono, personal communication, 1988), a paper by Berlucchi (1944) can be considered crucial in determining the end of scientific interest in character by Italian psychologists. Berlucchi, reviewing studies on personality, stressed the extent to which the temperament concept is useless and unacceptable insofar as it is too reductive. In fact it does not take into account the complex mixture of elements within each type. Furthermore, according to Berlucchi, even a genetic theory of personality should take into account the fact that multiple factors, including instincts as well as motivations, intelligence as well as feelings, influence it from the very early ages in a continuous interactive process between psychological life and the environment.

FROM TYPES TO STEREOTYPES

The above criticisms of the concept of temperament, the influence of American psychology, mainly of behaviourism, and the democratic ideology and milieu brought postwar Italian psychologists in the 1950s to reject the concept of temperament and character and to focus on the extent to which environmental, social and cultural conditions (indigence, climate), and ethnic and group stereotypes influence personality development. Iacono (1968), for example, studied the influence of environmental conditions on the character of southern Italian people; Fonzi (1956), the formation of stereotypes related to southern people; Piro (1956), the influence of stereotypes on personality development (by means of a longitudinal study on mulattos living in Naples, from birth to 12 years of age); and De Rita and Iacono (1964), the effects of indigence on peasants' personality.

Temperament has been studied only as a part of personality, which is in any case investigated by means of scales and questionnaires imported from the United States, such as the TAT by Murray, the Zulliger Z-Test, the Rorschach, the Rosenzweig test, and the PARI by Schaefer and Bell (Nencini, 1959; Nencini & Misiti, 1956). Some empirical studies on temperament were carried out but just in order to gain further evidence on non-Italian typologies such as that of Sheldon and Stevens (1942) – based on the relations between morphological and psychological variables (endomorphism–viscerotony; mesomorphism–somatotony; ectomorphism–cerebrotony (De Grada, 1958). Original contributions and conceptualizations were lacking, even though interest in temperament was proved by some handbooks on character reviewing (mainly non-Italian) methods for assessing it in children (Falorni, 1967).

RECENT STUDIES ON TEMPERAMENT

A renewed interest in basic personality traits is very recent and is characterized by temperament studied as an intervening variable or as part of a causal loop affecting social behaviour and human development. No attention is paid in these studies to neurological and/or physiological correlates of temperamental characteristics, nor to pathological deviations.

On the basis of the assumption that to assess how relationships vary with the characteristics of participants is one way of understanding the interconnection between relationships and individual characteristics, temperament is studied by us as an intervening variable affecting and being affected by the nature of relationships which children form in different contexts with different partners (mother, father and siblings at home; peers and teachers at preschool).

The Interface Between Temperament and Relationships: An Italian Study

Temperament, Development and Cultural Variability

In our study temperament – conceptualized according to the contribution by Thomas and Chess (1977) – was assessed by means of questionnaires (the Behavioral Style Questionnaire, BSQ; McDevitt & Carey, 1978) given to mothers and to fathers. By using a North American scale many culturally related problems had to be faced in advance. These problems concerned the assessment of the construct validity of the BSQ in a country other than the United States and the cultural variability of human behaviour, style of behaviour and expectations concerning the 'norm' of behaviour.

The BSQ was translated by us, and validated and standardized on an Italian population of 327 children aged between 3 and 7 years (M = 153, F = 174). Questionnaires were sent to mothers living in three different Italian towns. There were 84 parents in Turin (a northern Italian town), 177 in Rome (a central Italian town) and 66 in Naples (a southern Italian town). The age distribution of the children was as follows: 3.0–3.11, n = 50; 4.0–4.11, n = 78; 5.0–5.11, n = 86; 6.0–6.11, n = 70; 7.0–7.6, n = 43. All the parents belonged to middle or low-middle social class.

Thirty-three items were eliminated from the BSQ since they were not homogeneous at our correlation matrices and factorial analysis. Children's temperamental dimensions were not perceived by Italian mothers in terms of item configurations similar to those perceived by American mothers. Furthermore, Italian children's temperaments differed slightly from those found by McDevitt and Carey in their American children: Italian children seem to be more active (mean = 4.51 vs 3.56), less intense (mean = 4.01 vs 4.52), less adaptable (mean = 2.85 vs 2.55) and more sensitive (Sensory-Perceptual Threshold: mean = 4.62 vs 3.98) than American children (Attili, Alcini & Travaglia, in press).

Within the 3- to 7-year age-span considered above, some changes in temperament category mean scores were found. Comparing children aged 6–7 years (n = 113) and 3 years (n = 50) we found that older children tended to be more intense (mean = 4.06 vs 3.80) and more moody (mean = 3.37 vs 3.25), but more persistent (mean = 2.88 vs 3.07) and less distractible (mean = 3.71 vs 3.94) as well. Several interpretations can be given of these changes, from linking them to maturational factors to explaining them in terms of an increasing socializing effect of school (all subjects had been attending preschool and were in their first grade when they were 6 years old). We believe interaction of both factors to be the better explanation, with maturation leading to more effective socialization and contributing to the structuring of personality traits (Attili et al., in press).

Being a Difficult Child in Italy

Ratings of temperamental characteristics and their conceptualization inevitably reflect points of view and expectations by raters and by scholars as to what constitutes a norm according to the desiderata of their culture. This is even more true if we consider the concept of 'difficult child'. Indeed, according to most American scholars studying temperament, the diagnostic 'difficult' profile is based on temperamental traits which might not be considered elements of difficultness when found in children belonging to a different culture. Conversely, behaviours and behaviour styles, which are not considered symptoms of difficultness in the United States, might contribute to the picture of a difficult child when found in another country.

In order to assess the 'meaning' of a child's 'difficultness' to Italian parents, 327 Italian mothers were sent adapted BSQs to which two further items had been added:

(1) 'According to you, is your child a difficult or an easy child?'
(2) 'If you think your child is difficult, tell us why in two or three sentences.'

On the six-point scale of the BSQ 60% of the mothers gave general difficultness ratings above point 2 and only 20% above point 3. When we categorized the difficultness characteristics expressed by the mothers the following categories were the most frequent: non-malleability and assertiveness (50%), demandingness and low threshold (35%), intensity (12%), persistence and mood (5%), distractibility, impulsivity, hyperactivity and withdrawal (3%), non-persistence (2%). These categories are based on the replies given by 60 mothers who rated their children's difficultness above point 3. The general difficultness ratings given by the mothers correlated significantly with only three of the dimension scores which on the basis of the suggestions by Thomas and Chess are used to form the 'difficult profile': Adaptability (−.38), Mood (.24) and Intensity (.16) (the last just for boys).

The utilization of instruments elaborated for culturally different countries brings the risk of basing the profile 'difficult' just on the five categories, Rhythmicity, Approach, Adaptability, Intensity and Mood which have been suggested by Thomas and Chess and indicated in their BSQ by McDevitt and Carey, and to neglect taking into consideration characteristics such as non-malleability or demandingness which might be perceived as symptoms of difficultness in other countries (Attili, Travaglia, Alcini, Vermigli & Felaco, 1988b).

Temperament, Raters' Perceptions and Relationships

We were next concerned with the covariance between the nature of the relationships children form with family members at home and with peers and teachers in preschool and children's as well as mothers' individual characteristics. In a subsample of 34 children aged 46–52 months (M = 19, F = 15) we assessed the quality of children's relationships by means of direct observations at home and in preschool. We decided to consider mothers' characteristics in terms of their mood which was assessed by means of a self-report scale for the assessment of irritability,

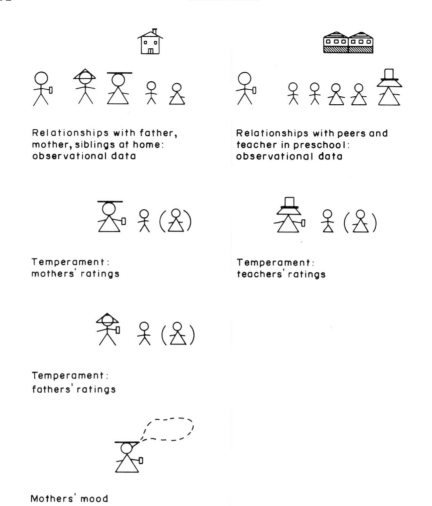

Relationships with father,
mother, siblings at home:
observational data

Relationships with peers and
teacher in preschool:
observational data

Temperament:
mothers' ratings

Temperament:
teachers' ratings

Temperament:
fathers' ratings

Mothers' mood

FIGURE 3   Dialectic between interpersonal relationships, temperamental characteristics
and mother's mood in preschoolers.

depression and anxiety (IDA scale by Snaith, Constantopoulos, Jardine &
McGuffin, 1978) (Figure 3).

So far the following preliminary aspects have been analyzed: the agreement
between fathers' and mothers' ratings of their children's temperamental characteristics, the associations between children's temperamental characteristics – separately
rated by each parent – and fathers' and mothers' behaviour towards their children;
the interface between mothers' mood, children's temperament, relationships with
peers and a particular aspect of home relationships, i.e. that of children being
consistently ignored and/or receiving irrelevant replies from their parents.

Due to the small sample size the correlation coefficients are given below with
some reservation. Nevertheless it should be stressed that direct, systematic and

extensive observations in natural settings and their coding are very time-consuming and do not allow for big samples. Furthermore the need for observer reliability places limitations on the possible number of experimenters involved in observational research projects. Correlations were computed using Spearman's rho.

Parents agreed on temperament categories (Activity .35, and Distractibility .41) less affected by interactional variables and on the Difficulty (.42) of their children. Furthermore, they agreed more on what their daughters were like than their sons (they agreed on the Intensity (.51) and Mood (.76) of their daughters). Rating differences might be due to a dialectic between parental behavioural style and children's behaviour: the former might be affected by parent's perception of their children's behaviour and in turn might produce differences in the way children behave towards them (Attili, Alcini & Felaco, 1988a).

In accordance with the individuals' cultural and biological expectations concerning their children's sex, temperamental characteristics correlated differently to fathers' and mothers' behaviour according to the sex of the children. Within parent–child relationships, activity, for example, correlated with mothers' behavior (who were less positive (–.70) and at the same time less controlling (–.41)) when with sons, but not with fathers'. Conversely fathers did not comply with requests (–.52), did not start interactions (–.80) and were not involved in neutral conversation (–.68) with their highly active daughters. Withdrawing boys had mothers who did not take the initiative in interactions with them (–.45), who did not talk to them in a friendly way (–.52), and who did not teach them (–.46). Fathers were even hostile to them (.42). Conversely no significant correlation was found between girls' 'shyness' and mothers' behaviour but mothers were less positive to them (–.53). By contrast fathers were often involved in conversation with their withdrawing daughters (.80), complied with their requests (.89), and started interactions with them (.54). We can expect that these feedback mechanisms contribute to the formation of stable individual characteristics (Attili, Felaco & Alcini, 1989).

Children's Temperamental Characteristics and Mothers' Mood

Children's temperamental characteristics correlated with some aspects of mothers' mood. Correlation coefficients differed according to children's sex and reflected a higher interdependency between mothers and daughters.

Mothers' mood correlated positively more with daughters' temperamental characteristics than with sons': mothers' anxiety correlated to sons' non-persistence (.40), and to daughters' activity and intensity (.55 and .68). Mothers' outward irritability correlated with sons' intensity and with daughters' withdrawal from new physical and social environments (–.44 and .55). Mothers' depression, by contrast, correlated only with daughters' temperamental characteristics such as activity (.50), intensity (.68) and difficulty (.78); and mothers' inward irritability correlated with daughters' activity (.60) and difficulty (.77).

It is of course hard to speak about these results (as well as about those mentioned above) in terms of a cause–effect relation. An explanation in terms of feedback mechanisms is the best one. Still the results by Wolkind and De Salis (1982), who found a positive association between mothers' ratings of difficultness of their 4-month-olds and mothers' depression and anxiety scored when their children were 14 months of age, might lead to our results being interpreted in terms of children's temperament influencing mothers' mood.

Temperament and Children's Behaviour in Preschool

Temperamental characteristics, such as mediating factors between home variables and children's behaviour towards peers in preschool, were considered. Observed behaviour towards peers associated more with girls' individual characteristics than with boys'. Girls who were slow in adapting to new social and physical environments were mostly disconfirming of their peers, that is they treated their peers as though they did not exist. Disconfirmation of peers was also associated with girls' individual characteristics such as being intense and highly active. Furthermore it was found that boys who scored low in approaching new social environments tended to be individuals disconfirming peers. Both boys' and girls' intensity and persistence plus girls' adaptability and mood correlated with frequency of initiations of interactions and of being involved in neutral conversation with peers (Attili, in press).

CONCLUSION

The history of temperament in Italy is the history of the different ideologies underlying psychology in this country and of the loans from disciplines other than psychology. It is also the history of a neglected field with very few original contributions coming from studies on adults and almost none from studies on infants and on children. The renewed interest in temperament is very new. Recent contributions are within a framework which focuses on the feedback mechanisms between individual characteristics and the nature of relationships children are part of.

ACKNOWLEDGMENTS

I am very grateful to Professor Gustavo Iacono who greatly helped me during the writing of this paper with his suggestions and information based partly on his own memories concerning the history of Italian psychology. This chapter is dedicated to him.

REFERENCES

Attili, G. (in press). Emotional factors affecting social skills within peer relationships: The interplay between mothers' mood, children's temperament and their home and school relationships. *Rassegna di Psicologia.*

Attili, G., Alcini, P. & Felaco, R. (1988a). Differenze madre–padre nella valutazione di caratteristiche temperamentali dei bambini. *Giornale Italiano di Psicologia,* **15**, 269–285.

Attili, G., Alcini, P. & Travaglia, G. (in press). Il questionario di McDevitt e Carey per la misura dello stile comportamentale da 3 a 7 anni: versione italiana. *Bollettino di Psicologia Applicata.*

Attili, G., Felaco, R. & Alcini, P. (1989). Temperamento e relazioni interpersonali: L'interfaccia tra caratteristiche individuali e la natura delle relazioni madre–bambino e padre–bambino. *Età Evolutiva*, **32**, 39–49.

Attili, G., Travaglia, G., Alcini, P., Vermigli, P. & Felaco, R. (1988b). The difficult child: Cultural determinants of a difficult concept. Paper presented at the ISSBD Third European Conference on Developmental Psychology, Budapest.

Berlucchi, C. (1944). Malati sintonici e malati autisti, caratteri aperti e caratteri chiusi, temperamenti ciclotimici e temperamenti schizotimici, tipi estravertiti e tipi introvertiti, soggetti integrati e soggetti sinestesici nella moderna psichiatria e caratterologia. *Archivio di Psicologia, Neurologia, Psichiatria e Psicoterapia*, **5**, 161–214.

Bonaventura, E. (1930). Contributo alla psicopatologia dei fanciulli 'instabili'. *Rivista di Psicologia Normale e Patologica*, **26**, 248–258.

Bonaventura, E. (1936). Lo studio sperimentale del carattere nel bambino lattante. *Rivista di Psicologia Normale e Patologica*, **32**, 36–53.

Colucci, C. (1907). Simulazione di nevrosi consecutive e trauma in soggetto isterico (Periziogiudiziale). In *Rivista sugli Infortuni del Lavoro*, Vol. 8, pp. 106. Roma.

De Giovanni, A. (1891). *Morfologia del corpo umano*, Milano: U. Hoepli.

De Grada, E. (1958). Aspetto fisico e personalità: ricerca suelle correlazioni somato-psichiche descritte da W.H. Sheldon. *Contributi dell'Istituto Nazionale di Psicologia del CNR 1956–1959*, 22–46.

De Rita, L. & Iacono, G. (1964). Aspetti psicologici dei meridionali in rapporto ai problemi déll'immigrazione. *Studi di Sociologia*, **2**(2), 170–177.

De Sanctis, S. (1925). *Neuropsichiatria infantile: Patologia e diagnostica*. Roma: A. Stock.

Falorni, M.L. (1967). *Lo studio psicologico del carattere e delle attitudini.* Firenze: Giunti.

Ferrari, G.C. (1914). La psicologia dei giovanetti criminali. *Rivista de Psicologia*, **11**, 333–357.

Fonzi, A. (1956). Sullo stereotipo del meridionale italiano. *Rivista di Psicologia Sociale*, **4**, 279–300.

Gemelli, A. (1930). Costituzione, carattere e temperamemto in psichiatria. *Rivista Sperimentale di Freniatria e di Medicina Legale*, **30**, 125–150.

Gemelli, A. (1931). Sulla natura e sulla genesi del carattere. *Contributi del Laboratorio di Psicologia*, serie V, 175–202.

Gemelli, A. (1948). *La personalità del delinquente.* Milano: Giuffre.

Gemelli, A. & Zunini, G. (1947). *Introduzione alla psicologia.* Milano: Vita e Pensiero.

Iacono, G. (1968). An affiliative society facing innovation. *Journal of Social Issues*, **24**, 125–132.

Kretschmer, E. (1951). *Koerperban und Character.* Heidelberg: Springer Verlag.

Lombroso, C. (1876). *L'uomo delinquente studiato in rapporto all'antropologia, alla medicina e alle discipline carcerarie.* Roma: Fratelli Bocca editore.

Lombroso, C. (1893). *Le più recenti scoperte ed applicazioni della psichiatria e antropologia criminale.* Roma: Fratelli Bocca editore.

Lombroso, C. (1894). *Prefazione a Saggi di psicologia del bambino di P. Lombroso.* Torino: Le Roux.

Lombroso, C. & Bianchi, A.G. (1905). *Il caso di Alberto Olivo.* Milano: Hoepli.

McDevitt, S.C. & Carey, W.B. (1978). The measurement of temperament in 3–7 year old children. *Journal of Child Psychology and Psychiatry and Allied Disciplines*, **19**, 245–253.

McGuffin, P. (1978). A clinical scale for the self assessment of irritability. *British Journal of Psychiatry*, **132**, 164–171.

Metelli, F. (1950). *Introduzione alla caratterologia moderna.* Siciliana: Editrice Liguori.

Nencini, R. (1959). Effetti di alcuni atteggiamenti materni sulla personalità dei figli. *Contributi dell'Istituto Nazionale di Psicologia del CNR, 1956–1959*, 3–39.

Nencini, R. & Misiti, R. (1956). Contributo alla identificazione di 'tipi' psicologici sulla base delle reazioni al P.F.T. di Rosenzweig. *Contributi dell'Istituto Nazionale di Psicologia del CNR, 1956–1959*, 48–74.

Pende, N. (1939). *Tratto di biotipologia umana*. Milano: Vallardi.

Pende, N. (1947). *La scienza moderna della persona umana*. Milano: Garzanti.

Pilo, M. (1892). *Nuovi studi sul carattere*. Milano: Hoepli.

Piro, S. (1956). Studio psicologico e psicopatologico sui fanciulli mulatti. *Acta Neurologica*, 13, 212–226.

Sheldon, W.H. & Stevens, S.S. (1942). *The varieties of temperament*. New York: Harper.

Snaith, R.P., Constantopoulos, A.A., Jardine, M.Y. & McGuffin, P. (1978). A clinical scale for the self-assessment of irritability. *British Journal of Psychiatry,* 132, 164–171.

Thomas, A. & Chess, S. (1977). *Temperament and development*, New York: Brunner/Mazel.

Viola, M. (1906). *L'antropometria come base di classificazione delle costituzioni individuali*. Torino: Bocca.

Wolkind, S.N. & De Salis, W. (1982). Infant temperament, maternal mental state and child behavioural problems. In R. Porter & G.M. Collins (Eds), *Temperamental differences in infants and young children*, Ciba Foundation Symposium (pp. 221–239). London: Pitman.

33

Temperament and Character: The French School

GENEVIÈVE BALLEYGUIER
University Francois Rabelais, Tours

CONCEPTS: A HISTORICAL REVIEW

In France, throughout the Middle Ages and up to modern time, the Greek theory of the four temperaments was generally accepted. With the development of medical science in the nineteenth century, new systems were elaborated in order to relate temperament to physiological activity. In a rapid overview, we describe: constitutional systems which start from somatic differences and end up with temperaments or character types; Wallon's theory which insists on the development of character and looks for its biological substratum; studies on tonico-motor types; and a more recent study on temperament and character.

The Morphological School

From the eighteenth to the beginning of the twentieth century, the morphological French school, mostly composed of physicians (Hallé, Sigaud, Rostan, Cabanis), measured differences in the development of body (head, thorax, abdomen, etc.) or facial parts, established relationships between them and biological functions (respiratory, digestive, etc.) or some internal fluids or chemicals, and related them to temperament types. Temperament was seen as the behavioral expression of the somatic constitution, which was considered hereditary.

With the development of neurology, at the beginning of the twentieth century, temperament was explained by physiological processes: i.e. the rapidity and mobility of nervous activity (Fouillée, 1895), the balance between sympathetic and parasympathetic processes (Mounier, 1946), and the general metabolism of the organism which commands the potential output of energy (Manouvrier, 1896). These authors described an active, motor or sthenic type as opposed to a sensory,

Temperament in Childhood   Edited by G.A. Kohnstamm, J.E. Bates and M.K. Rothbart
© 1989 John Wiley & Sons Ltd

vegetative or hyposthenic type, with some intermediary types, but their systems were more philosophical than scientific.

Physiologists refused to accept the causal link between physiological mechanisms and behavioral characteristics assumed by these theories. In consequence, the word temperament acquired an unscientific connotation.

During the first half of this century, French interest focused on descriptions of character. A very popular school, *La caractérologie*, took as its starting point the theory of the Dutch psychologists Heymans and Wiersma. It was taught at the Sorbonne by Le Senne (1945), and applied to adolescents and children by Le Gall (1950). In theory, a difference was made between the two concepts: temperament referred to constitutional and therefore hereditary somatic dispositions; character, to general behavior, which was thought to be strongly influenced by environment; but, in fact, we find the same definitions and physiological explanations under both names. For Le Senne, character was the stable, hereditary part of personality, the ensuing types resulting from different combinations of the three Dutch factors – activity, emotionality, primary–secondary function – being equivalent to temperaments. Le Gall assumed that each character factor had a different physiological basis: emotionality being the result of the balance of the autonomic nervous system which commands the activity of the endocrine glands; activity depending on the energy released by the subcortical nervous centers; and primary–secondary function depending on the rapidity of the chemical recovery of the nerve cells.

The real change lay in the way of describing individual differences. Their fixed and hereditary component was questioned, even for temperament (Zazzo, 1969). Character was defined as the general way of feeling and reacting, the formal part of behavior and not its content (Berger, 1950; Voutsinas, 1961).

The Biological Processes of Emotion: Wallon's Theory

Another course was followed by the French physician and psychologist, Wallon (1925, 1934). He used the neurological discoveries of his time and linked the affective component of personality to its biological origins. He did not like the word temperament, because of its connotation of unchangeability. He preferred to describe the progressive building of character, and relate it to its biological basis, seen as the maturing process of hierarchically ordered nervous centers. For him, character was synonymous with individual regulation of emotional processes. He turned to infant study and described the neurological and developmental 'origins of character' (Wallon, 1934). His theory became, and still serves as, the basis for many French studies. His theory was brought up to date, using more recent neurological discoveries, by Nguyen Thi (1976).

The excitation necessary for neurological functioning comes not only from the external stimulation of the senses, but also and primarily from internal sensations; these originate in the smooth muscles (visceral sensations), in the striated muscles and their articulations (kinesthetic sensations), and in the internal ear (labyrinthic sensations). The excitation produced by all these sensations is brought together in the ascending reticular formation, which links the medulla to the cortex. This excitation is regulated by hierarchically organized centers; the lower ones (bulb, cerebellum, thalamus) are very primitive, and function even before birth; the higher ones (the cortex and within it the forebrain) need many years to become completely functional. These centers integrate the afferent impulses coming from different pathways and command the efferent systems which activate motor and vegetative functioning.

Activation puts all the muscles, smooth and striated, under tension. It creates tonus, which is necessary as a preparation for action and even perception (which always involves some kind of activity). Apart from a general strengthening of the tonus, depending on the intensity of the activation, there are also specific 'postural attitudes', according to the present or anticipated activity. The tonus may be discharged through the vegetative system (smooth muscles, endocrine activity) or through the relational system (striated muscles performing activity). Since there are sensitive cells inside all kinds of muscles, the postural attitudes are linked with different sensations, but most of them produce only an affective tone, with no precision concerning the origin of the stimulation. For Wallon, the tonus was the substratum of the emotions, which correspond to specific postural attitudes, vegetative activity, and affective tone.

He described three innate emotions present at birth. The first, *rage*, is produced when the nervous system is overexcited and the discharge possibilities are insufficient; tension is great and overloads all discharge systems, causing spastic body movements; the affective tone is negative. The second, *pleasure*, is created when the excitation can be discharged through activity; it is the exact balance between excitation and discharge capacities which gives the sensation of pleasure. The third, *fear*, is the result of a sudden stimulation which renders the previous postural attitude inadequate. For the newborn, this happens when he loses his balance (labyrinthic sensations); later in life, fear is produced when there is uncertainty as to which postural attitude to take (an unknown situation, an ambiguous stimulus).

Emotions diversify with age for different reasons. The maturation of the nervous system provides new possibilities for discharging tension through adapted activities; it multiplies the modalities of discharge. Emotions are very easily conditioned; with growing interest in the external world, they become associated with specific stimuli or situations and anticipate them by creating the postural attitudes necessary to adapt to them. For example, the anticipation of a pleasurable situation increases tension and prepares the body for responding to it; this creates desire. When this anticipation is fulfilled, the tension is relieved through adapted actions and the sensation of joy follows. Conversely, when the anticipation is frustrated, the tension increases but discharges globally through the tonus system and uncoordinated movements result: the child puts on a tantrum. When there is uncertainty as to which posture to adopt, the tonus is high but cannot be discharged; the strong inner sensations give the unpleasant feeling of anxiety.

With the maturation of the cortical centers, the excitation coming from the subcortical levels is partly inhibited; movements and emotional expressions become controlled. Parents make use of this growing capacity in socializing the child's behavior. When the control is very strong, however, and forbids any adapted discharge of tension, the tonus becomes too high and gives way to cramps, spasms, and vegetative dysfunctioning.

Wallon described the affective development as the progressive control of more elaborate organizations (due to the maturation of higher centers) over the more primitive ones. It runs through four periods: the impulsive period, when the newborn reacts mainly through reflex activity; the emotional period, when he communicates with the environment through emotions; the sensorimotor period, when he can better differentiate the external elements of the environment and establishes social relations (e.g. imitation); and finally the projective period, when conscious aims and deliberate thinking reduce emotional expressions.

Although the individual's reactions vary with the situations encountered, character is defined as the general behavior pattern. It stabilizes early, since it depends on the maturation of the subcortical centers. Two adult types (emotional and sentimental) are distinguished according to the importance of emotional expression or its reduction by symbolic thought.

Following this theory, Malrieu (1952) described in detail, using many examples of normal children, the diversification and organization of the emotions during the first 3 years. He showed how this development is associated with psychomotor and symbolic progress, and the constitution of the sense of identity.

Wallon and Malrieu relied on the detailed description of individual cases; they were mostly interested in general processes of development and described those in a holistic way (with motor, emotional, intellectual, and verbal dimensions). More recent studies have introduced some form of measurement, with the aim of showing more systematically the early individual differences. They concentrate on tonico-motor development and its different types.

The Tonico-Motor Types

The observation of newborn and young children has revealed important differences in tonus. These can be evaluated (André-Thomas & Ajuriaguerra, 1949) through the intensity of the reflexes, the muscular rigidity, and the extensibility of the inferior limbs measured by two angles (adductor and popliteal). Stambak and Ajuriaguerra (1958) described three periods in the development of extensibility in the first year. During the first months, the limbs are very contracted, gradually becoming more relaxed until around the age of 12 months, and become more tonic again thereafter. Individual differences are best appreciated at the age at which the largest angle is obtained, and throughout the duration of the period of great extensibility. Using these criteria, children can be divided into hypo, medium, or hypertonic types.

After having studied 55 children from birth until the age of 3 years, Stambak (1963) compared their muscular extensibility with their degree of activity, the amount and kind of stereotyped movements they exhibited, and their Development Quotient (DQ; evaluated by the Brunet–Lezine test). On the basis of her discovery of significant correlations, she contrasted two motor types. The hypertonic is less extensible, stands and walks earlier, is more active, but manipulates things later and shows violent self-stimulating movements (swinging, self-aggression). The hypotonic is more extensible, stands and walks later, is less active, but manipulates things earlier, and stimulates himself smoothly (body exploration, thumb-sucking). There is no statistical difference between the DQ of the two types, but the hypertonic has a more advanced postural development, while the hypotonic shows better hand-eye coordination and verbal development. Their relational attitudes also differ:

> Hypotonics cry less, they are more fearful, more affectionate and more dependent towards their parents while hypertonics put on more frequent and violent tantrums and follow their parents less. (Stambak, 1963, p. 114)

These differences closely resemble those described in Schaffer and Emerson's (1964) cuddlers and non-cuddlers and Escalona's (1968) active and passive children.

Ajuriaguerra, Harrisson, and Lézine (1967) studied 50 children cared for in a day-center during their first year; they evaluated their tonus, experimented with their pattern of reaction to different physical stimuli, and observed their emotional reactions during routine situations. They also questioned the mother on the child's behavior in the same situations at home. They found some relationship between the child's tonico-motor type and his emotional reactions. They classified the children into four types (active–brisk, active–slow, excited–stiff, passive–stiff).

Although focused on motor style, the four studies mentioned above also described its relation with emotional, social, and intellectual development.

More recently, research has been undertaken, under the direction of Montagner, to study the specific behaviors of extremely hypotonic or hypertonic 5- to 6-year-old children. The children's behavioral (attention, communication, and stereotyped movements) and biological (cardiac frequency) rhythms at school have been studied, and they have been observed during the period of change from nursery to elementary school (Soussignan, Koch & Montagner, in press).

A Recent Study on Temperament and Character

In line with Wallon's theory, but also influenced by Thomas, Chess, Birch, Hertzig, and Korn (1963), Balleyguier (1981a) differentiates between temperament and character and develops appropriate measurement techniques. Temperament is defined as the emotional style, which is the individual expression of the regulation of the arousal process and its preferential channels of discharge. It is measured with scales for tension (degrees of excitation shown by the degree of activity and emotional involvement), control (degree of muscular and emotional restraint), mood (affective tone), and orientation of behavior (passivity; disoriented discharges such as cries, fussiness, etc.; orientation towards things; orientation towards people; defensive reactions such as fleeing or inhibition). Temperament does not include social attitudes, which are specific ways to establish and maintain relations with other people. They begin with attachment and diversify into many kinds of relationships: affection, imitation, aggression, obedience, autonomy. The individual pattern of temperament *and* social relationships can be called character.

Balleyguier followed 39 children from birth onward. They were observed at home in ten experimental situations, and the mothers were questioned about their child's behavior in 70 everyday situations. The data for the first 3 years were quantified according to the aforementioned system. The social attitudes of the members of the family (father, mother, sibling) towards the child were also measured. Principal component analyses (one for each 6-month period) involving the most discriminating variables of the child's temperament and social attitudes showed a close association between the two sets of variables. The same clusters of individual differences were found at each period. They showed four character types: the difficult child (very tense, weak control, aggressive relations), the sthenic child (moderately tense, good control, positive and aggressive relations), the easy child (balanced tension, moderate control, positive rather than negative relationships), and the passive child (low tension, weak control, relationships poorly developed). The two extremes (difficult and passive) resemble the 'difficult' and 'slow to warm up' types described by Thomas, Chess, and Birch (1968).

The same method, somewhat simplified (only 50 situations), is used as a test (Balleyguier, 1979) which has been standardized on 1025 French children with means and standard deviations for each variable given for each month during the first 3 years. This test is used as a clinical tool, showing individual's deviations outside the normal range over a series of 41 variables, as well as giving a global indication of character.

TEMPERAMENT AND DEVELOPMENT

Two topics will be discussed here: first, the development of manifestations of temperament; second, individual stability versus changeability.

The Development of Manifestations of Temperament

Since temperament is thought to be closely linked to neurological functioning, its manifestations should greatly change with maturation.

The development of the postural tonus, which increases until the child is able to walk, has been described by André-Thomas and Ajuriaguerra (1949), and the development of the extensibility of the limbs, by Stambak and Ajuriaguerra (1958). The growth of motor coordination must also be taken into account. The combination of these different developments explains the motor characteristics specific to certain periods: the global and diffuse movements of the newborn (when awake), the relative passivity generally accorded to the baby during its first year, the motor explosion of the second year, and the more controlled and adapted activity from the third year on.

Using the data of her longitudinal study Balleyguier (1986) divided the development of temperament during the first 3 years into four periods. First comes the infant colic (first 3 months), with much alternation between high and low tension (changing rapidly from low to high), rare moments of moderate tension, low control (few adapted movements), many disoriented discharges (crying, diffuse movements). Next comes the grace period (3–8 months), with less variations between high and low tension (less sleep and less crying), more self-stimulation and more activities oriented toward things or persons. During the tantrum period (9–24 months) high tension increases again and is demonstrated through tantrums, although moderate tension also increases (more adapted activity); almost all activities are oriented toward things or persons, with a decrease in self-stimulation. In the third year, when high tension decreases (less crying and tantrums), moderate tension takes over, and the motor and emotional control (silent tears, verbal instead of physical aggression) becomes much stronger. This development confirms the results of two previous studies (Goodenough, 1931; Lézine, 1964) observing a tantrum period during the second year with a peak around 18 months.

The rapid and non-linear development of manifestations of temperament during the first 3 years makes it necessary to compare a child with other children of his age in order to evaluate his temperament. What evidence do we have that the individual differences are stable?

Individual Stability Versus Changeability

This is a much disputed issue. Wallon (1934) thought that although emotions greatly depend on the situations encountered, each person has an individual way of reacting, which is relatively constant. Ajuriaguerra et al. (1967) found, in their prospective study, that 80% of their subjects kept their behavioral type between 2 and 15 months. Some changed as a result of a special circumstance (e.g. a surgical operation) but came back to their previous style after a few months. The modification lasted longer for some children whose environment changed in some way (such as being put in a day-care center). But Balleyguier (1981a) did not find such a strong stability. Of the 35 children followed during their first 36 months, only 2 always showed the same temperament, 19 showed small or transient changes, and 14 changed completely. The larger number of changes occurred during the end of the first, and at the beginning of the second years. Balleyguier concluded that, as a result of the regulation of dynamic processes, temperament is not fixed from birth on; it very often changes during the first year, gaining in stability with the progressive adaptation of the child to his environment's demands. Temperament may be relatively constant from the third year on, thus giving the impression of having always been fixed to those researchers who study older subjects. It may also be more stable when there is a neurological impairment from birth on. This is confirmed by the study of clinical cases.

TEMPERAMENT AND CLINICAL SYNDROMES

Wallon (1925) described individual pathological cases of strongly retarded and impulsive children, epileptic children, choreic children, etc. in the tradition of studies which use pathologic deviation to give more insight into normal development. He related their dysfunctioning to the impairment of some higher nervous center.

Lézine (1958) followed, from birth to the age of 4 years, 127 premature babies and compared them to 122 full-term babies. She measured their DQ and inquired about their behavioral difficulties. She found that premature babies have poor motor coordination, which makes food intake difficult. Their sucking rhythm is irregular; this often leads to anorexia. They also have sleep disturbances, and although they may be very inhibited they put on more frequent and violent tantrums. This could be explained as a difficulty in regulating their tension. The difficulty tends to decrease after the age of 1 year, but Lézine shows how it heightens the mother's anxiety, and may lead to real behavior problems when caretakers do not take into account the child's difficulties.

Stambak (1968) studied the psychomotor characteristics of mentally retarded children (mean age: 9 years) and compared them to those of normal children of the same chronological or mental age. She used graphic tasks requiring precision and rapidity. She found two 'motor styles' corresponding to two types of mental retardation. In the first, the children have very low efficiency but great persistence; they are slow to learn and do not abandon a task easily; they have different symptoms of neurological impairment; and they come from all socioeconomic classes. In the second type, the children have normal efficiency but are rather unstable; their results depend more on their task motivations. Their neurological examination gives normal results; they come from the lowest socioeconomic class. This study shows that the same degree of retardation may have different origins, which also leads to different patterns of activity. The clinical results are used for vocational guidance of mentally retarded adolescents.

TEMPERAMENT AND TYPES OF CHILD CARE

Lézine and Stambak (1959) questioned the mothers of 24 children, followed during the first 3 years, on their behavior in everyday situations and the emotional reactions of their children. They found three maternal types: liberal, strict, and incoherent. The children's emotional adaptation varied in accordance with these types. With a liberal form of child care, the children had few problems, were not fearful, and had good psychomotor development. The children of strict mothers had more sleeping problems, had crying fits during the first year, but later were rather inhibited and very dependent on their mother. The children of incoherent mothers were the most difficult; they cried more, had sleeping and feeding problems, were very dependent and opposing toward their mother and were very fearful; their psychomotor development regressed during the periods of strong opposition. The authors also compared types of maternal care with the children's motor behavior. They found that children with the same behavior could be easy or difficult – the hypotonic could be quiet or apathetic; the hypertonic lively or very irritable – depending on the type of maternal behavior.

Herren and Herren (1980) think that the environment should act differently according to the child's temperament – e.g. not to be too stimulating with a tense child – and even try to compensate its tendencies when they are extreme, in order to help the child find a good equilibrium. They proposed an infant-stimulation program suggesting that the hypertonic infant should have smooth and relaxing exercises while the hypotonic infant should be more actively stimulated.

Balleyguier (1981a) also found relations between the child's temperament and the family's way of raising the child (difficult children with overstimulating parents; easy children with an affectionate family; passive children with an understimulating family; etc.). In another study (1981b, 1988) she inquired if the mode of day-care had an influence on the child's character. The test described above was used. She found that there were some differences: the children in a day-care center were more passive and less autonomous than those staying home; those cared for by a child-minder being intermediate. This was true at 9 months and at 2 years. But after they all went to the same type of nursery school, at the age of 4, the previous modes of day-care did no longer make much difference. Balleyguier concluded that the child's behavior changes with the style of its caretaker – the same child even behaving differently at home and at his day-care place – but will change again when the conditions of his upbringing are modified. The young child is very adaptable indeed!

CURRENT TRENDS

In France, the word temperament is presently still laden with its unscientific connotation of the past. The word is not used for conferences and symposia as is the case in the US and in some other countries.

However, research on the same lines as what elsewhere is called temperament research continues. Results obtained with different techniques (questionnaire, observation) are being compared in order better to evaluate the extent of the informant's subjectivity. The stability of the child's reactions to specific situations is being examined (Meudec, 1986). A more general problem is being raised: what are the different strategies developed by young children in order to regulate their tension – which is experienced as having pleasure and avoiding unpleasant feelings – as they have to adapt with their temperament to different situations and caretaker attitudes.

REFERENCES

Ajuriaguerra, J. de, Harrisson, A. & Lézine, I. (1967). Etude sur quelques aspects de la réactivité émotionnelle dans la première année. *Psychiatrie de l'Enfant,* **10**, 293–380.

André-Thomas & Ajuriaguerra, J. de (1949). *Etudes sémiologiques du tonus musculaire.* Paris: Flammarion.

Balleyguier, G. (1979). *Test pour l'évaluation du caractère de l'enfant et des attitudes éducatives de l'entourage.* Issy-les-Moulineaux (France): Editions Scientifiques et Psychologiques. (An English translation is available when writing to the author.)

Balleyguier, G. (1981a). *La formation du caractère pendant les premières années.* Issy-les-Moulineaux. (France): Editions Scientifiques et Psychologiques.

Balleyguier, G. (1981b). *Le caractère de l'enfant en fonction de son mode de garde pendant les premières années.* Paris: Centre National del la Recherche Scientifique.

Balleyguier, G. (1986). The transformations of temperament during the first three years. Individual evaluation. Paper presented at Third World Congress of Infant Psychiatry and Allied Disciplines, Stockholm.

Balleyguier, G. (1988). What is the best mode of day care for young children: A French study. *Early Child Development and Care,* **33**, 41–65.

Berger, G. (1950). *Traité pratique d'analyse du caractère.* Paris: Presses Universitaires de France.

Brunet, O. & Lézine, I. (1951). Le développement psychologique de la première enfance. Paris: Presse Universitaires de France.

Escalona, S. (1968). *The roots of individuality.* Chicago: Alding.

Fouillée, A. (1895). *Le tempérament et le caractère selon les individus, les sexes et les âges.* Paris: Félix Alcan.

Goodenough, F. (1931). *Anger in young children.* Minneapolis: University of Minnesota Press.

Herren, H. & Herren, M.P. (1980). *La stimulation psychomotrice du nourrisson.* Paris: Masson.

Le Gall, R. (1950). *Caractérologie des enfants et des adolescents.* Paris: Presses Universitaires de France.

Le Senne, R. (1945). *Traité de caractérologie.* Paris: Presses Universitaires de France.

Lézine, I. (1958). Problèmes éducatifs du jeune prématuré. *Enfance,* **3**, 213–243.

Lézine, I. (1964). *Psychopédagogie du premier âge,* 2nd edn. Paris: Presses Universitaires de France.

Lézine, I. & Stambak, M. (1959). Quelques problèmes d'adaptation du jeune enfant en fonction de son style moteur et du régime éducatif. *Enfance,* **2**, 95–115.

Malrieu, P. (1952). *Les émotions et la personnalité de l'enfant.* Paris: Vrin.

Manouvrier, L. (1896). Le tempérament. *Revue mensuelle de l'Ecole d'Anthropologie de Paris.*

Meudec, M. (1986). Direct observations of the behavioral stability of six months old children. Paper presented at the ISSBD Second European Conference on Developmental Psychology, Rome.

Mounier, E. (1946). *Traité du caractère.* Paris: Seuil.

Nguyen Thi, T.H. (1976). *La formation des attitudes affectives.* Paris: Vrin.

Schaffer, H.R. & Emerson, P.E. (1964). Patterns of response to physical contacts in early human development. *Journal of Child Psychology,* **5**, 1–13.

Soussignan, R., Koch, P. & Montagner, H. (1988). Cardiovascular and behavioral changes in children moving from kindergarten to elementary school. *Journal of Child Psychology and Psychiatry,* **29**, 321–333.

Stambak, M. (1963). *Tonus et psychomotricité dans la première enfance.* Neuchâtel (Switzerland): Delachaux et Niestlé.

Stambak, M. (1968). La motricité des débiles mentaux. *Psychiatrie de l'enfant,* **10**, 293–380.

Stambak, M. & Ajuriaguerra, J. de (1958). Evolution de l'extensibilité depuis la naissance jusqu'à l'âge de deux ans. *La Presse Médicale,* **66**, 24–27.

Thomas, A., Chess, S. & Birch, H.G. (1968). *Temperament and behavior disorders.* New York: University Press.

Thomas, A., Chess, S., Birch, H.G., Hertzig, M.E. & Korn, S. (1963). *Behavioral individuality in early childhood.* New York: University Press.

Voutsinas, D. (1961). Tempérament, constitution, caractère. *Bulletin de Psychologie de l'Université de Paris,* **15**, 26–40.

Wallon, H. (1925). *L'enfant turbulent.* Paris: Alcan.

Wallon, H. (1934). *Les origines du caractère chez l'enfant.* Paris: Boivin.

Zazzo, R. (1969). *Croissance de l'enfant, genèse de l'homme,* Vol. 1, *Des garçons de six à douze ans.* Paris: Presses Universitaires de France.

34

Temperament Research in Scandinavia

ANNE MARI TORGERSEN
University of Oslo

Even though Scandinavia often is referred to as a unity, the different Scandinavian countries – Finland, Sweden, Norway and Denmark – have had different and separate traditions in developmental psychology as well as in psychology in general. In Norway, developmental psychology has been strongly influenced by psychoanalytic theories and clinical practice, while in Sweden and Finland studies of children were always much more related to education. In Finland, trends can be more frequently traced to Soviet theories, while other European traditions were more prevalent in the other Scandinavian countries. Influence from American research has increased over the last two decades in the Scandinavian countries.

While initial interest in temperament was motivated by the need for concepts to differentiate infants in their early individuality in behavior, this soon developed into an interest in the interactional process between the infant and its environment. Developmental theories were changed by these studies, and researchers in developmental psychology became also interested in temperament as it changes through childhood and adolescence.

The first temperament studies, all on infants, started independently of each other (Persson-Blennow and McNeil; Hagekull and Bohlin; Torgersen; Huttunen) in the late 1960s and early 1970s. In search of methods to describe infant individuality, the researchers all discovered publications from the New York Longitudinal Study (NYLS) by Thomas and Chess and co-workers. They then pursued their aims using different methods. Torgersen translated the interview used by Thomas and Chess (Thomas, Chess & Birch, 1968; Thomas, Chess, Birch, Hertzig & Korn, 1963) into Norwegian. Huttunen translated the first Carey questionnaire (Carey, 1970) into Finnish, and the two Swedish groups developed their own questionnaires, both with Carey's revised questionnaire as the starting point. The methodology was of great concern to them: how could temperamental individuality be measured in a reliable and valid way?

Temperament in Childhood   Edited by G.A. Kohnstamm, J.E. Bates and M.K. Rothbart
© 1989 John Wiley & Sons Ltd

These workers received inspiration from direct contact with Thomas and Chess, who visited Scandinavia several times in the 1970s. In 1979, they also met for the first time with Carey, McDevitt and Rothbart at a Child Development conference in Lund, where the first occasional temperament conference in the USA was planned. Torgersen attended a temperament conference in Warsaw in 1974, and Rutter gave a paper at a Scandinavian conference on psychiatry in 1972 which also supported the interest of early temperamental individuality. The initiative of Kohnstamm to invite us to a small international temperament meeting in Leiden in 1981 was also of importance to maintain motivation.

The interaction process between infant and mother was of main importance to others who wanted to work more directly with the mother–infant dyad. In Scandinavia these studies started in Denmark by Munck and co-workers (Munck, Mirdal & Marner, 1988), who used the Brazelton Neonatal Behavioral Assessment Scale (NBAS) (Brazelton, 1973) to study both developmentally and clinically oriented questions. Mathiessen (1982) worked in Norway in the same frame of reference.

In two different large-scale studies of aggression in children by Pulkkinen in Finland (Pulkkinen, 1987) and by Olweus in Norway and Sweden (Olweus, 1978), temperament was introduced as part of their understanding of the developmental process which leads to aggressive behavior. Typically, temperament was not their main interest, but they included the concept and found temperament, at least in their later works, to be of importance for a fuller understanding of development.

Other developmental psychologists have had the same secondary interest in temperamental individuality and included temperamental measurements as part of their studies on other topics. This has been done within clinical studies (Faleide *et al.*, 1985), in several studies of different types of day-care for preschool children (Arajärvi, Malmivaara, Martelin, Salerius-Laine & Turunen, 1987; Hwang, Lamb & Broberg, 1988; Munter, 1987) and in a study of non-vulnerable children of schizophrenic mothers (Schulsinger, 1976).

Twin studies have been of special interest in Scandinavia due to the existing twin registers. This tradition formed the background for Torgersen's early study of the genetic influence on temperament (Torgersen, 1987). The twin registers are also the main reason for American interest in collecting data in Scandinaiva.

Finally, the acknowledgment of temperament as an important issue in child psychiatric practice should also be mentioned, even if this is mainly clinical work and not research.

TEMPERAMENTAL INDIVIDUALITY: METHODOLOGICAL PROBLEMS

Three studies in Scandinavia have had as their primary goal the development of methods of measurement of temperamental individuality in infants: the studies of Torgersen (Torgersen & Kringlen, 1978), Persson-Blennow and McNeil (1979, 1980) and of Hagekull and Bohlin (1981; Hagekull, Bohlin & Lindhagen, 1984).

With the main interest in a broad description of infant's individuality and a belief in mother's reports from the home environment, the only satisfactory method in 1969 was the interview used in the NYLS (Thomas *et al.*, 1963). This interview was adapted to obtain additional information, specific for twins, and used in Torgersen's first data collection (Torgersen, 1973). This group of twins subsequently was followed at four different ages: 2 months, 9 months, 6 years and 15 years. What follows is a summarizing description.

A Norwegian Twin Study

Fifty-three pairs of same-sexed twins were seen 3 days after birth, and mothers were interviewed in their home when the twins were 2 and 9 months of age. As in the NYLS, detailed, objective descriptions of each child's behavior in different routine situations of daily life were obtained. Rules for scoring were developed in more detail than in the NYLS. Rather than a mere sentence-by-sentence analysis of the interview, several topics were covered, which also included some specific differences at the two ages, and reliability was tested and found to be satisfactory when translated interview protocols were double-scored by the author and trained raters from the NYLS.

Despite obvious problems with the method – problems with the accuracy of definitions; the same behavior scored for different temperamental variables; the change in behavior descriptions of the same variable from 2 to 9 months – individual differences on the nine dimensions were found to be close to normal distribution and to have a wide range. The exceptions were the J-curve distribution of Distractibility at both ages, and the shortage of situations in which Attention span at age 2 months could be rated. The fact that monozygotic (MZ) twins were significantly more similar than dizygotic (DZ) twins could, in addition to supporting the hypothesis of genetic influence, also be seen as a test of the reliability of the method (Torgersen & Kringlen, 1978). With the exception of Mood and Distractibility, all the variables were significantly stable from 2 to 9 months. Activity, Rhythmicity and Intensity were the most stable ($P < .01$).

The same interview method as in infancy was used for assessment of temperament when the twins were 6 years of age. One hundred and forty-seven items relating to the nine temperamental categories and scorable on a five-point scale were identified. The items were grouped under each of the nine categories according to the criteria of the NYLS. The items within each temperamental category which had satisfactory inter-rater reliability were then factor analyzed by means of principal component analysis. Items on the first factors which had factorial loadings lower than .30 were excluded, and the remaining 51 items were utilized for further analyses.

The internal consistency (Cronbachs alpha) was satisfactorily high for all temperamental variables except Distractibility and Rhythmicity (.64 to .73), and the final number of items within each of the other variables varied from four to nine (Torgersen, 1981).

At the 15-year follow-up the same procedure was followed. Items this time were chosen to be as close as possible to those of age 6, only with age-appropriate changes. All temperamental variables except Distractibility and Rhythmicity showed satisfactory internal consistency (.64 to .89). The number of items ranged from four to eleven (Torgersen, 1987).

Swedish Scale Construction

Discussing methodological problems in temperamental assessment, McNeil (1976) made several critical comments on the NYLS in an unpublished, but frequently quoted paper. He questioned several aspects of the NYLS, mainly the representativeness of its main sample, and the statistical significance of the published stabilities of its dimension scores. He expressed doubt as to whether certain temperament patterns could significantly identify disturbed groups *before* the onset of symptoms. He pointed to problems that still are discussed in the field of temperament research.

Persson-Blennow and McNeil started their study of temperamental individuality in infants with the intention of controlling some of these limitations. They tried to improve the reliability of the method and chose a more representative sample balanced for the different social classes. They also switched from interviews to parental questionnaires.

Three questionnaires were developed to measure the nine NYLS temperament variables in children, at 6 months, 1 year and 2 years of age. Basically the items developed for the 6-month sample were used at all ages, but some changes were made to make the questions age-specific. Items with a low percentage of valid answers (50%) and with skewed distributions (5%/80%) were excluded. Some new items were formulated, but most were derived from the NYLS interview and from Carey's questionnaire (Persson-Blennow and McNeil, 1980).

The Malmö-based authors standardized their questionnaires in a follow-up study of a group of 160 (147 at 2 years) children at the three ages. After statistical analysis of the answers, they ended up with 44, 49 and 47 items respectively for the three ages, with three to seven items for each variable.

Reliability of the questionnaires was measured by a retest after 2-4 weeks. A mean retest correlation of between .63 and .70 was found, which was regarded as satisfactory compared to other studies within the temperament field (Persson-Blennow & McNeil, 1982).

At all three ages satisfactory distributions and ranges were found for the different temperament variables with only one exception: Adaptability could not be measured at 2 years. The most stable variables over the three ages were Rhythmicity, Activity, Mood and Adaptability.

After factor analysis on the variable scores at the three separate ages, the authors suggested two temperamental clusters: (a) Mood, Approach and Adaptability, and (b) Activity and Intensity.

Few sex differences were found. Boys were slightly more adaptable at 6 months and 1 year, and more active and less distractible at 6 months.

The Uppsala Studies

Bohlin and Hagekull started their cooperation in 1974 with the translation of the first Carey questionnaire. After pilot projects with infants in different age groups, they skipped some items and added some, partly due to the distributions of given answers, partly to avoid general questions and keep them specific in terms of behavior and situation. Two parent questionnaires were developed for the infancy period (Bohlin, Hagekull & Lindhagen, 1981; Hagekull, Lindhagen & Bohlin, 1980). The first inventory, the Baby Behavioral Questionnaire (BBQ), covers the behaviors of infants aged 3–10 months, while the Toddler Behavior Questionnaire (TBQ) is suitable for 11- to 15-month-old children. For details see Chapter 15 by Hagekull.

Factor analysis was performed on questionnaire data from the two different age groups in order to establish broad dimensions of behavioral individuality. Altogether, 791 children were rated on the BBQ, and 357 children were rated on the TBQ, of which 90% also participated in the BBQ test.

In short, a seven-factor solution and an eight-factor solution were chosen to represent the behavioral repertoire of the 3- to 10-month-old and the 11- to 15-month-old infants respectively. Interpretations of the factors showed the dimensional structures in the two age groups to be highly similar to, but not identical with, the NYLS dimensions.

Reliability was tested by temporal stability over a short time period and internal consistency by using Cronbach's coefficient alpha. The coefficients for both instruments were considered to be within the range usually found for personality scales (r range: .63 to .93, alpha range: .51 to .77).

Stability analysis of the 322 children that formed the longitudinal part of the study was done separately. Assessment was made of the stability of individual children's relative position within the same behavioral dimensions at the two different ages. On the nine-month interval the stability of Activity/Intensity was substantial (r = .50), but Manageability and Approach–Withdrawal were found to have almost negligible stability (r = .20, .24).

Sex differences were only found as tendencies in the youngest age group. However, the temperament changed by age and was typical for the age group (Hagekull & Bohlin, 1981).

Validation attempts for the BBQ and TBQ involved different criterion measures. Statistically significant coefficients for all dimensions were found between parental BBQ ratings and parental direct observations of their children in three different studies (Hagekull et al., 1984).

The concurrent validity of the TBQ has been assessed by investigating the agreement between the mother's and father's ratings of their child. Agreements were significant for some of the dimensions (Approach, Sensory Sensitivity, Manageability) but close to zero for others (Intensity/Activity, Attentiveness and Regularity). The authors concluded that further studies of the validity of these TBQ scales are needed (Hagekull, 1985).

The TBQ seemed to be of more interest than the BBQ in a later study where the TBQ/BBQ dimensions were related to newborn behavior assessed with the NBAS. Forty-four newborn infants were tested on the first and third day after birth with the NBAS, at 4 months with the BBQ and at 1 year with the TBQ. More TBQ than BBQ dimensions were predicted by NBAS clusters. Regularity, Sensory Sensitivity and Manageability at 1 year could be predicted by different NBAS scales (Hagekull, 1985).

Mother–infant interaction in 30 dyads (aged 15 months) was observed in a 15-minute, structured home situation and compared with the infant's temperament

(TBQ). Parent-rated Manageability could be further validated since the observed behavior was close to the TBQ value on this dimension (Hagekull & Bohlin, 1986). Also it was clear that Manageability was the single best predictor of observed behavior in mother–child interaction. This supported the author's impressions that Manageability is largely a scale that measures parent–child interactions.

These authors now think that they have an instrument they can trust and use in new projects, focusing on questions regarding the relations between temperament and other developmental factors, of which types of interaction with parents and types of attachment are central aspects.

Finally, Hagekull and Bohlin started in 1985 a longitudinal study in which temperament will be studied prospectively in a group of 120 infants from birth to the age of 4 years. Behavior problems at 4 years will be studied in relation to early temperament, attachment and interaction between child and parents. The results will be compared with similar studies in other countries (see Chapter 16, by van den Boom, and Chapter 17, by Bates).

Too Many Different Instruments

As we have seen, the early temperament studies in Scandinavia, with different assessment methods and different concepts, have all been able to demonstrate that temperamental individuality can be reliably assessed from infancy onward.

However, the results from the different Scandinavian studies can not easily be compared. Even if some problems can be solved by reliability tests, and by deletion of bad items and non-replicated factors, the factors one ends with are dependent on the initial item selections. When it comes to comparing results from studies with different items, there is only one good criterion: their usefulness in explaining other aspects of behavior and interaction, notably the practical clinical usefulness, and the usefulness of the theoretical concepts in understanding the developing personality.

During the last years these two aspects have been considered in several studies in Scandinavia and will be presented separately.

The different instruments for assessing temperamental individuality have been almost as many as the number of studies. Methods that have been used are in addition to the above mentioned: Questionnaire by Rothbart (Hwang *et al.*, 1988), Bates (Mathiessen, 1982), Carey (Arajärvi & Huttunen, 1981; Arajärvi *et al.*, 1987; Huttunen, 1989; Huttunen & Nyman, 1982), Plomin (Hagekull, see Chapter 15) or self-made scales, by Pulkkinen, Olweus, Schulsinger and Faleide.

LONGITUDINAL STUDIES

Heritability of Temperament

Although Thomas and Chess explicitly do not speculate about the reasons for individual differences in temperament, it is quite common to regard temperament as 'the' inherited part of personality. Twin studies have a strong tradition in Scandinavia. Mainly due to the existing twin registers it has been possible to work

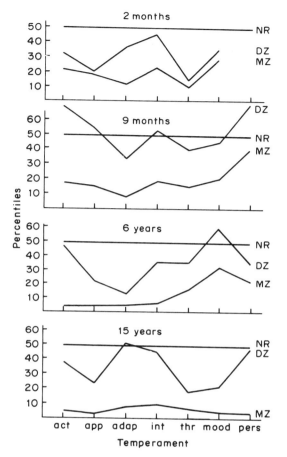

FIGURE 1   Median within-pair differences in temperament in monozygotic (MZ) and dizygotic (DZ) twins and in non-relative (NR) pairs presented as percentiles of the distribution of within-pair differences in NR. Groups were compared at 2 months, 9 months, 6 years and 15 years of age. (From Torgersen, 1987, p. 148.)

with representative groups. In other countries, like the USA, one is often dependent on twin clubs for the selection of samples. Parents who become members of such clubs tend to be interested in similarities in both zygosity groups. For this reason American researchers are interested in Scandinavian twins. See for example the newly started study by Nancy Pedersen and co-workers on temperament and personality in Swedish twins reared apart. Some interesting results are reported from this study (Plomin, Pedersen, McClearn, Nesselroade & Bergeman, 1987), but since this is on an adult population it will not be referred to here.

In my own initial study mentioned above the results showed substantial genetic influence on temperament development (Figure 1). Even if the group of twins studied (34 MZ, 16 DZ) was not large, the results were convincing in that identical twins (MZ) were much more alike than fraternals (DZ) at four different ages: 2

months, 9 months, 6 years and 15 years (Torgersen, 1981, 1987; Torgersen & Kringlen, 1978).

Although these results suggest that genetic influence becomes stronger at later ages, the minor problems with the twin method in infancy make the evidence of genetic influence in the infancy part of the study the most convincing – for several reasons:

(1) Most parents had no opinion regarding their twin's zygosity; only one pair of MZ twins was correctly diagnosed by the parents when the twins were 9 months old.

(2) At this early age the two twin groups were as often dressed alike.

(3) From birth on, MZ twins were as different in birth-weight and in individual birth complications as DZ twins.

(4) The person who did the scorings was not informed about the twin's zygosity.

(5) Mutual imitation is expected to start only after the age of 9 months.

Different environmental factors obviously exert more influence at later ages. At 6 years, MZ twins spend significantly more time together, and more often have the same friends than DZ twins. At 15 years, one reason for DZ twins to be more dissimilar in temperament is that pubertal development is more dissimilar in DZ pairs, which in turn correlates significantly with two of the temperament variables Adaptability and Attention span (Torgersen, 1989).

The stability of temperament was moderately high between 2 and 9 months, low from infancy to later years and surprisingly high between 6 and 15 years.

Several authors (Buss & Plomin, 1975; Goldsmith, 1983; and see Chapters 4 and 7) have concluded that evidence for differential genetic factors is strongest for sociability, emotionality and activity dimensions. In my own study activity is clearly among the most genetically influenced variables, both at separate ages and developmentally. That the same also holds for Approach is of special interest, not only because Approach seems close to a sociability factor, but also because of the similarity of this variable with other measures of reactions of individuals when confronted with novel stimuli or challenging situations. Several studies have found stability in such behavior from infancy onward (Fagan, 1985; Kagan, Reznick, Clarke, Snidman & Garcia-Coll, 1984; Sroufe, 1984; Suomi, 1987; and see Chapter 8 by Kagan, Reznick & Snidman). As for the reasons for this stability, however, there is less agreement. That Mood was found to be a variable with substantial change and low genetic influence is important to note. However, while emotionality in a broad sense is probably associated with the Mood scale we used, the two concepts are not identical.

Recent conclusions from developmental behavior genetics show little or no effects of differences between families on the variation of personality differences. Shared environmental influences create differences rather than similarities among family members (Scarr & Kidd, 1983). Such findings do not mean that shared environmental factors are of less importance for behavior development, but tell something of the importance of an interactional view on development. Inter-actional effects between shared environment and temperament have been found in this study even though the main focus has been on the assessment of temperament. With the prime effort directed toward the assessment of shared environmental factors as well as temperamental individuality, much evidence of interactional effects would be expected (Torgersen, 1989).

A Finnish Longitudinal Study of Aggression

The Finnish developmental psychologist Lea Pulkkinen was trained in personality and learning psychology. In a longitudinal study she traced the development of different ways of coping with conflicts as outcomes of different methods of parental caregiving (Pitkanen, 1969). The aggressive and non-aggressive behavior was measured by peer descriptions and teacher ratings of 369 children at the age of 8 years. At the age of 14, 95% of the group were seen again. At this age a selected group (77 girls, 77 boys) was studied more closely. Parents and adolescents were interviewed, and different types of childcare were rated by lengthy parental interviews. At the age of 20 the selected sample was interviewed again, and at the age of 26, 87% of the sample.

A two-dimensional model was developed to depict differences in behavior in a threatening situation. *Social Activity/Passivity* and *Strong/Weak Control of Behavior* were used to define four patterns of behavior, and, on the basis of factor scores, six extreme groups of children were identified.

Significant behavioral continuity was obtained between the three ages 8, 14 and 20 years, with a mean correlation of .44 between factor scores at the different age levels. It was interpreted as a *heterotypic* continuity, which means that a particular attribute is predictive of a phenotypically different but theoretically related attribute in terms of an impulse control model. Uncontrolled expression of impulse, i.e. aggressive behavior at age 8, was for example related to relatively higher dependence on peers than parents at age 14, and consequently, to gathering in the streets, early experiments with tobacco and alcohol, etc., and to reveling behavior at age 20 years. At age 26, disinhibition including use of tobacco and alcohol correlated with the earlier manifestations of weak control of behavior.

Also, when data from the official criminal register were obtained for the whole group (n = 369) at ages 20 and 26, it was shown that reliable predictions could be made from the children's behavior at age 8, defined by the six extreme groups identified at that age (Pulkkinen, 1983, 1987).

The style of child-rearing (child- or adult-centeredness) proved to be of great importance in explaining later criminal tendencies in behavior. The strong or weak control dimension was highly associated with type of family interactions: child-centered guidance with strong control. The other dimension however, the active versus passive dimension, was not associated at all with type of child-rearing.

In order to study the earlier formation of children's individuality Pulkkinen studied a group of preschool children. Differences in socialization as well as in temperamental characteristics were studied to understand the interindividual differences found. She was influenced by the Steiner schools which exist in some North-West European countries, where temperamental differences are taken as a central basis for differential teaching methods. Accordingly, Pulkkinen chose the classic four temperaments – sanguine, choleric, melancholic and phlegmatic – in developing SACHOMEPH, a scale of 52 gener.il behavioral descriptions. However, these four temperamental categories were not used as a basis for categorizing individuals, but as a basis for a two-dimensional system resulting from factor analyzing the items.

Caregivers in day-care centers rated the temperament of 231 children, aged 1.5–7.5 years, in six age groups of approximately 40 children each (Pulkkinen, 1983).

The first two varimax-rotated temperament factors explained most of the variance and were strongly bipolar. The first of these factors was interpreted as characterizing a choleric vs phlegmatic temperament according to the conception of Eysenck and Eysenck (1964). The second factor described a melancholic vs sanguine temperament. When stability of the factorial structures through the different age groups in her sample were studied, Pulkkinen discovered that some of the items showed a typical pattern of change over age. These items were related to prosocial behavior, which develops strongly during the age period studied.

When a three-factor rotation was made, the first two factors were the same as before and depicted temperamental variations independent of social development. The third factor could be interpreted as a prosocial vs antisocial behavior factor and as reflecting the process of socialization.

To verify this hypothesis Pulkkinen tested 72 children (aged 1.5–4.5 years) on different variables in social maturity and imagination, and interviewed their parents with regard to types of caregiving. She found the classic categories of temperament valuable in classifying individual differences in children's behavior, but insufficient to cover interindividual variations in social behavior, where social maturity appeared as a third dimension. The findings were interpreted in terms of the crystal model presented in Figure 2.

Pulkkinen describes each child with regard to his/her temperamental orientation to the world. Possibilities for prosocial as well as antisocial development are in every child. The parents play a crucial role as promoters of the child's development. Because of the differences in temperament, different children contribute to different types of social interaction problems.

In a discussion of the role of impulse control Pulkkinen (1986) concluded that:

> The two dimensional model confounds the construct of temperament and the process of socialization. Problems of social behavior in children correlate with parental social-ization practices. However, the educability of a child may depend on his or her temperamental characteristics. For example, it is difficult to teach self-control to an easily excitable child ... When this temperamental characteristic occurs with inadequate parenting, children have an especially strong risk for adopting unorganized, impulsive behavior. (Pulkkinen, 1986, pp. 170–171)

A Swedish-Norwegian Longitudinal Study of Aggression

Olweus, a Swedish reseacher living in Norway, has developed another model of development of aggressive behavior in which temperament is also an underlying factor. His primary interest was bully/victim problems among schoolchildren. In the early 1970s Olweus studied a large group of boys (nearly 1000), 13 to 16 years of

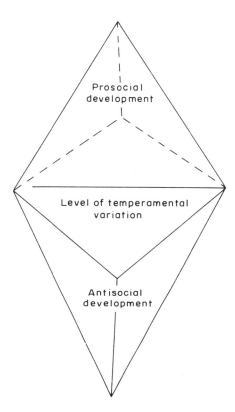

FIGURE 2   A crystal model of individual differences in social behavior as a function of temperament and socialization. (From Pulkkinen, 1983.)

age, in Sweden. About 5% of the boys showed typical aggressive behavior patterns across situations and stable over time (Olweus, 1977, 1978). The bullies were characterized by strong aggressive tendencies, weak control of such tendencies if activated, and strong needs for self-assertion and dominance. They were also fairly popular, fearless, non-anxious and tough, and had a positive attitude toward themselves.

In search for explanations of this type of behavior, Olweus made a closer study of two subgroups of the boys (76 at the age of 13 and 51 at the age of 16) (Olweus, 1980). The boys' level of aggressiveness was measured by highly reliable peer ratings on three aggression dimensions (Start fights, Verbal protest, and Tease).

Extensive retrospective interviews were carried out with the boys' parents. The parents' early handling of the child was assessed, as were the temperamental characteristics of the boys in the early years. Two temperament-related, open-ended questions were asked, relating to the boys' early childhood. One was related to the boys' general activity level; the other, to general intensity of temperament. The two questions correlated .56 and .62 in the two groups and thus were combined in one variable, scored from 1 (calm) to 5 (active, hot-headed).

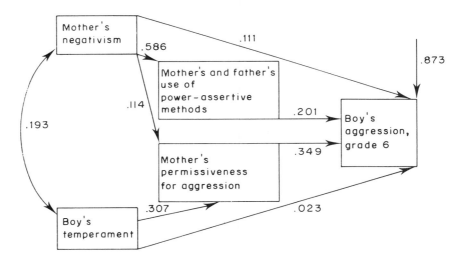

FIGURE 3   Path diagram for basic causal model. (From Olweus, 1980, p. 650.)

Olweus found four factors to be of special importance in partly explaining the development of aggressive behavior. Three of them supported earlier studies of aggression (Lefkowitz, Eron, Walder & Huesman, 1977; Martin, 1975; McCord, McCord & Howard, 1961; Sears, Maccoby & Levin, 1957) and were related to (a) mother's negativism in the child's first 3–4 years, (b) mother's permissiveness for aggression, and (c) parent's use of power-assertive methods in upbringing.

What made the Olweus study new and different from the earlier ones was, in addition to his use of a causal model (path analysis), that he included temperament as an additional causal factor (Olweus, 1980). His model and results for a subgroup at age 13 are presented in Figure 3. As can be seen from this model, early temperament had both a direct and indirect influence on aggressive behavior in the 13-year-old boys. The results from the other age group were found to be fairly similar and lend additional support to the conclusions drawn above.

Olweus concluded that a considerable amount of the variance in the aggression level of adolescent boys can be explained by means of the temperamental and early family factors included in the model.

A Danish Longitudinal Study of Schizophrenia

Another example of a new interest in temperament applied to an earlier longitudinal, developmental study is the work by Schulsinger in Denmark. A prospective longitudinal study of children at risk was started in 1962 (Mednik & Schulsinger, 1965, 1974). A total of 207 children of schizophrenic mothers and 104 of parents without mental illness were studied at the age of 10–19 years. Data on typical behavior from infancy and early childhood were collected through retrospective parental interviews and information from the teachers in addition to clinical interviews.

When the group was seen again, 10 years later, Schulsinger and her associates found that, of the 173 children in the at-risk group, 13 had developed schizophrenia and 29 borderline schizophrenia (Schulsinger, 1976).

Those children who later developed schizophrenia or borderline schizophrenia were, as babies, significantly more passive and had a shorter span of attention during play with familiar toys than did the at-risk children who did not develop any schizophrenic disorder. The former children were more often restless and disruptive in the school situation (Parnas *et al.*, 1982).

Schulsinger (1976) was interested in the 'non-vulnerable' of these children, those who did not develop any symptoms. Searching for premorbid characteristics of these children, she had also developed a temperament score from all the retrospectively available information from the children's early behavior. She composed a general temperament score after factor analyzing correlations between the different elements of information. Her temperament concept is influenced by Rutter's concept of 'good temperament' (Rutter, 1972) and can be described as a common sense temperamental quality. The extreme end of the scale is characterized by unconcentrated, intensive sudden emotional outbursts, and emotional instability.

Preliminary findings relating to the temperamental data suggest that children in the at-risk group who did not develop any symptoms had 'easier' or 'better' temperament than the mean of the whole group of low-risk children. They equalized *the best* in the low-risk group, with scores above the mean in unselected population samples (H. Schulsinger, personal communication, 1988).

In the studies of both Olweus and Schulsinger, temperament has been assessed retrospectively, and based on the authors' particular concepts of temperament. Thus it is difficult to compare their results with other studies of temperament in children. However, irrespective of type of definition and measurement, the results seem of great interest for further studies.

Clinical and Practical Studies

Finland has carefully and long kept population registers and a network of mother and well-baby clinics. This has given exceptional opportunities for epidemiological studies, and Huttunen has taken advantage of this. His main interest has been to look at the influence of maternal stress on the behavioral development of the offspring. In 1974 Huttunen and his co-workers started a prospective study of all infants born during one year in Helsinki (Arajärvi & Huttunen, 1981). At their monthly visits to outpatient clinics pregnant women were asked to fill out self-rating scales of their subjective symptoms of stress and altered mood in the previous month. When the infants were 6–8 months old, the mother rated their temperament on the first questionnaire developed by Carey. At present, Huttunen is engaged in a follow-up study of these children.

Temperament data were collected for 1855 infants, while only 240 of the mothers completed each of the monthly stress scales during pregnancy. The mothers' subjective stress ratings during the first, but not the second and third, trimester of pregnancy, correlated statistically significantly with some of the temperamental variables in the infants. Of interest is that some of the variables typical for the 'difficult child' showed the strongest relations. These were Withdrawal, Adaptability, Mood, Distractibility and Intensity (Huttunen, 1989).

In my own Norwegian longitudinal twin study, relations between behavior problems and temperamental individuality were studied when the children were 6 years old. Although some relations were found between difficult temperament and behavior problems, both assessed at 6, this was true for some symptoms and not for others. As expected, conduct disorders correlated significantly (r = .47) with difficult temperament, while psychosomatic complaints were only related to negative mood, and anxiety to low threshold. The fact that social stress was also slightly related to difficult temperament indicates an interactional effect (Torgersen, 1984).

Also of importance seem the tendencies of several of the 'difficult child' characteristics (Mood, Adaptability, Rhythmicity) to be influenced most by environmental factors (Torgersen, 1982). Behavior problems are also being studied in the twins at the age of 15, but the results are not yet available.

Temperament as one of several risk factors for asthmatic development in children is being studied in a prospective Norwegian longitudinal study by Faleide, Unger and Watten (1987). While preliminary results from the first two assessments of 161 children at 4 months and 4 years seem to be promising, the predictions rely more on global and clinical evaluations than on specific temperamental ratings or observations.

Temperament ratings at 4 months were obtained with only selected items from the ITQ. Slight but statistically significant relations were found between immunologic qualities of blood which are thought to be related to asthma (immunoglobulin E level) and higher activity and sensitivity scores (Faleide *et al.*, 1985).

Day-Care Studies

Behavior problems in children with different day-care experiences have also been related with temperament. Day-care arrangements seem to attract special attention in Scandinavia; the number of public day-care centers is steadily growing, in particular in Finland, but also in Sweden.

After a preliminary testing of Rothbart's Infant Behavior Questionnaire (IBQ) (see Chapter 12) on a group of preschool children, this method was evaluated as reliable and valid to measure Swedish children's temperamental individuality (Lamb, Frodi, Hwang & Frodi, 1983). Subsequently the IBQ was used in a study of the effect of day-care for preschool children (Hwang *et al.*, 1988). Other measures included contextual life events and family circumstances and several aspects of personality and intellectual development.

A total of 140 firstborn children whose parents all wanted them to be admitted to center-based day-care were first studied in the period before placement between 11 and 24 months and subsequently after they had been 1 and 2 years in three different types of day-care: center-based, family day-care home or at home with their own parents.

The parents completed the IBQ questionnaire at the first assessment. Only one composite measure was used in the analysis: temperamental difficulty was computed by adding the IBQ score for Anger/Frustration to the inverse of the scores for Positive Emotionality and Soothability (Frodi *et al.*, 1982). One of the results of interest here was that Griffith scores at different ages were not related with earlier temperament; they were best predicted by Caldwell's Home Scale.

Easy temperament was found to be among the predictors of later personality development, assessed with the Q-sort by Block and Block (1979, 1980). Social skills and negative peer relations, however, were not associated with earlier measures of temperament.

Different day-care influences on the child's emotional development have also been studied in Finland. The child psychiatric unit at Helsinki University was asked by the government in 1977 to lead a major investigation of the influence of different day-care settings on the child's development. Arajärvi was the head of this large-scale study in which 336 children were followed longitudinally at five ages (6 months, 9 months, 1, 2 and 3 years). The main results published from this study (Arajärvi *et al.*, 1987) showed that the influences from the home environment, and the relations between the parent and the child were of far more importance than the different kinds of childcare. Temperament was assessed with the Carey question-naire, translated by Huttunen, and rated by parents, health personnel and day-care workers. As yet no results are available. M.M. Turunen, who works with the temperament part of this study, is planning a follow-up study of these children at the age of 10 years, and temperament will again be one of the variables studied.

Also in Finland, Munter (1987) seeks to find out how temperamentally different children (0–3 years) adapt to the new routines in a day-care center. She uses the temperament questionnaire developed by Pulkkinen, rated by herself, the parents and the day-care workers.

Two Studies of Mother–Child Interaction

In her work with firstborn babies and their mothers, the Danish psychologist Munck observed that different babies had different influences on the mother–child interaction. In cooperation with Mirdal and Marner she started in 1975 a study of mother–child interactions. Twenty-eight dyads were studied at a maternity ward. In addition to the NBAS, a standardized 24-hour diary was kept by the mothers from the fourth day after birth. After 6 weeks the mothers were interviewed about their babies' soothability, attention and irritability (Munck *et al.*, 1988).

Munck's present work focuses on the interactional process between mothers and their premature infants, partly through a close follow-up of a small group of premature children, but also through a follow-up of 330 premature children at the age of 4 years. Several of the measures are of a temperamental nature: active–passive, helpless–self-assertive, withdrawn–outgoing, mood and sociability. Two experienced professionals rate the children independently on different aspects of interaction during a 3-hour visit in the homes.

The Norwegian psychologist Mathiessen was interested in how the quality of the contact between mother and infant influences the infant's attentive behavior (Mathiessen, 1982). At birth 11 firstborn infants were assessed with the NBAS. At

3, 7 and 12 months they were videotaped in interaction with their mothers. Temperament was assessed by asking the mothers to rate their child at the three ages using the ICQ by Bates. The four factors of the ICQ, as identified by Bates, showed varying degrees of stability. The most stable was Unadaptability. All four NBAS scales predicted the fussy–difficult factor at 12 months. This factor was not predicted by either the child's attention score or the overall interaction score at earlier ages. If a child was low in social responsivity ('dull') at 12 months, this was related with its attentiveness at 3 and 6 months, as well as with the interaction scores at those two ages, but not with any of the neonatal NBAS scores. Mother–child interaction ratings at 12 months had no relation with any of the foregoing measures apart from attention scores at ages 3 and 7 months.

CONCLUDING REMARKS

In the field of child development research in Scandinavia there has been a growing interest in temperamental individuality during the last 20 years. Some groups have had temperament as their primary interest and have worked towards a better understanding of this topic through methodological improvements. Others have used existing methods with temperament only as one of several studied aspects of childrens' behavior. Both approaches are still in operation.

While infants were the focus of interest in most of the earlier studies, there has been a growing interest in longitudinal studies over the last few years. Several of such studies are presently being carried out (and also some that are not reported in this chapter because they have just started). Another change of interest now taking place is that methods from different theoretical frames of reference, like the 'Strange Situation' and the Brazelton scales, are used in combination with measurements of temperament. For a long time these approaches have been kept separate in spite of the shared interest in the interaction between the child and its environment. The thought of a genetic core of temperament still seems to be the main reason for some to avoid further contact with this field. This might change when it is realized that better knowledge of aspects of behavior explained by genetic variance gives us a better possibility of studying in more detail the interactional process between the individual child and its individual environment.

REFERENCES

Arajärvi, T. & Huttunen, M.O. (1981). Pregnancy and birth complications in the aetiology of psychiatric disorders with a special reference to the temperament of the children: A description of the Finnish prospective epidemiological study. In S.A. Mednick & A.E. Baert (Eds), *Prospective longitudinal research: An empirical basis for the primary prevention of psychological disorders* (pp. 43–47). Oxford: University Press.

Arajärvi, T., Malmivaara, K., Martelin, L., Salenius-Laine, K. & Turunen, M.M. (1987). Working mothers and day-care in the development of 0–3 year old children: A study of child development and disorders in children and families. *Psychiatrica Finnica*, **18**, 9–19.

Block, J.H. & Block, J. (1979). Instructions for the California child-Q-set. Unpublished manuscript, Institute of Human Development, University of California at Berkeley.

Block, J.H. & Block, J. (1980). The role of ego-control and ego-resiliency in the organization of behavior. In W.A. Collins (Ed.), *Minnesota symposium on child psychology*, Vol. 13 (pp. 39–101). New York: Erlbaum.

Bohlin, G., Hagekull, B. & Lindhagen, K. (1981). Dimensions of infant behavior. *Infant Behavior and Development*, **4**, 83–96.

Brazelton, T.B. (1973). *Neonatal Behavioral Assessment Scale*. Clinics in Developmental Medicine No. 50. London: Heineman; Philadelphia: Lippincott.

Buss, A.H. & Plomin, R. (1975). *A temperament theory of personality development*. New York: Wiley.

Carey, W.B. (1970). A simplified method for measuring infant temperament. *Journal of Pediatrics*, **77**, 188–194.

Eysenck, H.J. & Eysenck, S.B.G. (1964). *Manual of the Eysenck Personality Inventory*. London: University of London Press.

Fagan, J.F. (1985). A new look at infant intelligence. In D.K. Determan (Ed.), *Current topics in human intelligence*, Vol. 1, *Research methodology* (pp. 223–246). Norwood, NJ: Ablex.

Faleide, A.O., Unger, S.E., Aas, K., Leegaard, J., Sande, H.A., Sten, J. & Watten, R. (1985). Psychosocial factors in asthma and atopic allergy in childhood: A preliminary report. In *Proceedings from the 8th World Conference on Psychosomatic Medicine*. Chicago: University of Chicago.

Faleide, A.O., Unger, S.E. & Watten, R.G. (1987). Psychosocial factors in bronchial asthma and allergy in childhood. In *Proceedings from the 16th European Conference on Psychosomatic Research*. London: Plenum.

Frodi, A., Lamb, M.E., Hwang, C.P., Frodi, M., Forstrom, B. & Corry, T. (1982). Stability and change in parental attitudes following an infant's birth into traditional and non-traditional Swedish families. *Scandinavian Journal of Psychology*, **23**, 53–62.

Goldsmith, H.H. (1983). Genetic influences on personality from infancy to adulthood. *Child Development*, **54**, 331–355.

Hagekull, B. (1985). The Baby and Toddler Questionnaires: Empirical studies and conceptual considerations. *Scandinavian Journal of Psychology*, **26**, 110–122.

Hagekull, B. & Bohlin, G. (1981). Individual stability in dimensions of infant behavior. *Infant Behavior and Development*, **4**, 97–108.

Hagekull, B. & Bohlin, G. (1986). Mother–infant interaction and perceived infant temperament. *International Journal of Behavioral Development*, **9**, 297–313.

Hagekull, B., Bohlin, G. & Lindhagen, K. (1984). Validity of parental reports. *Infant Behavior and Development*, **7**, 77–92.

Hagekull, B., Lindhagen, K. & Bohlin, G. (1980). Behavioral dimensions in one-year-olds and dimensional stability in infancy. *International Journal of Behavioral Development*, **3**, 351–364.

Huttunen, M.O. (1989). Maternal stress during pregnancy and the behavior of the offspring. In S. Doxiadis (Ed.), *Early influences shaping the individual*. New York/London: Plenum.

Huttunen, M.O. & Nyman, G. (1982). On the continuity, change and clinical value of infant temperament in a prospective epidemiological study. In R. Porter & G.M. Collins (Eds), *Temperamental differences in infants and young children* (pp. 240–247). Ciba Foundation Symposium No. 89. London: Pitman.

Hwang, C.P., Lamb, M.E. & Broberg, A. (1988). The development of social and intellectual competence in Swedish preschoolers raised at home and in out-of-home care facilities. In K. Kreppner & R.M. Lerner (Eds), *Family systems and lifespan development*. Hillsdale, NJ: Erlbaum.

Kagan, J., Reznick, J.S., Clarke, C., Snidman, N. & Garcia-Coll, C. (1984). Behavioral inhibition to the unfamiliar. *Child Development*, **55**, 2212–2225.

Lamb, M., Frodi, A.M., Hwang, C.P. & Frodi, M.E. (1983). Interobserver and test–retest reliability of Rothbart's Infant Behavior Questionnaire. *Scandinavian Journal of Psychology*, **24**, 153–156.

Lefkowitz, M.M., Eron, L.D., Walder, L.O. & Huesman, L.R. (1977). *Growing up to be violent*. New York: Pergamon.

Martin, B. (1975). Parent–child relations. In F.D. Horowitz, E.M. Hetherington, S. Scarr-Salpatek & G.M. Siegel (Eds), *Review of child development research*, Vol. 4. Chicago: Chicago University Press.

Mathiessen, B. (1982). Mother–child interaction and the development of attentive behavior in the first year of life. Paper presented at the 10th International Congress of the International Association for Child and Adolescent Psychiatry and Allied Professions, Dublin.

McCord, W., McCord, J. & Howard, A. (1961). Familial correlates of aggression in nondelinquent male children. *Journal of Abnormal and Social Psychology, 62*, 79–93.

McNeil, T.F. (1976). Temperament revisited: A research-oriented critique of the New York Longitudinal Study of Temperament. Unpublished manuscript, Psykiatriska institution, Universitetet i Lund, S-214 01 Malmo, Sweden.

Mednick, S.A. & Schulsinger, F. (1965). A longitudinal study of children with a high risk for schizophrenia: A preliminary report. In S. Vandenberg (Ed.), *Methods and goals in human behavior genetics* (pp. 255–296). New York: Academic Press.

Mednick, S.A. & Schulsinger, F. (1974). Studies of children at high risk for schizophrenia. In S.A. Mednick, F. Schulsinger, J. Higgins & B. Bell (Eds), *Genetics, environment and psychopathology* (pp. 103–116). Amsterdam/New York: North Holland/American Elsevier.

Munck, H., Mirdal, G. & Marner, L. (1988). Mother–infant interaction in Denmark. To appear in J.K. Nugent, M.B. Lester & T.B. Brazelton (Eds), *Cultural context of infancy*. New York: Ablex.

Munter, H. (1987). Psychophysical loading of children in Finnish day care centers. Unpublished manuscript. Department of Psychology, University of Jyvaskula, Finland.

Olweus, D. (1977). Aggression and peer acceptance in adolescent boys: Two short term longitudinal studies of ratings. *Child Development, 48*, 1301–1313.

Olweus, D. (1978). *Aggression in the schools*. New York: Wiley.

Olweus, D. (1980). Familial and temperamental determinants of aggressive behavior in adolescent boys: A causal analysis. *Developmental Psychology, 16*, 644–660.

Parnas, J., Schulsinger, F., Schulsinger, H., Mednick, S.A., Thomas, W. & Teasdale, M.A. (1982). Behavioral precursors of the schizophrenia spectrum. *Archives of General Psychiatry, 39*, 658–664.

Persson-Blennow, I. & McNeil, T.F. (1979). A questionnaire for measurement of temperament in six-month old infants: Development and standardization. *Journal of Child Psychology and Psychiatry, 20*, 1–13.

Persson-Blennow, I. & McNeil, T. (1980). Questionnaire for measurement of temperament in one- and two-year old children. *Journal of Child Psychology and Psychiatry, 21*, 37–46.

Persson-Blennow, I. & McNeil, T.F. (1982). New data on test–retest reliability for three temperament scales. *Journal of Child Psychology and Psychiatry, 23*, 181–183.

Pitkanen, L. (1969). A descriptive model of aggression and nonaggression with applications to children's behaviour. Jyvaskyla Studies in Education, Psychology and Social Research No. 19. University of Jyvaskyla, Finland.

Plomin, R., Pedersen, N.L., McClearn, G.E., Nesselroade, J.R. & Bergeman, C.S. (1987). EAS temperament during the last half of the life span: Twins reared apart and twins reared together. *Psychology and Aging, 3*, 43–50.

Pulkkinen, L. (1983). Interindividual differences in social behavior as a function of temperament and socialization. Paper presented at the symposium 'Interindividual differences in social development: The role of socialization and temperament'. International Society for the Study of Behavioral Development.

Pulkkinen, L. (1986). The role of impulse control in the development of antisocial and prosocial behavior. In D. Olweus, J. Block & M. Radke-Yarrow (Eds), *Development of antisocial and prosocial behavior*. New York: Academic Press.

Pulkkinen, L. (1987). A two-dimensional model as a framework for interindividual differences in social behavior. In S.B.G. Eysenck & D.H. Saklofske (Eds), *Individual differences in children and adolescents. International perspectives*. London: Hodder & Stoughton.

Pulkkinen, L. (1987). An eighteen year longitudinal study of social development. In *Proceedings of the IXth Biennial Meeting of the International Society of Behavioral Development,* July 1987, Tokyo.

Rutter, M. (1972). Relationships between child and adult psychiatric disorders. *Acta Psychiatrica Scandinavica,* **48**, 3–21.

Scarr, S. & Kidd, K.K. (1983). Developmental behavior genetics. In: P.H. Mussen (Ed.), *Handbook of child psychology,* Vol. 2. New York: Wiley.

Schulsinger, F. (1976). A ten-year follow-up of children of schizoprehnic mothers: Clinical assessment. *Acta Psychiatrica Scandinavica,* **53**, 371–386.

Sears, R.R., Maccoby, E.E. & Levin, H. (1957). *Patterns of child rearing.* Evanston, IL: Row Peterson.

Sroufe, L.A. (1984). Infant–caregiver attachment and patterns of adaptation in preschool: The roots of maladaption and competence. In M. Permutter (Ed.), *Minnesota Symposium in Child Psychology,* Vol. 16. Hillsdale, NJ: Erlbaum.

Suomi, S.J. (1987). Genetic and maternal contributions to individual differences in rhesus monkey biobehavioral development. In N. A. Krasnegor, E. M. Blass, M. A. Hofer & W. P. Smotherman (Eds), *Perinatal development: A biological perspective.* Academic Press.

Thomas, A., Chess, S. & Birch, H.G. (1968). *Temperament and behavior disorders in children.* New York: New York University Press.

Thomas, A., Chess, S., Birch, H.G., Hertzig, M.E. & Korn, S. (1963). *Behavioral individuality in early childhood.* New York: New York University Press.

Torgersen, A.M. (1981). Genetic factors in temperamental individuality. *Journal of the American Academy of Child Psychiatry,* **20**, 701–711.

Torgersen, A.M. (1982). Temperamental differences in infants and young children. In R. Porter & G.M. Collins (Eds), *Temperament differences in infants and young children.* Ciba Foundation Symposium No. 89. London: Pitman.

Torgersen, A.M. (1984). Relations between temperament, stress and behavior symptoms in the development from birth to six years. Paper presented at Advanced Study Institute meeting on 'Human assessment: advances in measuring cognition and motivation'. Athens, Greece.

Torgersen, A. M. (1987). Longitudinal research on temperament in twins. *Acta Geneticae Medicae et Gemellologiae.,* **36**, 145–154.

Torgersen, A.M. (1989). Genetic and environmental influences on temperamental development: A longitudinal study of twins from infancy to adolescence. In S. Doxiadis (Ed.), *Early influences shaping the individual.* New York/London: Plenum.

Torgersen, A.M. & Kringlen, E. (1978). Genetic aspects of temperamental differences in infants. *Journal of the American Academy of Child Psychiatry,* **17**, 433–444.

Trevarten, C. (1977). Descriptive analysis of infant communicative behaviour. In H.R. Schaffer (Ed.), *Studies in mother–infant interaction.*

Author Index

All author names appearing in the chapters are included, with the exception of names appearing in the lists of references.

Subject Index

With the exception of names of instruments, the items in this index are limited to the concepts appearing in paragraph headings and subheadings, table headings and subheadings, summaries, etc. Concepts closely connected with a particular author can be located using the author index. Where the discussion of an item extends over several pages only the first page number is given.